Sociological Methods

Sociological
Methods
A Sourcebook

Edited by
Norman K. Denzin

Routledge
Taylor & Francis Group

LONDON AND NEW YORK

First published 1970 by Transaction Publishers

Published 2017 by Routledge
2 Park Square, Milton Park, Abingdon, Oxon OX14 4RN
711 Third Avenue, New York, NY 10017, USA

Routledge is an imprint of the Taylor & Francis Group, an informa business

Library of Congress Catalog Number: 2005053823

Library of Congress Cataloging-in-Publication Data

Sociological methods : a sourcebook / Norman K. Denzin, editor.
    p. cm.
    Originally published: Chicago : Aldine Pub. Co., 1970. (Methodological perspectives)
    Includes bibliographical references and index.
    ISBN 0-202-30840-5 (pbk. : alk. paper)
    1. Sociology—Methodology. 2. Sociology—Research. I. Denzin, Norman K. II. Methodological perspectives.

HM511.S654 2006   2005053823
301.'072—dc22

ISBN 13: 978-0-202-30840-1 (pbk)

Acknowledgments

I am indebted to Alexander J. Morin and Richard J. Hill for their comments and suggestions in the preparation of this sourcebook, and for Kris Dymond's assistance in the arduous task of assembling the materials for publication.

My greatest debt is to Sheila M. Welch and Frances Jackson, the two editors who saw this sourcebook and *The Research Act* through to publication. Without their efforts these two books would still be unpublished.

Contents

INTRODUCTION

THE ENTERPRISE of sociology rests on three interrelated activities: theory, research, and substantive interest. In the main the discipline has reflected this three-part division. Texts, monographs, and readers separately display concerns for theory, research methods, and substantive speciality, be that deviance, organizations, small groups, or the family. This division has had an unfortunate consequence: It has created a breach between these inseparable components of the sociological act. Theory cannot be judged independent of research methods, and substantive speciality is of little value if it is not firmly embedded within a theoretical framework and based upon sound research strategies. The separation of theories and methods now characterize sociology—indeed, the discipline has separate specialists in theory, methods, and substantive areas. Seldom are the three combined into a common individual mind let alone a common professional perspective.

This condition sets this book's theme—that the separate elements of the sociological act must be brought back together. My selection of readings was made with this in mind. Each reading, in its own way, demonstrates how the doing of sociology demands a general view of sociology's three activities.

ELEMENTS OF THE RESEARCH ACT: AN OVERVIEW

My focus is on the research act—those endeavors of the sociologist that take him from theory to the empirical world and back again. Accordingly, I have broken this act into several rather arbitrary but discrete phases. The first is theory itself. I assume that the only justification for an empirical observation is the refinement, development, or refocusing of social theory. Sound sense of what social theory is and a knowledge of how theory guides the research process must be grasped. The readings in Parts I and II take up this problem.

As the sociologist moves from theory to concrete observations, a first problem demanding resolution is what to observe, the province of research design and sampling theory. Part III details the various strategies available to the observer who commits himself to the sampling of theoretically relevant units from a social structure. A social theory dictates certain types of observation, and I take it to be an axiom of modern sociology that persons at various levels and in various types of social structures must be sampled, that the sampling of persons aggregately distributed within a social community is no longer adequate. Thus, I have selected for Part III readings which indicate how elements and properties of social organization may be sampled.

Having selected his units of observation, the sociologist must next wrestle with the problem of how to measure or observe those units. Part IV treats various aspects of the measurement act. The problems of maintaining continuity with previous researchers are treated, as is the old issue of relating attitudes, or predispositions to act with overt actions. Various measurement instruments are reviewed and each is assessed in terms of its ability to predict concrete behavior. A last problem taken up is how the researcher undertakes to develop a new instrument.

In a wide variety of instances, the research act first comes alive during the interview, when the researcher is forced to confront his observational units on a direct, face-to-face basis. He must convince persons they should be interviewed, get them to set time aside for the interview, and keep them conscious of what the interview is about. Silent, deviant, hostile, or overly verbal respondents are problems; several of the readings in Part V treat these kinds of respondents, but the main thrust is to show in what ways the sociological interview is a special form of symbolic interaction, one relatively new within the horizon of human contacts, yet, a form that furnishes many of the foundations of modern sociology.

Part VI moves to the problem of data analysis. Here I ask how the researcher formulates sound causal explanations: explanations which display covariance between the independent and dependent variables, which demonstrate time order, and which stand up under the explanatory threat of alternative causal variables. I assume that there are three basic strategies for forging causal propositions — multivariate analysis, the experimental model, and analytic induction. The strengths and weaknesses of each are assessed. I take the position that an adequate causal model must permit the developmental and sequential analysis of events over time.

Parts VII through XI treat in progressive order what I regard as the five major research methods of the sociologist: social experiments, surveys, participant observation, life histories, and unobtrusive methods. My intent is to present the major forms of each method, to assess their strengths and weaknesses, and to present the interactional problems that arise when a researcher uses them. Each method creates special interactional problems, since each represents a different way of approaching the empirical world and opening that world to study. Properly speaking, these five parts focus on the social psychology of the research act.

Part XII offers a synthesis and critique of the five methods. I suggest that no single method is free from flaws — that no single method will adequately handle all of the problems of causal analysis — and that no single method will yield all the data necessary for a theory's test. Consequently, the researcher must combine his methods in a process termed triangulation; that is, empirical events must be examined from the vantage provided by as many methods as possible. The papers in Part XII alternatively assess and show how surveys, experiments, and participant observation may be combined and evaluated from a common perspective.

Part VIII gives an overview of the contingencies and problems that may arise during any of the earlier phases of the research act. Problems of theory, access to certain kinds of data, pressures that arise from granting agencies, and the difficulties of forging an ethical contract with subjects are treated. Once again the human, interactional side of doing research is shown, and the dilemma of the sociologist emerges: An imperfect human is studying other humans in situations where nothing approaching ideal control can be exerted. Values, ideologies, and idiosyncratic preferences make the sociological act less than perfect. This can not be escaped. It can be only recognized and openly stated. From that point each researcher is on his own.

The selections in Part XIII bring the reader full circle. Beginning with theory, he ends with ethics and interactional contingencies. Each element of the sociological act emerges within a social context. The acts of doing theory, of sampling, of measuring, of interviewing, and of analyzing are social acts, a symbolic act, the synthesis of which becomes what sociology is: a special form of interaction carried on between a very unique organism and the empirical world.

A NOTE ON THE ORGANIZATION OF READINGS

Readers may quarrel with my conception of the research act. By breaking it into several discrete phases, I do injustice to the fluid interactive process that must characterize empirical inquiry. It is obvious, for example, that many researchers will have conceptions of their measurement instruments and analytic strategies before a sampling model is selected. My only defense is that these readings, in whatever order they might have been arranged, cover the major features of the research act.

Any set of readings must be more than a bare collection of articles sequentially arranged. The editor of a sourcebook has an obligation to offer his reasons for gathering the readings he has. Accordingly, I have supplied introductions to each part that give my interpretation of selections and that offer reviews of issues only tangentially mentioned in certain readings. Since limitations of space prohibited the inclusion of some selections I would have liked to include, I have indicated, either in my introductions or in the suggested readings, what these selections were.

One last point: *The main focus of this book is on the problems involved in developing social theory and carrying out valid empirical inquiry; the theme is pragmatic.* As the readings will evidence, I have placed these problematic elements of theory and research within a social perspective. While the reader may reject my perspective, I do not think he can overlook the problems raised.

PART ONE

The Naturalistic Perspective

INTRODUCTION

THIS FIRST part borrows its title from a major theme underlying symbolic interaction research: the study and analysis of the empirical world in its natural settings.[1] The empirical world sets the tone, shapes the theories, and indicates the uses made of research methods. It is this world to which all theories, methods, and substantive specialties must return. It is this world that furnishes the final evaluation of the sociological act. If investigators are unsuccessful in explaining the nature of this world, they have failed in their efforts.

1. Very briefly to indicate the nature of the symbolic interactionist perspective, it is a point of view that gives heavy emphasis to man's ability to guide and direct his own activities, that lodges the source of human activity in ongoing units of social organization, most commonly social groups, and that stresses the importance of symbols, languages, and gestures in the formation of social action. Yet it always returns to the point of view of the acting person. A cardinal feature of this perspective is the assumption that the interaction process is a potentially emergent event; an event that must be studied over time in natural situations. For a major statement of this point of view, the reader is directed to the fuller source of Blumer's work. The readings by Kuhn and McPartland, Glaser and Strauss, Benny and Hughes, Becker, and Olesen and Whittaker also point up aspects of symbolic interactionism.

SOCIOLOGY'S REWARD STRUCTURE

Richard J. Hill's paper suggests that the current reward structure in sociology favors a separation of theory, method, and research activities. This structure has significant negative consequences: that is, the methodologist and the theorist are hindered in going to the empirical world and opening that world to analysis because they have separated themselves from each other. The result is a continued isolation of each speciality, with few students now being trained in the skills and practices necessary for the grounding and development of social theory. Hill's article offers a review of issues to be taken up in subsequent parts. He touches on the problems involved in current sampling theory, indicates how many of the traditional sociological methods are reactive in nature, and suggests that new ways of studying the empirical world need to be developed. This anticipates the readings in Part XII, which indicate how nonreactive and unobstrusive research methods can be employed. Hill's paper calls for a redefinition of the role currently given the methodologist. Because this role has become insulated from other aspects of the research and sociological act, Hill suggests that it be abolished, and that each sociologist should at once become his own theorist and methodologist. Such is the stance dictated by the naturalistic perspective, and in this sense Hill is justified in calling for an end to the role of methodologist.

THE NATURE OF EMPIRICAL INQUIRY

Hill's position is broadened and elaborated in Herbert Blumer's essay. For perhaps the first time, the full implications of the naturalistic stance are spelled out. Working from the symbolic interactionist perspective, Blumer takes the position that the research and methodological act encompasses all of the aspects of doing sociology. The cardinal feature of any science is its grounding in the empirical world. Consequently, the research process becomes but one aspect of the scientific enterprise. Theory, method, research, and substantive interest intertwine to produce and shape the creative act. The ultimate test of these actions is their ability to reveal and explain the empirical world — a world studied in its natural settings, not in simulated contexts. Perhaps the most significant scientific error is to assume that research actions can be separated; that they can be judged by separate criteria.

Blumer reviews the major ways by which the contemporary sociologist judges his research activity. These are seen to involve reliance

on scientific protocol, valuing replication studies, giving heavy emphasis to hypothesis testing and developing operational definitions
of the phenomena at hand. Each of these criteria are seen by Blumer
as having severe restrictions. He suggests, for example, that relying
on a scientific protocol that does not admit open analysis of the
empirical world is of little use in building a naturalistic empirical
science, as are operational definitions couched in terms of technical
rather than empirical contingencies. To illustrate his view of naturalistic research, Blumer cites the work of Charles Darwin, perhaps the
greatest naturalistic scientist. Darwin's work is seen as involving a
dual emphasis on the acts of exploration and inspection.

EXPLORATION AND INSPECTION

The naturalistic perspective breaks research activity into six interrelated processes: the use of a series of images or prior pictures
about the events to be studied; the formulation of questions and
problems about those events; the determination of what data are to
be gathered and how they are to be gathered; the ascertaining of
relationships between those data within an evolving theoretical
perspective; and, last, the use of concepts. A commitment to the
naturalistic perspective carries with it a number of implications. The
researcher necessarily begins his studies as an outsider. Seldom is he
intimately familiar with the groups, organizations, or persons being
studied — but the naturalistic stance demands such a familiarity.
Lacking this prior acquaintance, the sociologist is prone to develop
his own images and sterotypes. Too frequently these images bear
little relationship to what is being studied. Blumer cites studies on
intelligence as a case in point. Few social groups, he suggests, rank
their members by scores on an I.Q. test, yet many groups judge their
member's intelligence. The researcher must grasp these diverse
sources and points of evaluation; failing to do so opens him to the
fallacy of objectivism, to the belief that because his formulations are
theoretically or methodologically sound they must have relevance in
the empirical world. This may not be the case and in these situations
a reliance on the activities of exploration and inspection will be
useful, indeed necessary. Exploration involves a very free and relatively unstructured set of observational activities. The scientist will
admit any data that are ethically allowable and will employ any
methods, be they surveys, experiments, interviews, direct observation, or even introspection, that reveal aspects of the problem he is
studying. A critical attitude will characterize his activities in this
phase. He will be searching for negative cases which refute his

hypothesis, and he will be examining his problem from as many perspectives as possible. But most important, he will be assessing his knowledge of the events at hand. He must be constantly aware that his images and hypotheses may be irrelevant. Persons with insight into the situations he is studying will be sought, and often he will be led to forsake rules of scientific protocol concerning the representativeness of his samples – in order to discover data that provide him with new understanding. A notebook can and should be kept that is filled only with observations that refute his theory, or framework. In this way a constant interactive relationship is built up between himself and the empirical world. He progressively learns more and more about his problem, and the point where little new knowledge is forthcoming, the act of inspection begins.

This involves locating the major analytic concepts and elements relevant to the problem. It is complete once the scientist has discovered how those elements interrelate in an explanatory or theoretical scheme. Like a detective, the observer at this point is seeking to discover how and why something occured. To this end all points of view and all kinds of data are admitted into analysis. This phase is complete once an explanation that stands up under all data and all "negative cases" is forged. Unless such an explanation is developed, the scientific act is incomplete.

Both Blumer and Hill indicate how sociological researchers must learn to interact with the empirical world. The naturalistic or empirical position at the base of their statements may be taken as radical by many readers, for Hill and Blumer are developing a point of view that is currently out of favor among many methodologists. The reader must develop his own methodological stance, however, and this section concludes with suggested readings that present other points of view. It would of course be a mistake to assume that all the authors reprinted in this book share all of the views of Blumer and Hill, though their works, can easily be fitted within a perspective that calls for a new synthesis of theory, research, and methodology.

Suggested Readings. Paul F. Lazarsfeld and Morris Rosenberg's reader, *The Language of Social Research* (Glencoe, Ill.: Free Press, 1955), presents a view of theory and methodology that is heavily couched in the "variable language" approach to social research, and that focuses almost exclusively on the survey as a method. The reader should consult it because it details another major conception of the research act and of the organization of sociology. A recent continuation of this perspective, although one which covers other methods besides the survey, is Hubert and Ann Blalock's *Methodology in Social Research* (New York: McGraw-Hill, 1968). Consisting of original essays, this sourcebook stresses the quantitative and formal aspects of theory and method. A book that focuses strictly on the formal aspects of theory is Berger, Zelditch, and Anderson's *Sociological Theories in Progress* (Boston: Houghton Mifflin, 1966). It should be explicitly examined in the context of Part II of this volume. Gideon Sjoberg and Roger Nett's *A Methodology for Social Research* (New York: Harper and Row, 1968) presents a sociology of knowledge approach to theory and method. Its perspective largely complements the one contained in this volume. Irving Louis Horowitz' *Professing Sociology* (Chicago: Aldine Publishing Company, 1968) details in a highly critical fashion the current state of sociological practice. It is an important extension of the position stated by Hill and Blumer, and should be read in that light.

For an overview of sociological theories in general and of the various philosophical positions that underly each perspective, Don Martindale's *The Nature and Types of Sociological Theory* (Boston: Houghton Mifflin, 1960) is recommended. William J. Catton's *From Animistic to Naturalistic Sociology* (New York: McGraw-Hill, 1966) examines the logic and argument for a naturalistic perspective in sociology. Other positions are also reviewed by Catton, and his book provides a convenient and historical analysis of the naturalistic point of view. Scott Greer's *The Logic of Social Inquiry* (Chicago: Aldine Publishing Company, 1969) is an excellent analysis of sociology as seen from the inside. Greer discusses the nature of social theory, various conceptions of the empirical world, and the role of values and metaphors in sociological practice. He presents a convincing argument for intergrating the various components of the sociological act. Walter Wallace's *Sociological Theory* (Chicago: Aldine Publishing Company, 1969) gives probably the best analysis of the many theories now employed in sociology. It should be read in conjunction with Martindale's and Catton's books. Wallace's book also has the advantage of offering basic readings from diverse sociological theories.

1. On The Relevance of Methodology

RICHARD J. HILL

BORROWING a theme from the present generation of dissident students, I will argue that the "traditional" stance taken by sociologists regarding methodology has decreasing relevance for research activity in our discipline. I am convinced that the characteristic definitions of both "the methodologist" and "methodology" within many academic settings never were totally appropriate to the sociological enterprise. Further, given the current nature of the enterprise, these typical definitions of methodology rapidly are becoming anachronisms.

I take it that many, perhaps most, methodologists would agree with the distinction that has been made by Robert K. Merton between methodology and theory. Merton wrote as follows:

> At the outset we should distinguish clearly between sociological theory, which has for its subject matter certain aspects and results of the interaction of men and is therefore substantive, and methodology, or

the logic of scientific procedure. The problems of methodology transcend those found in any one discipline, dealing either with those common to groups of disciplines or, in more general form, with those common to all scientific inquiry. Methodology is not peculiarly bound up with sociological problems, and, though there is a plenitude of methodological discussions in books and journals of sociology, they are not thereby rendered sociological in character. Sociologists, in company with all others who essay scientific work, must be methodologically wise; they must be aware of the design of investigation, the nature of inference, the requirements of a theoretic system. But such knowledge does not contain or imply the particular *content* of sociological theory. There is, in short, a clear and decisive difference between *knowing how to test* a battery of hypotheses and *knowing the theory* from which to derive hypotheses to be tested.[1]

At an analytic and highly abstract level, there can be little disagreement with Merton's position. On the other hand, the distinction is totally artificial at the level of actual research. Further, I am convinced that the established predilection of methodologists to accept the distinction and view their speciality as something apart from substance has been dysfunctional for sociology and especially for the development of a methodology which has a high degree of utility to the investigation of crucial sociological problems.

At another point in the essay cited above, Merton describes a hiatus between theory and research.[2] Despite the score of years that has elapsed since the first edition of Merton's analyses, there continues to be less relationship between theory and research than most sociologists believe to be necessary to a respectable science.

If anything, the general condition of our discipline seems to be in a state of more serious disorder than that which Merton described. Not only has the separation between theory and research continued, but a new division is developing. As ridiculous as this may appear to some, there is a growing separation between research and methodology. Further, the emerging trichotomy that increasingly divides our discipline leads to other conditions which, if maintained, can only impede the rate of our development.

I wish to consider first certain consequences of this division for methodology and methodologists. Courses in methodology have proliferated in most major universities. Given the rapid growth of the

1. Robert K. Merton, *Social Theory and Social Structure*, revised and enlarged ed. (Glencoe, Ill.: Free Press, 1957), 86–87. Merton does blur the distinction slightly by a reference to the work of Pierre Duhem. (See footnote 2, p. 87.)

2. *Ibid.*, p. 85.

area since World War II, a strong justification for such proliferation can be forwarded. After all, when important, specialized and technical bodies of knowledge grow, the typical academic response is to expand the curriculum in those areas. This expansion, in my opinion, has not solved the problems of sociological methodology; on the contrary, it has widened the separation between the methodologist and his disciplinary colleagues. Consider but one example. In the current catalogue of one major university, the department of sociology lists a staff of 16 members. In that same catalogue, the same department of sociology also lists 12 courses in methodology, nine of which are at the graduate level. On the basis of my acquaintance with the department in question, I know that these courses are the responsibility of three men. If the courses are to be taught with any regularity, the departmental methodologists obviously can teach little but methodology. Further, under such conditions, a graduate student wishing to become a "methodologist" must take a very heavy concentration in his chosen area. Unless he has considerable stamina and an unusual ability to defer gratification, such a student will receive less exposure to the substantive problems of the discipline than will his "non-methodological" peer.[3]

The explosion of knowledge in what are now considered to be methodological areas also places unrealistic role requirements on those defined as methodologists. To be a general expert in the area, the methodologist now must have a working knowledge of dominance matrices, computer simulation, cononical correlations, discriminant analysis, game theory, non-metric spaces, multi-dimensional measurement, Markov chains, Bayesian probabilities, and so on, even forever. There is now some indication that these unrealistic expectations will bring about the demise of the "general methodologist." Younger scholars are focusing their attention on a more restricted set of interests. They are experts on Markov processes *or* computer simulation *or* multi-dimensional measurement models *or* some other speciality which is viewed by many of their colleagues as esoteric scientism having little relevance for the general substantive problems of sociology. Thus, the division widens. The non-methodologist sees little relevance in what the methodologist is about; the methodologist finds an ever decreasing number of men who can serve as his colleagues in an intellectually supporting fashion.

3. Young methodologists frequently are *over*-trained. For a discussion of the negative consequences of technical training, see C. Wright Mills, *The Sociological Imagination* (New York: Oxford University Press, 1959), esp. p. 211 ff.

I believe that the above description of the current state of affairs is essentially correct at least for a significant number of large departments. I also am convinced that this condition has contributed to still another disciplinary development. There now exist groups of scholars who "do sociology" but who reject the standard model of natural science and the traditional methods of investigation. Many of our disciplines' current heroes are those who write insightful treatises on obviously significant problems but who rely on their own professional judgment with respect to procedure and truth.

Consider but one recent example of this tendency to move away from standard methods. In their most provocative work on "grounded theory," Glaser and Strauss argue for the essential superiority of something called "theoretical sampling" over the sampling procedures that methodologists have worked so hard to master.[4] To many, it seems to make little difference that there are serious limitations in "theoretical sampling." It also makes little difference, apparently, that the considerations forwarded by Glaser and Strauss could be reformulated in a way that would permit the strategy of "theoretical sampling" to be combined with probability considerations. The pursuasive argument of Glaser and Strauss is taken as sufficient grounds to reject the relevance of more traditional sampling theory.[5]

If Glaser and Strauss were lonely voices in the wilderness, then perhaps they could be ignored. Such is not the case, and "standard methodology" is now fair game for a growing number of very articulate critics. Cicourel tells us that we really do not have the necessary knowledge to ask even basic questions in a way that permits the valid interpretation of the responses we obtain.[6] Sjoberg and Nett argue that all of methodology must be reviewed in a framework of the sociology of knowledge.[7] Rosenthal and Freidman even challenge the validity of our experimental efforts.[8] Such attacks on what I believe are considered to be standard methodological strategies are

---

4. Barney G. Glaser, and Anselm L. Strauss, *The Discovery of Grounded Theory* (Chicago: Aldine Publishing Company, 1967).

5. I do not wish to attribute a total rejection of statistical sampling theory to Professors Glaser and Strauss; however, some of their readers have used their work to defend such a rejection.

6. Aaron V. Cicourel, *Method and Measurement in Sociology* (New York: Free Press, 1964). See esp. chap. 4.

7. Gideon Sjobert and Roger Nett, *A Methodology for Social Research* (New York: Harper and Row, 1968).

8. Robert Rosenthal, *Experimenter Effects in Behavioral Research* (New York: Appleton-Century-Crofts, 1966), and Neil Freidman, *The Social Nature of Psychological Research* (New York: Basic Books, 1967).

increasing. This criticism is coming from a variety of sources, and it is having a growing influence on our total enterprise.

Criticism of methodological practice is not a new parlor game but a well-established form of professional recreation. Two types of response to such criticism continue to be typical of the devotee of standard methodological practice. We either ignore such nonsense, or if we notice it at all, we dismiss it with arrogant disdain. Thus, Sorokin's attack on the "psychosocial disciplines" and their methodology was labeled "rather demogogic than scholarly,"[9] and large portions of the ethnomethodological approach of Garfinkel were categorized as being either "trivial" or a "major disaster."[10]

Arrogance is no longer an appropriate response; in fact, it never was. Current methodological practice is not impeccable. Many of our measures are "reactive,"[11] and we ought to be cognizant of such contamination. Replication continues to be an unrewarded research activity, and we ought to be actively engaged in altering such an unscientific reward structure.[12] The standard survey is based on a design that has inherent weaknesses, and we ought to be more concerned with its basic limitations than with the technical details which are the subjects of most textbooks on research procedures.[13] The issues of tests of statistical significance, the power of analytic induction, the adequacy of simulation models, the development of reliable social indicators, and the robustness of statistical rituals are but examples of the problems which continue to require more convincing and definitive solutions. I suggest that the solutions to these and other problems will not be convincing if they are offered only in the context of abstract models. As methodologists, we must address these issues in the context of the substantive and theoretical prob-

9. Donald Horton, "Review of Peterim A. Sorokin, *Fads and Foibles in Modern Sociology and Related Sciences,*" *American Journal of Sociology,* vol. 62, no. 3, p. 338. For an interesting reintroduction of Sorokin's central theme, see Edgar F. Borgatta, "Prologue: The Current Status of Methodology in Sociology," in Edgar F. Borgatta, ed., *Sociological Methodology: 1969,* (San Francisco: Jossey-Bass, 1969).

10. James S. Coleman, "Review Symposium of Harold Garfinkel, *Studies in Ethnomethodology,*" *American Sociological Review,* vol. 33, no. 1, pp. 126–30.

11. See Eugene J. Webb, Donald T. Campbell, Richard D. Schwartz, and Lee Sechrest, *Unobtrusive Measures: Non-reactive Research in the Social Sciences* (Chicago: Rand McNally, 1966).

12. For a particularly cogent discussion of the function of replication, see Santo F. Camilleri, "Theory, Probability, and Induction in Social Research," *American Sociological Review,* vol. 27, no. 2, pp. 170-78.

13. For a lucid discussion of the limitations of the standard survey design, see Donald T. Campbell and Julian C. Stanley, "Experimental and Quasi-experimental Designs for Research and Teaching," in N. L. Gage, ed., *Handbook of Research on Teaching* (Chicago: Rand McNally, 1963).

lems that constitute the only justification for the existence of our methods. Our substantively oriented colleagues are impatient with solutions based on unbiased coins, urns full of marbles, perfect dice and the evaluation of the effect of fertilizers on corn production. Frankly, I am forced to admit that their impatience has at least a modicum of justification.

The above assessment has led me to the opinion that the definition of the role of the methodologist must undergo a radical alteration. Again borrowing from the rhetoric of the dissident, I make the very serious charge that the methodologist has a pronounced tendency to be "uninvolved" in the crucial work of our discipline. As a consequence, I suspect that many contemporary methodologists lack the necessary perspective to deal with the relevant. A man's work in methodology tends to be appraised in terms of its precision, its simple elegance, and its logical consistency. These are appropriate criteria for judging the work of a mathematician or a logician. They are not fully adequate to evaluate the efforts of a methodologist working within sociology. Within sociology, methodological developments ought to be judged in terms of their contribution to the solution of the theoretical and substantive problems of the discipline rather than in terms of their abstract elegance. If my position has merit, then it seems obvious that methodologists must become more directly engaged in work on those substantive and theoretical problems. The increased involvement of the methodologist seems to require two types of action: (1) a restructuring of the graduate curriculum, and (2) an effort to alter the professional image of the methodologist. Fortunately, these two courses of action are interrelated, and achieving one goal would facilitate the attainment of the other.

Methodological training ought to be more fully integrated with courses dealing with theoretical and substantive issues. I question the efficacy of highly-specialized, substantively-free, graduate level training in methods. At the level at which the researcher employs methodological strategies, the applicability of a method obviously is not substantively unrestricted. A course in laboratory methods is of limited relevance to the student of macrosociology, and such a student will find little about the nature of a Solomon Four-group Design which is directly pertinent to his concerns. Requiring such a student to take such a course is akin to the antiquated demand that all Ph.D.'s have a reading knowledge of German. There are methods that are of fundamental importance to the development of an understanding of macrosociological phenomena, but it makes no pedogogical sense to teach these procedures in isolation from the discussion of the phenomena themselves.

The complaint may be made that the integration of methods in the fashion I have just suggested would require a fundamental alteration in the graduate curriculum. In response to such a complaint, I would argue that such revision is long overdue. I have failed to notice any remarkable, recent improvement in the power, precision and methodological sophistication that characterizes our professional literature. Apparently the procedures that we find intriguing as methodological specialists are not having the desired impact on research. I suspect that the reason for this is not that methodologists are poor teachers of methods but that we cannot communicate the substantive relevance of the tools we so admire. Further, I suspect that we cannot demonstrate the relevance of our methods because we are not intimately acquainted with the substantive problems which intrigue our colleagues.

With respect to the relationship of the methodologist to his colleagues, I have suggested previously that I find a growing separation of interests. Part of the reason for this division is, I believe, a matter of professional expectations. One common dimension contained within the role definition of the department methodologist is the expectation that he will provide technical consultation. We are often approached by colleagues who are concerned with substantive problems which are of no compelling interest to us. On occasion, we are asked for advice about data-gathering techniques. If such advice is to be sound, we must first understand in detail the nature of the problem. In more instances than I like to admit, I have outlined what I saw as beautiful observational strategies to a colleague only to have him respond in something like the following words: "That is very interesting but I really would like to talk about my problems now." I take such remarks to be a polite way for a colleague to indicate that because of my failure to understand his problem, I could not bring my talents to bear upon the problem as he, in his own area of competence, defined that problem. It is totally unrealistic to expect the methodologist to be acquainted with the complexities and subtilities of the range of substantive problems that are now of professional interest. Any methodologist who acts the part of the complete expert is either a charlatan or a fool. We can know in detail only certain strategies, and we must learn where those strategies are applicable. Further, we must convince the profession that those strategies do make a difference in terms of the power, precision and generality of the *substantive* conclusions that result from research efforts.

A second element in the professional image of the methodologist is that he must act as a kind of magician. This element of the image is invoked by the colleague who arrives at our door with the intellectual equivalent of a bushel-basket of data. The question asked of us is some variant of the following: "What do you think I should do with these data?" If we were honest, our reply should be, "Have you thought about burning them?" All too often, we shy away from such frankness, and instead we try to create a scientifically respectable edifice out of a junk pile. We must convince our colleagues that methodological expertise should be introduced at the beginning of a research undertaking and not at mid-course. Again, we can only accomplish this by demonstrating that such early involvement has consequences that are substantively significant. Further, as methodologists, we ought to have the courage to shun involvement in activities directed to questions that are unrelated to our own substantive interests.

A final element in the professional image of the methodologist which I wish to consider very briefly is that of the methodologist as critic. It is my position that the methodologist is not professionally qualified to act as the guardian of the gates at scientific prestige. Methodological criticism that is not informed by an intimate knowledge of substantive considerations is likely to be as sterile as much of medieval philosophical debate. For example, suppose we criticize Lindesmith for failing to study a random sample of addicts.[14] What contribution have we made by demanding the impossible? In what way have we assisted Lindesmith in designing his next research project? Our criticism is as pertinent to the development of substantive understanding as is the question, "How many angels can dance on the point of a needle?"

Some of the members of the methodological fraternity now will have the feeling that I would advocate a termination of the role of "general methodologist." They are absolutely correct. I do not believe that such a role is viable under currect conditions. I look forward to the day when the category of "general methodologist" is a null class. Then, perhaps, we can turn our attention to ridding the discipline of another anachronism: the "general theorist."

14. Alfred R. Lindesmith, *Opiate Addiction* (Bloomington, Ind.: Principia Press, 1947).

2. Methodological Principles of Empirical Science

HERBERT BLUMER

I AM DEALING with symbolic interactionism not as a philosophical doctrine[1] but as a perspective in empirical social science – as an approach designed to yield verifiable knowledge of human group life and human conduct. Accordingly, its methodological principles have to meet the fundamental requirements of empirical science. What are these requirements? Current thought and discussion of methodology in the social and psychological sciences are marked by much misunderstanding and confusion on these matters. I find it advisable to sketch several basic principles.

From Herbert Blumer, *Symbolic Interactionism: Perspective and Method*, pp. 21–47. © 1969. Reprinted by permission of Prentice-Hall, Inc., Englewood Cliffs, New Jersey.

1. Symbolic interactionism provides the premises for a profound philosophy with a strong humanistic cast. In elevating the "self" to a position of paramount importance and in recognizing that its formation and realization occur through taking the roles of others with whom one is implicated in the joint activities of group life, symbolic interactionism provides the essentials for a provocative philosophical scheme that is peculiarly attuned to social experience. The outlines of this philosophy are sketched especially in the writings of George Herbert Mead and John Dewey.

I shall begin with the redundant assertion that an empirical science presupposes the existence of an empirical world. Such an empirical world exists as something available for observation, study, and analysis. It *stands over against* the scientific observer, with a character that has to be dug out and established through observation, study, and analysis. This empirical world must forever be the central point of concern. It is the point of departure and the point of return in the case of empirical science. It is the testing ground for any assertions made about the empirical world. "Reality" for empirical science exists only in the empirical world, can be sought only there, and can be verified only there.

The proper picture of empirical science, in my judgment, is that of a collective quest for answers to questions directed to the resistant character of the given empirical world under study. One has to respect the obdurate character of *that* empirical world—this is indeed the cardinal principle of empirical science. Empirical science pursues its quest by devising images of the empirical world under study and by testing these images through exacting scrutiny of the empirical world. This simple observation permits us to put the topic of methodology in proper focus. Methodology refers to, or covers, the principles that underlie and guide the full process of studying the obdurate character of the given empirical world. There are three highly important points implied by this conception of methodology: (1) methodology embraces the entire scientific quest and not merely some selected portion or aspect of that quest; (2) each part of the scientific quest, as well as the complete scientific act itself, has to fit the obdurate character of the empirical world under study; therefore, methods of study are subservient to that world and should be subject to test by it; and (3) the empirical world under study and not some model of scientific inquiry provides the ultimate and decisive answer to the test. I wish to elaborate each of these three points.

1. To my mind a recognition that methodology applies to and covers all parts of the scientific act should be self-evident. The point needs to be asserted only because of an astonishing disposition in current social science to identify methodology with some limited portion of the act of scientific inquiry, and further, to give that portion a gratuitous parochial cast. Today "methodology" in the social sciences is regarded with depressing frequency as synonymous with the study of advanced quantitative procedures, and a "methodologist" is one who is expertly versed in the knowledge and use of such procedures. He is generally viewed as someone who casts study in terms of quantifiable variables, who seeks to establish

relations between such variables by the use of sophisticated statistical and mathematical techniques, and who guides such study by elegant logical models conforming to special canons of "research design." Such conceptions are a travesty on methodology as the logical study of the principles underlying the conduct of scientific inquiry. The method of empirical science obviously embraces the full scope of the scientific act, including the starting premises as well as the full round of procedural steps contained in that act. All of these components are essential to scientific study and all of them need to be analyzed and respected in developing the principles of methodology. To understand this matter, let me identify the more important parts of scientific inquiry, parts that are indispensable to inquiry in empirical science.

(a) *The Possession and Use of a Prior Picture or Scheme of the Empirical World under Study.* As previously mentioned, this is an unavoidable prerequisite for any study of the empirical world. One can see the empirical world only through some scheme or image of it. The *entire act* of scientific study is oriented and shaped by the underlying picture of the empirical world that is used. This picture sets the selection and formulation of problems, the determination of what are data, the means to be used in getting data, the kinds of relations sought between data, and the forms in which propositions are cast. In view of this fundamental and pervasive effect wielded on the entire act of scientific inquiry by the initiating picture of the empirical world, it is ridiculous to ignore this picture. The underlying picture of the empirical world is always capable of identification in the form of a set of premises. These premises are constituted by the nature given either explicitly or implicitly to the key objects that comprise the picture. The unavoidable task of genuine methodological treatment is to identify and assess these premises.

(b) *The Asking of Questions of the Empirical World and the Conversion of the Questions into Problems.* This constitutes the beginning of the act of inquiry. It is obvious that the kind of questions asked and the kind of problems posed set and guide the subsequent lines of inquiry. Accordingly, it is highly important for the methodologist to examine carefully and appraise critically how problems are selected and formulated. Superficiality, humdrum conventionality, and slavish adherence to doctrine in the selection and setting of problems constitute a well-known bane in empirical science.

(c) *Determination of the Data to be Sought and the Means to be Employed in Getting the Data.* Obviously, the data are set by the problem — which indicates the importance of being sure of the satisfactory character of the problem. Even though set by the problem, the data need to be constantly examined to see if they require a revision or rejection of the problem. Beyond this, it is important to recognize that the means used to get the data depend on the nature of the data to be sought. A reverse relation of allowing the method used in securing data to determine the nature of the data vitiates genuine empirical inquiry. These few observations suggest the clear need for careful and critical consideration of how data are to be determined and collected.

(d) *Determination of Relations Between the Data.* Since the establishment of connections between the data yield the findings of the study, it is highly important to be aware of how such connections are reached. This is true whether one arrives at the connections through judicious reflection on what one conceives might be significant relations or whether one relies on a mechanical procedure such as factorial analysis or a scheme of computer correlation.

(e) *Interpretation of the Findings.* This terminal step carries the scientist beyond the confines of the problem he has studied, since in making interpretations he has to relate his findings to an outside body of theory or to a set of conceptions that transcend the study he has made. This important terminal step particularly merits methodological scrutiny in the case of social and psychological science. It is at this point, speaking metaphorically, that new cards may be slipped into the deck, conferring on the interpretation an unwarranted "scientific" status merely because the preceding steps of the study have been well done. The outside body of theory or set of conceptions used to frame the interpretation may be untested and may be false.

(f) *The Use of Concepts.* Throughout the act of scientific inquiry concepts play a central role. They are significant elements in the prior scheme that the scholar has of the empirical world; they are likely to be the terms in which his problem is cast; they are usually the categories for which data are sought and in which the data are grouped; they usually become the chief means for establishing relations between data; and they are usually the anchor points in interpretation of the findings. Because of such a decisive role in scientific inquiry, concepts need especially to be subject to methodological scrutiny.

Any treatment of methodology worthy of its name has to cover the above matters since they are clearly the essential parts of the act of empirical inquiry in science. They must be covered not in the sense of advancing a given scheme of the empirical world, outlining a set of problems in it, deciding on the data and how they are to be secured, prefiguring the lines of connection to be sought, sketching the framework to be employed in making interpretations, and identifying the concepts to be used. Instead, they must be covered in the sense of developing the principles to be observed in doing these things in such a way as to respect and come to grips with the obdurate character of the empirical world under study.

2. Recognizing that methodology embraces all of the important parts of the act of scientific inquiry, I wish now to state and stress a point of even greater importance for methodology. Every part of the act of scientific inquiry — and hence the full act itself — is subject to the test of the empirical world and has to be validated through such a test. Reality exists in the empirical world and not in the methods used to study that world; it is to be discovered in the examination of that world and not in the analysis or elaboration of the methods used to study that world. Methods are mere instruments designed to identify and analyze the obdurate character of the empirical world, and as such their value exists only in their suitability in enabling this task to be done. In this fundamental sense the procedures employed in each part of the act of scientific inquiry should and must be assessed in terms of whether they respect the nature of the empirical world under study — whether what they signify or imply to be the nature of the empirical world is actually the case. Thus the underlying scheme of the empirical world used in the act of scientific inquiry needs to be critically examined to see whether it is true; the problems set for study need to be critically studied to see whether they are genuine problems *in the empirical world;* the data chosen need to be inspected to see if in fact they have in the empirical world the character given to them in the study; similarly, the empirical world has to be examined, independently of the study, to see if the relations staked out between the data are found in their asserted form; the interpretations of the findings, particularly since they arise from sources outside the study, need to be given empirical testing; and the concepts used throughout the course of the study are in special need of scrutiny to see if they match in the empirical world what they purport to refer to. Nothing less than this is called for in methodological treatment.

Yet it is evident that such scrutiny and assessment of scientific inquiry are rare in what is advanced today as methodology in the social and psychological sciences. Premises, problems, data, relations, interpretations, and concepts are almost always accepted as given and so spared direct examination in terms of the empirical world. Instead, current methodology stresses other ways of trying to establish the empirical validity of the schemes, problems, data, relations, concepts, and interpretations. These other ways that are advocated and widely used are the following: (a) adhering to a scientific protocol, (b) engaging in replication of research studies, (c) relying on the testing of hypotheses, and (d) employing so-called operational procedures.

Undoubtedly, the chief means used in present-day social and psychological science to establish the empirical validity of one's approach is the testing of hypotheses. The reasoning here is simple. One starts with the construction of a scheme, theory, or model of the empirical world or area under study. The scheme, theory, or model represents the way in which one believes the empirical world to be structured and to operate. One then deduces from this scheme an assertion as to what one would expect to happen under such and such a set of empirical circumstances. This assertion is the hypothesis. One then arranges a study of a given empirical area that represents these circumstances. If the findings from such a study verify the hypothesis one assumes that the scheme, the model, or the theory from which the hypothesis has been drawn is empirically valid. Logically, this view rests on an "as if" notion; that is, one approaches the empirical world *as if* it had such and such a makeup, deduces narrow specific consequences as to what one would find if the empirical world had the makeup attributed to it, and then sees if in fact such consequences are to be found in the empirical world.

There is a measure of truth in this view—but only (a) if the hypothesis genuinely *epitomizes* the model or the theory from which it is deduced; and (b) if the testing of the hypothesis is followed by scrupulous search for negative empirical cases. All too frequently these conditions are not met in the social and psychological sciences. The hypothesis rarely embodies or reflects the theory or model so crucially that the theory or model rises or falls with the fate of the hypothesis being tested. Further, the testing of the hypothesis is distinctly inadequate if it is limited to the particular empirical situation that is circumscribed by the hypothesis; it is necessary to see whether it holds up in a series of other relevant empirical situations, varied as much as possible in their settings. Unless these two specified conditions are met, one is merely testing the hypothesis and not the model or theoretical scheme from which it is deduced.

The final type of procedure—the so-called operational procedure—is even less suitable for establishing the empirical validity of key anchor points in the act of scientific inquiry. "Operational procedure" rests on the idea that a theoretical assertion or a concept can be given both empirical reference and validation by developing a specific, regularized procedure for approaching the empirical world. The given procedure or operation may be the use of a test, a scale, a measuring instrument, or a standardized mode of inquiry. The procedure "operationalizes" the theoretical proposition or concept. If the given operation meets tests of reliability the operation is taken as a sound instrument for disengaging specific empirical data. In turn, these data are thought to be valid empirical referents of the concept or proposition that is operationalized. The use of intelligence tests is a classic example of operational procedure — the tests are reliable and standardized instruments; they yield clean-cut empirical data capable of replication; and the data (the intelligence quotients) can be justly regarded as constituting sound and valid empirical references of the concept of intelligence. Actually, a little careful reflection shows that operational procedure is not at all an empirical validation of what is being operationalized. The concept or proposition that is being operationalized, such as the concept of intelligence, refers to something that is regarded as present in the empirical world in diverse forms and diverse settings. Thus, as an example, intelligence is seen in empirical life as present in such varied things as the skillful military planning of an army general, the ingenious exploitation of a market situation by a business entrepreneur, effective methods of survival by a disadvantaged slum dweller, the clever meeting of the problems of his world by a peasant or a primitive tribesman, the cunning of low-grade delinquent-girl morons in a detention home, and the construction of telling verse by a poet. It should be immediately clear how ridiculous and unwarranted it is to believe that the operationalizing of intelligence through a given intelligence test yields a satisfactory picture of intelligence. To form an empirically satisfactory picture of intelligence, a picture that may be taken as having empirical validation, it is necessary to catch and study intelligence as it is in play in actual empirical life instead of relying on a specialized and usually arbitrary selection of one area of its presumed manifestation. This observation applies equally and fully to all instances of so-called operational procedures. If the concept or proposition that is being operationalized is taken to refer to something that is present in the empirical world, one cannot, as a true empirical scientist, escape the necessity of covering and studying representative forms of such empirical presense. To select (usually arbitrarily) some one form of empirical reference and to assume that the operationalized study of this one form catches the full empirical coverage of the concept or proposition is, of course, begging the question. It is this deficiency, a deficiency that runs so uniformly through operational procedure, that shows that operationalism falls far short of providing the empirical validation necessary to empirical science.

3. It is no wonder that the broad arena of research inquiry in the social and psychological sciences has the character of a grand display and clash of social philosophies. Instead of going to the empirical social world in the first and last instances, resort is made instead to a priori theoretical schemes, to sets of unverified concepts, and to canonized protocols of research procedure. These come to be the governing agents in dealing with the empirical social world, forcing research to serve their character and bending the empirical world to their premises. If this indictment seems unwarranted I merely call attention to the following: the array of conflicting schemes as to the nature and composition of human society and the conspicuous ease with which the adherents of each scheme "validate" the scheme through their own research; the astonishing fact that the over-whelming proportion of key concepts have not been pinned down in their empirical reference in the proper sense that one can go to instances in the empirical world and say safely that this is an in-stance of the concept and that is not an instance (try this out with such representative concepts as mores, alienation, value, integration, socialization, need-disposition, power, and cultural deprivation); the innumerable instances of scholars designing and pursuing elegant schemes of research into areas of social life with which they have little if any familiarity; and an endless parade of research studies that consist of no more than applying an already devised instrument, such as a scale or test, to a different setting of group life. Without wishing to be overly harsh, I believe one must recognize that the prevailing mode in the social and psychological sciences is to turn away from direct examination of the empirical social world and to give prefer-ence, instead, to theoretical schemes, to preconceived models, to arrays of vague concepts, to sophisticated techniques of research, and to an almost slavish adherence to what passes as the proper protocol of research inquiry. The fact that such theories, such models, such concepts, such techniques, and such a scientific protocol are brought to bear on the empirical world means little in itself. If the application were done systematically to test the empirical validity of the theory, the model, the concept, the technique, and the scientific protocol, all would be well. But this is not the order of the day. The prevailing disposition and practice is to allow the theory, the model, the con-

cept, the technique, and the scientific protocol to coerce the research and thus to bend the resulting analytical depictions of the empirical world to suit their form. In this sense, much current scientific inquiry in the social and psychological sciences is actually social philosophizing.

I repeat once more that what is needed is to gain empirical validation of the premises, the problems, the data, their lines of connection, the concepts, and the interpretations involved in the act of scientific inquiry. The road to such empirical validation does not lie in the manipulation of the method of inquiry; it lies in the examination of the empirical social world. It is not to be achieved by formulating and elaborating catchy theories, by devising ingenious models, by seeking to emulate the advanced procedures of the physical sciences, by adopting the newest mathematical and statistical schemes, by coining new concepts, by developing more precise quantitative techniques, or by insisting on adherence to the canons of research design. Such preoccupations, without prejudice to their merit in other respects, are just not headed in the direction that is called for here. What is needed is a return to the empirical social world.

I find it necessary to make clear what I mean by the exhortation to turn to a direct examination of the empirical social world.

Let me begin by identifying the empirical social world in the case of human beings. This world is the actual group life of human beings. It consists of what they experience and do, individually and collectively, as they engage in their respective forms of living; it covers the large complexes of interlaced activities that grow up as the actions of some spread out to affect the actions of others; and it embodies the large variety of relations between the participants. This empirical world is evidenced, to take a few examples, by what is happening in the life of a boy's gang, or among the top management of an industrial corporation, or in militant racial groups, or among the police confronted by such groups, or among the young people in a country, or among the Catholic clergy, or in the experience of individuals in their different walks of life. The empirical social world, in short, is the world of everyday experience, the top layers of which we see in our lives and recognize in the lives of others. The life of a human society, or of any segment of it, or of any organization in it, or of its participants consists of the action and experience of people as they meet the situations that arise in their respective worlds. The problems of the social and psychological sciences necessarily arise out of, and go back to, this body of on-going group life. This is true whether the problems refer to what is immediately taking place, as in the case of a student riot, or to the background causes of such a riot, or to the organization of institutions, or to the stratified relations of people, or to the ways in which people guide their lives, or to the personal organization of individuals formed through participation in group life. Ongoing group life, whether in the past or the present, whether in the case of this or that people, whether in one or another geographical area, is the empirical social world of the social and psychological sciences.

Several simple yet highly important observations need to be made with regard to the study of this world. The first is that almost by definition the research scholar does not have a firsthand acquaintance with the sphere of social life that he proposes to study. He is rarely a participant in that sphere and usually is not in close touch with the actions and the experiences of the people who are involved in that sphere. His position is almost always that of an outsider; as such he is markedly limited in simple knowledge of what takes place in the given sphere of life. This is no accusation against research scholars; it is a simple observation that applies to all human beings in their relation to an area of life that they do not know closely through personal association. The sociologist who proposes to study crime, or student unrest in Latin America, or political elites in Africa, and the psychologist who undertakes to study adolescent drug use, or aspirations among Negro school children, or social judgments among delinquents exemplify this almost inevitable absence of intimate acquaintance with the area of life under consideration. The initial position of the social scientist and the psychologist is practically always one of lack of familiarity with what is actually taking place in the sphere of life chosen for study.

This leads me to a second simple observation, namely, that despite this lack of firsthand acquaintance the research scholar will unwittingly form some kind of a picture of the area of life he proposes to study. He will bring into play the beliefs and images that he already has to fashion a more or less intelligible view of the area of life. In this respect he is like all human beings. Whether we be laymen or scholars, we necessarily view any unfamiliar area of group life through images we already possess. We may have no firsthand acquaintance with life among delinquent groups, or in labor unions, or in legislative committees, or among bank executives, or in a religious cult, yet given a few cues we readily form serviceable pictures of such life. This, as we all know, is the point at which stereotyped images enter and take control. All of us, as scholars, have our share of common stereotypes that we use to see a sphere of empirical social life that we do not know. In addition, the research scholar in the social sciences has another set of pre-established images that he uses. These images are constituted by his theories, by the beliefs current in his own professional circles, and by his ideas of how the empirical world must be set up to allow him to follow his research procedure. No careful observer can honestly deny that this is true. We see it clearly in the shaping of pictures of the empirical world to fit one's theories, in the organizing of such pictures in terms of the concepts and beliefs that enjoy current acceptance among one's set of colleagues, and in the molding of such pictures to fit the demands of scientific protocol. We must say in all honesty that the research scholar in the social sciences who undertakes to study a given sphere of social life that he does not know at first hand will fashion a picture of that sphere in terms of pre-established images.

There is no quarrel with this natural disposition and practice if the given research inquiry is guided by a conscientious and continuous effort to test and revise one's images, but this is not the prevailing motif in present-day social and psychological science. Theoretical positions are held tenaciously, the concepts and beliefs in one's field are gratuitously accepted as inherently true, and the canons of scientific procedure are sacrosanct. It is not surprising, consequently, that the images that stem from these sources control the inquiry and shape the picture of the sphere of life under study. In place of being tested and modified by firsthand acquaintance with the sphere of life they become a *substitute* for such acquaintance. Since this is a serious charge let me explain it.

To begin with, most research inquiry (certainly research inquiry modeled in terms of current methodology) is not designed to develop a close and reasonably full familiarity with the area of life under study. There is no demand on the research scholar to do a lot of free exploration in the area, getting close to the people involved in it, seeing it in a variety of situations they meet, noting their problems and observing how they handle them, being party to their conversations, and watching their life as it flows along. In place of such exploration and flexible pursuit of intimate contact with what is going on, reliance is put on starting with a theory or model, posing a problem in terms of the model, setting a hypothesis with regard to the problem, outlining a mode of inquiry to test that hypothesis, using standardized instruments to get precise data, and so forth. I merely wish to reassert here that current designs of "proper" research procedure do no encourage or provide for the development of firsthand acquaintance with the sphere of life under study.[2] Moreover, the scholar who lacks that firsthand familiarity is highly unlikely to recognize that he is missing anything. Not being aware of the knowledge that would come from firsthand acquaintance, he does not know that he is missing that knowledge. Since the sanctioned scheme of scientific inquiry is taken for granted as the correct means of treatment and analysis, he feels no need to be concerned with firsthand familiarity with that sphere of life. In this way, the established protocol of scientific inquiry becomes the unwitting substitute for a direct examination of the empirical social world. The questions that are asked, the problems that are set, the leads that are followed, the kinds of data that are sought, the relations that are envisioned, and the kinds of interpretations that are striven towards—all these stem from the scheme of research inquiry instead of from familiarity with the empirical area under study.

There can be no question that the substitution of which I write takes place. The logical question that arises is, "So what?" Why is it important or necessary to have a firsthand knowledge of the area of social life under study? One would quickly dismiss this as a silly question were it not implied so extensively and profoundly in the social and psychological research of our time.[3] So the question should be faced. The answer to it is simply that the empirical social world consists of ongoing group life and one has to get close to this life to know what is going on in it.

The metaphor that I like is that of lifting the veils that obscure or hide what is going on. The task of scientific study is to lift the veils that cover the area of group life that one proposes to study. The veils

2. See how far one gets in submitting proposals for exploratory studies to fund-granting agencies with their professional boards of consultants, or as doctoral dissertations in our advanced graduate departments of sociology and psychology! Witness the barrage of questions that arise: Where is your research design? What is your model? What is your guiding hypothesis? How are you operationalizing the hypothesis? What are your independent and dependent variables? What standard instruments are you going to use to get the data for your variables? What is your sample? What is your control group? And so on. Such questions presume in advance that the student has the firsthand knowledge that the exploratory study seeks to secure. Since he doesn't have it the protocolized research procedure becomes the substitute for getting it!

3. Kudos in our fields today is gained primarily by devising a striking theory, or elaborating a grand theoretical system, or proposing a catchy scheme of analysis, or constructing a logically neat or elegant model, or cultivating and developing advanced statistical and mathematical techniques, or executing studies that are gems of research design, or (to mention something I am not treating in this essay) engaging in brilliant speculative analysis of what is happening in some area of social life. To study through firsthand observation what is actually happening in a given area of social life is given a subsidiary or peripheral position—it is spoken of as "soft" science or journalism.

are not lifted by substituting, in whatever degree, preformed images for firsthand knowledge. The veils are lifted by getting close to the area and by digging deep into it through careful study. Schemes of methodology that do not encourage or allow this betray the cardinal principle of respecting the nature of one's empirical world.

How does one get close to the empirical social world and dig deeply into it? This is not a simple matter of just approaching a given area and looking at it. It is a tough job requiring a high order of careful and honest probing, creative yet disciplined imagination, resourcefulness and flexibility in study, pondering over what one is finding, and a constant readiness to test and recast one's views and images of the area. It is exemplified among the grand figures of the natural sciences by Charles Darwin. It is not "soft" study merely because it does not use quantitative procedure or follow a pre-mapped scientific protocol. That it is demanding in a genuinely rigorous sense can be seen in the analysis of its two fundamental parts. I term these parts respectively as "exploration" and "inspection." These two modes of inquiry clearly distinguish the direct naturalistic examination of the empirical social world from the mode of inquiry espoused by current methodology. I wish to sketch what is involved in exploration and inspection.

Exploration. Exploratory study of human group life is the means of achieving simultaneously two complementary and interknit objectives. On the one hand, it is the way by which a research scholar can form a close and comprehensive acquaintance with a sphere of social life that is unfamiliar and hence unknown to him. On the other hand, it is the means of developing and sharpening his inquiry so that his problem, his directions of inquiry, data, analytical relations, and interpretations arise out of, and remain grounded in, the empirical life under study. Exploration is by definition a flexible procedure in which the scholar shifts from one to another line of inquiry, adopts new points of observation as his study progresses, moves in new directions previously unthought of, and changes his recognition of what are relevant data as he acquires more information and better understanding. In these respects, exploratory study stands in contrast to the prescribed and circumscribed procedure demanded by current scientific protocol. The flexibility of exploratory procedure does not mean that there is no direction to the inquiry; it means that the focus is originally broad but becomes progressively sharpened as the inquiry proceeds. The purpose of exploratory investigation is to move toward a clearer understanding of how one's problem is to be posed, to learn what are the appropriate data, to develop ideas of what are significant lines of relation, and to evolve one's conceptual tools in the light of what one is learning about the area of life. In this respect it differs from the somewhat pretentious posture of the research scholar who under established scientific protocol is required in advance of his study to present a fixed and clearly structured problem, to know what kinds of data he is to collect, to have and hold to a prearranged set of techniques, and to shape his findings by previously established categories.

Because of its flexible nature, exploratory inquiry is not pinned down to any particular set of techniques. Its guiding maxim is to use any ethically allowable procedure that offers a likely possibility of getting a clearer picture of what is going on in the area of social life. Thus, it may involve direct observation, interviewing or people, listening to their conversations, securing life-history accounts, using letters and diaries, consulting public records, arranging for group discussions, and making counts of an item if this appears worthwhile. There is no protocol to be followed in the use of any one of these procedures; the procedure should be adapted to its circumstances and guided by judgment of its propriety and fruitfulness. Yet a few special points should be borne in mind in such exploratory research. One should sedulously seek participants in the sphere of life who are acute observers and who are well informed. One such person is worth a hundred others who are merely unobservant participants. A small number of such individuals, brought together as a discussion and resource group, is more valuable many times over than any representative sample. Such a group, discussing collectively their sphere of life and probing into it as they meet one another's disagreements, will do more to lift the veils covering the sphere of life than any other device that I know of.

It is particularly important in exploratory research for the scholar to be constantly alert to the need of testing and revising his images, beliefs, and conceptions of the area of life he is studying. Part of such testing and revision will come from direct observation and from what informants tell him, but since his task extends to a probing into areas beneath those known to his informants, he should cultivate assiduously a readiness to view his area of study in new ways. Darwin, who is acknowledged as one of the world's greatest naturalistic observers on record, has noted the ease with which observation becomes and remains imprisoned by images. He recommends two ways of helping to break such captivity. One is to ask oneself all kinds of questions about what he is studying, even seemingly ludicrous questions. The posing of such questions helps to sensitize

the observer to different and new perspectives. The other recommended procedure is to record all observations that challenge one's
working conceptions as well as any observation that is odd and
interesting even though its relevance is not immediately clear; Darwin has indicated from his personal experience how readily such
observations disappear from memory and that, when retained and
subjected to reflection, they usually are the pivots for a fruitful
redirection of one's perspective.

The aim of exploratory research is to develop and fill out as comprehensive and accurate a picture of the area of study as conditions
allow. The picture should enable the scholar to feel at home in the
area, to talk from a basis of fact and not from speculation. The picture
provides the scholar with a secure bearing so that he knows that the
questions he asks of the empirical area are meaningful and relevant
to it, that the problem he poses is not artificial, that the kinds of data
he seeks are significant in terms of the empirical world, and that the
leads he follows are faithful to its nature. Considering the crucial
need and value of exploratory research in the case of the social and
psychological sciences, it is an odd commentary of these sciences
that their current methodological preoccupations are practically mute
on this type of research.

It should be pointed out that the mere descriptive information
unearthed through exploratory research may serve, in itself, to provide the answers to theoretical questions that the scholar may have
in mind with regard to what he is studying. All too frequently, the
scholar confronted with an unfamiliar area of social life will fabricate, in advance, analytical schemes that he believes necessary to
account for the problematic features of the area. One of the interesting values of exploratory study is that the fuller descriptive account that it yields will frequently give an adequate explanation of
what was problematic without the need of invoking any theory or
proposing any analytical scheme. However, the picture of the sphere
of social life that is formed through effective exploration does not
terminate what is required by careful direct examination of the empirical social world. Such direct examination sets the need for another procedure that I find it convenient to label "inspection."

Inspection. The direct examination of the empirical social world is
not limited to the construction of comprehensive and intimate accounts of what takes place. It should also embody analysis. The
research scholar who engages in direct examination should aim at
casting his problem in a theoretical form, at unearthing generic
relations, at sharpening the connotative reference of his concepts,

and at formulating theoretical propositions. Such analysis is the proper aim of empirical science, as distinguished from the preparation of mere descriptive accounts. How is scientific analysis to be undertaken in the *direct* examination of the empirical social world, especially in the case of the account of that world yielded by exploration? The common answer is to apply to that account the scheme of scientific analysis espoused in current methodology. This scheme has the following form: Start with a theory or model that is framed in terms of relations between concepts or categories; use the theory to set up a specific problem in the area under study; convert the problem into specific kinds of independent and dependent variables that represent concepts or categories; employ precise techniques to get the data; discover the relations between the variables; and use the theory and model to explain these relations. To apply this conventional scheme to the account yielded by exploration would certainly be a gain over what is usually done, in that one would be working with data derived from what is actually happening rather than from what one imagines to be happening. Yet, in my judgment, this conventional protocol of scientific analysis is not suitable or satisfactory for the kind of analysis that is needed in direct examination of the empirical social world. Even though using the more realistic data yielded by exploration, the conventional protocol of scientific analysis still forces such data into an artificial framework that seriously limits and impairs genuine empirical analysis. Scientific analysis requires two things: clear, discriminating analytical elements and the isolation of relations between these elements. The conventional protocol does not pin down in an exact way the nature of the analytical elements in the empirical social world nor does it ferret out in an exacting manner the relation between these analytical elements. A different analytical procedure is necessary. I think that "inspection" constitutes this necessary procedure.

By "inspection" I mean an intensive focused examination of the empirical content of whatever analytical elements are used for purposes of analysis, and this same kind of examination of the empirical nature of the relations between such elements. Let me explain this abstract statement. By analytical elements I have in mind whatever general or categorical items are employed as the key items in the analysis, such as integration, social mobility, assimilation, charismatic leadership, bureaucratic relation, authority system, suppression of dissent, morale, relative deprivation, attitudes, and institutional commitment. As the examples suggest, such analytical elements may refer to processes, organization, relations, networks of relations, states of being, elements of personal organization, and happenings. These analytical elements may be cast in differing degrees of generality, ranging from something very broad such as integration to something more restricted such as mobility aspiration in the case of urban Negro adolescents. The procedure of inspection is to subject such analytical elements to meticulous examination by careful flexible scrutiny of the empirical instances covered by the analytical element. The empirical instances are those that appear in the area under study; their careful flexible scrutiny is done in the context of the empirical area in which they take place. Thus in the case of an analytical element such as assimilation, referring let us say to the assimilation of girls into organized prostitution, the empirical instances would consist, of course, of the separate careers of girls undergoing the assimilation. The careful scrutiny of such instances with an eye to disengaging the generic nature of such assimilation represents what I have in mind by "inspection."

As a procedure, inspection consists of examining the given analytical element by approaching it in a variety of different ways, viewing it from different angles, asking many different questions of it, and returning to its scrutiny from the standpoint of such questions. The prototype of inspection is represented by our handling of a strange physical object; we may pick it up, look at it closely, turn it over as we view it, look at it from this or that angle, raise questions as to what it might be, go back and handle it again in the light of our questions, try it out, and test it in one way or another. This close shifting scrutiny is the essence of inspection. Such inspection is not preset, routinized, or prescribed; it only becomes such when we already know what it is and thus can resort to a specific test, as in the case of a technician. Instead, inspection is flexible, imaginative, creative, and free to take new directions. This type of examination can be done also in the case of a social object, or a process, or a relationship, or any one of the elements used in the theoretical analysis of a given area or aspect of empirical social life. One goes to the empirical instances of the analytical element, views them in their different concrete settings, looks at them from different positions, asks questions of them with regard to their generic character, goes back and re-examines them, compares them with one another, and in this manner sifts out the nature of the analytical element that the empirical instances represent. This pinning down of the nature of the analytical element is done through scrutiny of the empirical life itself, by discovering what that empirical life yields when subjected to such a careful, flexible probing. I know of no other way to determine the nature of an analytical element that one proposes to use in the analysis of a given empirical area of social life and still be sure that the analytical element is both germane and valid for such use.

It should be clear that inspection as a mode of inquiry is the antithesis of scientific inquiry as outlined in current methodology in the social and psychological sciences. Inspection is not tied down to a fixed mode of approach and procedure; it does not start with analytical elements whose nature has been set in advance and never tested or revised in the course of their use; and it develops the nature of the analytical elements through the examination of the empirical world itself. Inspection is the opposite of giving a "nature" to the analytical element by operationalizing the element (for example, defining intelligence in terms of the intelligence quotient). It seeks, instead, to identify the nature of the analytical element by an intense scrutiny of its instances in the empirical world. Because of the failure to employ the procedure of inspection, the use of analytical elements in current social science research is somewhat scandalous. Nowhere is this more evident than in the state of our concepts, which in the last analysis are our analytical elements. The preponderant majority of our concepts are conspicuously vague and imprecise in their empirical connotation,[4] yet we use them right and left in our analyses, without concern about elaborating, refining, or testing their empirical connotation. The needed improvement of their empirical meaning is not accomplished in any degree whatsoever by "operationalizing" the concepts. It can be done only by the careful inspection of their empirical instances, in the course of which one disengages and refines their character.

Inspection is also the appropriate procedure for carrying out the other part of social analysis — the isolation of relations between analytical elements. Such a relation presumes the existence of a meaningful connection between the components *in the empirical world.* As something so presumed, the relation stands in need of scrutiny in that world, just as much as is true of assertions about the empirical connotation of analytical elements. The asserted relation needs to be pinned down and tested by careful, flexible scrutiny of its empirical

4. In order that this charge not be left hanging in the air, the reader is invited to try to pin down the empirical meaning of the following representative array of commonly used social science concepts: mores, integration, social role, alienation, socialization, attitude, value, anomie, and deviance. Empirical meaning is not given by a definition that merely serves the purpose of discourse; it exists instead in a specification that allows one to go to the empirical world and to say securely in the case of any empirical thing that this is an instance of the concept and that is not. Let the reader try his hand at doing this with the above concepts in observing what happens around him.

instances. Without this inspection one is captive to one's prior image or conception of the relation, without the benefit of knowing whether that conception is empirically valid and without the means of refining and improving the conception through a meticulous examination of empirical instances.

Exploration and inspection, representing respectively depiction and analysis, constitute the necessary procedure in direct examination of the empirical social world. They comprise what is sometimes spoken of as "naturalistic" investigation — investigation that is directed to a given empirical world in its natural, ongoing character instead of to a simulation of such a world, or to an abstraction from it (as in the case of laboratory experimentation), or to a substitute for the world in the form of a preset image of it. The merit of naturalistic study is that it respects and stays close to the empirical domain. This respect and closeness is particularly important in the social sciences because of the formation of different worlds and spheres of life by human beings in their group existence. Such worlds both represent and shape the social life of people, their activities, their relations, and their institutions. Such a world or sphere of life is almost always remote and unknown to the research scholar; this is a major reason why he wants to study it. To come to know it he should get close to it in its actual empirical character. Without doing this he has no assurance that his guiding imagery of the sphere or world, or the problem he sets forth for it, or the leads he lays down, or the data he selects, or the kinds of relations that he prefigures between them, or the theoretical views that guide his interpretations are empirically valid. Naturalistic inquiry, embracing the dual procedures of exploration and inspection, is clearly necessary in the scientific study of human group life. It qualifies as being "scientific" in the best meaning of that term.

My presentation has set forth rather sharply the opposition between naturalistic inquiry, in the form of exploration and inspection, and the formalized type of inquiry so vigorously espoused in current methodology. This opposition needs to be stressed in the hope of releasing social scientists from unwitting captivity to a format of inquiry that is taken for granted as the naturally proper way in which to conduct scientific study. The spokesmen for naturalistic inquiry in the social and psychological sciences today are indeed very few despite the fact that many noteworthy studies in the social sciences are products of naturalistic study. The consideration of naturalistic inquiry scarcely enters into the content of present-day methodology. Further, as far as I can observe, training in naturalistic inquiry is soft-pedaled or not given at all in our major graduate departments. There is a widespread ignorance of it and an accompanying blindness to its necessity. This is unfortunate for the social and psychological sciences since, as empirical sciences, their mission is to come to grips with their empirical world.

PART TWO

The Nature of Social Theory

INTRODUCTION

IT MAY be argued that all phases of the research act exist for only one reason: the creation of social theory. It is in social theory that the major goals of the sociologist are achieved. Here descriptions, explanations and predictions of the empirical world are developed. Theory, then, sets the foundations for the research act.

THEORY DEFINED

It is necessary for the researcher to have a sound understanding of what social theory is. Additionally, he must grasp how theory is to be interwoven with all other phases of research. George Caspar Homans' article offers a definition of theory that stems from the classical sciences. Theory for Homans represents a deductive system of propositions that are interrelated in a way that permits some to be derived from others. When such a system exists the theorist can claim to have explained the phenomena at hand. Theory is nothing,

Homans says, if it is not explanation. Accordingly, Homans breaks a theoretical system into its constituent elements. Concepts, variables and prositions are all defined. A major thesis of Homans' article is the need for sociologists to develop propositions that express interactive relationships between social events. He suggests that propositions that only explain how one or more events directly influence the other are insufficient. Interaction is the fact of social life. Consequently, researchers must learn how to build schemes that explain the continual interplay of several events with one another. For example, situations open to such explanations would include how a person gauges his actions in terms of another's responses to him; the response of one person calls forth a new response from the original initiator of action — neither person is the total cause of the other's conduct, each shapes and produces his and the other's response. In such explanatory schemes the traditional distinction between independent and dependent variables becomes meaningless. At one point in time one variable is a cause and at another it is an effect. (The nature of interactive propositions is further elaborated in the readings in Part VI, where different models of analysis are reviewed.) It is important to note that this conception of the explanatory process closely fits the naturalistic perspective, which calls for theories relevant to the happenings of the empirical world. Homans clearly states the steps for implementing this type of methodology, and he offers a basic rule for theory development. Concrete, empirical data must always furnish the foundations of theory. When all else fails, the theorist returns to the empirical world.

INDUCTION, SAMPLING, AND THEORY VERIFICATION

In a tightly woven paper requiring several readings, Camilleri offers a conceptualization of theory testing that touches on the problems of how theories are ordered, how samples are drawn, the relevance of significance tests, and the sources of error that arise during the observational process. In several senses his paper defies classification, for it reviews issues taken up in subsequent parts of this book on sampling and analysis. The reader should be aware that Camilleri's position on theory expands Homans' statements, but it also anticipates the views of Glaser and Strauss on sampling, Campbell on errors in experimental design, and Turner on analytic induction and probabilistic models of proof. Because of its heavy emphasis on theory it deserves special attention.

Camilleri assumes that the scientist has two main functions: to create and to provide empirical support for his own theories. This assumption supports Blumer, Homans, and Glaser and Strauss's position that every theorist is responsible for grounding his own formulations. It should be clear that this stance closely weds theory, research, and substantive interest. Camilleri suggests that a theory has a formal aspect; that is, that it consists of a deductively constructed set of propositions that can be tested by the rules of logic. This test could be applied to Durkheim's theory of suicide presented by Homans. The analyst need only ask if illogical deductions were made within Durkheim's propositional system. If they were, the theory is not formally valid. Theories have an empirical aspect as well, and in this sense they must be closely linked to concrete observations. If a theory does not permit empirical observations it fails as a theory.

Camilleri notes that theories may be of two general types: deterministic or probabilistic. A deterministic theory, often grounded through the use of analytic induction, claims to have explained all the cases analyzed. A deterministic statement is of the sort that the addition of a third person to a dyadic relationship always produces a splintering of relationships such that an isolate will invariably be created. A probabilistic statement applies to a proportion of the events that will be explained within any theory. Thus it might be predicted that in 95 out of 100 relationships the introduction of a third party will produce an isolate. Many theories contain probability statements, and Camilleri suggests that the term "intrinsic probability" be applied to the ordering of such formulations.

These considerations lead Camilleri to consider the function of sampling in the testing of theories. The researcher employs a sampling model when he is working within a probabilistic theory. Deterministic theories do not need probabilistic sampling models because the theorist can assume that all of his cases will be explained. This is a point that gives rise to arguments among sampling theorists (although Glaser and Strauss in Part III sanction such a position), but it is justified, Camilleri suggests, because all sampling must be theoretically directed. If it is not, generalizations to one's theory are hindered because the observed units may bear little relationship to that theory.

My own view favors the use of probabilistic sampling models, regardless of the type of theory being tested. Future researchers must know the procedures used when one selected his observational units, and a probabilistic sampling model insures that those units will have some degree of representativeness in the broader population. In this way the researcher begins to answer the problem

Campbell raises in his paper in Part VI, namely, the resolution of external validity. This question asks to what populations one may generalize his observations. It also asks whether unique features of those sampled may not be producing the results observed.

Too frequently investigators employ what Camilleri calls "convenience samples," in which the concern is less with how representative the sample is, more with obtaining the largest sample possible, an unsatisfactory strategy for two reasons. First, unless such samples are huge, they will not permit enough observations along the variables being examined. Second, they are not likely to be representative of any particular sample, and consequently, generalizations to other groups, communities, or settings will be severely restricted. The theory's test is situation-specific, and statements beyond that test cannot be made with any confidence.

As an alternative, Camilleri offers the technique of judgment sampling. This closely parallels Glaser and Strauss's concept of theoretical sampling and involves the deliberate search for groups and situations which will permit the maximum test of one's theory.

Camilleri next considers the functions of probability sampling models when the researcher randomly assigns subjects to observational groups. He offers a review of the logic of experimental design, but argues that unless subjects are sampled with a probabilistic model, the method of randomization is of little value because the researcher still lacks any confidence concerning his sample's representativeness.

Turning next to the verification of theories, Camilleri notes that every theory should direct its own empirical test. A problem may arise however, when observations are gathered. The act of making an observation can produce the differences observed. (This parallels Campbell's concern for internal validity which is detailed in Part VI.)

When the researcher undertakes to test statistical hypotheses, he must confront the fact that formal or logical tests, which are appropriate for deterministic propositions, are of limited use. Now he must demonstrate within certain confidence intervals that his proposition has been confirmed or disconfirmed, which raises the problem of how one determines what that level of confidence will be. At this point the statistical test of significance enters the picture, for it supposedly offers the investigator a rule for judging when a hypothesis has been adequately tested. But there are two problems with such tests. First, the choice of the level of significance is typically made in an arbitrary fashion, although there are certain canons or standards commonly accepted—typically, .05. Most important, the test of significance is only another construct that intervenes between the theory-building and the theory-testing process. It must not be taken as so sacred that it becomes an end in itself. The aim of any verification process is to subject a theory to as many relevant and critical tests as possible, and the test of significance is only a guide in this process.

As an alternative to the test of significance, Camillari offers the criterion of systematic import. This forces the theorist to ask what effect any specific empirical test is going to have upon his total theory. Rather than assuming, as the test of significance procedure does, that a series of investigators are going to replicate and retest one's hypotheses, Camilleri's position demands that every theorist have a well worked out deductive system before he begins testing specific hypotheses. In Camillari's scheme, the process of testing a hypothesis is not an infinitely repeated act. The purpose of testing any given hypothesis is to gather data relevant for an entire theory. All data must be conceptually relevant, or have systematic import.

An important feature of Camilleri's position is that the investigator must have a firm grasp of his total theoretical system when he begins the process of hypothesis testing. This is the deductive view of theory and research and it runs somewhat counter to the more open and interactive relationship between theory and research stressed by Blumer, and by Glaser and Strauss. Yet it keeps the sociologist ever mindful of theory, and this, in my judgment, is its chief contribution. Camilleri recognizes this point when he notes that astonishingly little is known about the process of theory development. He also notes that no theory ever springs forth in an elegantly developed deductive and logical fashion. His is a system, then, that offers a series of very specific rules and procedures for the research act. Theory must dictate the sampling and analysis phases of this act, but more to the point, every scientist is accountable for developing and testing his own theories. The division between theorists and researchers is again seen as indefensible.

THE THEORETICAL CONCEPT

In his paper "What Is Wrong with Social Theory?" Herbert Blumer focuses on what he regards as the major deficiency of modern social theory. The aim of theory, according to Blumer, is the construction of valid schemes of explanation relevant to natural happenings in the empirical world. This is the essence of the naturalistic perspective discussed in Part I. Blumer charges current social theorists with three basic errors. Their theories have become divorced from the empirical world; they have rested heavily on the importation of images, models, and metaphors from other sciences; they are incapable of utilizing available empirical observations. That many current theories borrow models from other disciplines is evident in the emphasis given such concepts as cybernetic systems, organic unity, equilibrium, drive, and need. The naturalistic perspective demands the use of models and images that come from the empirical world dictated by one's science.

Theory has become an end in and of itself. Theory feeds on theory, not on empirical fact. This buttresses Hill's position that the discipline needs to dispense with the term "general theorist." Several methods have been introduced to improve theory, but each is unacceptable from Blumer's perspective. They include the construction of new definitions for old concepts; engaging in endless logical analysis of others' theories; developing refined measuring instruments to examine concepts which remain ill-defined; and gathering mountains of empirical data which still resist theoretical synthesis.

The heart of the difficulty, Blumer suggests, lies in the current status and use of the sociological concept. A concept must meet three simple rules: (1) it must clearly point to a class of objects; (2) it must permit distinctions between that class and other classes; and (3) it must direct empirical activity. When these rules are met the concept serves three important functions: (1) it opens areas of empirical inquiry; (2) it directs concrete observations through the use of different research methods; and (3) it opens the door for theoretical development. By permitting data to be gathered, data that are conceptually relevant, hypotheses can be put to test.

Many theorists and researchers, sensing dissatisfaction with their concepts, have taken the line of the operational definition and the definitive concept, but in Blumer's judgment the operational or definitive strategy sidesteps the more basic question of how one is to work with concepts that are necessarily vague and elusive. He notes that the basic concepts of sociology (as expressed in terms such as "role," "value," "norm," "system," "assimilation," defy rigorous definitions and observations.

The sociologist is forced to ask why this is the case. For Blumer, the natural world of empirical events presents itself to the researcher in distinct forms. With forms that are distinct and different because the situation of occurence produces such differences, the sociologist is led to adopt a sensitizing approach in the use of his concepts. He must accept the distinct features of his concepts while he grapples to uncover what they have in common across diverse situations. A sensitizing concept does not direct immediate empirical activity, but it suggests leads, opens avenues for observation, and offers strategies for analysis. Initially, however, it stands elusive. Its empirical qualities only come forth within the research act—not before, as is so often the case with the definitive or operational definition. Obviously a sensitizing strategy must lead to concrete empirical observations. This was the thrust of Blumer's discussion of exploration and inspection in Part I: to show how the researcher committed to the sensitizing approach engages in empirical observations. This method demands an intimate familiarity with the empirical world. It dictates a sensitive awareness of negative cases. It forces the judicious collection of illustrative instances that reflect one's concepts. The reader will find illustrations of this method in the articles by Glaser and Strauss in Part III and by Becker in Part XI. The researcher is led to search for as many instances of his concepts as possible; he employs any and all methods relevant to such analysis—but he is ever mindful that his empirical activity is conceptually and theoretically directed.

The sensitizing approach has the great virtue of overcoming the major flaw of our current theories. By grasping the empirical world in terms of all its peculiarities, the researcher is forced to wed his observations to his theories.

PROBLEMS OF ABSENT THEORY

The researcher must realize that many times he will enter the field with little or no theory, and that on other occasions he will find himself conducting research in an area characterized by a great deal of theoretical contradiction. What is he to do? Obviously if theory is lacking, research is likely to go undirected. Too often one of three strategies is followed. Rigid, or what C. Wright Mills termed "abstracted" empiricism occurs; the researcher simply forgets theory and gathers data. Or perhaps he selects what propositions he can find and works with them. Or perhaps creates his own propositions.

Each of these strategies has its weaknesses: rigid empiricism serves no function if theory is absent; the selection of what propositions one can find has the potential of ignoring other more relevant formulations; and developing a new set of propositions is fine only as far as it goes, but too many researchers develop such propositions

after the data are collected, and limited after-the-fact theories prolife-
rate while the area of inquiry remains largely unconceptualized.

In an article not included in this book, "Toward Closer Relations
Between Theory and Research: A Procedure and an Example,"
American Sociological Review 22 (April 1957), 149-54, Frank R.
Westie has presented a five-step proposal that speaks to the problems
enumerated above. Westie proposes that the researcher first review
the literature relevant to his speciality and list all the possible propositions he can formulate. For each proposition he then lists all the
possible interpretations each would suggest. The actual research is
then conducted to determine which of the above propositions can be
identified and supported. Those that fail the empirical test are
thrown out, as are their interpretations. Through additional empirical
inquiry, the best, or most firmly grounded explanations are constructed and refined. The end product gives the researcher, and all future
investigators, a set of interpreted findings that are expressed propo-
sitionally.

In several senses Westie details what all researchers should be
doing — that is, simultaneously searching for and developing theory
relevant to one's empirical activity. His method offers a way of
moving from crude observations to more refined, deductive theory,
and this is the goal Camilleri sets forth.

In brief, the readings of Part II set the stage for all phases of the
research act. They show how theory is developed, how it is tested,
and how it often goes astray. Readings in subsequent sections build
upon these formulations by detailing the actual movements required
when the researcher moves from theory to the empirical world.

Suggested Readings. Robert K. Merton's classic formulations on
middle-range theory are presented in his *On Theoretical Sociology*
(New York: Free Press, 1967). Merton's essays also offer reviews of
Talcott Parsons' position on grand theory. A biting attack on the
Parsons' position is contained in C. Wright Mills' *The Sociological
Imagination* (New York: Oxford University Press, 1959). Barney Glaser and Anselm Strauss's *The Discovery of Grounded Theory* (Chicago: Aldine Publishing Company, 1967) offers a review of the veri-
ficational approach to theory given in Hans Zetterberg's *On Theory
and Verification in Sociology* (Totawa, N.J.: Bedminister Press,
1965). Glaser and Strauss's work spells out in detail the full implications of a naturalistic approach to theory development. The reader
will find in these works additional references to other statements on
theory.

3. Contemporary Theory in Sociology

GEORGE CASPAR HOMANS

CONTEMPORARY sociologists have been preoccupied with "theory," yet have seldom tried to make clear what a theory *is*. My first task, therefore, will be to describe the essential features of a theory. I shall then consider the intellectual confusions and practical difficulties that get in the way of the construction of theories in sociology. Next, I shall examine the differences between the main types of sociological theory. Since there are few areas of sociological investigation that have not claimed to be theoretical, I shall confine myself to the theories that pretend to be "general," especially structural, functional, and psychological theories. I shall end with a few remarks about the relations between theory and research.

WHAT IS A THEORY?

We sociologists show our confusion about the nature of theory both

Reprinted by permission from George Caspar Homans, "Contemporary Theory in Sociology," in R. E. L. Farris, ed., *Handbook of Modern Sociology*, pp. 951–959, 973–977. Copyright © 1964 by Rand McNally & Company.

by what we say about theory in general and by the kinds of theories we actually produce. In what follows I shall not simply accept as theory what various sociologists have called by that name, but assess the degree to which different theories meet the requirements of a classical definition. This is the definition that identifies a theory of a phenomenon with an explanation of it by means of a deductive system. See especially Braithwaite (1953) and Nagel (1961).

I cannot go further without putting an example of a theory before us, so let me take a famous one. It is Durkheim's (1951, pp. 152–170) theory of the low suicide rate in Spain:

1. In any social grouping, the suicide rate varies directly with the degree of individualism (egoism).

2. The degree of individualism varies with the incidence of Protestantism.

3. Therefore, the suicide rate varies with the incidence of Protestantism.

4. The incidence of Protestantism in Spain is low.

5. Therefore, the suicide rate in Spain is low.

I do not ask of this example, or of others I shall use, whether it is a true theory and whether its logic is absolutely watertight, but only what its general characteristics as a theory are. It consists, first, of a set of concepts or *conceptual scheme*. Some of the terms in the scheme I call *descriptive* concepts, serving to show what the theory is about: "individualism," "suicide," "Protestantism." Others I call *operative* concepts or properties of nature: "suicide *rate*," "*incidence* of Protestantism." These latter properties are variables, and the variables may be probabilities. In some cases, as in the example, the variables are treated as continuous; in others, the variables take only two values, in the sense that the property in question is either present or absent. A conceptual scheme alone is insufficient to constitute a theory.

A theory consists, second, of a set of *propositions*, each stating a relationship, such as "varies directly with," between at least two of the properties, and the propositions form a *deductive system*. That is, each proposition may be represented symbolically by signs like x, y, and $=$. The set of propositions forms a calculus, and according to the rules for the manipulation of the calculus, which are here taken to be those of simple logic, proposition 3 is said to be derived or deduced from propositions 1 and 2 and proposition 5 in turn from 3 and 4. When propositions are so derived they are said to be explained. A theory is nothing if it is not an explanation.

A deductive system also provides grounds for prediction. If, for instance, one did not know what the suicide rate in Eire was, but did know that the incidence of Protestantism was low, this proposition, together with proposition 3, would allow one to predict that the suicide rate there was low, too.

Third, some of the propositions of a scientific theory must be *contingent*, in the sense that experience is relevant to their truth or falsity or to that of propositions derived from them (Braithwaite, 1953, p. 24). In my example, all the propositions are of this sort. I shall not go into the problem of testing the truth of propositions, which is of course crucial for the acceptance or rejection of theories, but which seems to me to fall within the province of methodology rather than that of theory per se.

In some deductive systems, but not the present example, noncontingent propositions like $(x + y) (x - y) = (x^2 - y^2)$ are introduced into the calculus for convenience in making deductions. They are noncontingent in that experience is irrelevant to their truth or falsity. Rather they are logically necessary, like the propositions of mathematics, as following from axioms and postulates assumed a priori. Remember that a scientific theory does not consist solely of noncontingent propositions.

The propositions in a deductive system need not always differ in generality, but they often do, and the differences in generality may be of different kinds. In the example, proposition 5 is clearly less general than proposition 1 in that it applies to only one social unit, Spain, rather than to the universe of social groupings as does proposition 1. In a different way, and less clearly, proposition 2 might be considered less general than proposition 1 if we had reason to believe (as we do) that the degree of individualism varied with other properties besides the incidence of Protestantism. In what follows the more general propositions will also be called higher-order ones and the less general, lower-order or empirical ones. A theory need not contain, as my example does, only one highest-order proposition.

The deductive system I have used as an example is, in form, a theory of the low suicide rate in Spain. Since it explains only one empirical proposition, most scholars would not consider it a theory at all. Usually we speak of a theory only when it deals with a class of phenomena, such as all variations in suicide rates. In this sense of the word a theory consists of a cluster of deductive systems, differing of course in their lower-order propositions, including the propositions to be explained, but containing one or more of the same higher-order ones. When we speak of the "power" of a theory, we refer to the fact that a wide variety of empirical propositions may be derived

from a few higher-order propositions under different given conditions. This, indeed, is the justification for calling the higher-order
propositions more general.

I think it idle to claim that any theory is ever complete. In the first
place, the most general propositions in the theory as formulated may
themselves be explainable by another, still more general set of propositions. When they are so explained, they are often said to be
reduced to the more general set. I think proposition 1 in our example
could be reduced to a set of psychological propositions, though
Durkheim might not have agreed (Durkheim, 1927, p. 125). And
even if at any given time the most general propositions are not
reducible, the possibility is always open that at some future time
they will be, as Newton's law of gravitation was shown to follow
under specific limiting conditions from the theory of relativity.

In the second place, some of the lower-order propositions in a
theory are often themselves explainable by deductive systems,
though the theorist for one reason or another may not want to bother
to explain them. Take, for instance, proposition 4 in our example:
The incidence of Protestantism in Spain is low. This could certainly
be explained, but the deductive system would be long and intricate,
bringing in, in principle, nothing less than the whole history of
Spain. Under these circumstances, a theorist who is concerned with
suicide and not with the history of Spain, and who does not have all
the time in the world, may be pardoned if he treats proposition 4 as
simply given, and leaves it unexplained. In practice he is more apt to
do so if he regards the incidence of Protestantism in Spain as a
parameter, that is, as an independent variable, which is not itself
dependent on some other variable in his system, and whose value is
temporarily constant. In what follows I shall call propositions like 4
givens or *given conditions*. Though a theory may be treated for
convenience as if it were complete or closed, it is never so in fact.
Instead it is open to the universe both at the top, so to speak, and at
the sides.

The example used, like those used hereafter, was obviously a very
simple deductive system. Much depends on what one wants to explain or predict. If, for instance, one wants to explain, not why the
suicide rate in Spain is low but why the rate in some particular year
was some particular figure, one might have to introduce other "factors" besides religion, and the factors might not be independent of
one another. When the higher-order propositions in a theory are
many, when the relationships between the variables are intricate,
when, for instance, the values of several variables cannot be taken as
given but are functions of other variables in the system, then the

deductive system may have to use mathematics, and a computer may be required to solve the equations for the values of the unknowns. The deductive systems of sociology are increasingly likely to have these features. My only excuse for using simple examples is that the general requirements of a theory do not change just because it is complex.

The Definition of Concepts. I have yet to deal with the most difficult problem in characterizing a theory. The calculus representing the theory must be interpreted: In ordinary language, its terms must be defined, and the problem in question arises because they may be defined in two different ways. Some are defined directly by the criteria according to which observations are classed under the concept and measured. In our example, suicide rates are defined by the ways in which deaths are classified as suicides in vital statistics and their numbers counted. Such concepts are directly, explicitly, or, if you like, operationally defined (Bridgman, 1946, p. 5). More important, the operations defining such concepts are independent of those defining others.

But concepts of another kind are also apt to appear in deductive systems, concepts that are not defined in this way but that nevertheless play an important part in the systems. The classic example is that of *force* in mechanics as it appears in the equation: $f = ma$. In the interpretation of this equation, force is not defined independently of *mass (m)* and *acceleration (a)*. Yet *force* plays a useful part in the theory of mechanics, if only because a number of different force-functions, such as that of gravitation, may be substituted for f, and the deductive systems that contain these new equations can explain a wide variety of empirical propositions. Such a concept is said to be implicitly defined (see Braithwaite, 1953, p. 77). There are many other examples in physical science.

In sociology I think *individualism* in our example may be such a concept. But I am not sure, so let me take a case of which I am more sure, the concept of *value* as it occurs, for instance, in the proposition: The more valuable to a man the reward he gets from another man or the environment, the more often he will emit activity that gets him that reward. The two variables here are: (1) the frequency of emission of the activity and (2) the value of the reward. Now there are cases in which *value* can be operationally defined: the value of food to a man may be operationally defined by the length of time a man has gone without food, and this definition satisfies the proposition, for the longer a man has gone without food, the more activity that will get him food he is indeed apt to put out.

But this definition of value deals only with a single kind of reward, food, whose value is measured by the degree to which a man has been deprived of it. The problem of definition is more difficult when the theorist has to deal with the situation in which a man has to choose between two kinds of rewards, and the degree of deprivation cannot be used as a measure of value. Thus a sociologist might say: a thirsty Chinese finds tea more valuable than milk, and so, by the proposition cited above, will do more to get tea than to get milk. I need not point out that this kind of choice among values is of great importance to sociology.

The question then arises how the relative values of tea and milk are to be measured, that is, how *value* in this situation is to be defined. If we rule out the operation of asking the Chinese which he prefers, and many sociologists do rule out this sort of operation as unreliable, what are we left with? Our only way of measuring the relative value of milk and tea to a Chinese is to observe whether he will do more work (or pay more money) to get the one than to get the other. In this case, the proposition we started with becomes, not a proposition in which each of two variables is independently defined, but a proposition like $f = ma$ in mechanics in which one of the variables is only defined implicitly.

Then we may well ask why it is worthwhile introducing the concept of value at all. Why not simply drop it out and keep the empirical proposition: Chinese will do more to get tea than to get milk? This proposition is not a tautology, since both "being Chinese" and "doing more" can be independently and explicitly defined. The trouble is that the conditions leading a man to do more to get one reward than another are infinite in kind and number. "Being Chinese" is one, but so is "being unskilled" or "being out in the rain," and so on. It is impossible to enumerate them all, and new ones are forever being discovered. Under these circumstances, it is convenient to state the high-order proposition: "The more valuable the reward, the more a man will do to get it," and leave the various conditions that create differences in value in particular circumstances to be described by lower-order propositions in the various deductive systems that have the high-order proposition at their head. This procedure secures the advantages of generality, since from the high-order proposition true empirical conclusions may be derived, whether value is defined in terms of deprivation or in terms of such things as being Chinese. This is the procedure Braithwaite has in mind when, discussing the fitting of a symbolic calculus to a deductive system, he writes:

The implicit empirical definition of the theoretical terms in a scientific deductive system consists in the fitting of the calculus to the system from the bottom upwards. This is done by first fitting derived formulae of the calculus to the empirical generalizations which are the lowest-level hypotheses in the deductive system, and then working backwards so that the formulae containing the theoretical terms are interpreted as representing those higher-level hypotheses from which the lowest-level hypotheses logically follow in the scientific deductive system (Braithwaite, 1953, pp. 78-79).

If this procedure is adopted, as Braithwaite points out, "the hypotheses of the theory will be logically deducible from the empirical generalizations which they were put forward to explain" (1953, p. 67). And how, then, can we speak of explanation? On the other hand, the procedure has the advantage of allowing the theory to be extended to take account of empirical generalizations as yet unknown, and this is an important advantage in the present case, since the conditions that may create differences in value may be innumerable. Explicit definition, Braithwaite says, does not allow such extension. His demonstration is long; I urge students to read it for themselves (1953, Ch. 3); only his final statement can be quoted here:

> A theory which it is hoped may be expanded in the future to explain more generalizations than it was originally designed to explain must allow more freedom to its theoretical terms than would be given them were they to be logical constructions out of observable entities. A scientific theory which, like all good scientific theories, is capable of growth must be more than an alternative way of describing the generalizations upon which it is based, which is all it would be if its theoretical terms were limited by being explicitly defined (Braithwaite, 1953, p. 76).

The problem of implicit definition comes up again and again in the theories of social science. Thus the *cohesiveness* of a group plays a part in some theories of social psychology similar to the one *value* plays in the example I have used (see Festinger, Schachter, & Back, 1950, p. 164). The issue at stake is also, I think, that of nominal versus real definitions of concepts, which has exercised some sociologists (Bierstedt, 1959; Zetterberg, 1954, p. 30). Thus *cohesiveness* might be defined nominally by the high-order proposition: The more cohesive a group, the more often its members will take part in its activities. This is a proposition similar to the one defining *value* in the sense that there is no single measure of cohesiveness independent of the participation of the members. Instead, various lower-order propositions are brought into the theory, each stating what makes for cohesiveness under particular circumstances: the number of sociometric choices within a group, the value of the rewards obtained from the activities of the group, and the like. In terms of the distinction between nominal and real, these are the real definitions of cohesiveness.

Mathematical Models. The set of propositions that constitute a theory may be represented symbolically by a calculus, and the derivations made according to the rules for the manipulation of the calculus. When the symbols and the rules are those of mathematics, we say that the calculus is a mathematical model of the theory (see Lazarsfeld, 1954; Solomon, 1960). But remember always that a mathematical model, like a theory itself, must contain some contingent propositions (equations), even though they are stated in the language of mathematics. If it contains none, it is mathematics and not a mathematical model of a theory. The usual trouble with mathematical models in sociology is that they contain too few contingent equations to enable them, however beautiful the mathematics, to explain the empirical facts in any detail.

To set up a mathematical model, moreover, it is not enough to translate contingent propositions into mathematical symbols. The calculus must actually be used to derive new propositions. As Braithwaite says:

> "No calculus without calculation;" the mere translation of tendency statements into mathematical language (as, for example, in Kurt Lewin's *Principles of Topological Psychology*, 1936) is not sufficient to make a quasi-deductive system out of them. The essence of mathematics is not its symbolism, but its methods of deduction (Braithwaite, 1953, p. 300).

A model, then, is no more than a representation of a theory. The exception to this statement occurs when to the highest-order concepts of the theory may be attributed properties irrelevant to the theory, as when models of chemical theory represented atoms as if they were hard round balls. The model may then become misleading. But I do not think this feature is characteristic of current mathematical models in sociology.

The effort to represent a theory in the form of a mathematical model has many advantages. It forces the theorist to make explicit how his variables are to be defined. It forces him to state the relationships between variables—the functions relating one to another —much more specifically than theories stated in verbal form usually do. The model enables him to avoid the fallacies in making deductions to which reasoning in ordinary language is notoriously subject. Above all, it enables him, in the case of complicated theories to make deductions, especially new and unsuspected ones, that reasoning in ordinary language would be incapable of attaining at all. Let mathematical models flourish, then, especially those rich in the representation of contingent propositions.

In ending this description of the characteristics of theory let me make one statement as firmly as I can. As an ideal, the nature of theory, of explanation, is no different in the social sciences from what it is in the physical sciences, though some social scientists have talked as if it were. The two fields differ of course in the nature of the propositions that enter their deductive systems but not in the assumption that when they talk about theories deductive systems are what they mean.

THE DIFFICULTIES OF THEORY
CONSTRUCTION IN SOCIOLOGY

There are few theories in sociology — and perhaps no so-called general theories — that meet the definition given above of what a theory ought to be. I turn now to the practical difficulties and intellectual confusions that get in the way of theory-construction in sociology.

Many of the deductive systems in sociology, if spelled out in full, would be long and complicated. In practice, even the best of theorists, to save time and avoid boring their readers, leave out some of the steps in their arguments, take them for granted. The result is that they produce not explanations, but what Hempel (1959, p. 351) calls "explanation sketches." They write out their arguments, moreover, in ordinary discursive English, whose logic is apt to be slippery. The result is that, even when the theorist does have a deductive system latent in his mind, his readers have difficulty working it out for themselves. One remedy for this condition would be to present the theories in mathematical form. But even short of mathematics some measure of formalization would be a great help. At crucial points in his argument let the theorist state as precisely as he can what he believes to be the general propositions of his theory and draw attention to them by numbers or italics. Let him then spell out the steps in logic by which he draws empirical conclusions from the general propositions. No single procedure would do more to eliminate or resolve our interminable arguments and confusions about sociological theories. We might at least be able to decide what we were arguing about and, especially, whether we were dealing with deductive systems at all.

Some sociologists sound as if they do not know what a theory is. If, in what follows, I single out Talcott Parsons as an example of confusion, I do so only because he is the most famous of contemporary theorists, so I cannot be accused of hitting a man when he is down. In his most recent work (Parsons, Shils, Naegele & Pitts, 1961, vol. I, p. 32), he seems to be taking a more sensible view of theory, but his earlier doctrine may have led some of us astray. He wrote: "A theoretical system in the present sense is a body of logically interdependent generalized concepts of empirical reference" (Parsons et al., 1949, p. 17); and Robert Merton echoed him by saying that "the term *sociological theory* refers to logically interconnected conceptions which are limited and modest in scope, rather than all-embracing and grandiose" (Merton, 1957, p. 5). The two men differed in degree of modesty but not in their view of theory as "logically interdependent concepts."

I shall return to logic later, but what about the notion of theory as consisting of concepts? It seems to assume that a conceptual scheme is a theory. Concepts and their definitions are certainly part of a theory, but they are not sufficient by themselves to constitute a theory. Concepts are names for properties of nature, and a theory does not even begin to exist until propositions are stated about contingent relationships of the general form *x* varies as *y* between the properties. The reason is obvious: A theory is a deductive system, and no deductions can be made from concepts alone; propositions are absolutely necessary. All sociologists should know this, but it still badly needs saying.

None of this means that a conceptual scheme is useless. A scheme with clear criteria may allow investigators to identify instances of significant properties of nature, and the elaboration of such a scheme may be a useful preliminary to the construction of a theory. It may accordingly be called theoretical work; but it is not theory per se.

Much official sociological theory consists in fact of concepts and their definitions: it provides the dictionary of a language that possesses no sentences. Parsons is particularly good at practicing what he preaches. It would be going too far to say that his theories contain no propositions. He often slips at the lower or empirical levels. But at the higher ones, and since he claims to be "general," this means the very highest his theories seem to me to consist largely of conceptual schemes. In Zetterberg's (1958) terms, he is a "dimension-sit." In fairness to Parsons it must be said that his schemes include most of the sorts of terms that need to enter into sociological theory. All that is lacking are contingent propositions about their relationships.

Let me now consider the claim that the concepts of a theory are "logically interdependent." What do statements like this mean? If they mean that lower-order propositions in a theory can be deduced under the rules of logic from the higher-order ones, then all is well. But if they mean that logic enters in any other way they are in trouble. The highest-order propositions in a theory are not "logically" related to one another. Though in my example proposition 3 can be logically derived from the conjuncture of propositions 1 and 2, the two latter are not themselves "logically interdependent." More important, the contingent relationships between concepts in a theory are not "logically necessary" like those of mathematics. Nature, if you like, and not logic makes them what they are.

What Parsons has in mind when he speaks of the "logical interdependence" of concepts seems to be this: Concepts may be names for classes of observations, and Parsons often claims that his classifications "are exhaustive of the relevant logical possibilities" at a particular level of analysis (Parsons, 1951, p. 66). But anyone can always set up a logically exhaustive conceptual scheme in this sense. What he does is to define a class X and then say that everything else falls into the class Non-X, giving each of the classes a name, and then he has a logically exhaustive conceptual scheme. He can readily complicate the scheme, making it a fourfold or an n-fold one, by intersecting the first two classes with new ones like Y and Non-Y and calling the result a paradigm if he likes. But none of this work makes the conceptual scheme a theory, for it implies no contingent relationships between properties of nature. Only if, for instance, actual instances of X turned out also to be instances of Y, or instances of Non-X, instances of Non-Y would such a relationship be implied. You can make a conceptual scheme as exhaustive as you like and in any way you like, but it still remains only a conceptual scheme.

Yet Parsons claims he can make deductions or derivations from his conceptual scheme. In *Economy and Society*, for instance, he and Smelser say that their first chapter "established a presumption in favor of our thesis that economic theory is a special case of the general theory of social systems" (Parsons & Smelser, 1956, p. 296). They go on: "This presumption rested on two grounds: (1) the point-for-point correspondence of the logical structures of the two conceptual schemes, and (2) the fact that the goal of the economy is *less general* than societal goals." Now there is just one condition that must be met if one theory is to be called a special case of another: the propositions of the special theory must be derived in a deductive system from the propositions of the other. It is in this sense that the theory of the tides may be called a special case of Newtonian mechanics. Parsons and Smelser have not met this condition. Economic theory certainly possesses propositions, but Parsons and Smelser have not derived a single one of them through any deductive system. Instead they seem to feel that a special theory is derived from a general one if some "correspondence" can be found—and it is seldom hard to find—between the concepts of the general theory and those of the special one. But it is the deduction of propositions, not the translation of words, that counts. As for their second argument, it amounts to saying that a theory of the whole ought to be more general than a theory of a part. Indeed it ought to be, but the problem remains of demonstrating that it is.

Even when sociological theories do state relationships. between properties of nature, they often do not state very much. To say that there is some relationship, but not to go any further, to allow the propositions to take the form that x is some function of y without futher specifying the function, is to say something but not much that can take its place in a deductive system, for from the conjuncture of such propositions little can be deduced. Thus, Parsons (1951, p. 38) puts forward a "double contingency" paradigm of social behavior: When two men are interacting, the actions of each are rewards or punishments (sanctions) for the actions of the other. To say this is to say that variables characterizing the behavior of each man are functions of variables characterizing the behavior of the other. And to say this is certainly to say something: It is, I think, the statement from which our understanding of social behavior begins. But it is not to say much that can take its place in a theory. Only when the proposition is strengthened so as to say, for instance, that the more often the activity of one man rewards the activity of the other, the more often the other emits the activity—only when some beginning is made at specifying the functions relating the variables has anything been said from which conclusions can be drawn in a deductive system. When it does not consist of conceptual schemes, much sociological theory consists of statements like this one of Parsons. Again, it is theoretical work—I call it descriptive work—without being theory.

The weakest propositions properly entering a deductive system state, like the one cited above, that x varies directly as y, that x is some monotonically increasing function of y. For more precise explanation and prediction we should like, of course, to go further in specifying the function and say, for instance, that $x = y^2$ or $x = \log y$. But generally we are unable to do so. In practice we tend to assume that x is a linear function of y until the testing of conclusions drawn from the proposition shows that the assumption is untenable. Even then we are more apt to correct the deductive system by introducing new variables (factors) than by changing the form of the function.

A more serious problem with sociological propositions than that the relationship between two variables is only very roughly specified is that the propositions are suspected of holding good only under certain conditions. It is not just that the proposition holds good "other things equal," but that what the "other things" are and where they are "equal" is unknown. Braithwaite (1953, pp. 361–366) calls such propositions *tendency statements*. The use of tendency statements in a deductive system can lead to a sort of difficulty that may be illustrated from electricity. Suppose we were studying electrical circuits for the first time and had reason to believe the two separate propositions that current, I, tended to vary directly with electromotive force, E, and that E in turn tended to vary with resistance, R. We might be tempted to conclude that I varied directly with R; and we should be wrong, for the facts are summed up in the single proposition

$$I = \frac{E}{R} \ .$$

That is, I varies as E only under the condition that R is constant, and E with R only under the condition that I is constant.

Many sociological propositions, particularly those made by induction from observations in the field where the effects of "third variables" are uncontrolled, are tendency statements. Some people claim that tendency propositions from field research should not even be stated. They are quite wrong, for a proposition not stated is a proposition that cannot be retested, and unless it is tested and retested, the conditions in which it holds good or fails to do so cannot be discovered. Braithwaite (1953) suggests just this policy with regard to tendency statements. Construct a deductive system in which they are provisionally treated as if they were not tendency statements but fully general. Test the lowest-order propositions, the empirical conclusions of the system, against observation. Both the successes and the failures of such tests will provide information about the unknown limiting conditions. This is what sensible sociologists actually do.

THE RELATIONS BETWEEN
THEORY AND RESEARCH

I turn last and briefly to the relations between theory and research.

In this field sociologists have felt especially guilty. On the one hand they feel that theory ought to guide research, and, if it does not, that they are in danger of becoming mere factgatherers. On the other hand, they feel that research should contribute cumulatively to the development of a body of general theory and that something is wrong if theory keeps on going with a life of its own impervious to research. It may help matters if I try to clear away some of the less justifiable sources of guilt.

Theorists are fond of saying complacently, "Nothing is more practical than a good theory." Like many old chestnuts this is a tautology, for a theory is no good unless it is practical in the only sense in which a theory can be practical. If you are aware of a theory that will explain and predict a number of the known facts, then a research strategy makes obviously good sense if it is designed to work out the further implications of the theory—what it implies under different given conditions. A mathematical model of the theory is a great advantage here, as it may enable you to grind out the further implications mechanically, as it were. In this case, theory is properly guiding research. But note: you have to have the theory first.

There are theorists who will tell you that sociology possesses such a theory and that accordingly it should guide research. Parsons writes: "Heretofore [sociology] has not enjoyed the kind of integration and directed activity which only the availability and common acceptance and employment of a well-articulated generalized theoretical system can give to a science. The main framework of such a system is, however, now available, though the fact is not as yet very generally appreciated . . ." (Parsons, 1949, p. 17). Can the system in question be Parsons' own? No doubt it is available, but is it practical in the sense given above? In the absence of evidence that it is so, I regard the claim that it ought to guide research as presumptuous. Yet according to Merton, Parsons makes such claims: "Talcott Parsons has observed that numerical data are scientifically important only when they can be fitted into analytical categories and that 'a great deal of current research is producing facts in a form which cannot be utilized by any current generalized analytical scheme'" (Merton, 1957, p. 113). The only possible comment is, "So much the worse for the scheme."

Researchers are sometimes told that they should investigate the effects of "theoretically relevant variables." But relevant to what theory? And does the researcher have any reason to feel confidence in it? I should have thought it obvious that the only variables of any importance whatever were the actually relevant variables. If the effects of some empirical variable can be predicted from a proposition about some generalized variable in a deductive system, then all is well. (See what I had to say above about the nominal and real definitions of concepts on pp. 55f.) But if they cannot, then the actual variable may not be disregarded, whatever its theoretical status.

There are few cases in sociology in which a developed deductive system has actually guided research. The reason is that there are few such deductive systems and still fewer among "general" theories. Let the sociologist feel guilty about that if he likes, but not about the lack of theoretical guidance. It makes sense to have theory guide research only if there is some reason for having confidence in the theory, and the theorist's own assertion is not sufficient reason. In the absence of such confidence, the researcher should feel free to do anything he pleases, so long as he studies men. Indeed he could do worse than indulge in "mere data collection."

In trying to allay one form of guilt, I do not want to increase another. I have argued that the researcher should feel free not to accept theoretical guidance. But even if he does allow himself to be guided by ideas that turn out to be inadequate theoretically, the fact will not necessarily hurt his research and may do it much good. I speak here of broad theoretical orientations rather than of actual deductive systems. Good theories in this sense need not lead to good researches, and bad theories certainly need not lead to bad ones. Thus I have shown the difficulties of using notions like *function* and *equilibrium* in sociological deductive systems. But if holding a functional theory implies the research maxim "Look for the consequences of institutions, near and remote, good or bad, intended or unintended," and if holding an equilibrium theory implies the maxim "Look for the way institutions work together to promote something like social stability," then these theories are apt to lead to the discovery of true propositions, even though the propositions may eventually turn out to be best explained neither through function nor through equilibrium. To use functional language, theories have other functions than theoretical ones.

Finally, some sociologists confuse the way a theory looks when it is completed—and it is never more than provisionally completed—with the way a theory is arrived at. Since a completed theory works downward, so to speak, from general propositions to less general empirical ones, they feel that the process of theory-building should work downward, too, starting from very general considerations like "the action frame of reference" and hoping eventually to reach the data. My general doctrine is that good science has been done by some of the damnedest methods, and that some of the methods scientists have said they used were not the ones they actually used. Accordingly I cannot rule out the possibility that good sociological theories will be reached by the downward-moving strategy of theory-construction.

But there is another strategy, and one that the history of science suggests is more likely to be successful in a new science like ours. This is the strategy well described by Willard Gibbs in his statement: "It is the office of theoretical work to give the form in which the results of experiment may be expressed" (Rukeyser, 1942, p. 232). Here there is no complaining that empirical research does not investigate "theoretically relevant variables." The strategy starts with the empirical findings themselves and seeks to invent the more general propositions from which these same findings, and, under different conditions, other findings may be derived. This is the strategy by which deductive systems are inductively arrived at.

This strategy has already proved its worth in sociology in the sense that our best theories, those that most nearly meet my requirements for being deductive systems, have stayed close to the empirical findings. In Merton's (1957, p. 9) terms, these are our theories of "the middle range." But I think that this strategy, which has sometimes been called *codification*, could be made more effective if it were made more explicit.

Codification begins with the assumption that the "mere empirical generalizations" of sociology are our most precious possessions and, like precious stones, least likely to change. But they exist in large numbers and great variety, and they are stated in a number of different terminologies. Collect, as far as possible, the propositions within any given field, say that of small groups. Reduce their number as far as possible by asking whether some of them do not state the same proposition under different words. This will entail examining how the named variables were actually measured and how far the methods of measurement were similar. Reduce the number of propositions at a particular level of generalization still further by asking whether some of them do not follow from the others as corollaries under specific limiting conditions. When you have reduced your set of propositions as far as you dare, ask what propositions of a higher level of generality still your set might in turn be derived from. Invent the higher-order propositions if you must; be a Newton. But I do not think that in sociology you will have to take action as drastic as that. You will find the propositions already invented for you in behavioral psychology.

Note that in arriving at deductive systems (explanations) in this way, you will have been an ex post facto explainer: you will have explained the findings after the findings are in, and there are sociologists who will be ready to tell you that ex post facto explanations are somehow illegitimate. Never fear; both Newton and Darwin were ex post facto explainers so you will be in good company. It is true that a proposition invented to explain a single empirical finding is not worth much. But it need not stop at a single finding. If it will explain at least two different findings under different given conditions, it will have done better than most theories in sociology, even if the explanation is ex post facto. Though it will do still better if it successfully predicts the truth of some proposition as yet untested, prediction is not the crucial step. All science begins with ex post facto explanations and without them could not get off the ground.

Naturally I believe that what I have said here is true. But the most important advice I can give contemporary sociologists has nothing to do with the validity of my arguments. It is this: You do not have to believe anything about theory or methodology that is told you pretentiously and sanctimoniously by other sociologists — including myself. So much guff has gotten mixed with the truth that, if you cannot tell which is which, you had better reject it all. It will only get in your way. No one will go far wrong theoretically who remains in close touch with and seeks to understand a body of concrete phenomena.

REFERENCES

ABERLE, D. E., COHEN, A. K., DAVIS, A. K., LEVY, M. J., JR., AND SUTTON, F. X. *The functional prerequisites of a Society, Ethics*, 60 (1950), 100–111.

BECKER, H., AND BOSKOFF, A., eds., *Modern Sociological Theory in Continuity and Change* (New York: Holt, Rinehart and Winston, 1957).

BIERSTEDT, R. *"Nominal and Real Definitions in Sociological Theory,"* in L. Gross, ed., *Symposium on Sociological Theory* (Evanston, Ill.: Row, 1959).

BLACK, M., ed., *The Social Theories of Talcott Parsons* (Englewood Cliffs, N.J.: Prentice-Hall, 1961).

BLAU, P. M., *"Structural Effects,"* *American Sociological Review*, 26 (1960), 178–93.

BORGATTA, E. F., AND MEYER, H. J., eds., *Sociological Theory* (New York: Knopf, 1956).

BRAITHWAITE, R. B., *Scientific Explanation* (Cambridge: Cambridge University Press, 1953).

BRIDGMAN, P. W., *The Logic of Modern Physics* (New York: Macmillan, 1946).

COSER, L. A., AND ROSENBERG, B., eds. *Sociological Theory* (New York: Macmillan, 1957).

DAVIS, K., "The Myth of Functional Analysis as a Special Method in Sociology and Anthropology," *American Sociological Review*, 24 (1959), 757–73.

DURKHEIM, E., *Les Régles de la Methode Sociologique*, 8th ed. (Paris: Alcan, 1927).

DURKHEIM, E., *The Division of Labor in Society* (Glencoe, Ill.: Free Press, 1947).

DURKHEIM, E., *Suicide*, G. Simpson, ed. (Glencoe, Ill.: Free Press, 1951).

FESTINGER, L., SCHACHTER, S., AND BACK, K. *Social Pressures in Informal Groups* (New York: Harper, 1950).

GARDINER, P., ed., *Theories of History* (Glencoe, Ill.: Free Press, 1959).

GROSS, L., ed., *Symposium on Sociological Theory* (Evanston, Ill.: Row, 1959).

HEMPEL, C. G., "Explanations and Laws," in P. Gardiner, ed., *Theories of History* (New York: Free Press, 1958ff, p. 344–56.

HOMANS, G. C., *The Human Group* (New York: Harcourt, 1950).

HOMANS, G. C., *Social Behavior: Its Elementary Forms* (New York: Harcourt, 1961).

HOMANS, G. C., AND SCHNEIDER, D. M., *Marriage, Authority, and Final Causes* (Glencoe, Ill.: Free Press, 1955).

LAZARSFELD, P. F., ed., *Mathematical Thinking in the Social Sciences* (Glencoe, Ill.: Free Press, 1954).

LEVY, M. J., JR., *The Structure of Society* (Princeton, N.J.: Princeton University Press, 1952).

LEWIN, K., *Principles of Topological Psychology* (New York: McGraw-Hill, 1936).

LOOMIS, C. P., AND LOOMIS, Z. K., *Modern Social Theories* (Princeton, N.J.: Van Nostrand, 1961).

LUCE, R. D., AND RAIFFA, H., *Games and Decisions* (New York: Wiley, 1957).

MACH, E., *The Science of Mechanics* (LaSalle, Ill.: Open Court Publishing Co., 1942).

MARTINDALE, D. *The Nature and Types of Sociological Theory* (Boston: Houghton Mifflin, 1960).

MERTON, R. K., *Social Theory and Social Structure*, rev. ed. (Glencoe, Ill.: Free Press, 1957).

MURDOCK, G. P., *Social Structure* (New York: Macmillan, 1949).

NAGEL, E., *The Structure of Science* (New York: Harcourt, 1961).

NEEDHAM, R., *Structure and Sentiment* (Chicago: University of Chicago Press, 1962).

PARSONS, T., *Essays in Sociological Theory Pure and Applied* (Glencoe, Ill.: Free Press, 1949).

PARSONS, T., *The Social System* (Glencoe, Ill.: Free Press, 1951).

PARSONS, T., "General Theory in Sociology," in R. K. Merton, L. Broom, and L. S. Cottrell, Jr., eds., *Sociology Today* (New York: Basic Books, 1959).

PARSONS, T., SHILS, E., NAEGELE, K. D., AND PITTS, J. R., eds. *Theories of Society* (New York: Free Press of Glencoe, 1961), 2 vols.

PARSONS, T., AND SMELSER, N. J., *Economy and Society* (Glencoe, Ill.: Free Press, 1956).

RADCLIFFE-BROWN, A. R., *Structure and Function in Primitive Society* (Glencoe, Ill.: Free Press, 1952).

REX, J., *Key Problems of Sociological Theory* (London: Routledge and Kegan Paul, 1961).

ROSE, A. M., "A Systematic Summary of Symbolic Interaction Theory," in A. M. Rose, ed., *Human Behavior and Social Processes* (Boston: Houghton Mifflin, 1962).

RUKEYSER, M., *Willard Gibbs* (New York: Doubleday, Doran, 1942).

SCRIVEN, M., "Truisms as the Grounds for Historical Explanations," in P. Gardiner, ed., *Theories of History* (Glencoe, Ill.: Free Press, 1959).

SOLOMON, H., ed., *Mathematical Thinking in the Measurement of Behavior* (Glencoe, Ill.: Free Press, 1960).

THIBAUT, J. W., AND KELLEY, H. H., *The Social Psychology of Groups* (New York: Wiley, 1959).

TIMASHEFF, N. S., *Sociological Theory* (New York: Doubleday, 1955).

VON NEUMANN, J., AND MORGENSTERN, O., *Theory of Games and Economic Behavior* (Princeton, N.J.: Princeton University Press, 1944).

ZETTERBERG, H. L., *On Theory and Verification in Sociology* (New York: Tressler Press, 1954).

ZETTERBERG, H. L., "Review of Becker and Boskoff (1957)," *American Sociological Review*, 23 (1958), 95–96.

ZETTERBERG, H. L., *Social Theory and Social Practice* (New York: Bedminster Press, 1962).

4. Theory, Probability, and Induction in Social Research

SANTO F. CAMILLERI

MOST social researchers employ probability concepts in their research either explicitly or implicitly whether or not they are aware of it. The chief notable exceptions are those who are proponents of what has come to be called "analytic induction,"[1] a rationale that explicitly excludes certain probability formulations. But these are small minorities in the sociological society. Most of us, in one way or another, are probability oriented in our research. Yet, for all this collective commitment to the use of probability, there is a great deal of confusion and obscurity about its nature and use in research.

The disagreements connected with the use of probability in social research stem from many sources. There is a general failure to recognize the different purposes probability reasoning has served, with

1. For a description and analysis of this school of thought see William S. Robinson, "The Logical Structure of Analytic Induction," *American Sociological Review*, 16 (December 1951), 812–18.

the result that critics and defenders of probability often are talking about different things. A perhaps even more important source of difficulty lies in an inadequate understanding of the nature of science and the proper business of the scientist. Without presuming to be definitive, the present paper undertakes to make a contribution to the clarification of these basic issues. We shall discuss briefly some aspects of scientific theory and the verification of scientific hypotheses. In the course of this we shall distinguish three basic uses of probability: intrinsic, auxiliary, and inductive.[2] In a critical analysis of inductive probability we shall introduce the concept of systematic import as a part of the inductive process.

THE DUAL RESPONSIBILITY OF THE SCIENTIST

Discussions about science usually begin with a statement to the effect that the purpose of science is to make predictions for the purpose of control. We agree with these objectives, but they do not clearly reflect what we believe is the chief function of the scientist: to create and provide empirical support for a particular means of making predictions, viz., systematic theory. Our contention is that the scientist has a direct responsibility to both these tasks, the creation of theory and the providing of empirical support for theory, and that to fail to meet either responsibility is to fail fundamentally.

SOME ASPECTS OF SCIENTIFIC THEORY

Formal and Empirical Truth. Scientific theory has a formal aspect.[3] It consists of statements of fact in propositional form which are connected by explicit rules. These rules provide an objective, communicable means of operating on some of these propositions to produce additional "lower level" propositions or theorems. The *formal truth* of a theorem rests essentially on a demonstration that it has been generated by a correct application of the rules (has been correctly inferred).

Scientific theory has an empirical aspect, as well. To make the theory "say something" about reality it has to be interpreted or given empirical content. This is accomplished by means of a set of coordi-

2. The present discussion owes much to Lancelot Hogben, who treated this topic at great length in his important book, *Statistical Theory* (New York: W. W. Norton, 1958.

3. For a valuable recent treatment of the logical structure of scientific theories, see Richard B. Braithwaite, *Scientific Explanation* (New York: Cambridge University Press, 1955).

nating definitions that are essentially rules for identifying the empirical referents of the theorems. The *empirical truth* of a theorem refers to the judged correspondence of its interpreted assertion with the observed state of affairs. In their narrow conception, operational definitions serve as an important type of coordinating definition.[4]

Generality. The propositions embodied in the theory refer to all instances of the phenomena to which they are linked by the coordinating definitions. By *all* we mean literally those that occurred in the past, those that now exist, and those that may yet occur in the future. That is, the universes to which the propositions refer are always infinite and hence conceptual. Their elements never all exist at one time. Connected with this is the requirement that the coordinating definitions must not contain time or place specifications, except as these factors are variables in the system. For example, a proposition connecting vote with residence must not be interpreted so as to refer only to the voters in a given election who reside at that time in a given community. This conception of the universe and the correlated restriction on the coordinating definitions provide the system with its predictive relevance with regard to future events and its explanatory relevance with regard to events which have already occurred.[5]

Deterministic and Probabilistic Theories. The propositions of a theory can be arranged in a hierarchy based upon their order in the deductive evolvement of the theory. A deterministic theory is one whose propositions at all levels within the hierarchy express universal relationships of the sort "All A is B." A probabilistic theory is one that contains at least one highest level proposition that expresses a probability relationship between some classes of the elements referred to by the theory. The reason that such a proposition must be a highest level one is that probability statements can be *inferred* only from probability statements, so if they appear at all in a theory, they must appear at a highest level.[6]

When probability propositions are so incorporated in a theory, they express a fundamental property of the phenomena to which they refer. To remove this kind of proposition from a theory literally involves reconceptualizing the phenomena itself. We shall therefore refer to probability statements within a theory as *intrinsic* probability

4. Cf. Carl G. Hempel, "A Logical Appraisal of Operationism," in Phillip G. Frank, ed., *The Validation of Scientific Theories* (Boston: The Beacon Press, 1956).

5. These properties of scientific universes are not well recognized. For some discussion of them, see Karl R. Popper, *The Logic of Scientific Discovery* (New York: Basic Books, Inc., 1959), esp. chap. 1, and Braithwaite, *op. cit.*, p. 123.

6. Braithwaite, *op cit.*, chap. 6.

and speak of the intrinsic use of probability. It is especially important to maintain a distinction between the intrinsic use of probability
and the use of probability to deal with the conditions of observation,
which we shall treat presently.

SAMPLING AND EXPERIMENTATION

Discussions about whether sociology can ever be a science and
about whether it can be a science without experimentation often
center around the competitive advantages of surveys and controlled
experiments. In the former, probability considerations enter in the
context of sampling from finite, existent populations, and in the latter
they enter in the design and interpretation of randomized experiments. In the typology we are presenting here, these are auxiliary probability applications since they both refer primarily to the
process of observation. The present concern is with the implications
of each for theory and with the scope of induction they permit by
virtue of being sampling procedures.

Sampling from Finite, Existent Populations. The mathematical
theory of sampling from finite populations does not require any
assumptions about the population sampled except that it remain
fixed (or change predictably) during the course of our interest. We do
not, for example, have to say anything about the way in which the
population came into being. Given its existence and access to it, we
can draw samples from the population by a method that has been
previously verified to produce sampling distributions with predictable characteristics, and on the basis of this we can make some
statements about the population by inspecting the sample. In doing
so, we introduce the possibility of the two types of errors with which
we are familiar. But it is conceivable that we can avoid sampling
altogether by making a complete inspection of the population since it
is finite and existent. To see the scientific relevance of a sample from
such a population, then, we must understand how to use the information obtained by the complete inspection. It is clear that we must
know the scientific relevance of the population itself.

In the context of theory construction we would regard any statement of fact about the population as a proposition deducible from a
theory, i.e., as a hypothesis. In addition, since that statement is
treated as a hypothesis, the elements to which it refers are designated by the coordinating definitions. Thus, the finite, existent population is interpreted as a collection of instances of the kind referred
to by the coordinating definitions. By this interpretation the charac-

teristics of the population become evidence for or against a hypothesis. Without some theoretical context, however, and without suitably generalized coordinating definitions, the statement of fact about the population has as yet no scientific relevance. It is merely a descriptive statement.

If some systematic theory is at issue and if the phenomenon is properly identified, we might resort to sampling as an efficiency measure. The scope of the induction provided by the sampling is, however, limited to the finite set of elements upon which the sampling procedure was employed. There is no procedure for *selecting* a probability sample from the infinite hypothetical universe specified by the coordinating definitions. To extend the scope of the sampling induction to the hypothetical universe requires us to *postulate* explicitly a specific connection between the existent elements and the hypothetical universe.

Since the connection between existing and future cases is a matter of postulation, whether a probability sampling scheme is required in choosing cases to observe depends upon the nature of the theory involved. If the theory is deterministic, the primary concern would be with choosing cases having the appropriate values of the independent variables specified by the theory. There is no need to know the proportionate representation of cases having those values; therefore, there is no need for probability sampling at all. For example, if the hypothesis asserts that all A is B, then any subset of A is also included in B, and so it is a matter of convenience how we chose the subset of A's to observe. If it were our interest to know how many A's there are in the existing population, then, of course, we might choose to estimate this by a probability sampling procedure, but that number itself would have to be somehow consequential for a theory.

If the theory is probabilistic, we would be interested not only in making sure that the cases exhibit the appropriate values of the variables specified by the theory, but, in addition, we would be interested in the proportionate representation of the cases having these values, because it provides sample values of the probabilities at issue. We are obliged therefore to postulate a statistical relationship between the existing cases and the hypothetical pool. By virtue of this postulate a complete inspection of the existing cases would be interpreted as a probability sample of the hypothetical population. A probability sample of the existing cases would also be appropriate.[7]

It is virtually impossible in most social research to obtain such

7. For a discussion of this type of sampling, see W. Edwards Deming, *Some Theory of Sampling* (New York: Wiley, 1950), pp. 252–59.

samples, however, and in practice the usual procedure is to get one's subjects as best one may, being as much concerned about the number of subjects as by the manner in which they are selected. These "convenience" samples are unsatisfactory from both standpoints: the representation of variables and the representation of populations. Unless these samples are huge they will usually not contain enough of the right combinations of variable values to make an adequate test of the theory. In addition, since they are not usually chosen by a randomizing procedure, they cannot be considered as probability samples representative of the existing population.

If we cannot afford both kinds of representation, the present writer feels that it is better to choose our cases so as to be sure to get the right combinations of variable values. Such sampling is termed judgment sampling and is usually eschewed on the advice of statisticians, but there seems to be no practicable way to improve on this in most instances. Such a procedure would greatly facilitate the direct replication of studies by keeping the sample size within reasonable limits and by an explicit statement of conditions, apart from possible selection biases, that would make the studies comparable.

Randomized Experimentation. A fundamental criticism of Mill's methods of experimental inquiry is that to use them to discover the causes of a phenomenon or to prove that a particular factor is the cause of a phenomenon requires that *a priori* assumption that all the possible causes are known and examinable. R. A. Fisher flatly denied the possibility of an exhaustive enumeration of possible effective factors and proposed a formal argument, based upon the physical act of randomizing treatment, to account for the effects of all relevant factors, know or unknown, that might be present in the experimental situation.[8]

In a Fisherian experiment the experimenter exposes the experimental units or subjects to a pattern of treatment which has been randomly selected by the experimenter from all the possible patterns of treatment to which he might have exposed them. This universe of possible patterns of treatment is, of course, hypothetical in that it exists only symbolically. Once a particular pattern has been applied to a set of subjects its effects cannot (usually) be erased so that the same subjects may be given another selected pattern of treatment. If this could be done, there would be no need to randomize treatment if the objective is to satisfy the form of Mill's canons. The formal argument by which the effects of the randomized and controlled factors are accounted for includes a specification of the form of the

8. R. A. Fisher, *The Design of Experiments* (London: Oliver and Boyd, 1949).

functional relationships between the factors and the effects, for example the often referred to "linear hypothesis."

It is also relatively a matter of course to postulate a fundamental, irreducible variation in the experimental units. That is, an intrinsic statistical proposition is postulated, but the variation due to this is not usually separable from errors of observation or other probabilistic errors in conducting the experiment. As a matter of fact, a number of combinations of deterministic and statistical propositions could lead to the same deductions, and which is to be preferred among these is precisely the task involved in constructing any theory.

We see then, that a Fisherian experiment involves a particular theoretical conception. This conception is by no means appropriate to all phenomena, but this fact has been obscured by the great attention paid to the act of randomization.

The scope of generalization or induction that is due to the act of randomization can only be subjects like those used in the experiment and under the conditions of the experiment, whatever they were. If the experimenter cannot provide us with the identifying characteristics of like subjects and of the same conditions, we cannot know where to apply the conclusions of the experiment.[9] The scope of the induction can be increased by choosing subjects at random from an existent population of subjects, and by choosing environmental conditions from an existent population of these, but then the induction from sampling would apply only to those finite, existent populations. Predictions to situations other than the sampled existent ones must be made on other grounds. This will require the *explicit* specification of conditions, or the adoption of some assumption to the effect that conditions will be presented (but not by a voluntary act of selection) to the experimenter in a random fashion. This all amounts to the assertion of a complex probabilistic theory which is to be verified by the experimentation. Without such a theory the act of randomization is useless.

9. In this connection Cochran and Cox wrote, ". . . agricultural and field experiments are often repeated both at a number of places and for a number of years. . . . In experimental programs of this type, it is usually hoped that the places and years constitute a representative sample of the population of places and years to which the results will be applied. There are obvious practical difficulties in choosing places and years that can confidently be asserted to be such a representative sample, and sometimes little effort is made to ensure that this will be so. The hard fact is that any statistical inference made from an analysis of the data will apply only to the population (if one exists) of which the experiments are a random sample. If this population is vague and unreal, the analysis is likely to be a waste of time, at least from the strictly practical point of view." William G. Cochran and Gertrude M. Cox, *Experimental Designs*, (New York: Wiley, 1950), p. 411.

THE VERIFICATION OF HYPOTHESES

The Specification of Conditions. In a sense, a theory says every-thing it has to say all at once, and to make it say something about a specific instance some parts of the theory have to be pinned down. This is accomplished by specifying the values of some of the vari-ables in the theory and thereby deriving a specific consequence.[10] The examples given to illustrate this point are usually taken from physics (the law of freely falling bodies is asserted under the condi-tion that the falling is done in a vacuum; the boiling point of water depends upon the pressure of the water, etc.), but it is possible to find examples from social research. In general, whenever a relation-ship between two variables is affected by a third variable, that vari-able becomes a condition for the relationship.

The significance of these remarks is that any test of a theory requires the specification of conditions under which certain results are expected. The researcher must ascertain that those conditions did in fact exist when the test was made, and to do this he must make observations on the conditioning variables. Thus observations enter into the testing situation at two points: the empirical determination of the specified conditions and the empirical determination of the hypothesized results.

Errors of Observation. The fact that the act of making observations may introduce errors into the testing setting serves to complicate the task of verification. A hypothesis may be mistakenly rejected or accepted because of error introduced either in the empirical certifi-cation of the conditions or of the results or both. To deal with this we must learn something about the possible errors that may obscure the phenomena or make them appear different and thereby lead us astray in evaluating our hypotheses.

These errors, if they exist, are as much phenomena to be explained as the events to which they are connected. We proceed in the ex-planation of errors in the same way we do in the explanation of the phenomena of primary interest, i.e., by the formulation and veri-fication of propositions about the errors. This does not mean that the propositions formed to explain the errors have to be the same as those formed to explain the phenomenon studied. In fact, the ex-planation of errors may be formally independent of the substantive theory, so that a statistical theory of errors may be employed in the testing of deterministic hypotheses and so on, for all the com-

10. Popper, *op. cit.*, sect. 28.

binations of types of errors and types of hypotheses. The theory of errors is auxiliary to the substantive theory of primary concern.

The intrusion of errors of observation makes for peculiar difficulties in the process of verification in that the same data are used to disentangle the workings out of two distinct theories. To cope with the complexities added by the intrusion of errors of observation, we must deal with the fundamental problem of verifying hypotheses in general. We shall, therefore, restrict ourselves to the brief comments we have already made about these errors and return to the main trend of our discussion.

The Empirical Implications of Deterministic and Probabilistic Hypotheses. The hypotheses tested empirically make assertions about the specific situation being observed. If the hypothesis is deterministic it asserts something of this sort: All A is B. From this we infer that if the instance before us is in fact A, then it must also be B. If, having determined that the instance is in fact A, we observe that it is not also B, we have a clear, logical contradiction of the hypothesis and would, therefore, regard it as false. If the instance is in fact both A and B, we would regard this as *consistent* with the hypothesis, but not as logical proof that the hypothesis is true, because the hypothesis refers to *all* instances of this kind and we have examined only one (or some) of them. From the standpoint of formal proof, nothing is changed if we should multiply the number of instances observed (i.e., enlarge the sample); the hypothesis is only not contradicted.

The testing of statistical hypotheses is even less definitive, for it turns out that they are not even formally refutable on material grounds. A statistical hypothesis asserts something about the proportion of an infinite collection of samples (or elements) that are of each possible sample type, but nothing at all about the order in which they will exist. All that a statistical hypothesis implies about *any particular sample* is that it be one of the logically possible ones, but not which one. For example, to assert that the probability of heads for a given coin is p implies no more about the empirical events than that any sample of tosses of the coin will consist of some proportion (*any* proportion, from zero to one) of heads. Thus, any result, any sample proportion of heads is formally consistent with the hypothesis and none is formally inconsistent with it. If matters were left at this, we should have to conclude that experience is irrelevant to the testing of statistical hypotheses and by virtue of this they would not be acceptable as scientific hypotheses.

It is clear that if statistical hypotheses are to be admitted as scientific propositions, they can be made empirically responsible only by a logically arbitrary decision to regard certain empirical results as consistent and confirming and to regard other empirical results as contradictory and disconfirming, even though all these empirical results are *logically* consistent with the respective hypotheses. The problem becomes one of finding a reasonable plan for determining which results shall be considered contradictory and which consistent and of justifying that plan with respect to scientific objectives.

Inductive Probability. Because of the empirical uncertainty stemming from errors of observation and intrinsic statistical formulations, and because no scientific hypothesis can be established conclusively, the entire process of verification has become regarded as probabilistic. In a broad construction, inductive probability has been construed as appropriate to the verification of any hypothesis, deterministic as well as statistical. This conception leads to statements asserting that it is probably true that all A is B (in the deterministic case) or it is probably true that the probability of B given A is p (in the statistical case).

To the extent that the probability-of-hypotheses conception is primarily an expression of the attitude toward induction that the verification of any hypothesis is always provisional and depends upon future observation, there seems to be nothing seriously objectionable about it. More than this is intended, however, for there is some general connotation that hypotheses are more or less likely to be refuted in the future depending upon the *degree* of verification in the past. This in itself seems reasonable enough, except that the idea has been pursued further by various schemes to quantify the degree of verification in probability terms, and these have been far from consistent with each other, much less universally acceptable.

The Test of Significance. The modern theory of statistical inference, however, while still a probabilistic policy of induction, has avoided the idea of the probability of a hypothesis in its program of dealing with statistical hypotheses. It concerns itself instead with the *probability of a correct decision* regarding a hypothesis tested.

The rationale of a test of significance is, in effect, this: If we adopt a rule to reject a statistical hypothesis whenever certain of the logically possible results occur and not to reject it when any of the other logically possible results occur, then if we test the hypothesis over and over again *indefinitely* and evaluate it each time by this rule, we should find that we have made the correct decision in a predictable proportion of the tests, provided the hypothesis is in fact true. There will be, then, as many rejections as there are events of the first kinds and as many failures to reject as there are events of the remaining kinds, if the events in fact occur as the hypothesis specified.

There is a fundamental difficulty with the theory of tests of significance. The probability of error is a hypothetical construct referring to a hypothetical population of tests. The empirical interpretation usually given this conception suggests to us that we can attain a desired level of accuracy in deciding the truth of a hypothesis is we test the hypothesis over and over again indefinitely. But this amounts to a commitment to test the same hypothesis forever, regardless of the previous outcomes. Thus the decision to reject or not to reject a hypothesis seems to be no more than to hang a "tag" on the hypothesis and to have no consequence for our future behavior with regard to that hypothesis.

This is patently absurd and not in fact what scientists do. They do not test the same hypothesis over and over again. Rather, a great many hypotheses will eventually be tested various finite numbers of times by a great number of researchers. The argument for tests of significance is that it is the proportions of *these* tests to which the level of significance is referred. Unfortunately this construction does not solve the problem, for it merely exchanges a sample space of tests of a single hypothesis for a sample space of tests of a large number of hypotheses. The latter sample space is a composite of all the separate spaces of the respective hypotheses. The "batting average" associated with the test of significance is still a hypothetical construct referring to an infinite number of tests.

There is another problem associated with the test of significance. The particular level of significance chosen for an investigation is not a logical consequence of the theory of statistical inference. We are free to choose whatever level seems appropriate. To cope with this arbitrariness (from the formal point of view) we are informed to consider a second kind of error, that of failing to reject the hypothesis tested when it is in fact false. That is, we are informed to choose a level of significance that balances the probability of the first kind of error against the probability of the second kind of error by a consideration of the costs attendant upon them and the costs of more sensitive research designs.

In many practical applications, for example the control of quality in manufacturing, the various costs can be expressed in terms of money or time or some such firm criterion. But in scientific research the calculation of costs is more complicated. To be sure we can compute the costs of taking various kinds and sizes of samples, but how are we to compute the costs of making an incorrect decision about a scientific hypothesis? Which should we fear most, rejecting a true hypothesis or failing to reject a false one and thereby rejecting a true alternative? There is as yet no firm criterion of costs, and in view of this the levels of significance so often used in sociological research (the 5 per cent and the 1 per cent levels) can hardly be the outcome of objective calculations of costs.

We must be explicit in disclaiming a possible interpretation of our criticism of statistical inference as implying that we abandon probability statements altogether. The fact is that the success of other sciences in using intrinsic and auxiliary probability statements and the promising results of their application in learning theory and small groups research argue against any categorical exclusion of statistical hypotheses in social science.

We can see no alternative to considering the probability of occurrence of certain consequences assuming that a hypothesis tested is true as *relevant* to the decision to regard that hypothesis as true in fact. Still this does not lead inevitably to the imperative criteria expressed in the test of significance. The precision and empirical concreteness often associated with the test of significance are illusory, and it would be a serious error to predicate our actions toward hypotheses on the test of significance as if it were a reliable arbiter of truth.

The Criterion of Systematic Import. Much of social research is informed by the strategy of searching for reliable empirical generalizations which, because of their empirical constancy, must be included as propositions within any theory that might later be formed to deal with the phenomena.[11] In this strategy the test of significance is often viewed as a means of determining which generalizations have that compelling empirical property. Thus we encounter statements to the effect that the test of significance tells us whether in a particular study there is anything to explain, i.e., whether a relationship between variables "exists" and so whether there is anything to theorize about. In view of the interpretive and pragmatic ambiguities involved in the test of significance this seems to be a very risky policy.

If we take as our objective the construction and verification of systematic theory, then the inductive policy we adopt should be

11. This discussion is a highly selected and simplified version of a complex point of view. Braithwaite and Popper offer comprehensive statements of the position. For an earlier and perhaps most understandable statement, see Homer H. Dubs, *Rational Induction*, (Chicago: The University of Chicago Press, 1930).

measured also against this criterion. We suggest the following considerations as an essential part of the inductive policy that sociologists might adopt in pursuit of this objective.

In the development of systematic theory, the purpose of research is not primarily to determine the empirical adequacy of a particular hypothesis. Its purpose is to test the coordinated formal system that produced the hypothesis as a theorem. The question of testing a hypothesis thus would not occur until that hypothesis had been set in an explicit deductive context. In this framework the process of testing a hypothesis is not an infinitely repeated act whose outcome is the accumulation of "verdicts," as is implied in the literal interpretation of the test of significance. The empirical truth of the particular hypotheses the researcher checks upon is valuable chiefly for its instrumental use in determining what he should do with the deductive system by which he produced the hypothesis. It is this conceptual relevance that we refer to as the systematic import of an empirical result.

It is clear that in this formulation, the process of induction intimately involves the verification of hypotheses, but it would be too simple to regard it as solely this. The history of science clearly indicates that theories do not emerge full grown from the brow of Jove and present themselves in their entirety to be tested, but rather that the construction of verified theory is a crescive process. Often research is undertaken not to test a theory, in the sense of trying to reject it, but to extend it, to determine its scope of applicability or to enlarge this scope by the introduction of modifications in the theory.[12]

Thus to test a theory in the present framework means that there must be some conception of how the theory is to be treated as a result of the test. The alternative courses of action dependent upon the results of empirical investigation are seen as alternative steps in the process of theory construction and not simply the acceptance or rejection of a particular formulation. This implies that the contrasted alternatives in a test situation be constructive ones, for if induction were merely the elimination of alternatives we would establish any hypothesis by testing it against absurd or surely false formulations.

To the extent that we are comparing systems of hypotheses, the research situation can be made as finely structured as need be to decide between the systems. This is because many consequences can be deduced from each system and the comparison is made over

12. Dubs, *op. cit., chap.* 7.

all of these. We would never be in a position of deciding between alternatives on the basis of a single hypothesis.

These considerations would seem to be essential aspects of the process of induction, but they could only be a part of the process. What more is required has only partly been determined. For example, although a great deal has been written about the nature of theory and its role in induction, astonishingly little attention has been given the process of theory development itself.[13]

SUMMARY AND CONCLUSIONS

In attempting to clarify the role of probability in sociological research we have been led into a discussion of the nature of scientific theory and induction. We have tried to articulate the principle that since scientific induction is accomplished through the construction and verification of deductive theories, the primary concern of the social scientist ought to be the development of such theories.

We distinguish three major uses of probability in science: in intrinsic statistical hypotheses; in auxiliary statistical hypotheses, including the theory of errors of observation, sampling from finite populations, and randomized experimentation; and thirdly in inductive probability policies, particularly the theory of tests of significance.

We have tried to show that the hypothetical character of the risk probabilities associated with the level of significance and the pragmatic ambiguities of the rationale for choosing any particular level of significance seriously undermine its value in the evaluation of statistical hypotheses.

It is our belief that the great reliance upon tests of significance so often found in sociologists is chiefly an attempt to provide scientific legitimacy to empirical research without adequate theoretical significance. Lest we be misunderstood we wish to emphasize the point that the construction of deductive theory is *developmental*, involving an *accumulation* of research experience. But it also involves formal reasoning, and the task of the scientist is to expose his thinking to a formal reconstruction, to formalize it as well as he can, so that it can contribute to the construction of a deductive system of some size and scope.

13. For an important contribution to the understanding of the development of theory, see *Types of Formalization in Small Group Research* by Joseph Berger, Bernard P. Cohen, J. Laurie Snell, and Morris Zelditch (Boston: Houghton Mifflin, 1962).

5. What Is Wrong with Social Theory?

HERBERT BLUMER

MY CONCERN is limited to that form of social theory which stands or presumes to stand as a part of empirical science.[1]

The aim of theory in empirical science is to develop analytical schemes of the empirical world with which the given science is concerned. This is done by conceiving the world abstractly, that is, in terms of classes of objects and of relations between such classes.

Reprinted by permission from the *American Sociological Review*, 19 (February 1955), pp. 3–10. Copyright © 1955 American Sociological Association.

1. There are two other legitimate and important kinds of social theory which I do not propose to assess. One of them seeks to develop a meaningful interpretation of the social world or of some significant part of it. Its aim is not to form scientific propositions but to outline and define life situations so that people may have a clearer understanding of their world, its possibilities of development, and the directions along which it may move. In every society, particularly in a changing society, there is a need for meaningful clarification of basic social values, social institutions, modes of living and social relations. This need cannot be met by empirical science, even though some help may be gained from analysis made by empirical science. Its effective fulfillment requires a sensitivity to new dispositions and an appreciation of new lines along which social life may take shape. Most social theory of the past and a great deal in the

Theoretical schemes are essentially proposals as to the nature of such classes and of their relations where this nature is problematic or unknown. Such proposals become guides to investigation to see whether they or their implications are true. Thus, theory exercises compelling influence on research – setting problems, staking out objects and leading inquiry into asserted relations. In turn, findings of fact test theories, and in suggesting new problems invite the formulation of new proposals. Theory, inquiry and empirical fact are interwoven in a texture of operation with theory guiding inquiry, inquiry seeking and isolating facts, and facts affecting theory. The fruitfulness of their interplay is the means by which an empirical science develops.

Compared with this brief sketch of theory in empirical science, social theory in general shows grave shortcomings. Its divorcement from the empirical world is glaring. To a preponderant extent it is compartmentalized into a world of its own, inside of which it feeds on itself. We usually localize it in separate courses and separate fields. For the most part it has its own literature. Its lifeline is primarily exegesis – a critical examination of prior theoretical schemes, the compounding of portions of them into new arrangements, the translation of old ideas into a new vocabulary, and the occasional addition of a new notion as a result of reflection on other theories. It is remarkably susceptible to the importation of schemes from outside its own empirical field, as in the case of the organic analogy, the evolutionary doctrine, physicalism, the instinct doctrine, behaviorism, psychoanalysis, and the doctrine of the conditioned reflex. Further, when applied to the empirical world social theory is primarily an interpretation which orders the world into its mold, not a studious cultivation of empirical facts to see if the theory fits. In terms of both origin and use social theory seems in general not to be geared into its empirical world.

present is wittingly or unwittingly of this interpretative type. This type of social theory is important and stands in its own right.

A second type of theory might be termed "policy" theory. It is concerned with analyzing a given social situation, or social structure, or social action as a basis for policy or action. It might be an analysis of communist strategy and tactics, or of the conditions that sustain racial segregation in an American city, or of the power play in labor relations in mass production industry, or of the morale potential of an enemy country. Such theoretical analysis is not made in the interests of empirical science. Nor is it a mere application of scientific knowledge. Nor is it research inquiry in accordance with the canons of empirical science. The elements of its analysis and their relations have a nature given by the concrete situation and not by the methods or abstractions of empirical science. This form of social theorizing is of obvious importance.

Next, social theory is conspicuously defective in its guidance of research inquiry. It is rarely couched in such form as to facilitate or allow directed investigation to see whether it or its implications are true. Thus, it is gravely restricted in setting research problems, in suggesting kinds of empirical data to be sought, and in connecting these data to one another. Its divorcement from research is as great as its divorcement from its empirical world.

Finally, it benefits little from the vast and ever growing accumulation of "facts" that come from empirical observation and research inquiry. While this may be due to an intrinsic uselessness of such facts for theoretic purposes, it also may be due to deficiency in theory.

These three lines of deficiency in social theory suggest that all that is needed is to correct improper preoccupations and bad working practices in theorizing. We hear repeatedly recommendations and injunctions to this effect. Get social theorists to reduce drastically their preoccupation with the literature of social theory and instead get in touch with the empirical social world. Let them renounce their practice of taking in each other's washing and instead work with empirical data. Let them develop their own conceptual capital through the cultivation of their own empirical field instead of importing spurious currency from alien realms. Get them to abandon the practice of merely interpreting things to fit their theories and instead test their theories. Above all, get them to cast their theory into forms which are testable. Have them orient their theory to the vast bodies of accumulated research findings and develop theory in the light of such findings.

These are nice injunctions to which all of us would subscribe. They do have a limited order of merit. But they neither isolate the problem of what is basically wrong with social theory nor do they provide means of correcting the difficulties. The problem continues to remain in the wake of studies made with due respect to the injunctions. There have been and there are many able and conscientious people in our field alone who have sought and are seeking to develop social theory through careful, sometimes meticulous preoccupation with empirical data — Robert E. Park, W. I. Thomas, Florian Znaniecki, Edwin Sutherland, Stuart Dodd, E. W. Burgess, Samuel Stouffer, Paul Lazarsfeld, Robert Merton, Louis Wirth, Robin Williams, Robert Bales and dozens of others who equally merit mention. All of these people are empirically minded. All have sought in their respective ways to guide research by theory and to assess their theoretical propositions in the light of empirical data. Practically all of them are familiar with the textbook canons of empirical research. We cannot correctly accuse such people of indifference to the empirical world, or of procedural naivete, or of professional incompetence. Yet their theories and their work are held suspect and found wanting, some theories by some, other theories by others. Indeed, the criticisms and countercriticisms directed to their respective work are severe and box the compass. It is obvious that we have to probe deeper than the level of the above injunctions.

In my judgment the appropriate line of probing is with regard to the concept. Theory is of value in empirical science only to the extent to which it connects fruitfully with the empirical world. Concepts are the means, and the only means of establishing such connection, for it is the concept that points to the empirical instances about which a theoretical proposal is made. If the concept is clear as to what it refers, then sure identification of the empirical instances may be made. With their identification, they can be studied carefully, used to test theoretical proposals and exploited for suggestions as to new proposals. Thus, with clear concepts theoretical statements can be brought into close and self-correcting relations with the empirical world. Contrariwise, vague concepts deter the identification of appropriate empirical instances, and obscure the detection of what is relevant in the empirical instances that are chosen. Thus, they block connection between theory and its empirical world and prevent their effective interplay.

A recognition of the crucial position of concepts in theory in empirical science does not mean that other matters are of no importance. Obviously, the significance of intellectual abilities in theorizing, such as originality and disciplined imagination, requires no highlighting. Similarly, techniques of study are of clear importance. Also, bodies of fact are necessary. Yet, profound and brilliant thought, an arsenal of the most precise and ingenious instruments, and an extensive array of facts are meaningless in empirical science without the empirical relevance, guidance and analytical order that can come only through concepts. Since in empirical science everything depends on how fruitfully and faithfully thinking intertwines with the empirical world of study, and since concepts are the gateway to that world, the effective functioning of concepts is a matter of decisive importance.

Now, it should be evident that concepts in social theory are distressingly vague. Representative terms like mores, social institutions, attitudes, social class, value, cultural norm, personality, reference group, social structure, primary group, social process, social system, urbanization, accommodation, differential discrimination and social control do not discriminate cleanly their empirical instances. At best they allow only rough identification, and in what is so roughly identified they do not permit a determination of what is covered by the concept and what is not. Definitions which are provided to such terms are usually no clearer than the concepts which they seek to define. Careful scrutinizing of our concepts forces one to recognize that they rest on vague sense and not on precise specification of attributes. We see this in our common experience in explaining concepts to our students or outsiders. Formal definitions are of little use. Instead, if we are good teachers we seek to give the sense of the concept by the use of a few apt illustrations. This initial sense, in time, becomes entrenched through the sheer experience of sharing in a common universe of discourse. Our concepts come to be taken for granted on the basis of such a sense. It is such a sense and not precise specifications that guides us in our discipline in transactions with our empirical world.

This ambiguous nature of concepts is the basic deficiency in social theory. It hinders us in coming to close grips with our empirical world, for we are not sure what to grip. Our uncertainty as to what we are referring obstructs us from asking pertinent questions and setting relevant problems for research. The vague sense dulls our perception and thus vitiates directed empirical observation. It subjects our reflection on possible relations between concepts to wide bands of error. It encourages our theorizing to revolve in a separate world of its own with only tenuous connection with the empirical world. It limits severely the clarification and growth that concepts may derive from the findings of research. It leads to the undisciplined theorizing that is bad theorizing.

If the crucial deficiency of social theory, and for that matter of our discipline, is the ambiguous nature of our concepts, why not proceed to make our concepts clear and definite? This is the nub of the problem. The question is how to do this. The possible lines of answer can be reduced a lot by recognizing that a great deal of endeavor, otherwise conscientious and zealous, does not touch the problem. The clarification of concepts is not achieved by introducing a new vocabulary of terms or substituting new terms—the task is not one of lexicography. It is not achieved by extensive reflection on theories to show their logical weaknesses and pitfalls. It is not accomplished by forming or importing new theories. It is not achieved by inventing new technical instruments or by improving the reliability of old techniques—such instruments and techniques are neutral to the concepts on behalf of which they may be used. The clarification of concepts does not come from piling up mountains of research findings. As just one illustration I would point to the hunreds of studies of attitudes and the thousands of items they have yielded; these thousands of items of findings have not contributed one iota of clarification to the concept of attitudes. By the same token, the mere extension of research in scope and direction does not offer in itself assurance of leading to clarification of concepts. These various lines of endeavor, as the results themselves seem abundantly to testify, do not meet the problem of the ambiguous concept.

The most serious attempts to grapple with this problem in our field take the form of developing fixed and specific procedures designed to isolate a stable and definitive empirical content, with this content constituting the definition or the reference of the concept. The better known of these attempts are the formation of operational definitions, the experimental construction of concepts, factoral analysis, the formation of deductive mathematical systems and, although slightly different, the construction of reliable quantitative indexes. Although these attempts vary as to the kind of specific procedure that is used, they are alike in that the procedure is designed to yield through repeated performances a stable and definitive finding. A definition of intelligence as being the intelligence quotient is a convenient illustration of what is common to these approaches. The intelligence quotient is a stable and discriminating finding that can be checked through a repetition of clearly specified procedures. Ignoring questions as to the differential merit and the differential level of penetration between these approaches, it would seem that in yielding a specific and discriminating content they are the answer to the problem of the ambiguous concept in social theory. Many hold that resolute employment of one or the other of these methods will yield definitive concepts with the consequence that theory can be applied decisively to the empirical world and tested effectively in research inquiry.

So far, the suitability of these precision endeavors to solving the problem of the ambiguous concept remains in the realm of claim and promise. They encounter three pronounced difficulties in striving to produce genuine concepts related to our empirical world.

First, insofar as the definitive empirical content that is isolated is regarded as constituting by itself the concept (as in the statement that, "X is the intelligence quotient"), it is lacking in theoretic possibilities and cannot be regarded as yielding a genuine concept. It does not have the abstract character of a class with specifiable attributes. What is "intelligence quotient" as a class and what are its properties? While one can say that "intelligence quotient" is a class made up of a series of specific intelligence quotients, can one or does one point out common features of this series—features which, of course, would characterize the class? Until the specific instances of empirical content isolated by a given procedure are brought together in a class with common distinguishing features of content, no concept with theoretic character is formed. One cannot make proposals about the class or abstraction or relate it to other abstractions.

Second, insofar as the definitive empirical content that is isolated is regarded as qualifying something beyond itself (as in the statement that, "Intelligence is the intelligence quotient," wherein intelligence would now be conceived as including a variety of common sense references such as ability to solve business problems, plan campaigns, invent, exercise diplomatic ingenuity, etc.), the concept is constituted by this something which is beyond the definitive empirical content. But since this "something beyond" is not dealt with by the procedure yielding the definitive empirical content, the concept remains in the ambiguous position that originally set the problem. In other words, the concept continues to be constituted by general sense or understanding and not by specification.

Third, a pertinent question has to be faced as to the relation of the definitive empirical content that is isolated, to the empirical world that is the concern of the discipline. One has to have the possibilities of establishing the place and role of the specific content in the empirical world in order for the empirical content to enter into theory about the world. A specific procedure may yield a stable finding, sometimes necessarily so by the internal mechanics of the procedure. Unless this finding is shown to have a relevant place in the empirical world under study, it has no value for theory. The showing of such relevancy is a critical difficulty confronting efforts to establish definitive concepts by isolating stable empirical contents through precise procedures. Incidentally, the establishment of such relevancy is not accomplished by making correlations. While classes of objects or items covered by concepts may be correlated, the mere establishment of correlations between items does not form concepts or, in other words, does not give an item as an instance of a class, a place or a function. Further, the relevance of an isolated empirical content to the empirical world is not established merely by using the concept to label given occurrences in the empirical world. This is a semantic pit into which scores of workers fall, particularly those working with operational definitions of concepts or with experimental construction of concepts. For example, a careful study of "morale" made in a restricted experiment may yield a stable finding; however, the mere fact that we customarily label many instances in our empirical world with the term "morale" gives no assurance whatsoever that such an experimental construct of "morale" fits them. Such a relation has to be established and not presumed.

Perhaps these three difficulties I have mentioned may be successfully solved so that genuine definitive concepts of theoretic use can be formed out of the type of efforts I have been considering. There still remains what I am forced to recognize as the most important question of all, namely whether definitive concepts are suited to the study of our empirical social world. To pose such a question at this point seems to move in a reverse direction, to contradict all that I have said above about the logical need for definitive concepts to overcome the basic source of deficiency in social theory. Even though the question be heretical I do not see how it can be avoided. I wish to explain why the question is very much in order.

I think that thoughtful study shows conclusively that the concepts of our discipline are fundamentally sensitizing instruments. Hence, I call them "sensitizing concepts" and put them in contrast with definitive concepts such as I have been referring to in the foregoing discussion. A definitive concept refers precisely to what is common to a class of objects, by the aid of a clear definition in terms of attributes or fixed bench marks. This definition, or the bench marks, serve as a means of clearly identifying the individual instance of the class and the make-up of that instance that is covered by the concept. A sensitizing concept lacks such specification of attributes or bench marks and consequently it does not enable the user to move directly to the instance and its relevant content. Instead, it gives the user a general sense of reference and guidance in approaching empirical instances. Whereas definitive concepts provide prescriptions of what to see, sensitizing concepts merely suggest directions along which to look. The hundreds of our concepts—like culture, institutions, social structure, mores, and personality—are not definitive concepts but are sensitizing in nature. They lack precise reference and have no bench marks which allow a clean-cut identification of a specific instance, and of its content. Instead, they rest on a general sense of what is relevant. There can scarcely be any dispute over this characterization.

Now, we should not assume too readily that our concepts are sensitizing and not definitive merely because of immaturity and lack of scientific sophistication. We should consider whether there are

other reasons for this condition and ask particularly whether it is due
to the nature of the empirical world which we are seeking to study
and analyze.

I take it that the empirical world of our discipline is the natural
social world of every-day experience. In this natural world every
object of our consideration—whether a person, group, institution,
practice or what not—has a distinctive, particular or unique character
and lies in a context of a similar distinctive character. I think that it is
this distinctive character of the empirical instance and of its setting
which explains why our concepts are sensitizing and not definitive.
In handling an empirical instance of a concept for purposes of study
or analysis we do not, and apparently cannot meaningfully, confine
our consideration of it strictly to what is covered by the abstract
reference of the concept. We do not cleave aside what gives each
instance its peculiar character and restrict ourselves to what it has in
common with the other instances in the class covered by the concept. To the contrary, we seem forced to reach what is common by
accepting and using what is distinctive to the given empirical instance. In other words, what is common (i.e., what the concept refers
to) is expressed in a distinctive manner in each empirical instance
and can be got at only by accepting and working through the distinctive expression. All of us recognize this when we commonly ask,
for instance, what form does social structure take in a Chinese peasant community or in an American labor union, or how does assimilation take place in a Jewish rabbi from Poland or a peasant from
Mexico. I believe that you will find that is is true in applying any of
our concepts to our natural empirical world, whether it be social
structure, assimilation, custom, institution, anomie, value, role, stratification or any of the other hundreds of our concepts. We recognize
that what we are referring to by any given concept shapes up in a
different way in each empirical instance. We have to accept, develop
and use the distinctive expression in order to detect and study the
common.

This apparent need of having to make one's study of what the
concept refers to, by working with and through the distinctive or
unique nature of the empirical instance, instead of casting this
unique nature aside calls, seemingly by necessity, for a sensitizing
concept. Since the immediate data of observation in the form of the
distinctive expression in the separate instances of study are different,
in approaching the empirical instances one cannot rely on bench
marks or fixed, objective traits of expression. Instead, the concept
must guide one in developing a picture of the distinctive expression,

as in studying the assimilation of the Jewish rabbi. One moves out from the concept to the concrete distinctiveness of the instance instead of embracing the instance in the abstract framework of the concept. This is a matter of filling out a new situation or of picking one's way in an unknown terrain. The concept sensitizes one to this task, providing clues and suggestions. If our empirical world presents itself in the form of distinctive and unique happenings or situations and if we seek through the direct study of this world to establish classes of objects and relations between classes, we are, I think, forced to work with sensitizing concepts.

The point that I am considering may be put in another way, by stating that seemingly we have to *infer* that any given instance in our natural empirical world and its content are covered by one of our concepts. We have to make the inference from the concrete expression of the instance. Because of the varying nature of the concrete expression from instance to instance we have to rely, apparently, on general guides and not on fixed objective traits or modes of expression. To invert the matter, since what we infer does not express itself in the same fixed way, we are not able to rely on fixed objective expressions to make the inference.

Given current fashions of thought, a conclusion that concepts of social theory are intrinsically sensitizing and not definitive will be summarily dismissed as sheer nonsense by most people in our field. Others who are led to pause and give consideration to such a conclusion may be appropriately disquieted by what it implies. Does it mean that our field is to remain forever in its present state of vagueness and to forego the possibilities of improving its concepts, its propositions, its theory and its knowledge? This is not implied. Sensitizing concepts can be tested, improved and refined. Their validity can be assayed through careful study of empirical instances which they are presumed to cover. Relevant features of such instances, which one finds not to be covered adequately by what the concept asserts and implies, become the means of revising the concept. To be true, this is more difficult with sensitizing concepts than with definitive concepts precisely because one must work variable instead of fixed forms of expression. Such greater difficulty does not preclude progressive refinement of sensitizing concepts through careful and imaginative study of the stubborn world to which such concepts are addressed. The concepts of assimilation and social disorganization, for instance, have gained more fitting abstraction and keener discrimination through insightful and realistic studies, such as those of W. I. Thomas and Robert E. Park. Actually, all that I am saying here is that careful and probing study of occurrences in our natural social world provides the means of bringing sensitizing concepts more and more in line with what such study reveals. In short, there is nothing esoteric or basically unusual in correcting and refining sensitizing concepts in the light of stubborn empirical findings.

It should be pointed out, also, that sensitizing concepts, even though they are grounded on sense instead of on explicit objective traits, can be formulated and communicated. This is done little by formal definition and certainly not by setting bench marks. It is accomplished instead by exposition which yields a meaningful picture, abetted by apt illustrations which enable one to grasp the reference in terms of one's own experience. This is how we come to see meaning and sense in our concepts. Such exposition, it should be added, may be good or poor—and by the same token it may be improved.

Deficiency in sensitizing concepts, then, is not inevitable nor irremediable. Indeed, the admitted deficiency in our concepts, which certainly are used these days as sensitizing concepts, is to be ascribed to inadequacy of study of the empirical instances to which they refer, and to inadequacy of their exposition. Inadequate study and poor exposition usually go together. The great vice, and the enormously widespread vice, in the use of sensitizing concepts is to take them for granted—to rest content with whatever element of plausibility they possess. Under such circumstances, the concept takes the form of a vague stereotype and it becomes only a device for ordering or arranging empirical instances. As such it is not tested and assayed against the empirical instances and thus forfeits the only means of its improvement as an analytical tool. But this merely indicates inadequate, slovenly or lazy work and need not be. If varied empirical instances are chosen for study, and if that study is careful, probing and imaginative, with an ever alert eye on whether, or how far, the concept fits, full means are provided for the progressive refinement of sensitizing concepts.

Enough has been said to set the problem of what is wrong with social theory. I have ignored a host of minor deficiencies or touched them only lightly. I have sought to pin-point the basic source of deficiency. This consists in the difficulty of bringing social theory into a close and self-correcting relation with its empirical world so that its proposals about that world can be tested, refined and enriched by the data of that world. This difficulty, in turn, centers in the concepts of theory, since the concept is the pivot of reference, or the gateway, to that world. Ambiguity in concepts blocks or frustrates contact with the empirical world and keeps theory apart in a corresponding unrealistic realm. Such a condition of ambiguity seems in general to be true of concepts of social theory.

How to correct this condition is the most important problem of our discipline insofar as we seek to develop it into an empirical science. A great part, if not most, of what we do these days does not touch the problem. Reflective cogitation on existing theory, the formulation of new theory, the execution of research without conceptual guidance or of research in which concepts are accepted uncritically, the amassing of quantities of disparate findings, and the devising and use of new technical instruments — all these detour around the problem.

It seems clear that there are two fundamental lines of attack on the problem. The first seeks to develop precise and fixed procedures that will yield a stable and definitive empirical content. It relies on neat and standardized techniques, on experimental arrangements, on mathematical categories. Its immediate world of data is not the natural social world of our experience but specialized abstractions out of it or substitutes for it. The aim is to return to the natural social world with definitive concepts based on precisely specified procedures. While such procedures may be useful and valuable in many ways, their ability to establish genuine concepts related to the natural world is confronted by three serious difficulties which so far have not been met successfully.

The other line of attack accepts our concepts as being intrinsically sensitizing and not definitive. It is spread the logical difficulties confronting the first line of attack but at the expense of forfeiting the achievement of definitive concepts with specific, objective bench marks. It seeks to improve concepts by naturalistic research,[2] that is, by direct study of our natural social world wherein empirical instances are accepted in their concrete and distinctive form. It depends on faithful reportorial depiction of the instances and on analytical probing into their character. As such its procedure is markedly different from that employed in the effort to develop definitive concepts. Its success depends on patient, careful and imaginative life study, not on quick shortcuts or technical instruments. While its progress may be slow and tedious, it has the virtue of remaining in close and continuing relations with the natural social world.

The opposition which I have sketched between these two modes of attack sets, I believe, the problem of how the basic deficiency of social theory is to be addressed. It also poses, I suspect, the primary line of issue in our discipline with regard to becoming an empirical science of our natural social world.

2. I have not sought in this paper to deal with the logic of naturalistic research.

PART THREE

Sampling Techniques: Strategies for Observing Elements of Theory and Social Structure

INTRODUCTION

SEVERAL of the themes in this part were anticipated in Camilleri's article in the previous part—chiefly, how does the investigator move from his theory to empirical observations which will permit the best possible test of that theory? Camilleri noted several different strategies, including probability, convenience, and judgment samples. Before the problems surrounding each of these methods can be discussed, however, the general process of sampling must be placed in proper focus.

THE NATURE OF SAMPLING

As the observer moves from theory to data he confronts two problems: what units to observe, and whether or not those units will permit generalizations to other cases and instances of the same phenomena. The observations must permit theoretical analysis, and in this simple sense all acts of observation must be theoretically directed. Of equal importance, however, is the assumption that the observations will permit descriptions and explanations of how individuals are linked to, shaped by, and—in turn—create features of social structure. The sociologist must be able to move from his observations to features of social structure, be these descriptions of how individuals enter into and are influenced by social relationships, social groups, or entire communities.

The logic for sampling must be established. It is seldom feasible or possible for a researcher to observe all the units or events relevant to his theory. Problems of access to such units, restrictions of time, money, and even personnel limit total observations. When testing a theory, for instance, the investigator seldom gathers data relevant to every hypothesis. He assumes that by testing certain key hypotheses, generalizations regarding the other propositions are possible. Or when studying a social organization he will find that it is simply impossible to interview every member. The strategy of observing a portion of some total set of events, or objects is termed "sampling"; sampling is a fact of social research.

WHAT TO OBSERVE

Depending on his theory, interests, and proclivities, the researcher may observe one or any combination of the following: (1) time and its organization and passage; (2) features from a theory; (3) social situations; (4) persons aggregately distributed over time and space; (5) interactive collectivities of persons as seen in social groups, relationships, encounters, organizations, communities, or entire societies. The three readings in this section alternatively treat these elements. Glaser and Strauss indicate how properties of a theory may be sampled; Coleman reviews strategies for sampling persons in various states of social organization; Lipset, Trow, and Coleman present a discussion of the problems involved in making statements about an entire social organization. They present features of their sampling model and indicate the costs and consequences of each phase of the sampling and observational act.

SOME SAMPLING PRINCIPLES

A number of assumptions underlie sampling activity. First, the researcher must insure that his observations are theoretically directed. Second, he must be able to locate and ennumerate those units which constitute his sampling frame. This may involve listing hypotheses from a theory, or—under more difficult conditions—determining the names of every member of an organization. From this total set of events a sample will then be drawn. This sample must be representative of that population in the sense that members of the sample do not differ significantly from the population. If differences appear, they must be recognized, for they can serve to restrict generalizations to that population.

Fourth, drawing on Glaser and Strauss, it is possible to hold up the criterion of sampling until a grounded theory is developed. The investigator must remain in the field until he has adequately tested or formulated his theory. A sense of ongoing inclusion thus underlies the sampling act. Sampling, theory, and hypothesis testing continually interact in the production of new theory.

Fifth, the investigator must attempt to sample natural empirical events, or natural data outcroppings. The naturalistic perspective presented by Blumer demands the sampling and analysis of behavior as it occurs in its natural settings, not in settings of the investigator's choosing or construction. Such units would include work groups, athletic teams, marriages, and even street gangs. Sampling of this order insures that observations directly relevant to theory will be collected.

Sixth, whenever possible, sampling should be comparative in nature. Observations should not be restricted to one group, setting, or process. A comparative focus increases the possibilities of locating strategic data which may refute emerging hypotheses. If just one data source is sampled, the investigator runs the risk of observing only events that will confirm his hypotheses. A theory must always be put to the severest possible test. Comparative sampling facilitates such tests.

Seventh, the investigator must make every step in the sampling process public. He must carefully record how he selected his units, why he chose some and not others, and he should detail the problems encountered when he began his observations. Unless a public record is given, future researchers are restricted in their ability to build upon and replicate earlier studies. The research act must be a public act.

SAMPLING MODELS

The researcher may employ two basic types of sampling models. The first is noninteractive and the second is interactive. Noninteractive models restrict analysis of how natural social units interrelate. These are often variations on the simple random sample, wherein the observed objects are assumed to be independent of one another. Noninteractive sampling typically proceeds in terms of such variables as social class position, age, sex, educational attainment, or religious preference. Such samples are often statistically rigorous, as the Glaser and Strauss, and Lipset, Trow, and Coleman selections indicate. There are several varieties of the noninteractive model: the simple random, the stratified random, the cluster technique, and the multistage, stratified cluster sample. Coleman offers a critique of these models, as do Glaser and Strauss.

Interactive sampling models explicitly focus on natural behavioral units and offer strategies for uncovering how such units interrelate and influence one another. These include techniques for sampling social relationships, social groups, organizations, and cliques.

It is frequently the case that the user of an interactive sampling model is forced to violate certain assumptions underlying the noninteractive method. It is often impossible to completely ennumerate the population from which the natural unit is drawn. For example, how many relationships are contained within a small community? This is a relevant question if the researcher desires to make generalizations concerning, for example, the effects of social relationships upon individual attitudes. Of course the assumption that the sampled units do not interrelate, which is integral to the simple random sample, has to be violated.

It is clear, then, that the use of interactive sampling models demands a reconceptualization of the traditional standards of sampling evaluation. This is the problem taken up by Glaser and Strauss. They state that the researcher must not permit formal rules of method to stand in the way of theory construction. Their solution is the use of theoretical sampling, a technique that directs the researcher to collect, code, analyze, and test hypotheses *during* the sampling process.

A commitment to theoretical sampling, which in my judgment is a variation on the use of interactive strategies, suggests a number of basic differences between the interactive and noninteractive methods. Theoretical sampling does not end until theory has been adequately grounded. Statistical, or noninteractive, sampling ends when a predetermined sample has been observed. Theoretical samples are judged by the quality of theory. Statistical samples are judged by the extent to which they conform to the rigorous rules of statistical sampling theory.

RELEVANT STRATEGIES

Theoretical sampling raises such basic questions as what groups to observe, when to stop observing, and what data to gather. These questions lead Glaser and Strauss to discuss how a researcher selects "slices of data" and how he determines when "saturation" has occurred. The general rule is that one ceases to sample when no new data are forthcoming. Their use of theoretical sampling parallels Blumer's conception of the exploration phase of research and should be understood in that light. The researcher will collect any and all data relevant to his problems, will carefully record all negative cases, and will continuously monitor his data for their theoretical relevance. The selection from Glaser and Strauss extends Blumer's position and offers more explicit directives for implementing the naturalistic perspective.

Coleman's criticism of the traditional survey and the sampling method complements Glaser and Strauss's article. The Coleman selection has the advantage of indicating how the researcher can work within the survey method and still develop generalizations concerning properties of social structure. His discussion of pair, clique, and homogeneity analysis suggests how interactions within natural social units may be undertaken.

The selection from the highly influential *Union Democracy* by Lipset, Trow, and Coleman raises a series of critical issues that any researcher must resolve when he undertakes the observation and analysis of a social organization. The authors suggest that a basic question involves whether the analysis is going to be particularistic and relevant only to the organization selected for study, or whether it is going to be general. If the latter, then steps must be taken to permit generalizations to the class of objects from which the single case was drawn. Though their aim was to study the International Typographical Union so that generalizations to union politics could be developed, they admit that their own study does not clearly fall into either category.

When a generalizing and comparative study is undertaken, three problems must be confronted. First, what dimensions and units of analysis are going to be selected for attention? Second, how are those going to be observed (i.e., sampled and measured)? Third, how are they going to be interrelated so that systematic theory can be developed? In Table 8.1 Lipset *et al.* present the levels of analysis employed in *Union Democracy*. It also pinpoints the types of data taken from each level. As can be seen, generalizations were developed at three levels: the union as a total system, the workshops, and the individual workers. In one sense, the unit of analysis was the entire union, but at other levels it was the shops and the attitudes of the workers. As a point of analysis, Lipset, Trow, and Coleman took specific sets of behaviors (a given vote in an election) and attempted to work from these behaviors to the total system. They note that no firm strategy can be given for such analyses. Their method had restrictions, for statements about the workers' attitudes were limited.

In their study the reader is offered explanations that move from the organizational to the interactional and the individual levels. The complexity of the union as a social organization clearly emerges from the data. Their study has great relevance for the sampling process because it indicates the variety of problems that must be resolved before a single observation is gathered. It also shows how sampling can proceed in a multistage fashion — shifting at appropriate points from level to level. *Union Democracy* sets a high standard for all organizational studies. It also shows how the sampling process must continually interact with the development of theory. Lipset, Trow, and Coleman were engaging in a sophisticated form of structural analysis. Social organization clearly emerges as an interactional concern within their data and interpretations.

The readings in this section offer the reader a glimpse of how theory, data, sampling, and hypothesis interact to produce the synthetic analysis of social organization. Sociology is nothing if it is not the study of social interaction and social organization, hence the intent of this section: to show how such studies may be implemented.

Suggested Readings. A highly statistical treatment of modern sampling theory is presented in Leslie Kish's *Survey Sampling*, (New York: Wiley, 1965). This book must be read for a more comprehensive understanding of statistical sampling theory. It should be read in the context of Glaser and Strauss' *The Discovery of Grounded Theory* (Chicago: Aldine Publishing Company, 1967), which, as the selection from it in this part indicates, presents the logic for an alternative view of the sampling process.

Because of space limitations three highly relevant papers were excluded from this section: Peter M. Blau, "Structural Effects," *American Sociological Review* 25 (April 1960), 178-93; Linda Brookover and Kurt W. Back, "Time Sampling as a Field Technique," *Human Organization* 25 (Spring, 1966), 64-70; and Elihu Katz and Paul F. Lazarsfeld, "Choice of a City," from the 1964 Free Press paperback edition of *Personal Influence*, pp. 335-39. The Blau discussion offers a useful model for discerning the relationship between individual attributes and structural characteristics. The Brookover and Back article presents one of the few analyses of time sampling techniques. Katz and Lazarsfeld detail the steps a survey researcher passes through when he selects a city for study.

6. Theoretical Sampling

BARNEY G. GLASER AND
ANSELM L. STRAUSS

THEORETICAL sampling is the process of data collection for generating theory whereby the analyst jointly collects, codes, and analyzes his data and decides what data to collect next and where to find them, in order to develop his theory as it emerges. This process of data collection is *controlled* by the emerging theory, whether substantive or formal. The initial decisions for theoretical collection of data are based only on a general sociological perspective and on a general subject or problem area (such as how confidence men handle prospective marks or how policemen act toward Negroes or what happens to students in medical school that turns them into doctors). The initial decisions are not based on a preconceived theoretical framework.

The basic question in theoretical sampling (in either substantive or formal theory) is: *what* groups or subgroups does one turn to *next*

Reprinted from Barney G. Glaser and Anselm L. Strauss, *The Discovery of Grounded Theory* (Chicago: Aldine Publishing Company, 1967), pp. 45, 47, 62–71. Copyright © 1967 by Barney G. Glaser and Anselm L. Strauss.

in data collection? And for *what* theoretical purpose? In short, how does the sociologist select multiple comparison groups? The possibilities of multiple comparisons are infinite, and so groups must be chosen according to theoretical criteria.

THEORETICAL AND STATISTICAL SAMPLING

It is important to contrast theoretical sampling based on the saturation of categories with statistical (random) sampling. Their differences should be kept clearly in mind for both designing research and judging its credibility. Theoretical sampling is done in order to discover categories and their properties, and to suggest the interrelationships into a theory. Statistical sampling is done to obtain accurate evidence on distributions of people among categories to be used in descriptions or verifications. Thus, in each type of research the "adequate sample" that we should look for (as researchers and readers of research) is very different.

The adequate theoretical sample is judged on the basis of how widely and diversely the analyst chose his groups for saturating categories according to the type of theory he wished to develop. The adequate statistical sample, on the other hand, is judged on the basis of techniques of random and stratified sampling used in relation to the social structure of a group or groups sampled. The inadequate theoretical sample is easily spotted, since the theory associated with it is usually thin and not well integrated, and has too many obvious unexplained exceptions. The inadequate statistical sample is often more difficult to spot; usually it must be pointed out by specialists in methodology, since other researchers tend to accept technical sophistication uncritically.

The researcher who generates theory need not combine random sampling with theoretical sampling when setting forth relationships among categories and properties. These relationships are suggested as hypotheses pertinent to direction of relationship, not tested as descriptions of both direction and magnitude. Conventional theorizing claims generality of scope; that is, one assumes that if the relationship holds for one group under certain conditions, it will probably hold for other groups under the same conditions.[1] This assumption of persistence is subject only to being disproven—not proven—when other sociologists question its credibility. Only a reversal or disappearance of the relationship will be considered by

1. See discussion on this in Hans L. Zetterberg, *On Theory and Verification in Sociology* (Totowa, N.J.: Bedminster Press, 1963), pp. 52–56.

sociologists as an important discovery, not the rediscovery of the same relationship in another group, since once discovered, the relationship is assumed to persist. Persistence helps to generalize scope but is usually considered uninteresting, since it requires no modification of the theory.

Furthermore, once discovered the relationship is assumed to persist in direction no matter how biased the previous sample of data was, or the next sample is. Only if the hypothesis is disproven do biases in the sample come under question. For generating theory these biases are treated as conditions changing the relationship, which should be woven into the analysis as such. Thus, random sampling is not necessary for theoretical sampling, either to discover the relationship or check out its existence in other groups.[2] However, when the sociologist wishes also to describe the magnitude of relationship within a particular group, random sampling, or a highly systematic observation procedure done over a specified time is necessary. For example, after we discovered the positive relationship between the attention that nurses gave dying patients and the nurses' perceptions of a patient's social loss, we continually found this relationship throughout our research and were quick to note conditions altering its direction. But we could never state the precise magnitude of this relationship on, say, cancer wards, since our sampling was theoretical.

Another important difference between theoretical and statistical sampling is that the sociologist must learn when to stop using the former. Learning this skill takes time, analysis and flexibility, since making the theoretically sensitive judgment about saturation is never precise. The researcher's judgment becomes confidently clear only toward the close of his joint collection and analysis, when consid-

2. We have taken a position in direct opposition to Udy, who says: "Any research of any type whatsoever which seeks to make generalizations beyond the material studied involves problems of sampling. . . . [The researcher] is implicitly identifying a larger population, of which his cases purport to be a representative sample, and contending that certain relationships observed in his sample could not have occurred there by chance. It is simply not true that one can avoid sampling problems by proceeding in words instead of numbers or by avoiding the use of statistical techniques, though it is unfortunately true that by avoiding such methods one can often keep sampling problems from becoming explicit." Udy's gross, categorical position could be modified to compatibility with ours, we believe, if he thought rather in terms of diverse purposes of research and the degree to which each purpose requires a relationship to be described in terms of its various properties: existence, direction, magnitude, nature, and conditions, etc. In any event, a few lines later he then admits that "one cannot really solve them" (problems of representativeness). Stanley H. Udy, Jr., "Cross Cultural Analysis: A Case Study," in Phillip Hammond, ed., *Sociologists at Work* (New York: Basic Books, 1964), pp. 169–70.

erable saturation of categories in many groups to the limits of his data has occurred, so that his theory is approaching stable integration and dense development of properties.

By contrast, in statistical sampling the sociologist must continue with data collection no matter how much saturation he perceives. In his case, the notion of saturation is irrelevant to the study. Even though he becomes aware of what his findings will be, and knows he is collecting the same thing over and over to the point of boredom, he must continue because the rules of accurate evidence require the fullest coverage to achieve the most accurate count. If the researcher wishes to diverge from his preplanned research design because of conceptual realizations and implicit analyses, he must hold his wish in abeyance or laboriously integrate his new approach into the research design, to allow a new preplanned attack on the total problem. He must not deviate from this new design either; eventually it leads him back into the same "bind."[3]

SLICE OF DATA

In theoretical sampling, no one kind of data on a category nor technique for data collection is necessarily appropriate. Different kinds of data give the analyst different views or vantage points from which to understand a category and to develop its properties; these different views we have called *slices of data*. While the sociologist may use one technique of data collection primarily, theoretical sampling for saturation of a category allows a multi-faceted investigation, in which there are no limits to the techniques of data collection, the way they are used, or the types of data acquired.[4] One reason for this openness of inquiry is that, when obtaining data on different groups, the sociologist works under the diverse structural conditions of each group: schedules, restricted areas, work tempos,

3. For example, Udy says, "The coding operation proved to be very tedious 'dog work' in the worst sense of the terms. I . . . was now attempting to resist, rather than encourage flights of imagination. I had to accept the fact that there were gaps in the data about which I could do nothing" (*op. cit.*, pp. 178–79). To avoid this bind, many sociologists hire data collectors and coders in preplanned research for description and verification. Then, however, discoveries are made too late to effect changes in data collection. See the tug-of-war waged between Riesman and Watson on this bind: Riesman continually wanted to break out and Watson wanted to maintain tight control; David Riesman and Jeanne Watson, "The Sociability Project: A Chronicle of Frustration and Achievement," in Hammond, *op. cit.*, pp. 269–84.

4. For examples of multifaceted investigations, see in Hammond, *op. cit.*: the research chronicles of Renee Fox, "An American Sociologist in the Land of Belgian Research"; Dalton; and Seymour M. Lipset, "The Biography of a Research Project: Union Democracy."

the different perspectives of people in different positions, and the availability of documents of different kinds. Clearly, to succeed he must be flexible in his methods and in his means for collecting data from group to group.[5]

The result is, of course, a variety of slices of data that would be bewildering if we wished to evaluate them as accurate evidence for verifications. However, for generating theory this variety is highly beneficial, because it yields more information on categories than any one mode of knowing (technique of collection). This makes the research very exciting to the sociologist, providing motivation to keep him at his task. The different ways of knowing about a category virtually force him to generate properties as he tries to understand the differences between the various slices of data, in terms of the different conditions under which they were collected.[6] But it must be remembered that this comparative analysis of different slices of data should be based on the researcher's theoretical understanding of the category under diverse conditions, not on methodological differences and on standard problems of the diverse techniques he has used.

Among the many slices of data that may be collected, which one is the best to obtain? The answer is, of course, the collection technique that best can obtain the information desired, provided that conditions permit its use in some manner.[7] For an extreme example, Dalton had to bribe a secretary in order to see secret personnel records so that he could find out the ethnic composition of an executive hierarchy, rather than trying to guess its composition from names.[8]

Most often, however, the sociologist's strategy will be constrained by such structural conditions as who is available to be observed, talked with, overheard, interviewed, or surveyed, and at what times. He should realize that no matter what slices of data he is able to obtain, comparing their differences generates properties, and most

5. Compare the flexibility in ethics of Dalton, *op. cit.*, pp. 59–62, with the ethical problems of Riesman and Watson, *op. cit.*, pp. 260–69.

6. Lipset said he wished to test his theory of union democracy by a survey of the International Typographers' Union. What actually happened when he compared this new slice of data to the formed theory was not testing but coming to terms with differences. Thereby more theory on union democracy was generated. See Seymour M. Lipset in Hammond, *op. cit.*, pp. 107–119.

7. Thus, any discussion about whether survey data are better or worse than field data is usually meaningless. Often the researcher is forced to obtain only one kind—and when theory is the objective, both kinds are useful. Only under particular conditions of a group which allows both does the question arise: which method would give the best data on the information desired? The answer is technical, not doctrinaire.

8. Dalton, *op. cit.*, pp. 66 and 67.

any slice can yield the same necessary social-structural information. For example, no matter whom the sociologist observes or talks with in a situation where someone is dying (patient, nurse, doctor, chaplain or family member), he will soon know what type of awareness context is operating. Possibly his theory will receive considerable development from any information that happens his way; even subtantively "trivial" data can help, if it yields useful information on a relevant category. For example, one can gain useful data on the life styles of professionals by examining, for this group, a national market-research survey about meat consumption (done for the meat-packing industry). The data need not be important in themselves; only the category which they indicate must be theoretically relevant. Similarly, a down-to-earth article on illness and pain by a nurse or patient may yield very useful information to a researcher who is studying the management of pain in hospitals.

Another slice of data that should be used is the "anecdotal comparison." Through his own experiences, general knowledge, or reading, and the stories of others, the sociologist can gain data on other groups that offer useful comparisons. This kind of data can be trusted if the experience was "lived." Anecdotal comparisons are especially useful in starting research and developing core categories. The researcher can ask himself where else has he learned about the category and make quick comparisons to start to develop it and sensitize himself to its relevancies.

As everyone knows, different people in different positions may offer as "the facts" very different information about the same subject, and they vary that information considerably when talking to different people. Furthermore, the information itself may be continually changing as the group changes, and different documents on the same subject can be quite contradictory. Some sociologists see these circumstances as presenting an unbounding relativism of facts — no data are accurate. Since such a situation is unbearable to those who wish to verify or describe, they tend to claim that only their method can give the "accurate" evidence. Other methods that they might use only yield biased or impressionistic data, and so can be discounted.[9]

9. For example, "The significance of the quantitative case study, then, is (1) that it stimulates the kind of theoretical insights that can be derived only from quantitative analysis as well as the kind that results from close observation of an empirical situation, and (2) that it provides more severe checks on these insights than an impressionistic study and thus somewhat increases the probably validity of conclusions." Peter Blau, "The Research Process in the Study of the Dynamics of Bureaucracy," in Hammond, *op. cit.*, p. 20.

Using this argument, they take only one slice or mode of knowing as giving the "facts." Since they do not seek other modes, they remain untroubled. For example, in one noted study of adolescents in high school, only the adolescents were surveyed; and in a study of workers in a factory, only workers were observed and interviewed.[10]

But when different slices of data are submitted to comparative analysis, the result is *not* unbounding relativism. Instead, it is a proportioned view of the evidence, since, during comparison, biases of particular people and methods tend to reconcile themselves as the analyst discovers the underlying causes of variation. This continual correction of data by comparative analysis gives the sociologist confidence in the data upon which he is basing his theory, at the same time forcing him to generate the properties of his categories. The continual correction of data also makes the sociologist realize clearly an important point: when used elsewhere, theory generated from just one kind of data never fits, or works as well, as theory generated from diverse slices of data on the same category. The theory based on diverse data has taken into consideration more aspects of the substantive or formal area, and therefore can cope with more diversity in conditions and exceptions to hypotheses.

If the sociologist has two slices of data (such as field and survey data), but does not engage in comparative analysis, he will generate his theory from one mode of collection and ignore the other completely when it disproves his theory – although he may selectively use confirmatory pieces of the other data as supporting evidence. Thus, when no comparative analysis is done, different slices of data are seen as tests of each other, not as different modes of knowing that must be explained and integrated theoretically. The result is that, without comparative analysis, even men who generate theory tend to use and fall into the rhetoric of verification.[11] They miss out on the rich diversity of modes of knowing about their categories. And they fail to tell their readers of their other data, since they believe, quite wrongly, that it disproves their theory, when it would have actually enriched it immensely.

10. James Coleman, "Research Chronicle: The Adolescent Society," in Hammond, *op. cit.*, pp. 198-204; and James Coleman, *The Adolescent Society* (New York: Free Press of Glencoe, 1961), and see, for the study of workers, Donald Roy, "Efficiency and the Fix: Informal Intergroup Relations in a Piecework Machine Shop," *American Journal of Sociology*, 60 (1954), 255-66.

11. These same sociologists tend to be debunkers who try to dig up something out of their own reading to disprove the theory presented by their colleague. They do not understand they are merely offering a new slice of data that under comparative analysis would enrich his theory by providing or modifying properties and categories.

DEPTH OF THEORETICAL SAMPLING

The *depth* of theoretical sampling refers to the amount of data collected on a group and on a category.[12] In studies of verification and description it is typical to collect as much data as possible on the "whole" group. Theoretical sampling, though, does not require the fullest possible coverage on the whole group except at the very beginning of research, when the main categories are emerging—and these tend to emerge very fast.[13] Theoretical sampling requires only collecting data on categories, for the generation of properties and hypotheses.

Even this kind of selective collection of data, however, tends to result in much excess data, from which new and related categories emerge. For example, after a full day in the field, when the field worker is tired and jammed with dozens of incidents to report in his field notes, he need only dictate data about his categories. Going through his categories also helps him to remember data he may have forgotten during his full day. With these categories firmly in mind, directing his attention, the field worker can focus on remembering the details of his day's observations with the confidence that the notes will be implicitly guided by his categories. Any additional information he decides to note afterwards is "gravy" for theoretical consideration, not a required chore for the fullest coverage. Theoretical sampling, therefore, can save much time in note-taking.

It is not too difficult to compare as many as forty groups on the basis of a defined set of categories and hypotheses (not on the basis of the "whole" group), and when groups within groups are compared (*e.g.*, different and similar wards within different types of hospitals). These groups can be studied one at a time, or a number can be studied simultaneously. They can also be studied in quick succession, to check out major hypotheses before too much theory is built around them. Without theoretical sampling, the field worker, or the writer of a survey questionnaire, collects as much data as he can and hopes that this full coverage will "catch enough" that later will prove relevant. Probably, though, it will prove too thin a basis for a developed theory.[14] Theoretical sampling reduces the mass of data that otherwise would be collected on any single group. Indeed, without

12. See the instructive discussion on "depth" by Udy, *op. cit.*, pp. 164–65.
13. For examples on the quick emergence of relevant categories see Blanche Geer, "First Days in the Field," in Hammond, *op. cit.*; and Blau, *op. cit.*, pp. 33–34. Blau discovered the significance of the "consultation" pattern within a week after starting his field research.
14. For example see Riesman and Watson, *op. cit.*, p. 295.

theoretical sampling for categories one could not sample multiple groups; he would be too bogged down trying to cover just one.

The depth to which a category should be sampled is another matter. The general idea is that the sociologist should sample a category until confident of its saturation, but there are qualifications. All categories are obviously not equally relevant, and so the depth of inquiry into each one should not be the same.[15] *Core* theoretical categories, those with the most explanatory power, should be saturated as completely as possible. Efforts to saturate less relevant categories should not be made at the cost of resources necessary for saturating the core categories. As his theory develops and becomes integrated, the sociologist learns which categories require the most and least complete saturation, and which ones can be dropped. Thus, the theory generates its own selectivity for its direction and depth of development.

In actual practice, even the saturation of core categories can be a problem. In field work especially, the tendency always is to begin collecting data for another category before enough has been collected on a previous one. The sociologist should continue to saturate all categories until it is clear which are core categories. If he does not, he risks ending up with a vast array of loosely integrated categories, none deeply developed. This results in a thin, unbalanced theory. Since stable integration of the theory requires dense property development of at least some core categories, it then becomes difficult to say which of the array are the core categories; that is, those most relevant for prediction and explanation.

TEMPORAL ASPECTS OF THEORETICAL SAMPLING

When generating theory through joint theoretical collection, coding, and analysis of data, the temporal aspects of the research are different from those characteristic of research where separate periods of work are designated for each aspect of the research. In the latter case, only brief or minor efforts, if any, are directed toward coding and analysis while data are collected. Research aimed at discovering theory, however, requires that all three procedures go on simultaneously to the fullest extent possible; for this, as we have said, is the underlying operation when generating theory. Indeed, it is impossible to engage in theoretical sampling without coding and analyzing at the same time.

15. Edward A. Shils, "On the Comparative Study of New States," in Clifford Geertz, ed., *Old Societies and New States* (New York: Free Press, 1963), pp. 5, 9.

Theoretical sampling can be done with previously collected research data, as in secondary analysis, but this effort requires a large
mass of data to draw on in order to develop a theory of some density
of categories and properties. The sociologist engages in theoretical
sampling of the previously collected data, which amounts to collecting data from collected data. Also. he is bound to think of ways to
make quick, brief data-collection forays into other groups, to find
additional relevant comparative data. Therefore, in the end, theoretical sampling and data collection for discovering theory become
simultaneous, whether the sociologist uses collected data or collects
his own data, or both. How much time and money are available is
important in deciding to what degree the data to be sampled will
have been collected previously by the researcher or anyone else who
compiles data.

7. Relational Analysis: The Study of Social Organizations with Survey Methods

JAMES S. COLEMAN

SURVEY research methods have often led to the neglect of social structure and of the relations among individuals. On the other hand, survey methods are highly efficient in bringing in a large volume of data—amenable to statistical treatment—at a relatively low cost in time and effort. Can the student of social structure enjoy the advantages of the survey without neglecting the relationships which make up that structure? In other words, can he use a method which ordinarily treats each individual as an isolated unit in order to study social structure?

The purpose of this paper is to describe some important developments in survey research which are giving us a new way of studying social organization.

It is useful to trace briefly the history of survey research, to indicate how it has grown from "polling" to the point where it can now study problems involving complex human organization. A look at this history indicates two definite stages. The first was a polling stage which was concerned with the *distribution* of responses on any one

Reprinted from *Human Organization*, 16 (Summer 1958), pp. 28–36. Copyright © 1958 by the Society for Applied Anthropology.

item: What proportion favored Roosevelt in 1936? What proportion was in favor of labor unions? This type of concern continues even today among pollsters, and to the lay public it is still the function of surveys to "find out what people think" or to see just how many feel thus and so.

Among sociologists, however, this purely descriptive use of survey research was soon supplanted by an *analytical* one. First there began to be a concern with how different subgroups in the population felt or behaved. From this, the analysts moved on to further cross-tabulations. Finally, some survey analysts began, through cross-tabulations and correlations, to study complicated questions of why people behaved as they did. By relating one opinion item to another, attitude configurations and clusters of attitudes emerged; by relating background information to these attitudes, some insight was gained into the *determinants* of attitudes. It was in this analytical stage, then, beyond the simple description of a population, that survey research began to be of real use to social science.

But throughout all this one fact remained, a very disturbing one to the student of social organization. The *individual* remained the unit of analysis. No matter how complex the analysis, how numerous the correlations, the studies focused on individuals as separate and independent units. The very techniques mirrored this well: Samples were random, never including (except by accident) two persons who were friends; interviews were with one individual, as an atomistic entity, and responses were coded onto separate IBM cards, one for each person. As a result, the kinds of substantive problems on which such research focused tended to be problems of "aggregate psychology," that is, *within*-individual problems, and never problems concerned with relations between people.

Now, very recently, this focus on the individual has shown signs of changing, with a shift to groups as the units of analysis, or to networks of relations among individuals. The shift is quite a difficult one to make, both conceptually and technically, and the specific methods used to date are only halting steps toward a full-fledged methodology. Nevertheless, some of these methods are outlined below, to indicate just how, taken together, they can even now provide us with an extremely fruitful research tool. This tool has sometimes been used for the study of formal organization but more often for the study of the informal organization which springs up within a formal structure. In both cases, it shows promise of opening to research, problems which have been heretofore the province of speculation.

PROBLEMS OF DESIGN AND SAMPLING

The break from the atomistic concerns of ordinary survey analysis requires taking a different perspective toward the individual interview. In usual survey research and statistical analysis, this interview is regarded as *independent* of others, as an entity in itself. All cross-tabulations and analyses relate one item in that questionnaire to another item in the same questionnaire. But, in this different approach, an individual interview is seen as a *part* of some larger structure in which the respondent finds himself: his network of friends, the shop or office where he works, the bowling team he belongs to, and so on. Thus, as a part of a larger structure, the individual is *not* treated independently. The analysis must somehow tie together and interrelate the attributes of these different parts of the structure.

So much for the basic change in perspective — away from the atomistic treatment of the individual interview, and toward the treatment of each interview as a part of some larger whole. This basic perspective has several implications for the kind of data collected and for the sample design. Perhaps the most important innovation in the kind of data collected is sociometric-type data in the interview, that is, explicit questions about the respondent's relation to other specific individuals. Each person may be asked the names of his best friends, or the names of his subordinates in the shop upon whom he depends most, or any one of a multitude of *relational* questions. For example, in a study of two housing projects by Merton, Jahoda, and West,[1] one way to map out the informal social structure in the community was to ask people who their best friends were. Having obtained such data from all the families in the project, so that each family could be located in the network of social relations in the community, it was then possible to examine the relation between this social structure, on the one hand, and various values and statuses on the other. Specifically, this information allowed these authors to show that in one housing project social ties were based very largely on similarities in background and religion; in the other, social relations were more often built around common leisure interests and participation in community organizations.

More generally, the incorporation of sociometric-type data into survey research allows the investigator to *locate* each interviewed

1. Robert K. Merton, Patricia S. West, and Marie Jahoda, *Patterns of Social Life: Explorations in the Sociology of Housing*, forthcoming.

individual within the networks of voluntary relations which surround him. In some cases, these networks of voluntary relations will be superimposed on a highly articulated formal structure. In a department of a business, for example, there are numerous hierarchical levels and there are numerous work relations which are imposed by the job itself. In such cases, sociometric-type questions can be asked relative to these formal relations, e.g.: "Which supervisor do you turn to most often?" or, "Which of the men in your own workgroup do you see most often outside of work?" or, "When you want X type of job done in a hurry to whom do you go to get it done?" or, "When you need advice on such-and-such a problem, whom do you usually turn to?"

Another kind of data is that which refers to some larger social unit. For example, in some research on high schools currently being carried out at The University of Chicago, it is necessary to find the paths to prestige within a school, so that the boys are asked: "What does it take to be important and looked up to by the other fellows here at school?". Then the responses to this question—aggregated over each school separately—can be used to characterize the *school* as well as the individual. Because of this, the question itself makes explicit reference to the school.

But apart from the kinds of data collected, there are also important *sampling* considerations. In this kind of research, it is no longer possible to pull each individual out of his social context and interview him as an independent entity. It is necessary to sample parts of that context as well or, to say it differently, to sample explicitly with reference to the social structure. There are numerous ways of doing this; only a few, which have been successfully tried, are mentioned below.

Snowball sampling. One method of interviewing a man's immediate social environment is to use the sociometric questions in the interview for sampling purposes. For example, in a study of political attitudes in a New England community, Martin Trow has used this approach: first interviewing a small sample of persons, then asking these persons who their best friends are, interviewing these friends, then asking *them* their friends, interviewing these, and so on.[2] In this way, the sampling plan follows out the chains of sociometric relations in the community. In many respects, this sampling technique is like that of a good reporter who tracks down "leads" from one person to another. The difference, of course, is that snowball

2. Martin A. Trow, "Right Wing Radicalism and Political Intolerance: A Study of Support for McCarthy in a New England Town." Unpublished Ph.D. disseration, Columbia University, 1957.

sampling in survey research is amenable to the same scientific sampling procedures as ordinary samples. Where the population in ordinary samples is a population of individuals, here it is two populations: one of individuals and one of *relations* among individuals.

Saturation sampling. Perhaps a more obvious approach is to interview *everyone* within the relevant social structure. In a study of doctors in four communities, *all* the doctors in these communities were interviewed.[3] Sociometric-type questions were then used to lay out the professional and social relations existing among these doctors. This "saturation" method or complete census was feasible there, because the total number of doctors in these communities was small—less than three hundred. But in the study mentioned earlier which used snowball sampling, such an approach would have been practically impossible, for the community was about 15,000 in size. Thus this "saturation sampling" is only feasible under rather special circumstances. A borderline case is the study of high schools mentioned earlier. There are 9,000 students in the ten schools being studied. Only because students are given self-administered questionnaires, rather than interviews, is it possible to use a saturation sample, and thereby characterize the complete social structure.

Dense sampling. Another approach is to sample "densely." This is a compromise between the usual thinly-dispersed random sample and the saturation sample. An illustration will indicate how this may be useful. In a study of pressures upon the academic freedom of college social science teachers, carried out by Paul Lazarsfeld, at least *half* of the social science faculty in every college in the sample was interviewed.[4] Thus, by sampling densely, enough men were interviewed in each college so that the climate of the college could be characterized, as well as the attitudes of the individual respondent.

Multi-stage sampling. Any of the above approaches to sampling can be combined with an element found in many sample designs: the multi-stage sample. For example, in the academic freedom study referred to above, it would have been impossible to have a dense sample of social science teachers in *all* the colleges in the United States, so a two-stage sample was used: first sampling colleges, and then teachers within colleges. In doing this, of course, the crucial question is what balance to maintain between the sampling of colleges and the sampling of teachers within colleges. Enough colleges

3. J. S. Coleman, E. Katz, and H. M. Menzel, "Diffusion of an Innovation Among Physicians," *Sociometry*, XX (Dec. 1957).

4. P. F. Lazarsfeld and Wagner Thielens, *The Academic Man: Social Scientists in a Time of Crisis*, The Free Press, Glencoe, Ill.: 1956.

are needed to have representativity, yet few enough so that the sampling within each one can be dense. In a study of union politics, reported in *Union Democracy*,[5] we perhaps made a wrong decision: we interviewed in 90 printing shops, spreading the interviews so thinly that only one man out of three—at most—was interviewed within the shop. This meant that we had only a very few interviews in each shop, and could not use the interview material to characterize the climate or atmosphere of the shops, except in the very largest ones.

These sampling procedures are, of course, not the only possible ones. An infinite degree of variation is possible, depending upon the problem and upon the kind of social structure involved. The most important point is that the individual interview can no longer be treated as an independent entity, but must be considered as a part of some larger whole: in the sampling, in the questions asked, and in the subsequent analysis.

ANALYTICAL METHODS

The real innovations in this new kind of research are in the techniques of analysis. I will mention several of these with which I am most familiar, to give an indication of the kinds of problems this research examines and the way it examines them.

Contextual analysis. The first, and the one closest to usual survey research, might be termed contextual analysis. In essence, it consists of relating a characteristic of the respondent's social context—and the independent variable—to a characteristic of the individual himself.[6] A good example of this occurred in *The American Soldier*, where the attitudes of inexperienced men, in companies where most others were inexperienced, were compared to attitudes of similarly inexperienced men in companies where most others were veterans. It was found that inexperienced men in green companies felt very differently about themselves, and about combat, than their counterparts in veteran companies. That is, when men were characterized by both individual characteristics and by their social surroundings, the latter were found to have an important effect on their attitudes.

5. S. M. Lipset, M. A. Trow, and J. S. Coleman, *Union Democracy* The Free Press, Glencoe, Ill.: 1956.

6. Peter Blau has emphasized the importance of such analysis in formal organizations for locating the "structural effects" of a situation upon the individuals in it. See his "Formal Organization: Dimensions of Analysis," *American Journal of Sociology*, LXIII (1957), 58-69.

In the union politics study mentioned above, one of the major elements in the analysis was an examination of the effect of the shop context on the men within the shop. We had access to voting records in union political elections for these shops, and these made it possible to characterize the shop as politically radical or politically conservative and as high or low in political consensus. Then we could examine the different behavior or attitudes of men in different kinds of shops and compute a "shop effect." An example is given in Table 7.1. Each man is in a shop of high or low political consensus, depending on whether the men in the shop vote alike or are evenly split between the radical and conservative parties. And each man has a certain degree of political activity. In this table, the shop's political consensus and the man's political activity are related. The table indicates that in shops of high consensus, men are politically more active than in shops of low consensus. The inference might be that high consensus provides a kind of resonance of political beliefs which generates a greater interest in politics. In any case, the table exemplifies the use of an attribute of a *shop* related to an attribute of a *man* in the shop. This general kind of analysis, which bridges the gap between two levels of sociological units—the individual and his social context—seems to be a very basic one for this "structural" approach to survey research.

TABLE 7.1.

		Shops of high political consensus	Shops of low political consensus
Per cent of men active in union politics		29%	7%
	N	(125)	(28)

Boundaries of homogeneity. A second kind of analysis attempts to answer the question: How homogeneous are various groups in some belief or attitude? In a medical school, for example, are a student's attitudes toward medicine more like those of his fraternity brothers or more like those of his laboratory partners? This question, incidentally, has been posed in a study of medical students presently being carried out at Columbia University.[7] The answer is, in the

___

7. Some of the work in this study (though not the work mentioned here) is reported in P. F. Kendall, R. K. Merton, and G. S. Reader, eds., *The Student Physician*, (New York: Commonwealth Fund, 1957).

particular medical school being studied, that his attitudes are far more like those of his fraternity brothers. In other words, in this medical school, the "boundaries of homogeneity" of certain attitudes about medicine coincide very largely with fraternity boundaries.

The major problems in answering questions of group homogeneity are problems of index construction. Consider the above example: each student has twenty or thirty fraternity brothers, but only three laboratory partners in anatomy lab. How can the effects of variability between groups, due to small numbers in a group, be separated out from the actual tendency toward homogeneity of attitude? It can be done, and indices have been developed to do so. The indices, incidentally, are much like the formulas by which statisticians measure the effects of clustering in a random sample.

An example of group homogeneity may indicate more concretely how this approach can be useful in research. In the study of doctors in four connumities mentioned earlier, we were interested in the social processes affecting the physicians' introduction of a new drug into their practices. Through interviewing all doctors and asking sociometric questions in the interview, we were able to delineate seven "cliques" of doctors who were sociometrically linked together. (How to reconstruct such cliques is another problem, which will be considered shortly.) The question, then, became this: At each point in time after the drug was marketed, were cliques homogeneous or not in their members' use or non-use of the drug? If they were homogeneous, then this was evidence that some kind of social influence or diffusion was going on in relation to the measured sociometric ties. If not, this indicated that the cliques delineated on the basis of questions in the interview had little relevance to drug adoption. Table 7.2 shows, for several time periods, just how much homogeneity there was in the cliques, beyond that which would arise by chance. An index value of 1.0 means each clique is completely homogeneous in its use or non-use of the drug. An index value of 0 means there is no more homogeneity than would arise through chance variation between groups.

Table 7.2 shows that there was no homogeneity until around seven months after the drug was introduced, that is, until over 50 percent of the doctors had used the drug. The maximum homogeneity was reached at about eleven months, when three-fourths of the doctors had begun to use the drug. Then after that, the homogeneity receded to zero again.

This result helped to reinforce a conclusion derived from other findings in the study: that the social networks measured in the study

TABLE 7.2.

Months after drug was marked	Amount of clique homogeneity	Percent of doctors who had used the drug
1 months	no homogeneity	14 %
3	no "	32
5	no "	49
7	.07	66
9	.12	71
11	.18	76
13	.03	83
15	no homogeneity	86

were effective as paths of diffusion at certain times but not at others. However, apart from the substantive results of the study, this example indicates how such analysis of the boundaries of homogeneity may be useful for the study of the functioning of various social organizations.

Pair analysis. Neither of the above kinds of analysis has required the use of sociometric-type data. An important kind of analysis which does use such direct data on relationships is the analysis of *pairs*. Here, the pair formed by A's choosing B becomes the unit of analysis. Speaking technically, "pair cards" may be constructed for each sociometric choice, and then these cards used for cross-tabulations. In other words, instead of cross-tabulating a man's attitude toward Russia with his attitude toward the United Nations, we can cross-tabulate the man's attitude toward Russia with the attitude toward Russia of the man he eats lunch with at the cafeteria.

One of the most important problems which has been studied in this way is the similarity or difference in attitudes or backgrounds between the two members of a pair. That is, do people have friendship relations with those who are like them politically, with people of the same age, with persons in the same occupation?

This kind of problem can be illustrated by Table 7.3, which contains hypothetical data. This table, which looks very much like an ordinary contingency table, must be treated in a slightly different fashion. It allows us to raise the question: Do boys tend to choose boys more than would be expected by chance? and, do girls tend to choose girls more than would be expected by chance? The answer, of course, depends upon what we take as chance. However, chance models have been worked out, so that one can assign measures of the tendency to choose others of one's own kind. For the above example,

Table 7.3.

	Chosen		
	boy	girl	
boy	45	15	60
girl	20	20	40
			100

Chooser

this measure (varying between 0 and 1) says that the tendency to in-choice for boys is .38 and that for girls is .17. By comparing such indices for numerous attributes, one could get a good glimpse into the informal social organization of the group. For example, in the medical study mentioned earlier which is being carried out at Columbia University, the values of in-choice tendency for friends shown in Table 7.4 were found:

Table 7.4.

Subgroups	Tendencies toward in-choice
Class in school	.92
Fraternity	.52
Sex	.33
Marital Status	.20
Attitudes toward national health insurance	.37

By looking at the relative sizes of these index values, we get an idea of just how the informal social relations — that is, the friendship choices — at this medical school mesh with the formal structure, and with the distribution of attitudes.

In the study mentioned above of drug introduction by doctors, these pair relations were used as the major aspect of the analysis: By examining how close in time a doctor's first use of a new drug was to the first use of the doctor he mentioned as a friend, it was possible to infer the functioning of friendship networks in the introduction of this drug.

These examples or pair analysis give only a crude picture of the kinds of problems which can be studied in this fashion. The important matter is to break away from the analysis of *individuals* as units to the study of *pairs* of individuals. To be sure, this involves technical IBM problems and problems of index construction along with conceptual problems, but the difficulties are not great.

Partitioning into cliques. Another important kind of problem is the partitioning of a larger group into cliques by use of sociometric choices. This problem is a thorny one, for it involves not only the delineation of cliques, but, even prior to this, the *definition* of what is to constitute a clique. Are cliques to be mutually exclusive in membership, or can they have overlapping memberships? Are they to consist of people who all name one another, or of people who are tied together by more tenuous connections? Such questions must be answered before the group can be partitioned into cliques.

A good review of some of the methods by which cliques and subgroups can be treated is presented in Lindzey and Borgotta.[8] The two most feasible of these are the method of matrix multiplication[9] and the method of shifting rows and columns in the sociometric choice matrix until the choices are clustered around the diagonal.[10] This last technique is by far the more feasible of the two if the groups are more than about twenty in size. When the groups are on the order of a hundred, even this method becomes clumsy. And IBM technique was successfully used in the study of doctors and the study of medical students, both mentioned above, in which the groups were 200-400 in size. At The University of Chicago, a program has been developed for Univac, using a method of shifting rows and columns in a matrix, which can handle groups up to a thousand in size.[11] The necessity for some such method becomes great when, for example, one wants to map out systematically the informal organization of a high school of a thousand students.

CONCLUSION

These four kinds of analysis, contextual analysis, boundaries of homogeneity, pair analysis, and partitioning into cliques, are only four of many possibilities. Several other approaches have been used, but these four give some idea of the way in which survey analysis can come to treat problems which involve social structure. In the long run, these modes of analysis will probably represent only the initial halting steps in the development of a kind of structural re-

8. G. Lindzey ed., *Handbook of Social Psychology*, Addison-Wesley, Cambridge, 1956, Chap. II.

9. See L. Festinger, "The Analysis of Sociograms Using Matrix Algebra," *Human Relations*, II, No. 2 (1949), 153-58 and R. D. Luce, "Connectivity and Generalized Cliques in Sociometric Group Structure," *Psychometrika*, XV (1950), 169-90.

10. C. O. Beum and E. G. Brundage, "A Method for Analyzing the Sociomatrix," *Sociometry*, XIII (1950), 141-45.

11. A description of this program, written by the author and Duncan McRae, is available upon request from the author and the program itself is available for copying, for those who have access to a Univac I or II.

search which will represent a truly sociological methodology. In any case, these developments spell an important milestone in social research, for they help open up for systematic research those problems which have heretofore been the province of the theorist or of purely qualitative methods.

There is one new development which should be mentioned, although the frontier is just opened, and not at all explored. This development is the construction of electronic computers with immediate-access storage capacities a hundred times the size of an 80-column IBM card. Such computers make it possible, for the first ime, to lay out a complex social structure for direct and systematic examination. Instead of examining the similarity of attitudes between socially-connected pairs, after laborious construction of "pair cards," it becomes possible to trace through a whole structural network, examining the points in the network where attitudes or actions begin to diverge. Methods for doing this have not yet been developed but, for the first time, the technical facilities exist, and it is just a matter of time until analytical methods are developed. IBM cards and counter-sorters were methodologically appropriate for the individualistic orientation which survey research has had in the past; electronic computers with large storage capacities are precisely appropriate for the statistical analysis of complex social organization.

Unfortunately, it has not been possible here to present any of the tools discussed above fully enough to show precisely how it is used. In giving a broad overview of a number of developments, my aim has been to point to an important new direction in social research, one which may aid significantly in the systematic study of social organization.

8. Organizational Analysis

SEYMOUR MARTIN LIPSET,
MARTIN TROW, AND JAMES S. COLEMAN

GENERAL PROBLEMS

WHEN an empirical analysis of a single case (in this instance, the typographical union's political system) is to be carried out, it can be of either of two general types, as follows:

(a) Description and explanation of the single case, to provide information concerning its present state, and the dynamics through which it continues as it does. This may be called a *particularizing* analysis.

(b) The development of empirical generalizations or theory through the analysis of the single case, using it not to discover anything about *it* as a system but as an empirical basis either for generalization or theory construction. This may be called a *generalizing* analysis.

The crucial element which distinguishes these two types of analysis is the way they treat general laws and particular statements about the single case. The first kind of analysis *uses* general laws or regularities in order to carry out the analysis of the particular case, much as a metallurgist utilizes his knowledge of general chemical properties in analyzing a sample of ore. That is, it uses previously known generalizations in order to help make particular statements. The second kind of analysis is just the reverse of this: Much as a biologist focuses his microscope on a living and growing fruit fly in order to make generalizations about processes of growth, the social scientist in this kind of analysis attempts to utilize the particular case in developing general statements. The particular statement and the general law trade places in these two types of analysis. In the former, the law is used to aid in making particular statements; in the second, the particular statements are used to develop the law.

Both these kinds of analysis have long and honorable traditions in the social sciences, as they have in the natural sciences,[1] perhaps the best-known case of the first in social research is Max Weber's *Protestant Ethic;* a good example of the second is Michel's *Political Parties*.[2] In the former, Weber used general, well-accepted relations between values and behavior in order to partially explain the genesis of capitalism. In the latter, Michels examined many aspects of the German Social Democratic Party over a period of time, not to make statements about that party, but to make statements about political parties in general.

The present analysis is not clearly in either of these categories; it always attempts to be in the second, though it sometimes goes no further than the first. Many statements refer to the ITU rather than to organizations in general, but at the same time there is usually implicit extension to organizations other than the ITU.

Since it is the second kind of analysis which is attempted here (though not always with success) several problems specific to this kind of analysis arise in the study.

1. Some men have suggested that all of social science must be a particularizing or "idiographic" science, as contrasted to the generalizing or "nomothetic" natural sciences. The most influential of these was Wilhelm Rickert; many social philosophers, since his time have spent much effort in refuting him. See, for example, Ernst Cassirer: *An Essay on Man* (New York: Doubleday, 1953), p. 235; and his *Substance and Function* (New York: Dover Publications, 1953), pp. 226 ff.

2. Perhaps better examples of the second type can be given if the analyses under consideration are not restricted to a single case analysis, as we have restricted them. Durkheim in *Suicide* (Glencoe, Ill.: Free Press, 1951) used particular cases of suicide (or more accurately, rates of suicide) occurring in many social situations, and abstracted from those situations the properties which they held in common and which appeared to be relevant to suicide. This allowed him to make general statements about social organization and suicide, or more generally, certain kinds of deviant behavior.

MULTIPLE-LEVEL ANALYSIS:
THE PROBLEM OF UNITS AND PROPERTIES

In an analysis of the second kind, a generalizing one, several requirements arise which a particularizing analysis need not meet. An important one is the necessity of delineating *units* of analysis and characterizing the units according to certain general *concepts* or *properties*.

If, as is possible in a particularizing analysis, nothing more than a vivid picture is to be given of the system being analyzed, this problem need not arise. A faithful recording of events as they occur can fulfill the task of the particularizing analysis, much as a documentary film does, without once using general sociological concepts. But in order to make generalizations which may be applied to other organizations, general sociological concepts must be used. In the present analysis, this means characterizing several different "sizes" or "levels" of units. The man, his immediate social environment (e.g., his shop), the local, and the ITU as a whole are a minimum set of units which it is necessary to characterize. In this study the union as a whole was characterized in terms of certain structural and environmental properties: for example, the degree of stratification in the occupation, the political structure of the union, the issues which have existed at various times, the union's policies, the kind of employer attitudes toward the union.

It was necessary to characterize the New York local as well by these same kinds of variables. For example, the difference in types of policy problems at the local and international levels was documented, and this was related to an important difference in voting behavior of some men on the two levels (i.e., the predominance of wage-scale problems in local politics leads to interest voting which often unseats the incumbent).

Besides these properties of the New York union which are observable in the perspective of the union as a whole, the random sample allowed characterization of the New York union in terms of some parameters of the distribution of the men's attributes. The average age of printers, the number of men who have other printers as their best friends, and the proportion of men who work nights are examples of this. Such attributes characterize the union as a whole, even though they are based on data gathered from individual men. The interview data were used for characterizing an intermediate social unit as well, the man's direct social environment. His shop and his chapel chairman were both characterized by means of the sample data (and by the actual records of the shop's vote). Finally, the greatest amount of data characterized the man himself: his attitudes, his background, his behavior, etc.

The kinds of observations made and the properties by which the various units were characterized are indicated in Table 8.1, which summarizes the above discussion. In the cells of the table are listed the kinds of properties by which these units were characterized. This table suggests the complexity of the analysis, for properties in each cell must be related to those in other cells in propositions or generalizations.

TABLE 8.1. *Types of Data Gathered, Types of Units Being Characterized, and Types of Resulting Properties*

		KINDS OF DATA				
	TOTAL SYSTEM	*INTERMEDIATE UNITS*			*INDIVIDUALS*	
Unit Being Characterized	*Issues; Data on Occupation; Union Laws; Policies; Historical Data; Convention Reports*	*Local's Histories and Voting Records; Issues on Local Level; Size of Locals*	*Shops' Voting Records; Shop Size*	*Interviews with Leaders*	*Interviews of the Sample of Men*	
ITU as a whole	*Structural, environmental, behavioral properties*	*By inference; communication network (structural)*				
Locals	*Behavioral properties (militancy, etc.)*	*Behavioral properties, size*	*By inference: communication network (structural)*	*Structural, environmental, behavioral properties*	*Distributions of individual properties*	
Shops			*Behavioral properties, and size*		*Distributions of individual properties*	
Other immediate social environment of men	*The social climate, by inference from dominant issues and election outcome*	*The social climate, by inference from dominant issues and election outcome*			*Chapel chairman's attributes, friends' attributes*	
Men	*By inference: dominant values and interests*	*By inference: values, interests, and loyalties (e.g., to local over international)*	*By inference: values, interests, and loyalties (e.g., to shop over local)*	*By inference: values*	*Behavior, background, values, attitudes*	

This complexity raises a number of problems in the design of a study. Some of the most important of these, in the present study, were those related to the interview data. These data were perhaps the most important in the study. It was a primary means of characterizing at least three of the units in the analysis: (1) The population of the New York local union as a whole, in order to make statements like: "X per cent of the members have good friends among other printers off the job."[3] (2) The immediate social environment of the individual, including his shop, the clubs to which he belongs, his close circle of friends, etc. Such characterizations are used in this study primarily for locating the effect of differing social environments on the individual. (3) The man, in order to determine relations between various properties of the man: his values and his vote, his background and his values, etc.

This study is weakest in its characterization of the immediate social environment. We could have attempted explicitly to characterize shops by interviewing all or almost all of the men in them, and by asking questions more specifically directed toward finding the man's relation to his shopmates and to the employer. But such concentration would have been made at the expense of other gains: Interviewing more men in each shop would have meant interviewing each man less thoroughly or else covering fewer shops, thus gaining knowledge about shops at the expense of knowledge about either individuals or the union as a whole.

What this really means is that not all values can be maximized at once, and that such studies as the present one must include in their design a decision as to what units it is most important to characterize with the interview data. As suggested above, the experience of the study suggests that in a single case analysis like this, it is more important to characterize the man and his immediate social environment than to characterize the union itself, that is, the single case being analyzed.

However, this is not the end of the sampling or design problems related to the interview data. Given some decision on the problem above, it is still necessary to decide whether some manner of random sampling is best (taking into account social environments, as indicated above, by two-stage sampling), or systematic sampling determined by the social or political structure of the union. We want to locate the elements which affect these men's political decisions. But do we consider all men's decisions equally important? Are not the decisions of some active men more important in influencing the

---

3. Such statements are ordinarily used in comparison of the union with another, or with itself at another time. If a comparative analysis . . . were being carried out, this would be a more important kind of statement than it is in this single-case analysis.

outcome of union elections than are those of the followers? And is this criterion of "importance to the outcome" the optimum criterion for our purpose? These are questions which this study only begins to answer. At the same time, they are questions whose answers are important in the design of research.

One possible answer has been suggested in the analysis: to develop a provisional model of the political system, conceived as a structure of interlocking decision (e.g., union officers, party leaders, convention delegates, voters), and to accurately measure the influences on each of these decisions. This would entail a rather complex research design, one which equalizes the accuracy with which each decision point in the system is analyzed.

MULTIPLE-LEVEL ANALYSIS:
RELATIONS BETWEEN DIFFERENT UNITS

The second major problem concerning units at different levels is the problem of relating them by means of generalizations. This problem is an important one, for it is such generalizations which are the fruits of the analysis. The problem in its simplest aspects may be posed in this way: Certain properties of one unit (e.g., the total union) are determinants of behavior at another level (e.g., the individual). Yet how is it possible to really bridge the gap between the units? For example, to say that a certain political climate characterizes the union does not mean that this climate is felt by all printers alike. The climate makes itself felt more strongly by some men than others, depending upon their social and political locations.

When an analysis is not one of this multiple-level sort, then such a problem never exists: Analysis relates an individual's political dispositions to his vote, or an organization's size to its bureaucratization. Both properties being related are attributes of the same unit (e.g., the individual, the organization), and there is no problem of bridging the gap between units at different levels.

We said above that relating two different levels is only the simplest case of the general problem. This certainly is so, for even if we succeed in relating properties of diverse social units to a man's vote decision, this is not at all the end of the analysis. The aim of this study is to be able to make statements about political systems as wholes, not statements about the determinants of individual vote decisions.

What we have done in focusing upon this individual vote decision has been to enter the system at a particular point and to work outward from there. . . .

But is this the best strategy for analyzing a social or political system? The point at which we entered is probably a very important one in the system, but would it have been better to proceed differently? For example, having a tentative *model* of the political system . . . the way is pointed to certain *variables* or concepts (which are simply the properties as outlined in Table 8.1) and certain *processes* which seem important in the operation of the system. Only one of these processes concerns the vote decision; others concern the policy decisions of the administrative leaders, and the decision of the oppositionists or potential oppositionists. Perhaps the best mode of analysis, given that the aim is to analyze the system as a whole, would be to start with a crude model . . . and to focus upon each of the processes postulated in that model. An example of the way that such an analysis would be of aid is the following: The model indicates that one important decision point in the system is the president's policy decisions. In particular, it suggests that to know the constraints placed by the organization upon the president is important. Thus it directs one to ask such questions as: What restrained Scott (the ITU president) from sending in strikebreakers to New York in 1919? And why was George Berry, the Pressmen president (who did send in strikebreakers for the same strike by the printing pressmen) not restrained in the same way?

If we had focused in this study on the several decision points, and on the communication processes, rather than entering the system at a particular point, the results might have been far superior to those obtained. However, this is a matter as yet unresolved, and we intend only to raise the problem: What is the most advantageous way to carry out a study of the dynamics of a social or political system?

THE PARADOX: HOW TO GENERALIZE FROM A SINGLE CASE

Another difficult problem arises in studies of organizations or social systems rather than individuals. Often, only a single case is analyzed, as is done here. This is in strong contrast to the usual statistical procedure with studies of individual behavior, where the number of cases is relatively great. The fact that the present study includes a sample of individuals from the union, and that part of the analysis is one of individual behavior, must not be allowed to confuse this issue. Clearly in this study these individuals are not themselves the focus of the analysis; it is the union as an organization which is the center of interest. This focus upon a single case rather than the statistical study of individual behavior implies a quite different kind of analysis. Perhaps some of the differences can be suggested by an analogy.

If a chemist is developing a theory or set of laws concerning the equilibrium system existing inside a test tube containing water, sodium hydroxide, and hydrochloric acid, he may utilize many kinds of data, but all from the single system which he has before him; tests of acidity, of electrical conductivity, examination of precipitate, and general knowledge about the reactivity of sodium, hydrogen, chlorine, and hydroxyl ions. He would not need to examine a thousand replications of this little test-tube system, but would analyze the internal dynamics of the single system, using these various types of data. From these he would build up knowledge about what reactions were taking place. He would conclude, among other things, that these chemicals reacted rather rapidly to form salt and water.

However, if the same chemist were concerned with finding the chemical properties of various metals and their relative positions on a scale of activity, he would need to carry out a comparative analysis, subjecting each of the metals to similar tests and noting the differences in their reactivity.

This analogy indicates that both internal analyses and comparative analyses have a place in research, and that neither is unilaterally superior. In the present study there was a choice between the two types: an intensive analysis of this single case, or an extensive and more superficial examination of many cases. The first was chosen and the latter discarded. Can we say anything about what was gained by this choice and what lost, that is, the differences between the two models of investigation?

The outcome of both such types of analysis is the same kind of generalizations. For example, "The more highly stratified an occupation is, the more intense and rigid will be its political cleavages if its union has democratic politics." A comparative analysis seeks to develop such generalizations in the obvious manner, by comparing occupations which differ with respect either to the independent or the dependent variable and then testing whether they also differ with respect to the other variable. The "internal analysis" attempts to establish the same generalization in one of two fashions:

1. It uses variations which occur *within* the system, either (*a*) over a period of time (e.g., at one time, there was stratification between a politically important group of Mailers and the majority, typogra-

phers; at the same time, rigid cleavage between these groups occurred); or *(b)* between different parts of the system (e.g., while
there is little stratification within the union as a whole, there is
economic stratification between officers and men; these create issues
between the membership and the administration . . .). The internal
analysis thus substitutes variations within the one system for variations between systems. This is in essence what an experimentalist
does when he varies the conditions under which a particular system
exists, or when he observes the evolution of an object over a period
of time.

2. An internal analysis can operate in a different way. By going
behind the over-all generalization to the processes through which it
is presumed to exist, the internal analysis may validate the generalization by validating these processes. For example, the generalization above, relating economic stratification to the rigidity and
intensity of political cleavage, can be either observed to hold true
statistically or built up through more fundamental generalizations, to
wit: *(a)* the economic motivation is an overriding one, which will be
a very strong determinant of one's decision if economics are involved; *(b)* the policy decisions in a stratified union involved economic matters which will differentially affect persons at different
economic levels. By proving that these two statements are true, one
can prove, by inference, the original statement about stratifications
and rigidity of cleavage. Thus internal analysis, which, in some
cases, cannot directly prove a generalization, may prove it by indirection through proof of the generalizations underlying it.

An internal analysis will not ordinarily be as exhaustive of the
important elements which affect a particular variable as will a comparative analysis, simply because certain things are invariant for the
single system as a whole. Certain kinds of issues may never occur in
this union, though they occur in others; certain aspects of the particular system are so invariant that situations common in other systems are simply absent in the ITU. These invariances can lead to
overgeneralization; for example, some of Michels' generalizations
from the German Social Democratic Pary to organizations in general
are seriously in error for certain kinds of organizations which diverge
too much from the single case Michels examined.

But except for these difficulties, it seems that internal analysis has
no great disadvantages with respect to comparative analysis. It may,
in fact, have one important advantage: By taking simple comparative
correlation out of the reach of the investigator, it focuses his attention
upon the underlying processes which operate within the system. In

this way the internal analysis may lead to a deeper explanation of the phenomenon and to generalization of a more fundamental kind.

But whether an internal analysis has more advantages or disadvantages with respect to a comparative analysis, it is important to realize that these two kinds of analyses of organizations both exist in social science, and a choice must be made between them in any research. The problem which begs for resolution here is the problem of spelling out the two different logics of analysis for these two methods, and of providing diagnostic indicators which will tell the relative merits of the two methods for a particular research problem.

These problems discussed above are three which seem to be of increasing importance as social research moves from description into analysis, and as it moves from focus upon individuals to a focus upon social units: voluntary organizations, the social system of communities, industrial plants, and so on. We have not attempted to give answers to the problems, but only to state them, in the hope that this will stimulate a search for the answers.

PART FOUR

Problems and Strategies of Measurement

INTRODUCTION

HAVING selected a theoretically relevant sample, the investigator must next decide how to measure or observe those units. The resolution of this question cuts to the core of a theory, for if valid and reliable measurements are not taken, a theory's empirical grounding is considerably weakened. The standards for evaluating the measurement act must be made to fit the theorist's conception of the empirical world. If a theory requires data on the dynamics of face-to-face interaction, then all measurements must be assessed by that requirement. That is, do they reflect aspects of the interaction process?

The measurement process assumes that observations of concepts can be transformed into statements concerning the degree to which a concept (or aspect of a concept) is present or absent in a given empirical instance. Measurements that transform concepts into variables, or statements of greater or less, are quantitative. Measurements that vary only in kind and not quantity are qualitative. A man may be Catholic or Protestant, but he may not be both.

Levels of measurement can be distinguished. These are commonly reflected in scale types and include nominal, ordinal, interval, and ratio levels. Nominal measurements place objects in mutually exclusive categories, while ordinal measurements rank-order observations. Thus a person could be given a score on a scale reflecting his involvement in a religion, perhaps ranging from high involvement on the one hand, to no or low involvement on the other. When the distance between categories on a scale can be measured, interval measurement is attained. Ratio scales exist when the investigator can demonstrate how much greater one object is than another on his scales. A ratio scale assumes the location of a zero point as seen on scales of weight or temperature.

Corresponding to each level of measurement are appropriate statistical tests which can be applied to those data. These range from nonparametric to complex parametric techniques. The article by Tittle and Hill offers a useful review of these scale types, and presents the steps by which the most popular scales are developed (the Likert, Guttman, Thurstone, and Semantic-Differential scales).

It is relevant to ask what the investigator may measure. The answer is quite simple: any object which can be theoretically conceived and empirically located. These objects will range from time and its variations, to social situations, attitudes of individuals in various situations, the actions of individuals, or the interactions between individuals as seen in relationships or groups.

A more crucial question is how one evaluates his measurements. I offer the following criteria. First, the measured objects must be theoretically relevant. Second, because no measurement instrument is free from flaws or restrictions, combined strategies must be employed (this is termed the process of triangulation and is more fully discussed in parts X and XI). Third, the researcher must assess his instruments in terms of their ability to be employed in the field situation. He may find, for example, that an instrument developed on college sophomores cannot be given to lower class blacks. If this is the case, he must adopt his measuring instrument to the field situation.

Fourth, and closely related to the third criterion, is the principle that directs the researcher to frame his measurements and observations in the language of those studied. If little or no corresponsence exists between the researcher's perspective and those studied, then valid observations are restricted. The two parties are simply not communicating. Unless meaningful communication is present, the links between theory and data are limited. The investigator must adapt his perspective to the empirical world.

Fifth, all measurements must be as reliable and valid as possible. Techniques for assessing these two criteria are offered by Tittle and Hill and by Kuhn and McPartland. Reliability asks to what extent the investigator can repeat his observations. Perfect reliability is reflected in the same group of subjects giving the same answers on the same scale at two points in time. There are several reasons why perfect reliability is seldom achieved. The instrument may change from observation to observation, thus precluding parallel results. This would result from in the researcher changing or reordering his questions. The researcher may change over time, as may the subject, and these changes will obviously restrict reliability. The researcher may change his conception of his instrument, may adopt different views of his subjects, may become fatigued, bored, or more skilled in asking questions. Any of these factors will alter the measurement results. The instrument, or measurement procedure, may induce, shape, or reshape existing attitudes held by the subject. Additionally, the investigator may, during his application of a scale or instrument, give certain cues or signals that lead the subject to respond in special ways. These may bring out socially desirable statements which would otherwise not be elicited. On the other hand, the researcher may create feelings of hostility and in this way provoke the subject into answers he otherwise would not express.

These problems suggest that the interaction between an investigator and subject can itself produce variations in reliability. Because each is responding to the other, making indications to himself and formulating new lines of action in accordance with the other's previous actions, this interchange can preclude anything approaching perfect reliability. It must be concluded that while an instrument, scale, index, or technique may be reliable, those who apply and respond to scales may not be themselves reliable. Reliability must be seen in interactional terms. It adheres as much to the situations and persons observed as it does to the instruments of observation.

The validity of an instrument refers to its ability to measure what the investigator purports to measure. Tittle and Hill review the major techniques of validation. These include using behavioral criteria, known groups, and theoretical relevance. Kuhn and McPartland also offer a review of the standard tests of validity.

Little can be added to their discussions. I would only note that all measurements can be assessed in terms of their ability to capture the emergent features of the interaction process (as was noted above in the context of reliability). The researcher must ask if his measurements of a subject's attitudes actually reflect what a subject will do in a situation that calls forth that attitude. The process of interaction may reshape, create, or even destroy an existing attitude. In such cases the attitude scale is likely to bear little resemblance to the observed behavior. This provides another argument for combining measurement techniques. The investigator could, for example, employ both behavioral and attitudinal measurements, or he could use several different scales.

It is possible to distinguish two basic measurement strategies. Closed-ended techniques offer respondents a fixed set of categories as a basis for response. The rationale for this approach is criticized by Kuhn and McPartland when they state that such approaches may force the subject to express an opinion he does not hold. It may also force him to answer in a way that does not reflect the complexity of his opinion. It may also simply be uninterpretable within his frame of reference. For these reasons, open-ended strategies are often used. The "Who am I?" self-concept test rests on this logic. Kuhn and McPartland detail the steps they went through in developing this instrument.

In my judgment, the researcher should not restrict his use of measuring instruments to either the closed- or open-ended approach. He should be willing to employ both, but he should use them in situations that justify their use. If a stable population is observed where a fixed set of attitudes is known, then the closed-end strategy is appropriate. Additionally, if certain kinds of information are required from everyone, than a fixed approach would be called for. On the other hand, if the researcher is dealing with attitudes and behaviors that are not stabilized, or that resist fixed designations, then the open-ended approach must be used. This of course furnishes the fundamental logic of the "Who am I?" test.

When he engages in the research act, the investigator must be conscious of existing scales and techniques. Where possible he should endeavor to build upon those techniques that have preceded his research. This strategy insures a modicum of continuity between past and future research. It is continuity of this order that makes science an emergent, yet orderly process.

Unfortunately many sociologists avoid such a commitment. This is the clear implication of Bonjean, Hill, and McLemore's research. In a twelve-year period, 2,080 scales were reported in four major sociological journals. Of this astonishing number, only 47, or 2.26 per cent, were used more than five times. Sociologists are prone to ignore the work of their predecessors. (This point relates to a feature of the current reward structure in sociology, a feature noted in Hill's essay in Part I: Replication is not rewarded. If students of the future are to learn from the mistakes of the past, the situation must change.)

To summarize, the three readings in this section cover the problems of measurement continuity, the prediction of behavior from attitude scales, and the construction of new measurement instruments. Tittle and Hill's article reviews the logic of the major scales now used by sociologists. It also presents the relevant literature on the "behavior prediction" problem. Kuhn and McPartland's article presents the logic for a test that is grounded in symbolic interactionism. This test has become a major instrument in the study of the self. But of equal importance, this article reviews the major techniques of test validation. These readings set the stage for the next part on the interview, since the interview is the major way measurement strategies are implemented empirically. These readings also anticipate Part VI on design and analysis, since the data gathered via the scales and instruments reported in this part must be causally analyzed. Part VI shows how such analyses may proceed.

Suggested Readings. Aaron V. Cicourel's *Method and Measurement in Sociology* (New York: Free Press, 1964) presents a highly critical analysis of modern theories of measurement. His book should be examined because it directs the reader to the major works in measurement. It is also centrally relevant because it calls for a theory of measurement that fits a social theory of the empirical world. The reader interested in examining the many scales and instruments now employed by sociologists should examine the book from which the reading by Bonjean, Hill, and McLemore is taken, *Sociological Measurement* (San Francisco: Chandler, 1967), which presents the history, content, and logic of instruments employed over the past dozen or so years. A publication of the American Sociological Association, *Sociological Methodology*, annually presents recent developments in the areas of sociological methods and analysis.

9. Continuities in Sociological Measurement

CHARLES M. BONJEAN, RICHARD J. HILL, AND S. DALE McLEMORE

ONE OF the major themes in the development of contemporary sociology has been a steadily increasing interest in problems of measurement. Almost every issue of our journals reveals the development of new measures as well as new uses of old ones. This proliferation of measuring instruments has led some sociologists to express fear that sociology is becoming fragmented and to raise questions concerning continuity in social research. When the investigator tries to build continuity in his research, more often than not, he is faced with one or both of two major problems. So many different measures are available for some phenomena that the selection of a scale or index may itself be a research problem of no small magnitude.[1] In other cases, an extensive search through the literature may yield no ade-

From *Sociological Measurement: An Inventory of Scales and Indices,* pp. 1–9, by Charles M. Bonjean, Richard J. Hill, and S. Dale McLemore, published by Chandler Publishing Company, San Francisco. Copyright © 1967 by Chandler Publishing Co. Reprinted by permission.

1. Examples of such variously measured phenomena include achievement, alienation, segregation, socioeconomic status, and so on.

quate description of a scale or index to measure the phenomenon of concern to the investigator.[2] The purposes [here] are related to assessing this problem in social research more clearly and to offering some initial aids to its solution. . . .

CONTINUITIES IN MEASUREMENT, 1954–1965

Following Lazarsfeld and Rosenberg, ". . . we use the word 'index' when we are confronted with a combination of several indicators into one measurement."[3] This definition suggests that more than one dimension of a concept may be reflected by an index. The term "scale" as used here may be thought of generally as a special type of index which is designed to reflect only a single dimension of a concept; however, it is extremely difficult to draw a sharp distinction between an index and a scale, and no such effort will be made. Hagood and Price state in this regard that: "In sociological research the terms 'scale' and 'index' are used to refer to all sorts of measures absolute or relative, single or composite, usually indirect or partial. . . ."[4]

Measuring instruments which were classified as scales or indices for the purposes of this volume typically involved the use of more than one "piece" of information. For example, if an author measured religiosity by asking "How many times did you attend church last year?" the resulting numbers were regarded as indicators rather than as indices or scales, because they were based upon a single piece of information; and such indicators are, consequently, not included in this volume. If, on the other hand, religiosity was measured by combining information on church attendance, number of other church-related activities, proportion of income spent on religious matters, frequency of Bible reading, and so on, the measure has been included.

The most conspicuous exceptions to or departures from the above criterion for the acceptance of a measure as a scale or index occur in the bibliographies concerning "Societal Characteristics" and "Socioeconomic Status, Occupational." In the former case, marginal inclusions occur primarily because at the societal level it frequently is

2. Examples are numerous. Should the reader desire verification, he should attempt to find a *complete* description of a measure of social mobility or of conservatism in our major journals.
3. Paul F. Lazarsfeld and Morris Rosenberg (eds.), *The Language of Social Research* (Glencoe, Ill.: Free Press, 1955), p. 16.
4. Margaret Jarman Hagood and Daniel O. Price, *Statistics for Sociologists*, rev. ed. (New York: Henry Holt, 1952), p. 138.

not feasible for researchers to array or categorize societies in terms of more than a single piece of information. Technological development, for instance, may be measured in terms of per capita coal consumption or of median income. Of course, such information may represent some underlying combination of data. This same observation applies also to occupation as an index of socioeconomic status. Although only a single piece of information is utilized for classifying respondents or subjects, in most cases the occupational categories were constructed on the basis of additional information.[5]

The *American Journal of Sociology*, the *American Sociological Review*, *Social Forces*, and *Sociometry* were taken to be representative of the main research currents of American sociology. Every article and every research note in each issue of these four journals published from January, 1954, through December, 1965, was examined carefully. To check reliability, 20 per cent of the issues were examined independently by two readers. Still further, after the initial search was concluded all of the references cited were checked by the authors. Each attempt to measure an attribute or variable through the use of scales or indices was noted on a separate card listing the following: (1) a complete reference to the article in which the measure appeared, (2) the concept indicated by the measure employed, (3) the technique(s) of measurement employed, and (4) other uses and users of the same or similar techniques which were cited. The last point should be stressed here because even though this inventory was confined to articles published in the journals named above during a twelve-year period, the tables and bibliographies presented below reflect both a variety of other research publications and a much longer span of time.

The cards accumulated in the manner described were than classified according to (1) the concepts underlying the various measurements, and (2) the specific measures utilized. The conceptual classes employed were set up during the examination of the accumulated cards and have undergone several revisions.[6] Other concepts and criteria of classification might have been utilized. Thus, the reader is cautioned that generalizations based on the frequency of uses and citations of measures by concept as well as the number of different

5. For example, the North-Hatt (NORC) list of occupations by prestige was constructed from ratings by 2,920 respondents. See Cecil C. North and Paul K. Hatt, "Jobs and Occupations: A Popular Evaluation," *Opinion News*, 9 (September, 1947), 3-13.

6. An earlier summary of our findings, based on an analysis of the four journals cited above over a five-year time span, employs a somewhat different set of conceptual classes. See Charles M. Bonjean, Richard J. Hill, and S. Dale McLemore, "Continuities in Measurement, 1959-63," *Social Forces*, 43 (March, 1965), 532-36.

measures found are highly conditional. Obviously, different conceptual classes might yield different conclusions.

The criteria employed in constructing the classification scheme were (1) utility to the reader and (2) comprehensiveness. We have tried throughout to "take the role of the other" and to imagine the types of problems which would lead researchers to consult [our study]. Consequently, we have proceeded empirically and have constructed enough conceptual classes to minimize the number of entries which are treated as "Miscellaneous Categories." The result is one possible way of classifying the concepts which sociologists have found to be most useful in conducting their research. A consequence of our approach, which will become obvious to the reader, is that the constructed conceptual classes are not mutually exclusive. We hope that this departure from the strict rules of logical classification is made more palatable by the closer approximation of the classification scheme to common research interests and usage. . . .

Table 9.1 presents a frequency distribution of measures by concept as well as the number of different measures found for each concept. The 3,609 recorded uses and citations of the 2,080 scales and indices identified in the analysis are classified by categories within the 78 conceptual classes listed. . . . For reference purposes, they are listed alphabetically in Table 9.1.

TABLE 9.1. Classification and Frequency of Use and Citation of Scales and Indices, 1954–1965

Conceptual Class	Number of Scales and Indices	Number of Uses and Citations
1. Achievement	9	10
2. Achievement Motivation	12	45
3. Anomia and Alienation	24	71
4. Aspirations	35	46
5. Assimilation	16	16
6. Authoritarianism	6	61
7. Authority: Attitudes toward and Characteristics of	33	36
8. Class Consciousness	8	12
9. Cohesion	18	21
10. Community: Attitudes toward and Characteristics of	24	26
11. Complex Organizations: Attitudes toward and Perceptions of	42	45
12. Complex Organizations: Characteristics of	34	56
13. Complex Organizations: Informal Relations	36	46

Conceptual Class	Number of Scales and Indices	Number of Uses and Citations
14. Conformity and Deviance	23	29
15. Consensus	10	11
16. Crime and Delinquency	47	64
17. Education: Attitude toward and Perceptions of	16	18
18. Education: Behavior in and Characteristics of	11	12
19. Family: Interpersonal Relations and Authority	86	103
20. Family: Perceptions of and Attitudes toward	22	36
21. Family Cohesion	20	22
22. Health: Individual	10	15
23. Innovation and Diffusion	27	35
24. Interests	6	10
25. Intergroup Relations: Ethnocentrism	4	12
26. Intergroup Relations: Nonracial and Nonethnic	20	30
27. Intergroup Relations, Racial and Ethnic: Characteristics of	16	19
28. Intergroup Relations, Racial and Ethnic: Discrimination	19	26
29. Intergroup Relations, Racial and Ethnic: Geoup Belongingness	12	15
30. Intergroup Relations, Racial and Ethnic: Prejudice and Social Distance	37	74
31. Intergroup Relations, Racial and Ethnic: Stereotypes	4	18
32. Interpersonal Relations: Attitudes toward	23	30
33. Interpersonal Relations: Characteristics of	53	63
34. Job Satisfaction, Morale, and Related Measures	29	35
35. Leadership, Community and Organizational: Behavior and Characteristics of	17	32
36. Leadership, Community and Organizational: Identification of	13	54
37. Leadership, Small Group: Behavior and Characteristice of	39	52
38. Leadership, Small Group: Identification of	18	22
39. Marital Adjustment and Courtship	28	70
40. Marital and Family Roles	17	19
41. Medicine and Health: Attitudes toward	23	29
42. Medicine and Health: Behavior in and Characteristics of	34	49

43. Mental Ability	32	67
44. Miscellaneous Categories	29	
45. Neighborhood, Attitudes toward and Characteristics of	11	16
46. Norms	22	30
47. Occupational Roles	48	56
48. Personal Adjustment	63	100
49. Personality: General	34	61
50. Personality Traits: Creativity	4	8
51. Personality Traits: Dominance	6	23
52. Personality Traits: Masculinity-Femininity	7	14
53. Personality Traits: Motives and Needs	32	56
54. Personality Traits: Sociability-Withdrawal	9	17
55. Personality Traits: Various Categories	60	101
56. Political Attitudes	49	68
57. Political Behavior	17	27
58. Religion: Attitudes toward, Participation and Characteristics of	40	61
59. Self-Image, Self-Concept, and Related Measures	55	84
60. Small Groups: Attitudes toward, Identification with, and Perceptions of	41	59
61. Small Groups: Behavior and Interaction in	80	104
62. Small Groups: Status and Status Relations in	14	55
63. Social Mobility and Related Measures	29	71
64. Social Participation	39	71
65. Societal Characteristics	59	80
66. Socioeconomic Status: Composite, Objective	68	146
67. Socioeconomic Status: Composite, Subjective and Objective	6	8
68. Socioeconomic Status: Occupational	56	270
69. Socioeconomic Status: Reputational	2	11
70. Status Concern	4	10
71. Status Consistency and Related Measures	11	21
72. Urban Areas: Metropolitan Areas and Dominance	11	13
73. Urban Areas: Segregation	10	61
74. Urban Areas: Socioeconomic Status	27	65
75. Urban Areas: Urbanization (Family Status)	1	28
76. Urban Areas: Various Categories	19	31
77. Values	63	127
78. Work-Value Orientations	44	62
Totals	2,080	3,609

As a sociologist might expect, measures of socioeconomic status were used and cited with the greatest frequency during the twelve-year period investigated. In the four journals reviewed there were noted 435 attempts to measure socioeconomic status by techniques employing either occupational status or more than one piece of information.

Table 9.1 also indicates those areas characterized by the greatest amount of continuity in social research. Continuity is apparently most characteristic among investigations dealing with authoritarianism, racial and ethnic stereotypes, community leadership, occupational status, reputational status, and residential segregation. On the other hand, there seems to be little or no continuity in regard to the measurement of achievement, authority, community characteristics, attitudes toward and perceptions of complex organizations, consensus, and characteristics of education.

Indeed, Table 9.1 indicates that fragmentation, rather than continuity, is an important characteristic of measurement in social research. A comparison of the number of measures found for each conceptual class with the frequency of uses and citations of the measures indicates that most measures used and cited in the journals examined were developed or modified by the investigator for the specific research reported.

Continuity in social research may be assessed, at least roughly, by comparing the total number of measurement attempts to the total number of measures used and cited.[7] As noted above, there were 3,609 attempts to measure various phenomena by the use of scales or indices and 2,080 different measures were used. Of the measures used, only 589 (28.3 per cent of the total number of scales and indices) were used more than once. Even though the percentage figure is low, it may overestimate continuity in social research since in many cases a measure contrived by one investigator and used on data presented in one journal article was reported a second time by the same investigator using the same data in a different article.

The lack of continuity in social research is reflected further by the observation that of the 2,080 scales and indices appearing in the journals over the twelve-year period covered by the analysis, only 47, or 2.26 per cent, were used more than five times.

---

7. The assessment is termed "rough" because uses, although they greatly outnumbered citations, were not analyzed separately here.

10. Attitude Measurement and Prediction of Behavior: An Evaluation of Conditions and Measurement Techniques

CHARLES R. TITTLE AND
RICHARD J. HILL

THE DEGREE of relationship between measured attitude and other behavior continues to be investigated and debated.[1] Some social scientists now conclude that accurate prediction of behavior from attitude measures is not possible with the techniques generally employed. Green, for instance, states that "many investigations have found that specific acts or action attitudes often cannot be predicted very accurately from elicited verbal attitudes."[2] Deutscher recently reintroduced the issue in most general terms when he again ques-

Reprinted by permission from *Sociometry*, 30 (June 1967), pp. 199-213. Copyright © 1967, American Sociological Association.

1. Two more recent and noteworthy studies are: Pamela K. Poppleton and G. W. Piljington, "A Comparison of Four Methods of Scoring an Attitude Scale in Relation to Its Reliability and Validity," *British Journal of Social and Clinical Psychology*, 3 (February 1964), 36–39; and Lawrence S. Linn, "Verbal Attitudes and Overt Behavior: A Study of Racial Discrimination," *Social Forces*, 43 (March 1965), 353–64. For general discussions of the issue see: Donald T. Campbell, "Social Attitudes and Other Acquired Behavioral Dispositions," in Sigmund Koch, ed., *Psychology: A Study of a Science*, vol. 6 (New York: McGraw-Hill, 1963); and Melvin L. DeFleur and Frank R. Westie, "Attitude as a Scientific Concept," *Social Forces*, 42 (October 1963), 17-31.

2. Bert F. Green, "Attitude Measurement," in Gardner Lindzey, ed., *Handbook of Social Psychology* (Cambridge: Addison-Wesley, 1954), p. 340.

tioned the assumption that verbal responses reflect behavioral tendencies.[3] However, if the issue is examined on the basis of available evidence, no conclusion can be reached with a satisfactory degree of confidence.

In addition to conventional standards of research, adequate investigation of the problem appears to require that several methodological conditions be fulfilled. First, it would seem obvious that a particular attitude should be measured using a multi-item instrument constructed according to a replicable set of procedures and resulting in at least the objective ordering of respondents. The general superiority of multi-item instruments over single-item measures and introspective orderings of data has been discussed at length. The argument will not be reviewed here.[4]

Second, derivation of an appropriate criterion of non-attitudinal behavior would appear to necessitate consideration of action taking place under typical social circumstances. Preferably, a behavioral measure or index should refer to sets of acts indicative of consistent or patterned action. The concept of attitude usually implies some form of cognitive and affective organization in terms of which an individual responds to an aspect of the world.[5] Further, if attitudes are cognitive and affective organizations which result from normal socialization processes, it seems reasonable to assume that the correspondence between attitude and other behavior will be highest in those situations which the individual has come to define as normal and common. The individual encountering a situation which is characterized by unfamiliar contingencies is not likely to have a well-structured attitudinal organization relevant to behavior in that situation. Attitudinally influenced response is not seen as the equivalent of a deterministic reflex. Many situational contingencies enter into any particular action situation in ways which influence response. Given these considerations, attitude measures should be least predictive of behaviors occurring in situations which (1) are alien to the subject's customary behavioral context or (2) call for aberrant behavior in a familiar action context.[6] Attitude measures should be most

3. Irwin Deutscher, "Words and Deeds: Social Science and Social Policy," *Social Problems*, 13 (Winter, 1966), 235–54.

4. Cf. Clyde H. Coombs, "Theory and Methods of Social Measurement," in Leon Festinger and Daniel Katz, *Research Methods in the Behavioral Sciences* (Chicago: Holt, Rinehart and Winston, 1953) and Lee J. Cronbach, *Essentials of Psychological Testing*, 2nd ed. (New York: Harper and Row, 1960), pp. 130–31.

5. Daniel Katz and Ezra Stotland, "A Preliminary Statement to a Theory of Attitude Structure and Change," in Sigmund Koch, ed. , *Psychology: A Study of a Science*, vol. 3, (New York: McGraw-Hill, 1959).

6. Campbell, *op. cit.*

predictive of behavior in situations which occur repetitively within the common behavioral context of the individual. With respect to the general relationship, then, the criteria of most relevance should reflect those behaviors which are repetitious and which take place under usual social circumstances.

When studies designed specifically to evaluate the relationship between measured attitude and other behavior are examined with these considerations in mind, the degree of discrepancy is found to be partially a function of the methodological strategies employed. Table 10.1 summarizes the results of a review of previous research.[7] Studies were classified by the measurement instrument employed, the kind of behavioral criterion which was used, and the type of situation under which the behavior occurred. For purposes of this classification, several behaviors occurring over time, or the same behavior repetitively engaged in, were considered to constitute a configuration of patterned behavior. With respect to the behavioral circumstances, the studies were categorized into two groups—those that utilized a behavioral criterion representing normal action alternatives and those that employed unusual options. In some cases the research report indicated that the subjects probably defined the situation as atypical. For example, in the Kutner study, it was graphically illustrated that the subjects were dealing with an undefined situation. In instances where no detailed information was provided, we used our own judgment following the general prescription that laboratory situations represented unusual behavior contexts or options.

In addition, the studies were classified as to whether a low, moderate, or high relationship between attitude and the behavioral crite-

7. These studies include: Richard T. LaPiere, "Attitudes vs. Actions," *Social Forces,* 13 (December 1934), 230–37; Bernard Kutner, Carol Wilkins, and Penny Rechtman Yarrow, "Verbal Attitudes and Overt Behavior Involving Racial Prejudice," *Journal of Abnormal and Social Psychology,* 47 (July 1952), 649–52; Richard T. LaPiere, "Type-Rationalizations of Group Antipathy," *Social Forces,* 15 (December 1936), 232–37; Douglas W. Bray, "The Prediction of Behavior from Two Attitude Scales," *Journal of Abnormal and Social Psychology,* 45 (January 1950), 64–84; Stephen M. Corey, "Proffessed Attitudes and Actual Behavior," *Journal of Educational Psychology,* 38 (April 1937), 271–80; Michael Zunich, "A Study of the Relationship Between Child and Action: A Study in Validity of Attitude Measurement," *American Psychologist,* 4 (July 1949), 242; Herbert W. Rogers, "Some Attitudes of Students in the R.O.T.C.," *Journal of Educational Psychology,* 26 (April 1935), 291–306; Gardner Murphy, Barclay Murphy, and Theodore M. Newcomb, *Experimental Social Psychology,* (New York: Harper and Brothers, 1937), pp. 894–912 (three studies are reviewed); Gwynne Nettler and Elizabeth Havely Golding, "The Measurement of Attitudes Toward the Japanese in America," *American Journal of Sociology,* 52 (July 1946), 31639; and Poppleton and Pilkington, *op. cit.*

TABLE 10.1. *Summary of Studies of Correspondence Between Measured Attitude and Behavioral Patterns*

Study	Attitude Measure	Criterion	Circumstances	Correspondence
La Piere	Hypothetical single question	Single act	Unusual	Low
Kutner	Single question	Single act	Unusual	Low
La Piere	Stereotypical single question	Patterned behavior	Normal	Low
Bray	Summated rating scale	Single set of acts	Unusual	Low
Corey	Thurstone-Likert scale	Patterned behavior	Normal	Low
Zunich	Summated rating scale	Single set of acts	Unusual	Low
DeFleur	Summated differences scale	Single act	Unusual	Moderate
Linn	Intuitive scale	Single act	Unusual	Moderate
Pace	No indication	Patterned behavior	Normal	Low to Moderate
Rogers	Battery of single questions	Patterned behavior	Normal	High
Murphy (1)	Thurstone scale	Patterned behavior	Normal	High
Murphy (2)	No indication	Patterned behavior	Normal	High
Murphy (3)	No indication	Patterned behavior	Normal	High
Nettler	Thurstone scale	Patterned behavior	Normal	High
Poppleton	Thurstone, scored 4 ways	Patterned behavior	Normal	High

rion was observed. In cases where no actual measures of association were provided, the reported conclusions were taken as the basis of classification. Where measures of association were available, association below .35 were classified as showing little relationship, associations between .35 and .59 were considered to represent moderate association, and associations of .60 or above were classified in the high category.

Obviously, the results reported in Table 10.1 do not include all investigations concerned with the relationship between attitudes and other behaviors. For example, several consistency tests using "known groups" have been undertaken but are not reported here because the nature of the known groups was such that it was impossible to make inferences about individual behaviors as corresponding to individual attitudes.[8] In addition many other investigations have used certain kinds of attitude measures as predictors within specific substantive contexts. Such studies permit little direct inference about the general relationship of concern here. The research selected for inclusion deals specifically with attitudes and corresponding individual behavior. These studies are those most frequently cited in connection with the argument and to our knowledge are considered to be the crucial investigations of the problem.

It is apparent from Table 10.1 that the degree of correspondence between measured attitude and other behaviors varies not only with the measure of attitude used, but also with the criterion which is taken as an indicator of behavior. Of the four studies that most nearly fulfill the methodological requirements set forth above, three show attitude measures to be highly associated with behavioral patterns. Considering all fifteen studies with no regard for their limitations, six report little relationship, three report moderate (or low-to-moderate) relationship, and six report high relationship. In view of these results, Campbell's conclusion is apparently inescapable: "The degree of correspondence is, for the most part, yet to be discovered."[9] The above reconsideration suggests that the degree of correspondence observed is at least a function of (1) the measurement techniques employed, (2) the degree to which the criterion behavior constitutes action within the individuals' common range of experience, and (3) the degree to which the criterion behavior represents a repetitive behavioral configuration.

The investigation reported below had two purposes. The first con-

8. See Corey, *op. cit.* for a review of these studies.
9. Campbell, *op. cit.*, p. 162.

cern was to determine the degree of correspondence between measured attitude and other behavior which would be observed when (1) the technique employed to measure attitude consisted of a multi-item instrument constructed according to replicable procedures which result at least in the objective ordering of respondents, (2) the criterion behaviors occurred within the common behavioral context of the individual, and (3) the behavioral situation occurred repetitively in the life experience of the individual.

The second purpose was the evaluation of the relative predictive efficiency of four frequently used measurement techniques in terms of the degree to which these techniques result in the ability to predict behavioral configurations.

DEVELOPMENT OF ATTITUDE MEASURES

It was suggested above that adequate investigation of the first problem required utilization of multi-item instruments. But since several measuring techniques are in vogue, it seemed desirable to employ more than one of them. The techniques evaluated were: (1) Thurstone successive-interval technique, (2) a semantic differential procedure, (3) a summated-rating (Likert) technique, and (4) a Guttman type scale. In addition, a simple self rating of attitude was examined. The efficiency of each of the five measures was assessed in terms of its correspondence with five criteria of behavior. The assessment was made under the conditions discussed above. These conditions were expected to maximize the relationship between measured attitudes and criterion behaviors.

Others have argued that if one wishes to predict a particular set of behaviors he should attempt to measure an attitude that is specific for a given individual as he relates to that class of behavior.[10] Given this argument, maximizing the credibility of the present study required an attempt to measure a specific rather than a general attitude. One would not expect to predict an individual's personal behavior with respect to his own marriage from a measure of his attitude toward marriage as a social institution. In the present instance, attitude toward personal participation in student political activity was taken as an appropriate measurement objective.

One hundred forty-five statements thought to reflect such an attitude were placed on a successive interval continuum by 213 student judges. The statements were formulated by the authors and several

10. Linn, *op. cit.* and DeFleur and Westie, "Attitude as a Scientific Concept," *op. cit.*, p. 30.

graduate students, using the literature on political participation in the larger society for suggestive outlines. These items were oriented around eight possible channels of individual political activity: (1) voting in student elections, (2) belonging to student political groups, (3) taking part in student political party activities, (4) taking part in student campaign activities, (5) keeping informed about student politics, (6) contact with student government officials, (7) inter-personal discussion of student politics, and (8) personal office holding or seeking.

The panel of judges consisted of entire classes of students, selected to give a broad representation of the student population. The statements were printed in eight-page booklets with the pages arranged randomly, and were submitted for judging with the customary instructions.[11] Following the procedures discussed by Edwards, successive-interval scale and Q values for the statements were calculated.[12] Fifteen statements were selected so that the scale values were approximately evenly spaced on the continuum and Q values were minimal.[13] For the test sample, the median scoring technique was used.[14]

The summated rating scale was built from the same basic 145 statements. Four editors independently classified the statements as to their favorable or unfavorable content. Those statements about which all four agreed were submitted to a separate sample of 213 students. The subjects were asked to respond to each statement on a five-point scale: strongly agree, agree, undecided, disagree, strongly disagree. Responses were weighted in the standard Likert fashion from zero to four. The fifteen items that discriminated best between the top fifty and the bottom fifty subjects were selected for this scale.

A semantic differential employing nine adjectival pairs was constructed for five concepts: (1) voting in student elections, (2) discussing student political issues, (3) holding student political office, (4) helping in a student political campaign, and (5) keeping informed about student politics. The nine adjectival pairs utilized were: good-bad, valuable-worthless, clean-dirty, pleasant-unpleasant,

11. The Seashore and Hevner method of rating items was used. See Robert H. Seashore and Kate Havner, "A Time-Saving Device for the Construction of Attitude Scales," *Journal of Social Psychology*, 4 (August 1933), 366–72.

12. Allen L. Edwards, *Techniques of Attitude Scale Construction* (New York: Appleton-Century-Crofts, 1957), pp. 123–38. An internal consistency test yielded an Absolute Average Deviation of .034, a value slightly higher than usually reported when the method of successive intervals is used to scale stimuli.

13. This was not entirely possible, since only a few statements were found to have scale values near the middle of the continuum.

14. Edwards, *op. cit.*, p. 145.

wise-foolish, fair-unfair, complex-simple, active-passive, and deep-shallow. The first six pairs represent the evaluative or attitude dimension. They were interspersed with the remaining three to obscure the purpose of the measurement (a procedure recommended by the originators of the semantic differential).[15] Pairs were selected using the criteria suggested by Osgood and his associates. Scores on all five concepts were summed and a mean taken as an ordinal measure of attitude toward personal participation in student political activity.

A set of items constituting a Guttman scale was derived using the same responses as those utilized for constructing the summated rating scale. A random sample of 95 questionnaires was selected from the 213 respondents. The statements were examined for scalability using the Cornell technique. Ten items, six dichotomous and four trichotomous, were found to form a scale with a coefficient of reproducibility of .928 and a minimal reproducibility of .635. All error appeared to be random.

These Guttman attitude items were retested for scalability after being administered to the test sample (N=301). The items met the criteria of scalability for this sample but only when used in dichotomous form. Accordingly the four trichotomous items were collapsed into dichotomies. The final scale had a coefficient of reproducibility of .930 and a minimal marginal reproducibility of .751. Menzel's coefficient of scalability for these data was .717,[16] and Schuessler's Test I resulted in a probability of less than .001.[17]

Once the instruments were constructed they were incorporated into a questionnaire including items about the student's background, participation in student political activity, and his group affiliations on the campus. In addition, the questionnaire included an item eliciting a self-rating of attitude toward student politics on a continuum from zero to eight. This questionnaire was administered to two large sections of a course in marriage and the family, which was composed of a widely variant student population. Freshmen were eliminated from consideration as were students who failed to provide complete

15. Charles E. Osgood, George S. Suci, and Percy H. Tannenbaum, *The Measurement of Meaning* (Urbana: The University of Illinois Press, 1957). The same six evaluative pairs were used by Osgood and his associates in comparing the semantic differential with other measures of attitude. See pp. 192–95.

16. Menzel suggests the level of acceptance for scales at somewhere between .60 and .65. Cf. Herbert Menzel, "A New Coefficient for Scalogram Analysis," *Public Opinion Quarterly*, 17 (Summer 1953), 268–80.

17. Karl F. Schuessler, "A Note on the Statistical Significance of the Scalogram," *Sociometry*, 24 (September 1961), 312–18.

data. The final set of subjects was composed of 301 upper-class students.

DEVELOPMENT OF CRITERION MEASURES

The criterion behavior was indexed in several ways. First, the voting behavior of each subject was determined by inspecting student-voting records in an election held one week prior to the administration of the questionnaire. Second, the respondent's report of his voting behavior for the previous four elections was taken as a behavioral indicator. Third, an index of behavioral patterns was constructed by combining responses to questions about frequency of engagement in various types of student political activity. Eight activities were found to form a Guttman scale for the 301 subjects. These activities included frequency of participation in meetings of a student assembly, frequency with which the individual had written to or talked with a student representative concerning an issue, frequency of voting over the past four elections, frequency of engagement in campaign activities on behalf of a particular candidate, frequency of reading the platforms of candidates for student political office, and frequency of discussion of student political issues in talking with friends. When the items were dichotomized, the scale was characterized by a coefficient of reproducibility of .907 and a minimal marginal reproducibility of .698. Again error appeared to be random. Menzel's coefficient of scalability was .675 and Schuessler's Test I yielded a probability of less than .001.

The fourth index of student political participation was devised by summing, in Likert fashion, the categories of response concerning frequency of engagement in ten types of student political activity. These activities included the eight previously mentioned as well as the frequency of personal office seeking and response to an item indicating whether the respondent had ever written a letter of protest to the student newspaper. A fifth measure of participation was an adaptation of the standard Woodward-Roper index of political participation involving a modified scoring of five of the activities already listed.[18]

The five criterion indexes were designed to represent alternate methods of measuring the same behavioral patterns. The degree of association between the criterion measures is reported in Table 10.2.

18. See Julian L. Woodward and Elmo Roper, "Political Activity of American Citizens," *American Political Science Review*, 44 (December 1950), 872–85.

TABLE 10.2. Interrelationship Among Criterion Measures

	Vote over time	Guttman index	Likert index	Woodward-Roper Index
Vote in last election	.778	.559	.636	.632
Vote over time	___	.577	.757	.789
Guttman index of political participation	___	___	.850	.721
Likert index of political participation	___	___	___	.869

In general the magnitude of association is relatively high. All measures of association are in the expected direction and are significantly non-zero at a probability level less than .001. These results suggest that the various indexes measured approximately the same aspects of the students' political involvement.

The degree of interrelationship of the several attitude measures varied considerably (see Table 10.3). This points up the fact that various methods of measuring the same characteristic may result in the ordering of individuals quite differently. Presumably the variation is accounted for by error factors intrinsic to the measurement techniques. An assessment of the extent to which such factors affect the predictive power of the several instruments in this specific instance is presented below. Moreover, the present research design permitted certain inferences to be made about the nature of the error factors involved.

TABLE 10.3. Interrelationship Among Attitude Measures

	Guttman	Thurstone	Sem. Diff.	Self-Rating
Likert	.796	.588	.619	.511
Guttman	___	.445	.523	.476
Thurstone	___	___	.432	.337
Sem Diff	___	___	___	.387

The behavioral indexes included one "objective" indicator and several "reported" indicators of activity. This raises questions with respect to the adequacy of such a design for making the assessment here proposed. Specifically, it is known that reported behavior does not always correspond to actual behavior; and that the extent of error varies with kinds of information being reported.[19] In the present instance, it was possible to compare one report of a behavior with an independent record of that behavior. The subjects were asked if they had voted in the last student election. This report was compared with the voting records. In 11 per cent of the cases, the report and the record did not coincide. In 28 of the 33 instances of non-correspondence, subjects reported that they had voted when in fact they had not. In the remaining five cases, the subject's name was not included in the voting records. In these latter instances, it was not possible to determine whether the error resulted from in-adequacies of the student government's record-keeping procedures or whether the subjects had falsified their names. The degree of error observed corresponds closely to that reported in the analysis of the political behavior of other populations.[20] Thus, the self-reported data in this instance appear to provide a fairly close approximation to the actual behavior of the subjects. This conclusion is reinforced by the findings reported in Table 10.2, which indicate relatively high asso-ciation between recorded vote and four reported indexes of related behavior.

The present research design, then, permitted the assessment of the relative efficiency of scaling techniques by determining the corre-spondence of five measures of attitude to five measures of other behavior, including a single act and four indexes of reported con-figurations of behavior. All the criterion indexes were composed of, or referred to, behaviors occurring under normal social circum-stances, and they represented referents for specific non-hypothetical attitude components.

FURTHER PROCEDURES

The attitude measures and criterion indexes used in this study were treated as ordinal data. A frequency distribution for each attitude scale was obtained, and the categories were then collapsed into six ordered classes, following the convention of equalization of margin-als. The Guttman and Woodward-Roper indexes of participation also were collapsed into six categories. The seven categories of the sum-mated index of participation were maintained to prevent a serious

19. Hugh J. Parry and Helen M. Crossley, "Validity of Responses to Survey Ques-tions," *Public Opinion Quarterly*, 14 (Spring 1950), 61–80.

20. See Charles R. Tittle and Richard J. Hill, "The Accuracy of Self-Reported Data and Prediction of Political Activity," *Public Opinion Quarterly*, 31 (Spring 1967), pp. 103–06.

mal-distribution of category frequencies. The association between each scale and each index was measured by the Goodman-Kruskal gamma. Since gamma is somewhat sensitive to marginal distributions, and perhaps, the number of cells in a contingency table, care was taken to make comparisons across rows where tables with approximately equal cell numbers and marginal distributions were involved.

RESULTS

The results reported in Table 10.4 indicate that only a moderate degree of correspondence between measured attitude and other behavior can be observed when (1) scaling techniques are employed to measure attitude and (2) the behavioral criterion is based upon a consideration of a series of acts occurring under normal circumstances. On the other hand, the data do show that the degree of correspondence observed is at least in part a function of the methodological conditions which maintain.

TABLE 10.4. *Associations* Between Attitude Measures and Behavioral Indexes

	Attitude Measure					
Behavior Index	15-item Likert	10-item Likert	Guttman	Self	Sem. Diff.	Thurstone
Record vote	.504	.459	.391	.285	.350	.318
Vote over time	.493	.423	.329	.365	.309	.213
Guttman index	.553	.559	.421	.410	.335	.248
Likert index	.619	.612	.535	.495	.364	.257
W-R index	.548	.535	.419	.425	.335	.238
Mean association	.543	.518	.419	.396	.339	.255

*Gamma.

The data support the argument that greater correspondence between measured attitude and other benavior can be found when the behavioral criterion incorporates a wide range of activity with respect to the attitude object under consideration. Although the findings are not decisive, they do reveal that in five of six instances greatest association was found between the attitude measures and the Likert-type index which was derived from ten distinct kinds of behavior. The data also show, in general, lower association was found for the voting indexes than for the Guttman and Wood-ward-Roper indexes based respectively on eight and five kinds of activity. Such results support the contention that the appropriate criterion measure to use in evaluating the predictive efficacy of attitude measure is one that includes sets of acts indicative of con-sistent or patterned behavior.

With respect to the assessment of the alternative measurement strategies, the results indicate that there is wide variation in the predictive power of the various instruments. In this instance, the Likert scale was clearly the best predictor of behavior. It was most highly associated with every one of the five behavioral indexes. The Thurstone scale showed the poorest correspondence—in only one case did it produce better prediction than any of the other measures. In fact, in four of five instances a simple self-rating of attitude pro-vided better results than the elaborate Thurstone procedure.

DISCUSSION

On the basis of a reconsideration of the relevant literature, it was maintained that multi-item attitude instruments would have consid-erable utility as predictors of behavior when such behavior repre-sents a normal configuration of repetitive actions. The findings pro-vide only modest support for this contention.

It could be argued that these findings strengthen the indictment against attitude measures as predictive tools. It is clear that attitude measurement alone, as examined herein, is not totally adequate as a predictor of behavior. However, when it is possible to obtain an average association of .543 using a Likert scale in its crude form, it seems entirely possible that technical refinements and additional methodological considerations could increase predictive efficiency. Investigation of the performance of the various measuring in-struments suggests certain refinements and considerations meriting further exploration.

Analysis of the present data indicates that the differential pre-dictive power of the various measurement approaches may be at least partially attributable to differences in reliability. Split-half reliability coefficients based upon the Spearman-Brown correction formula[21] were as follows: the Likert scale—.95; the semantic

21. To this point, the data have been treated as ordinal. The use of the Spear-man-Brown procedure makes interval assumptions. However, to the authors' knowl-edge there exists no ordinally-based procedure which provides a reasonable alterna-tive to the Spearman-Brown approach.

differential measure — .87; the Guttman scale — .80; and the Thurstone scale — .67. While the order in terms of reliability does not correspond perfectly with the predictive ordering, it does place the Likert and Thurstone measures in the same relative positions. The Likert scale was found to be the best predictor and to exhibit the greatest reliability, while the Thurstone scale is the poorest predictor and the least reliable. The findings with respect to the range of reliability are similar to those reported in other studies using Likert and Thurstone procedures. In addition, the available evidence suggests that in cases where the two types of scales are of equal length, one can expect the Likert scale to exhibit higher reliability.[22]

Differential reliability, however, does not seem to be a complete explanation for the findings. The Guttman scale exhibits lower observed reliability than the semantic differential, yet it performs considerably better as a predictor. In like manner the single-item self-rating of attitude would reasonably be expected to be less reliable than the multiple-item semantic differential and Thurstone scales, yet it is found to be a better predictor than either of these two scales.

It might also be argued that the superiority of the Likert over the Guttman technique can be accounted for by the fact that the original Likert scale was composed of 15 items while the Guttman scale contained only ten items. Since in general the greater the length of a test, the higher is its reliability,[23] it seemed desirable to rescore the Likert scale using the ten "best" items rather than the 15 "best" items. The data in Table 10.4 show that this procedure had little effect on the results. The ten-item Likert scale was still superior to the ten-item Guttman scale as well as to each of the other attitude measures.

A second factor appears to be the differential extent to which the various scaling procedures result in the derivation of scales incorporating a specificity dimension. Although each scale was designed to measure the same specific attitude relating to personal participation in student political activity, the various scales do differ substantially with respect to the content specificity of the actual items incorporated. This observation is based on the assumption that response to an item is likely to be more specific for an individual if the item contains some self-reference. Thus, the larger the number of self-referent items included in a scale, the more specific is response likely to be. Comparison of the Likert, Guttman, and Thurstone

22. Edwards, *op. cit.*, pp. 159–69.

23. Harold Gulliksen, *Theory of Mental Tests* (New York: Wiley, 1950), pp. 74–86.

scales in terms of the proportion of self-referent items derived for the final measuring instrument revealed a ranking corresponding exactly to the predictive ranking. For this comparison, items containing the personal pronouns "I" or "me," were considered to be self-referent in content. The Likert scale is found to rank first with 87 per cent of the items self-referent, the Guttman scale is second with 60 per cent and the Thurstone scale is ordered last with only 20 per cent of the items including a reference to self.

There are other technical differences between the different measuring procedures which may have some bearing on the findings. In addition to the advantage of greater reliability and specificity, the Likert technique also seems to have the particular advantage of providing for the operation of an intensity factor. Because scoring is influenced by the degree as well as direction of response to each item, intense judgments weight the final score assigned to an individual. Hence, an ordering of subjects by the summated rating procedure is not only a ranking on a favorable-unfavorable dimension, but a ranking influenced by how strongly the subject feels. A respondent who holds a favorable attitude but who does not feel intensely about it will consequently be ranked lower than one who holds a favorable attitude and supports that attitude with intense feelings.

Development of efficient means for handling such components as intensity and specificity may offer recognizable advantages for improving the predictive efficiency of attitude scales. The Guttman procedure for intensity analysis represents one technique for handling an additional dimension. But as ordinarily practiced, it lacks the advantage of permitting individual scores to be "corrected" for intensity (other than in a gross dichotomous sense). There is nothing, however, to prevent some combination of content score and intensity score to derive a "total" score. Certainly such possibilities deserve more exploration.

The semantic differential as a measure of attitude appears to suffer a serious disadvantage. Subjects tend to respond in a set. They observe that "desirable" things appear on one side of a continuum and "undesirable" things appear on the other. The discriminal process then apparently becomes a matter of self-evaluating overall attitude and marking the scale accordingly, with little distinction between the various adjectival pairs. Interspersing reversed continua probably only serves to make the respondent's task more difficult without fundamentally altering the problem. In this instance, the tendency for subjects to adopt a response set probably accounts for the fact that the semantic differential procedure resulted in a measure having high reliability but low predictive validity.

The findings in regard to the Thurstone technique are somewhat contrary to general methodological thinking with respect to attitude measurement. The Thurstone scale has been considered by some as the standard against which other attitude measures are to be compared. In addition to the factors of reliability and item-specificity, the poor showing of the Thurstone scale might also be influenced by the existence of a hiatus between the scaling of items and the process of measuring attitudes once the items are scaled. The judging procedure itself introduces a number of perceptual variables, the total effect of which has not been fully explored. Moreover, the nature of the typical response to Thurstone scales raises questions about the general adequacy of the Thurstone procedure. It is a common observation that respondents do not always endorse contiguous items. Indeed, subjects often endorse a wide range of items.[24] This does not make sense in light of the rationale of the procedure, and it may be largely responsible for some degree of unreliability and unpredictability.

The data presented here and the results of previous research with attitude measures strongly suggest that the error factors accounting for the differential predictability are to some extent intrinsic to the several measurement procedures. This conclusion, of course, cannot be advanced as compelling since any particular instance of the application of a given measuring technique or instrument represents only one of many possible applications. As such it is subject to various random errors. The crucial questions concerning these measurement procedures can only be answered convincingly when the results of numerous applications are available.

24. George J. Dudycha, "A Critical Examination of the Measurement of Attitude Toward War," *Journal of Social Psychology*, 18 (November 1943), 383–92; Selltiz, *et al., op. cit.*, pp. 359–65; and Otis Monroe Walter, Jr., "The Improvement of Attitude Research," *Journal of Social Psychology*, 33 (February 1951), 143–46.

11. An Empirical Investigation of Self-Attitudes

MANFORD H. KUHN AND
THOMAS S. McPARTLAND

ALTHOUGH the self has long been the central concept in the symbolic interaction approach to social psychology, little if anything has been done to employ it directly in empirical research. There are several reasons for this, one of the most important of which is that there has been no consensus regarding the class of phenomena to which the self ought to be operationally ordered. The self has been called an image, a conception, a concept, a feeling, an internalization, a self looking at oneself, and most commonly simply the self (with perhaps the most ambiguous implications of all). One of these many designations of the self has been as *attitudes*. We do not have space here to discuss the theoretical clarification which results from the conscious conceptualization of the self as a set of attitudes[1] except to point out that this conceptualization is most consistent with Mead's view of the self as an object which is in most respects like all

Reprinted from *American Sociological Review*, 19 (February 1954), pp. 68–76. Copyright © 1964, American Sociological Association.

1. A paper dealing with this view is being prepared by the present authors for publication elsewhere.

other objects, and with his further view that an object is a plan of action (an attitude).

If, as we suppose, human behavior is *organized* and *directed*, and if, as we further suppose, the organization and direction are supplied by the individual's *attitudes toward himself*, it ought to be of crucial significance to social psychology to be able to identify and measure self-attitudes. This paper is intended to provide an initial demonstration of the advantages to empirical research from thus treating the self as attitudes.

PROBLEMS IN THE DEVELOPMENT OF A SELF-ATTITUDES TEST

The obvious first step in the application of self-theory to empirical research is the construction and standardization of a test which will identify and measure self-attitudes.

The initial consideration in designing such a test is the question of accessibility. Would people give to investigators the statements which are operative in identifying themselves and therefore in organizing and directing their behavior? Or would they be inclined to hide their significant self-attitudes behind innocuous and conventional fronts? Those following symbolic interaction orientation have apparently guessed the latter to be the case for they have seldom if ever asked direct questions regarding self-attitudes, and have tended to assemble self-attitudes of those they were studying from diverse kinds of statements and behavior through the use of long and dubious chains of inference.

One of the present authors, in an earlier attempt to identify and measure self-attitudes among groups of Amish, Mennonite and Gentile school children,[2] made the assumption that self-attitudes might be studied in a fairly direct manner by collecting statements of role preference and role avoidance, role expectations, models for the self, and the like. While this investigation yielded results which corresponded to the cultural differences involved, it was clear that the self-statements which the children gave were specific to the role situations asked for and that therefore *general* self-attitudes still had to be (somewhat tenuously) inferred from them.

2. Manford H. Kuhn, "Family Impact upon Personality," chap. 5 of *Problems in Social Psychology: An Interdisciplinary Inquiry*, J. E. Hulett, Jr. and Ross Stagner, eds. (Urbana: University of Illinois Press, 1953), esp. pp. 50–52. A more comprehensive report of this study is included in a symposium on culture and personality, edited by Francis L. K. Hsu (*Aspects of Culture and Personality.* New York: Abelard-Schuman, 1954).

Subsequent pilot studies were made comparing the contents of extended autobiographies of university students with paragraphs written in answer to the question "Who are you?" These paragraphs contained virtually all the items which were yielded by rough content analyses of the self-attitudes in their corresponding autobiographies. This applied to painful and self-derogatory materials as well as to self-enhancing materials. Thus we concluded that it might be profitable to construct a test which was aimed directly at self-attitudes.[3]

The device which we then used, and upon the use of which this research report is in major part based, consisted of a single sheet of paper headed by these instructions:

> "There are twenty numbered blanks on the page below. Please write twenty answers to the simple question 'Who am I?' in the blanks. Just give twenty different answers to this question. Answer as if you were giving the answers to yourself, not to somebody else. Write the answers in the order that they occur to you. Don't worry about logic or 'importance.' Go along fairly fast, for time is limited."

APPLICATION OF THE "TWENTY-STATEMENTS" TEST

This test was given to 288 undergraduate students at the State University of Iowa. It was administered during regular class meetings of introductory courses given in the Department of Sociology and Anthropology at various times during the spring of 1952. In a few classes the instructions were presented orally rather than in writing. In every instance students were given twelve minutes in which to complete the test. The students were naive in the sense that they had not received instruction in the area to which this research was directed.

The number of responses per respondent evoked by these instructions varied from the twenty requested to one or two (with the

3. The social scientist, unlike the Freudian, assumes that most human behavior is organized and directed by internalized but consciously held role recipes. See, for example, Newcomb, Theodore, *Social Psychology* (New York: Dryden, 1950), for his excellent discussion of the relation of attitudes and symbols to the *direction* of behavior (pp. 77–78, 82), and his discussion of the *directive* (versus the expressive) organization of behavior (pp. 343–344). Those absorbed in the present fashion of projective testing would seem to have the cart before the horse, for relatively few of their subjects have been studied in terms of their directive and overt attitudes. It would seem much more reasonable to run out the implications of findings from tests of such attitudes before attempting to uncover deeplying, unconscious or guarded attitudes. We have concluded that much time is wasted debating *in advance* to what extent people will hide their "true attitudes," whether they be self-attitudes or attitudes toward other objects or states of affairs.

median being seventeen responses). The responses took the general form "I am. . . ." Frequenty "I am" was omitted, the responses consisting of phrases (*e.g.,* "a student," "an athlete," "a blonde") or of single words (*e.g.,* "girl," "married," "religious.").

The responses were dealt with by a form of content analysis. They were categorized dichotomously either as *consensual* references or as *subconsensual* references.[4] These content categories distinguish between statements which refer to groups and classes whose limits and conditions of membership are matters of common knowledge, *i.e., consensual;* and those which refer to groups, classes, attributes, traits or any other matters which would require interpretation by the respondent to be precise or to place him relative to other people, *i.e., subconsensual.* Examples of the consensual variety are "student," "girl," "husband," "Baptist," "from Chicago," "pre-med," "daughter," "oldest child," "studying engineering"; that is, statements referring to consensually defined statuses and classes. Examples of the subconsensual category are "happy," "bored," "pretty good student," "too heavy," "good wife," "interesting"; that is, statements without positional reference, or with references to consensual classes obscured by ambiguous modifiers.

The assignment of responses to these dichotomous content categories was highly reliable between different analysts, differences in categorization between two judges occurring less than three times in one hundred responses.

When the content was dichotomized in this way several interesting and useful features emerged:

First, from the ordering of responses on the page it was evident that *respondents tended to exhaust all of the consensual references they would make before they made (if at all) any subconsensual ones;* that is, having once begun to make subconsensual references they tended to make no more consensual references (if indeed they had made any at all). This ordering of responses held whether a respondent made as many as nineteen consensual references or as few as one.

Second, the number of consensual references made by respondents varied from twenty to none. Similarly the number of subconsensual references made by respondents varied from twenty to none. However, the number of consensual and subconsensual references made by any given respondent did not stand in a simple arithmetic

4. The precise working definitions of the two categories are given in detail in Thomas S. McPartland, *The Self and Social Structure: An Empirical Approach,* Iowa City: State University of Iowa Library, 1953, p. 147, Ph.D. dissertation, microfilm.

relation (such as the number of consensual references plus the number of subconsensual references equals twenty). This resulted from the fact that many respondents made fewer than twenty statements. For example, a respondent might make ten consensual statements and then leave the remaining ten spaces blank, while another might make two consensual references, twelve subconsensual references, and then leave the last six spaces blank.[5] In the analysis on which this report is based, all consensual references are on one side of the dichotomy, while "no-responses" are combined with subconsensual references on the other. An individual's "locus score" is simply the number of consensual references he makes on the "Twenty-Statements" Test.

These characteristics of the responses to the "Twenty-Statements" Test satisfy the definition of a Guttman scale. "The scalogram hypothesis is that the items have an order such that, ideally, *persons who answer a given question favorably all have higher ranks on the scale than persons who answer the same question unfavorably.*"[6] In applying this criterion it is necessary to keep in mind that "a given question" refers in this case to a specified one (by order) of the twenty statements, and that a "favorable response" would refer to a statement with a consensual reference — one that places the individual in a social system.

"The items used in a scalogram analysis must have a special *cumulative property.*"[7] Again it must be kept in mind that "the items" must in this case be interpreted in terms of the content analysis and not in terms of the raw responses to the open-ended question. Since a person who, let us say, makes a consensual statement as his seventh has also (in more than 90 per cent of the instances) made consensual statements in his first six, and since "consensuality" or "locus" refers to anchorage or self-identification in a social system, a variable which is numerically cumulative, we may regard the criterion of cumulativeness as being satisfied in this test. Guttman states, "A third equivalent definition of a scale is the

5. The variables which result from these characteristics of responses to the "Twenty-Statements" Test are presently being utilized in further research with special reference to clinical use. There are some interesting indications that those with few if any *consensual* statements to make have symptoms of emotional disturbance, while those having few statements *of any kind* to make are of Riesman's "radar" type, taking their cues from each specific situation, and (in the phrase of John Gould) "taking their 'immediate others' to be their 'significant others.'"

6. S. A. Stouffer, L. Guttman, E. A. Suchman, P. F. Lazarsfeld, S. A. Star, and J. A. Clausen, *Studies in Social Psychology in World War II, Volume IV: Measurement and Prediction* (Princeton: Princeton University Press, 1950), p. 9.

7. *Ibid.,* p. 10.

one upon which our practical scalogram analysis procedures are directly based. It requires that each person's responses should be reproducible from the rank alone. A more technical statement of the condition is that each item shall be a simple function of the persons' ranks."[8] This is true for the test under consideration.

Scores can therefore be assigned which indicate not only *how many* consensual references were made by each respondent, but *which* of his responses fell into the consensual category. The coefficient of reproducibility for this scale, based on 151 respondents, is .903. The test-retest reliability of the scale scores is approximately +.85.

Both for convenience and because consensual references are references to subjective identification by social position we have called the consensual-subconsensual variable the *locus* variable. Table 11.1 is a summary of the "scale of locus," and shows among other things the number of respondents approximating each scale type. For example, the first row in Table 11.1 indicates that 19 respondents most closely approximated Scale Type 20, *i.e.*, making twenty statements of the consensual reference variety. Of their 380 responses there were 41 errors (that is, randomly distributed nonconsensual statements), giving a coefficient of reproducibility of .892 for this scale type. At the other end of the scale there were three respondents who belonged in Scale Type O, which is that of making no consensual statements, thus giving a perfect coefficient of reproducibility, 1.00.

VALIDITY OF THE TEST

The problem of validity of a test in a hitherto uninvestigated area is a difficult one. There are generally recognized to be two related but distinct methods of assessing validity. One is by examining the logical relatedness of the test with the body of theory on which it rests. This subsumes the test of validity by correlating test results with the criterion behavior indicated by the theory. The other method is through correlation of the results of the test with other (already standardized) tests of the problem under investigation. When—as in this case—an area has not been previously investigated by inductive research there are no other tests to use as correlational checks. We need not be held up unduly by this consideration, however, for this is apparently a very much misused method of assessing validity in the field of personality research.[9]

8. *Ibid.*, p. 62.

9. There has been a considerable tendency to validate each new personality test by correlating its results with those obtained by the already existent ones, without

TABLE 11.1. *The Scale of Locus, Showing Scale-Types, Frequency,
Total Responses° in Each Scale Type and the Coefficient
of Reproductibility for Each Scale Type*

Scale Type	Frequency	Total Response	Errors	C.R.
20	19	380	41	.892
19	5	100	13	.870
18	1	20	1	.950
17	4	80	7	.913
16	1	20	3	.850
15	6	120	24	.800
14	8	160	9	.937
13	8	160	19	.875
12	4	80	10	.875
11	13	260	21	.915
10	7	140	15	.893
9	9	180	19	.895
8	9	180	15	.912
7	7	140	9	.936
6	10	200	15	.925
5	11	220	24	.891
4	8	160	11	.932
3	12	240	24	.900
2	2	40	5	.875
1	4	80	8	.900
0	3	60	0	1.000
	151	3020	293	.903

° Includes failure to respond to a blank as a response.

inquiring into *their* validity. See Leonard W. Ferguson, *Personality Measurement,*
(New York: McGraw-Hill, 1952). Ferguson points out (p. 178) that the Bernreuter
Personality Inventory was validated by correlating its scales with scores on the Allport
Ascendance-Submission scale, the Bernreuter Self-Sufficiency Scale, the Laird In-
troversion-Extroversion Schedule and the Thurstone Personality Inventory. The correlations were high. But the Laird and Thurstone tests had been through *no validation
process whatsoever,* and the other two were unsatisfactorily validated! He points out,
later, that the Bell Adjustment Inventory was validated against the Allport, Thurstone
and Bernreuter tests (p. 232), thus pyramiding still another validation on the original
shaky base. And so it goes until people have completely forgotten all details of the
construction of the earliest tests on whose validity the whole series rests as far as this
variety of validation is concerned.

We should note parenthetically that we were not interested in validating this test
operation of ours against any of the existent personality tests not alone for the reasons
involved in the argument above, but more basically because these other tests were
designed from orientations quite foreign to ours. One has only to check the items on
any current personality test to see how seldom is there any logical relation to
self-theory.

There are two kinds of demonstration required to deal properly with the problem of the consistency of the test with its antecedent body of orientational theory. One is that of making explicit the chains of logic which went into the designing of the test, the test operations and the manipulations of the data obtained through its application. The other is that of showing that the test results correlate in some consistent patterns with the kinds of behavior which the orientation assets are related.

With respect to the first kind of demonstration we need indicate only that the question "Who am I?" is one which might logically be expected to elicit statements about *one's identity;* that is, his social statuses, and the attributes which are in his view relevant to these. To ask him to give these statements "as if to himself" is an endeavor to obtain from him *general* self-attitudes rather than simply ones which might be idiosyncratic to the test situation or those which might be uniquely held toward himself in his relation to the test administrator. The request in the test for as many as twenty statements of self-identity stems from a recognition by the investigators of the *complex* and *multifarious* nature of an individual's statuses, their curiosity regarding the question of whether the *ordering of responses* correlates with the individual's particular anchoring in society, and their interest in exploring the *range* of self-attitudes.

The manipulation of the responses by assigning them to dichotomous categories, that of consensual reference and that of subconsensual reference, rests on the self-theory view that the self is an interiorization of one's positions in social systems. One may assume from this orientation that variations in such self-identifications are equivalents of variations in the ways in which the individuals in a society such as ours have cast their lot within the range of possible reference groups.

There is an alternative hypothetical mechanism which might be advanced to explain the salience of the consensual reference statement. It is this: our society requires such a volume of census information from its citizens that the salience of consensual references in the replies to the "Twenty-Statements" Test is, according to this hypothesis, simply a superficial carryover from other questionnaires and forms. On this view those responses which are treated in our investigation as subconsensual are "deeper" self-attitudes, and hence those which lie closer to the "authentic individual."

We do not agree with this view. It is our belief that the ordering of responses is a reflection of the make-up of the self-conception.[10] The

10. In the ordering of responses we are dealing essentially with the dimension of *salience* of self-attitudes. Theodore Newcomb (in his *Social Psychology* [New York:

fact that the volume of consensual responses (corresponding to social anchorings) varies greatly from respondent to respondent is taken to give indirect confirmation of our position. Another and more direct empirical confirmation is to be found in the fact that three- and four-year-old children when asked "Who are you?" give, in addition to their names, their sex and occasionally their ages; in their instances one cannot allege a carry-over from the giving of census data. Of course only the pragmatic success or failure of the technique here under consideration will give a dependable answer, and the latter part of this report is devoted to an account of one such pragmatic test. This pragmatic test of the usefulness of the scale scores of the "locus" component of self-attitudes may serve also as the second kind of demonstration of the validity of the instrument.

VARIATIONS IN SELF-ATTITUDES BY "KNOWN GROUPS"

The behavior which we rested for correlation with locus scores derived from our self-attitudes test is that of differential religious affiliation. It is simply one of a multitude of possible investigations which now need to be undertaken to answer the larger question, "What values of this variable (locus) are related to what kinds of behavior and to what trains of social experience?"

Our orientation indicates that the self-conception should vary with differential social anchorage in (a) large, conventional, "respectable," accepted and influential groups; (b) small, weak or different, ambivalently viewed, marginal or dissident groups; or (c) no groups at all (in institutional areas in which a large fraction of the society's membership belongs and is identified by status in one or another of the existent groups). Religious groups and corresponding affiliation by our respondents fitted this model admirably so that we might check differentials in their self-attitudes against differentials in their

Dryden, 1950], p. 151) says of salience that it "refers to a person's readiness to respond in a certain way. The more salient a person's attitude the more readily will it be expressed with a minimum of outer stimulation. It seems reasonable to assume that a very salient attitude — one expressed with great spontaneity — has more importance for the person expressing it than does an attitude which he expresses only after a good deal of prodding or questioning. The weakness of direct questions is that they provide no way of measuring the salience of an attitude; we never know whether the attitude would have been expressed at all, or in the same way, apart from the direct question." Thus when a respondent in reply to the "Who am I?" question on the "Twenty-Statements" Test, writes "I am a man," "I am a student," "I am a football player," it is reasonable to believe that we have far more solid knowledge of the attitudes which organize and direct his behavior than if, on a checklist and among other questions, we had asked "Do you think of yourself as a man?" "Do you think of yourself as a student?" and "Do you think of yourself as an athlete?"

religious group affiliations. Some religious groups in our society are "majority groups," while others are groups whose subcultures contain norms which set their members at odds with the norms of the larger society. Then, too, a large fraction of the population either has no religious reference group or no religious group membership.

Reports of membership in religious groups in our sample were collected by means of the direct question: "What is your religious affiliation or preference?" The numbers of each variety of affiliation are given in the column under the heading "N" in Table 11.2. The mean locus scale scores were computed for each of these religious groups and are given in the next column. The mean scale scores ranged from 11.89 (for Catholics) to 5.75 (for "nones"). These scale scores are simply the mean number of consensual reference statements made by respondents in each of the religious groups.

TABLE 11.2. *Variations in Self-Attitudes by Religious Affiliation: The Significance of Observed Differences between Locus Scores of Affiliates of Various Religious Denominations*

Denomination	N[1]	Denominational Mean	Significance of Difference[2]	Significance of Difference[3]
Roman Catholic	38	11.89	..	P <.001
"Small Sects"[4]	20	11.00	not sig.	P <.001
"Protestant"	21	10.47	not sig.	P <.01
Congregationalist	13	10.30	not sig.	P <.01
Lutheran	33	10.09	not sig.	P <.01
"Christian"	11	9.81	not sig.	P <.02
Jewish	19	9.57	not sig.	P <.05
Methodist	73	8.94	P <.02	not sig.
Presbyterian	32	8.18	P <.01	not sig.
"None"	28	5.75	P<001[°]	..

[1] The total N is 288. These 288 include the 151 on whom the locus scale, reported in Table 1, was established, plus 137 cases obtained subsequently.

[2] Computed from the Roman Catholic group mean as the base.

[3] Computed from the group mean of "Nones" as the base.

[4] Includes Baptists, Espicopalians, Evangelicals, Mennonites, Nazarenes, Reorganized Latter Day Saints, Unitarians.

[°] While this and other measures of statistical significance of difference are such as to give great confidence that the differences are not due to chance, it will only be through repeated correlations of locus scores with other behavior with respect to representative samples that we will be able to discover the theoretical import of the *magnitude* of the difference.

Analysis of variance revealed a relation between religious affiliation and scale scores significant beyond the one per cent level. The differences between group means of Roman Catholics on the one hand and Methodists, Presbyterians, and persons reporting no affiliation on the other, were significant beyond the two per cent level. Taking the group reporting no affiliation as the base, we found significant differences between this group-mean and the group-means of Roman Catholics, "small sects," "Protestants," Congregationalists, Lutherans, Christians and Jews. Although the N's were relatively large, Methodists and Presbyterians did not differ significantly from "nones" at any usually accepted level of statistical significance. The results of this analysis appear in the last two columns in Table 11.2.

These results indicate clear differences in the relative strength of the more directly socially anchored component of the self-conception among affiliates of certain religious subcultures, but leave open the question of the antecedent correlates of these differences. If one postulates that Roman Catholics have in common with members of small Protestant denominations, Lutherans and Jews the characteristic that religious affiliation is picked out as "important" and differentiating, and that Methodists, Presbyterians, and "indifferentists" have in common the characteristic that religious affiliation is not "important" or that it is taken for granted, then the two clusters of denominations by scale scores make sense.

If this postulate is sound, then Roman Catholics, Jews and members of small sects should carry religious references more saliently in the self-conception. The "Twenty-Statements" Test provides data on this point.[11]

The salience of a self-reference may be understood as the relative spontaneity with which a particular reference will be used as an orientation in the organization of behavior.[12] In this research salience of religious reference in the self-conception was measured by the rank of religious reference (if any was made) on the page of twenty statements, mention of religious affiliation in first place being scored 20, mention in last place scoring 1, and omission of reference to religious affiliation arbitrarily scored zero.

The mean salience of religious references on the "Twenty-Statements" Test ranged from 7.4 for Roman Catholics to 1.82 for "Christians." Analysis of variance of religious references showed salience scores to be related to religious affiliation beyond the one

11. This, obviously, is a use of data from the "Twenty-Statements" Test in an altogether different way than through the use of them to obtain locus scores. There are, in fact, almost unlimited numbers of ways in which these self-statements may be treated, but each would constitute essentially a new test.

12. The comments and quotation in footnote 10 above apply equally here.

per cent level. The analysis of the significance of the difference between group means appears in Table 11.3.

TABLE 11.3. *Differential Self-Anchorage in Religious Groups: The Significance of Observed Differences between Mean Salience Scores of Religious References Among Affiliates of Various Religious Denominations*

Denomination	Denominational Mean	Significance of Difference°
Roman Catholic	7.39	..
Lutheran	7.09	not significant
"Small Sects"	7.04	not significant
Jewish	6.68	not significant
Congregationalist	5.54	not significant
Presbyterian	4.47	$P < .01$
Methodist	3.22	$P < .01$
"Christian"	1.82	$P < .01$

° Computed from the Roman Catholic group mean as a base.

A completely independent operation was conducted to test this finding of the relation between the social "importance" of group affiliation and "importance" in the self-conception; 116 undergraduates, whose religious affiliations were known, were asked to answer one of two alternative "reference-group" questions: "With what groups do you feel most closely identified?" or "I am proudest of my membership in ____." When respondents were cross-

TABLE 11.4. *Reference Group Evidence: The Dichotomous Division of 116 Respondents on the Basis of Religious Affiliation and Identification with Religious Groups*

	Religious Reference Present		Religious Reference Absent	
Catholics and Jews	13	(5.5)	7 (14.5)	20
All others	19	(26.5)	77 (69.5)	96
Total	32		84	116

Chi Square: 17.03
Q: .875
P less than .0001

classified (a) by religious affiliation and (b) by their giving or not giving religious affiliation references in response to these direct questions, Table 11.4 resulted. Since we had obtained, from the self-attitudes research done previously, an empirically derived gradient of "differentism," we used this to make a finer subdivision of these responses, which yielded Table 11.5.

TABLE 11.5. Reference Group Evidence on the Gradient of Differentism: The Dichotomous Division of Respondents by Religious Identification Against a Trichotomous Division by Religious Affiliation

	Religious Reference Present		Religious Reference Absent	
Catholics and Jews	13	(6.2)	7 (13.8)	20
"Small Sects"	9	(6.2)	11 (13.8)	20
"Large Denominations"	10	(19.6)	53 (43.4)	63
Total	32		71	103

Chi Square: 19.45
T: .37
P less than .0001

These independently derived data support the hypothesized relation between salience in the self-conception and socially defined importance of group membership at high levels of statistical significance.

CONCLUSIONS

The evidence provided by the "Twenty-Statements" Self-Attitudes Test and by its application to "known groups," in this case religious groups, gives support to the following empirically grounded inferences which have, in our view, rather large theoretical implications:

(1) The consensual (more directly socially anchored) component of the self-conception is the more salient component. Stated differently, consensually supported self-attitudes are at the top of the hierarchy of self-attitudes.

(2) Persons vary over a rather wide range in the relative volume of consensual and subconsensual components in their self-conceptions. It is in this finding that our empirical investigation has given the

greatest advance over the purely deductive and more or less literary formulations of George Herbert Mead. Stated in terms of the language of this test, people have locus scores which range from 0 to 20. The variable involved here is one which we can correlate with a wide variety of other attitudes and behavior.

(3) The variation indicated in (1) and (2) can be established and measured by the empirical techniques of attitude research — specifically, the Guttman scaling technique. This gives a dual advantage in that it furthers the presumption that the locus variable is a unitary one and also in that it facilitates the further manipulation of values of the variable with respect to other quantitative problems.

(4) Locus scores vary with religious affiliation, as our initial validation test shows, members of the "differentistic" religious groups having significantly higher locus scores than do members of the "conventional" religious groups (using an independent source of information to establish the fact of membership in religious groups).

(5) Religious affiliation references are significantly more salient among the self-attitudes of members of "differentistic" religious groups than among members of "majority" or conventional religious groups.

(6) Corroboratively, the religious group as a reference group appears far more frequently as an answer to a direct, reference-group type of question among those made by members of "differentistic" religious groups.

This is a first (and only partially completed) effort to build a personality test consistent with the assumptions and findings of social science. The social science view is that people organize and direct their behavior in terms of their subjectively defined identifications. These in turn are seen as internalizations of the objective social statuses they occupy, but for prediction we need to have the *subjective* definitions of identity, in view of the looseness between the social systems and the individual occupants of statuses in them in a society such as ours, characterized by alternatives, change, and collective behavior — in short, a society toward the secular end of the scale. Our test elicits these self-definitions.

To complete a comprehensive personality test on this basis we will need to know, in addition to the subjects' subjective identifications in terms of statuses, their roles, role preferences and avoidances and role expectations, their areas of self-threat and vulnerability, their self-enhancing evaluations, their patterns of reference-group election (their "negative others" as well as their "positive others"), and probably their self-dissociated attitudes. Questions such as "What do you do?" "Who do you wish you were?" "What do you intend to do?" "What do you take the most pride in?" "As a member of what groups or categories would you like to count yourself?" are a few of the indicated types in the directions suggested of building a soundly grounded approach to a science of personality and culture.

PART FIVE

The Sociological Interview: Problems and Strategies

INTRODUCTION

As NOTED earlier, the sociological interview represents those situations where previously reached sampling and measurement decisions come to life. It is at this point, when a subject is approached and induced to answer questions, that the information relevant to theory is gathered. Unfortunately, the process of gathering of such information is not clear-cut, nor is it well understood. Few interviewers perfectly follow an interview guide, and subjects seldom answer all the questions they are asked. The interview situation must be seen as an interactional sequence where one person asks questions and another answers. Yet it is an encounter which has a number of emergent properties about it. Mood, affect, and involvement have to be controlled. Embarassment has to be avoided. Public and socially desirable attitudes have to be probed. Suitable and sufficient time has to be arranged and set aside for asking the relevant questions. Introductions have to be made; entrance into homes, offices, or private settings has to be accomplished. Respondents who refuse to talk, who wander, or who become hostile have to be overcome and manipulated. Guards must be ever set against duping, lying, fabrication, or stereotyping. In short, interviewing is not easy. This part reviews many of the problems and strategies relevant to the production of a valid and reliable interview. The word "production" must be stressed. The interview is a conversational production, anticipated in the investigator's mind and imagination, but realized only in the world of conversational interaction. It is in this world that so often problems arise. The above list only partially covers the range of difficulties encountered as a single or corps of interviewers moves from the office into an organization, community, or group with the fervent hope of returning home with completed questionnaires or interviews.

SOME DISTINCTIONS

An interview is any face-to-face conversational exchange where one person elicits information from another, but a variety of types can be noted. There are those that rest on highly structured formats. Their logic is discussed by Benney and Hughes. Here, one set of questions, placed in the same order, is given all respondents. This strategy, which has the potential of eliciting common information from all respondents, rests on the assumption that questions can be worded and ordered in a way that will be understood by all respondents. As Benney and Hughes note, this assumption is often unfounded. Few respondents share the same perspective, and few words, terms, or concepts elicit the same response from different respondents.

A variation on the highly structured method is the focused interview, or the nonschedule standardized interview. Here, the interviewer works with a fixed list of questions or problems to be covered but alters that list for each respondent. He also rephrases questions for each respondent. This is a strategy which has the benefits of eliciting common information grounded in the perspective of those observed.

The last major interview form, the one reported by Riecken, employs neither fixed questions nor a predetermined order for asking questions. The investigator simply has a sense of what information is needed for his theory, and he attempts to gather that information. With this method there is a more fluid and constant interaction between hypothesis and questions. The investigator uses each respondent or subject as a source and test of hypotheses. Whenever a subject presents an opinion or reports an action that contradicts a previous hypothesis, reformulation is called for. This strategy closely fits the naturalistic method and is often formalized into the technique of analytic induction. It has problems (as Turner notes in Part VII). The researcher may neglect important data because he cannot fit them into his theoretical scheme. He may also be so informal as to preclude another researcher replicating his study. To guard against this, a list of questions should be made and a public record of how this list changed during the field research should be given.

The logic for employing each of these interview types was suggested in the previous part. When the investigator has to have the same data from all his respondents, then a fixed and structured interview is called for. When he is probing attitudes which are ill-defined, or when he encounters situations where diverse opinions are prevalent, an open and more unstructured method should be employed.

PROBLEMS AND STRATEGIES

One basic theme underlies the papers in this part—that the interview must be seen as a special interactional encounter. Benney and Hughes treat the evolution of this encounter is the history of man's relationship and note how it differs from such traditional relationships as those between the rich and poor, the educated and the ignorant, the lover and the loved, parent and child. They treat such problems as multiple role-playing, shifts in selves, and confusions over intent within the interview. They spell out the special problems surrounding affect and its display and note that paradoxically the interview rests on the respondent's expertise on the matters relevant to the interview guide. While the interviewer is the expert at asking the questions (presumably), the respondent is the expert on the answers. This creates a very unusual conversational sequence—a sequence that departs from normal, daily interactions.

Benney and Hughes discuss the fictions of equality and comparability that underly the interview. Those social differences sensed between the interviewer and respondent must be muted to maintain a sense of equality between the two. They note that of course this is a seldom realized fiction. (A highly relevant paper in this context is Peter Manning's "Problems in Interpreting Interview Data," *Sociology and Social Research*, 51 (April 1967), 302–16). The young, inexperienced graduate student interviewing a physician soon senses a great degree of social distance. In few senses can this encounter be seen as one between equals. This observation (as Manning discusses in his paper) furnishes part of an argument for viewing the interview in terms of the intersection of a number of social games — games which may shift from pure sociability, to information, or one-upmanship. The skilled interviewer must be capable of shifting game perspectives during his conversations.

The fiction of comparability supplies one of the rationales for the structured interview. As Benney and Hughes note, all interviews are seen as comparable happenings within a population of such occurences. While this aids certain kinds of statistical analyses, it overlooks the tremendous range of variations that can occur within a large number of interviews. The fiction of comparability hinders any meaningful analysis of what transpires within such encounters. A model of interaction and analysis relevant to the interview must be constructed. Benney and Hughes point in the direction of such a model.

Becker offers a strategy appropriate for many interview situations. This builds on Arnold Rose's proposal that the interviewer actively enter into his own interactions and experiments with the respondent. Becker reports how he varied his attitudes and questions so as to better probe the idealistic perspective of medical students. Experimentation within the interview is an underdeveloped technique. It has obvious relevance for any theory of the interview, for each interviewer can quickly check out the impact of certain mannerisms, questions, or strategies with his respondent.

Riecken's paper touches on issues central to participant observation when the observer remains unidentified. In such circumstances, asking questions central to one's theory becomes difficult. If the observer asks too many questions, he runs the risk of being uncovered, or challenged for not knowing what every other group member knows. The reactive effect of such questions cannot be ignored either. To ask a question is to call forth an opinion that may well be reinforced through the answering process. The unidentified interviewer occupies a very difficult position. He must guard against over-reactivity and identification while in the role. A number of strategies relevant to this role are discussed by Riecken, and are amplified in Part IX.

While the papers in this part point to many problems inherent in the interview method, it must be remembered, as Benney and Hughes note, that sociology rests in the ultimate analysis on the interview. The interview is, as they suggest, the ultimate flirtation with life. It remains, and rightfully so, the basic source of sociological data. It will be complemented by other methods, but never replaced. What is needed is a fuller understanding of the peculiarities surrounding its use. This is the intent of the papers in this section: to give the student a sense of what can go wrong in the interview, and to suggest possible corrective strategies.

Suggested Readings. The September 1956 issue of the *American Journal of Sociology* presents a series of papers all relevant to the analysis of the interview, and deserves special attention. Herbert Hyman's *Interviewing in Social Research* (Chicago: University of Chicago Press, 1954) presents findings from one of the first large-scale studies of the interview. It should be examined in the context of Richardson, Dohrenwend, and Klein's, *Interviewing: Its Forms and Functions* (New York: Basic Books, 1965), a work that offers an analysis of the three major interview types and discusses the effects of interviewer and respondent bias of interview data. *The Public Opinion Quarterly* should also be reviewed; it consistently publishes papers on the interview as a sociological method. The most recent analysis of the interview as interaction is contained in Gorden's *Interviewing: Strategy, Techniques and Tactics* (Homewood, Ill.: Dorsey, 1969). For a fuller understanding of the skills involved in interviewing, this work must be read. It also treats various views of the interview, but stresses the point that the interview must be seen as a communicative act.

12. Of Sociology and the Interview

MARK BENNEY AND
EVERETT C. HUGHES

SOCIOLOGY has become the science of the interview, and that in two senses. In the first sense the interview has become the favored digging tool of a large army of sociologists. The several branches of social study are distinguished from one another perhaps more by their predilection for certain kinds of data and certain instruments for digging them up than by their logic. While the essential features of human society have probably varied within fairly narrow limits in all times and places where men lived, certain of these features can be more effectively observed in direct contact with living people. Others may perhaps be best seen through the eyes of men who left documents behind them. Sociologists have become mainly students of living people. Some, to be sure, do still study documents. Some observe people *in situ;* others experiment on them and look at them literally *in vitro.* But, by and large, the sociologist of North America, and in a slightly less degree in other countries has become an interviewer. The interview is his tool; his works bear the marks of it.

Reprinted by permission from *American Journal of Sociology*, 62 (July 1956), pp. 137-142. © 1956 by The University of Chicago Press.

Interviews are of many kinds. Some sociologists like them standardized and so formulated that they can be "administered" to large groups of people. This can be done only among large homogeneous populations not too unlike the investigator himself in culture. Where languages are too diverse, where common values are too few, where the fear of talking to strangers is too great, there the interview based on a standardized questionnaire calling for a few standardized answers may not be applicable. Those who venture into such situations may have to invent new modes of interviewing. Some of the articles which follow deal with problems of large-scale standardized interviews; others tell of the peculiar problems of interviewing special kinds of people.

In the second sense sociology is the science of the interview in a more essential way. The subject matter of sociology is interaction. Conversation of verbal and other gestures is an almost constant activity of human beings. The main business of sociology is to gain systematic knowledge of social rhetoric; to gain the knowledge, we must become skilled in the rhetoric itself. Every conversation has its own balance of revelation and concealment of thoughts and intentions: Only under very unusual circumstances is talk so completely expository that every word can be taken at face value. The model of such exposition is the exchange of information among scientists. Each is pledged to tell all he knows of the subject in terms whose meanings are strictly denoted. Every member of any society knows from early childhood a number of such model situations and the appropriate modes of rhetoric. He knows them so well, in fact, that he can improvise new ones and can play at the game of keeping others guessing just what rhetoric he is using. We mention these subtleties of social rhetoric and social interaction, not to spin out analysis of them, but to sharpen the point that the interview, as itself a form of social rhetoric, is not merely a tool of sociology but a part of its very subject matter. When one is learning about the interview, he is adding to sociological knowledge itself. Perhaps the essence of the method of any science is the application, in quest of new knowledge, of what is already known of that science. This is certainly true of sociology; what we learn of social interaction — of the modes of social rhetoric — we apply in getting new knowledge about the same subject.

But the interview is still more than tool and object of study. It is the art of sociological sociability, the game which we play for the pleasure of savoring its subtleties. It is our flirtation with life, our eternal affair, played hard and to win, but played with that detachment and amusement which give us, win or lose, the spirit to rise up and interview again and again.

The interview is, of course, merely one of the many ways in which two people talk to each other. There are other ways. About a year ago Miss Margaret Truman was employed on Ed Murrow's "Person to Person" television show to interview her parents in their home, and the event proved to be a notable exercise in multiple role-playing. As a daughter, Miss Truman asked the kinds of questions that any daughter might ask of a parent: "Dad, how is the book coming?" As interviewer, she asked questions that bore the unmistakable stamp of the newspaperman: "So many people want to know what you do to relax, inasmuch as you don't fish, hunt, or play golf." And at the end of the interview she achieved a nice convergence of the two roles by asking, as interviewer, her parents' views about herself, as daughter. Now Miss Truman is by way of being both a professional daughter and a professional interviewer, and the happy idea that she should act in the one role in a situation and with people where the other role is conventionally to be expected takes us right to the center of our concern.

If we look at the variety of ways in which people in our culture meet together and talk, we will be struck not only by the range of expectations which subsume unique, particular encounters under a rubric of reciprocal roles but also by the different degrees of self-involvement that inform the playing of different roles. Much attention has been given to the range of intensity with which the individual plays his roles; much less attention has been paid to the degree of *expected* intensity. It is clear enough that along with more or less specific expectations of the appropriate behavior in a given role go other expectations about the degree of self-involvement. The general expectation is that Miss Truman should be more involved in the role of daughter than of interviewer; and certainly she managed to underline the family ties by very frequent use of such terms of address as "Dad" and "Mommie" and also by occasionally prefacing a question with the phrase, "Ed Murrow wanted me to ask. . . ." These differences of expected intensity are to some extent codified for us in such terms as "commandment," "law," "rule," "standard," "convention," "fashion." At the upper limits of intensity there is a total prescription of alternative roles—the priest must never be a lover, the citizen must never be a traitor: only minimal distinction is expected between the self and the role. At the lower limit there is still the expectation that, when roles conflict, the resolution shall favor one role rather than another—but, by their very semantics, such terms as "convention" or "fashion" operate in areas of life where ethical neutrality is acceptable and ambivalence frequent. Thus, Miss Truman could abandon the role of interviewer for that of daughter without our feeling that violence has been done to our ethos; she could not, if the two roles conflicted, abandon the role of daughter so easily.

The role of the interviewer, then, is one governed by conventions rather than by standards, rules, or laws; it is a role that is relatively lightly held, even by professionals, and may be abandoned in favor of certain alternative roles if the occasion arises. *What* alternative roles is another matter. The interview is a relatively new kind of encounter in the history of human relations, and the older models of encounter — parent-child, male-female, rich-poor, foolish-wise — carry role definitions much better articulated and more exigent. The interviewer will be constantly tempted, if the other party falls back on one of these older models, to reciprocate — tempted and excused. For, unlike most other encounters, the interview is a role-playing situation in which one person is much more an expert than the other, and, while the conventions governing the interviewer's behavior are already beginning, in some professional circles, to harden into standards, the conventions governing the informant's behavior are much less clearly articulated and known. Viditch and Bensman, discussing this aspect of the interview, give examples of the respondent's insecurity in his role:

> "In a difficult joint interview between a husband and wife, which required them to discuss certain problems, respondents would remind their spouses of failures to fulfill the instruction to "discuss" with the remark that "this is not what they wanted!" When couples failed to fulfill the instructions and saw that they had failed, they frequently apologized for their "ignorance" or ineptitude."[1]

Of course there is an enormous amount of preparatory socialization in the respondent role — in schools and jobs, through the mass media — and more and more of the potential respondents of the Western world are readied for the rap of the clipboard on the door. (In some places, perhaps, overreadied. There was a charming story in the London *News of the World* recently about a political canvasser who liked to demonstrate, on the backsides of young suburban mothers, how they could check the urge to delinquency in their offspring. During the ensuing prosecution it was suggested that the ladies had

---

1. A. Viditch and J. Bensman, "The Validity of Field Data," *Human Organization*, XIII, no. 1 (Spring 1954), 20–27.

become, through their experiences with interviewers, so docile as subjects of experiments that they were surprised at nothing.) Probably the most intensive presocialization of respondents runs in roughly the social strata from which interviewers themselves are drawn — the middle, urban, higher-educated groups, while at the top and bottom — though for different reasons — the appropriate role of the informant is apparently much less known. At the moment it is enough to say that where the parties to an interview are unsure of their appropriate roles they are likely to have recourse to other, more firmly delineated social roles that will turn the encounter into one where they feel more at home.

Two conventions characterize most interviews and seem to give this particular mode of personal encounter its uniqueness: These are the conventions of *equality* and *comparability*.

The view that information obtained under stress is likely to be unreliable is not universal, even in our own culture, as "third degree' practices by the police and some popular techniques of cross-examination in the law courts indicate. But in the research interview, at least — and we can regard this as archetypal — the assumption is general that information is the more valid the more freely given. Such an assumption stresses the voluntary character of the interview as a relationship freely and willingly entered into by the respondent; it suggests a certain promissory or contractual element. But if the interview is thought of as a kind of implicit contract between the two parties, it is obvious that the interviewer gains the respondent's time, attention, and whatever information he has to offer, but what the respondent gets is less apparent. A great many people enjoy being interviewed, almost regardless of subject, and one must assume, from the lack of tangible rewards offered, that the advantages must be totally subjective. Here Theodore Caplow's suggestion, in his article (The Dynamics of Information Interviewing, *American Journal of Sociology*, 62 [September, 1956], pp. 165–71), that the interview profits as a communication device from the contrast it offers to conversation in less formal situations might satisfy us until further evidence is available: that by offering a program of discussion, and an assurance that information offered will not be challenged or resisted, self-expression is facilitated to an unusual degree and that this is inherently satisfying. In this sense, then, the interview is an understanding between the two parties that, in return for allowing the interviewer to direct their communication, the informant is assured that he will not meet with denial, contradiction, competition, or other harassment. As with all contractual relations, the fiction or convention of equality must govern the situation. Whatever actual inequalities of sex, status, intelligence, expertness, or physique exist between the parties should be muted. Interviewing-training consists very largely of making interviewers aware of the kinds of social inequalities with which respondents are likely to be concerned and of teaching them how to minimize them. This is most important, perhaps, if the respondent is likely to see himself as inferior in some respect to the interviewer, and certainly this has been the most closely studied aspect of interviewer effect.

But what happens when, as increasingly happens, a run-of-the-mill, middle-class interviewer encounters a member of some financial, intellectual, or political elite? Our own impression is that such respondents contrive to re-establish equality in the interview by addressing themselves subjectively, not to the actual interviewer, but to the study director or even his sponsor. The different subjective uses to which respondents put these ghostly figures is something that might very profitably be looked into; certainly, people of superior status are more aware of them, and make more use of them, than others.

Evidently such a view of the interview has much in common with Simmel's view of sociability. Both in the interview as seen here and in the sociable gathering as seen by Simmel the convention of equality is a formal necessity and is achieved by excluding from immediate awareness all those attributes of the individual, subjective and objective, which make for inequalities in everyday life. But, as Simmel stresses, the objects of a sociable gathering can be achieved only within a given social stratum — "sociability among members of very different social strata often is inconsistent and painful."[2] The muting of minor social inequalities, such as age, sex, wealth, erudition, and fame, can be accomplished only by the physical elimination of the grosser subcultural differences. But the interview was designed to provide a bridge for communicating between the social strata precisely of the kind that sociability cannot provide (if it could, interviewing would be unnecessary). And this fact brings out another important difference between the interview as practiced and the sociable gathering as seen by Simmel — in the handling of affect. The identifications which bring people together easily in sociable gatherings are primarily established on an emotional basis, and, as Simmel stresses, any affective expression which runs counter to these emotional bonds is suppressed: it is, says Simmel, the essential function

2. Kurt Wolff, trans., *The Sociology of Georg Simmel* (Glencoe, Ill.: Free Press, 1950), p. 47.

of *tact* "to draw the limits, which result from the claims of others, of the individual's impulses, ego-stresses, and intellectual and material desires."[3] The only emotional expression tolerable in the sociable gathering is that which heightens the emotional bonds already established within the group. Psychologically, however, exclusion from these shared affective responses constitutes social inequality; and, if equality in the interview is to be established, it must at bottom be achieved by the interviewer's encouraging and accepting the affect as well as the information the respondent offers. (Hence the growing emphasis on "rapport" in the technical manuals dealing with the interview.) The problem of establishing equality in the interview, then, depends on the expression rather than the suppression of affective responses, on some encouragement of the private, idiosyncratic, and subjective dimensions of at least one of the personalities involved. True, the interview *tends* toward the form of the sociable conversation, in that, once the interviewer has been "cued" to the level of discourse a given respondent is capable of, and has adapted himself to it, communication is expected to approximate that which would take place between actual equals, so that the information carried away is assumed to be such as a man might give when talking freely to a friend. Thus students of the dynamics of interviewing find that there is in general an early release of affect, followed by a more equable flow of information.

Interviewing, then, is distinguished by the operations of the convention that both parties to the encounter are equals, at least for the purposes and duration of the encounter. But there is another important characteristic of the interview which serves to differentiate it from other modes of human interaction—the convention of *comparability*. The first operates primarily for the advantage of the respondent; the second, for the advantage of the interviewer and his employers. They are not completely compatible conventions, and the latent conflict between them is always threatening to become manifest.

Regarded as an information-gathering tool, the interview is designed to minimize the local, concrete, immediate circumstances of the particular encounter—including the respective personalities of the participants—and to emphasize only those aspects that can be kept general enough and demonstrable enough to be counted. As an encounter between these two particular people the typical interview has no meaning; it is conceived in a framework of other, comparable meetings between other couples, each recorded in such

3. *Ibid.*, p. 45.

fashion that elements of communication in common can be easily isolated from more idiosyncratic qualities. However vaguely this is conceived by the actual participants, it is the needs of the statistician rather than of the people involved directly that determine much, not only the content of communication but its form as well. Obviously, this convention conflicts with the psychological requirements for equality of affective interchange, and one can observe various attempts to resolve the problem, from interviewing in groups to interviewing in depth. At its most obvious the convention of comparability produces the "standardized" interview, where the whole weight of the encounter is placed on the order and formulation of the questions asked and little freedom is permitted to the interviewer to adjust the statistician's needs to the particular encounter. The statistician, indeed, seldom uses *all* the material collected; few reports, apparently, make use of more than 30 or 40 per cent of the information collected. But less obtrusively it enters into almost all interviewing, even psychiatric interviewing, as the possibilities of statistical manipulation of "data" force themselves on the attention of research-minded practitioners. Here technological advances such as the tape recorder are hastening the process—directly, by making available for comparison transcripts of psychiatric interviews hitherto unobtainable and, indirectly, by exposing more clearly to colleagues those purely personal and private (or "distorting" and "biasing") observations and interpretations which the practitioner brings into the interview with him. The very displacement of the older words "session" or "consultation" by the modern word "interview," to describe what passes between the psychiatrist and his patient, is a semantic recognition of this spread of the convention of comparability.

All this amounts to a definition of the interview as a relationship between two people where both parties behave as though they are of equal status for its duration, whether or not this is actually so; and where, also, both behave as though their encounter had meaning only in relation to a good many other such encounters. Obviously, this is not an exhaustive definition of any interview; it leaves out any reference to the exchange and recording of information, to the probability that the parties involved are strangers, and to the transitory nature of the encounter and the relationship. In any formal definition of the interview these elements must have a place.

A relationship governed by the conventions just discussed can occur, it is clear, only in a particular cultural climate; and such a climate is a fairly new thing in the history of the human race.

Anthropologists have long realized—if not always clearly—that the transitory interview, held with respondents who do not share their view of the encounter, is an unreliable source of information in itself. It is not until they have been in the society long enough to fit into one of its better-defined roles that they can "tap" a valid communication system and hear the kind of messages that the others in the culture hear. Equally, the climate which makes widespread interviewing possible in the West today is itself relatively novel. A century ago, when Mayhew pioneered in the survey by interviewing "some thousands of the humbler classes of society," the social distance between his readers and his subjects, though they largely lived in the same city, was such that he could best conceptualize his undertaking as an ethnological inquiry, seeking to establish that "we, like the Kaffirs, Fellahs and Finns, are surrounded by wandering hordes—the 'Sonquas' and the 'Fingoes' of this country." Mayhew was a newspaperman, and his survey was first published in a London newspaper. This fact serves to remind us that interviewing as we know it today was an invention of the mass-communications industry and, as a mode of human encounter, has much the same boundaries. On the other hand, the interview has become something very like a medium of mass communication in its own right, and one, on the whole, with less frivolous and banal concerns than related media. One might even make the point that newspapers, movies, radio, and television have been encouraged to pursue their primrose paths by delegating to the survey researchers and their interviewers most of the more serious functions of social communication. If this is so, the interviewer has ousted the publicist by virtue of the convention of comparability, and the ideological and social shifts which have made it possible for individuals willingly to populate the statistician's cells become as worthy of study as, say, the spread of literacy.

We can trace the spread of this convention from the time it was a radical idea in the mind of Jeremy Bentham and a few of his disciples until it became a habit of thought of all but the very top and bottom segments of our society. In like fashion we trace the growth of the convention of equality from the ideas of John Locke and his disciples to its almost total permeation of the American scene. To chart such changes in the way people relate themselves to one another is the historian's job rather than the sociologist's, and it is one requiring volumes rather than pages. But even a brief review of the course of such changes will tead to a sharper sense of the novelty and significance of the interview as a mode of human relationship and will perhaps aid in assessing its limits and potentialities in the future.

13. Interviewing Medical Students

HOWARD S. BECKER

THE VALUES of any social group are an ideal which actual behavior may sometimes approximate but seldom fully embodies. To deal with the tension between ideal and reality conceptually, there are two possible polar attitudes toward values. Individuals may be idealistic, accepting the values warmly and wholeheartedly, feeling that everyone can and should live up to them and that they are both "right" and "practical." Or they may be cynical, conceiving the values as impossibly impractical and incapable of being lived up to; they may feel that anyone who accepts these values wholeheartedly deceives himself and that one must compromise in meeting the exigencies of daily life. The distinction, only one among many which might be made, is useful in a discussion of certain problems of which I have become aware in studying the social-psychological development of medical students.[1]

Reprinted by permission from *American Journal of Sociology*, 62 (September 1956), pp. 199–201. © 1956 by The University of Chicago Press.

1. This study is sponsored by Community Studies, Inc., of Kansas City, Missouri, and is being carried out at the University of Kansas Medical Center, to whose dean and staff we are indebted for their wholehearted co-operation. Professor Everett C. Hughes of The University of Chicago is director of the project.

Probably most commonly, individuals feel both ways about the values of their group at the same time; or one way in some situations, the other way in others. In which of these moods are they likely to respond to the interviewer seeking sociological information? Or to turn attention to the interviewer himself: Which of these is he looking for in the people he talks to? Which kind of response is he concerned with eliciting?

Sociologists have had a penchant for the exposé since the days of muckraking. The interviewer is typically out to get "the real story" he conceives to be lying hidden beneath the platitudes of any group and is inclined to discount heavily any expressions of the "official" ideology. The search for the informal organization of a group reflects this, and Merton's dictum that sociology's distinctive contribution lies in the discovery and analysis of latent rather than manifest functions is a theoretical statement of this position.[2]

The interviewer must always remember that cynicism may underlie a perfunctory idealism. In many situations, interviewees perceive him as a potentially dangerous person and, fearing lest he discover secrets better kept from the outside world, resort to the "official line" in order to keep his inquisitiveness at bay in a polite way. The interviewer may circumvent such tactics by affecting cynicism himself, so that the interviewee is lulled into believing that the former accepts his own publicly disreputable view of things,[3] or by confronting him with the evidence of his own words or reported deeds which do not jibe with the views he has presented.[4] There may, perhaps, be other ways, for this area has not been well explored.

Convinced that idealistic talk is probably not sincere but merely a cover-up for less respectable cynicism, the interviewer strives to get beneath it to the "real thing." If he is using a schedule, he may be instructed or feel it necessary to use a "probe." An interview is frequently judged successful precisely to the degree that it elicits cynical rather than idealistic attitudes. A person interviewing married couples with an eye to assessing their adjustment would probably place less credence in an interview in which both partners insisted that theirs was the perfect marriage than he would in one in which he was told that "the honeymoon is over."

Important and justified as is the interviewer's preoccupation with

2. Robert K. Merton, *Social Theory and Social Structure* (Glencoe, Ill.: Free Press, 1949), p. 68.

3. See Arnold M. Rose, "A Research Note on Interviewing," *American Journal of Sociology*, LI (September 1945), 143-44.

4. See Howard S. Becker, "A Note on Interviewing Tactics," *Human Organization*, XII (Winter 1954), 31-32.

the problem, it creates the possibility that he will either misinterpret idealism sincerely presented to him or, by his manner of questioning, fashion a role for himself in the interview that encourages cynicism while discouraging idealism. For the interviewer's manner and role can strongly affect what the interviewee chooses to tell him, as can the situation in which the interview is conducted.

In what follows I speak largely from my current experiences in interviewing medical students.

In interviewing medical students, the difficulty does not lie in eliciting cynical attitudes; such statements are likely to be made without much help from the interviewer. The real problem is quite different—that of making sure that one does not prevent the expression of more idealistic attitudes but helps the interviewee to say such things if he has them to say. Using the semicynical approach I have elsewhere described as useful in piercing the institutional idealism of schoolteachers,[5] in interviewing the students informally and casually in the midst of the student groups among whom I have done my participant observation, I failed to allow them much opportunity to give vent to their hidden personal idealism.

By being warm and permissive, by expressing idealistic notions one's self, and subtly encouraging their expression on the part of the student, one might well gather a set of data which would picture the student as wanting to "help humanity," uninterested in the financial rewards of medical practice, intrigued by the mysteries of science, bedeviled by doubts about his ability to make sound judgments in matters of life and death—a set of data, in short, which would draw heavily on this part of the student's repertoire of mixed emotions. If one saw students alone and was not with them as they went through their daily routine, he would be even more likely to get such an impression. The student cannot well express such thoughts to his fellows or in front of them, for the students are almost ritualistically cynical, and, more important perhaps, their attention is focused on immediate problems of studenthood rather than on problems which will be forced into immediate awareness only when, as young doctors, they assume full medical responsibility. By playing his role properly, the interviewer can help the student express this submerged part of his medical self and become a sounding board for his repressed better half.

As I began my field work, I fell into a relationship with the students which would have inhibited their expressing idealistic sentiments to me, even had I been operating with an "idealistic" frame

5. *Ibid.*

of reference rather than the "realistic" one I in fact used. I was with them most of the time, attending classes with them, accompanying them on teaching rounds, standing by while they assisted at operations and in delivering babies, having lunch with them, playing pool and cards with them, and so on. This meant, in the first place, that I was with them mainly in larger groups where cynicism was the dominant language and idealism would have been laughed down; this fact colored more intimate and private situations. More subtly, in being around them so much, day after day, I was likely to see the inevitable compromises and violations of lofty ideals entailed by the student role. Could a student expect me to believe his statement that the patient's welfare should be a primary consideration for him (to take a hypothetical example) when he knew that I had seen him give less than his full time to his patients because of an impending examination?

My data give a quite different picture from that arrived at by our hypothetical "idealist" researcher. I finally became aware of the way I had been systematically underestimating the idealism of the men I was studying by finding evidences of it in my own field notes. Some men made almost continual implicit reference, in their comments about practicing physicians they had seen at work, to an extremely high and "impractical" standard of medical practice best typified by their clinical teachers. Others went to great lengths to acquire knowledge on specific topics required neither by their immediate practical interests as students nor by the more long-range material interests related to their medical futures. Particular patients seen on the hospital wards typified certain difficult dilemmas of medical idealism, and, faced with a concrete example, some students brought up their own heavily idealistic worries about what they might do if confronted with a similar dilemma when they became doctors.

Seeing this, I began deliberately encouraging the expression of such thoughts. I spent more time with students engaged in activities carried out alone, raising questions in a sympathetic fashion quite different from the manner I used in groups. I "kidded" them less, asked interestedly about topics in which they had an "impractical" interest, and so on. Not every student displayed strong "idealism"; a few, indeed, did not respond idealistically at all, no matter how hard I searched for it or what situations I attempted the search in. But I had now looked for it; if I missed it where it was in fact present, it was not because of aspects of my research role.

So, in the long run, I have both kinds of data on my interviewees. I have been fortunate in having long enough contact with them to get by another means the idealism I missed at first and so have ended with a picture of these men which includes both aspects of their selves. The technical moral to be drawn is perhaps that one might best assume that interviewees have both varieties of feelings about the values underlying the social relationships under study and be aware of and consciously manipulate those elements of role and situation which give promise of eliciting one sentiment or the other.

As always, the technical moral forces a theoretical moral as well. We may tend to assume too readily that our interviewees will be easily classified as "attitude types" and that they will be more or less consistent in their view of things germane to our study. It is, after all, such a theoretical assumption that accounts for the exposé, with its emphasis on uncovering the "real" attitudes, as well as for the opposite "Pollyanna" attitude, with its unquestioning belief that people are as good as they say they are. It may be more useful to start with the hypothesis that people may entertain each attitude, at one time or another, and let this notion inform a more flexible interviewing style.

14. The Unidentified Interviewer

HENRY RIECKEN

DURING a participant-observation study of an apocalyptic group,[1] the interviewers faced a number of difficulties in developing a suitable role for themselves. They sought to collect essential data but yet to remain ostensibly just ordinary members of the group of believers being studied. Furthermore, the observers tried to behave in such a way as to minimize the effect they might have on the members' beliefs and actions.

The group had gathered around a middle-aged housewife in a suburb of an American city. She believed that, through "automatic writing," she had received a number of messages from beings dwelling in outer space, forecasting the destruction of the earth by flood on a certain date. She made known this prediction among her acquaintances, and a number of people began calling on her regularly

Reprinted by permission from *American Journal of Sociology*, 62 (September 1956), pp. 210–212. © 1956 by The University of Chicago Press.

1. A complete account of the study [appears] . . . in a book by Leon Festinger, H. W. Riecken, and Stanley Schacter, *When Prophecy Fails* (Minneapolis: University of Minnesota Press, 1956). The present article draws upon the "Methodological Appendix" of this book.

to be instructed in the "lessons" from outer space and to discuss the possibilities of salvation. Most "members" were adult men and women, of between about twenty to about fifty-five years of age, of middle socioeconomic status and well educated, all but two having at least attended college. About twenty-five people at one time or another showed interest in the prophet's messages. During the last month before the flood was expected the most convinced believers (about a dozen people) often met in the living room of the prophet's home in what resembled social gatherings. No formal organization was ever established.

The study of the group was undertaken in order to test a hypothesis derived from the theory of dissonance.[2] That hypothesis can be stated as follows: Under certain specified conditions, when a belief or prediction is demonstrated to have been wrong, those who have held the belief not only will fail to relinquish it but will try even harder than before to convince others of its validity. Among the specified conditions are that the believers, before the predicted event, were sincerely *convinced* of the validity of their belief, and they must have taken some action, consistent with the belief, that is hard or impossible to revoke or undo (i.e., they must be *committed*). The major problem for the participant-observers in this study was to determine, for each believer, the degree of his *conviction*, the amount and kind of his *commitment*, and, of course, the extent of his *proselyting*. It was essential, of course, that the participant-observers obtain data on all three variables both before and after the crucial date.

Furthermore, it was important that the observers avoid exerting influence on the beliefs and actions of the members. We wished especially to avoid doing or saying anything that would affect the extent of proselyting; but we also wanted to avoid increasing or decreasing the conviction and the commitment of the members.

From our very first contact with the chief figures it was apparent that a study could not be conducted openly. The leaders had not yet adopted a policy of secrecy and exclusion, but they were at that time neither seeking publicity nor recruiting converts. Rather, their attitude can be best described as one of passive acceptance of individuals who came to call and seemed to be interested in the messages from outer space. Our observers were welcomed politely, and their questions were answered, for the most part, fully, but they were not

2. *Ibid.*, chap. 1. A full presentation of the theory and a number of derivations appear in a book by Festinger. (*A Theory of Cognitive Dissonance*, Stanford: Stanford University Press, 1957).

proselyted vigorously or enlisted to spread the word. To obtain entree and maintain contact with the group, our observers posed as ordinary inquirers and, later, as ordinary members who believed in the tenets of the group as the others did.

Because they took the part of ordinary members, the observers obviously could not play the usual role of interviewers. They were effectively prevented from using any kind of formal schedule of questions, and even attempts to cover a systematic list of topics by ordinary questions were not feasible. The only interviewing possible was necessarily conversational in style and carefully casual. In gathering the data on conviction, commitment, and proselyting, the observers tried to be non-directive, sympathetic listeners—passive participants who were inquisitive and eager to learn whatever others might want to tell them. But such a role was not without its difficulties.

In the first place, the passive-member role greatly hampered inquiry. Unable to take command of the situation as an interviewer ordinarily does, the observers were forced to maintain constant alertness for relevant data that members of the group spontaneously brought forth and had to be extremely tactful and skillful in following up leads so as not to appear too inquisitive. Second, while the attitude we strove for was easy enough for an observer to take during his first few contacts, it became increasingly difficult to maintain as he began to be seen as a "regular." Non-directive inquiry about others, while revealing little about one's own feelings or actions, is appropriate enough behavior for a newcomer, but, if prolonged, it tends to cast doubt on either the intelligence or the motives of interrogator. In ordinary social intercourse it is reasonably expected that the members of a group will give as well as receive information about beliefs, opinions, and actions relevant to their common purpose. But in the role we defined privately for ourselves such expectations did not fit.

Nearly every conversation he had with a member about his conviction, commitment, or proselyting presented the observer with an unsought opportunity to influence the other; for it is difficult, outside the interviewer's role, to inquire of an individual how he feels about a matter without having him return the question. Such reciprocal questioning was especially common in this group, because their beliefs concerned the future and the non-material world. Since the beliefs could not be validated (at least not until the cataclysm) by physical reality, the only confirmation available was from social reality—the beliefs and actions of fellows. The pressure on observers to take part in the process of mutual support and confirmation was ever present and often strong.

The alternatives for dealing with such pressures were all unattractive. Had the observers been completely truthful about their convictions, they would unquestionably have weakened the convictions of other members and would, in addition, have been in the absurd position of trying to maintain membership in a group whose beliefs they flatly denied. On the other hand, had they simulated the sincerity and depth of conviction of the regular members, they would have strongly reinforced conviction. A third choice, non-committal responses and evasive replies, soon became embarrassing and awkward, besides jeopardizing the observer's status in the group. The observers were forced, therefore, to present the appearance of agreement with the major beliefs of the group. While they avoided taking strong stands on these issues and never voluntarily or spontaneously spoke up to reinforce conviction, their general air of acceptance as well as their mere presence and interest in the affairs of the group undoubtedly had some strengthening effect on the conviction of the others. The goal of avoiding influence completely, proved unrealistic, for, in order to remain members and yet gather the necessary data, the observers had to offer some support to the members' convictions. And this, while indeed minimal, must have had some effect.

In the matter of commitment the effect of the observers is difficult to assess. Many members of the group committed themselves by spending appreciable amounts of money to attend meetings, by making public declarations of belief, at least among acquaintances and neighbors, by giving up friendship with skeptics, by giving away possessions, or by quitting their jobs. Until the week or two before the date of the expected flood, there was little or no pressure on observers to make or to report commitments, and, when the pressure to quit jobs grew, the observers were able to invent various reasons why they could not or should not quit their jobs. But even though they did not quit jobs, give away possessions, or make public declarations of faith, the observers must have appeared to the regular members to have committed themselves by spending both time and money to attend meetings. One observer may have seemed heavily committed, since he made a number of trips by air from a distant city to attend meetings; two others, who resided in the city where the group was located, devoted a great deal of time to its activities, not only attending all meetings but paying numerous additional calls at the home of the prophet. All the observers spent virtually full time at the prophet's home during the four days immediately preceding the date when the flood was expected.

It is hard to estimate the effect of this apparent commitment by the observers. On the one hand, it probably reinforced members' convictions and confidence that they had been right in making whatever commitments they had made; on the other hand, the observers' commitments may have made those of other members seem either more or less important. The perceived amount of the observers' commitment probably ranged from moderate to slight: There were at least two members whose commitment was less than that of any observer and at least four or five who exceeded that of any observer. For the latter, the lesser commitment of the observers probably made their own seem greater and more binding, whereas the former probably perceived their commitment to be even slighter in contrast to the observers'. In short, for most of the group the observers' investment in group activity was supportive, but the amount of support varied.

Only in proselyting were we able to avoid exercising any influence. During the greater part of the period of our observation, the attitude of the leaders and most of the members toward proselyting was ambivalent, and there had been at least one pronouncement by the prophet that proselyting was forbidden. Although this policy was not strictly adhered to, the observers were able to fall back on it as a convenient justification for their inactivity. During the brief time when potential converts were appearing at the prophet's home and asking for information and instruction, the observers managed to stay largely in the background and to observe rather than take part. On the one or two occasions when the observers were specifically asked to talk to an inquirer, they managed either to turn the occasion into an interview with the visitor or else to repeat only information that was already public knowledge and otherwise act in so uninformed a fashion that the inquirer quickly became bored and left the house.

In summary, then, the role that was forced on us as observers prevented us from achieving the unrealistic goal of avoiding *any* influence on conviction and commitment. That we were able to avoid any observer effect on the major dependent variable — proselyting — is of the utmost importance in judging the scientific value of the research, however, and our success here should not be overlooked. But, from our experience, it seems likely that observers cannot avoid exercising *some* influence on behavior and beliefs. The conflict in roles and its attendant consequences seem to be inherent in the process of doing a study such as this, although it may be possible to devise better ways of handling the conflict and of further reducing observer effect. Such inventions would indeed be welcome.

PART SIX

Problems of Design and Analysis

INTRODUCTION

THIS part reviews the three major strategies available to the researcher as he forges causal explanation. These methods, or models of inference and proof, are the experimental design, multivariate analysis, and analytic induction. It is important for the reader to fully understand the implications of each of these models as he examines the five specific methods presented in parts VII through XII. Each of the sociologist's methods (experiments, surveys, participant observation, life histories, unobstrusive measures) rest on one, or some combination, of these three models of inference. Success at theory construction is ultimately contingent of the sensitive and knowledgeable use of these models.

THE NATURE OF CAUSAL ANALYSIS

A theory is nothing, Homans says, if it is not explanation. Explanation, in turn, is nothing if it is not causally based. Causal analysis demands the demonstration of three properties. The researcher must show that the causal variables in his system produced variations in his dependent variables. He must also show that the causal variable occurs before his dependent, or caused, variable. And last he must show that his causal systems are not spurious, or not contingent on other variables not explicitly examined. There other variables may be *intrinsic* to the research act—as would be the case with variations produced by the investigator's self-conception or in his interactions with a subject—but some variables of this rival causal class may be *extrinsic* to the research process and represent other events that could be producing the observed events. For example, both over-involvement in one's self-presentation and the intrusion of outsiders can destroy a face-to-face encounter. Involvement and intrusion represent substantive causal factors; they are not factors intrinsic to the observational act.

A valid causal relationship is one that is not destroyed by either intrinsic or extrinsic test factors. When a relationship is found to be so contingent, two results can follow. On the one hand, the relationship may be spurious. That is, variation in the dependent variable simply is not caused by the variables the investigator claims are causal. A spurious relationship may be of two types. It may be intrinsic, or extrinsic. Demonstration of intrinsic spuriousness is damaging to all subsequent analysis because it lodges explanation in the research act. This means, in effect, that the researcher has failed. His own actions have produced his findings.

Extrinsic spuriousness is less damaging because it at least demonstrates what substantive variables are causing the observed variations. Under many conditions spuriousness will not be produced. Instead, contributory or contingent events will be uncovered that influence the observed relationship. They do not destroy that relationship, however. Thus, to take the above example of encounters, self-involvement and outside intrusions may together produce more collapsed encounters than either one would alone.

A fact of causal analysis must be noted. The researcher can never be unequivocally assured that his analysis has isolated all the relevant causal factors. He must ever be aware that rival factors—intrinsic or extrinsic—can be influencing his analysis. Causal inference thus becomes a fact of social research. Seldom will one cause or one effect ever be located within an explanatory system.

NATURALISTIC ANALYSIS

The naturalistic perspective assumes a very special view of causal analysis. Because social events interact through time, causal models which recognize interaction and process must be developed. Several examples could be offered. An infant, for example, does not enter the world with a fully developed self-concept; only through interactions with others does a self come into existence. One seldom falls in love and becomes married at the same time, nor does a person immediately become an opiate addict. Divorce does not immediately lead to remarriage. The possession of an advanced degree does not automatically secure a job. In each of these instances a series of steps, or phases, are passed through. Each phase may have a separate cause; the sum of these causes then produces a self-concept, marriage, addiction, or a desired job.

An additional feature of the naturalistic perspective is the commitment to the discovery of propositions which have the widest possible explanatory relevance. Commonly termed universal propositions, these explanations direct the researcher to search out negative cases as he develops his theory. These negative cases serve the functions of refocusing theory and refining observations. Their analysis places all subsequent explanations within a proper focus. The reader can quickly see what is and what is not explained. The study of the negative case pinpoints the weaknesses of theory and furnishes the grounds for future investigation.

THE THREE MODELS OF INFERENCE

The statistical method. Hirschi and Selvin's paper in this part is included in their very important book, *Deliquency Research: An Appraisal of Analytic Methods* (New York: Free Press, 1967), which reviews the most frequent claims of causal analysis in the field of delinquency. Their essay here is aimed primarily at the survey, statistical, or multivariate method of analysis. I have taken my criteria for causal analysis from their discussion. As they state, covariance, time order, and lack of spuriousness must be demonstrated for any explanation to be causally valid. A break in any one of these links establishes lack of causality.

Hirschi and Selvin's analysis of deliquency research leads to devestating conclusions. Few, if any, of the many theories and research reports produced to explain this phenomena are causally valid. Six false criteria of causality have guided past research. These range from a commitment to a single causative view of social events, to a misunderstanding of necessary and sufficient conditions, to a misconception of multivariate analysis generally.

Problems of inference and analysis cannot be restricted to one research area, or one research method. The Hirschi-Selvin critique could be applied to other specialities including organizational research, small group analysis, or the family.

The experimental method. Donald T. Campbell's paper presents what has become the accepted view of experimental design and control. Not only does he distinguish three categories of experimental design, but his treatment of external and internal validity points to alternative variables that can influence any causal analysis. By external validity, Campbell refers to those conditions or events that influence the generalizability of findings. Internal validity asks whether the specific treatment conditions caused the observed variations, or whether these differences are due to the experimental arrangements. His discussion distinguishes several categories of internal and external validity. These include changes in the subject or investigator arising from maturation, testing effects, or shifts in the measurement instrument to selective, or biasing features of the subjects.

It is important to note that external validity raises issues primarily resolved by one's sampling model. If a valid and probability-based model has been employed, then generalizations can be confidently formulated. In Campbell's judgment, however, the researcher must give greater attention to problems of internal validity, because internal validity points directly to aspects of the observational process. If variations are due to subject bias, observer reactivity, or the like, all results may be due to these factors, and not to the experimental variable.

I have rephrased Campbell's use of internal and external validity to specify factors intrinsic or extrinsic to the research process. This is more than a semantic distinction, for it is obvious that all models of causal inference can be assessed by these two factors. Campbell's distinctions are relevant to any and all research designs. By using the term "intrinsic test factor," I hope to stress the importance of examining one's own research situations as sources of causal variance. Similarly, the notion of "extrinsic test factor" extends beyond problems of generalization. It cuts to the heart of causal analysis. The investigator must always be aware that other causal conditions may be influencing his observations. These conditions, while outside the research act per se, demand a sensitivity to rival substantive propositions and theoretical schemes.

As Campbell notes, the true experimental design has two observational groups: one exposed to certain stimuli and the other not. Two observations are taken—before and after exposure to the treatment. The differences between the scores of the experimental and control group represent the effect of the experimental treatment. He distinguishes three designs which do not meet these minimum criteria: the one-shot case study, the one-group pre-test, post-test design, and the static-group comparison design. (These designs, in conjunction with the quasi-experimental designs, should be kept in mind when reading the papers in Part VIII on the survey method. While attempting to approximate the experiment, most, if not all, surveys fall into either the non-experimental or the quasi-experimental categories.)

It is relevant to compare some statistical strategies of analysis with the experimental model. By sorting observational groups into categories which differ on his independent and dependent variables, the survey analyst parallels his experimental counterpart who works with experimental and control groups. Unless two observations are taken on at least two groups, however, the experimental model is not achieved.

It can be seen that the survey method is largely a *strategy of analysis*, while the experiment is a *method of control*. Lacking the ability to control exposure or non-exposure to critical variables, the survey analyst must approximate the experiment through analysis only. This considerably weakens resulting causal conclusions.

Analytic induction. As with the survey, analytic induction proposes a strategy of design, as opposed to a method of control, for causal analysis. But there are several important differences between the two strategies. Users of analytic induction commonly employ participant observation or life histories as their major research strategy. In addition, the use of analytic induction demands that the researcher intimately familiarize himself with the field situation. He must penetrate the groups or situations under study. He must grasp the meaning implicit in their languages. He must learn to see the world through their eyes. (This is the essence of the naturalistic perspective earlier spelled out by Blumer.)

Such a stance permits the field worker to examine his processes as they unfold over time. He can study the natural history of a drug user's career; he can understand how a common group perspective arises among medical students to ward off excessive demands of their professors. By following events longitudinally, time order and covariance between independent and dependent variables can be discovered. It also becomes possible to sort through the multitude of rival causal factors relevant to the situation at hand. The observer is there in the field. He can assess the impact of his own presence, and he can detect changes in his subjects.

Analytic induction proposes the progressive formulation and testing of hypothesis through the observational process. As negative cases appear, they are made to fit the emergent hypothesis. If they cannot be explained, a revision of the hypothesis is demanded. This strategy is close to what Glaser and Strauss mean by theoretical sampling. Theory, data and hypothesis interrelate to produce explanations that explain every observed case.

Ralph Turner's article reviews the classic studies conducted within the method of analytic induction. He cites evidence from previous studies to show that frequently analytic induction fails to produce predictive hypotheses; instead, it offers definitions of the phenomena studied. Lindesmith's study of opiate addiction is criticized on these grounds; his theory does not state who will first take the drug, nor does it state at what level of withdrawal symptoms have to be sensed before the drug will be taken again. It also fails to state what an individual's pattern of behavior will be after he once becomes addicted.

Turner also notes that unless the field worker uncovers data that are universally shared by all his subjects, those data that do not must be rejected. Hence, since Lindesmith's opiate addicts varied in terms of education and social background, those variations had to be omitted from the final analysis. This leaves the reader with no knowledge of who those users were.

Turner's main criticism of analytic induction is its inability to handle factors which are extrinsic, or external, to a causal scheme. That is, the method proposes a closed system of analysis within which all relevant causal variables are contained, and in Turner's judgment the method must be made to handle rival causal factors which enter from the outside. Because such factors seldom have a uniform effect or distribution (e.g., class background), they will not have an universal causal impact. Consequently, analytic induction must be used together with the statistical method, which is better suited to the study of nonuniformly distributed events.

Turner's conclusions are well-displayed in Becker's analysis of data gathered with the observational method (see Part IX). Becker shows how simple forms of statistical analysis can be carried out on observational data, and he shows how such analysis can uncover negative cases, a strategy that responds to Turner's plea for the simultaneous use of analytic induction and the statistical method.

Becker's article, which will also be discussed in Part IX, has the advantage of detailing the steps necessary for an observational study. He notes how field evidence has to be analyzed by situational and intrinsic test factors (e.g. , the credibility of informants, the reactivity of the situation, and so on). He also offers a paradigm for analyzing such data. Of major importance is his stress on moving from observations to the study of a total organization. His remarks once again indicate how theory, sampling, observations, and analysis must be combined. Becker also stresses the importance of recording and making public every aspect of the research act. His paradigm suggests how the less rigorous method of analytic induction may be formalized and hence made public.

The reader must decide for himself what method of inference and proof he wants to work with, but whatever his choice, the canons of valid causal analysis cannot be ignored.

Suggested Readings. The general logic of multivariate analysis is elaborated in Section 2 of Lazarsfeld and Rosenberg's reader, *The Language of Social Research* (New York: Free Press, 1955). Lazarsfeld's paper, "Interpretation of Statistical Relations as a Research Operation," pp. 115–25, in this reader should be examined. Hirschi and Selvin's monograph, *Deliquency Research* (New York: Free Press, 1967), is recommended as well. Several of the papers in Hubert and Ann Blalock's reader, *Methodology in Social Research* (New York: McGraw-Hill, 1968), elaborate the general strategies of statistical and experimental analysis. I would suggest examining the articles by Siegel and Hodge, Blalock, Boudon, Ross and Smith, and Wiggins in it. Naroll's article on the comparative method in anthropology is relevant in the context of the field method and analytic induction, and Coleman's on mathematical models and the study of change should also be read.

The best combination of analytic induction and the quasi-statistical method is *Boys in White* (Chicago: University of Chicago Press, 1961) by Howard S. Becker, Blanche Geer, Everett C. Hughes and Anselm L. Strauss.

The reader should also examine Denton E. Morrison and Ramon E. Henkel's "Significance Tests Reconsidered," *American Sociologist*, 4 (May 1969), 131–40 for a review of the problems surrounding the use of significance tests in causal analysis. The same authors are editing a book, *The Significance Test Controversy: A Reader* (Chicago: Aldine Publishing Company, 1970), that details the controversies surrounding such tests. One of their conclusions is that between the years 1947 and 1967 a majority of the articles reported in the *American Sociological Review* incorrectly employed significance tests. That is, they were used in situations where a sample was unspecified beforehand, or where nonprobability sampling techniques were employed.

15. False Criteria of Causality in Delinquency Research

TRAVIS HIRSCHI AND HANAN C. SELVIN

Smoking per se is not a cause of lung cancer. Evidence for this statement comes from the thousands of people who smoke and yet live normal, healthy lives. Lung cancer is simply unknown to the vast majority of smokers, even among those who smoke two or more packs a day. Whether smoking is a cause of lung cancer, then, depends upon the reaction of the lung tissues to the smoke inhaled. The important thing is not whether a person smokes, but how his lungs react to the smoke inhaled. These facts point to the danger of imputing causal significance to superficial variables. In essence, it is not smoking as such, but the carcinogenic elements in tobacco smoke that are the real causes of lung cancer.[1]

The task of determining whether such variables as broken homes, gang membership, or anomie are "causes" of deliquency benefits from a comparison with the more familiar problem of deciding whether cigarette smoking "causes" cancer. In both fields many statistical studies have shown strong relations between these pre-

This is publication A-56 of the Survey Research Center, University of California, Berkeley. We are grateful to the Ford Foundation for financial support of the larger study from which this paper is drawn. An early account of this study, which does not include the present paper, is *The Methodological Adequacy of Delinquency Research*, Berkeley: Survey Research Center, 1962. Ian Currie, John Lofland, Alan B. Wilson, and Herbert L. Costner made useful criticisms of previous versions of this paper.

1. This is a manufactured "quotation;" its source will become obvious shortly.

sumed causes and the observed effects, but the critics of these studies often attack them as "merely statistical." This phrase has two meanings. To some critics it stands for the belief that only with experimental manipulation of the independent variables is a satisfactory causal inference possible. To others it is a brief way of saying that observing a statistical association between two phenomena is only the first step in plausibly inferring causality. Since no one proposes trying to give people cancer or to make them delinquent, the fruitful way toward better causal analyses in these two fields is to concentrate on improving the statistical approach.

In setting this task for ourselves we can begin with one area of agreement: all statistical analyses of causal relations in delinquency rest on observed associations between the independent and dependent variables. Beyond this there is less agreement. Following Hyman's reasoning,[2] we believe that these two additional criteria are the minimum requirements for an adequate causal analysis: (1) the independent variable is causally prior to the dependent variable (we shall refer to this as the criterion of "causal order"), and (2) the original association does not disappear when the influences of other variables causally prior to both of the original variables are removed ("lack of spuriousness").[3]

The investigator who tries to meet these criteria does not have an easy time of it.[4] Our examination of statistical research on the causes of delinquency shows, however, that many investigators do not try to meet these criteria but instead invent one or another new criterion of causality — or, more often, of noncausality, perhaps because noncausality is easier to demonstrate. To establish causality one must forge a chain of three links (association, causal order, and lack of spuriousness), and the possibility that an antecedent variable not yet considered may account for the observed relation makes the third link inherently weak. To establish noncausality, one has only to break any one of these links.[5]

2. Herbert H. Hyman, *Survey Design and Analysis* (Glencoe, Ill.: Free Press, 1955) chaps. 5–7.

3. Hyman appears to advocate another criterion as well: that a chain of intervening variables must link the independent and dependent variables of the original relation. We regard this as psychologically or theoretically desirable but not as part of the minimum methodological requirements for demonstrating causality in nonexperimental research.

4. Travis Hirschi and Hanan C. Selvin, "False Criteria of Causality in Delinquency Research," *Social Problems* 13 (Winter 1966), p. 254.

5. Popper calls this the asymmetry of verifiability and falsifiability. (Karl R. Popper, *The Logic of Scientific Discovery* [New York: Basic Books, 1959], esp. pp. 27–48). For a fresh view of the verification-falsification controversy, see Thomas S. Kuhn, *The Structure of Scientific Revolutions* [Chicago: University of Chicago Press, 1962]. Kuhn discusses Popper's views on pp. 145–46. Actually, it is harder to establish

Despite the greater ease with which noncausality may be demonstrated, many assertions of noncausality in the delinquency literature turn out to be invalid. Some are invalid because the authors misuse statistical tools or misinterpret their findings. But many more are invalid because the authors invoke one or another false criterion of noncausality. Perhaps because assertions of noncausality are so easy to demonstrate, these invalid assertions have received a great deal of attention.

A clear assertion that certain variables long considered causes of delinquency are not really causes comes from a 1960 *Report to The Congress:*

> Many factors frequently cited as causes of delinquency are really only concomitants. They are not causes in the sense that if they were removed delinquency would decline. Among these factors are:
> Broken homes.
> Poverty.
> Poor housing.
> Lack of recreational facilities.
> Poor physical health.
> Race.
> Working mothers.[6]

According to this report, all of these variables are statistically associated with delinquency, i.e., they are all "concomitants." To prove that they are not causes of delinquency it is necessary either to show that their relations with delinquency are spurious or that they are effects of delinquency rather than causes. Since all of these presumptive causes appear to precede delinquency, the only legitimate way to prove noncausality is to find an antecedent variable that accounts for the observed relations. None of the studies cited in the *Report* does this.[7] Instead, the assertion that broken homes, poverty,

noncausality than our statement suggests, because of the possibility of "spurious independence." This problem is discussed in Hirschi and Selvin, *op. cit.*, pp. 38–45, as "elaboration of a zero relation."

6. U.S. Department of Health, Education, and Welfare, *Report to The Congress on Juvenile Delinquency* (United States Government Printing Office, 1960), p. 21. The conclusion that "poor housing" is not a cause of delinquency is based on Mildred Hartsough, *The Relation Between Housing and Delinquency* (Federal Emergency Administration of Public Works, Housing Division, 1936). The conclusion that "poor physical health" is not a cause is based on Edward Piper's "unpublished Children's Bureau manuscript summarizing the findings of numerous investigators on this subject." Since we have not examined these two works, the following conclusions do not apply to them.

7. Yhe works cited are: broken homes, Negly K. Teeters and John Otto Reinemann, *The Challenge of Delinquency* (New York: Prentice-Hall, 1950), pp. 149–54; poverty, Bernard Lander, *Toward an Understanding of Juvenile Delinquency* (New York:

lack of recreational facilities, race, and working mothers are not causes of delinquency appears to be based on one or more of the following false "criteria":[8]

> 1. Insofar as a relation between two variables is not *perfect*, the relation is not causal.
> (a) Insofar as a factor is not a *necessary condition* for delinquency, it is not a cause of delinquency.
> (b) Insofar as a factor is not a *sufficient condition* for delinquency, it is not a cause of delinquency.
> 2. Insofar as a factor is not *"characteristic"* of delinquents, it is not a cause of delinquency.
> 3. If a relation between an independent variable and delinquency is found for a *single value of a situational or contextual factor*, then the situational or contextual factor cannot be a cause of delinquency.[9]
> 4. If a relation is observed between an independent variable and delinquency and if a psychological variable is suggested as *intervening* between these two variables, then the original relation is not causal.
> 5. *Measurable* variables are not causes.
> 6. If a relation between an independent variable and delinquency is *conditional* upon the value of other variables, the independent variable is not a cause of delinquency.

In our opinion, all of these criteria of noncausality are illegitimate. If they were systematically applied to any field of research, no relation would survive the test. Some of them, however, have a superficial plausibility, both as stated or implied in the original works and as reformulated here. It will therefore be useful to consider in some

Columbia University Press, 1954); recreational facilities, Ethel Shanas and Catherine E. Dunning, *Recreation and Delinquency* (Chicago: Chicago Recreation Commission, 1942); race, Lander, *op. cit.*; working mothers, Eleanor E. Maccoby, "Children and Working Mothers," *Children,* 5 (May-June, 1958), 83–89.

8. It is not clear in every case that the researcher himself reached the conclusion of noncausality or, if he did, that this conclusion was based on the false criteria discussed below. Maccoby's article, for example, contains a "conjectural explanation" of the relation between mother's employment and delinquency (i.e., without presenting any statistical evidence she suggests that the original relation came about through some antecedent variable), but it appears that the conclusion of noncausality in the *Report* is based on other statements in her work.

9. All of the foregoing criteria are related to the "perfect relation" criterion in that they all require variation in delinquency that is unexplained by the "noncausal" variable. A more general statement of criterion 3 would be: "if variable X is related to delinquency when there is no variation in variable T, then variable T is not a cause of delinquency." In order for this criterion to be applicable, there must be some residual variation in delinquency after T has had its effect.

Although both forms of this criterion fairly represent the reasoning involved in some claims of non-causality, and although both are false, the less explicit version in the text is superficially more plausible. This inverse relation between explicitness and plausibility is one reason for the kind of methodological explication presented here.

detail just why these criteria are illegitimate and to see how they appear in delinquency research.

FALSE CRITERION 1. INSOFAR AS A RELATION BETWEEN TWO VARIABLES IS NOT PERFECT, THE RELATION IS NOT CAUSAL.

> Despite the preponderance of Negro delinquency, one must beware of imputing any causal significance to race per se. There is no *necessary* concomitance between the presence of Negroes and delinquency. In Census Tracts 9-1 and 20-2, with populations of 124 and 75 Negro juveniles, there were no recorded cases of delinquency during the study period. The rates of Negro delinquency also vary as widely as do the white rates indicating large differences in behavior patterns that are not a function or effect of race per se. It is also of interest to note that in at least 10% of the districts with substantial Negro juvenile populations, the Negro delinquency rate is lower than the corresponding white rate.[10]

There are three facts here: (1) not all Negroes are delinquents; (2) the rates of Negro delinquency vary from place to place; (3) in some circumstances, Negroes are less likely than whites to be delinquent. These facts lead Lander to conclude that race has no causal significance in delinquency.

In each case the reasoning is the same: Each fact is another way of saying that the statistical relation between race and delinquency is not perfect, and this apparently is enough to disqualify race as a cause. To see why this reasoning is invalid one has only to ask for the conditions under which race *could be* a cause of delinquency if this criterion were accepted. Suppose that the contrary of the first fact above were true, that *all* Negroes are delinquent. It would then follow necessarily that Negro delinquency rates would not vary from place to place (fact 2) and that the white rate would never be greater than the Negro rate (fact 3). Thus in order for race to have "any" causal significance, all Negroes must be delinquents (or all whites non-delinquents). In short, race must be perfectly related to delinquency.[11]

10. Bernard Lander, *Towards an Understanding of Juvenile Delinquency*, (New York: Columbia University Press, 1954), p. 32. Italics in original. An alternative interpretation of the assumptions implicit in this quotation is presented in the discussion of criterion 6, below.

11. Strictly speaking, in this quotation Lander does not demand that race be perfectly related to delinquency, but only that all Negroes be delinquents (the sufficient conditions of criterion 1-b). Precedent for the "perfect relation" criterion of causality appears in a generally excellent critique of crime and delinquency research by Jerome

Now if an independent variable and a dependent variable are perfectly associated,[12] no other independent variable is needed: that is, perfect association implies single causation, and less-than-perfect association implies multiple causation. Rejecting as causes of delinquency those variables whose association with delinquency is less than perfect thus implies rejecting the principle of multiple causation. Although there is nothing sacred about this principle, at least at the level of empirical research it is more viable than the principle of single causation. All studies show that more than one independent variable is needed to account for delinquency. In this field, as in others, perfect relations are virtually unknown. The researcher who finds a less-than-perfect relation between variable X and delinquency should not conclude that X is not a cause of delinquency, but merely that it is not the *only* cause.[13]

For example, suppose that tables like the following have been found for variables A, B, C, and D as well as for X:

Delinquency by X, where X is neither a necessary nor a sufficient condition for delinquency, but may be one of several causes.

	X	Not X
Delinquent	40	20
Nondelinquent	60	80

The researcher using the perfect relation criterion would have to conclude that none of the causes of delinquency has yet been discovered. Indeed, this criterion would force him to conclude that

Michael and Mortimer J. Adler published in 1933: "There is still another way of saying that none of the statistical findings derived from the quantitative data yields answers to etiological questions. The findings themselves show that every factor which can be seen to be in some way associated with criminality is also associated with non-criminality, and also that criminality is found in the absence of every factor with which it is also seen to be associated. In other words, what has been found is merely additional evidence of what we either knew or could have suspected, namely, that there is a plurality of related factors in this field (*Crime, Law and Social Science* [New York: Harcourt Brace], p. 53)."

12. "Perfect association" here means that all of the cases fall into the main diagonal of the table, that (in the 2×2 table) the independent variable is both a necessary and a sufficient cause of the dependent variable. Less stringent definitions of perfect association are considered in the following paragraphs. Since Lander deals with ecological correlations, he could reject race as a cause of delinquency even if it were perfectly related to delinquency at the census tract level, since the ecological and the individual correlations are not identical.

13. We are assuming that the causal order and lack of spuriousness criteria are satisfied.

there are *no causes* of delinquency except *the* cause. The far-from-perfect relation between variable X and delinquency in the table above leads him to reject variable X as a cause of delinquency. Since variables A, B, C, and D are also far from perfectly related to delinquency, he must likewise reject them. Since it is unlikely that *the* cause of delinquency will ever be discovered by quantitative research, the researcher who accepts the perfect relation criterion should come to believe that such research is useless: All it can show is that there are *no* causes of delinquency.

FALSE CRITERION 1-A. INSOFAR AS A FACTOR IS NOT A NECESSARY CONDITION FOR DELINQUENCY, IT IS NOT A CAUSE OF DELINQUENCY.

The "not necessary" (and of course the "not sufficient") argument against causation is a variant of the "perfect relation" criterion. A factor is a necessary condition for delinquency if it must be present for delinquency to occur—e.g., knowledge of the operation of an automobile is a necessary condition for auto theft (although all individuals charged with auto theft need not know how to drive a car). In the following table the independent variable X is a necessary (but not sufficient[14]) condition for delinquency.

Delinquency by X, where X is a necessary but not sufficient condition for delinquency.

	X	Not X
Delinquent	67	0
Nondelinquent	33	100

The strongest statement we can find in the work cited by the Children's Bureau in support of the contention that the broken home is not a cause of delinquency is the following:

> We can leave this phase of the subject by stating that the phenomenon of the physically broken home is a cause of delinquent behavior is, in itself, not so important as was once believed. In essence, it is not

14. To say that X is a necessary condition for delinquency means that all delinquents are X (i.e., that the cell in the upper right of this table is zero); to say that X is a sufficient condition for delinquency implies that all X's are delinquent (i.e., that the cell in the lower left is zero); to say that X is a necessary and sufficient condition for delinquency means that all X's and no other persons are delinquent (i.e., that both cells in the minor diagonal of this table are zero).

that the home is broken, but rather that the home is inadequate, that really matters.[15]

This statement suggests that the broken home is not a necessary condition for delinquency (delinquents may come from intact but "inadequate" homes.). The variable with which the broken home is compared, inadequacy, has all the attributes of a necessary condition for delinquency: a home that is "adequate" with respect to the prevention of delinquency will obviously produce no delinquent children. If, as appears to be the case, the relation between inadequacy and delinquency is a matter of definition, the comparison of this relation with the relation between the broken home and delinquency is simply an application of the illegitimate "necessary conditions" criterion. Compared to a necessary condition, the broken home is "not so important." Compared to some (or some *other*) *measure* of inadequacy, however, the broken home may be very important. For that matter, once "inadequacy" is empirically defined, the broken home may turn out to be one of its important causes. Thus the fact that the broken home is not a necessary condition for delinquency does not justify the statement that the broken home is "not [a cause of delinquency] in the sense that if [it] were removed delinquency would decline."[16]

FALSE CRITERION 1-B. INSOFAR AS A FACTOR IS NOT A SUFFICIENT CONDITION FOR DELINQUENCY, IT IS NOT A CAUSE OF DELINQUENCY.

A factor is a sufficient condition for delinquency if its presence is invariably followed by delinquency. Examples of sufficient conditions are hard to find in empirical research.[17] The nearest one comes to such conditions in delinquency research is in the use of predictive devices in which several factors taken together are virtually sufficient for delinquency.[18] (The fact that several variables are required even

15. Teeters and Reinemann, *op. cit.*, p. 154.

16. *Report to The Congress*, p. 21. Two additional illegitimate criteria to causality listed above are implicit in the quotation from Teeters and Reinemann. "Inadequacy of the home" could be treated as an intervening variable which interprets the relation between the broken home and delinquency (criterion 4) or as a theoretical variable of which the broken home is an indicator (criterion 5). These criteria are discussed below.

17. In his *Theory of Collective Behavior* (New York: Free Press, 1963) Neil J. Smelser suggests sets of necessary conditions for riots, panics, and other forms of collective behavior; in this theory the entire set of necessary conditions for any one form of behavior is a sufficient condition for that form to occur.

18. In the Gluecks' prediction table, those with scores of 400 or more have a 98.1%

to approach sufficiency is of course one of the strongest arguments in favor of multiple causation.) Since sufficient conditions are rare, this unrealistic standard can be used against almost any imputation of causality.

> First, however, let us make our position clear on the question. Poverty per se is not a cause of delinquency or criminal behavior; this statement is evidenced by the courage, fortitude, honesty, and moral stamina of thousands of parents who would rather starve than steal and who inculcate this attitude in their children. Even in the blighted neighborhoods of poverty and wretched housing conditions, crime and delinquency are simply nonexistent among most residents.[19]
>
> Many mothers, and some fathers, who have lost their mates through separation, divorce, or death, are doing a splendid job of rearing their children.[20]
>
> Our point of view is that the structure of the family *itself* does not cause delinquency. For example, the fact that a home is broken does not cause delinquency, but it is more difficult for a single parent to provide material needs, direct controls, and other important elements of family life.[21]

The error here lies in equating "not sufficient" with "not *a* cause." Even if every delinquent child were from an impoverished (or broken) home — that is, even if this factor were a necessary condition for delinquency — it would still be possible to show that poverty is not a sufficient condition for delinquency.

In order for the researcher to conclude that poverty is a cause of delinquency, it is not necessary that all or most of those who are poor become delinquent.[22] If it were, causal variables would be virtually impossible to find. From the standpoint of social action, this criterion can be particularly unfortunate. Suppose that poverty were a necessary but not sufficient condition for delinquency, as in the table on page 227. Advocates of the "not sufficient" criterion would be forced to conclude that, if poverty were removed, delinquency would not

chance of delinquency. However, as Reiss has pointed out, the Gluecks *start* with a sample that is 50% delinquent. Had they started with a sample in which only 10% were delinquent, it would obviously have been more difficult to approach sufficiency. Sheldon Glueck and Eleanor Glueck, *Unraveling Juvenile Delinquency* (Cambridge: Harvard University Press, 1950), pp. 260–62; Albert J. Reiss, Jr., "Unraveling Juvenile Delinquency. II. An Appraisal of the Research Methods," *American Journal of Sociology*, 57:2, 1951, pp. 115–20.

19. Teeters and Reinemann, *op. cit.*, p. 127.

20. *Ibid.*, p. 154.

21. F. Ivan Nye, *Family Relationships and Delinquent Behavior* (New York: Wiley, 1958), p. 34. Italics in original.

22. We are of course assuming throughout this discussion that the variables in question meet what we consider to be legitimate criteria of causality.

decline. As the table clearly shows, however, removal of poverty under these hypothetical conditions would *eliminate* delinquency!

To take another example, Wootton reports Carr-Saunders as finding that 28% of his delinquents and 16% of his controls came from broken homes and that this difference held in both London and the provinces. She quotes Carr-Saunders' "cautious" conclusion:

> We can only point out that the broken home may have some in-fluence on delinquency, though since we get control cases coming from broken homes, we cannot assert that there is a direct link be-tween this factor and delinquency.[23]

Carr-Saunders' caution apparently stems from the "not sufficient" criterion, for unless the broken home is a sufficient condition for delinquency, there must be control cases (nondelinquents) from broken homes.

In each of these examples the attack on causality rests on the numbers in a single table. Since all of these tables show a non-zero relation, it seems to us that these researchers have misinterpreted the platitude "correlation is not causation." To us, this platitude means that one must go beyond the observed fact of association in order to demonstrate causality. To those who employ one or another variant of the perfect relation criterion, it appears to mean that there is something suspect in any numerical demonstration of association. Instead of being the first evidence for causality, an observed association becomes evidence against causality.

FALSE CRITERION 2. INSOFAR AS A FACTOR IS NOT "CHARACTERISTIC" OF DELINQUENTS, IT IS NOT A CAUSE OF DELINQUENCY.

> Many correlation studies in delinquency may conquer all these hur-dles and still fail to satisfy the vigorous demands of scientific causation. Frequently a group of delinquents is found to differ in a statistically significant way from a nondelinquent control group with which it is compared. Nevertheless, the differentiating trait may not be at all characteristic of the delinquent group. Suppose, for example, that a researcher compares 100 delinquent girls with 100 nondelinquent girls with respect to broken homes. He finds, let us say, that 10% of the nondelinquents come from broken homes, whereas this is true of 30% of the delinquent girls. Although the difference between the two groups is significant, the researcher has not demonstrated that the

23. Barbara Wootton, *Social Science and Social Pathology*, New York: Macmillan, 1959, p. 118.

broken home is characteristic of delinquents. The fact is that 70% of them come from unbroken homes. Again, ecological studies showing a high correlation between residence in interstitial areas and delinquency, as compared with lower rates of delinquency in other areas, overlook the fact that even in the most marked interstitial area nine tenths of the children do not become delinquents.[24]

This argument is superficially plausible. If a factor is not characteristic, then it is apparently not important. But does "characteristic" mean "important"? No. Importance refers to the variation accounted for, to the size of the association, while "being characteristic" refers to only one of the conditional distributions (rows or columns) in the table (in the table on page 258, X is characteristic of delinquents because more than half of the delinquents are X). This is not enough to infer association, any more than the statement that 95_ of the Negroes in some sample are illiterate can be really traceable to a plurality of causes," then some of these causes may well "characterize" a minority of delinquents. Furthermore, this "inconsistency" is empirical as well as logical: In survey data taken from ordinary populations it is rare to find that any group defined by more than three traits includes a majority of the cases.[25]

FALSE CRITERION 3. IF A RELATION BETWEEN AN INDEPENDENT VARIABLE AND DELINQUENCY IS FOUND FOR A SINGLE VALUE OF A SITUATIONAL OR CONTEXTUAL FACTOR, THAT SITUATIONAL OR CONTEXTUAL FACTOR, FACTOR CANNOT BE A CAUSE OF DELINQUENCY.

No investigation can establish the causal importance of variables that do not vary. This obvious fact should be even more obvious when the design of the study restricts it to single values of certain variables. Thus the researcher who restricts his sample to white Mormon

24. Milton L. Barron, *The Juvenile in Delinquent Society* (New York: Knopf, 1954), pp. 86–87.

25. There are two reasons for this: the less-than-perfect association between individual traits and the fact that few traits are simple dichotomies. Of course, it is always possible to take the logical complement of a set of traits describing a minority and thus arrive at a set of traits that does "characterize" a group, but such artificial combinations have too much internal heterogeneity to be meaningful. What, for example, can one say of the delinquents who share the following set of traits: not Catholic, not middle class, not of average intelligence?

The problem of "characteristic" traits arises only when the dependent variable is inherently categorical (Democratic; member of a gang, an athletic club, or neither) or is treated as one (performs none, a few, or many delinquent acts). In other words, this criterion arises only in tabular analysis, not where some summary measure is used to describe the association between variables.

boys cannot use his data to determine the importance of race, religious affiliation, or sex as causes of delinquency. Nevertheless, students of delinquency who discover either from research or logical analysis that an independent variable is related to delinquency in certain situations or contexts taken to say anything about the association between race and illiteracy in that sample without a corresponding statement about the whites. In the following table, although Negroes are predominantly ("characteristically") illiterate, race has no effect on literacy, for the whites are equally likely to be illiterate.

| | Race | |
	Negro	White
Literate	5	5
Illiterate	95	95

More generally, even if a trait characterizes a large proportion of delinquents and also characterizes a large proportion of nondelinquents, it may be less important as a cause of delinquency than a trait that characterizes a much smaller proportion of delinquents. The strength of the relation is what matters – that is, the *difference* between delinquents and nondelinquents in the proportion having the trait (in other words, the difference between the conditional distributions of the dependent variable). In the quotation from Barron at the beginning of this section, would it make any difference for the imputation of causality if the proportions coming from broken homes had been 40% for the nondelinquents and 60% for the delinquents, instead of 10% and 30% ... Although broken homes would now be "characteristic" of delinquents, the percentage difference is the same as before. And the percentage difference would still be the same if the figures were 60% and 80%, but now broken homes would be characteristic of *both* nondelinquents and delinquents!

The "characteristic" criterion is thus statistically irrelevant to the task of assessing causality. It also appears to be inconsistent with the principle of multiple causation, to which Barron elsewhere subscribes.[26] If delinquency is often conclude that these situational or contextual variables are not important causes of delinquency. Since personality or perceptual variables are related to delinquency in most kinds of social situations, social variables have suffered most from the application of this criterion:

26. Barron, *op. cit.*, pp. 81–83.

Let the reader assume that a boy is returning home from school and sees an unexpected group of people at his doorstep, including a policeman, several neighbors, and some strangers. He may suppose that they have gathered to welcome him and congratulate him as the winner of a nationwide contest he entered several months ago. On the other hand, his supposition may be that they have discovered that he was one of several boys who broke some windows in the neighborhood on Halloween. If his interpretation is that are a welcoming group he will respond one way; but if he feels that they have come to "get" him, his response is likely to be quite different. In either case he may be entirely wrong in his interpretation. *The important point, however, is that the external situation is relatively unimportant.* Rather, what the boy himself thinks of them [it] and how he interprets them [it] is the crucial factor in his response.[27]

There are at least three independent "variables" in this illustration: (1) the external situation—the group at the doorstep; (2) the boy's past behavior—entering a contest, breaking windows, etc.; (3) the boy's interpretation of the group's purpose. As Barron notes, variable (3) is obviously important in determining the boy's response. It does not follow from this, however, that variables (1) and (2) are unimportant. As a matter of fact, it is easy to see how variable (2), the boy's past behavior, could influence his interpretation of the group's purpose and thus affect his response. If he had not broken any windows in the neighborhood, for example, it is less likely that he would think that the group had come to "get" him, and it is therefore less likely that his response would be one of fear. Since Barron does not examine the relation between this situational variable and the response, he cannot make a legitimate statement about its causal importance.

Within the context of this illustration it is impossible to relate variable (1), the group at the doorstep, to the response. The reason for this is simple: This "variable" does not vary—it is fixed, given, constant. In order to assess the influence of a group at the doorstep (the external situation) on the response, it would be necessary to compare the effects of groups varying in size or composition. Suppose that there was no group at the doorstep. Presumably, if this were the case, the boy would feel neither fear nor joy. Barron restricts his examination of the relation between interpretation and response to a single situation, and on this basis concludes that what appears to be a necessary condition for the response is *relatively unimportant!*

27. Barron, *op. cit.*, pp. 87-88. Italics added.

In our opinion, it is sometimes better to say nothing about the effects of a variable whose range is restricted than to attempt to reach some idea of its importance with inadequate data. The first paragraph of the following statement suggests that its authors are completely aware of this problem. Nevertheless, the concluding paragraphs are misleading:

> We recognized that the Cambridge-Somerville area represented a fairly restricted socio-economic region. Although the bitter wave of the depression had passed, it had left in its wake large numbers of unemployed. Ten years after its onset, Cambridge and Somerville still showed the effects of the depression. Even the best neighborhoods in this study were lower middle class. Consequently, our results represent only a section of the class structure.
>
> In our sample, however [therefore], there is not a *highly* significant relation between "delinquency areas," or subcultures, and crime. If we had predicted that every child who lived in the poorer Cambridge-Somerville areas would have committed a crime, we would have been more often wrong than right. Thus, current sociological theory, by itself, cannot explain why the majority of children, even those from the "worst" areas, never became delinquent.
>
> *Social factors*, in our sample, were not strongly related to criminality. The fact that a child's neighborhood did not, by itself, exert an independently important influence may [*should not*] surprise social scientists. Undeniably, a slum neighborhood can mold a child's personality—but apparently only if other factors in his background make him susceptible to the sub-culture that surrounds him.[28]

FALSE CRITERION 4. IF A RELATION IS OBSERVED BETWEEN AN INDEPENDENT VARIABLE AND DELINQUENCY AND IF A PSYCHOLOGICAL VARIABLE IS SUGGESTED AS INTERVENING BETWEEN THESE TWO VARIABLES, THEN THE ORIGINAL RELATION IS NOT CAUSAL.

There appear to be two elements in this causal reasoning. One is the

---

28. William McCord and Joan McCord, *Origins of Crime*, New York: Columbia University Press, 1959, pp. 71 and 167.

In a study restricted to "known *offenders*" in which the dependent variable is the *seriousness* of the *first offense* Richard S. Sterne concludes: "Delinquency cannot be fruitfully controlled through broad programs to prevent divorce or other breaks in family life. The prevention of these would certainly decrease unhappiness, but it would not help to relieve the problem of delinquency." Since the range of the dependent variable, delinquency, is seriously reduced in a study restricted to *offenders*, such conclusions can not follow from the data. *Delinquent Conduct and Broken Homes*, (New Haven: College and University Press, 1964), p. 96.

procedure of *conjectural interpretation.*[29] The other is the confusion between *explanation,* in which an antecedent variable "explains away" an observed relation, and *interpretation,* in which an intervening variable links more tightly the two variables of the original relation. In short, the vanishing of the partial relations is assumed, not demonstrated, and this assumed statistical configuration is misconstrued.

This criterion is often encountered in a subtle form suggestive of social psychological theory:

> The appropriate inference from the available data, on the basis of our present understanding of the nature of cause, is that whether poverty, broken homes, or working mothers are factors which cause delinquency depends upon the meaning the situation has for the child.[30]
>
> It now appears that neither of these factors [the broken home and parental discipline] is so important in itself as is the child's reaction to them.[31]
>
> A factor, whether personal or situational, does not become a cause unless and until it first becomes a motive.[32]

The appropriate inference about whether some factor is a cause of delinquency depends on the relation between that factor and delinquency (and possibly on other factors causally prior to both of these). All that can be determined about meanings, motives, or reactions that *follow from* the factor and *precede* delinquency can only strengthen the conclusion that the factor is a cause of delinquency, not weaken it.

A different example may make our argument clearer. *Given* the bombing of Pearl Harbor, the crucial factor in America's response to this situation was its interpretation of the meaning of this event. Is one to conclude, therefore, that the bombing of Pearl Harbor was relatively unimportant as a cause of America's entry into World War II? Intervening variables of this type are no less important than variables further removed from the dependent variable, but to limit analysis to them, to deny the importance of objective conditions, is to

29. Like conjectural explanation, this is an argument, unsupported by statistical data, that the relation between two variables would vanish if the effects of a third variable were removed; here, however, the third variable "intervenes" causally between the original independent and dependent variables.

30. Sophia Robison, *Juvenile Delinquency* (New York: Holt, Rinehart and Winston, 1961), p. 116.

31. Paul W. Tappan, *Juvenile Delinquency* (New York: McGraw-Hill, 1949), p. 135.

32. Sheldon and Eleanor Glueck, *Family Environment and Delinquency* (Boston: Houghton-Mifflin, 1962), p. 153. This statement is attributed to Bernard Glueck. No specific reference is provided.

distort reality as much as do those who ignore intervening subjective states.[33]

This kind of mistaken causal inference can occur long after the original analysis of the data. A case in point is the inference in the *Report to The Congress*[34] that irregular employment of the mother does not cause delinquency. This inference appears to come from misreading Maccoby's reanalysis of the Gluecks' results.

Maccoby begins by noting that "the association between irregular employment and delinquency suggests at the outset that it may not be the mother's absence from home per se which creates adjustment problems for the children. Rather, the cause may be found in the conditions of the mother's employment or the family characteristics leading a mother to undertake outside employment."[35] She then lists several characteristics of the sporadically working mothers that might account for the greater likelihood of their children becoming delinquent. For example, many had a history of delinquency themselves. In our opinion, such conjectural "explanations" are legitimate guides to further study but, as Maccoby says, they leave the causal problem unsettled:

> It is a moot question, therefore, whether it is the mother's sporadic employment as such which conducted to delinquency in the sons; equally tenable is the interpretation that the emotionally disturbed and antisocial characteristics of the parents produced both a sporadic work pattern on the part of the mother and delinquent tendencies in the son.[36]

Maccoby's final step, and the one of greatest interest here, is to examine simultaneously the effects of mother's employment and mother's supervision on delinquency. From this examination she concludes:

> It can be seen that, whether the mother is working or not, the quality of the supervision her child receives is paramount. If the mother remains at home but does not keep track of where her child is and

33. "Write your own life history, showing the factors *really* operative in you coming to college, contrasted with the external social and cultural factors of your situation (Barron, *op. cit.*, p. 89)."

34. *Op. cit.*, p. 21.

35. Eleanor E. Maccoby, "Effects upon Children of Their Mothers' Outside Employment," in Norman W. Bell and Ezra F. Vogel, eds., *A Modern Introduction to The Family* (Glencoe, Ill.: Free Press, 1960), p. 523. In fairness to the Children's Bureau report it should be mentioned that Maccoby's argument against the causality of the relation between mother's employment and delinquency has a stronger tone in the article cited there (see footnote 7) than in the version we have used as a source of quotations.

36. *Ibid.*

what he is doing, he is far more likely to become a delinquent (within this highly selected sample), than if he is closely watched. Furthermore, if a mother who works does arrange adequate care for the child in her absence, he is no more likely to be delinquent . . . than the adequately supervised child of a mother who does not work. But there is one more lesson to be learned from the data: among the working mothers, a majority did not in fact arrange adequate supervision for their children in their absence.[37]

It is clear, then, that regardless of the mother's employment status, supervision is related to delinquency. According to criterion 3, employment status is therefore not a cause of delinquency. It is also clear that when supervision is held relatively constant, the relation between employment status and delinquency disappears. According to criterion 4, employment status is therefore *not* a cause of delinquency. This appears to be the reasoning by which the authors of the *Report to The Congress* reject mother's employment as a cause of delinquency. But criterion 3 ignores the association between employment status and delinquency and is thus irrelevant. And criterion 4 treats what is probably best seen as an intervening variable as an antecedent variable and is thus a misconstruction of a legitimate criterion. Actually, the evidence that allows the user of criterion 4 to reach a conclusion of noncausality is, at least phychologically, evidence of *causality*. The disappearance of the relation between mother's employment and delinquency when supervision is held relatively constant makes the "How?" of the original relation clear: Working mothers are less likely to provide adequate supervision for their children, and inadequately supervised children are more likely to become delinquent.

FALSE CRITERION 5. MEASURABLE VARIABLES ARE NOT CAUSES.

> In tract 11-1, and to a lesser extent in tract 11-2, the actual rate [of delinquency] is lower than the predicted rate. We suggest that these deviations [of the actual delinquency rate from the rate predicted from home ownership] point up the danger of imputing a causal significance to an index, per se, despite its statistical significance in a prediction formula. It is fallacious to impute causal significance to home ownership as such. In the present study, the author hypothesizes that the extent of home-ownership is probably highly correlated with, and hence constitutes a measure of community anomie.[38]

37. *Ibid.*, p. 524.
38. Lander, *op. cit.*, p. 71.

As a preventive, "keeping youth busy," whether through compulsory education, drafting for service in the armed forces, providing fun through recreation, or early employment, can, at best, only temporarily postpone behavior that is symptomatic of more deep-seated or culturally oriented factors. . . . Merely "keeping idle hands occupied" touches only surface symptoms and overlooks underlying factors known to generate norm-violating behavior patterns.[39]

The criterion of causation that, in effect, denies causal status to measurable variables occurs frequently in delinquency research. In the passages above, home ownership, compulsory education, military service, recreation, and early employment are all called into question as causes of delinquency. In their stead one finds as causes anomie and "deepseated or culturally oriented factors." The appeal to abstract as opposed to more directly measurable variables appears to be especially persuasive. Broad general concepts embrace such a variety of directly measurable variables that their causal efficacy becomes almost self evident. The broken home, for example, is no match for the "inadequate" home:

[T]he physically broken home as a cause of delinquent behavior is, in itself, not so important as was once believed. In essence, it is not that the home is broken, but rather that the home is inadequate, that really matters.[40]

The persuasiveness of these arguments against the causal efficacy of measurable variables has two additional sources: (1) their logical form resembles that of the legitimate criterion "lack of spuriousness"; (2) they are based on the seemingly obvious fact that "operational indices" (measures) do not *cause* the variations in other operational indices. Both of the following arguments can thus be brought against the assertion that, for example, home ownership causes delinquency.

Anomie causes delinquency. Home ownership is a measure of anomie. Anomie is thus the "source of variation" in both home ownership and delinquency. If the effects of anomie were removed, the observed relation between home ownership and delinquency would disappear. This observed relation is thus causally spurious.

Home ownership is used as an indicator of anomie, just as responses to questionnaire items are used as indicators of such things as "authoritarianism," "achievement motivation," and "religiosity." No one will argue that the responses to items on a questionnaire *cause*

39. William C. Kvaraceus and Walter B. Miller, *Delinquent Behavior: Culture and the Individual* (National Education Association, 1959), p. 39.

40. Teeters and Reinemann, *op. cit.*, p. 154.

race hatred, long years of self-denial, or attendance at religious services. For the same reason, it is erroneous to think that home ownership "causes" delinquency.

Both of these arguments beg the question. As mentioned earlier, conjectural explanations, although legitimate guides to further study, leave the causal problem unsettled. The proposed "antecedent variable" may or *may not* actually account for the observed relation.

Our argument assumes that the proposed antecedent variable is directly measurable. In the cases cited here it is not. If the antecedent variable logic is accepted as appropriate in these cases, all relations between measurable variables and delinquency may be said to be causally spurious. If anomie can "explain away" the relation between *one* of its indicators and delinquency, it can explain away the relations between *all* of its indicators and delinquency.[41] No matter how closely a given indicator measures anomie, the indicator is not anomie, and thus not a cause of delinquency. The difficulty with these conjectural explanations is thus not that they may be false, but that they are *non-falsifiable*.[42]

The second argument against the causality of measurable variables overlooks the following point: It is one thing to use a measurable variable as an indicator of another, not directly measurable, variable; it is something else again to assume that the measurable variable is *only* an indicator. Not owning one's home may indeed be a useful indicator of anomie; it may, at the same time, be a potent cause of delinquency in its own right.

The user of the "measurable variables are not causes" criterion treats measurable variables as epiphenomena. He strips these variables of all their causal efficacy (and of all their meaning) by treating them merely as indexes, and by using such words as *per se, as such,* and *in itself*.[43] In so doing, he begs rather than answers the important question: Are these measurable variables causes of delinquency?

41. As would be expected, Lander succeeds in disposing of all the variables in his study as causes of delinquency—even those he says at some points are *"fundamentally* related to delinquency."

42. While Lander throws out his measurable independent variables in favor of anomie, Kvaraceus and Miller throw out their measurable dependent variable in favor of "something else." "Series of norm-violating behaviors, which run counter to legal codes and which are engaged in by youngsters [delinquency], are [is] only symptomatic of something else in the personal make-up of the individual, in his home and family, or in his cultural milieu (*op. cit.,* p. 34)." The result is the same, as the quotations suggest.

43. The appearance of these terms in the literature on delinquency almost invariably signals a logical difficulty.

FALSE CRITERION 6. IF THE RELATION BETWEEN AN IN-
DEPENDENT VARIABLE AND DELIQUENCY IS CONDITIONAL
UPON THE VALUE OF OTHER VARIABLES, THE INDEPENDENT
VARIABLE IS NOT A CAUSE OF DELINQUENCY.

> The rates of Negro delinquency also vary as widely as do the white
> races indicating large differences in behavior patterns that are not a
> function or effect of race per se. It is also of interest to note that in at
> least 10 percent of the districts with substantial Negro juvenile popu-
> lations, the Negro delinquency rate is lower than the corresponding
> white rate.[44]
>
> The appropriate inference from the available data, on the basis of
> our present understanding of the nature of cause, is that whether
> poverty, broken homes, or working mothers are factors which cause
> delinquency depends upon the meaning the situation has for the
> child.[45]

Both of these quotations make the same point: The association
between an independent variable and delinquency depends on the
value of a third variable. The original two-variable relation thus
becomes a three-variable conditional relation. In the first quotation,
the relation between race and delinquency is shown to depend on
some (unspecified) property of census tracts. In the second quotation, each of three variables is said to "interact" with "the meaning
of the situation" to cause delinquency.

One consequence of showing that certain variables are only condi-
tionally related to delinquency is to invalidate what Albert K. Cohen
has aptly named "the assumption of intrinsic pathogenic qualities" — the assumption that the causal efficacy of a variable is, or can
be, independent of the value of other causal variables.[46] Invalidating
this assumption, which Cohen shows to be widespread in the literature on delinquency, is a step in the right direction. As many of the
quotations in this paper suggest, however, the discovery that a variable has no *intrinsic* pathogenic qualities has often led to the conclusion that it has no pathogenic qualities at all. The consequences
of accepting this conclusion can be shown for delinquency research
and theory.

Cloward and Ohlin's theory that delinquency is the product of lack
of access to legitimate means *and* the availability of illegitimate

44. Lander, *op. cit.*, p. 32. This statement is quoted more fully above (see footnote
10).
45. See footnote 30.
46. "Multiple Factor Approaches," in Marvin E. Wolfgang *et al.*, eds., *The Sociology
of Crime and Delinquency* (New York: Wiley, 1962,), pp. 78–9.

means assumes, as Palmore and Hammond have shown,[47] that each of these states is a necessary condition for the other — i.e. , that lack of access to legitimate and access to illegitimate means "interact" to produce delinquency. Now, if "conditional relations" are non-causal, neither lack of access to legitimate nor the availability of illegitimate means is a cause of delinquency, and one could manipulate either without affecting the delinquency rate.

Similarly absurd conclusions could be drawn from the results of empirical research in delinquency, since all relations between independent variables and delinquency are at least conceivably conditional (the paucity of empirical generalizations produced by delinquency research as a whole shows that most of these relations have already actually been found to be conditional).[48]

Although conditional relations may be conceptually or statistically complicated and therefore psychologically unsatisfying, their discovery does not justify the conclusion that the variables involved are not causes of delinquency. In fact, the researcher who would grant causal status only to unconditional relations will end by granting it to none.

Any one of the criteria of causality discussed in this paper makes it possible to question the causality of most of the relations that have been or could be revealed by quantitative research. Some of these criteria stem from perfectionistic interpretations of legitimate criteria, others from misapplication of these legitimate criteria. Still others, especially the argument that a cause must be "characteristic" of delinquents, appear to result from practical considerations. (It would indeed be valuable to the practitioner if he could point to some easily identifiable trait as the "hallmark" of the delinquent.) Finally, one of these criteria is based on a mistaken notion of the relation between abstract concepts and measurable variables — a notion that only the former can be the causes of anything.

The implications of these standards of causality for practical efforts to reduce delinquency are devastating. Since nothing that can be pointed to in the practical world is a cause of delinquency (e.g. , poverty, broken homes, lack of recreational facilities, working mothers), the practitioner is left with the task of combatting a nebulous

47. Erdman B. Palmore and Philip E. Hammond, "Interacting Factors in Juvenile Delinquency," *American Sociological Review*, 29 (December 1964), 848–54.

48. After reviewing the findings of twenty-one studies as they bear on the relations between twelve commonly used independent variables and delinquency, Barbara Wootton concludes: "All in all, therefore, this collection of studies, although chosen for its comparative methodological merit, produces only the most meager, and dubiously supported generalizations, *op. cit.*, p. 134)."

"anomie" or an unmeasured "inadequacy of the home"; or else he must change the adolescent's interpretation of the "meaning" of events without at the same time changing the events themselves or the context in which they occur.

Mills has suggested that accepting the principle of multiple causation implies denying the possibility of radical change in the social structure.[49] Our analysis suggests that rejecting the principle of multiple causation implies denying the possibility of *any* change in the social structure — since, in this view, nothing causes anything.

49. C. Wright Mills, "The Professional Ideology of Social Pathologists," *American Journal of Sociology,* 44 (September 1942), 165–80, esp. 177–72.

16. Factors Relevant to the Validity of Experiments in Social Settings

DONALD T. CAMPBELL

WHAT do we seek to control in experimental designs? What extraneous variables which would otherwise confound our interpretation of the experiment do we wish to rule out? The present paper attempts a specification of the major categories of such extraneous variables and employs these categories in evaluating the validity of standard designs for experimentation in the social sciences.[1]

Validity will be evaluated in terms of two major criteria. First, and as a basic minimum, is what can be called *internal validity*: Did in fact the experimental stimulus make some significant difference in this specific instance? The second criterion is that of *external valid-*

Reprinted by permission from *Psychological Bulletin*, 54 (July 1957), pp. 297–311. Copyright 1957, American Psychological Association.

1. A dittoed version of this paper was privately distributed in 1953 under the title "Designs for Social Science Experiments." The author has had the opportunity to benefit from the careful reading and suggestions of L. S. Burwen, J. W. Cotton, C. P. Duncan, D. W. Fiske, C. I. Hovland, L. V. Jones, E. S. Marks, D. C. Pelz, and B. J. Underwood, among others, and wishes to express his appreciation. They have not had the opportunity of seeing the paper in its present form, and bear no responsibility for it. The author also wishes to thank S. A. Stouffer (33) and B. J. Underwood (36) for their public encouragement.

ity, representativeness, or *generalizability:* To what populations, settings, and variables can this effect be generalized? Both criteria are obviously important although it turns out that they are to some extent incompatible, in that the controls required for internal validity often tend to jeopardize representativeness.

The extraneous variables affecting internal validity will be introduced in the process of analyzing three preexperimental designs. In the subsequent evaluation of the applicability of three true experimental designs, factors leading to external invalidity will be introduced. The effects of these extraneous variables will be considered at two levels: As simple or main effects, they occur independently of or in addition to the effects of the experimental variable; as interactions, the effects appear in conjunction with the experimental variable. The main effects typically turn out to be relevant to internal validity, the interaction effects to external validity or representativeness.

The following designation for experimental designs will be used: X will represent the exposure of a group to the experimental variable or event, the effects of which are to be measured: O will refer to the process of observation or measurement, which can include watching what people do, listening, recording, interviewing, administering tests, counting lever depressions, etc. The Xs and Os in a given row are applied to the same specific persons. The left to right dimension indicates temporal order. Parallel rows represent equivalent samples of persons unless otherwise specified. The designs will be numbered and named for cross-reference purposes.

THREE PRE-EXPERIMENTAL DESIGNS AND THEIR CONFOUNDED EXTRANEOUS VARIABLES

The One-Shot Case Study. As Stouffer (32) has pointed out, much social science research still uses Design 1, in which a single individual or group is studied in detail only once, and in which the observations are attributed to exposure to some prior situation.

X   O   1. One-Shot Case Study

This design does not merit the title of experiment, and is introduced only to provide a reference point. The very minimum of useful scientific information involves at least one formal comparison and therefore at least two careful observations (2).

The One-Group Pretest-Posttest Design. This design does provide for one formal comparison of two observations, and is still widely used.

$O_1 \, X \, O_2$ 2. One-Group Pretest-Posttest Design

However, in it there are four or five categories of extraneous variables left uncontrolled which thus become rival explanations of any difference between O_1 and O_2, confounded with the possible effect of X.

The first of these is the main effect of *history*. During the time span between O_1 and O_2 many events have occurred in addition to X, and the results might be attributed to these. Thus in Collier's (8) experiment, while his respondents[2] were reading Nazi propaganda materials, France fell, and the obtained attitude changes seemed more likely a result of this event than of the propaganda.[3] By history is meant the specific event series other than X, i.e., the stimuli. Relevant to this variable is the concept of experimental isolation, the employment of experimental settings in which all extraneous stimuli are eliminated. The approximation of such control in much physical and biological research has permitted the satisfactory employment of Design 2. But in social psychology and the other social sciences, if history is confounded with X the results are generally uninterpretable.

The second class of variables confounded with X in Design 2 is here designated as *maturation*. This covers those effects which are systematic with the passage of time, and not, like history, a function of the specific events involved. Thus between O_1 and O_2 the respondents may have grown older, hungrier, tireder, etc., and these may have produced the difference between O_1 and O_2, independently of X. While in the typical brief experiment in the psychology laboratory, maturation is unlikely to be a source of change, it has been a problem in research in child development and can be so in extended experiments in social psychology and education. In the form of "spontaneous remission" and the general processes of healing it becomes an important variable to control in medical research, psychotherapy, and social remediation.

There is a third source of variance that could explain the difference between O_1 and O_2 without a recourse to the effect of X. This is the effect of *testing* itself. It is often true that persons taking a test for the second time make scores systematically different from those taking the test for the first time. This is indeed the case for intelligence tests, where a second mean may be expected to run as much as five IQ points higher than the first one. This possibility

---

2. In line with the central focus on social psychology and the social sciences, the term *respondent* is employed in place of the terms *subject, patient,* or *client.*

3. Collier actually used a more adequate design than this, an approximation to Design 4.

makes important a distinction between *reactive* measures and *non-reactive* measures. A reactive measure is one which modifies the phenomenon under study, which changes the very thing that one is trying to measure. In general, any measurement procedure which makes the subject selfconscious or aware of the fact of the experiment can be suspected of being a reactive measurement. Whenever the measurement process is *not* a part of the normal environment it is probably reactive. Whenever measurement exercises the process under study, it is almost certainly reactive. Measurement of a person's height is relatively nonreactive. However, measurement of weight, introduced into an experimental design involving adult Americal women, would turn out to be reactive in that the process of measuring would stimulate weight reduction. A photograph of a crowd taken in secret from a second story window would be nonreactive, but a news photograph of the same scene might very well be reactive, in that the presence of the photographer would modify the behavior of people seeing themselves being photgraphed. In a factory, production records introduced for the purpose of an experiment would be reactive, but if such records were a regular part of the operating environment they would be nonreactive. An English anthropologist may be nonreactive as a participant-observer at an English wedding, but might be a highly reactive measuring instrument at a Dobu nuptials. Some measures are so extremely reactive that their use in a pretest-posttest design is not usually considered. In this class would be tests involving surprise, deception, rapid adaptation, or stress. Evidence is amply present that tests of learning and memory are highly reactive (35, 36). In the field of opinion and attitude research our well-developed interview and attitude test techniques must be rated as reactive, as shown, for example, by Crespi's (9) evidence.

Even within the personality and attitude test domain, it may be found that tests differ in the degree to which they are reactive. For some purposes, tests involving voluntary self-description may turn out to be more reactive (especially at the interaction level to be discussed below) than are devices which focus the respondent upon describing the external world, or give him less latitude in describing himself (e.g., 5). It seems likely that, apart from considerations of validity, the Rorschach test is less reactive than the TAT or MMPI. Where the reactive nature of the testing process results from the focusing of attention on the experimental variable, it may be reduced by imbedding the relevant content in a comprehensive array of topics, as has regularly been done in Hovland's attitude change studies (14). It seems likely that with attention to the problem, observational and measurement techniques can be developed which are much less reactive than those now in use.

Instrument decay provides a fourth uncontrolled source of variance which could produce an $O_1 - O_2$ difference that might be mistaken for the effect of X. This variable can be exemplified by the fatiguing of a spring scales, or the condensation of water vapor in a cloud chamber. For psychology and the social sciences it becomes a particularly acute problem when human beings are used as a part of the measuring apparatus, as judges, observers, raters, coders, etc. Thus O_1 and O_2 may differ because the raters have become more experienced, more fatigued, have acquired a different adaptation level, or have learned about the purpose of the experiment, etc. However infelicitously, this term will be used to typify those problems introduced when shifts in measurement conditions are confounded with the effect of X, including such crudities as having a different observer at O_1 (3 O_2, or using a different interviewer or coder. Where the use of different interviewers, observers, or experimenters is unavoidable, but where they are used in large numbers, a sampling equivalence of interviewers is required, with the relevant N being the N of interviewers, not interviewees, except as refined through cluster sampling considerations (18).

A possible fifth extraneous factor deserves mention. This is statistical *regression*. When, in Design 2, the group under investigation has been selected for its extremity on O_1, $O_1 - O_2$ shifts toward the mean will occur which are due to random imperfections of the measuring instrument or random instability within the population, as reflected in the test-retest reliability. In general, regression operates like maturation in that the effects increase systematically with the $O_1 - O_2$ time interval. McNemar (22) has demonstrated the profound mistakes in interpretation which failure to control this factor can introduce in remedial research.

The Static Group Comparison. The third pre-experimental design is the Static Group Comparison.

$$\frac{X\ O_1}{O_2}\quad 3.\ \text{The Static Group Comparison}$$

In this design, there is a comparison of a group which has experienced X with a group which has not, for the purpose of establishing the effect of X. In contrast with Design 6, there is in this design no means of certifying that the groups were equivalent at some prior time. (The absence of sampling equivalence of groups is symbolized by the row of dashes.) This design has its most typical occurrence in the social sciences, and both its prevalence and its weakness have been well indicated by Stouffer (32). It will be recognized as one form of the correlational study. It is introduced here to complete the list of confounding factors. If the Os differ, this difference could have come about through biased *selection* or recruitment of the persons making up the groups; i.e., they might have differed anyway without the effect of X. Frequently, exposure to X (e.g., some mass communication) has been voluntary and the two groups have an inevitable systematic difference on the factors determining the choice involved, a difference which no amount of matching can remove.

A second variable confounded with the effect of X in this design can be called experimental *mortality*. Even if the groups were equivalent at some prior time, O_1 and O_2 may differ now not because individual members have changed, but because a biased subset of members have dropped out. This is a typical problem in making inferences from comparisons of the attitudes of college freshmen and college seniors, for example.

TRUE EXPERIMENTAL DESIGNS

The Pretest-Posttest Control Group Design. One or another of the above considerations led psychologists between 1900 and 1925 (2, 30) to expand Design 2 by the addition of a control group, resulting in Design 4.

$O_1 \, X \, O_2$ 4. Pretest-Posttest Control Group Design
$O_3 \quad O_4$

Because this design so neatly controls for the main effects of history, maturation, testing, instrument decay, regression, selection, and mortality, these separate sources of variance are not usually made explicit. It seems well to state briefly the relationship of the design to each of these confounding factors, with particular attention to the application of the design in social settings.

If the differences between O_1 and O_2 were due to intervening historical events, then they should also show up in the O_3-O_4 comparison. Note, however, several complications in achieving this control. If respondents are run in groups, and if there is only one experimental session and one control session, then there is no control over the unique internal histories of the groups. The O_1-O_2 difference, even if not appearing in O_3-O_4, may be due to a chance distracting factor appearing in one or the other group. Such a design, while controlling for the shared history or event series, still confounds X with the unique session history. Second, the design implies a simultaneity of O_1 with O_3 and O_2 with O_4 which is usually impossible. If one were to try to achieve simultaneity by using two experimenters, one working with the experimental respondents, the other with the controls, this would confound experimenter differences with X (introducing one type of instrument decay). These considerations make it usually imperative that, for a true experiment, the experimental and control groups be tested and exposed individually or in small subgroups, and that sessions of both types be temporally and spatially intermixed.

As to the other factors: If maturation or testing contributed an $O_1 - O_2$ difference, this should appear equally in the $O_3 - O_4$ comparison, and these variables are thus controlled for their main effects. To make sure the design controls for instrument decay, the same individual or small-session approximation to simultaneity needed for history is required. The occasional practice of running the experimental group and control group at different times is thus ruled out on this ground as well as that of history. Otherwise the observers may have become more experienced, more hurried, more careless, the maze more redolent with irrelevant cues, the lever-tension and frictional diminished, etc. Only when groups are effectively simultaneous do these factors affect experimental and control groups alike. Where more than one experimenter or observer is used, counterbalancing experimenter, time, and group is recommended. The balanced Latin square is frequently useful for this purpose (4).

While regression is controlled in the design as a whole, frequently secondary analyses of effects are made for extreme pretest scorers in the experimental group. To provide a control for effects of regression, a parallel analysis of extremes should also be made for the control group.

Selection is of course handled by the sampling equivalence ensured through the randomization employed in assigning persons to groups, perhaps supplemented by, but not supplanted by, matching procedures. Where the experimental and control groups do not have this sort of equivalence, one has a compromise design rather than a true experiment. Furthermore, the $O_1 - O_3$ comparison provides a check on possible sampling differences.

The design also makes possible the examination of experimental mortality, which becomes a real problem for experiments extended over weeks or months. If the experimental and control groups do not differ in the number of lost cases nor in their pretest scores, the experiment can be judged internally valid on this point, although mortality reduces the generalizability of effects to the original population from which the groups were selected.

For these reasons, the Pretest-Posttest Control Group Design has been the ideal in the social sciences for some thirty years. Recently, however, a serious and avoidable imperfection in it has been noted, perhaps first by Schanck and Goodman (29). Solomon (30) has expressed the point as an *interaction* effect of testing. In the terminology of analysis of variance, the effects of history, maturation, and testing, as described so far, are all *main* effects, manifesting themselves in mean differences independently of the presence of other variables. They are effects that could be added on to other effects, including the effect of the experimental variable. In contrast, interaction effects represent a joint effect, specific to the concomitance of two or more conditions, and may occur even when no main effects are present. Applied to the testing variable, the interaction effect might involve not a shift due solely or directly to the measurement process, but rather a sensitization of respondents to the experimental variable so that when X was preceded by O there would be a change, whereas both X and O would be without effect if occurring alone. In terms of the two types of validity, Design 4 is internally valid, offering an adequate basis for generalization to other sampling-equivalent *pretested* groups. But it has a serious and systematic weakness in representativeness in that it offers, strictly speaking, no basis for generalization to the *unpretested* population. And it is usually the *unpretested* larger universe from which these samples were taken to which one wants to generalize.

A concrete example will help make this clearer. In the NORC study of a United Nations information campaign (31), two equivalent samples, of a thousand each, were drawn from the city's population. One of these samples was interviewed, following which the city of Cincinnati was subjected to an intensive publicity campaign using all the mass media of communication. This included special features in the newspapers and on radio, bus cards, public lectures, etc. At the end of two months, the second sample of 1,000 was interviewed and the results compared with the first 1,000. There were no differences between the two groups except that the second group was somewhat more pessimistic about the likelihood of Russia's cooperating for world peace, a result which was attributed to history rather than to the publicity campaign. The second sample was no better informed about the United Nations nor had it noticed in particular the publicity campaign which had been going on. In connection with a program of research on panels and the reinterview problem, Paul Lazarsfeld and the Bureau of Applied Social Research arranged to have the initial sample reinterviewed at the same time as the second sample was interviewed, after the publicity campaign. This reinterviewed group showed significant attitude changes, a high degree of awareness of the campaign and important increases in information. The inference in this case is unmistakably that the initial interview had sensitized the persons interviewed to the topic of the United Nations, had raised in them a focus of awareness which made the subsequent publicity campaign effective for them but for them only. This study and other studies clearly document the possibility of interaction effects which seriously limit our capacity to generalize from the pretested experimental group to the unpretested general population. Hovland (15) reports a general finding which is of the opposite nature but is, nonetheless, an indication of an interactive effect. In his Army studies the initial pretest served to reduce the effects of the experimental variable, presumably by creating a commitment to a given position. Crespi's (9) findings support this expectation. Solomon (30) reports two studies with school children in which a spelling pretest reduced the effects of a training period. But whatever the direction of the effect, this flaw in the Pretest-Posttest Control Group Design is serious for the purposes of the social scientist.

The Solomon Four-Group Design. It is Solomon's (30) suggestion to control this problem by adding to the traditional two-group experiment two unpretested groups as indicated in Design 5.

$$O_1 \quad X \quad O_2$$
$$O_3 \qquad\quad O_4 \qquad \text{5. Solomon Four-Group Design}$$
$$\quad X \quad O_5$$
$$\qquad\quad O_6$$

This Solomon Four-Group Design enables one both to control and measure both the main and interaction effects of testing and the main effects of a composite of maturation and history. It has become the new ideal design for social scientists. A word needs to be said about the appropriate statistical analysis. In Design 4, an efficient single test embodying the four measurements is achieved through computing for each individual a pretest-posttest difference score which is then used for comparing by t test the experimental and control groups. Extension of this mode of analysis to the Solomon Four-Group Design introduces an inelegant awkwardness to the otherwise elegant procedure. It involves assuming as a pretest score for the unpretested groups the mean value of the pretest from the first two groups. This restricts the effective degrees of freedom, violates assumptions of independence, and leaves one without a legitimate base for testing the significance of main effects and interaction. An alternative analysis is available which avoids the assumed pretest scores. Note that the four posttests form a simple two-by-two analysis of variance design:

	No X	X
Pretested	O_4	O_2
Unpretested	O_6	O_5

The column means represent the main effect of X, the row means the main effect of pretesting, and the interaction term the interaction of pretesting and X. (By use of a t test the combined main effects of maturation and history can be tested through comparing O_6 with O_1 and O_3.)

The Posttest-Only Control Group Design. While the statistical procedures of analysis of variance introduced by Fisher (10) are dominant in psychology and the other social sciences today, it is little noted in our discussions of experimental arrangements that Fisher's typical agricultural experiment involves no pretest: equivalent plots of ground receive different experimental treatments and the subsequent yields are measured.[4] Applied to a social experiment as in testing the influence of a motion picture upon attitudes, two randomly assigned audiences would be selected, one exposed to the movie, and the attitudes of each measured subsequently for the first time.

$$A \ X \ O_1$$
$$A \quad O_2$$

6. Posttest-Only Control Group Design

In this design the symbol A had been added, to indicate that at a specific time prior to X the groups were made equivalent by a random sampling *assignment*. A is the point of selection, the point of allocation of individuals to groups. It is the existence of this process that distinguishes Design 6 from Design 3, the Static Group Comparison. Design 6 is not a static cross-sectional comparison, but

4. This is not to imply that the pretest is totally absent from Fisher's designs. He suggests the use of previous year's yields, etc., in covariance analysis. He notes, however, "with annual agricultural crops, knowledge of yields of the experimental area in a previous year under uniform treatment has not been found sufficiently to increase the precision to warrant the adoption of such uniformity trials as a preliminary to projected experiments" (10, p. 176).

instead truly involves control and observation extended in time. The sampling procedures employed assure us that at time A the groups were equal, even if not measured. A provides a point of prior equality just as does the pretest. A point A is, of course, involved in all true experiments, and should perhaps be indicated in Designs 4 and 5. It is essential that A be regarded as a specific point in time, for groups change as a function of time since A, through experimental mortality. Thus in a public opinion survey situation employing probability sampling from lists of residents, the longer the time since A, the more the sample underrepresents the transient segments of society, the newer dwelling units, etc. When experimental groups are being drawn from a self-selected extreme population, such as applicants for psychotherapy, time since A introduces maturation (spontaneous remission) and regression factors. In Design 6 these effects would be confounded with the effect of X if the As as well as the Os were not contemporaneous for experimental and control groups.

Like Design 4, this design controls for the effects of maturation and history through the practical simultaneity of both the As and the Os. In superiority over Design 4, no main or interaction effects of pretesting are involved. It is this feature that recommends it in particular. While it controls for the main and interaction effects of pretesting as well as does Design 5, the Solomon Four-Group Design, it does not measure these effects, nor the main effect of history-maturation. It can be noted that Design 6 can be considered as the two unpretested "control" groups from the Solomon Design, and that Solomon's two traditional pretested groups have in this sense the sole purpose of measuring the effects of pretesting and history-maturation, a purpose irrelevant to the main aim of studying the effect of X (25). However, under normal conditions of not quite perfect sampling control, the four-group design provides in addition greater assurance against mistakenly attributing to X effects which are not due it, inasmuch as the effect of X is documented in three different fashions (O_1 vs. O_2, O_2 vs. O_4, and O_5 vs. O_6). But, short of the four-group design, Design 6 is often to be preferred to Design 4, and is a fully valid experimental design.

Design 6 has indeed been used in the social sciences, perhaps first of all in the classic experiment by Gosnell, *Getting Out the Vote* (11). Schanck and Goodman (29), Hovland (15) and others (1, 12, 23, 24, 27) have also employed it. But, in spite of its manifest advantages of simplicity and control, it is far from being a popular design in social research and indeed is usually relegated to an inferior position in discussions of experimental designs if mentioned at all (e.g., 15, 16, 32). Why is this the case?

In the first place, it is often confused with Design 3. Even where Ss have been carefully assigned to experimental and control groups, one is apt to have an uneasiness about the design because one "doesn't know what the subjects were like before." This objection must be rejected, as our standard tests of significance are designed precisely to evaluate the likelihood of differences occurring by chance in such sample selection. It is true, however, that this design is particularly vulnerable to selection bias and where random assignment is not possible it remains suspect. Where naturally aggregated units, such as classes, are employed intact, these should be used in large numbers and assigned at random to the experimental and control conditions; cluster sampling statistics (18) should be used to determine the error term. If but one or two intact classrooms are available for each experimental treatment, Design 4 should certainly be used in preference.

A second objection to Design 6, in comparison with Design 4, is that it often has less precision. The difference scores of Design 4 are less variable than the posttest scores of Design 6 if there is a pretest-posttest correlation above .50 (15, p. 323), and hence for test-retest correlations above that level a smaller mean difference would be statistically significant for Design 4 than for Design 6, for a constant number of cases. This advantage to Design 4 may often be more than dissipated by the costs and loss in experimental efficiency resulting from the requirement of two testing sessions, over and above the considerations of representativeness.

Design 4 has a particular advantage over Design 6 if experimental mortality is high. In Design 4, one can examine the pretest scores of lost cases in both experimental and control groups and check on their comparability. In the absence of this in Design 6, the possibility is opened for a mean difference resulting from differential mortality rather than from individual change, if there is a substantial loss of cases.

A final objection comes from those who wish to study the relationship of pretest attitudes to kind and amount of change. This is a valid objection, and where this is the interest, Design 4 or 5 should be used, with parallel analysis of experimental and control groups. Another common type of individual difference study involves classifying persons in terms of amount of change and finding associated characteristics such as sex, age, education, etc. While unavailable in this form in Design 6, essentially the same correlational information can be obtained by subdividing both experimental and control groups in terms of the associated characteristics, and examining the experimental-control difference for such subtypes.

For Design 6, the Posttest-Only Control Group Design, there is a class of social settings in which it is optimally feasible, settings which should be more used than they now are. Whenever the social contact represented by X is made to single individuals or to small groups, and where the response to that stimulus can be identified in terms of individuals or type of X, Design 6 can be applied. Direct mail and door-to-door contacts represent such settings. The alternation of several appeals from door-to-door in a fund-raising campaign can be organized as a true experiment without increasing the cost of the solicitation. Experimental variation of persuasive materials in a direct-mail sales campaign can provide a better experimental laboratory for the study of mass communication and persuasion than is available in any university. The well-established, if little-used, split-run technique in comparing alternative magazine ads is a true experiment of this type, usually limited to coupon returns rather than sales because of the problem of identifying response with stimulus type (20). The split-ballot technique (7) long used in public opinion polls to compare different question wordings or question sequences provides an excellent example which can obviously be extended to other topics (e.g., 12). By and large these laboratories have not yet been used to study social science theories, but they are directly relevant to hypotheses about social persuasion.

Multiple X designs. In presenting the above designs, X has been opposed to No-X, as is traditional in discussions of experimental design in psychology. But while this may be a legitimate description of the stimulus-isolated physical science laboratory, it can only be a convenient shorthand in the social sciences, for any No-X period will not be empty of potentially change-inducing stimuli. The experience of the control group might better be categorized as another type of X, a control experience, an X_c instead of No-X. It is also typical of advance in science that we are soon no longer interested in the qualitative fact of effect or no-effect, but want to specify degree of effect for varying degrees of X. These considerations lead into designs in which multiple groups are used, each with a different X_1, X_2, X_3, X_n, or in multiple factorial design, as X_{1a}, X_{1b}, X_{2a}, X_{2b}, etc. Applied to Designs 4 and 6, this introduces one additional group for each additional X. Applied to 5, The Solomon Four-Group Design, two additional groups (one pretested, one not, both receiving X_n) would be added for each variant on X.

In many experiments, X_1, X_2, X_3, and X_n are all given to the same group, differing groups receiving the Xs in different orders. Where the problem under study centers around the effects of order or combination, such counterbalanced multiple X arrangements are, of course, essential. Studies of transfer in learning are a case in point (34). But where one wishes to generalize to the effect of each X as occurring in isolation, such designs are not recommended because of the sizable interactions among Xs, as repeatedly demonstrated in learning studies under such labels as proactive inhibition and learning sets. The use of counterbalanced sets of multiple Xs to achieve experimental equation, where natural groups not randomly assembled have to be used, will be discussed in a subsequent paper on compromise designs.

Testing for effects extended in time. The researches of Hovland and his associates (14, 15) have indicated repeatedly that the longer range effects of persuasive Xs may be qualitatively as well as quantitatively different from immediate effects. These results emphasize the importance of designing experiments to measure the effect of X at extended periods of time. As the misleading early research on reminiscence and on the consolidation of the memory trace indicate (36), repeated measurement of the same persons cannot be trusted to do this if a reactive measurement process is involved. Thus, for Designs 4 and 6, two separate groups must be added for each posttest period. The additional control group cannot be omitted, or the effects of intervening history, maturation, instrument decay, regression, and mortality are confounded with the delayed effects of X. To follow fully the logic of Design 5, four additional groups are required for each posttest period.

True experiments in which O is not under E's control. It seems well to call the attention of the social scientist to one class of true experiments which are possible without the full experimental control over both the "when" and "to whom" of both X and O. As far as this analysis has been able to go, no such true experiments are possible without the ability to control X, to withhold it from carefully randomly selected respondents while presenting it to others. But control over O does not seem so indispensable. Consider the following design.

A X O_1
A O_2 6.   Posttest Only Design, where O
   (O)   cannot be withheld from any
   (O)   respondent
   (O)

The parenthetical Os are inserted to indicate that the studied groups, experimental and control, have been selected from a larger universe all of which will get O anyway. An election provides such an O, and using "whether voted" rather than "how voted," this was Gosnell's design (11). Equated groups were selected at time A, and the experimental group subjected to persuasive materials designed to get out the vote. Using precincts rather than persons at the basic sampling unit, similar studies can be made on the content of the voting (6). Essential to this design is the ability to create specified randomly equated groups, the ability to expose one of these groups to X while withholding it (or providing X_2) from the other group, and the ability to identify the performance of each individual or unit in the subsequent O. Since such measures are natural parts of the environment to which one wishes to generalize, they are not reactive, and Design 4, the Pretest-Posttest Control Group Design, is feasible if O has a predictable periodicity to it. With the precinct as a unit, this was the design of Hartmann's classic study of emotional vs. rational appeals in a public election (13). Note that 5, the Solomon Four-Group Design, is not available, as it requires the ability to withhold O experimentally, as well as X.

FURTHER PROBLEMS OF REPRESENTATIVENESS

The interaction effect of testing, affecting the external validity or representativeness of the experiment, was treated extensively in the previous section, inasmuch as it was involved in the comparison of alternative designs. The present section deals with the effects upon representativeness of other variables which, while equally serious, can apply to any of the experimental designs.

The interaction effects of selection. Even though the true experiments control selection and mortality for internal validity purposes, these factors have, in addition, an important bearing on representativeness. There is always the possibility that the obtained effects are specific to the experimental population and do not hold true for the populations to which one wants to generalize. Defining the universe of reference in advance and selecting the experimental and control groups from this at random would guarantee representativeness if it were ever achieved in practice. But inevitably not all those so designated are actually eligible for selection by any contact procedure. Our best survey sampling techniques, for example, can designate for potential contact only those available through residences. And, even of those so designated, up to 19 per cent are not contactable for an interview in their own homes even with five callbacks (37). It seems legitimate to assume that the more effort and time required of the respondent, the larger the loss through non-availability and noncooperation. If one were to try to assemble experimental groups away from their own homes, it seems reasonable to estimate a 50 per cent selection loss. If, still trying to extrapolate to the general public, one further limits oneself to docile pre-assembled groups, as in schools, military units, studio audiences, etc., the proportion of the universe systematically excluded through the sampling process must approach 90 per cent or more. Many of the selection factors involved are indubitably highly systematic. Under these extreme selection losses, it seems reasonable to suspect that the experimental groups might show reactions not characteristic of the general population. This point seems worth stressing lest we unwarrantedly assume that the selection loss for experiments is comparable to that found for survey interviews in the home at the respondent's convenience. Furthermore, it seems plausible that the greater the cooperation required, the more the respondent has to deviate from the normal course of daily events, the greater will be the possibility of nonrepresentative reactions. By and large, Design 6 might be expected to require less cooperation than Design 4 or 5, especially in the natural individual contact setting. The interactive effects of experimental morality are of similar nature. Note that, on these grounds, the longer the experiment is extended in time the more respondents are lost and the less representative are the groups of the original universe.

Reactive arrangements. In any of the experimental designs, the respondents can become aware that they are participating in an experiment, and this awareness can have an interactive effect, in creating reactions to X which would not occur had X been encountered without this "I'm a guinea pig" attitude. Lazarsfeld (19), Kerr (17), and Rosenthal and Frank (28), all have provided valuable discussions of this problem. Such effects limit generalizations to respondents having this awareness, and preclude generalization to the population encountering X with nonexperimental attitudes. The direction of the effect may be one of negativism, such as an unwillingness to admit to any persuasion or change. This would be comparable to the absence of any immediate effect from discredited communicators, as found by Hovland (14). The result is probably more often a cooperative responsiveness, in which the respondent accepts the experimenter's expectations and provides pseudoconfirmation. Particularly is this positive response likely when the respondents are self-selected seekers after the cure that X may offer.

The Hawthorne studies (21) illustrate such sympathetic changes due to awareness of experimentation rather than to the specific nature of X. In some settings it is possible to disguise the experimental purpose by providing plausible façades in which X appears as an incidental part of the background (e.g., 26, 27, 29). We can also make more extensive use of experiments taking place in the intact social situation, in which the respondent is not aware of the experimentation at all.

The discussion of the effects of selection on representativeness has argued against employing intact natural preassembled groups, but the issue of conspicuousness of arrangements argues for such use. The machinery of breaking up natural groups such as departments, squads, and classrooms into randomly assigned experimental and control groups is a source of reaction which can often be avoided by the use of preassembled groups, particularly in educational settings. Of course, as has been indicated, this requires the use of large numbers of such groups under both experimental and control conditions.

The problem of reactive arrangements is distributed over all features of the experiment which can draw the attention of the respondent to the fact of experimentation and its purposes. The conspicuous or reactive pretest is particularly vulnerable, inasmuch as it signals the topics and purposes of the experimenter. For communications of obviously persuasive aim, the experimenter's topical intent is signaled by the X itself, if the communication does not seem a part of the natural environment. Even for the posttest-only groups, the occurrence of the posttest may create a reactive effect. The respondent may say to himself, "Aha, now I see why we got that movie." This consideration justifies the practice of disguising the connection between O and X even for Design 6, as through having different experimental personnel involved, using different façades, separating the settings and times, and embedding the X-relevant content of O among a disguising variety of other topics.[5]

Generalizing to other Xs. After the internal validity of an experiment has been established, after a dependable effect of X upon O has been found, the next step is to establish the limits and relevant dimensions of generalization not only in terms of populations and

5. For purposes of completeness, the interaction of X with history and maturation should be mentioned. Both affect the generalizability of results. The interaction effect of history represents the possible specificity of results to a given historical moment, a possibility which increases as problems are more societal, less biological. The interaction of maturation and X would be represented in the specificity of effects to certain maturational levels, fatigue states, etc.

settings but also in terms of categories and aspects of X. The actual X in any one experiment is a specific combination of stimuli, all confounded for interpretative purposes, and only some relevant to the experimenter's intent and theory. Subsequent experimentation should be designed to purify X, to discover that aspect of the original conglomerate X which is responsible for the effect. As Brunswik (3) has emphasized, the representative sampling of Xs is as relevant a problem in linking experiment to theory as is the sampling of respondents. To define a category of Xs along some dimension, and then to sample Xs for experimental purposes from the full range of stimuli meeting the specification while other aspects of each specific stimulus complex are varied, serves to untie or unconfound the defined dimension from specific others, lending assurance of theoretical relevance.

In a sense, the placebo problem can be understood in these terms. The experiment without the placebo has clearly demonstrated that some aspect of the total X stimulus complex has had an effect; the placebo experiment serves to break up the complex X into the suggestive connotation of pill-taking and the specific pharmacological properties of the drug—separating two aspects of the X previously confounded. Subsequent studies may discover with similar logic which chemical fragment of the complex natural herb is most essential. Still more clearly, the sham operation illustrates the process of X purification, ruling out general effects of surgical shock so that the specific effects of loss of glandular or neural tissue may be isolated. As these parallels suggest, once recurrent unwanted aspects of complex Xs have been discovered for a given field, control groups especially designed to eliminate these effects can be regularly employed.

Generalizing to other Os. In parallel form, the scientist in practice uses a complex measurement procedure which needs to be refined in subsequent experimentation. Again, this is best done by employing multiple Os all having in common the theoretically relevant attribute but varying widely in their irrelevant specificities. For Os this process can be introduced into the initial experiment by employing multiple measures. A major practical reason for not doing so is that it is so frequently a frustrating experience, lending hesitancy, indecision, and a feeling of failure to studies that would have been interpreted with confidence had but a single response measure been employed.

Transition experiments. The two previous paragraphs have argued against the *exact* replication of experimental apparatus and measurement procedures on the grounds that this continues the confounding of theory-relevant aspects of X and O with specific artifacts of unknown influence. On the other hand, the confusion in our literature generated by the heterogeneity of results from studies all on what is nominally the "same" problem but varying in implementation, is leading some to call for exact replication of initial procedures in subsequent research on a topic. Certainly no science can emerge without dependably repeatable experiments. A suggested resolution is the *transition experiment*, in which the need for varying the theory-independent aspects of X and O is met in the form of a multiple X, multiple O design, one segment of which is an "exact" replication of the original experiment, exact at least in those major features which are normally reported in experimental writings.

Internal vs. external validity. If one is in a situation where either internal validity or representativeness must be sacrificed, which should it be? The answer is clear. Internal validity is the prior and indispensible consideration. The optimal design is, of course, one having both internal and external validity. Insofar as such settings are available, they should be exploited, without embarrassment from the apparent opportunistic warping of the content of studies by the availability of laboratory techniques. In this sense, a science is as opportunistic as a bacteria culture and grows only where growth is possible. One basic necessity for such growth is the machinery for selecting among alternative hypotheses, no matter how limited those hypotheses may have to be.

SUMMARY

In analyzing the extraneous variables which experimental designs for social settings seek to control, seven categories have been distinguished: history, maturation, testing, instrument decay, regression, selection, and mortality. In general, the simple or main effects of these variables jeopardize the internal validity of the experiment and are adequately controlled in standard experimental designs. The interactive effects of these variables and of experimental arrangements affect the external validity of generalizability of experimental results. Standard experimental designs vary in their susceptibility to these interactive effects. Stress is also placed upon the differences among measuring instruments and arrangements in the extent to which they create unwanted interactions. The value for social science purposes of the Posttest-Only Control Group Design is emphasized.

REFERENCES

1. ANNIS, A. D. AND MEIER, N. C. *The Induction of Opinion Through Suggestion by Means of Planted Consent,"* Journal of Social Psychology, 5 (1934), 65–81.
2. BORING, E. G., *"The Nature and History of Experimental Control,"* American Journal of Psychology, 67 (1954), 573–89.
3. BRUNSWIK, E, *Perception and the Representative Design of Psychological Experiments* (Berkeley: University of California Press, 1956).
4. BUGELSKI, B. R, *"A Note on Grant's Discussion of the Latin Square Principle in the Design and Analysis of Psychological Experiments,"* Psychology Bulletin, 46 (1949), 49–50.
5. CAMPBELL, D. T, *"The Indirect Assessment of Social Attitudes,"* Psychology Bulletin, 47 (1950), 15–38.
6. CAMPBELL, D. T., *"On the Possibility of Experimenting with the Bandwagon Effect,"* International Journal of Opinion Attitude Research, 5 (1951), 251–60.
7. CANTRIL, H., *Gauging Public Opinion* (Princeton: Princeton University Press, 1944).
8. COLLIER, R. M., *"The Effect of Propaganda upon Attitude Following a Critical Examination of the Propaganda Itself,"* Journal of Social Psychology, 20 (1944), 3–17.
9. CRESPI, L. P., *"The Interview effect in Polling,"* Public Opinion Quarterly, 12 (1948), 99–111.
10. FISHER, R. A., *The Design of Experiments* (Edinburgh: Oliver and Boyd, 1935).
11. GOSNELL, H. F., *Getting out the Vote: An Experiment in the Stimulation of Voting* (Chicago: The University of Chicago Press, 1927).
12. GREENBERG, A., *"Matched Samples,"* Journal Marketing, 18 (1953–54).
13. HARTMAN, G. W., *"A Field Experiment on the Comparative Effectiveness of Emotional and Rational Political Leaflets in Determining Election Results,* Journal of Abnormal Social Psychology, 31 (1936), 99–114.
14. HOVLAND, C. E., JANIS, I. L., AND KELLEY, H. H., *Communication and Persuasion* (New Haven: Yale University Press, 1953).
15. HOVLAND, C. I., LUMSDAINE, A. A., AND SHEFFIELD, F. D., *Experiments on Mass Communication* (Princeton University Press, 1949).
16. JAHODA, M., DEUTSCH, M., AND COOK, S. W. *Research Methods in Social Relations* (New York: Dryden Press, 1951).
17. KERR, W. A., *"Experiments on the Effects of Music on Factory Production,"* Applied Psychology Monographs, 1945, no. 5.
18. KISH, L., *"Selection of the Sample,"* In L. Festinger and D. Katz, eds., Research Methods in the Behavioral Sciences (New York: Dryden Press, 1953).
19. LAZARSFELD, P. F., *"Training Guide on the Controlled Experiment in Social Research,"* dittoed (Columbia University Bureau of Applied Social Research, 1948).

20. LUCAS, D. B., AND BRITT, S. H., *Advertising Psychology and Research* (New Yrok McGraw-Hill, 1950).
21. MAYO, E., *The Human Problems of an Industrial Civilization* (New York Macmillan, 1933).
22. MCNEAR, Q., *"A Critical Examination of the University of Iowa Studies of Environmental Influences upon the IQ,"* Psychology Bulletin, 37 (1940), 63–92.
23. MENEFEE, S. C., *"An Experimental Study of Strike Propaganda,"* Social Forces, 16 (1938), 574–82.
24. PARRISH, J. A., AND CAMPBELL, D. T., *"Measuring Propaganda with Direct and Indirect Attitude Tests,"* Journal of Abnormal Social Psychology, 48 (1953), 3–9.
25. PAYNE, S. L., *"The Ideal Model for Controlled Experiments"* Public Opinion Quarterly, 15 (1951), 557–62.
26. POSTMAN, L., AND BRUNER, J. S., *"Perception under Stress,"* Psychology Review, 55 (1948), 314–22.
27. RANKIN, R. E., AND CAMPBELL, D. T., *"Galvanic Skin Response to Negro and White Experimenters,"* Journal of Abnormal Social Psychology, 51 (1955), 30–33.
28. ROSENTHAL, D., AND FRANK, J. O., *"Psychotherapy and the Placebo Effect,"* Psychology Bulletin, 53 (1956), 294–302.
29. SCHANCK, R. L., AND GOODMAN, C. *"Reactions to Propaganda on Both Sides of a Controversial Issue,"* Public Opinion Quarterly, 3 (1939), 107–12.
30. SOLOMON, R. W., *"An Extension of Control Group Design,"* Psychology Bulletin, 46 (1949), 137–150.
31. STAR, S. A., AND HUGHES, H. M., *"Report on Educational Campaign: The Cincinnati Plan for the United Nations,"* American Journal of Sociology, 55 (1949), 389.
32. STOUFFER, S. A., *"Some Observations on Study Design,"* American Journal of Sociology, 55 (1949–50), 355–361.
33. STOUFFER, S. A., *"Measurement in Sociology,"* American Sociology Review., 18 (1953), 591–97.
34. UNDERWOOD, B. J., *Experimental Psychology* (Appleton-Century-Crofts, 1949).
35. UNDERWOOD, B. J., *"Interference and Forgetting,"* Psychology Review, 64 (1957), 49–60.
36. UNDERWOOD, B. J., *Psychological Research* (New York: Appleton-Century-Crofts, 1957).
37. WILLIAMS, R., *"Probability Sampling in the field: A Case History,"* Public Opinion Quarterly, 14 (1950), 316–30.

17. The Quest for Universals in Sociological Research

RALPH H. TURNER

IN A BOOK which has maintained attention and perhaps increased in influence over two decades, Florian Znaniecki describes the method he names "analytic induction," and designates it as *the* method which should be adopted in all sociological research.[1] Analytic induction is merely a special name for one formulation of a basic philosophy that research must be directed toward generalizations of *universal* rather than *frequent* applicability.[2] But Znaniecki's statement is unusually unequivocal and is specifically oriented toward sociological research. Hence it makes an excellent point of departure for a study of contrasting methodologies.

Znaniecki's position has recently been challenged by W. S. Robinson, who depicts analytic induction as an imperfect form of the

Reprinted by permission from *American Sociological Review*, 24 (June 1953), pp. 605-611.

1. Florian Znaniecki, *The Method of Sociology* (New York: Farrar and Rinehart, 1934).

2. This point is brought out by Alfred R. Lindesmith in his comments in the *American Sociological Review*, 17 (August 1952), 492.

method Znaniecki calls enumerative induction.[3] Robinson's contentions are further discussed by Alfred Lindesmith and S. Kirson Weinberg in replies to his paper.[4] The three discussions extend our understanding of the method, but leave some questions unanswered.

Methodological advance requires more than the mere tolerance of alternative methods. Any *particular* methodology must be examined and assessed in the light of the total process of research and theory formulation.[5] Accordingly, the objective of the present paper is to offer a definition of the place of the search for universals in the total methodology for dealing with non-experimental data. The procedure will be to examine specific examples of empirical research employing the analytic induction (or similar) method, to note what they do and do not accomplish, to establish logically the reasons for their distinctive accomplishments and limitations, and on these grounds to designate the specific utility of the method in relation to probability methods.

EMPIRICAL PREDICTION

Robinson's contention that actual studies employing the method of universals do not afford a basis for empirical prediction appears sound. However, it is only when the method is made to stand by itself that this limitation necessarily applies. Furthermore, the reason for the limitation is more intimately linked to the intrinsic logic of the method than the incidental fact that investigators using the method have tended to neglect the right-hand side of the four-fold table.[6] These statements may be substantiated and elaborated by an examination of selected studies.

Lindesmith's well-known study of opiate addiction will serve as a

3. W. S. Robinson, "The Logical Structure of Analytic Induction,"*American Sociological Review*, 16 (December 1951), 812-18. Robinson's argument may not altogether escape a logical pitfall. He first makes a careful description of the analytic induction procedure, but does it by describing its elements within the framework of statistical method. Any such operation necessarily slights any aspects of the first framework which lack counterparts in the second. The conclusion that analytic induction is a special but imperfect form of statistical procedure would then be inherent in the operation itself rather than a legitimate finding.

4. "Two Comments on W. S. Robinson's 'The Logical Structure of Analytic Induction,' " *American Sociological Review*, 17 (August 1952), 492-95.

5. Lindesmith's statement that, "Statistical questions call for statistical answers and causal questions call for answers within the framework of the logic of causal analysis" (*ibid.*, p. 492), seems to be an evasion of the problems of *why* and *when* each type of question should be asked. "Methodological parallelism" is of dubious fruitfulness.

6. Robinson, *op. cit.*, pp. 814-16. The writer doubts that this limitation inheres logically in the conception of analytic induction as described by Znaniecki.

useful first case. The causal complex which is essential to the process of addiction involves several elements. The individual must use the drug, he must experience withdrawal distress, he must identify these symptoms or recognize what they are, he must recognize that more of the drug will relieve the symptoms, and he must take the drug and experience relief.[7]

From the standpoint of predicting whether any given individual will become an addict or not, the formulation has certain limitations. First, it does not tell who will take the drug in the first place, nor give any indication of the relative likelihood of different persons taking the drug.[8] Second, the thesis itself affords no cue to variability in intensity of withdrawal symptoms, nor any guide to instances in which the symptoms will be mild enough not to result in addiction. Third, the theory does not provide a basis for anticipating who will recognize the symptoms and the means of securing relief. Fourth, personal and social factors involved in taking or not taking the drug to relieve the identified distress are not indicated. We cannot predict in an empirical instance unless there is some way of anticipating which people, given exposure to the drug, will recognize the nature of the withdrawal symptoms, will identify the means of relief, and will take that means of relief.[9] Finally, Lindesmith's theory does not indicate to us what will be the pattern of the addict's behavior, since this is determined by the cultural definition and treatment of the drug and its addicts. In sum, Lindesmith provides us with a causal complex which is empirically verified *in retrospect*, but which does not in itself permit prediction that a specific person will become an addict nor that a specific situation will produce addiction.

Donald R. Cressey's statement regarding the violation of financial trust likewise is posited as a system of universal generalizations and

---

7. Alfred R. Lindesmith, *Opiate Addiction* (Bloomington: Principia Press, 1947), pp. 67-89, *et passim*.

8. Some of Lindesmith's argument with current theories of drug addiction (*ibid*., pp. 141-64) rest upon a difference of purpose. Some of the theories he criticizes can be defended if reworded in terms of likelihood of first taking the drug in other than a medical treatment situation, rather than in terms of the likelihood of becoming addicted.

9. Lindesmith does not overlook these considerations in his descriptive treatment of the process. However, his treatment of them remains anecdotal and impressionistic rather than systematic and they are not integrated into the rigorous statement of his theory. The nearest he comes to a systematic statement concerning one of these variables is his observation that "as long as a patient believes he is using the drugs solely to relieve pain, and regards it as a 'medicine,' he does not become an addict." (*ibid*, p. 56). Weinberg suggests the use of measurement in some of these connections (*op. cit.*, p. 493).

is similar to Lindesmith's in format.[10] Three elements are essential to trust-violation. The person who will violate a financial trust has, first, a "non-sharable financial problem," a difficulty which he feels he cannot communicate to others. Second, he recognizes embezzlement as a way of meeting this problem. And third, he rationalizes the prospective embezzlement, justifying it to himself in some way.

First, the points at which Lindesmith's and Cressey's statement are parallel and points at which they are not parallel may be noted. The withdrawal symptoms and the non-sharable problem can be equated as the conditions which require some relief which cannot be secured through conventional channels. There is also a parallel between recognition that the drug will relieve the distress and recognition of embezzlement as a possible solution to the non-sharable problem. On the other hand, because drug addiction ensues from but one type of problem, withdrawal distress, Lindesmith can specify the taking of an opiate as essential. Cressey can specify no specific "first step" because of the variety of problems which may come to be non-sharable. The rationalization stage is absent from Lindesmith's formulation though he discusses it as a *frequent* phenomenon.

It is difficult to find a logical reason why rationalization should be *essential* in the one instance and merely *frequent* in the other. Perhaps the explanation lies, not in the logic of the phenomena themselves, but in the conditions necessary for a sense of closure on the part of the investigators. Since Lindesmith is explaining the existence of a continuing psychological state, it is sufficient for his purposes that the prospective addict be carried from a particular state of recognition (the symptoms and role of the drug) to an overt act with specific psychological consequences (relief by taking the drug). Cressey, however, is explaining a single action and so he seeks to fill the gap more fully between the particular state of recognition (that embezzlement will solve a non-sharable problem) and the act of embezzling, which he does with the rationalization.[11]

In light of the parallels between the two schemes, it is not surprising that the same limitations with regard to empirical prediction

10. *Other People's Money* (Glencoe: The Free Press, 1953). A brief statement of the theory also appears as, "Criminal Violation of Financial Trust," *American Sociological Review*, 15 (December 1950), 738–43.

11. Perhaps there is an object lesson indicated by this comparison. If the perspective of the investigator can determine what will be necessary for inclusion as the *essential* elements, there may be no theoretical limit to the number of such perspectives and consequently to the variations in what is considered essential. Such an observation would make Znaniecki's dictum that the investigator can arrive at a point beyond which no new knowledge about a class can be added difficult to defend. (Cf. Znaniecki, *op. cit.*, p. 249.

268 PART VI : *Problems of Design and Analysis*

apply to Cressey's statement as did to Lindesmith's. The theory does not indicate who will have non-sharable problems, what specific conditions will make a problem non-sharable and in what circumstances a problem may cease to be non-sharable. Nor do we have a guide to the circumstances surrounding recognition of embezzlement as a solution to the problem. And, finally, there are no systematic indicators of who will be able to rationalize and who will not.

There are perhaps two general reasons why the Lindesmith and Cressey studies do not produce empirical prediction, reasons which are applicable because of the very specifications of their method itself. One of these reasons has already been extensively illustrated, namely, that there is no basis for determining beforehand whether the conditions specified as necessary will exist in a particular instance.

The second general reason for lack of empirical prediction is that the alleged *preconditions* or essential causes of the phenomenon under examination cannot be fully specified apart from observation of the condition they are supposed to produce. In any situation in which variable "A" is said to cause variable "B," "A" is of no value as a predictor of "B" unless we establish the existence of "A" apart from the observation of "B." This limitation is in particular applicable to Cressey's study. Is it possible, for example, to assert that a problem is non-sharable *until* a person embezzles to get around it? If a man has not revealed his problem to others today, can we say that he will not share it tomorrow? The *operational* definition of a non-sharable problem is one that has not been shared up to the time of the embezzlement. Similarly, Cressey must be referring to some *quality* in the recognition of embezzlement as a solution which may not be identifiable apart from the fact that under appropriate conditions it eventuates in embezzlement. With embezzlement techniques and tales of successful embezzlement a standard part of the folklore of banks, offices handling public and private payrolls, and the like, mere recognition of embezzlement as a solution to problems is probably a near-universal characteristic of persons in a position to be able to embezzle. Similarly, rationalizations of embezzlement are part of the folklore and their use is standard joking behavior among persons in such positions. Consequently both recognition of embezzlement as a potential solution and ability to rationalize the act only become discriminating conditions when some sort of qualitative or quantitative limitation is imposed upon them. But under the present formulation it is only possible to identify what is a sufficient recognition or a sufficient ability to rationalize by the fact that they eventuate in embezzlement.

Lindesmith's theory, though less subject to this limitation, reveals the same vulnerability. Since withdrawal distress varies in degree according to size of dose and the number of shots taken, and since several shots may precede the existence of addiction as Lindesmith defines it, definition of the point at which the individual is taking the drug *to relieve withdrawal distress* as distinct from the point at which he is simply taking another shot must be arbitrary in some cases. But the distinction is crucial to Lindesmith's theory, since before this point the individual is not addicted and presumably may interrupt the process, while after this point he is addicted and the process is complete. Hence, the identification of what constitutes an effective recognition of the relief the drug will bring can only ultimately be determined by the fact that addiction follows such recognition.[12]

As a final case, we shall refer to a study which is in important respects rather different, but which is couched in terms of a parallel logic. In Robert C. Angell's well-known study of fifty families that suffered a serious reduction in income during the Depression, he attempted to work out a set of categories which could be applied to a family before the Depression which would predict how it would respond to the drop in family income. On the basis of assessments of "integration" and "adaptability," Angell "predicts" the response to financial crisis in terms of a "vulnerability-invulnerability" continuum and a "firm-readjustive-yielding" continuum.[13] Through his designation of a presumably comprehensive pair of concepts for describing those characteristics of the family which are essential in predicting his post-crisis variables, Angell follows an analytic induction model, though his variables are not simple attributes as are those of Lindesmith and Cressey.

On the surface, Angell's formulation looks a good deal more like a device for empirical prediction since he provides categories which can be assessed before the process of responding to the Depression gets under way and without reference to the consequences. A careful examination of the nature and manner of assessment of the two essential variables will indicate whether the impression is justified.

The idea of integration seems to refer to the degree to which a family is a unit, which is a fact not observable in the same direct

12. Lindesmith admits some vagueness on the matter of what genuinely constitutes knowledge that an opiate will relieve withdrawal distress, but regards the vagueness as a present limitation of his knowledge rather than an intrinsic limitation of his method. Cf. *op. cit.*, p. 77.

13. Robert C. Angell, *The Family Encounters the Depression* (New York: Scribner's Sons, 1936).

sense as the fact of taking a drug, for example. Integration conveys a meaning or feeling which is recognized by a number of symptoms, such as affection, common interests, and sense of economic interdependence. Integration in practice, then, is identified by an impressionistic assessment of several observable variables.[14] Of these variables there is no single one by which alone integration can be identified, nor is there any single "symptom" which may not be lacking in families classified as highly integrated.

The prediction which is provided by this scheme is *theoretical* prediction according to an analytic induction model. But the theoretical prediction cannot be converted into empirical prediction unless integration can be assessed beforehand. The assessment is made by an implicitly statistical operation, a mental weighting of several items of observation. In order, then, to gain *empirical* prediction the investigator shifts over to an "enumerative induction" procedure.

The concept of adaptability is both more important[15] and more complex, combining two elements as Angell uses the term. First, if a family has been flexible in the face of minor crises or problems that have occurred in the past, it is said to be adaptable and the prediction that it will maintain its unity in the face of a larger crisis is consequently made. This, of course, is merely an application of the principle that there is a constancy in the response of a given system to situations of the same sort, and has no causal significance. The other aspect of adaptability consists of a number of criteria, such as commitment to material standards, concerning which the same comments apply as in the case of integration.

Thus in the three cases cited empirical prediction is not provided by statements of universally valid relationships taken alone. What, then, do such efforts accomplish?

ANALYTIC INDUCTION AS DEFINITION

What the method of universals most fundamentally does is to provide definitions. Not all definitions are of equal value for deriving scientific generalizations, and the definitions produced by the analytic

14. Not only is the weighting of the various data of observation impressionistic but these criteria are themselves impressionistic. The implicitly statistical nature of Angell's operation has been noted before and his documents subjected to a restudy under Social Science Research Council auspices. In the restudy, scales for the measurement of integration and adaptability were devised to objectify ratings and translate them into numerical values. Ruth Cavan, *The Restudy of the Documents Analyzed by Angell in "The Family Encounters the Depression,"* unpublished.

15. Reuben Hill, *Families Under Stress* (New York: Harper & Row, 1949), p. 132, citing Cavan, *op. cit.*

induction procedure are intended to be characterized by causal homogeneity.

The effort at causal homogeneity is evident in the refinements of definition that accompany the method. In the process of attempting to generalize about addiction Lindesmith had to distinguish between those drugs that produce withdrawal distress and those that do not. Early in his work he concluded that it would be futile to seek a single theory to explain both types. Cressey points out that he could not study everyone who is legally defined as an embezzler. Unless he restricted his subjects, for example, to those who entered the situation in good faith, he could not form valid generalizations having universal applicability. Angell also rules out certain types of families. He recognized that some of his families were units merely in a formal sense, and that he could not observe uniform principles which would be applicable to the latter.

Saying that the principal accomplishment of the search for universals is to make definitions depends upon showing that the generalizations which it produces are deducible from the definitions. This is clearest in the case of Lindesmith's theory. In Lindesmith's presentation he has outlined the essential stages in becoming addicted by the time that he has arrived at his full definition of the phenomenon. The essential stages are implicit in the concept of addiction as he presents it.[16]

In place of the empirical attributes viewed essential by Lindesmith, Angell constructs two theoretical categories to which he ascribes the character of essentiality. But Angell is really getting the definition of his causal variables from the dependent or effect variables which he set up. Adaptability seems to correspond to the firm-yielding dimension and integration to the vulnerability dimension. Adaptability and integration are the logically deducible counterparts to the dependent variables.

Cressey's formulation is less completely amenable to this interpretation. The recognition of embezzlement as a solution is a logically deducible component, since one cannot perform a purposive self-conscious act unless its possibility is recognized. By definition the subjects of Cressey's study possessed long standing conceptions of themselves as law-abiding individuals, and were socially recognized as such at the time of the offense. While perhaps not from the

---

16. W. S. Robinson has suggested this in his "Rejoinder to Comments on 'The Logical Structure of Analytic Induction,'" *American Sociological Review,* 17 (August 1952), 494.

definition alone, at least from the body of established theory which is implicit in the definition, it follows that the individuals must at the time of the crime in some way reconcile their behavior with their law-abiding self-conception. Indeed, we cannot help wondering whether failure to report rationalization could be entirely independent from the criteria by which an investigator would exclude some subjects from his study on grounds of doubting the honesty of their initial intentions.

The non-sharable problem, however, is probably only partially deducible. Given the fact that all people have problems that might be solved by stealing, given the fact that these subjects were mature individuals, and recognizing that they must, by definition, have resisted situations in the past which could have been improved by stealing, then it would seem to follow that a very distinctive type of problem would be required for people to deviate from their established life-patterns. The non-sharability of the problem might be deducible as a *frequent* characteristic, but probably not as a universal characteristic.

Thus, with the exception of non-sharability, the theories that have been examined serve chiefly to delimit a causally homogeneous category of phenomena, the so-called essential causes of the phenomenon being deducible from the definition.

It is, of course, not accidental but the crux of the method that these generalizations should be deducible. It is through the causal examination of the phenomenon that its delimitation is effected. The operation in practice is one which alternates back and forth between tentative cause and tentative definition, each modifying the other, so that in a sense closure is achieved when a complete and integral relation between the two is established. Once the generalizations become self-evident from the definition of the phenomenon being explained, the task is complete.

THE INTRUSIVE FACTOR

The next step in our argument must be to ask why the search for universals does not carry us beyond formulating a definition and indicating its logical corollaries, and why it fails to provide empirical prediction. The answer may be that there are no universal, uniform relations to be found except those which constitute logical corollaries of conceptual definition. The positing of operationally independent causal variables, empirically assessible prior to the existence of the postulated effect, always seems to result in relationships of statistical probability rather than absolute determination.[17]

A minor reason for these limited findings is the fact of multiple determination, with which analytic induction is rather ill-equipped to cope. When such complex phenomena as family integration, rather than individual behavior, are examined, the method very rapidly shifts into the ideal-type technique, which is no longer subject to the sort of straight-forward empirical verification as analytic induction. As in Angell's study, the logic of the method is preserved but the empirical problems become quite different.

But as the central thesis of this paper we shall call attention to another explanation for the absence of universal, uniform relations which are not logical corollaries of definitions. The "closed system," which is the core of Znaniecki's statement and whose isolation is the objective and accomplishment of the method, is a causally self-contained system. As such, it is not capable of activation from within, but only by factors coming from outside the system. While, by definition, uniform relations exist within closed causal systems, uniform relations do not exist, *between* any causal system and the external factors which impinge on it. *External variables operating upon any closed system do not have a uniform effect because they have to be assimilated to the receiving system in order to become effective as causes.* The outside variable has to be translated, in a sense, into a cause relevant to the receiving system. Normally there will be alternate ways in which the same external variable may be translated depending upon the full context within which it is operative. The situation in which a man finds himself, for example, can only activate the closed system of the embezzlement process when it becomes translated into a non-sharable problem. Cressey finds no type of problem, phenomenologically speaking, which necessarily and uniformly becomes a non-sharable problem.

The external factor which activates a system may be referred to as an *intrusive* factor. This idea is taken from Frederick Teggart's discussion of what he calls an "event." "We may then define an event as an intrusion from any wider circle into any circle or condition which may be the object of present interest."[18] There are always

17. These remarks and some of the subsequent observations must be qualified by noting that Cressey's "non-sharable problem" is an apparent exception. If the statements in this paragraph are correct, we should expect further research to eventuate either in some modification of the concept, "violation of financial trust," or in the re-evaluation of the non-sharable problem as a *frequent* rather than essential characistic.

18. Frederick J. Teggart, *Theory of History* (New Haven: Yale University Press,

intrusive factors which are accordingly not predictable in terms of the causal system under examination, but which serve to activate certain aspects of the system. The same idea may be thought of as levels of phenomena. There are no uniform relations between levels of phenomena, only within levels.

Empirical prediction always concerns the way in which one closed system is activated by various intrusive factors. Hence empirical prediction always requires some statistical or probability statements, because there is some uncertainty or lack of uniformity in the *way* in which the intrusive factors will activate the causal system and even in *whether* they will activate the system.

UNIVERSALS AND STATISTICAL METHOD

The utility of defining universals within closed systems lies in the translation of *variables* into *concepts*. A variable is any category which can be measured or identified and correlated with something else. A concept is a variable which is part of a theoretical system, implying causal relations. That correlations among variables, of themselves, do not provide a basis for theory, or even for anticipating future correlations, is well known. Analytic induction fails to carry us beyond identifying a number of closed systems, and enumerative induction fails to go beyond the measurement of associations. The functions of the two methods are not only distinct; they are complementary. When the two methods are used together *in the right combination*,[19] they produce the type of findings which satisfies the canons of scientific method.

What the identification of closed systems does is to provide a basis for organizing and interpreting observed statistical associations. For example, valid research would probably reveal some correlation between liking-to-run-around-with-women and embezzlement. Cressey's findings do not discredit such an observation but afford a basis for interpreting it. In the light of certain American mores such a behavior pattern is likely, in some circumstances, to create a problem which would be difficult to discuss with others. The crucial aspect of this behavior for the determination of embezzlement would be its creation of a non-sharable problem.

1925), p. 149. Quoted by Clarence Marsh Case in "Leadership and Conjuncture: A Sociological Hypothesis," *Sociology and Social Research*, 17 (July, 1933), 513.

19. In no sense can those research reports which devote a section to statistical findings and another section to case study findings be said to illustrate the thesis of this paper. In most cases such contrasting categories refer only to the method of data *collection*, the method of *analysis* being enumerative in both cases, but precise in the former and impressionistic in the latter.

With the closed system described it is possible to take the various correlations and get order from them. Identification of the closed system also gives us guides to significant variables, correlations that would be worthy of test. At the present point it should be profitable to search for the kinds of situations which most often become non-sharable problems, the characteristics which are correlated with the ability to rationalize an activity which would normally be regarded as contrary to the mores of society, the personal and situational characteristics associated with taking opiates (other than by medical administration) sufficiently to experience withdrawal symptoms. A study of correlations between certain sex patterns and the acquisition of non-sharable problems would build cumulatively in a way that a study of correlation between the former and embezzlement would not do. Some quantitative measure of such correlation would in turn provide the basis for using the closed system formulation for empirical prediction.[20]

One useful indication of the way in which a statement of universals can function in the total research operation is afforded by Edwin Sutherland's "differential association" theory of criminality.[21] While this theory is not the product of a specific empirical research operation of the sort that Lindesmith or Cressey undertook, the form of Sutherland's proposition is that of the analytic induction model. He employs a felicitous term in stating his theory. Differential association, he says, is "the specific causal process' in the genesis of systematic criminal behavior. He does not say that differential association is *the* cause or the *only* one; poverty and the like may be in some sense causes. But differential association is the specific causal process through which these other factors, or more removed causes, must operate. Poverty and other correlated factors only facilitate criminal behavior because they affect the person's likelihood of learning a pattern of criminality from a model of criminality which is presented to him. The differential association theory identifies a hypothesized closed system, in terms of which the many correlated variables gain their meaning.

There are many theories already extant which have this same

20. Cressey proposes a study of such related conditions in much the same manner as is indicated here, but does not clarify whether this should be by a further extension of the method he has used or by the measurement of probabilities. Cf. *Other People's Money*, chap. V.

21. Edwin H. Sutherland, *Principles of Criminology* (Chicago: J. B. Lippincott, 1939), pp. 4–9. The third edition of Sutherland's work is cited here because he has modified the features of his theory most relevant to the argument of this paper in his fourth edition (1947).

character, but which have not always been viewed as logical counterparts to the analytic induction method. Edwin Lemert's proposition that, "The onset of insanity coincides with the awareness of one's behavior as being invidiously different from that of all other people's," points to the same sort of *specific causal process* in the genesis of insanity, or "secondary psychotic deviation."[22] And Sorokin's interpretation of Durkheim's theory of suicide follows the same form.[23]

Statements of this sort are devices for placing in bold outline the meaningful components of the phenomenon under study. In order to achieve the form of a universally valid generalization the investigator either states his causes as inferential variables (Angell), or states empirically continuous variables as attributes (Lindesmith, Cressey). In the latter case, the dividing point between the two phases of the crucial attribute is identifiable only retrospectively on the basis that the specified sequence is or is not completed. But if the essential components of the causal complex are viewed as continuous variables, capable of measurement independently of completion of the hypothesized sequence, the *essential degree* of the components will vary from instance to instance. Hence, in the process of designating the essential causes in a manner susceptible to empirical identification prior to their expected effect, the investigator must recast his thesis in terms of probability rather than uniform and universal relations.

A danger of the serach for universals lies in the inadequate utilization of much valuable data. Cressey has information on the types of backgrounds his subjects came from, but because these are not universals the information has been filed away, or handled impressionistically. Lindesmith likewise secured abundant information which he uses only to demonstrate that absolute uniformity does not exist. Angell describes the frequent characteristics of the integrated and the adaptable family, but he does not systematize this material because such aspects of it are not universals. In these cases the imposition of particular methodological restrictions has limited what can be found out about the phenomenon under examination.

Analytic induction or some logical counterpart of the method is an essential aspect of research directed toward accumulating an ordered body of generalizations. But, for the reasons developed in this paper, Znaniecki's statement that, "analytic induction ends where enumera-

22. Edwin M. Lemert, *Social Pathology* (New York: McGraw-Hill, 1951), p. 428.
23. Pitirim A. Sorokin, *Society, Culture and Personality* (New York: Harper, 1947), pp. 8–13.

tive induction begins; and if well conducted, leaves no real and soluble problems for the latter,"[24] represents an untenable position. It is through conceiving the "essential" conditions in a closed system as the avenues through which correlated factors can operate as causes, that generalizations about closed systems can escape their self-containment and probability associations may be organized into meaningful patterns.

24. Florian Znaniecki, *The Method of Sociology*, p. 250.

PART SEVEN

The Social Experiment: Uses and Problems

INTRODUCTION

THE READINGS in this part have a single focus: the social and interactional problems inherent in the experimental method. I take it as
axiomatic that the experiment represents a situation of interaction, a
situation wherein every action and reaction of the experimenter has
the possibility of shaping the behaviors of the subject.

It is unnecessary to establish the logic of the experiment. This was
done in Part VI by Campbell, and was also indicated in the selection
by Camilleri. It is now necessary to treat the interactional nature of
experimental research.

Orne's paper sets the theme for Leik's article. The behaviors of the
experimenter, and indeed the experimental situation itself, produce
definitions, or demand characteristic effects, that shape the subject's
conduct. For a variety of reasons, some economical, other humanitar-
ian, scientific, or social, subjects approach the experiment with special conceptions of what is expected of them. They interpret the
cues, gestures and utterances of the experimenter in this light, ever
attempting to discover the "true" intent of the study. Having once

formed their interpretation, they then construct lines of action that will implement those definitions. A self-fulfilling prophecy is created and often carried to completion. The experimenter's study, or hypothesis, can be validated simply because the subject has read the experimenter's intentions correctly. This raises Orne's major hypothesis that behavior in any experiment will be the product of at least two variables: the experimental conditions, and the subject's definition of the situation. (Orne's call for research that will identify the conditions under which demand characteristic effects are greater or less is partially answered in a study by Susan Roth Sherman on attitude change, "Demand Characteristics in an Experiment on Attitude Change." *Sociometry*, 30 (September 1967), 246–61. Suggesting that traditional studies of attitude change within the experimental situation may have been effected by the subject's readiness to be influenced by the experimenter, Sherman designed a typology of potential subject reactions. There are those subjects who think the investigator wants favorable change and acts accordingly. Others may think no change is desired and act to implement that definition. Some may rebel against the experimenter's intentions either by changing in an unfavorable direction, or by refusing to change favorably. This typology suggests that while the experimenter's results may be confirmed by a subject's behavior, confirmation stems from diverse psychological sources which are not directly attributable to the experimental design. Sherman's findings were not clear-cut; that is, favorable cues from the experimenter produced the greatest change among persons scoring high on the other-directed measures only when other relevant cues suggested favorable change. However, empirical support is given the Orne hypothesis. Investigators can no longer ignore the social and interactional factors present in their experimental design.)

Another facet of Orne's hypothesis suggests that extensions of the experimenter as seen in stooges, or confederate subjects, may also influence the subject's behavior. That is, just because a person dresses or talks like other subjects, his behavior may produce unwanted effects. While the use of stooges in experimental settings has a long history in small group research, few systematic studies have been conducted to assess the effects of varying certain aspects of the stooge's behavior upon subsequent results.

Leik's paper examines the influence of a stooge's behavior that are irrelevant to the experimental purpose. Two features of the stooge's behavior were varied: his dress, whether sloppy or neat, and his demeanor, whether confident or hesitant. This classification produced four experimental conditions. The data indicated that while attire, or dress, contributed to variations in the subject's behavior, demeanor had a greater effect.

These findings are provocative. They suggest ways of systematically studying the effects aspects of self-presentation have upon face-to-face interactions. They suggest that the way a person presents himself influences the subsequent reactions of others to him. A commonplace observation, but one that has seldom been examined experimentally.

THE RELEVANCE OF THE EXPERIMENT

Aside from the fact that the experiment is the most rigorous method of causal analysis, the findings of Orne and Leik point to an aspect of the experiment that demands future exploitation. These studies suggest how interactionally oriented researchers may bring their theory into the laboratory. With the elaborate features now present in most laboratories it is possible to systematically examine the dynamics of face-work, dress, demeanor, deference, gestures, and other components of interaction. The construction of lines of action toward problematic objects can also be researched. The movements and shifts between selves when conflict appears can be studied. The list of potential topics is endless.

Such studies will serve two aims. On the one hand, interaction theory can only be improved by research of this order, but—of equal importance—the methodology of experimental design stands to gain a great deal by the systematic exploration of social interaction. If, as Orne and others have argued, the experiment is an interactional situation, then studies of the above order can no longer be delayed.

Suggested Readings. The research of Robert Rosenthal on experimenter effects in the experiment must be read. His book, *Experimenter Effects in Behavioral Research* (New York: Appleton-Century-Crofts, 1966), presents some of his findings on this dimension of experimental design. Neil Friedman's *The Social Nature of Psychological Research* (New York: Basic Books, 1967) is of equal importance. Tapes of experimental sessions are presented to show how a researcher's attitudes and dress influence a subject's conduct. The work of Orne, Rosenthal, and Friedman, in conjunction with the formulations of Donald T. Campbell, have significantly influenced the direction of experimental research in the last five years. An understanding of their perspective is demanded for any subsequent experimental research.

As often happens when a new perspective emerges within a discipline, counter-reactions are produced, reactions that call for a rejection of the new perspective. Such is the case with the research cited above. The reader should examine the recent work of T. X. Barber and associates who have reanalyzed the Rosenthal data. The *Journal of Consulting and Clinical Psychology* (volume 33, No. 1, 1969) presents some of their findings. Their position is followed by reactions from Leon Levy and others more favorably disposed to the interactional conclusions offered in this part.

18. On the Social Psychology of the Psychological Experiment: With Particular Reference to Demand Characteristics and Their Implications

MARTIN T. ORNE

It is to the highest degree probable that the subject['s] ... general attitude of mind is that of ready complacency and cheerful willingness to assist the investigator in every possible way by reporting to him those very things which he is most eager to find, and that the very questions of the experimenter ... suggest the shade of reply expected. ... Indeed ... it seems too often as if the subject were now regarded as a stupid automaton. ...

A. H. PIERCE, 1908[1]

Since the time of Galileo, scientists have employed the laboratory experiment as a method of understanding natural phenomena. Generically, the experimental method consists of abstracting relevant variables from complex situations in nature and reproducing in the laboratory segments of these situations, varying the parameters involved so as to determine the effect of the experimental variables. This procedure allows generalization from the information obtained

Reprinted by permission from *American Psychologist,* 17 (November 1962), pp. 776–783. Copyright 1962, American Psychological Association.

This paper was presented at the Symposium, "On the Social Psychology of the Psychological Experiment," American Psychological Association Convention, New York, 1961.

The work reported here was supported in part by a Public Health Service Research Grant, M-3369, National Institute of Public Health.

I wish to thank my associates Ronald E. Shor, Donald N. O'Connell, Ulric Neisser, Karl E. Scheibe, and Emily F. Carota for their comments and criticisms in the preparation of this paper.

1. See reference list (Pierce, 1908).

in the laboratory situation back to the original situation as it occurs in nature. The physical sciences have made striking advances through the use of this method, but in the behavioral sciences it has often been difficult to meet two necessary requirements for meaningful experimentation: reproducibility and ecological validity.[2] It has long been recognized that certain differences will exist between the types of experiments conducted in the physical sciences and those in the behavioral sciences because the former investigates a universe of inanimate objects and forces, whereas the latter deals with animate organisms, often thinking, conscious subjects. However, recognition of this distinction has not always led to appropriate changes in the traditional experimental model of physics as employed in the behavioral sciences. Rather the experimental model has been so successful as employed in physics that there has been a tendency in the behavioral sciences to follow precisely a paradigm originated for the study of inanimate objects, i.e., one which proceeds by exposing the subject to various conditions and observing the differences in reaction of the subject under different conditions. However, the use of such a model with animal or human subjects leads to the problem that the subject of the experiment is assumed, at least implicitly, to be a *passive responder* to stimuli—an assumption difficult to justify. Further, in this type of model the experimental stimuli themselves are usually rigorously defined in terms of what *is done* to the subject. In contrast, the purpose of this paper will be to focus on what the human subject *does* in the laboratory: what motivation the subject is likely to have in the experimental situation, how he usually perceives behavioral research, what the nature of the cues is that the subject is likely to pick up, etc. Stated in other terms, what factors are apt to affect the subject's reaction to the well-defined stimuli in the situation? These factors comprise what will be referred to here as the "experimental setting."

Since any experimental manipulation of human subjects takes place within this larger framework or setting, we should propose that the above-mentioned factors must be further elaborated and the parameters of the experimental setting more carefully defined so that adequate controls can be designed to isolate the effects of the experimental setting from the effects of the experimental variables. Later in this paper we shall propose certain possible techniques of control which have been devised in the process of our research on the nature of hypnosis.

2. Ecological validity, in the sense that Bruswik (1947) has used the term: appropriate generalization from the laboratory to nonexperimental situations.

Our initial focus here will be on some of the qualities peculiar to psychological experiments. The experimental situation is one which takes place within the context of an explicit agreement of the subject to participate in a special form of social interaction known as "taking part in an experiment." Within the context of our culture the roles of subject and experimenter are well understood and carry with them well-defined mutual role expectations. A particularly striking aspect of the typical experimenter-subject relationship is the extent to which the subject will play his role and place himself under the control of the experimenter. Once a subject has agreed to participate in a psychological experiment, he implicitly agrees to perform a very wide range of actions on request without inquiring as to their purpose, and frequently without inquiring as to their duration.

Furthermore, the subject agrees to tolerate a considerable degree of discomfort, boredom, or actual pain, if required to do so by the experimenter. Just about any request which could conceivably be asked of the subject by a reputable investigator is legitimized by the quasi-magical phrase, "This is an experiment," and the shared assumption that a legitimate purpose will be served by the subject's behavior. A somewhat trivial example of this legitimization of requests is as follows:

A number of casual acquaintances were asked whether they would do the experimenter a favor; on their acquiescence, they were asked to perform five push-ups. Their response tended to be amazement, incredulity and the question "Why?" Another similar group of individuals were asked whether they would take part in an experiment of brief duration. When they agreed to do so, they too were asked to perform five push-ups. Their typical response was "Where?"

The striking degree of control inherent in the experimental situation can also be illustrated by a set of pilot experiments which were performed in the course of designing an experiment to test whether the degree of control inherent in the *hypnotic* relationship is greater than that in a waking relationship.[3] In order to test this question, we tried to develop a set of tasks which waking subjects would refuse to do, or would do only for a short period of time. The tasks were intended to be psychologically noxious, meaningless, or boring, rather than painful or fatiguing.

For example, one task was to perform serial additions of each adjacent two numbers on sheets filled with rows of random digits. In order to complete just one sheet, the subject would be required to perform 224 additions! A stack of some 2,000 sheets was presented to

3. These pilot studies were performed by Thomas Menaker.

each subject—clearly an impossible task to complete. After the instructions were given, the subject was deprived of his watch and told, "Continue to work; I will return eventually." Five and one-half hours later, the *experimenter* gave up! In general, subjects tended to continue this type of task for several hours, usually with little decrement in performance. Since we were trying to find a task which would be discontinued spontaneously within a brief period, we tried to create a more frustrating situation as follows:

Subjects were asked to perform the same task described above but were also told that when finished the additions on each sheet, they should pick up a card from a large pile, which would instruct them on what to do next. However, every card in the pile read,

> You are to tear up the sheet of paper which you have just completed into a minimum of thirty-two pieces and go on to the next sheet of paper and continue working as you did before; when you have completed this piece of paper, pick up the next card which will instruct you further. Work as accurately and as rapidly as you can.

Our expectation was that subjects would discontinue the task as soon as they realized that the cards were worded identically, that each finished piece of work had to be destroyed, and that, in short, the task was completely meaningless.

Somewhat to our amazement, subjects tended to persist in the task for several hours with relatively little sign of overt hostility. Removal of the one-way screen did not tend to make much difference. The postexperimental inquiry helped to explain the subjects' behavior. When asked about the tasks, subjects would invariably attribute considerable meaning to their performance, viewing it as an endurance test or the like.

Thus far, we have been singularly unsuccessful in finding an experimental task which would be discontinued, or, indeed, refused by subjects in an experimental setting.[4],[5] Not only do subjects continue to perform boring, unrewarding tasks, but they do so with few errors and little decrement in speed. It became apparent that it was extremely difficult to design an experiment to test the degree of social control in hypnosis, in view of the already *very high degree of control in the experimental situation itself.*

The quasi-experimental work reported here is highly informal and

4. Tasks which would involve the use of actual severe physical pain or exhaustion were not considered.

5. This observation is consistent with Frank's (1944) failure to obtain resistance to disagreeable or nonsensical tasks. He accounts for this "primarily by S's unwillingness to break the tacit agreement he had made when he volunteered to take part in the experiment, namely, to do whatever the experiment required of him" (p. 24).

based on samples of three or four subjects in each group. It does, however, illustrate the remarkable compliance of the experimental subject. The only other situations where such a wide range of requests are carried out with little or no question are those of complete authority, such as some parent-child relationships or some doctor-patient relationships. This aspect of the experiment as a social situation will not become apparent unless one tests for it; it is, however, present in varying degrees in all experimental contexts. Not only are tasks carried out, but they are performed with care over considerable periods of time.

Our observation that subjects tend to carry out a remarkably wide range of instructions with a surprising degree of diligence reflects only one aspect of the motivation manifested by most subjects in an experimental situation. It is relevant to consider another aspect of motivation that is common to the subjects of most psychological experiments: high regard for the aims of science and experimentation.

A volunteer who participates in a psychological experiment may do so for a wide variety of reasons ranging from the need to fulfill a course requirement, to the need for money, to the unvoiced hope of altering his personal adjustment for the better, etc. Over and above these motives, however, college students tend to share (with the experimenter) the hope and expectation that the study in which they are participating will in some material way contribute to science and perhaps ultimately to human welfare in general. We should expect that many of the characteristics of the experimental situation derive from the peculiar role relationship which exists between subject and experimenter. Both subject and experimenter share the belief that whatever the experimental task is, it is important, and that as such no matter how much effort must be exerted or how much discomfort must be endured, it is justified by the ultimate purpose.

If we assume that much of the motivation of the subject to comply with any and all experimental instructions derives from an identification with the goals of science in general and the success of the experiment in particular,[6] it follows that the subject has a stake in the outcome of the study in which he is participating. For the volunteer subject to feel that he has made a useful contribution, it is necessary for him to assume that the experimenter is competent and that he himself is a "good subject."

6. This hypothesis is subject to empirical test. We should predict that there would be measurable differences in motivation between subjects who perceive a particular experiment as "significant" and those who perceive the experiment as "unimportant."

The significance to the subject of successfully being a "good subject" is attested to by the frequent questions at the conclusion of an experiment, to the effect of, "Did I ruin the experiment?" What is most commonly meant by this is, "Did I perform well in my role as experimental subject?" or "Did my behavior demonstrate that which the experiment is designed to show?" Admittedly, subjects are concerned about their performance in terms of reinforcing their self-image; nonetheless, they seem even more concerned with the utility of their performances. We might well expect then that as far as the subject is able, he will behave in an experimental context in a manner designed to play the role of a "good subject" or, in other words, *to validate the experimental hypothesis.* Viewed in this way, the student volunteer is *not* merely a passive responder in an experimental situation but rather he has a very real stake in the successful outcome of the experiment. This problem is implicitly recognized in the large number of psychological studies which attempt to conceal the true purpose of the experiment from the subject in the hope of thereby obtaining more reliable data. This maneuver on the part of psychologists is so widely known in the college population that even if a psychologist is honest with the subject, more often than not he will be distrusted. As one subject pithily put it, "Psychologists always lie!" This bit of paranoia has some support in reality.

The subject's performance in an experiment might almost be conceptualized as problem-solving behavior; that is, at some level he sees it as his task to ascertain the true purpose of the experiment and respond in a manner which will support the hypotheses being tested. Viewed in this light, the totality of cues which convey an experimental hypothesis to the subject become significant determinants of subjects' behavior. We have labeled the sum total of such cues as the *"demand characteristics of the experimental situation"* (Orne, 1959a). These cues include the rumors or campus scuttlebutt about the research, the information conveyed during the original solicitation, the person of the experimenter, and the setting of the laboratory, as well as all explicit and implicit communications during the experiment proper. A frequently overlooked, but nonetheless very significant source of cues for the subject lies in the experimental procedure itself, viewed in the light of the subject's previous knowledge and experience. For example, if a test is given twice with some intervening treatment, even the dullest college student is aware that some change is expected, particularly if the test is in some obvious way related to the treatment.

The demand characteristics perceived in any particular experiment will vary with the sophistication, intelligence, and previous experience of each experimental subject. To the extent that the demand characteristics of the experiment are clear-cut, they will be perceived uniformly by most experimental subjects. It is entirely possible to have an experimental situation with clear-cut demand characteristics for psychology undergraduates which, however, does not have the same clear-cut demand characteristics for enlisted army personnel. It is, of course, those demand characteristics which are perceived by the subject that will influence his behavior.

We should like to propose the heuristic assumption that a subject's behavior in any experimental situation will be determined by two sets of variables: (a) those which are traditionally defined as experimental variables and (b) the perceived demand characteristics of the experimental situation. The extent to which the subject's behavior is related to the demand characteristics, rather than to the experimental variable, will in large measure determine both the extent to which the experiment can be replicated with minor modification (i.e., modified demand characteristics) and the extent to which generalizations can be drawn about the effect of the experimental variables in nonexperimental contexts (the problem of ecological validity [Brunswik, 1947]).

It becomes an empirical issue to study under what circumstances, in what kind of experimental contexts, and with what kind of subject populations, demand characteristics become significant in determining the behavior of subjects in experimental situations. It should be clear that demand characteristics cannot be eliminated from experiments; all experiments will have demand characteristics, and these will always have some effect. It does become possible, however, to study the effect of demand characteristics as opposed to the effect of experimental variables. However, techniques designed to study the effect of demand characteristics need to take into account that these effects result from the subject's *active* attempt to respond appropriately to the *totality* of the experimental situation.

It is perhaps best to think of the perceived demand characteristics as a contextual variable in the experimental situation. We should like to emphasize that, at this stage, little is known about this variable. In our first study which utilized the demand characteristics concept (Orne, 1959b), we found that a particular experimental effect was present only in records of those subjects who were able to verbalize the experimenter's hypothesis. Those subjects who were unable to do so did not show the predicted phenomenon. Indeed we found that whether or not a given subject perceived the experimenter's hypothesis was a more accurate predictor of the subject's actual performance than his statement about what he thought he had done on the experimental task. It became clear from extensive interviews with subjects that response to the demand characteristics is not merely conscious compliance. When we speak of "playing the role of a good experimental subject," we use the concept analogously to the way in which Sarbin (1950) describes role playing in hypnosis: namely, largely on a nonconscious level. The demand characteristics of the situation help define the role of "good experimental subject," and the responses of the subject are a function of the role that is created.

We have a suspicion that the demand characteristics most potent in determining subjects' behavior are those which convey the purpose of the experiment effectively but not obviously. If the purpose of the experiment is not clear, or is highly ambiguous, many different hypotheses may be formed by different subjects, and the demand characteristics will not lead to clear-cut results. If, on the other hand, the demand characteristics are so obvious that the subject becomes fully conscious of the expectations of the experimenter, there is a tendency to lean over backwards to be honest. We are encountering here the effect of another facet of the college student's attitude toward science. While the student wants studies to "work," he feels he must be honest in his report; otherwise, erroneous conclusions will be drawn. Therefore, if the subject becomes acutely aware of the experimenter's expectations, there may be a tendency for biasing in the opposite direction. (This is analogous to the often observed tendency to favor individuals whom we dislike in an effort to be fair.)[7]

Delineation of the situations where demand characteristics may produce an effect ascribed to experimental variables, or where they may obscure such an effect and actually lead to systematic data in the opposite direction, as well as those experimental contexts where they do not play a major role, is an issue for further work. Recognizing the contribution to experimental results which may be made by the demand characteristics of the situation, what are some experimental techniques for the study of demand characteristics?

As we have pointed out, it is futile to imagine an experiment that could be created without demand characteristics. One of the basic

7. Rosenthal (1961) in his recent work on experimenter bias, has reported a similar type of phenomenon. Biasing was maximized by ego involvement of the experimenters, but when an attempt was made to increase biasing by paying for "goods results," there was a marked reduction of effect. This reversal may be ascribed to the experimenters' becoming too aware of their own wishes in the situation.

characteristics of the human being is that he will ascribe purpose and meaning even in the absence of purpose and meaning. In an experiment where he knows some purpose exists, it is inconceivable for him not to form some hypothesis as to the purpose, based on some cues, no matter how meager; this will then determine the demand characteristics which will be perceived by and operate for a particular subject. Rather than eliminating this variable then, it becomes necessary to take demand characteristics into account, study their effect, and manipulate them if necessary.

One procedure to determine the demand characteristics is the systematic study of each individual subject's perception of the experimental hypothesis. If one can determine what demand characteristics are perceived by each subject, it becomes possible to determine to what extent these, rather than the experimental variables, correlate with the observed behavior. If the subject's behavior correlates better with the demand characteristics than with the experimental variables, it is probable that the demand characteristics are the major determinants of the behavior.

The most obvious technique for determining what demand characteristics are perceived is the use of postexperimental inquiry. In this regard, it is well to point out that considerable self-discipline is necessary for the experimenter to obtain a valid inquiry. A great many experimenters at least implicitly make the demand that the subject not perceive what is really going on. The temptation for the experimenter, in, say, a replication of an Asch group pressure experiment, is to ask the subject afterwards, "You didn't realize that the other fellows were confederates, did you?" Having obtained the required, "No," the experimenter breathes a sigh of relief and neither subject nor experimenter pursues the issue further.[8] However, even if the experimenter makes an effort to elicit the subject's perception of the hypothesis of the experiment, he may have difficulty in obtaining a valid report because the subject as well as he himself has considerable interest in appearing naive.

Most subjects are cognizant that they are not supposed to know any more about an experiment than they have been told and that excessive knowledge will disqualify them from participating, or, in the case of a postexperimental inquiry, such knowledge will invalidate their performance. As we pointed out earlier, subjects have a real stake in viewing their performance as meaningful. For this reason, it is commonplace to find a pact of ignorance resulting from the intertwining motives of both experimenter and subject, neither

8. Asch (1952) himself took great pains to avoid the pitfall.

wishing to create a situation where the particular subject's perform-ance needs to be excluded from the study.

For these reasons, inquiry procedures are required to push the subject for information without, however, providing in themselves cues as to what is expected. The general question which needs to be explored is the subject's perception of the experimental purpose and the specific hypotheses of the experimenter. This can best be done by an open-ended procedure starting with the very general question of, "What do you think that the experiment is about?" and only much later asking specific questions. Responses of "I don't know" should be dealt with by encouraging the subject to guess, use his imagina-tion, and in general, by refusing to accept this response. Under these circumstances, the overwhelming majority of students will turn out to have evolved very definite hypotheses. These hypotheses can then be judged, and a correlation between them and experimental performance can be drawn.

Two objections may be made against this type of inquiry: (a) that the subject's perception of the experimenter's hypotheses is based on his own experimental behavior, and therefore a correlation be-tween these two variables may have little to do with the determi-nants of behavior, and (b) that the inquiry procedure itself is subject to demand characteristics.

A procedure which has been independently advocated by Riecken (1958) and Orne (1959a) is designed to deal with the first of these objections. This consists of an inquiry procedure which is conducted much as though the subject had actually been run in the experiment, without, however, permitting him to be given any experimental data. Instead, the precise procedure of the experiment is explained, the experimental material is shown to the subject, and he is told what he would be required to do; however, he is not permitted to make any responses. He is then given a postexperimental inquiry as though he had been a subject. Thus, one would say, "If I had asked you to do all these things, what do you think that the experiment would be about, what do you think I would be trying to prove, what would my hypothesis be?" etc. This technique, which we have termed the pre-experimental inquiry, can be extended very readily to the giving of pre-experimental tests, followed by the explanation of ex-perimental conditions and tasks, and the administration of post experimental tests. The subject is requested to behave on these tests as though he had been exposed to the experimental treatment that was described to him. This type of procedure is not open to the objection that the subject's own behavior has provided cues for him as to the purpose of the task. It presents him with a straight problem-solving situation and makes explicit what, for the true experimental subject, is implicit. It goes without saying that these subjects who are run on the pre-experimental inquiry conditions must be drawn from the same population as the experimental groups and may, of course, not be run subsequently in the experimental condition. This technique is one of approximation rather than of proof. However, if subjects describe behavior on the pre-inquiry conditions as similar to, or identical with, that actually given by subjects exposed to the experimental conditions, the hypothesis becomes plausible that demand characteristics may be responsible for the behavior.

It is clear that pre- and postexperimental inquiry techniques have their own demand characteristics. For these reasons, it is usually best to have the inquiry conducted by an experimenter who is not acquainted with the actual experimental behavior of the subjects. This will tend to minimize the effect of experimenter bias.

Another technique which we have utilized for approximating the effect of the demand characteristics is to attempt to hold the demand characteristics constant and eliminate the experimental variable. One way of accomplishing this purpose is through the use of simulating subjects. This is a group of subjects who are not exposed to the experimental variable to which the effect has been attributed, but who are instructed to act *as if* this were the case. In order to control for experimenter bias under these circumstances, it is advisable to utilize more than one experimenter and to have the experimenter who actually runs the subjects "blind" as to which group (simulating or real) any given individual belongs.

Our work in hypnosis (Damaser, Shor, & Orne, 1963; Orne, 1959b; Shor, 1959) is a good example of the use of simulating controls. Subjects unable to enter hypnosis are instructed to simulate entering hypnosis for another experimenter. The experimenter who runs the study sees both highly trained hypnotic subjects and simulators in random order and does not know to which group each subject belongs. Because the subjects are run "blind," the experimenter is more likely to treat the two groups of subjects identically. We have found that simulating subjects are able to perform with great effectiveness, deceiving even well-trained hypnotists. However, the simulating group is not exposed to the experimental condition (in this case, hypnosis) to which the given effect under investigation is often ascribed. Rather, it is a group faced with a problem-solving task: namely, to utilize whatever cues are made available by the experimental context and the experimenter's concrete behavior in order to behave as they think that hypnotized subjects might. Therefore, to the extent that simulating subjects are able to behave identically, it is possible that demand characteristics, rather than the altered state of consciousness, could account for the behavior of the experimental group.

The same type of technique can be utilized in other types of studies. For example, in contrast to the placebo control in a drug study, it is equally possible to instruct some subjects not to take the medication at all, but to act as if they had. It must be emphasized that this type of control is different from the placebo control. It represents an approximation. It maximally confronts the simulating subject with a problem-solving task and suggests how much of the total effect could be accounted for by the demand characteristics — assuming that the experimental group had taken full advantage of them, an assumption not necessarily correct.

All of the techniques proposed thus far share the quality that they depend upon the active cooperation of the control subjects, and in some way utilize his thinking process as an intrinsic factor. The subject does *not* just respond in these control situations but, rather, he is required *actively* to solve the problem.

The use of placebo experimental conditions is a way in which this problem can be dealt with in a more classic fashion. Psychopharmacology has used such techniques extensively, but here too they present problems. In the case of placebos and drugs, it is often the case that the physician is "blind" as to whether a drug is placebo or active, but the patient is not, despite precautions to the contrary; i.e., the patient is cognizant that he does not have the side effects which some of his fellow patients on the ward experience. By the same token, in psychological placebo treatments, it is equally important to ascertain whether the subject actually perceived the treatment to be experimental or control. Certainly the subject's perception of himself as a control subject may materially alter the situation.

A recent experiment in our laboratory illustrates this type of investigation (Orne & Scheibe, 1964). We were interested in studying the demand characteristics of sensory deprivation experiments, independent of any actual sensory deprivation. We hypothesized that the overly cautious treatment of subjects, careful screening for mental or physical disorders, awesome release forms, and, above all, the presence of a "panic (release) button" might be more significant in producing the effects reported from sensory deprivation than the actual diminution of sensory input. A pilot study (Stare, Brown, & Orne, 1959), employing pre-inquiry techniques, supported this view. Recently, we designed an experiment to test more rigorously this hypothesis.

This experiment, which we called Meaning Deprivation, had all the *accoutrements* of sensory deprivation, including release forms and a red panic button. However, we carefully refrained from creating any sensory deprivation whatsoever. The experimental task consisted of sitting in a small experimental room which was well lighted, with two comfortable chairs, as well as ice water and a sandwich, and an optional task of adding numbers. The subject did not have a watch during this time, the room was reasonably quiet, but not soundproof, and the duration of the experiment (of which the subject was ignorant) was four hours. Before the subject was placed in the experimental room, 10 tests previously used in sensory deprivation research were administered. At the completion of the experiment, the same tasks were again administered. A microphone and a one-way screen were present in the room, and the subject was encouraged to verbalize freely.

The control group of 10 subjects was subjected to the identical treatment, except that they were told that they were control subjects for a sensory deprivation experiment. The panic button was eliminated for this group. The formal experimental treatment of these two groups of subjects was the same in terms of the objective stress — four hours of isolation. However, the demand characteristics had been purposively varied for the two groups to study the effect of demand characteristics as opposed to objective stress. Of the 14 measures which could be quantified, 13 were in the predicted direction, and 6 were significant at the selected 10% alpha level or better. A Mann-Whitney U test has been performed on the summation ranks of all measures as a convenient method for summarizing the overall differences. The one-tailed probability which emerges is $p = .001$, a clear demonstration of expected effects.

This study suggests that demand characteristics may in part account for some of the findings commonly attributed to sensory deprivation. We have found similar significant effects of demand characteristics in accounting for a great deal of the findings reported in hypnosis. It is highly probable that careful attention to this variable, or group of variables, may resolve some of the current controversies regarding a number of psychological phenomena in motivation, learning, and perception.

In summary, we have suggested that the subject must be recognized as an active participant in any experiment, and that it may be fruitful to view the psychological experiment as a very special form of social interaction. We have proposed that the subject's behavior in an experiment is a function of the totality of the situation, which includes the experimental variables being investigated and at least one other set of variables which we have subsumed under the heading, demand characteristics of the experimental situation. The study and control of demand characteristics are not simply matters of good experimental technique; rather, it is an empirical issue to determine under what circumstances demand characteristics significantly affect subjects' experimental behavior. Several empirical techniques have been proposed for this purpose. It has been suggested that control of these variables in particular may lead to greater reproducibility and ecological validity of psychological experiments. With an increasing understanding of these factors intrinsic to the experimental context, the experimental method of psychology may become a more effective tool in predicting behavior in nonexperimental contexts.

REFERENCES

ASCH, S. E., *Social Psychology* (New York: Prentice Hall, 1952).
BRUNSWIK, E., *Systematic and Representative Design of Psychological Experiments with Results in Physical and Social Perception*, (Berkeley: University of California Press, 1947, Syllabus Series, no. 304.
DAMASER, ESTHER C., SHOR, R. E., AND ORNE, M. T., "Physiological Effects During Hypnotically-Requested Emotions," *Psychosomatic Medicine*, 4 (1963), 334–43.
FRANK, J. D., "Experimental Studies of Personal Pressure and Resistance: I. Experimental Production of Resistance. *Journal of General Psychology*, 30 (1944), 33–41.
ORNE, M. T., "The Demand Characteristics of an Experimental Design and their Implications," paper read at American Psychological Association, Cincinnati, 1959a.
ORNE, M. T., "The Nature of Hypnosis: Artifact and Essence," *Journal of Abnormal Social Psychology*, 58 (1959b), 277–99.
ORNE, M. T., AND SCHEIBE, K. E., "The Contribution of Nondeprivation Factors in the Production of Sensory Deprivation Effects: The Psychology of the 'Panic Button,' " *Journal of Abnormal Social Psychology*, 68 (1964), 3–12.
PIERCE, A. H., "The Subconscious Again," *Journal of Philosophy, Psychology, and Scientific Method*, 5 (1908), 264–71.
RIECKEN, H. W., "A Program for Research on Experiments in Social Psychology," paper read at Behavioral Sciences Conference, University of New Mexico, 1958.

ROSENTHAL, R., *"On the Social Psychology of the Psychological Experiment: With Particular Reference to Experimenter Bias,"* paper read at American Psychological Association, New York, 1961.

SARBIN, T. R., *"Contributions to Role-taking Theory: I. Hypnotic Behavior,"* *Psychological Review,* 57 (1950), 255–70.

SHOR, R. E., *"Explorations in Hypnosis: A Theoretical and Experimental Study,"* unpublished doctoral dissertation, Brandeis University, 1959.

STARE, F., BROWN, J., AND ORNE, M. T., *"Demand Characteristics in Sensory Deprivation Studies,"* unpublished seminar paper, Massachusetts Mental Health Center and Harvard University, 1959.

19. "Irrelevant" Aspects of Stooge Behavior: Implications for Leadership Studies and Experimental Methodology

ROBERT K. LEIK

THE STUDY reported here is an outgrowth of various inquiries into the validity of the use of stooges in small-group experiments. Many articles report carefully conceived experiments which have used stooges, i.e., persons trained by the experimenter to interject needed experimental conditions into the interaction under study.[1] Aside from instruction of these confederates, however, the experimenter seldom concerns himself with whether the stooge is in fact interjecting only that which was intended. Might presumably "irrelevant" aspects of the stooge's behavior or appearance cause unanticipated and perhaps unobserved changes in the behavior of naive subjects?

1. Two classical examples of the use of stooges are S. E. Asch, "Effects of Group Pressure upon the Modification and Distortion of Judgments," in H. Guetzkow, ed., *Groups, Leadership and Men* (Pittsburgh: Carnegie Press, 1951), and S. Schacter, "Deviation, Rejection and Communication," *Journal of Abnormal and Social Psychology*, 46 (April, 1951), 190–207.

Early in these methodological inquiries it became apparent that not only was the answer to the foregoing question affirmative, but that important questions about the well-known distinction between "task" and "social-emotional" leadership were raised. This study, then, is focused on aspects of a stooge's behavior, irrelevant to the experimental purpose, which nevertheless may affect the naive subjects' impressions of the stooge and hence their evaluation of his behavior as well as the likelihood of their considering him likeable or a source of good ideas in the discussion.

PROCEDURE

Four subjects, one of them a stooge, were brought into the laboratory and so seated that three subjects were side by side behind one table while the fourth was seated alone behind another table facing the three. The experimenter sat near the table of three, facing the lone subject. Subjects were told that they were going to play Twenty Questions, a fairly well-known game in which players try to deduce what the game master has in mind by asking no more than 20 yes-or-no questions. The subject seated alone played the game first by himself. As he asked each question, the other three subjects rated that question on a five-point scale ranging from "very good" to "very poor." When he finished his game, he exchanged positions with one of the three remaining subjects who then played a new game. Each of the four subjects, in turn, played one game and was rated question-by-question by the remaining three. To standardize the rate at which questions were asked, the subject had to wait 15 seconds after a question had been answered before he could ask the next question. Upon being told that the next question was due, he had to ask the question within five seconds, or forfeit it and begin a new 15-second cycle.

When all subjects had played the game, they were seated around one table and told to discuss for ten minutes the best strategy to employ when trying to win at Twenty Questions. After the discussion, each subject completed a 12-item semantic-differential rating of each of the other three subjects, then ranked all four (including self) on who had contributed the best ideas to the discussion, and ranked the other three on his liking of them. The semantic-differential items included pairs of terms descriptive of appearance, such as "sloppy-neat," and of behavior, such as "confident-hesitant."

The stooge was always given the same topic to try to deduce, and was trained to ask exactly the same 16 questions each session. (The answer was "guessed" on question 16.) The same male stooge was used in all sessions. During the discussion, he contributed a specific set of three ideas plus fairly standard small talk. Thus in the *content* of his behavior, the stooge performed identically from session to session. Also, he was always seated between two naive subjects at the outset of the session so that he always played his game in third position, and he took the same seat each time in the discussion. The only exceptions to these controls occurred in two sessions for which one naive subject failed to appear. In these cases the stooge was second rather than third.

A total of 16 sessions was conducted, not counting pre-test sessions. Forty-six naive subjects participated, both male and female, all of whom were students in a group-behavior course. Because the stooge was also a student in the course, naive subjects had no reason to suspect his authenticity. Later discussions indicated no awareness during the study that one of the subjects was a stooge.

Four treatments were employed, each being used for four sessions. One dimension of treatment variation was the apparent confidence or hesitancy of the stooge in asking questions and in contributing to the discussion. In the confident treatment, the stooge asked the questions as if he were following up a promising hypothesis; he then looked as if he had expected whatever answer was given, whether it was yes or no. In the hesitant treatment, however, the stooge asked questions somewhat haltingly, as if they were vague guesses, then looked puzzled at the answers. As stated previously, the questions were identical across all treatments.

The second dimension of treatment variation involved the attire of the stooge. In one-half of the sessions, the stooge wore slacks, white shirt, tie and coat. Alternately he wore old jeans, a somewhat disreputable-looking sweat shirt, and tennis shoes. For convenience, the four treatments can be designated as (1) confident-neat, (2) hesitant-neat, (3) confident-sloppy, and (4) hesitant-sloppy.

Analysis of Question Ratings. With small frequencies, only 11 or 12 naive subjects per treatment, it is quite possible that the average rating standards of the naive subjects would vary somewhat from treatment to treatment. To avoid such a contamination of the effects being analyzed, each subject's rating of the performance of the other two naive subjects was used as a basis for analyzing his rating of the stooge's performance. First, the five possible ratings of each question, from "very good" to "very bad," were assigned numerical values from +2 to −2. The assumption of equal intervals was justified by the fact that the rating consisted of placing a check on a horizontal line divided into five equal segments, the outer segments being labelled as indicated. These numerical values were then averaged across all questions asked by one subject and rated by another. Such an average constitutes an over-all assessment of one subject's perception of how well another subject played the game. Since a given naive subject rated two other naive subjects, the mean of his two naive-subject mean ratings was subtracted from his mean rating of the stooge. This difference indicates any increase or decrease in evaluation of the stooge's performance over the same rater's evaluation of other performances. Variation in raters is therefore controlled.

Clarification of "Relevant." Before examining the effects of demeanor and dress on ratings of the stooge's performance, it is appropriate to ask what were the "relevant" aspects of his performance, and did they affect the ratings. For the purposes of this experiment, "relevant" refers to actual quality of the questions asked. Did ratings vary between good questions (those which logically progressed from previous information gained) and poor questions (those which were haphazard, illogical, or repetitious)?

It is not necessary to examine data from the immediate study to answer this question due to the fact that a series of earlier studies had used the same pattern of 16 questions asked by the stooge. From these earlier studies the following conclusions are possible:

1. There is a high degree of agreement among naive subjects on the *relative* evaluation of the questions asked. Thus, although mean ratings may vary by treatment, the ranking of the questions by mean rating remains highly stable from treatment to treatment. For various treatments in previous studies, the intraclass correlation by ranks (mean evaluations of questions ranked within treatment over all 16 questions) is significant beyond .0005.[2]

2. Question-by-question predictions by the naive subjects of the total number of questions the stooge would need to ask in order to guess the answer (assuming he had no limit on the number of questions he could ask) were related to the evaluations of the questions themselves. Thus the overall performance predictions varied as the question-by-question performance rating varied.[3] Over-all pre-

2. R. K. Leik, "Effects of Comparison and Visibility on Evaluation of Behavior," manuscript in preparation, University of Washington, 1965.
3. R. K. Leik, "Evaluation and Trend: Bases of Naive Predictions of Behavior," manuscript in preparation, University of Washington, 1965.

dictions were not requested of the naive subjects in the study to be reported here.

Although these conclusions are not basic to the points to be made in the present study, they serve to clarify what is meant by "irrelevant." Clearly, the demeanor and dress of the stooge are non-content factors which are not relevant to the *actual* quality of the questions which he asked, although they may affect naive subject *perceptions* of the quality of his questions.

RESULTS

A one-way analysis of the differences in rating by treatment is significant beyond the .01 level. Table 19.1 shows the mean differences by treatment as well as the analysis of variance data. It is possible, however, that a second contaminating variable could influence these observed differences by treatment. If the naive subjects were, on the average, less effective performers in some treatments than in others, then the stooge would appear better by comparison regardless of the effect of treatment variation. To check such a possibility, the stooge's rating of the three naive subjects per session was averaged by treatment. The extent to which treatment average differed from over-all average was relatively small, ranging from +.13 to −.10. Mean ratings of the stooge by treatment, adjusted for naive subject variability, show essentially the same pattern as Table 19.1.

TABLE 19.1. *Mean Rating and Analysis of Variance, of Stooge Questions by Treatment*

Confident-neat	Hesitant-neat	Confident-sloppy	Hesitant-sloppy
.39	−.05	.43	−.34

Source	Sum of Squares	df	Mean Square
Between	4.6216	3	1.5405
Within	14.9560	42	.3563
Total	19.5776	45	—

F = 4.32; $p < .01$.

Although the confidence-hesitance variation shows the expected pattern of higher ratings for the confident performance (both means are positive) than for the hesitant performance (both means are negative), the neat-sloppy variation is not so direct in its effects. Evidently, attire (at least for the population represented by these 46 students) serves as an augmenting variable. If the actor apparently knows what he is doing but is sloppy in his dress, perhaps the sloppiness indicates some sort of "brain" who does not worry about conforming to social niceties. On the other hand, if he performs poorly, sloppiness simply furthers the impression of an inadequate person. This interpretation of the data must be highly tentative, however, because the effects of dress are not large. In fact, if separate *t* tests are performed on pairs of mean ratings, the only two non-significant tests involve confident-neat versus confident-sloppy, and hesitant-neat versus hesitant-sloppy. This question will be addressed later when other data are examined.

It is important to remember in considering these data that the objective performance of the stooge in terms of content was identical in all sessions, and, of course, the same individual was used for the stooge in all sessions. Ostensibly, the performance ratings were of an identical set of questions asked by the stooge, yet the irrelevant factors of demeanor and attire clearly altered the ratings. The difference between the confident-sloppy treatment and the hesitant-sloppy treatment, in fact, is nearly 20 per cent of the total range of possible ratings (mean difference of .77 on a scale with a range of 4). Evidently, as any good symbolic interactionist should have predicted, the irrelevant factors are by no means irrelevent but carry considerable information.[4]

Best Ideas and Liking. Table 19.2 indicates the extent to which being assigned top-idea rank is related to the four treatments. Interestingly, only the lowest rated treatment, hesitant-sloppy, shows less than half the naive subjects choosing the stooge as top-idea man. Perhaps three standardized ideas exceeded the average contribution of naive subjects. It is also possible that his generally good performance in the group-behavior class predisposed naive subjects in his favor, a bias which would be constant for all treatment.

Clearly, the confident treatments show a higher proportion of top rank for ideas than do the hesitant treatments. When combined for this distinction, the data show an association between confidence and top-idea rank of $Q = .79$. Fisher's Exact Test indicates that the

---

4. Although his concern is somewhat different from that of this paper, for a good discussion of the appearance variable as a part of symbolic interaction, see G. P. Stone, "Appearance and Self," in A. M. Rose, ed., *Human Behavior and Social Processes* (Boston: Houghton Miffin Company, 1962).

TABLE 19.2, *Stooge Rank on Ideas by Treatment*

Rank on Ideas	C-N	C-S	H-N	H-S	Total
High (1)	10	10	7	3	30
Low (2-4)	1	2	5	8	16
Total	11	12	12	11	46

x^2 (corrected) = 8.74; $p <.05$.

probability of such association under the null hypothesis equals .005. The other dimension, neat versus sloppy, does not appear by itself strongly associated with idea ranking. If the apparent augmenting effect of sloppiness which was mentioned earlier is present, however, then the lumping of the two types of neat versus the two types of sloppy treatment would be internally contradictory. That is, sloppiness increased mean rating when associated with confidence, but decreased mean rating when associated with hesitance, thus washing out any over-all effect of dress upon the ranking. Such a contradiction is readily apparent in comparing the confident-sloppy treatment with the hesitant-sloppy treatment. The association between idea ranking and these two extreme treatments is $Q = .93$, with a Fisher's Exact Test showing a probability under the null hypothesis of .008.[5]

Being best liked does not appear to be related to the treatments. As Table 19.3 indicates, very little difference by treatment or by either dimension of treatment is apparent. Interestingly, however, being best liked is strongly associated with being ranked highest on ideas. This relationship, shown in Table 19.4 is not in full accord with the division of leadership hypothesis of Bales and Slater.[6] There is only one case out of 18 rankings of the stooge as best liked which did not have concomitant ranking of him as top idea man. On the other hand, being ranked top in ideas carried a little better than an even chance of concomitant ranking as best liked. It will be necessary to examine more fully related perceptions of the stooge to determine the meaning of these findings.

5. The larger value of p in this comparison of extreme types compared to the general comparison of confidence versus hesitance, does not imply a weaker relationship, due to the fact that n is only half as large.

6. R. F. Bales, and P. E. Slater, "Role Differentiation in Small Decision Making Groups," chap. 5 in T. Parsons and R. F. Bales, eds., *Family, Socialization and Interaction Process* (Glencoe: Free Press, 1955); and P. E. Slater, "Role Differentiation in Small Groups," *American Sociological Review*, 20 (June 1955), 300–310.

TABLE 19.3. *Stooge Rank on Liking by Treatment*

Rank on Liking	C-N	C-S	H-N	H-S	Total
High (1)	5	5	5	3	18
Low (2-3)	6	7	7	8	28
Total	11	12	12	11	46

x^2 (corrected) = .39; .90 $p <$ .95.

TABLE 19.4. *Relationship Between Rank on Ideas and Liking*

Rank on Liking	Rank on Ideas High (1)	Low (2-4)	Total
High (1)	17	1	18
Low (2-3)	13	15	28
Total	30	16	46

Q = .90; p (Fisher's Exact Test)=.008.

Semantic Differential Scales. Rather than attempt to analyze all of the semantic-differential items separately, they were examined for response patterns which allowed construction of scales subsuming a number of items. As noted previously, items pertained either to appearance or to behavior. Analysis revealed two Guttman-type scales involving respectively five and four items. The remaining three items did not fit either scale and will not be discussed.

Scale 1 consisted of the following items: interesting-dull, confident-hesitant, brilliant-uninspired, aggressive-passive, and individualistic-conforming. This scale has a coefficient of reproducibility of .94 with minimum marginal reproducibility of .57.[7] The basic dimension appears to be that of task-area leadership qualities; hence, although the term is not sufficiently comprehensive, the dimension will be called competence.

The small frequencies involved require that the scale be collapsed into high and low competence. Dichotomizing the total distribution of scale types (including both naive subjects and stooge) provides 73 high-competence ratings and 60 low-competence ratings. When only the ratings of the stooge are considered, however, it becomes appar-

7. Not all pairs were worded in the order stated. Because the semantic differential involved seven intervals on a continuum between the indicated extremes, items were dichotomized according to response frequencies. Continua were divided between categories 3 and 4 for the first four items listed, and between 4 and 5 for the fifth item.

ent that he was evaluated as more competent than his average co-participant, even in the hesitant treatment. As shown in Table 19.5, the only low-competence ratings received by the stooge were in the hesitant variations. Since the competence scale is designed to measure essentially what this experimental variation was intended to produce, some evidence of experimental success is indicated by this one-sided relationship. Similar to earlier data, the neat-sloppy variation has virtually no relationship to experimental treatment. The relationships between competence and ratings of stooge questions, idea rank and likeability will be explored after discussion of the second scale.

TABLE 19.5. Scale 1 (Competence) by Treatment: Stooge Only*

Competence	C-N	H-N	C-S	H-S	Total
High	12	9	11	7	39
Low	0	3	0	3	6
Total	12	12	11	10	45

* One naive subject inadequately completed the semantic-differential items, reducing n to 45 for all tables involving those items. Theoretical frequencies are too small to compute x^2.

Scale 2 consisted of the following items: tastefully dressed-poorly dressed, careless-careful, plain-good looking, and sloppy-neat, again not all worded in that order. The scale has a coefficient of reproducibility of .895 with minimum marginal reproducibility of .615. The basic dimension of this scale appears to be attractiveness with some implications of tidiness, hence the term attractiveness will be used. Dichotomizing into high and low attractiveness is based on the total distribution of scale types, encompassing naive subjects and stooge.

When attractiveness of the stooge is examined with respect to treatment, as seen in Table 19.6, further evidence of the success of the experimental variations is apparent. Although there is no relationship between attractiveness and confidence, the association between attractiveness and the neat-sloppy dimension is $Q = .89$ with a probability far less than .001. Clearly, attire made an observable difference to the naive subjects whether or not it was evident in the initial examination of ratings of stooge questions.

To proceed with the question of the relationship between the scales and the variables of question rating, ideas and liking, a joint-scale locus will be useful. The two scales provide the following types: competent-attractive, competent-unattractive, incompetent-attractive, and incompetent-unattractive. Of course the

TABLE 19.6. Scale 2 (Attractiveness) by Treatment: Stooge Only

Attractiveness	C-N	H-N	C-S	H-S	Total
High	10	11	4	2	27
Low	2	1	7	8	18
Total	12	12	11	10	45

x^2 (corrected) = 12.38; $p < 01$.

prefixes *in* and *un* are relative, not necessarily implying derogation. Due to the very few low-competence ratings, the last two categories contain only two and four entries respectively. Table 19.7 indicates the mean rating of stooge questions, as measured earlier (Table 19.1), by joint-scale type.

TABLE 19.7. Mean Rating, and Analysis of Variance, of Stooge Questions by Joint-Scale Type

Joint Type	Mean Rating	n
Competent-Attractive	.328	25
Competent-Unattractive	−.006	14
Incompetent-Attractive	−.275	2
Incompetent-Unattractive	−.753	4

Source	Sum of Squares	df	Mean Square
Between	4.6469	3	1.5490
Within	14.5282	41	.3543
Total	19.1751	44	—

F = 4.36; $p < 0$

It is quite clear that variation in joint-scale type results in different mean ratings of the stooge's questions. One important difference between Table 19.7 and Table 19.1 should be noted. Previously the effect of sloppy attire was to increase ratings when associated with confidence. The parallel case of unattractiveness, however, effectively decreases ratings regardless of the perceived competence. If the type of interpretation suggested earlier is correct, then there may be two contradictory social types, or perhaps stereotypes, operative here. One type suggests that sloppiness coupled with confidence denotes a somewhat asocial intellectual, perhaps a "beat." Sloppiness here implies a likelihood of better performance. The other contrasting type suggests that competence and attractiveness, both more general terms, tend to be coincident.[8] Sloppiness in this context would imply incompetence. The first social type is likely to be peculiar to a collegiate population, having little currency in the larger culture, while the second is presumably a more common phenomenon. Probably, therefore, the same experiment using non-college subjects would result in Table 19.1 being more in accord with Table 19.7.

The foregoing discussion suggests that lack of association between treatment and being best liked may be a result of counter-balancing effects. Since liking is related to ideas, it should occur that liking is related to perceived competence. Under one of the above hypothesized social types, however, competence is enhanced by sloppiness, while under the other type it is enhanced by neatness. Assuming that some of the naive subjects used one typological criterion and others used its opposite, the peculiar patterns in the data on liking would be understandable.

While it is not possible to determine typological concepts used by the subjects, it is possible to examine how each of the scales relates to the rankings on ideas and liking. Scale 1, as shown in Table 19.8, is strongly related to top rank on ideas. This result is, of course, to be expected. Of greater interest is the fact that competence and liking are also related, as suggested above. Apparently, if the stooge was perceived as competent, he was liked best approximately half the time; but in none of the six cases of perceived low competence was he ranked highest on liking. These data are precisely in accord with the relationship between liking and ideas shown in Table 19.4.

TABLE 19.8. Rank on Ideas and Liking by Competence: Stooge Only

	Rank on Ideas		Rank on Liking	
Competence	*1*	*2-4*	*1*	*2-3*
High	30	9	19	20
Low	1	5	0	6
	$Q = .89, p = .008.$		$Q = 1.00, p = .028.$	

8. Scales 1 and 2 show an association for all subjects of $Q = .58, p < .005$. For stooge only, $Q = .56$, but is not significant due to extreme marginals. It would seem that, even when experimental design has precluded an objective association of competence and attractiveness, they are perceived by the naive subjects as associated traits.

To complete the analysis, Table 19.9 presents the relationship of attractiveness to ranking on liking and ideas. In support of the above discussion of contradictory effects, attractiveness shows virtually no relationship to rank on ideas; but being best liked is associated with attractiveness. Again it should be remembered that the only difference underlying the attractiveness dimension is the change in clothing worn by the stooge. Yet this has a strong effect of the extent to which naive subjects liked him.

TABLE 19.9. *Rank on Ideas and Liking by Attractiveness: Stooge Only*

	Rank on Ideas		Rank on Liking	
Attractiveness	*1*	*2-4*	*1*	*2-3*
High	19	8	15	12
Low	12	6	4	14
		$Q=.09.$		$Q = .63; p = .027.$

DISCUSSION

It is apparent that variables which have no objective relationship either to the content of ideas contributed to the discussion or to properties of interaction which are normally assumed to underlie interpersonal attraction have affected (1) perception of performance, (2) perception of ideas contributed, and (3) perceived likeability. The fact that similar questions pertaining to ideas and to likeability constitute the basis for much of the leadership studies in small-group research means that serious questions need to be raised about just what is being measured in these studies. Assuming that both the present research and the large body of existing leadership studies are valid, what hypotheses can be advanced which will satisfy the data?

First, it is likely that much leadership choice among groups of strangers is based on superficial impressionistic evidence. That initial leadership is subject to later attack and potential upset has been noted previously by Heinicke and Bales.[9] Similarly, Newcomb[10] has demonstrated that initial friendships break up and re-form over time when more salient information about others becomes available.

9. C. Heinicke and R. F. Bales, "Developmental Trends in the Structure of Small Groups," *Sociometry*, 16 (February 1953), 7–38.
10. T. M. Newcomb, *The Acquaintance Process* (New York: Holt Rinehart and Winston, 1961).

Thus, the superficiality which this study suggests may underlie much early leadership could be expected to gradually give way to more stable, factual leadership. Studies of longer duration than the usual one-shot laboratory group are needed to examine such a process.

A second hypothesis is that the social types suggested earlier may have a degree of truth to them. If superficial traits of confidence and dress represent with some accuracy actual competence and potential likeability, then to assign leadership on the basis of these traits is a convenient and economical procedure. Leadership studies have noted some tendencies for demonstrated leaders to display such traits.[11]

Regardless of the validity of the above hypotheses, there is the important fact that instrumental leadership and expressive leadership, had they been assigned on the basis of the idea and likeability rankings from this study, would have overlapped to a considerable degree. The treatment of these facets of leadership as separate, generally being allocated to different individuals, is therefore questionable.[12] Recent studies in family groups have suggested that there is far less distinction between instrumental and expressive leadership in family interaction than earlier small-group research would indicate.[13] Perhaps the problems lies with the extent to which the group is primarily a task-oriented group versus being primarily oriented to interpersonal relationships. Specialized leadership is less relevant, and perhaps less workable, if specific tasks are subordinate to general interpersonal relations.

Fianlly, an observation relevant to experimental methodology is in order. As noted, the data presented in this paper strongly indicate that aspects of the stooge which were not related to the content of his behavior were nevertheless operative in his relationships with naive subjects. In retrospect, it may be tempting to say "of course, but any

11. For example, Zeleny found self-confidence a distinguishing trait of leaders, and Stogdill found appearance related to leadership. L. D. Zeleny, "Characteristics of Group Leaders," *Sociology and Social Research*, 24 (November 1939), 140–49; and R. M. Stogdill, "Personal Factors Associated with Leadership: A Survey of the Literature," *Journal of Psychology*, 25 (January 1948), 35–71.

12. See Bales' discussion of the Hypothesis of Two Complementary Leaders: R. F. Bales, "Task Roles and Social Roles in Problem Solving Groups," in Maccoby, *et al.*, *op. cit.*, pp. 437–47. Although an hypothesis of complementarity of leadership areas is theoretically valuable, there is good reason to be cautious about inferring the allocation of these areas to separate persons.

13. See R. K. Leik, "Instrumentality and Emotionality in Family Interaction," *Sociometry*, 26 (June 1963), 131–45; and G. Levinger, "Task and Social Behavior in Marriage," *Sociometry*,

competent experimenter would know this and guard against it."
Such an assertion is of doubtful validity. There is almost no concern
expressed in the various studies which have used stooges with any
guarantee or even any checks on non-content aspects of the stooge or
his behavior. An extreme case of unexpected stooge effects might be
discovered because of unexplainable patterns in the relationships
under study. More subtle effects, however, are likely to pass unnoticed, either augmenting or washing out otherwise moderate interrelationships of variables. As with other convenient but unexplored
techniques in research, the use of experimental stooges seems to
involve more faith than knowledge about the precise nature of the
introjected "controls."

PART EIGHT

The Social Survey: Uses and Problems

INTRODUCTION

THE SURVEY, in conjunction with the interview, statistical sampling models, and multivariate analysis, has become the favorite method of the sociologist. Unlike the recent research surrounding the experiment, however (as evidenced in the preceding part), few studies have been undertaken to uncover the problems inherent in the method, nor are there many studies aimed at improving its rigor.

Any research method must confront and solve a fundamental problem: It must permit valid causal analysis, and this in the face of the interactional contingencies inherent in its application. Thus the experiment, while permitting the most rigorous situation for causal analysis, is flawed because of the demand characteristics emanating from the experimenter.

Such is the case with the survey. Multivariate analysis as a strategy of analysis can be a powerful tool for uncovering causal relationships, yet the gathering of data via interviews or questionnaires opens the method to problems arising from respondent bias, interviewer effect, and the like. The papers in this part examine these two problems. Demming's article on errors in the survey presents a paradigm of potential problems that are present whenever a survey is executed. He notes 13 errors, ranging from poor, or leading questions, variations in sampling models, bias from the interviewer or respondent, and processing or coding errors to errors of causal interpretation.

Zeisel presents an informative comparison of cross-sectional and panel surveys. A panel design represents any survey situation where more than one interview is given to the same set of respondents at two different points in time. The advantages of this strategy are several. When events are followed over time, through reinterviewing or continuous observation, the problem of establishing time order and convariance between variables is greatly reduced. Similarly, the memory distortion surrounding past issues, or topics that are emotionally laden can be overcome through reinterviewing. Repeated interviews also yield more information from the respondent, which in turn permits a more clear-cut analysis of changes and shifts in opinion and action.

On the other hand, panel data suffer from two basic difficulties: mortality, or the differential loss of respondents from interview to interview, and reinterviewing bias. This latter factor again points to the demand characteristic effect of face-to-face observations. As Zeisel notes, the fact that one has been repeatedly interviewed can itself produce changes. (Susan Roth Sherman's findings — cited in the introduction to Part VII — within the experiment are relevant in this context.) Studies need to be conducted which indicate how respondents vary in their readiness to be influenced by an interviewer. Available data suggest that the attitudes of the interviewer as given off in his speech and style of dress can significantly shape a respondent's perspective. This is noted in Demming's article. As one test of this effect, Zeisel suggests the use of a control sample that is not reinterviewed.

Pelz and Andrews continue the examination of the panel method by offering methods for detecting causal relationships with such data. Their article offers a brief review of multivariate analysis, but focuses primarily on the method of correlational analysis.

Examples of this method are offered on a variety of data, and the methods limitations are presented. It is important to note that this system works with small numbers of variables. In a typical survey, many factors will be analyzed. This method would be repeated for each two-variable combination.

In general, this strategy reflects a commitment to "the variable analysis" approach earlier criticized by Blumer. Strict variable analysis often overlooks the problems inherent in the measurement process. That is, it quickly moves from measurement to analysis and does not focus on the problems surrounding the collection of data. Nor does the method fully consider situations where variables can not be easily quantified. These limitations must be kept in mind. Obviously, however, survey data have to be analyzed, and Pelz and Andrews present a causally sound method for such analysis.

A number of problems inherent in the survey are not treated here — these include the use of theoretical sampling, the construction of sequential analytic models, and the movement from aggregate, individual data to levels of social organization. For these, readings from previous sections warrant reexamination. Coleman's article (Part III) on adapting the survey to the study of social organization is of central relevance. Lipset, Trow, and Coleman's discussion of their methods of analysis in *Union Democracy* are also relevant in this context. Because the survey rests on some form of the interview, the readings in Part V are relevant here also. They point to many of the interactional contingencies inherent in the collection of survey data. It would also be useful to reread Hirschi and Selvin's critique (Part VI) of delinquency research.

Because the above sources constitute much of the core literature in the area of survey analysis, this part does not conclude with a list of suggested readings, but the student is encouraged to follow up the references given in the readings for this part.

20. On Errors in Surveys

W. EDWARDS DEMING

I. PURPOSE

There are thirteen different factors that affect the usefulness of surveys. The chief aim of this article is to point out the need for directing effort toward all of them when planning a survey, and the futility of concentrating on only one or two of them. Another aim is to point out the need for theories of bias and variability in response; such theories would correlate the vast amount of experience that is accumulating and would make comparability possible between different methods of collecting data. Biased methods could then be utilized in circumstances where they are more reliable and cheaper, just as biased samples are sometimes used for gains in reliability.

In the planning of a survey, effort should be directed toward the reduction of all of the errors that it is possible to reduce, but the effort should be apportioned with a view to producing the greatest possible usefulness with the funds available. As a matter of fact, consideration of all the errors that will effect the ultimate usefulness

Reprinted by permission from *American Sociological Review*, 19 (August 1944), pp. 359–369. Copyright 1944, American Sociological Association.

of a survey largely determines whether it should be taken at all; and then, when the decision is made to go ahead, the same considerations should form the basis of planning. Burden of response, public relations, and availability of personnel and facilities are also governing factors.

There will also be occasion in this article to point out

(a) That the errors arising from some of the factors are larger than is commonly supposed;

(b) The need for wider coverage and integrated research programs in the theoretical and empirical evaluations of some of the errors with the aim of (i) finding ways of reducing them; (ii) discovering the limitations that some of these errors place on the accuracy of a survey;

(c) That precisions sometimes specified in the administrative requirements of a proposed survey are altogether unnecessary, and owing to noncompensating errors and biases have not in the past been realized;

(d) That to eliminate sampling errors by taking a complete count will be a bad investment if other sources of error could be reduced and sufficient reliability attained at less cost;

(e) That there is a special responsibility in presenting the data of a survey to give an account of all the difficulties of response and collection, in order that errors of interpretation and utilization may be reduced.

II. CLASSIFICATION OF FACTORS AFFECTING THE ULTIMATE USEFULNESS OF A SURVEY

The thirteen factors referred to are not always distinguishable and there are other ways of classifying them, but the following list has been found useful.

1. Variability in response;
2. Differences between different kinds and degrees of canvass;
   (a) Mail, telephone, telegraph, direct interview;
   (b) Intensive vs. extensive interviews;
   (c) Long vs. short schedules;
   (d) Check block plan vs. response;
   (e) Correspondence panel and key reporters;
3. Bias and variation arising from the interviewer;
4. Bias of the auspices;
5. Imperfections in the design of the questionnaire and tabulation plans;

(a) Lack of clarity in definitions; ambiguity; varying meanings of same word to different groups of people; eliciting an answer liable to misinterpretation;

(b) Omitting questions that would be illuminating to the interpretation of other questions;

(c) Emotionally toned words; leading questions; limiting response to a pattern;

(d) Failing to perceive what tabulations would be most significant;

(e) Encouraging nonresponse through formidable appearance;

6. Changes that take place in the universe before tabulations are available;

7. Bias arising from nonresponse (including omissions);

8. Bias arising from late reports;

9. Bias arising from an unrepresentative selection of date for the survey, or of the period covered;

10. Bias arising from an unrepresentative selection of respondents;

11. Sampling errors and biases;

12. Processing errors (coding, editing, calculating, tabulating, tallying, posting and consolidating);

13. Errors in interpretation;

(a) Bias arising from bad curve fitting; wrong weighting; incorrect adjusting;

(b) Misunderstanding the questionnaire; failure to take account of the respondents' difficulties (often through inadequate presentation of data); misunderstanding the method of collection and the nature of the data;

(c) Personal bias in interpretation.

The foregoing factors will be ranked in importance one way for one type of survey and another way for another type. Thus, in a survey asking farmers their intentions to plant a certain crop next spring, the date of the survey would be especially important. For a survey of farm income the definition of farm income might easily be the most important factor.

Kendall[1] in a recent paper has stated that respondent bias and questionnaire construction are outstanding problems toward which statistical research must be directed. We ought to find out for example whether estimates of crops always tend to over-estimate low yields and under-estimate high ones, and how much. We ought to

1. M. G. Kendall, "On the Future of Statistics," *Journal of the Royal Statistical Society* CV (1942), 69–91. See pp. 74 and 85 in particular.

know the relation between snap judgments and considered judgments, and between long and short questionnaires, and different plans of interview and follow-up. Many biased methods of eliciting information are cheaper and quicker and show smaller variability than so-called unbiased methods. If the relation between biased and unbiased results were known (predictable), the biased techniques would sometimes be preferable. There is need for workable theories of bias and variability in response just as much as there ever was need for theories of sampling bias and sampling errors. A considerable amount of brilliant work has been done, but some of the best of it remains unpublished and uncoordinated. Scattered measurements of bias and variability here and there are not enough. A thorough-going plan of theoretical and experimental investigation into the nature of bias and variability in response is needed. It should include research into the bias of nonresponse, various ways of constructing questionnaires and writing instructions to respondent and interviewer, selection and training of personnel for interviewing. Such a program would pay dividends in money, not to speak of dividends in scientific self-respect of the statistician. A great deal has already been done, of course, an example being the research reported by Jessen[2] in the line of memory bias, and an outstanding summary by Gladys L. Palmer[3] on differential response in labor-market inquiries. Certain other good examples are cited in Part II, although the aim of this article is not to present a bibliography nor a compendium of experimental results.

The attainment of greater economy and reliability through studies of bias and variability of response will open up new realms of usefulness for the statistician jointly with his colleagues in sociology, marketing, and political science.

III. REMARKS ON THE VARIOUS FACTORS[4]

1. *Variability in Response.* There are two kinds of variability in response, different descriptions of the same situation (i) given by the same person at two different times, (ii) given by different persons. Both kinds of error are often much greater than is ordinarily supposed, and both can be controlled to some extent by the drafting of

2. Raymond J. Jessen, "Statistical Investigation of a Sample Survey for Obtaining Farm Facts," *Research Bulletin*, 304, Agriculture Experiment Station, Ames (June 1942), 27–32 in particular.

3. Gladys L. Palmer, "The Reliability of Response in Labor Market Inquiries," *Technical paper No. 22* (Bureau of the Budget, Washington, July 1942).

4. For convenience, the sections in Part III will be numbered to correspond with the enumeration of factors in Part II.

the questionnaire and the training of the interviewers. In a continuing survey the cooperation and education of the respondent may often be fostered so as to decrease the first type. However, it must be recognized that respondents under repeated questioning often change their characteristics.

It might be thought that factual data such as age could be collected with little error, and that only data with looser definition such as employment status and education are subject to wide variation. An extensive study carried out by Gladys L. Palmer,[5] however, shows that variation in response is indeed large in all these characteristics, and that age is certainly no exception. Yet what property could be more objective? In a recanvass of 8,500 people in Philadelphia, after an interval of only eight to 10 days, 10 percent of the ages were different by one year or more when reported by the same respondent in both canvasses (an example of the first kind of variability), and 17 percent of the ages were different by one year or more when reported by different respondents (an example of the second kind of variability).

Another example of the second kind of variability in response is furnished by Katherine D. Wood[6] who exhibited tables showing the discrepancies between duplicate reports of the occupations of 4500 workers, one report coming from the worker himself or some member of the household, and the other report coming from the worker's employer. Table I in her article shows that when the occupations are broken into only nine major occupational groups, 21.7 percent of the total number of duplicate reports are in disagreement—i.e., fall in a different one of the nine broad groups. Her Table 2 shows that when the classification of occupations is broken down into 233 groups, the difference jumps to 35.5 percent. It would be useful to understand the mechanism by which such variability operates, so that the approximate magnitude of the discrepancies could be allowed for in the interpretation of surveys on occupations.

It should be pointed out that the net effect of variability in reporting is not always as bad as might be surmised. One reason is that many errors can be caught in a careful job of editing. For instance, in processing the reports on the annual production of lumber which are sent into the Census from sawmills, every effort is made to diminish the net effect of variability and carelessness in response. Each report

5. Gladys L. Palmer, "Factors in the Variability of Response in Enumerative Studies," *Journal of the American Statistical Association*, 38 (1943), 143–52.

6. Katherine D. Wood, "The Statistical Adequacy of Employers' Occupational Records," *Social Security Bulletin*, 2 (May 1939), 21–24.

is carefully compared with the previous annual report from that mill. To expert editors who know the lumber business, the respondent's difficulty and the consequent correction of an erroneous report are often obvious. When not obvious, the case may be turned over to the Forest Service which in turn may initiate correspondence or send a local representative to the mill to discover what difficulty if any exists. A second reason is that the poorest reporting on production and sales often occurs in the small establishments, which all told contribute only a small fraction of the total of the annual production or sales. The larger establishments keep records and can make better reports. For a third reason there is an element of randomness in reporting dictated by the accident of circumstance. The weather, time of day, the particular person providing the information, the route followed by the interviewer, and many other factors are accidental in nature and affect the results. As a result, some reports (of age, number of board-feet of wood cut, sales, and stocks) are accidentally higher and others are accidentally lower than they might have been under other circumstances. This random element is compensating on a probability basis, the net effect being, that the final tabulations may portray distributions that are reasonably independent of the random element of variability and able to serve many useful purposes. Random errors have less chance of cancelling each other if the tabulations are made in fine classes.

It is a mistake, however, to take refuge in the assumption that errors in response are going to cancel each other, and thus to excuse poorly designed questionnaires and inexpert interviewing. Too often the responses possess not merely a random element, but a bias as well. The random element may wash out, but a bias is different; it is not necessarily partially or wholly compensated by another bias in the opposite direction. For instance, in spite of variability in the reporting of age, frequencies showing characteristics of the population by age will usually turn out to be remarkably independent of the random errors in reporting, but will clearly show the downward and upward heaping toward the fives and tens. Likewise, the random errors that occur in taking inventories of canned peas in a number of grocery stores may pretty well cancel each other, leaving only the effect of (a) the downward bias that arises from failures to look in the basement or out-of-the-way places for peas, and (b) the downward or upward bias that arises from the natural tendency to undercount or overcount, whichever it may be.

In view of errors in response, not to speak of the other factors that affect the usefulness of a survey, it is obvious that a complete coverage can not give absolute accuracy. As a matter of fact, absolute accuracy is nondefinable and must be replaced by something else. A useful and practical replacement arises from the fact that repeated surveys, whether taken by sample or complete count, will not give identical results for any category, but varying results. In place of the mythical term "absolute accuracy" it is profitable to speak of the tolerance band within which 99 percent of the results for a particular category (age by sex class) are expected to fall by random variation in repeated surveys. The limits that are allowable will depend on the funds available and the requirements of precision which are dictated by the uses that are to be made of the data.

In this connection I am reminded of a conversation with Mr. Frederick F. Stephan. He was once asked how big a sample would be required to measure within 5 percent the extent of unemployment in the country. This was in 1934 when plans for a sample census of unemployment were being considered. His reply was that even a 100 percent sample could not give 5 percent accuracy because of differing ideas regarding definitions of unemployment and the interpretation of the questions. Even with the elimination of sampling errors, there would remain unsettled differences between various alternative definitions of unemployment. There would remain, moreover, errors of enumeration (variability in response; housewife doesn't know the answer but answers anyhow; some families missed; some refuse; etc.). Before it is profitable to talk of reducing sampling errors to 5 percent, it is necessary to reduce both the variability in response (by sharpening the definition) and the error of enumeration to magnitudes comparable with 5 percent accuracy.

2. *Differences Between Different Kinds and Degrees of Canvass.* Too little is known in regard to the differences in results obtained from mail, telephone, telegraph, and interview canvasses, or the results obtained from different plans of questionnaire.[7] The problem is not whether differences exist but how great are the differences, and why do they exist, and what effect will they have on the uses that are made of the data? Theory and more extensive empirical evaluations are needed so that comparability can be obtained between different methods, and so that the cheaper methods may have greater utility.

3. *Bias and Variation Arising from the Interviewer.* In 1914 Rice[8]

7. It is important not to confuse (a) the differences in response elicited from different kinds and degrees of canvass, with (b) the different proportions of response that will be obtained.

8. Stuart A. Rice, "Contagious bias in the interview, "*American Journal of Sociology,*" vol. 35 (1929), pp. 420–23.

in a social study of 2000 destitute men found that the reasons given by them for being down and out carried a strong flavor of the interviewer. Results recorded by a prohibitionist showed a strong tendency for the men that he interviewed to ascribe their sorry existence to drink; those interviewed by a man with socialist learnings showed a strong tendency to blame their plight on industrial causes. Quantitative measures of the interviewer bias in this particular survey turned out to be amazingly large. The men may have been glad to please anyone that showed an interest in them.

Variation attributable to the interviewer arises from many factors: the political, religious, and social beliefs of the interviewer; his economic status, environment, and education. Also, perhaps most interviewers can not help being swayed in the direction of their employers' interests. But how much? What is the effect on the tabulations? Different interviewers will record different descriptions of the same situation and will record different interpretations to identical statements from a respondent. When is a house in need of major repairs? The definitions given to the enumerators in the Census were as definite as possible, yet variability in interpretation must be expected. One interviewer will say yes, and another will say no for the same house. Nevertheless the tabulations of the returns from many interviewers concerning many houses may be satisfactory owing to compensation. Certainly such figures as those produced by the 1940 Census of Housing are valuable in indicating the variation around locally accepted norms.

One source of bias and variability arising from the interviewer has its roots in lack of understanding of the subject and purpose under investigation, without which the interviewer can not evaluate a situation or properly record the respondent's statements.

Part of the variation attributable to the interviewer arises from the different moods into which different interviewers cast their respondents. The interviewer may make the respondent gay or despairing, garrulous or clammish. Some interviewers unconsciously cause respondents to take sides with them, some against them. This kind of variability is difficult to distinguish from the error of response.

A small corps of interviewers can be trained to a high level of homogeneity; hence in sample surveys and other partial coverages it is possible to diminish differences between interviewers to a degree not attainable in large scale surveys. In particular, partial coverages repeated at intervals may possess an enchanced degree of comparability from one survey to another.

Training will sometimes introduce biases in a corps of interviewers, depending on how they are trained. A corps of enumerators with less training and greater variability might come nearer to finding out what a social scientist really wishes to know about. Bias produced by training partakes of bias of the auspices (q.v.), and it is sometimes difficult to make the distinction.

4. *Bias of the Auspices.* Any change in the method of collecting or processing data can be expected to show a change in results. A shift in the sponsoring organization is no exception. Bias of the auspices likely stems from a conscious or unconscious desire on the part of the respondent to take sides for or against the organization sponsoring the survey, but perhaps more to protect his own interests which may vary with the sponsoring agency. Everyone supposes, for instance, that the replies concerning income and work status are different, on the whole, when elicited by an agent of a relief organization than when elicited by a government agency such as the Census, but evidence regarding the exact magnitude of such differences is still far from satisfactory. Bias of the auspices is so well recognized that both government and private organizations have sometimes attempted to hide their identities by contracting and subcontracting the collection of the data, so that the respondents would be unaware of the sponsoring agency.

As integrated research program designed to give empirical evaluations of this bias in many fields of enquiry and under a variety of conditions is needed for aid in planning and interpreting data.

5. *Imperfections in the Design of the Questionnaire and Tabulation Plans.* Faulty design of the questionnaire can be the cause of considerable bias. Faulty design often arises from lack of knowledge of the subject matter. It is not sufficient merely to elicit answers to questions somehow or other related to the subject. The questions must attack the root of the problem by discovering what are the significant underlying causes (geographic location, economic level, size of family, size of establishment, and the like) so that these causes can be differentiated, qualified, and related to particular classes of the universe. Without some pretty good idea what the analysis is going to show it will be impossible to design the questionnaire so that any useful proportion of these aims will be accomplished. An understanding of the subject is accordingly demanded as one of the qualifications for planning a survey.

Likewise the tabulation program (which really should precede the questionnaire but usually does not) demands enough knowledge of the problem to see what tables are going to be needed and which ones will be significant.

6. *Changes That Take Place in the Universe Before Tabulations Are*

Available. The conditions that are described by a survey may have changed by the time the tabulations are ready for processing. These changes detract from the utility of the survey. The complete count requires a longer time than a sample for processing — so much longer, in fact, that often because of changes in conditions, it is merely a historical record by the time it is ready. As a basis for action (the only excuse for taking a survey) a sample or a "cut-off" (section 10) will therefore often be more reliable because of the shorter collecting and processing time.

7. *Bias Arising from Nonresponse (Including Omissions).* Nonresponses and omissions may cause serious bias unless they are too few to cause trouble, or unless the user can readjust his weights after demonstrating that acceptable limits to the bias arising from the nonresponses from various strata can be set without special investigation. A partial coverage offers advantages here also. The follow-up can start sooner, and more expensive and more effective methods can be used, such as telegrams, individual letters, or even personal interviews. Whether a partial coverage or a complete count is used, the bias of the nonresponses if not known should be measured by a small program of interviews, specially designed to measure the differences between the people or establishments that respond and those that do not. A distinct advance in survey technique has been made by my colleagues Messrs. Hansen and Hurwitz in the Census by determining the optimum number of questionnaires to be mailed initially, and the optimum amount of follow-up of nonresponse to be carried out by direct interview for a given allowable cost. The solution will be published eventually, but it has already been written up for use in the 1943 coverage of lumber production (a joint undertaking between the Census, the Forest Service, and the Tennessee Valley Authority).

The volume of nonresponse is often unnecessarily large owing to formidable appearance of the questionnaire. The volume of nonresponse in some subjects is a strong function of the date on which the questionnaire is received, and the date the follow-up letter is received. No attempt can be made here to summarize points of good practice in questionnaire format and timing. A great deal of research has been published, and still more has been done but not yet published.

It is not sufficiently appreciated that a 70 percent response on a complete coverage may yield data that are unusable, whereas a smaller bundle of returns representing 95 percent response on a 10 percent sample may yield results of great reliability. In other words, a carefully controlled small sample may be far preferable to a careless complete count.

8. *Bias Arising from Late Reports.* In any survey, the office processing of the data must commence on a certain date. Reports coming in after the deadline can not be included in the tabulations. The reports received late may be biased. How much? As with the nonresponses, a sample study may answer the question adequately. Again, a partial coverage offers advantages over a complete count in the control of late reports because effective pressure can be exerted to decrease them.

At first sight it may seem that the nonresponses and omissions must be cousins-german of the late reports, and that both present the same problems. There are differences, however, arising in the causes, among which carelessness and press of other work are common factors. In addition, however, nonresponse and omission are often caused by inability or unwillingness to furnish the data required.

9. *Bias Arising from an Unrepresentative Selection of Date for the Survey, or of the Period Covered.* A single-time coverage of weekly household purchases would hardly be representative during any week in December. A passenger-traffic survey would not be representative near the 4th of July or Labor Day, unless the peak load is to be measured. The choice of date is often a difficult problem, especially when a survey must serve several purposes. One purpose is often served best by one date, and another purpose best by some other date; and one or both must take a loss when both purposes are covered in one survey. Then, too, the urgency of the information often forces a compromise: Rather than wait for the most advantageous week in the year it may be wiser from the standpoint of framing a course of action in the immediate future to take the survey at once. Sometimes the seasonal correction is known satisfactorily, in which case data taken at an unrepresentative date can be corrected. During rapid changes the answer may lie in recurring surveys, monthly or quarterly. The dangers of selecting an unrepresentative date are recognized pretty generally, with the result that biases arising from this source are controlled much better than most of the other factors on the list.

10. *Bias Arising from an Unrepresentative Selection of Respondents.* The definition of the universe to be covered in the survey goes hand in hand with the statement of the purpose of the survey. Unfortunately, however, the universe is sometimes elusive. Too frequently no accurate and up-to-date list is available by which the

universe can be covered completely or sampled satisfactorily. Various schemes of partial coverage are then often devised, with the hazard of dangerous biases. If there is time, a preliminary survey can be taken to establish a sample list and remove the bias.

Even when a complete list is available, a short-cut to some of the advantages of sampling is often taken by covering only the most important portion of the universe by a plan called the "cut-off,"which is accomplished by including only the biggest establishments and "cutting off" the myriads of small ones that all totogether contribute possibly only 5 or 10 percent of the actual business or inventory that is to be studied. This plan gives a picture of the main part of the business but is biased to an unknown extent by the omission of the smaller establishments, often by misassignment of weights, and also by the changing proportion of large establishments with time. The "cut-off plan bears resemblance to sampling by giving heavy representation to the biggest establishments and light representation to the smallest ones, but a sample does not go so far as to cut the small ones out entirely; it gives them the proper representation for maximum reliability by drawing a small percentage of them into the sample. Of course, if the list is badly incomplete at the lower end, or if the reporting at the lower end is bad,[9] the "cut-off" is perhaps as near an approach to sampling as can be devised, or may be even better until more is known about the bias in the reporting at the lower end.

A less satisfactory partial coverage is the "invitation questionnaire," which is obtained by the familiar device used by some business houses (restaurants, air lines, department stores) when they provide their patrons with simple check-box questionnaires enquiring whether this or that item or service is satisfactory, why they bought what they bought, and why they bought it here. The returns show only the extremes in satisfaction and vexation, and at that only from the articulate. Such devices do serve some useful if limited purposes, but if interpreted as representative the results may be disastrous. A small investment in even a very small sample, even though taken at a much higher cost per schedule, will give information really worth while by comparison. The "invitation questionnaire" is justified only in attempts to discover the possible range of response.

It may be interesting to note that in a partial coverage of this kind there will be not only heavy biases present, but also the much lighter

9. Cf. the quotation form the *Production of Lumber* cited in Part V; particularly the sentence, "Among the smaller mills. . . ."

chance errors of sampling, for it is through the vagaries of chance that a well satisfied or sorely vexed customer fills in a questionnaire or fails to do so. Some acquaintance coming along at a crucial moment, or the realization that it is almost 2 o'clock, will sidetrack the intention to fill out a questionnaire; while some accidental irritation will induce him to go ahead and fill it out and voice complaints, as he was half-way in the mood to do anyhow.

An unrepesentative choice of respondents often arises as a matter of convenience to the interviewer. He has perhaps been told to talk to 10 people in some age and economic group, so he talks to 10 people close to home who will submit to an interview and in filling his quota introduces a respondent bias that may take on considerable magnitude. It can be eliminated by adopting inflexible rules for selecting the respondents. Such rules may take the form of specific addresses, with designation of a particular member of the family to be interviewed. The same purpose is served by specifying the block and some rule for picking out certain households within it for the interviewers.

11. *Sampling Errors and Biases.* One often hears objections to sampling because of sampling errors. Such objections can be sustained only if, after consideration of the other inaccuracies, the elimination of sampling errors seems to be a wise investment. Sampling errors have the favorable characteristics of being controllable through the size and design of the sample. It is now possible to lay out sample designs in many types of surveys whereby one can state in advance the width of a band that will contain 99 percent or any other percent of the sampling errors. Sampling errors, even for small samples, are often the least of the errors present.

The next step in the direction of greater reliability of surveys must lie along the line of further research like that called for in Part II. At present, sampling errors are the only errors that are in satisfactory condition so far as theoretical and experimental knowledge is concerned.

12. *Processing Errors.* A review of the codes assigned on a schedule is oftentimes not a matter of correcting wrong codes, but merely a matter of honest differences of opinion between coder and reviewer. Two coders will often find themselves in disagreement on the correct codes to assign to a response. Two coders working on the same set of schedules are going to turn out two different sets of results; likewise two sections of coders working on the same set of schedules are going to turn out two different sets of results. A *fortiori*, two sections of coders working under slightly different instructions will

show still greater differences, even though the two sets of instructions supposedly say the same thing in different words. The two sets of results may however produce distributions so nearly alike that in most problems they would lead to the same action, and that is what counts. Research needs to be carried out to show the extent of the differences to be expected from various shades of wording of instructions for coding, editing, and field work. The conclusion seems inevitable that unless it is merely a matter of transcription (such as 1 for male and 2 for female) it is impossible to define a perfect job of coding except in terms of the distributions produced because there is no way of determining whether the individual codes have been assigned correctly. One can only say that two different sets of instructions or two differents sets of coders produced substantially the same distributions. In view of this fact it seems to follow that when the work of a coder or editor or punch operator is uniformly good enough so that his errors are relatively insignificant compared with the other errors (such as variability of response) it is only necessary to perform enough review of his work (preferably by sampling methods) to be assured of the continuity of control.[10] Workers who can not qualify for sample review should be transferred.

Machine and tally errors are often supposed to be negligible or nonexistent but the actual situation is otherwise. These errors can be held at a reasonable minimum, however, by machine controls and other checks, especially with a force of workers in which there are a few key people with seasoned experience.

A sample study or other partial coverage possesses a distinct advantage in the processing for the same reason that it does in the interviewing, viz., the smaller force required to do the work, and the consequent better control that is possible.

13. *Errors in Interpretation.* In any study made for the analysis of causes, preliminary to formulating a course of action for the future, there must be inferences drawn from empirical data. There are bound to be errors of inference, arising from difficulties of interpretation. A familiar example is the picture of a labor situation presented by management, as opposed to the picture presented by labor organizations.

10. Two reports dealing with a small amount of research in the frequency of punching errors and the sample review of office processing are contained in papers by the author and colleagues: (1) W. Edwards Deming, Leon Geoffrey, and Benjamin J. Tepping, "On Errors in Card Punching," *Journal of the American Statistical Association*, vol. 37, pp. 525–35; (2) W. Edwards Deming and Leon Geoffrey "On Sample Inspection in the Processing of Census Returns," *Journal of the American Statistical Association*, vol. 36, pp. 351–60.

Errors and differences in interpretation sometimes arise from misunderstanding the questionnaire or failure to take into consideration the form of the questions as written on it or as actually used in the interview. Without some recognition of the problems involved in carrying out the survey both from the standpoint of the collecting agency and the respondent, sizeable errors in interpretation are almost sure to arise. The more important the survey, the more important are the errors of interpretation. For careful interpretation it is necessary to be acquainted with the field work; not just with the instructions which tell how the field work should have been carried out, but with the procedure as actually followed. (See the quotation from *The Production of Lumber* farther on.)

Even with the best of intentions there will be a personal and professional bias in interpretation. This fact is so well known that it would be superfluous to go into the subject here or to point out the magnitude of the differences that can exist purely on the grounds of personal differences in education, experience, and environment.

IV. A WORD ON SAMPLE STUDIES OF
COMPLETE RETURNS

There often arises the problem of selecting a sample of reports from files of complete returns, which might be waybills, tax forms, census returns, wage reports, hospital records, relief records, consumers' accounts, or the like. There is sometimes reluctance to adopt sampling methods because of a commendable pride in traditional accuracy. But let us look at the problem in its entirety and see just how far this accuracy goes. If the study were purely for accounting purposes, a complete count with an attempt at perfect processing would be justified or even demanded. It should be borne in mind that the purpose is not accounting, however, unless the action to be taken is with respect to each respondent by reason of the data on his response; an income tax report is an example. Most studies are for purposes of analysis, wherein the ultimate aim is policy and action for the future, not the past. For purposes of analysis, even though the office work such as coding, editing, transcribing, and tabulation were 100 percent perfect there would still remain the errors of response, the bias of nonresponse, late reports, imperfections arising in the tabluation plans, bias from an unrepresentative date, changes taking place in the universe before tabulations become available, and errors of interpretation. No 100 percent perfect job of processing a study of waybills, wage reports, or other kinds of returns can eliminate these errors.

V. DESCRIPTION OF ERRORS AND DIFFICULTIES
REQUIRED IN PRESENTATION OF DATA[11]

In the presentation of data the omission of an adequate discussion of all the errors present and the difficulties encountered constitutes a serious defect in the data and is sure to lead to misinterpretation and misuse (error No. 13). It is common in a sample study to point out the sampling errors, as should always be done. There are several ways of doing this. The paragraph below appears in many of the reports published from the *Sixteenth Census* (1940) on the basis of the 5 percent sample.

> The statistics based on the sample tabulations are expected to differ somewhat from those which would have been obtained from a complete count of the population. An analysis of the statistics based on the tabulations of the 5 percent sample of the population for items that were obtained also for the total population indicates that in 95 percent of the cases the sample statistics differ from the complete census statistics by less than 5 percent of all numbers of 10,000 or more, by less than 10 percent for numbers between 5,000 and 10,000 and by less than 20 percent for numbers between 2,000 and 5,000. Somewhat larger variation may be expected in numbers below 2,000. Even for these small numbers, however, the majority of the differences between the sample and the complete census statistics are less than 10 percent, although much larger differences occasionally occur.

The statement of a standard deviation or probable error or band of variation in the form of a plus and minus (e.g. 1123 ± 42), along with *the number of independent sampling units* on which the calculation is based, is a common way of calling attention to the sampling errors.

Unfortunately there is no simple way of indicating the possible magnitudes of the other errors, but it can be done in one way or another. As an example it is a pleasure to cite a few lines from the *Production of Lumber, by States and by Species;* 1942 (Bureau of the Census, November 1943), published under the direction of Mr. Maxwell R. Conklin, Chief of the Industry Division.

> These statistics are based on a mail canvass, supplemented by a field enumeration conducted by the U. S. Forest Service and the Tennessee Valley Authority. In the field enumeration, Forest Service and TVA representatives interviewed mills that did not respond to the mail canvass, and, in addition, conducted an intensive search for mills.... Among the smaller mills, bookkeeping is generally inadequate. Even the total cut for a mill may be an estimate, and the species breakdown

11. Chapter III in Shewhart's *Statistical Method from the Viewpoint of Quality Control* (Gradiste School, Department of Agriculture, Washington, 1939) should be read in connection with these remarks.

for such a mill, particularly in areas of diversified growth, must frequently be estimated by the mill operator or by the enumerator. . . . Difficulties in enumeration because of lack of adequate mill records were overcome in many cases where the mill disposed of its total cut through a concentration yard. In such instances enumerators were able to obtain information for individual mills from the yard operator, particularly in the South and Southeast where concentration yards are an important factor in the distribution of lumber. This approach was not satisfactory, however, when an operator sold his lumber to several different yards in the course of the year, and where the records at the concentration yard did not indicate clearly whether the cut was for 1942 or 1941. . . . Mills engaged solely in remanufacturing, finishing, or otherwise processing lumber were excluded. . . . In a number of cases, the mill reports were in terms of dressed or processed lumber, since many integrated mills, i.e., those both sawing and dressing, were able to report only on a finished basis. The discrepancy, which is of unknown magnitude, is equivalent to the amount of waste in processing. In canvassing integrated mills, however, the cut was counted at only one point in the processing operation, so that no duplication occurred. . . . An ever-present complicating factor in the canvass was the extreme mobility of the smaller mills. . . .

VI. USEFUL ACCURACY OFTEN ATTAINABLE IN SPITE OF ERRORS

It is not to be inferred from the foregoing material that there are grounds for discouragement or that the situation is entirely hopeless with regard to the attainment of useful accuracy. My point is that the accuracy supposedly required of a proposed survey is frequently exaggerated — is in fact often unattainable — yet the survey when completed turns out to be useful in the sense of helping to provide a rational basis for action. Why? Because both the accuracy and the need for accuracy were overestimated.

Fortunately the errors in a survey are not always additive, as has been pointed out. It should also be remembered that often it is ratios between frequencies that are of interest and not the absolute values of the frequencies themselves. Many of the biases cancel out of the ratios, which are thus determined much more accurately than the absolute frequencies. Similar remarks apply to comparability between results obtained in recurring surveys; the pattern of month to month change is more accurately determined percentagewise than the absolute values of the frequencies involved.

There is no excuse for complacency in the fact that exaggerated claims of accuracy are often compensated by exaggerated requirements of accuracy.

VII. SAMPLING IN THE GOVERNMENT SERVICE

In the government service there must be special insistence that a survey, if it is to be carried out at all, produce the greatest possible usefulness for the money expended. The increased use of sampling in government service seen in recent years is in accordance with these demands. The same consideration also demands that sampling facilities operated by and for government agencies be constructed along lines that will minimize not only the errors of sampling but also (in particular) the bias in the selection of respondents. The development of sampling theory for government surveys must continue to keep pace with government requirements of economy and reliability. An obligate symbiotic relationship is necessary in the development of theory and practice, and the government service provides practice on a large enough scale, both in magnitude and variety, to give proper nourishment to the required theory. Private industry and research organizations are of course not bound to the same obligations.

In conclusion it is a pleasure to express appreciation to many friends for helpful suggestions, in particular my colleague Dr. Margaret Gurney of the Bureau of the Budget.

21. The Panel

HANS ZEISEL

MOST of the data that come into the office of the survey analyst are
based on one interview with each member of a group of people. But
sometimes one interview is not enough. It is of great advantage in
many studies, to interview people more than one time.

Various individuals may be asked what soap they are using for
washing dishes; six months later the same question may be asked of
them again. Several months before an election, people may be interviewed about their political views and how they intend to vote; two
months later they may be interviewed again, and the day before the
election a third time.

When interviews are obtained in this way from the same group of
people on two or more occasions, we call the group involved a panel.

From pp. 215–219, "The Panel," in *Say It with Figures*, Rev. 4th Ed., by Hans
Zeisel. Copyright © 1957 by Harper & Row, Publishers, Incorporated. By permission
of the author and publishers.

[Here] we want to discuss the technique of the panel, how it is handled and what it is good for.[1]

PANEL VERSUS MEMORY

Attempts are frequently made to obtain information involving facts or experiences during the course of time from a single contact with the respondent. Such questions as, "For whom did you intend to vote four months ago?" or "Have you recently made a change in the soap you use?" may be asked. But experience shows that such questions are very often unsatisfactory. The memory of the respondents may be inadequate for the question, it may be deceptive, or both.

The panel technique of repeated interviews with the same respondents, however, is not needed if the event or opinion to be traced is easily remembered, or if the time lapse involved is comparatively short. For example, most people can easily remember which make of automobile they bought before their present one. Yet, for such items as cereals or passing opinions, people may find it difficult to recall accurately what they bought or felt as short ago as one week. And certainly no one could give from memory an accurate record of small expenditures over a greater period of time.

Through the use of the panel technique, the doubtful validity of such questions as, "How long have you been using this brand?" etc., is replaced by objective records of actual purchases.[2]

Memory is deceptive when there are conscious or unconscious desires of the respondent to distort the past. It is well known, for example, that the question, "For whom did you vote?" asked one day after election will result in a surprisingly low figure for the loser, because people like to claim that they voted for the winner.

The projection of answers into the future is no more reliable. The question, "Will you sell your car within the next six months?" can never mean more than "Do you (now) think that you will sell your car . . . etc.?"

The panel is thus undoubtedly a superior tool when we study attitudes or behavior habits that extend over a period of time.

1. The first systematic presentation of this technique was published in 1938: Paul F. Lazarsfeld and Marjorie Fiske, "The Panel as a New Tool for Measuring Opinion," *Public Opinion Quarterly*, vol. 2, no. 4, pp. 596–612. Ever since that time the Bureau of Applied Social Research at Columbia University has led the field in the development and refinement of the panel technique.

2. Alfred R. Root and Alfred C. Welch, "The Continuing Consumer Study: A Basic Method for the Engineering of Advertising," *Journal of Marketing*, VII (July 1942), p. 7.

PANEL VERSUS REPEATED CROSS-SECTIONS

Trends are sometimes studied by means of repeated interviews, but often a new group of respondents is interviewed each time the investigator goes back into the field. The best known examples of such repeated surveys are the public opinion polls of Gallup and Roper. But here again, there are a number of important advantages in the use of the panel, that is, in the re-interviewing of the respondents who were originally interviewed. The following is a brief synopsis of these advantages. . . . :

1. RECORDING CHANGES

Cross-Sections

In comparing, for example, the "Proportion of users of XX-soap" at two different periods, one obtains the difference in the total proportion of users at each interview: the net change.

Panel

In addition to the net change, one obtains an accurate picture of the number and the direction of individual shifts which, when added together, account for the "net change."

2. REASONS FOR OBSERVED CHANGES

Cross-Sections

Whether or not, for instance, a certain type of propaganda has influenced a person's political attitude, is difficult to ask and to answer.

Panel

By analyzing separately those who were exposed to a certain piece of propaganda and those who were not, the panel can ascertain whether the number and the direction of attitude changes are different for the two groups.

3. AMOUNT OF COLLECTED INFORMATION

Cross-Sections

Since the respondents differ from survey to survey, one does not know more about each one respondent than what can be gathered in any one interview.

Panel

Repeated interviews with the same respondents yield an ever increasing amount of information. In a three interview panel study we can get "2 or 3 hours worth" of information about each member of our panel.

4. DATA REFERRING TO TIME PERIODS

Cross-Sections

One-interview surveys will yield accurate results if the question refers to the time *instrant* at which the interview takes place. If the respondent is to recall events which extend over a time *period* one must rely on memory. Such data are most always required if certain research concepts are to be defined:

If we want to find out a person's "reading habits" or whether he is a "regular listener" to a certain radio program, we must rely entirely on the respondent's memory and judgment.

Panel

Only through the panel can one avoid reliance on the respondent's memory, if one aims at data which refer to an extended period of time. Repeated interviews yield objective data on the consistency and fluctuations of habits and attitudes. Such distinctions as that of "regular" vs. "non-regular" listener can be made with accuracy and reliability.

5. RELIABILITY OF RESULTS

Cross-Sections

The statistical significance of observed changes from survey to survey depends upon the size and the structure of the particular sample.

Panel

In most cases an observed change in a panel will be a higher statistical significance than a change of equal size observed in repeated cross-sections that equal the panel in size and structure.

In brief outline these five points mark out the realm of the panel's superiority over consecutive samples, which are independent of each other. But there are two basic difficulties inherent in the panel technique: the mortality of the sample, and the bias of repeated interviews.

(1) *Mortality* is the loss of panel members due to the difficulty of reaching the same person for two or more contacts, or due to the refusal of their continuous co-operation. Since different sections of the panel may show a different mortality rate, there arises some danger of a biased sample.

(2) *Re-Interviewing Bias* is the effect of repeated discussions on certain topics on the respondent's behavior or attitude towards these very topics. Thus, the fact of being repeatedly interviewed may in itself induce changes of opinion habits.

22. Detecting Causal Priorities in Panel Study Data

DONALD C. PELZ AND FRANK M. ANDREWS

A GOAL of much scientific research is to identify variables which, when they change themselves, influence other variables. Such influences among variables may be called "causal relationships."

Numerous philosophical difficulties are involved in a formal definition of "cause." Suffice it to note, as do Simon[1] and Blalock,[2] that "the really essential aspect of a causal relationship is that it is asymmetrical in nature...."[3]

When data derive not from experiments but from surveys or other observations of an ongoing system, one can readily determine whether two variables A and B are related, but to determine the direction of causation (if any) is difficult.

Reprinted by permission from *American Sociological Review*, 29 (December 1964), pp. 836–48. Copyright 1964, American Sociological Association.

1. Herbert A. Simon, "Spurious Correlation: A Causal Interpretation," *Journal of the American Statistical Association*, 49 (September, 1954), 467–79.

2. Hubert M. Blalock, Jr., "Four Variable Causal Models and Partial Correlations," *American Journal of Sociology*, 68 (September, 1962), 182–94.

3. *Ibid*, p. 183.

PREVIOUS APPROACHES FOR IDENTIFYING CAUSAL RELATION-
SHIPS

One previous approach is to introduce other variables that have been
measured at the same time as A and B. This approach, when treated
elegantly, leads to some form of "path analysis." Wright advocated
this in 1920,[4] and it has received recent theoretical discussion by
Simon,[5] Turkey,[6] and Blalock.[7] Miller and Stokes[8] recently used a
form of path analysis to determine whether the voting behavior of
Congressmen in the House of Representatives with respect to civil
rights legislation was more strongly controlled by the representatives' own attitudes or by their perception of their constituencies'
attitudes.

As applied by Blalock, the method consists of setting up a variety
of models differing with respect to which variables are presumed to
influence others. Different predictions are made for the models, and
a choice among the models is made on the basis of which model
comes closest to fitting the observed data.

A second approach to the problem of identifying causal relationships involves the panel study — i.e. taking the same measurements
on the same people on at least two different occasions. Lazarsfeld[9]
has developed a method using a 16-fold table to display frequencies
for each of two dichotomous variables measured on two occasions. In
one example, this allowed him to determine whether it was primarily
respondents' political affiliations that determined their preferences
among candidates in the 1940 presidential election, or their candidate preferences that determined their political affiliations.

4. Sewall Wright, "Correlation and Causation," *Journal of Agricultural Research*, 20
(January 1921), 557–85.

5. Simon, *op. cit.*

6. John W. Tukey, "Causation, Regression, and Path Analysis," in Oscar Kemp-
thorne, ed., *Statistics and Mathematics in Biology* (Ames: Iowa State College Press,
1954).

7. Blalock, *op. cit.*, and "Evaluating the Relative Importance of Variables," *American Sociological Review*, 26 (December 1961), 866-874; "Correlation and Causality:
the Multivariate Case," *Social Forces*, 39 (March 1961), 246–51; "Spuriousness versus
Intervening Variables: The Problem of Temporal Sequence," *Social Forces*, 40 (May
1962), 330–336; *Causal Inferences in Nonexperimental Research* (Chapel Hill: University of North Carolina Press, 1964).

8. Warren E. Miller and Donald E. Stokes, "Constituency Influence in Congress,"
American Political Science Review, 57 (March 1963), 45–56.

9. Paul F. Lazarsfeld, "Mutual Effects of Statistical Variables," paper read at Dartmouth Seminar on Social Process, Hanover, N.H., July 1954; Seymour M. Lipset,
Paul F. Lazarsfeld, Allen H. Barton, and Juan Linz, "The Psychology of Voting: An
Analysis of Political Behavior," in Gardner Lindzey, ed., *Handbook of Social Psychology* (Cambridge, Mass.: Addison-Wesley, 1954), pp. 1124–75.

When continuous rather than dichotomous variables are available, Campbell[10] has suggested that the logic of the 16-fold table may be retained. Instead of examining frequencies, Campbell compares various correlation coefficients between the two variables measured on two occasions. Because it is analogous with lagged cross-correlations, as used by economists in analyses of time series data, Campbell suggests "cross-lagged panel correlation" as an appropriate name for this approach. He has applied the cross-lagged panel correlation to several sets of data treated initially by Lazarsfeld in terms of the 16-fold table, and obtained consistent results.

Although it was developed independently, Campbell's approach turns out to be identical with the one we have explored for causal analysis using correlational data.

THE METHOD OF "DIFFERENTIAL IN CROSS-LAGGED PANEL CORRELATIONS"

The basic idea is simple. Imagine a population characterized by two variables A and B (both subject to measurement error). From time to time variable A changes (as a result of forces that need not concern us, except that they are not attributable to B). Whenever A changes, the increment (or decrement) in A at time t produces a related increment (or decrement) in B within a certain "interval of causation."[11] We may assume that B is also subject to effects of other factors.

In such a system A and B are measured for all individuals at time t and again at t + k (k = arbitrary remeasurement interval). From the four measurements, six correlation coefficients (or other measures of association) can be obtained (Figure 22.1).

The vertical (or simultaneous) correlations 1 and 2 will both be positive and about the same magnitude (the magnitude depending on errors in measurement, and the extent to which other factors affect B). The horizontal (or lagged) correlations 3 and 4 will reflect the consistency in each variable over time.

10. Donald T. Campbell, "From Description to Experimentation: Interpreting Trends as Quasi-Experiments," in Chester W. Harris, ed., *Problems in Measuring Change* (Madison, Wis.: University of Wisconsin Press, 1963), pp. 212–42; Donald T., Campbell and Julian C. Stanley, "Experimental and Quasi-Experimental Designs for Research on Teaching," chap. 5 in Nathaniel L. Gage, ed., *Handbook of Research on Teaching* (Chicago: Rand McNally, 1963), pp. 171–246.

11. Philosophically of course causation must be "instantaneous"—the causal factor must be present when the effect occurs. Intention to buy a car, for example, must exist at the time of actual purchase. The intention, however, often arises (and can be measured) several months before the purchase.

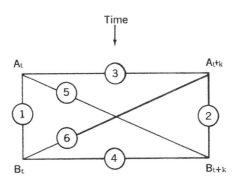

Fig. 22.1–Six Correlations among Two Variables Measured Twice.

Suppose now that we have chosen a remeasurement interval k which is close to the causal interval needed for a change in A to effect a change in B. It then seems to us plausible that *the state of A at times t should be more strongly associated with the state of B at time t + k, than the state of B at time t is associated with the state of A at time t+ k.* That is to say, the diagonal (i.e., cross-lagged) correlation 5, between A_t and B_{t+k}, should be relatively large, while the opposite diagonal correlation 6, between B_t and A_{t+k}, should be relatively small. A clear *difference* between the two diagonals should appear.[12]

Intuition also suggests that the cross-lagged correlation 5 $(A_t B_{t+k})$ should be larger than either simultaneous correlation 1 or 2 $(A_t B_t$ or $A_{t+k} B_{t+k})$, if k is close to the causal interval.

Since the logic of correlations is complex, we shall not attempt a full algebraic defense of this intuition; our case rests essentially on the empirical tests described below. But as a start toward a rational argument, we invite the reader to consider a highly simplified model consisting of a population of individuals with scores on two vari-

12. Thus Campbell and Stanley, *op. cit.*, pp. 238-40, observed that if variable X could be said to cause variable O, then "the 'effect' should correlate higher with a prior 'cause' than with a subsequent 'cause,' i.e., r $_{102}$ $r_{x2 01}$." An example of the same reasoning is cited by Joseph de Revira, *American Psychologist*, 17 (October 1962), 695, from an unpublished senior honors thesis by Thomas K. Landauer and C. T. Lane ("The Political Influence of Economic Aid," Dartmouth College, 1962). They observed a correlation of +.49 between our per capita foreign aid to a country and the extent to which the country voted with us in the United Nations, but also noted that UN voting correlated more highly with aid given in the previous year (+.54) than in the year following the voting (+.44).

ables, A and B. Let small changes in A occur at successive intervals, 1, 2,..., and let each individual's score on A at time t completely determine his score on B one interval later. As the simplest case let $A_t = B_{t+1}$, and the correlation $A_t B_{t+1} = 1.00$.

Assume furthermore that the changes in A are small relative to the total range; an individual low or high on A at time 1 will tend to remain low or high (respectively) at time 2. Thus the correlation $A_1 A_2$ is positive but less than unity (for illustration, call it .70). Let us take another measurement at time 3. Assuming that increaes or decreases in each person's A score occur in a random fashion, then the longer the interval of remeasurement, the lower should be the correlation between the two A measurements. For illustration, let the correlation $A_1 A_3 = .50$.

Now in terms of the algebra of correlations, if one measures three variables on the same set of objects, and two of these variables are perfectly correlated, it follows that both of them must have an identical correlation with the third variable.[13] Hence if $A_1 B_2 = 1.00$, and $A_1 A_3 = .50$, $B_2 A_3$ must $= .50$. Also (since $A_1 A_2 = .70$), the simultaneous correlation $A_2 B_2$ must $= .70$.

In such a system, all cross-lagged correlations $A_t B_{t+1}$ will $= 1.00$; all simultaneous cross-correlations $A_t B_t$ will $= .70$, and all cross-lagged correlations along the opposite diagonal $B_t A_{t+1}$ will $= .50$.

Even if one has selected an interval of remeasurement larger or smaller than the causal interval, there is reason to believe the predicted inequalities will appear, providing that A is reasonably consistent over time. Suppose the causal interval is 1 as before, but our interval of remeasurement (k) is 2. The correlation $A_1 B_3$ will now be fixed by the product $(A_1 B_2)(A_2 B_3) = (.70)(1.00) = .70$; while the most probable value of $B_1 A_3$ will be given by the product $(B_1 A_1)(A_1 A_3) = (.70)(.50) = .35$. Hence the *difference* in cross-lagged diagonals will probably appear, although the major diagonal $A_t B_{t+1}$ will not necessarily exceed the simultaneous correlation $A_t B_t$.

What if our interval of remeasurement is too small? Since our

13. The correlations among three variables must have a certain consistency even if none of them is unity. If two of the correlations are given (say, r_{12} and r_{13}), the third (r_{23}) must lie within these limits:

$$r_{12}r_{13} + \sqrt{1 - r^2_{12} - r^2_{13} + r^2_{12}r^2_{13}}.$$

Cf. Quinn, McNemar, *Psychological Statistics* (New York: Wiley, 1949), p. 142. If two correlations among three variables are known, the most probable estimate of the third (in the absence of other knowledge) is simply the product of these two.

model does not permit any shorter interval than 1, let us assume that the causal interval actually is 2 (i.e., $A_1B_3 = 1.00$), while $k = 1$; let the other values remain as before, and we measure (say) at times 2 and 3 only. The correlation A_2B_3 is now fixed by: $(A_1A_2)\ (A_1A_3) = (.70)\ (1.00) = .70$. The opposite diagonal B_2A_3 has a probable value of $(A_1B_2)\ (A_1A_3) = (.70)\ (.50) = .35$; again the differential appears.

As an early step in testing these ideas, artificial data-systems were set up and allowed to operate over several intervals; the cross-lagged differentials at various points were then examined. In one system, individuals were distributed over a five-value variable A and made to fluctuate by random changes of +1 at successive times; identical changes were made to occur in B four time-units later. The predicted differences appeared clearly, even when the interval of remeasurement varied from two to eight time-units; maximal difference occurred when causal interval $k = 4$.

Hence if the correlations in Figure 1 are observed to stand in this order: $5 > (1 = 2) > 6$, we have reason to prefer the hypothesis $A \longrightarrow B$ ("A causally prior to B") over the hypothesis $B \longrightarrow A$. But if $5 = (1 = 2) = 6$, then we cannot assert any priority; perhaps both influence each other ($A \longleftrightarrow B$), or both are determined by a third factor ($A \longleftarrow C \longrightarrow B$). Note that in the real world of multiple influences, the method will not establish A as the *sole* cause of B (or vice versa). It will simply indicate which of the two hypotheses is more plausible – i.e., which variable (if either) is "causally prior" to the other.

Even if we do not observe $5 > (1 = 2)$, but do observe $5 > 6$, it is still plausible that $A \longrightarrow B$, although the interval of remeasurement k may not match the true causal interval.

ASSUMPTIONS

What minimum assumptions must be met if this model is to work? One of the simplest – perhaps so obvious that it need not be mentioned – is that *changes* constantly occur in the state of variable A for each individual. If each person's A value became constant (A_tA_{t+1} approaching unity), then (by the algebra of the previous footnote) all cross-correlations among any A or B would approach whatever value exists for A_tB_{t+k}; all four cross-correlations 1, 2, 5 and 6 in Figure 1 would approach identity.

A second assumption is that the causal effect of A on B is not immediate, but occurs over a certain *interval*.[14] Suppose B changed simultaneously when A changed. Under our model, the correlation

14. See fn. 11.

$A_t B_t$ would equal 1.00. Assuming moderate consistency in A as before ($A_t A_{t+1} = B_t B_{t+1} = .70$), it would then follow that both of the cross-lagged correlations $A_t B_{t+1}$ and $B_t A_{t+1}$ must equal .70. The two diagonals would be equal and less than the simultaneous correlations.

While we must assume that A is not completely consistent over time, it is also necessary to assume that A is *not markedly inconsistent*. As one case let $A_t A_{t+1}$ = zero, while $A_t B_{t+1}$ = 1.00 as before. No problem arises so long as the interval of remeasurement k correctly matches the causal interval. But suppose k = 2. Then the most probable estimate of $A_1 B_3 = (A_1 A_2) (A_2 B_3) = (.00) (1.00)$ = zero; and by similar logic the most probable estimates of the simultaneous correlations $A_t B_t$ and of the opposite diagonal $B_1 A_3$ are likewise zero.

Take an even more extreme case in which the correlation $A_t A_{t+1}$ is negative — that is, individuals tend to fluctuate between opposite scores. Again no problem arises if we have correctly judged the causal interval. But say this is 1, as before, and our k = 2. If for illustration we let $A_1 A_2 = -.50$, and $A_2 B_3$ (as before) = +1.00, the cross-lagged diagonal $A_1 B_3$ will be −.50. It is entirely possible that the opposite diagonal $B_1 A_3$ will be less negative than this. Hence if there are marked fluctuations in A, and if the interval of remeasurement differs from the interval of causation, it is quite possible that the cross-lagged correlations will be negative, and the direction of the difference, opposite to what we have predicted.

Such a situation appears to have arisen in another of our artificial systems. Variables A and B each took one of two states ("high" and "low"), which persisted until a random flip to the opposite state. Superimposed on this random pattern was a causal connection: whenever A flipped, B took the corresponding "high" or "low" value one unit later (and persisted in that state until its next random flip, or until a change caused by A). After this system was allowed to operate for some time, the simultaneous relationships (phi coefficients) approached .40, and the diagonals diverged as predicted (average phi $A_t B_{t+1} = .50$, $B_t A_{t+1} = .36$). But we found that with k = 2 the difference in diagonals reversed sign, and as k increased, the relationship $A_t B_{t+k}$ became increasingly negative!

Other assumptions may turn out to be necessary. With real data, if the consistency of A or of B over time were changing (A or B becoming progressively more stable, or less stable), the method might run into difficulty. Or if A showed greater variation at time t + k than at time t, or other factors affecting B varied more at one time than at another, the predicted inequalities might not hold. In a stable system one would expect the simultaneous correlations to be steady over time ($A_tB_t = A_{t+k}B_{t+k}$). If they are not, this fact may signal instabilities that might upset the predicted inequalities. And finally, of course, if A and B are related in a non-linear fashion, the use of product-moment correlations is inappropriate.

Faced with these complexities, we felt an urgent need for empirical tests. Let the method be confronted with some actual data in which the causal priorities were clear. Would it work, or not?

Such empirical tests might resolve further uncertainties. How large a difference must appear between the diagonals, in order to favor the A⟶B hypothesis over B⟶A or A⟷B? How well would it work if the variables changed in an unidirectional rather than reversible fashion?

SOME PRELIMINARY APPROACHES

Our interest in this procedure was first stimulated by a working paper of Victor H. Vroom, in which he compared "static" correlations (between measures taken at a single point in time) with "dynamic" correlations (between changes in successive measurements of the same individuals), using data from an organizational study.[15] Vroom did not attempt to answer the question of causal priority, but his correlations among changes did suggest that other procedures with the same data might do so.[16]

Given measures of two variables on the same individuals at two points in time, A_1, A_2, B_1, B_2, one can compute the increase or decrease in each variable (A_{2-1} and B_{2-1}), and from this set of six measures obtain nine cross-correlations. Two of these were used in the method described above (A_1B_2 and B_1A_2), which proved useful in subsequent tests.

It also seemed plausible at the time that if A⟶B, we should observe four additional inequalities among the correlations involving *changes*, such as $A_1B_{2-1} > B_1A_{2-1}$. While these relationships showed some promise, they were inferior to our main method. (See the "postscript" at the end of the article.)

The several methods were tried out on artificial systems as described above; results suggested that the main scheme worked well when applied to mild variations along continuous scales, even when

15. Internal memo, untitled, Survey Research Center, University of Michigan, December 1958, hectograph.

16. Donald C. Pelz, on "Teasing Causal Connections out of 'Dynamic' Correlations," internal memo, Survey Research Center, University of Michigan, March 1959, hectograph.

the remeasurement interval k departed substantially from the causal interval. Thus encouraged, we next sought sets of real data in which causal direction could be judged *a priori*.

HEIGHT AND WEIGHT IN CHILDREN

Two unidirectional and highly correlated variables are height and weight in growing children. Both are determined by common factors, such as chronological age, heredity, and diet. For testing our method, though, one may suppose an asymmetrical causal priority. An increase in height is accompanied by a larger bony mass that almost certainly will increase weight. But weight can change in terms of fat and muscle without an immediate effect on height. Therefore the hypothesis H⟶W is more plausible than the hypothesis W⟶H.

Data on the height and weight of 100 unrelated male children were obtained, recorded within a few months of, these boys' 6th, 7th, 8th, and 11th birthdays.[17] If H⟶W is more plausible than W⟶H, we should observe these differences in measures of association:

$$H_1W_2 > (H_1W_1 = H_2W_2) > W_1H_2$$

Table 22.1. Zero-Order Correlations Between Height and Weight at Birth Dates of 100 Boys Ages 6 to 11

Age at measurement		Cross- correlations		Lagged self- correlations		Cross-lagged correlations		
First	Second	H_1W_1	H_2W_2	H_1H_2	W_1W_2	H_1W_2	W_1H_2	Difference
6	7	.79	.80	.96	.94	.79	.76	.03
6	8	.79	.75	.93	.90	.77	.72	.05
6	11	.79	.72	.89	.83	.71	.67	.04
7	8	.80	.75	.95	.94	.75	.75	.00
7	11	.80	.72	.90	.88	.68	.70	.02
8	11	.75	.72	.94	.90	.69	.69	.00
					Mean	.73	.72	.01

The first results, shown in Table 22.1, were dismal. The pairs of cross-lagged relationships between height and weight were not

17. We are indebted to Dr. Byron O. Hughes for making available these data from records of the University Elementary School. Data were recorded in terms of

different, and they were slightly lower than the simultaneous correlations. Perhaps even a k of one year was too long to match the causal interval (if indeed a causal asymmetry existed).

But it was also clear that our scheme was operating under a formidable constraint—the extreme consistency of the height and weight measures over time. These lagged self-correlations were all .90 or more except for the interval between ages 6 and 11.

As we discussed earlier, if variable A is highly consistent (A_tA_{t+k} approaches 1.00), then all cross-correlations (A_tB_t, A_tB_{t+k}, B_tA_{t+k}) must take very similar values, and the predicted difference in the two diagonal correlations has little opportunity to appear.

Could the diagonal relationships be freed from this constraint? The technique of partial correlation appeared a reasonable way to do so. What is the effect (if any) of height at age 6 on weight at age 7, *over and above* what one could predict simply from weight at age 6? Similarly, what is the effect of weight at age 6 on height at age 7, over and above what is predictable from height at age 6?

Table 22.2. A First-Order Partial Correlation for Cross-Lagged Relationships (N = 100)

Time 1	Time 2	$H_1W_2 \cdot W_1$	$W_1H_2 \cdot H_1$	Difference
6	7	.25*	.02	.23**
6	8	.22*	−.07	.29**
6	11	.15	−.11	.26**
7	8	.01	−.06	.07
7	11	−.06	−.06	.00
8	11	.04	−.08	.12
	Mean	.10	−.06	.16

* Differs significantly from zero at .05 level of confidence (one-tailed).
** Difference in partial r's is statistically significant at .05 level (one-tailed).

The partial correlations given in Table 22.2 showed, in five of six comparisons, a small but consistent difference in the predicted direction (and in no case a difference opposite to prediction). The average difference was .16, and three of the six differences were statistically

"height-age" and "weight-age"—transformations which express height and weight in terms of the age (in months) at which a given height or weight is normal in this population. Since this transformation has little effect on the correlations, we shall call the measures simply "height" and "weight."

significant. Five of the six partial H_1W_2 correlations were positive, while five of the opposite diagonals were negative.[18]

Thus, even with highly consistent variables that were increasing in one direction, and a remeasurement interval that was probably too long, the scheme confirmed (in five of six trials) the common-sense expectation that the causal hypothesis $H \rightarrow W$ was more plausible than $W \rightarrow H$.

A TEST USING ECONOMIC ATTITUDES AND BEHAVIOR

To explore further the cross-lagged correlation method, we applied it to a set of panel data dealing with economic behavior. In a series of studies conducted by the Survey Research Center's Economic Behavior Program with support from the Ford Foundation, a national sample of approximately 800 urban families was interviewed in November 1954, and again in November 1955. From the interviews we selected the 12 variables listed in Table 22.3.

Since the same variables have appeared in many studies conducted by the Survey Research Center, there is much information about their interrelationships. Intentions to purchase a car are strongly related to subsequent car purchases;[19] intentions to buy household durables are reasonably good predictors of subsequent purchases of household durables;[20] and actual change in family income is a reasonably good predictor of a six-item index of economic optimism, which in turn (together with income change) predicts subsequent car purchases.[21]

While these findings have been of great interest to economic forecasters, they did not answer our need for an *a priori* determination as to which of two variables has the major causal priority over the other. While one might suppose that an attitude or an expectation precedes actual behavior, a case can be made for the reverse (on the basis of Festinger's cognitive dissonance theory,[22] for example).

18. Donald T. Campbell (personal communication) has suggested an alternative technique: from all four measures extract by factor analysis a single factor ("size?"), partial out this factor, and then examine cross-lagged correlations among residuals.

19. George Katona, Charles A. Lininger, and Richard F. Kosobud, *1962 Survey of Consumer Finances* (Ann Arbor, Mich.: Survey Research Center, University of Michigan, 1963).

20. A. M. Okum, "The Value of Anticipations Data in Forecasting National Product," in National Bureau of Economic Research, *The Quality and Economic Significance of Anticipations Data* (Princeton: Princeton University Press, 1960).

21. Eva Mueller, "Ten Years of Consumer Attitude Surveys: Their Forecasting Records," *Journal of the American Statistical Association*, 58 (December 1963), 899–917.

22. Leon Festinger, A *Theory of Cognitive Dissonance* (Evanston, Ill.: Row, Peterson, 1957).

We therefore asked three members of the Survey Research Center's Economic Behavior Program to judge the probable direction of causal priority between pairs of specified variables. (In such complex matters, of course, the judgment even of experts is not a certain guide to the "real" priorities.) Each judge worked independently and indicated for each pair a choice between hypotheses A⟶B, B⟶A, or neither (causal priority believed to be absent, or bidirectional, or ambiguous). Two judges were asked to consider ten pairs, while one judge considered all 66 possible pairs among the 12 variables.[23]

On six of the ten common pairs, all three judges agreed as to the direction of primary determining influence. On the remaining four pairs, agreement varied.[24] Figure 22.2 is a composite of the predictions.

Many of the arrows (or absence of arrows) in Figure 22.2 were based on the decisions of only one judge. Where all three judges considered a given pair, an arrow was drawn only if at least two judges agreed on the direction of priority.

RESULTS

Since many of the scales in these economic data were sharply skewed, and many have lacked interval properties, we used the non-parametric measure of association *gamma*, rather than a product-moment correlation.[25]

23. The analysis actually went through two phases. In the first, tests were run on the ten pairs submitted to two judges. These preliminary results suggested that all 12 variables might be arranged in a mutually consistent network (see Figure 22.3). For further predictions, a third judge was added, and 25 additional pairs tested.

24. All judges agreed as to direction of AB, CD, EF, GI, GJ, and HI. Two judges agreed, the third abstained on HJ.

25. Leo A. Goodman and William H. Kruskal, "Measures of Association for Cross-Classifications," *Journal of the American Statistical Association*, 49 (September 1954), 732–64. The statistical tests of gamma were based on a critical ratio technique in which the numerator of gamma (Kendall's S) was compared to its standard error. E. J. Burr, "The Distribution of Kendall's Score S for a Pair of Tied Rankings," *Biometrika*, 47 (June 1960), 151–71, discusses the computation of the standard error of S; and Robert H. Somers, "A New Asymmetric Measure of Association for Ordinal Variables," *American Sociological Review*, 27 (December 1962), 799–811, notes that the technique may appropriately be applied to gamma. Leo A. Goodman and William H. Kruskal, "Measures of Association for Cross Classifications; III: Approximate Sampling Theory," *Journal of the American Statistical Association*, 58 (June 1963), 310–64, have recently developed the sampling theory for gamma more fully.

We also applied the method of partial relationship described under the height-weight data, using partial gammas. A partial gamma between two variables may be obtained by computing a separate gamma within each classification of a third variable, and then (provided the separate values are not too far apart) determining the weighted average.

*Table 22.3. Variables Used from Ford Panel Studies**

Buying intentions	*Question asked*
A. Number of household durables R was "quite certain" or had a "fair chance" of buying (0, 1, 2, 3, 4 or more).	"Are there any special expenditures you would really like to make in the next twelve months?" "You mentioned a .... Would you say that you are quite certain of buying it, or that there is a fair chance, a slight chance, or no chance at all that you'll be buying it during the next 12 months?"
C. Whether R planned to buy a TV set (with certainty of "fair chance" or higher).	(Derived from questions under A.)
E. Whether R planned to buy a car (4-point scale of certainty).	"Do you people expect to buy a car during the next 12 months or so?"

Purchases

B. Number of household items bought (0, 1, 2, 3, 4 or more).	"How about these large items for the house—during the past 12 months did you buy a refrigerator, TV set, washing machine, cooking range, air conditioner, furniture? Did you buy other large household appliances?"
D. Whether R bought a TV set.	(Derived from questions under B.)
F. Whether R bought a car.	"Did you or anyone else in the family buy a car for your own personal use during the last 12 months?"

Income

G. Expected change in family income (5-point scale).	Percentage change calculated from: "We talked about your total family income for 1955; what is your best estimate for the family's income for 1956?"
I. Actual change in family income (more, same, less).	(Derived from questions on income received.)

Attitudes

H. Expected change in financial well-being (3-point scale).	"Now looking ahead, do you think that a year from now you people will be better off financially, or worse off, or just about the same as now?"

J. Change in financial well-being 3-point scale). "Would you say that you and your family are better off or worse off financially than you were a year ago?"

I. Climate for buying household durables (3-point scale). "Now about things people buy for their homes—I mean furniture, house furnishings, refrigerator, stove, TV, and things like that—do you think now is a good or bad time to buy such large household items?"

L. Expected economic climate (5-point scale). "Do you think that during the next 12 months we'll have good times financially, or bad times, or what?"

* November-December 1954 and November-December 1955. Where question wording differed slightly, that used in 1955 is shown.

Six pairs on which judges agreed. Since Figure 22.2 involves many pairs where only a single judge was asked to make a prediction, we examined separately the six pairs on which all three judges agreed as to causal priority. (These are listed in Table 22.4). The predicted "causes" were all expectations about future events or experiences; the predicted "results" were statements about past experience or behavior.

The predicted difference in cross-lagged relationships appeared for five of the six pairs. Interestingly, the partials, while showing the same trends, were slightly less sensitive indicators than the zero-order gammas—contrary to our findings on height and weight.

In one pair (HI) the cross-lagged differential suggested a mild priority opposite to the judges' prediction: change in family income over the past year   expected change in future financial well-being, rather than the reverse.

Overall results. For 25 more pairs of variables, one judge predicted causal priorities. Data for the additional pairs are not tabulated, but they are pictured in Figure 22.3.

Among the total set of 31 pairs, the results *agreed* with the prediction in 15 pairs (seven showed strong priorities, three mild, and five ambiguous—as predicted). Results were *opposite* to prediction in only two pairs—both mild. In six cases, a direction was predicted but not found, and in eight cases the prediction was ambiguous but a direction was found (four strong, four mild). This indicates considerable, though by no means complete, agreement between the observed results and the composite predictions in Figure 22.2.[26]

26. It is reasonable to ask whether our criteria for clear priority (see footnote in Table 22.4) were statistically justified. Using gammas we have as yet no convenient

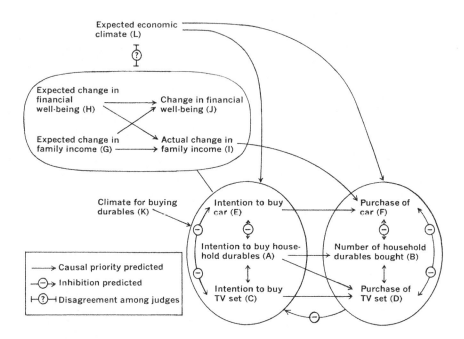

Figure 22.2–Composite Prediction of Causal Priorities among 12 Variables of Economic Behavior and Attitudes. Arrows to or from an Ellipse Apply to All Variables within the Ellipse. Where No Connection is Indicated the Priority is Predicted to be "Ambiguous."

Consistency in network of priorities. Figure 22.3 presents another view of the cross-lagged differential technique. Diagrammed here is a network of causal priorities among the 35 pairs of variables tested. The 23 directed connections form a consistent network in which almost all the directional arrows proceed from left to right. The only reversal involved plans to purchase a TV set, which was very unevenly split. This was the only clear inconsistency in the entire set of 35 connections.[27]

test of the statistical significance of difference between diagonals. For the diagonals themselves, however, the "major diagonal" X_1Y_2 (where X   Y) was significant in 19 of the 23 "directed" pairs, while the "minor diagonal" was not.

27. This network of causal priorities is not a complete map of causal connections. The true picture is undoubtedly much more complicated; two or more variables may jointly determine a third; complex interaction effects may exist. All the diagram does is to map priorities among various *pairs* of variables. Note that the network has the

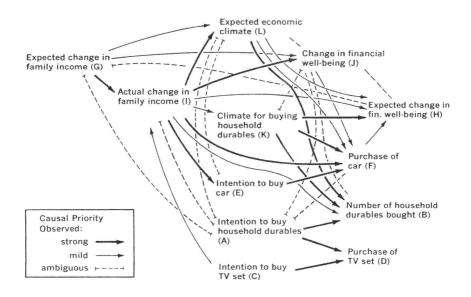

Figure 22.3–Network of Causal Priorities Based on 35 Pairs among 12 Variables of Economic Behavior and Attitudes.

The network has some interesting characteristics from a sociological standpoint. Dominating almost all the other variables as a determinant was actual change in family income (I). Preceding this was expected change in income (G). (For most families, apparently, income change could be accurately anticipated.)

Just as clearly, variables of actual behavior (purchase of car and other durables, F, B, D) appeared on the right as "resultants." "Intervening variables" standing in the middle included various expectations as to future climate (L and K) together with buying intentions (E, A, C).

formal characteristics of a "directed graph;" conceivably the propositions of graph theory may be useful in analyzing its properties. See Frank Harary, Robert Z. Norman, and Dorwin Cartwright, *An Introduction to the Theory of Directed Graphs* (New York: Wiley, 1964).

Table 22.4. Predicted and Observed Directions of Causal Priority among Six Pairs of Economic Variables where Three Judges Agreed[a]

Predicted direction[b]	Observed direction[c]	Zero-order gammas			Partial gammas		
		X_1Y_2	Y_1X_2	Diff.	$X_1Y_2Y_1$	$Y_1X_2X_1$	Diff.
A⟶B	⟶ (strong)	.33*	.09	.24	.30	.07	.23
C⟶D	⋯⟶ (strong)	.75*	−.57	1.32	d	d	d
E⟶F	⟶ (strong)	.59*	.20*	.39	.60	.26	.34
G⟶I	⋯⟶ (strong)	.32*	.04	.28	.29	.06	.23
G⟶H	⟶ (mild)	.22*	.04	.18	.16	.09	.07
H⟶I	⟵ (mild)	.14*	.24*	−.10	.11	.18	−.07
Mean (omitting pair CD)		.32	.12	.20	.29	.13	.16

[a] X_1 and Y_1 refer to 1954 data, X_2 and Y_2 to 1955.
[b] Arrow shows causal priority as predicted in Figure 2.
[c] "Strong:" both differences were .20 or more, or one difference .30 or more; 'mild ': one difference was at least .10, the other at least .05; 'ambiguous ': neither of above.
[d] Indeterminate. Because there were no cases in one cell, only one of the two values necessary for the partial gamma could be computed. Families who bought a TV set last year rarely planned to buy a set next year.
* Statistically significant at .05 level (test applied to zero-order gammas only, not to differences nor to partials).

Note especially the two items on felt change in being "well off" financially – both recent experience (J) and future expectation (H). These are matters of *satisfaction*. And just as satisfaction of industrial employees may have little effect on performance, it appeared from this network that financial satisfaction is not a determinant of behavior (contrary to the judges' anticipation), nor even an intervening variable, but simply a resultant.

TIME SERIES ANALYSIS AND CYCLICAL DATA

Since our method superficially resembles a time series analysis, certain difficulties in the latter ought to be considered here. In a time series analysis one takes aggregate data on two variables (such as crop prices and rainfall), and correlates the values of variable A at successive times t, with corresponding values of B after a time lag k. If A$\longrightarrow$B, then the lagged time-series correlation A_tB_{t+k} should be greater than the simultaneous cross-correlation A_tB_t, and greater than B_tA_{t+k}.

A potential difficulty arises when both variables show a periodic cyclical fluctuation. Imagine a population of individuals for whom variable A changes over a regular cycle, returning to exactly the same value after (say) ten time-units; suppose that for each individual, variable B follows the identical pattern five units later. (All individuals need not rise or fall at the same time, but the length of the cycle must be about the same for all.) In such a model, A_tB_{t+5} will be 1.00 — but so will B_tA_{t+5}. (And of course at any given time A and B will take diametrically opposite values, so that $A_tB_t = -1.00$.) Is the method of cross-lagged differentials inappropriate, then, with cyclical data?

Remember that our model assumes only moderate consistency of A. Suppose each person's A score returns only approximately to the same value after the periodic interval. (In the real world we seldom expect perfect periodicity!) In our model let $A_0A_{10} =$ less than unity, say .70. What then will be the correlation B_5A_{10}? Not 1.00, but the product (A_0B_5) $(A_0A_{10}) = (1.00)$ $(.70) = .70$. Hence the difference in diagonals will still appear.

The presence of such inconsistencies — one source of which is individual "measurement error" — leads us to expect differences in the cross-lagged correlations to appear even when there is an underlying periodicity in both variables. This expectation needs to be tested with empirical data, however. In time series analysis, of course, the aggregation of data tends to eliminate these and other irregularities, and the more complete the elimination, the more a time series analysis is subject to the difficulty noted above.

A different kind of difficulty may arise, however, when the interval of remeasurement differs markedly from the interval of causation. In the above model, A and B measured either at the same time or ten units apart will tend to take opposite values; the correlations A_tB_t and A_tB_{t+10} will be strongly negative; hence cross-lagged correlations over too short or too long an interval (say, A_0B_1 or A_0B_9) will also be negative. The opposite diagonals B_0A_1 or B_0A_9 might possibly be less so. If we have reason to expect periodicity, then, the presence of strong negative correlations should signal caution in applying the method.

POSTSCRIPT: FOUR OTHER METHODS

Social scientists sometimes decry the fact that only "successful" analyses are published, while "failures" are quietly buried. We should therefore like to share the results of four other techniques — all of which seemed plausible at first — for establishing causal priority. These approaches all used *changes* in the A and B values (A_{2-1} and B_{2-1}) — preserving the sign, whether increase or decrease.

In our early thinking about ways to establish causal priority from panel data,[28] five distinct comparisons seemed worth exploring. These are sketched in Figure 22.4.

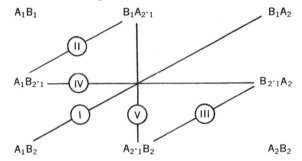

Figure 22.4—Five Possible Comparisons among Correlations Obtained from Two Panel Measurements on Variables A and B.

Comparison I formed the basis of our main method of simple cross-lagged correlations. If A⟶B, we would expect $A_1B_2 > B_1A_2$.

Comparison II. The initial value of each variable is correlated with the *change* in the other variable, obtaining the correlations A_1B_{2-1} and B_1A_{2-1}. Now if A⟶B (rather than B⟶A) ought we to expect any difference in these two correlations? Intuition suggested that A_1B_{2-1} should be greater than B_1A_{2-1}.

As a rationale, assume again the model used earlier, in which changes in variable A at time 1 completely determine changes in variable B one interval later. Necessarily in our model, $A_{1-0} = B_{2-1}$, and the correlation $A_{1-0}B_{2-1} = 1.00$.

Now let us make another assumption: that A has a finite range (A cannot increase nor decrease indefinitely). If so, most (but not all) individuals who stand high on A_1 are likely to have arrived there via an increase in A; and for this majority of high scorers, the change in B will be positive. The converse applies to individuals who stand

28. Pelz, *op. cit.*, fn. 16.

low on A_1; for the majority, the change in B will be negative. Hence the correlation A_1B_{2-1} should be strongly positive. (It will not be unity, since some individuals near the extremes will have decreased from even more extreme positions.)

What of the correlation B_1A_{2-1}? Under our model, B_1 is completely determined by the prior A_0; $A_0B_1 = 1.00$. We now need the connection of A_0 with A_{2-1}. Since A has a finite range, high initial values of A are likely to be followed by a drop, and low values by a rise (these are the typical regression effects). The correlation A_0A_{1-0} will hence be negative; and even after two intervals it is probable that the correlation A_0A_{2-1} will be slightly negative. Hence B_1A_{2-1} must equal $(A_0B_1)(A_0A_{2-1})$ or the same slightly negative value. We should, then, observe a very clear difference: $A_1B_{2-1} > B_1A_{2-1}$.

We shall not take the space to examine the remaining comparisons. Our first hunch was that terms along the left or bottom of Figure 22.4 should be larger than those along the right or top. Closer scrutiny justified the expectation of a slight difference in comparison IV: A_1B_{2-1} should exceed $B_{2-1}A_2$; but the other two were ambiguous. The chain of reasoning in each case depended on uncertain assumptions on size of regression effects (correlation between change and either the initial or the final value).

When we applied these methods to the height-weight data, we found that the changes were in fact strongly correlated with initial or with final values (for example, boys who were initially tall or heavy tended to gain more than those who were short or light). When such regression effects were held constant by partial correlations, comparisons II and IV came out in the direction expected, and as strongly as method I. Comparison III was ambiguous, and V was opposite to our initial hunch.

When the methods were applied to three variables from the economic data (G, I, and L), however, none of the comparisons generated differences of any size.

Still a sixth method could be applied if one had measures at *three* time points. One looks for differences in correlations between successive changes. If A⟶B, an initial change in A should have more effect on a subsequent change in B, than the reverse. We should observe $A_{2-1}B_{3-2} > B_{2-1}A_{3-2}$. When the method was tried on the height-weight data, results were inconclusive; all correlations were small. The time intervals may have been too long to permit the phenomenon (if present) to emerge.

Our conclusion was while comparisons II and IV held some promise, the empirical evidence was ambiguous. We found no reason to prefer methods using changes over method I, which used simple values.

Why did the change methods prove dubious? Note among other things that they necessarily involve the question of regression effects — and in our data these were often puzzling in size and direction. A further difficulty concerns measurement errors. The measured amount of change will be affected by errors both at time 1 and at time 2; hence measures of change will be doubly unstable.

SUMMARY

This paper describes a method for analyzing panel data to indicate which of two intercorrelated variables (A and B, each measured at time 1 and time 2) is more likely to have "causal priority" over the other. If in fact A determines B rather than the reverse, then the cross-lagged correlation A_1B_2 should exceed the cross-lagged correlation B_1A_2. Donald T. Campbell has independently suggested the same method.

In one test using highly stable heights and weights of boys measured at various ages from 6 to 11, the zero-order correlations did not show the expected differences, but they did appear (height causally prior to weight, rather than the reverse) when the initial state of the "resultant" variable was partialed out.

When the method was applied to panel data on 12 variables of economic behavior and attitudes, results were generally in agreement with predictions of three economists, using both zero-order and partial measures of association (gammas). The method also indicated some causal priorities not anticipated by the judges.

In a network of 35 connections among the set of 12 economic variables, 22 priorities were internally consistent, and only one inconsistent (the remainder were ambiguous).

Logical examination, and tests with artificial models, suggest that the method will not work if the variables involved are highly inconsistent over time *and* the interval of remeasurement does not match the underlying interval of causation, though either condition alone can be tolerated.

PART NINE
Participant Observation: Uses and Problems

INTRODUCTION

PARTICIPANT observation represents the avowed commitment on the part of the investigator to participate as intimately as possible in the experiences of those he studies. This demands that he learn their language and understand the actions surrounding their valued social objects. The meaning of their styles of dress and modes of gesturing must also be grasped. The observer must, to the extent of his abilities, learn to view the world of his subjects from their perspective. Preconceptions and stereotypes must be forsaken; a flexible and relativistic stance must be adopted.

The development of such a perspective suggests that no single method or field strategy will reveal all the relevant aspects of the phenomena at hand. The participant observer learns to employ multiple methods in his research activities. Documents are collected and analyzed; interviews are conducted; informants are sought out for their unique perspectives; and direct participation in the group's activities is employed. Introspection and direct observation are utilized as well. When appropriately conceived, participant observation

365

represents the simultaneous use of many methods; it becomes a triangulated methodology.

OBSERVATIONAL ROLES

Four varieties of the observational role can be distinguished. As Gold notes in his article in this part, these range from *complete participation*, wherein the observer never makes his true identity known, to the *complete observer*, as seen in the experiment where the researcher does not directly participate in the events studied. Between these two extremes are the *participant-as-observer* and the *observer-as-participant*. The latter role is best seen in the survey, where the interviewer only meets his respondent once in a fleeting, often stranger-like relationship. The participant-as-observer represents the most common use of the observational method. The observer makes his presence known, but attempts as fully as possible to become a "normal" and "acceptable" person within the group's activities.

OBSERVATIONAL PROBLEMS

Each of these roles have special problems. The difficulties of the observer-as-participant were presented in the preceding parts on the interview and survey. The complete observer's problems were seen in the context of Orne's and Leik's papers. Their data indicate that the complete observer may be more a participant in his own studies than heretofore recognized.

The papers in this part focus on the participant-as-observer and complete participation roles. The earlier reading from Riecken on the unidentified interview discusses issues involved in with the complete participant strategy.

In general, six specific problems characterize these two observational roles. These include gaining entry into the group to be studied, establishing and maintaining membership after entry has been achieved, avoiding altering by one's presence the behavior of those observed, maintaining objectivity in the face of new experiences, recording and analyzing the data—which are largely qualitative—and overcoming the ethical aspects of observation.

The analytic strategies involved in the observational method were presented in the earlier selection by Turner in Becker's article in this part. The reader should examine Turner's position. Becker's discussion presents the classic statement on this problem. The ethics of observation will be discussed in Part XIII.

STEPS IN THE OBSERVATIONAL PROCESS

Polsky, in an essay not reprinted here ("Research Methods, Morality, and Criminology," pp. 119–30 in his *Hustlers, Beats, and Others,* Aldine Publishing Company, 1967), offers what I regard as a convincing case for the observational and naturalistic technique. Couched specifically in the context of studying criminals, his position calls for the study of deviants in their natural settings, and he offers ten suggestions for implementing the participant-as-observer role. These range from learning how to listen and keeping one's mouth shut to learning the language of those studied. Polsky's comments on language are important. He suggests that special argots can only be seen as aspects of a subculture; they do not contain all the relevant objects and activities within those subcultures. He also notes that the frequent use of a term may not be an accurate index of the prevalence of the event so designated. Polsky suggests as one sampling and observational strategy the snowball method. In the context of field work this involves working from one informant to a chain of others who are known to the initial subject. Polsky suggests that the observer attempt to work downward from the highest status positions within a group. In my judgment, Polsky's most important recommendation is that the observer immediately and clearly establish his identity in the field.

Olesen and Whittaker detail four steps through which the participant-as-observer is likely to pass. Having once established entry, the observer has to develop a relationship with those studied. Once this relationship is formed, the observer is likely to become a provisional member of the group. Here a reciprocal interaction between the observed and observer can be noted. Both will be shaping the other's activities, attempting to forge a satisfactory relationship. The observer will be teaching subjects how to act toward him and the subjects will be doing the same. There is likely to be a constant tension between the two roles. This is seen in some of the field notes presented by Olesen and Whittaker. Frequently they found student nurses instructing them on proper behavior. If provisional membership is established, the observer moves into the status of categorical member. Now he is freely working within the group perspective, actively gathering and processing data. The last phase is movement out of the group. This exit process may be difficult, because subjects will be attempting to shape the investigator's final opinion of them. At this point ethical agreements and contracts established in earlier phases become central. The observer is bound to follow any and all such agreements and he must be careful not to have made commitments he can not meet.

Schwartz and Schwartz, in a paper not reprinted here ("Problems in Participant Observation," *American Journal of Sociology*, 55 [January 1955], 343–53), examine the effects of direct participation upon the observer and those observed. They note that an observer's presence in the field produces behaviors and actions that would not have appeared had the observer not located himself with the group. This suggests the principle that all acts of observation produce reactive effects upon the observed and the observer. These reactive effects point to elements intrinsic to the research act. They are always present, and they cannot be ignored. Every research method creates its own reactive effects, as does every researcher.

There are many ways to control and assess these effects, and the readings in Part XI discuss a method explicitly designed to minimize such effects, the unobstrusive method, which simply removes the observer from the field situation as an active agent. He passively observes. One of the problems inherent in passive observation, however, is the effect of participation on the observer's self. On the one hand, he may become so involved that objectivity is lost, a point stressed by Gold, but at the other extreme, empathetic participation can increase the observer's sensitivity to the field situation. He can intimately sense what his subjects are feeling. He can take their role and correctly apprehend the world from their perspective. This must be the goal toward which observers work.

EXPERIMENTATION WITHIN THE OBSERVATIONAL METHOD

It is possible for the researcher to systematically vary his activities in the field so that the effects of various variables can be assessed. He can change his style of dress, vary his speech patterns, talk to different persons, challenge accepted perspectives, act dumb, or act knowledgeable. He can leave the field for a period of time and reenter at a different point to assess his reactive influence. Each variation points to aspects of the researcher's activities that may be shaping the nature of his results. Because he is present and can continually experiment with his own activities, the participant observer is perhaps in a better position to assess the effect of these intrinsic variables than are his counterparts in the survey and experiment.

Lofland and Lejeune, in an article not reprinted here ("Initial Interaction of Newcomers in Alcoholics Anonymous: A Field Experiment in Class Symbols and Socialization," *Social Problems*, 8 [Fall 1960], 102–11), present the findings of a field experiment that rested on the complete participant method. By varying the dress and demeanor of field observers, Lofland and Lejeune assessed the effects of imputed social class upon interaction rates within Alcoholic Anonymous groups. Four experimental conditions were created and systematic observations recording the nature and duration of interaction at A.A. meetings were gathered. Hidden stop watches were employed, as were hidden observers. The members in each A.A. club never knew they were being studied. This strategy of course raises ethical issues and the study has been criticized on these grounds.

A single theme emerges from the papers in this part: The act of observation must be seen interactionally. Every gesture and utterance of the researcher displays the interactional quality of the observational process. Until investigators realize this and begin systematically to study the social features of their own conduct, few methodological advances will be forthcoming.

Suggested Readings. An excellent monograph that focuses on the interactional features of field work is Gerald D. Berreman's *Behind Many Masks*, monograph number 4 (1962), published by the Society for Applied Anthropology, Cornell University. Among other matters, Berreman treats the problems of learning a language, establishing residence, and working with different informants in the field. His analysis is framed in terms of Erving Goffman's dramaturgical perspective as seen in his *The Presentation of Self in Everyday Life*, (New York: Doubleday, 1959).

A reader by George J. McCall and J. L. Simmons, *Issues in Participant Observation, A Text-Reader* (Addison-Wesley, 1969), offers a basic review of the problems inherent in this method. A number of the classic readings in participant observation are presented in it. An earlier collection of readings on the field method is Adams and Preiss's *Human Organization Research: Field Relations and Techniques* (Chicago: Dorsey, 1960). This source is quite good because of its focus on organizational research. Severyn T. Bruyn's *The Human Perspective in Sociology: The Methodology of Participant Observation* (Englewood Cliffs, N. J.: Prentice-Hall, 1966) presents a synthesis and review of the major themes and literature surrounding this method.

23. Roles in Sociological Field Observations

RAYMOND L. GOLD

BUFORD Junker has suggested four theoretically possible roles for sociologists conducting field work.[1] These range from the complete participant at one extreme to the complete observer at the other. Between these, but nearer the former, is the participant-as-observer; nearer the latter is the observer-as-participant. As a member of Junker's research team, I shared in the thinking which led to conceptualization of these research roles. After the work of the team was completed, I continued the search for insight regarding processes of interaction learning in field observation in a special study of my own.[2] A considerable portion of this study was devoted to explor-

Reprinted by permission from *Social Forces*, 36 (March 1958), pp. 217–23. Copyright 1958, The University of North Carolina Press.

1. Buford Junker, "Some Suggestions for the Design of Field Work Learning Experiences," in Everett C. Hughes, *et al.*, *Cases on Field Work* (hectographed by The University of Chicago, 1952), part III-A.

2. Raymond L. Gold, "Toward a Social Interaction Methodology for Sociological Field Observation," unpublished Ph.D. dissertation, The University of Chicago, 1954.

ation of the dimensions of Junker's role—conceptions and their controlling effect on the product of field study.

My aim in this paper is to present extensions of Junker's thinking growing out of systematic interviews with field workers whose experience had been cast in one or more of these patterns of researcher-subject relationship. All of these field workers had gathered data in natural or nonexperimental settings. I would like in this paper to analyze generic characteristics of Junker's four field observer roles and to call attention to the demands each one places on an observer, as a person and as a sociologist plying his trade.

Every field work role is at once a social interaction device for securing information for scientific purposes and a set of behaviors in which an observer's self is involved.[3] While playing a field work role and attempting to take the role of an informant, the field observer often attempts to master hitherto strange or only generally understood universes of discourse relating to many attitudes and behaviors. He continually introspects, raising endless questions about the informant and developing field relationship, with a view to playing the field work role as successfully as possible. A sociological assumption here is that the more successful the field worker is in playing his role, the more successful he must be in taking the informant's role. Success in both role-taking and role-playing requires success in blending the demands of self-expression and self-integrity with the demands of the role.

It is axiomatic that a person who finds a role natural and congenial, and who acts convincingly in it, has in fact found how to balance role-demands with those of self. If need be he can subordinate self-demands in the interest of the role and role-demands in the interest of self whenever he perceives that either self or role is in any way threatened. If, while playing the role, someone with whom he is interacting attacks anything in which he has self-involvement, he can point out to himself that the best way to protect self at the moment is to subordinate (or defer) self-expression to allow successful performance in the role. In other words, he uses role to protect self. Also, when he perceives that he is performing inadequately in the role he can indicate to himself that he can do better by changing tactics. Here he uses self as a source of new behaviors to protect role.

3. To simplify this presentation, I am assuming that the field worker is an experienced observer who has incorporated the role into his self-conceptions. Through this incorporation, he is self-involved in the role and feels that self is at stake in it. However, being experienced in the role, he can balance role-demands and self-demands in virtually all field situations, that is, all except those to be discussed shortly.

The case of using role to protect self from perceived threat is one of acute self-consciousness, a matter of diminishing over-sensitivity to self-demands by introspectively noting corresponding demands of role. The case of using self to protect role from perceived threat is one of acute role-consciousness, a matter of diminishing over-sensitivity to role-demands by introspectively indicating that they are disproportionately larger than those of self. Both cases represent situations in which role-demands and self-demands are out of balance with each other as a result of perceived threat, and are then restored to balance by appropriate introspection.

Yet, no matter how congenial the two sets of demands seem to be, a person who plays a role in greatly varied situations (and this is especially true of a sociologist field observer) sometimes experiences threats which markedly impair his effectiveness as an interactor in the situation. When attempting to assess informational products of field work, it is instructive to examine the field worker's role-taking and role-playing in situations of perceived, but unresolved, threat. Because he defines success in the role partly in terms of doing everything he can to remain in even threatening situations to secure desired information, he may find that persevering is sometimes more heroic than fruitful.

The situation may be one in which he finds the informant an almost intolerable bigot. The field worker decides to stick it out by attempting to subordinate self-demands to those of role. He succeeds to the extent of refraining from "telling off" the informant, but fails in that he is too self-conscious to play his role effectively. He may think of countless things he would like to say and do to the informant, all of which are dysfunctional to role-demands since his role requires taking the role of the other as an informant, not as a bigot. At the extreme of nearly overwhelming self-consciousness, the field worker may still protect his role by getting out of the situation while the getting is good. Once out and in the company of understanding colleagues, he will finally be able to achieve self-expression (i.e., finally air his views of the informant) without damaging the field role.[4]

Should the situation be such that the field worker finds the informant practically inscrutable (i.e., a "bad" informant), he may decide to persevere despite inablity to meet role-taking and role-playing

4. An inexperienced field worker might "explode" on the spot, feeling that role and self are not congenial in this *or any other* situation. But an experienced field worker would leave such a situation as gracefully as possible to protect the role, feeling that role and self are not congenial in *this* situation only.

demands. In this situation he becomes acutely role-conscious, since he is hypersensitive to role-demands, hyposensitive to self. This partial breakdown of his self-process thwarts his drawing on past experiences and current observations to raise meaningful questions and perceive meaningful answers. At the extreme, a role-conscious field worker may play his role so mechanically and unconvincingly that the informant, too, develops role-and-self problems.

The following discussion utilized these conceptions of role and self to aid in analyzing field work roles as "master roles" for developing lesser role-relationships with informants.[5] While a field worker cannot be all things to all men, he routinely tried to fit himself into as many roles as he can, so long as playing them helps him to develop relationships with informants in his master role (i.e., participant-as-observer, etc).

COMPLETE PARTICIPANT

The true identity and purpose of the complete participant in field research are not known to those whom he observes. He interacts with them as naturally as possible in whatever areas of their living interest him and are accessible to him as situations in which he can play, or learn to play, requisite day-to-day roles successfully. He may, for example, work in a factory to learn about inner-workings of informal groups. After gaining acceptance at least as a novice, he may be permitted to share not only in work activities and attitudes but also in the intimate life of the workers outside the factory.

Role-pretense is a basic theme in these activities. It matters little whether the complete participant in a factory situation has an upper-lower class background or perhaps some factory experience, or whether he has an upper-middle class background quite divorced from factory work and the norms of such workers. What really matters is that he knows that he is pretending to be a colleague. I mean to suggest by this that the crucial value as far as research yield is concerned lies more in the self-orientation of the complete partici-

5. Lesser role-relationships include all achieved and ascribed roles which the field worker plays in the act of developing a field relationship with an informant. For example, he may become the "nice man that old ladies can't resist" as part of his over-all role-reportoire in a community study. Whether he deliberately sets out to achieve such relationships with old ladies or discovers that old ladies ascribe him "irresistible" characteristics, he is still a participant-as-observer who interacts with local old ladies as a "nice man." Were he not there to study the community, he might choose *not* to engage in this role-relationship, especially if being irrestible to old ladies is not helpful in whatever master role(s) brought him to town. (Cf. any experienced community researcher.)

pant than in his surface role-behaviors as he initiates his study. The complete participant realizes that he, and he alone, knows that he is in reality other than the person he pretends to be. He must pretend that his real self is represented by the role, or roles, he plays in and out of the factory situation in relationships with people who, to him, are but informants, and this implies an interactive construction that has deep ramifications. He must bind the mask of pretense to himself or stand the risk of exposure and research failure.

In effect, the complete participant operates continually under an additional set of situational demands. Situational role-and-self demands ordinarily tend to correspond closely. For this reason, even when a person is in the act of learning to play a role, he is likely to believe that pretending to have achieved this correspondence (i.e., fourflushing) will be unnecessary when he can actually "be himself" in the role. But the complete observer simply cannot "be himself"; to do so would almost invariably preclude successful pretense. At the very least, attempting to "be himself"—that is, to achieve self-realization in pretended roles—would arouse suspicion of the kind that would lead others to remain aloof in interacting with him. He must be sensitive to demands of self, of the observer role, and of the momentarily pretended role. Being sensitive to the set of demands accompanying role-pretense is a matter of being sensitive to a large variety of overt and covert mannerisms and other social cues representing the observer's pretended self. Instead of being himself in the pretended role, all he can be is a "not self," in the sense of perceiving that his actions are meaningful in a contrived role.

The following illustration of the pretense of a complete participant comes from an interview with a field worker who drove a cab for many moths to study big-city cab drivers. Here a field worker reveals how a pretended role fosters a heightened sense of self-awareness, an introspective attitude, because of the sheer necessity of indicating continually to himself that certain experiences are merely part of playing a pretended role. These indications serve as self-assurance that customers are not really treating *him* as they seem to do, since he is actually someone else, namely, a field worker.

> Well, I've noticed that the cab driver who *is* a cab driver acts differently than the part-time cab drivers, who don't think of themselves as real cab drivers. When somebody throws a slam at men who drive only part of the year, such as, "Well, you're just a goddamn cab driver!," they do one of two things. They may make it known to the guy that they are not a cab driver; they are something else. But as a rule, that doesn't work out, because the customer comes back with,

"Well, if you're not a cab driver what the hell are you driving this cab for?" So, as a rule, they mostly just rationalize it to themselves by thinking, "Well, this is not my role or the real me. He just doesn't understand. Just consider the source and drop it." But a cab driver who *is* a cab driver, if you make a crack at him, such as, "You're just a goddamn cab driver!" he's going to take you out of the back seat and whip you.

Other complete participant roles may pose more or less of a challenge to the field worker than those mentioned above. Playing the role of potential convert to study a religious sect almost inevitably leads the field worker to feel not only that he has "taken" the people who belong to the sect, but that he has done it in ways which are difficult to justify. In short, he may suffer severe qualms about his mandate to get information in a role where he pretends to be a colleague in moral, as well as in other social, respects.

All complete participant roles have in common two potential problems; continuation in a pretended role ultimately leads the observer to reckon with one or the other. One, he may become so self-conscious about revealing his true self that he is handicapped when attempting to perform convincingly in the pretended role. Or two, he may "go native," incorporate the role into his self-conceptions and achieve self-expression in the role, but find he has so violated his observer role that it is almost impossible to report his findings. Consequently, the field worker needs cooling off periods during and after complete participation, at which time he can "be himself" and look back on his field behavior dispassionately and sociologically.

While the complete participant role offers possibilities of learning about aspects of behavior that might otherwise escape a field observer, it places him in pretended roles which call for delicate balance between demands of role and self. A complete participant must continually remind himself that, above all, he is there as an observer: This is his primary role. If he succumbs to demands of the pretended role (or roles), or to demands of self-expression and self-intregity, he can no longer function as an observer. When he can defer self-expression no longer, he steps out of the pretended role to find opportunities for congenial interaction with those who are, in fact, colleagues.

PARTICIPANT-AS-OBSERVER

Although basically similar to the complete observer role, the participant-as-observer role differs significantly in that both field worker and informant are aware that theirs is a field relationship. This mutual awareness tends to minimize problems of role-pretending; yet, the role carries with it numerous opportunities for compartmentalizing mistakes and dilemmas which typically bedevil the complete participant.

Probably the most frequent use of this role is in community studies, where an observer develops relationships with informants through time, and where he is apt to spend more time and energy participating that observing. At times he observes formally, as in scheduled interview situations; and at other times he observes informally—when attending parties, for example. During early stages of his stay in the community, informants may be somewhat uneasy about him in both formal and informal situations, but their uneasiness is likely to disappear when they learn to trust him and he them.

But just when the research atmosphere seems ripe for gathering information, problems of role and self are apt to arise. Should field worker and informant begin to interact in much the same way as ordinary friends, they tend to jeopardize their field roles in at least two important ways. First, the informant may become too identified with the field worker to continue functioning as merely an informant. In this event the informant becomes too much of an observer. Second, the field worker may over-identify with the informant and start to lose his research perspective by "going native." Sould this occur the field worker may still continue going through the motions of observing, but he is only pretending.

Although the field worker in the participant-as-observer role strives to bring his relationship with the informant to the point of friendship, to the point of intimate form, it behooves him to retain sufficient elements of "the stranger" to avoid actually reaching intimate form. Simmel's distinction between intimate content and intimate form contains an implicit warning that the latter is inimical to field observation.[6] When content of interaction is intimate, secrets may be shared without either of the interactors feeling compelled to maintain the relationship for more than a short time. This is the

---

6. "In other words, intimacy is not based on the *content* of the relationship. . . . Inversely, certain external situations or moods may move us to make very personal statements and confessions, usually reserved for our closest friends only, to relatively strange people. But in such cases we nevertheless feel that this 'intimate' *content* does not yet make the relation an intimate one. For in its basic significance, the whole relation to these people is based only on its general, unindividual ingredients. That 'intimate' content, although we have perhaps never revealed it before and thus limit it entirely to this particular relationship, does nevertheless not become the basis for its form, and thus leaves it outside the sphere of intimacy." K. H. Wolff, ed., *The Sociology of Georg Simmel* (Glencoe, Illinois: Free Press, 1950), p. 127.

interaction of sociological strangers. On the other-hand, when form of interaction is intimate, continuation of the relationship (which is no longer merely a field relationship) may become more important to one or both of the interactors that continuation of the roles through which they initiated the relationship.

In general, the demands of pretense in this role, as in that of the complete participant, are continuing and great; for here the field worker is often defined by informants as more of a colleague than he feels capable of being. He tries to pretend that he is as much of a colleague as they seem to think he is, while searching to discover how to make the pretense appear natural and convincing. Whenever pretense becomes too challenging, the participant-as-observer leaves the field to re-clarify his self-conceptions and his role-relationships.

OBSERVER-AS-PARTICIPANT

The observer-as-participant role is used in studies involving one-visit interviews. It calls for relatively more formal observation than either informal observation or participation of any kind. It also entails less risk of "going native" than either the complete participant role or the participant-as-observer role. However, because the observer-as-participant's contact with an informant is so brief, and perhaps superficial, he is more likely than the other two to misunderstand the informant, and to be misunderstood by him.

These misunderstandings contribute to a problem of self-expression that is almost unique to this role. To a field worker (as to other human beings), self-expression becomes a problem at any time he perceives he is threatened. Since he meets more varieties of people for shorter periods of time than either the complete participant or the participant-as-observer, the observer-as-participant inclines more to feel threatened. Brief relationships with numerous informants expose an observer-as-participant to many inadequately understood universes of discourse that he cannot take time to master. These frustratingly brief encounters with informants also contribute to mistaken perceptions which set up communication barriers the field worker may not even be aware of until too late. Continuing relationships with apparently threatening informants offer an opportunity to redefine them as more congenial partners in interaction, but such is not the fortune of a field worker in this role. Consequently, using his prerogative to break off relationships with threatening informants, an observer-as-participant, more easily than the other two, can leave the field almost at will to regain the kind of role-and-self balance that he, being who he is, must regain.

COMPLETE OBSERVER

The complete observer role entirely removes a field worker from social interaction with informants. Here a field worker attempts to observe people in ways which make it unnecessary for them to take him into account, for they do not know he is observing them or that, in some sense, they are serving as his informants. Of the four field work roles, this alone is almost never the dominant one. It is sometimes used as one of the subordinate roles employeed to implement the dominant ones.

It is generally true that with increasingly more observation than participation, the chances of "going native" become smaller, although the possibility of ethnocentrism becomes greater. With respect to achieving rapport in a field relationship, ethnocentrism may be considered a logical opposite of "going native." Ethnocentrism occurs whenever a field worker cannot or will not interact meaningfully with an informant. He then seemingly or actually rejects the informant's views without ever getting to the point of understanding them. At the other extreme, a field worker who "goes native" passes the point of field rapport by literally accepting his informant's views as his own. Both are cases of pretending to be an observer, but for obviously opposite reasons. Because a complete observer remains entirely outside the observed interaction, he faces the greatest danger of misunderstanding the observed. For the same reason, his role carries the least chance of "going native."

The complete observer role is illustrated by systematic eavesdropping, or by reconnaissance of any kind of social setting as preparation for more intensive study in another field role. While watching the rest of the world roll by, a complete observer may feel comfortably detached, for he takes no self-risks, participates not one whit. Yet, there are many times when he wishes he could ask representatives of the observed world to qualify what they have said, or to answer other questions his observations of them have brought to mind. For some purposes, however, these very questions are important starting points for subsequent observations and interactions in appropriate roles. It is not surprising that reconnaissance is almost always a prelude to using that participant-as-observer role in community study. The field worker, feeling comfortably detached, can first "case" the town before committing himself to casing *by* the town.

CONCLUSIONS

Those of us who teach field work courses or supervise graduate students and others doing field observations have long been concerned with the kinds of interactional problems and processes discussed above. We find such common "mistakes" as that of the beginner who over-identifies with an informant simply because the person treats him compassionately after others have refused to grant him an interview. This limited, although very real, case of "going native" becomes much more understandable to the beginner when we have analyzed it for him sociologically. When he can begin utilizing theory of role and self to reflect on his own assets and shortcomings in the field, he will be well on the way to dealing meaningfully with problems of controlling *his* interactions with informants.

Beyond this level of control, sophistication in field observation requires manipulating informants to help them play their role effectively. Once a field worker learns that a field relationship in process of being structured creates role-and-self problems for informants that are remarkably similar to those he has experienced, he is in a position to offer informants whatever kind of "reassurances" they need to fit into their role. Certainly a field worker has mastered his role only to the extent that he can help informants to master theirs. Learning this fact (and doing something about it!) will eliminate nearly all excuses about "bad" or "inept" informants, since, willy-nilly, an informant is likely to play his role only as fruitfully or as fruitlessly as a field worker plays his.[7]

Experienced field workers recognize limitations in their ability to develop relationships in various roles and situations. They have also discovered that they can maximize their take of information by selecting a field role which permits them to adjust their own role-repertoires to research objectives. Objectively, a selected role is simply an expedient device for securing a given level of information. For instance, a complete participant obviously develops relationships and frames of reference which yield a somewhat different perspective of the subject matter than that which any of the other field work roles would yield. These subjective and objective factors come together in the fact that degree of success in securing the level of information which a field role makes available to a field worker is largely a matter of his skill in playing and taking roles.

Each of the four field work roles has been shown to offer advan-

---

7. In a recent article on interviewing, Theodore Caplow also recognizes the key role played by the field worker in structuring the field relationship. He concludes, "The quality and quantity of the information secured probably depend far more upon the competence of the interviewer than upon the respondent." "The Dynamics of Information Interviewing," *American Journal of Sociology*, LXII (September 1956), 169. Cf. also the studies by Junker and Gold, *op. cit.*

tages and disadvantages with respect to both demands of role and self and level of information. No attempt has been made in this report to show how a sociological conception of field work roles can do more than provide lines of thought and action for dealing with problems and processes of field interaction. Obviously, however, a theory of role and self growing out of study of field interaction is in no sense limited to that area of human activity. Learning to take and play roles, although dramatized in the field, is essentially the same kind of social learning people engage in throughout life.

In any case, the foregoing discussion has suggested that a field worker selects and plays a role so that he, being who he is, can best study those aspects of society in which he is interested.

24. Role-Making in Participant Observation: Processes in the Researcher-Actor Relationship

VIRGINIA L. OLESEN AND
ELVI WAIK WHITTAKER

The act of knowing includes an appraisal; and this personal coefficient, which shapes all factual knowledge, bridges in doing so the disjunction between subjectivity and objectivity. It implies the claim that man can transcend his own subjectivity and objectivity by striving passionately to fulfill his personal obligations to universal standards.[1]

ALTHOUGH recent essays about participant observation have extended our understanding of that research method and its problematic aspects, few methodologists have scrutinized intensively the processes by which roles are developed in this type of fieldwork or the relationship of role development to the data gathered. Our purpose in reviewing our own experiences as participant observers in long-

Reprinted by permission from *Human Organization*, 26 (1967), pp. 273–81. Copyright 1967, The Society for Applied Anthropology.

1. Michael Polanyi, *Personal Knowledge: Towards a Post-Critical Philosophy* (New York: Harper Torchbooks, 1964), p. 17.

itudinal study of baccalaureate student nurses is to explore these questions. We have also studied reports of the encounters of other researchers in participant observation. Using information from such experiences, we have tried to outline and interpret the characteristic processes of role defining in this type of research. We have restricted ourselves to consideration of fieldwork situations in which the involved parties are mutually aware of the research, thus avoiding the special problems of role definitions in hidden research.

THE PARTICIPANT OBSERVER EXPERIENCE

Our experiences as participant observers occurred during the data-gathering phase of a longitudinal fieldwork study in which questionnaires, interviews, psychological measures and participant observation were used to gather information on emergence of professional identity in baccalaureate student nurses. We and our purposes were fully known to and sanctioned by the administration and faculty. The students were aware from the beginning of our presence and our purposes, because we and they had arrived simultaneously at the school of nursing and we made our intentions known to them from the onset.

In company with male colleagues we observed some 38 members of the class of 1963 for the better part of their three year program, excluding vacation summers. We also observed members of adjacent classes, but not as extensively or intensively. We were with the students almost daily, frequently for the better part of the day and sometimes at night, too. We interacted with them under a variety of circumstances: in classroom discussion, ward work and on informal social occasions. Because we were not students or faculty and because we had emphasized from the start that we were researchers, we were not truly participants, yet time and again we would be drawn into active participation, for example, to help at a student party, to lend a hand with a patient, to give advice. Perhaps the best label for us is "participants-as-observers," Pearsall's term, which captures the intimacy and intensity of our prolonged relationship with these students.[2]

2. Marion Pearsall, "Participant Observation as Role and Method in Behavioral Research," *Nursing Research*, vol. 14, no. 1 (Winter 1965), 38. Findings based primarily on our observational data may be found in Fred Davis and Virginia L. Olesen, "Initiation into a Woman's Profession," *Sociometry*, Vol. 26, no. 1 (March 1963), 89-101, and Virginia L. Olesen and Elvi Waik Whittaker, "Adjudication of Student Awareness in Professional Socialization: The Language of Laughter and Silences," *The Sociological Quarterly*, vol. 7, no. 3 (Summer 1966), 381–96.

The students themselves were in general of Anglo-Saxon origin, native born and of middle and upper middle socio-economic origins. For the most part they had been reared in large and medium-sized cities in the American West. Their families were affiliated with the major Protestant denominations. Because the students were in their late teens and early twenties, they were younger by at least a decade then we, the researchers, who were closer in age to faculty members. Their previous academic work had included two years preparation at junior colleges or branches of the state university.

Throughout we shall refer to the students who were the subjects of the study as "actors" or "participants," which reflects our contention that research roles in participant observation are created, eroded or sustained jointly by the investigator and the actor. We regard participant observation as a mutual venture in which reciprocal interpersonal exchanges between the research investigator and the actor result in more or less mutually meaningful, well-understood, viable social roles. The process is that of role-making, in Ralph Turner's phraseology:

> Roles "exist" in varying degrees of concreteness and consistency, while the individual confidently frames his behavior as if they had unequivocal existence and clarity. The result is that in attempting from time to time to make aspects of the roles explicit he is creating and modifying roles as well as merely bringing them to light; the process is not only role-taking, but *role-making*.[3]

The phases through which role-making passes in the course of interaction in fieldwork are stages of definitions by investigator and actors around the research roles and also around life roles (age, sex, social class and other non-occupational roles). Each phase represents a distinctive segment of the role-making process and each is relevant for the establishment of mutual awareness, consensus on role meanings, and management of the ongoing interaction, as well as for data gathered. The four phases are:

1. *Surface encounter.* The initial contact with the other's research and life roles.

2. *Proffering and inviting.* The mutual exchange involved in offering definitions of one's self and the other while simultaneously asking for definitions of one's self and the other from the other party.

3. *Selecting and modifying.* The reciprocal selection of mean-

---

3. Ralph Turner, "Role-Taking: Process Versus Conformity," in Arnold Rose, ed., *Human Behavior and Social Processes* (Boston: Houghton-Mifflin, 1952), p. 20. (Italics in the original.)

ingful and viable portions of the research roles and life roles of participant and observer.

4. *Stabilizing and sustaining.* Achievement of a balance, albeit tentative, within and between the research and life roles, of meaningful definitions, and the refurbishing necessary to maintain the meaningful definitions that are proffered, invited, selected and stabilized.

Though they reflect the general flow of role-making, these phases are by no means cleanly and clearly delineated in the actual experience: They may in fact exist simultaneously or overlap. Thus a number of discrepancies between and among phases are likely. The actors and the investigator may not experience the phases simultaneously, nor will all actors necessarily be in the same phase with respect to the investigator at the same time. Moreover, either party, or both, may interact in one phase with respect to the research role, and in quite a different one regarding life roles. These discrepancies are shaped by structural and situational factors that will be discussed as we elaborate on the phases.

THE PHASES OF ROLE-MAKING

Surface Encounter. This phase is the apogee of researcher-actor relationships, encompassing as it does that fleeting period at the outset of fieldwork wherein the parties relate as almost total strangers. This brief period, like that described by Alfred Schutz in his insightful essay on "The Stranger," is one in which the participants locate and tolerate one another in terms of broad role categories which the other seems to occupy.[4] Definitions at this stage, as sometimes happens when one flirts with a handsome man or pretty woman who later turns out to be married, may be erroneous, but they permit limited interaction.

The categories open to the parties initially, with respect to the life roles, depend on the categories available in the field situation, or those known from past experience. The possibilities may be very limited, in which case some amusing placements can occur. Our notes show, for example, that we were categorized as students, regis-

4. Alfred Schutz, "The Stranger," in Arvid Brodersen, ed., *Collected Papers, Vol. II, Studies in Social Theory*, (The Hague: Martinus Nijhoff, 1964), pp. 91–105. See also Georg Simmel, "The Stranger," in Kurt Wolff, ed., *The Sociology of Georg Simmel*, (Glencoe, Ill.: Free Press, 1950), pp. 402–08; Mary Margaret Wood, *The Stranger, A Study in Social Relationships* (New York: Columbia University Press, 1934), Dennison Nash, "The Ethnologist as Stranger: An Essay in the Sociology of Knowledge," *Southwestern Journal of Anthropology*, vol. 19, no. 2 (Summer 1963), 149–67.

tered nurses or faculty. The period of initial location and tolerance, which we here call "surface encounter," is likely to be transitory. The duration may depend on the extent to which the actors are acquainted with research roles in general and the complexity of the social situation with respect to alternatives for life roles. Floyd Mann notes that because many people do not have a clear idea of research roles, the bases for understanding the researcher and presumably the bases for the onward flow of the interaction will be found in the researcher's life roles.[5] It is possible, therefore, that the less the actor knows of the research role and the greater the number of possibilities for placing the researcher in life roles, the sooner the parties will embark on the second phase of "proffering and inviting."

Proffering and Inviting. In this phase both involved parties seek to expand the meanings of their own roles and the roles of the other. This occurs primarily through a series of exchanges in which one party proffers a definition either of himself or the other persons for tentative acceptance, rejection or modification. Simultaneously, he invites from the other party definitions that have to do with himself or the other party. This process of proffering and inviting embraces both the research roles and the life roles of the actor and the participant observer.

In the early part of our study with student nurses, the students often tentatively asked us whether they were being used as subjects in an experiment. This type of question was an invitation to us to clarify our mutual research roles. Some of them went so far as to state explicitly that they thought they were being used as "guinea pigs," a declaration that constructed an offering of definitions, both of their research roles and ours. Likewise, they asked if we were faculty members, an invitation to clarify our research role. Some thought the study was part of the curriculum, thus offering us their definition of our research role. They also proffered and invited definitions about our research techniques (were we interviewers, observers, or what). This phase of proffered and invited definitions in which both we and the students participated allowed the students and us to shape the definitions of ourselves as investigators and the students as actors in research and life roles. Our experience was thus similar to Scott's in clarifying his research role with social workers.[6]

During this phase two types of interaction may first emerge and

5. Floyd C. Mann, "Human Relations Skills in Social Research," *Human Relations*, vol. 4, no. 4 (November 1951), 341.

6. W. Richard Scott, "Field Work in a Formal Organization: Some Dilemmas in the Role of Observer," *Human Organization*, vol. 22, no. 2 (Summer 1963), 163.

may perhaps continue throughout the fieldwork. The first, to use Strauss' phrase, is "coaching."[7] The second we have called "sponsoring." In "coaching," the investigator deliberately proffers or invites certain definitions from the actor, particularly concerning the research roles. The investigator then accepts, rejects or modifies these definitions and attempts to influence the actor to accept the investigator's definition. "Coaching," however, is not solely the investigator's prerogative, for actors, too, as Whyte recalls, "coach" the investigator. His "Corner Boys" let him know that they preferred that he not use profanity, thus indicating the role they wanted Whyte to take.[8] In our study, the student nurses were wont to "coach" us on our role and our role behaviors with patients, staff and students themselves. Their "coaching" tactics ranged from open advice to subtle gesture and expression, as in this incident:

> As I opened the door I caught sight of Mary Jones at the bedside of her patient, facing the direction in which I was looking. Mary caught sight of me and remarked so that I could hear, "We're having our bath now." I said that I was sorry to have disturbed them and would be back a while later. (First year notes, October 1960).

"Sponsoring" refers to the situation in which the actors give definitions of the investigator's research or life roles to persons not immediately involved in the research. Our students took it upon themselves to define us as researchers and persons to patients, doctors, nursing staff, faculty and faculty members, in a fashion not unlike that of Whyte's "Corner Boys," who had to certify that he was not a G-man.[9]

Consider this instance of student "sponsoring:"

> Joan (the student) drew the drapes away from the patient's bed and said, "Mr. Ross, I want to introduce you to a friend who is doing research on the nursing students." (First year notes, January 1961.)

Somewhat later in our research "sponsoring" took on a more intense quality:

> When I arrived at the class, the instructor said, "The students will sit up here and the observers will sit back there." I really didn't know what to do, because I didn't want to irritate this instructor, nor did I want to set in the back. While I was trying to decide what to do,

---

7. On "coaching," see Anselm Strauss, *Mirrors and Masks* (Glencoe, Ill.: Free Press, 1960), pp. 109–18.
8. W. F. Whyte, *Streetcorner Society* (Chicago: The University of Chicago Press, 1955), p. 304.
9. Whyte, *op. cit.*, p. 298.

Rebekah Stout said to the instructor in loud, agressive tones, "Well, she gets to sit up here with us." Other students then began chiming in, "Come up and sit with us." (Second year notes, November 1961.)

Proffering and inviting also occurs around life roles. In this phase, with respect to life roles, we presented ourselves as former students, as book lovers, ballet afficionadas, cooks, and the like. We also offered the student nurses definitions of themselves as music lovers, citizens, sports fans, hobbyists, and other appropriate roles. This was by no means one-sided. The students, too, proffered definitions of themselves as persons with interests and lives beyond the institutional confines, and they invited us to define ourselves in similar terms. Particularly in the early part of the fieldwork, but throughout the study, the many definitions of life roles seemed critical in humanizing the researcher:

> These students seemed very curious about the study and about my background. I told them again what we were and were not doing and then I talked about my own concerns about myself as a student. Recalling the student role seemed to be an effective way of relating with them, for a good many of them asked what degree I was working on, where I had gone to school and various other matters about being a student. (First year notes, September 1960.)

Others have pointed out this need to humanize investigator and actor in the process of prying and poking, questioning and doubting which is inherent in this type of fieldwork. Rosalie Wax, for instance, has noted:

> If I invade another human's privacy with long lists of questions, I will learn little unless I am genuinely curious; it is no more than common courtesy to reciprocate by satisfying the curiosity of my informant.[10]

Selecting and Modifying. The role definitions proffered and invited are the interpersonal materials for the succeeding phase of selection and modification. Fron the wide range of highly variegated definitions of both research and life roles exchanged between investigator and actor, a number are selected, some with little modification, others with considerable alteration. Which definitions will be selected and how they will be modified seems to turn on the degree of congruence between the definitions offered and the values, structure and ideology of the people associated with the research setting.

10. Rosalie Wax, "Reciprocity in Field Work," in Richard N. Adams and Jack J. Preiss, eds., *Human Organization Research* (Homewood, Ill.: Dorsey, 1960), p. 23.

With respect to the research role, the selection of meaningful definitions may be facilitated, as Robert Janes, Joseph Lohman and Herbert Gans have pointed out, if a comparable role exists in the situation or if actors are familiar with research roles.[11]

In our study the students were generally acquainted with research roles. Indeed, on their entering questionnaires, 58 percent indicated that they expected to have some or a great deal of contact during their nursing education with researchers. This awareness speeded the selection of definitions concerning our research role, for the role-making phase could spur the definition of researcher as participant observer and, within that special research role category, the refining of the nuances that characterized our approach. The following conversation, typical of such refinement efforts, occurred with a second-year student in the first week of our study. (Second-year students were also being observed and it was necessary to explain ourselves to them as well as to first-year students.)

> I told her (the student) about our purposes and then let her ask several questions ... I then explained the nature of participant observation ... She then wanted to know if I were living at the dorm. I said that I was not, because of the necessity to have some time away from the campus and to give the students a relief from me. She agreed with this and went on to relate a story she had heard in one of her anthropology classes about an observer who had gone native. (First year notes, September 1960.)

As this story suggests, we were also understandable to the students because some were acquainted, if only in the layman's way, with stated anthropological traditions of observational research.

Value configurations also play a significant part in the selection of mutually meaningful definitions. We could not define ourselves to the students as being too close to the more liberal, free-living aspects of academic and intellectual life, for these definitions would depart too fully from the more conservative values endorsed by the students, as this anecdote clearly shows:

> Janet told me that I should not mention to the other students that I had "beatnik" friends. When I wanted to know why, she replied, "Some of them are very young and narrow-minded." (First year notes, November 1960.)

11. Robert W. Janes, "A Note on the Phases of the Community Role of the Participant Observer," *American Sociological Review*, vol. 26, no. 3 (June 1961), 446–50; Joseph D. Lohman, "The Participant Observer in Community Studies," *American Sociological Review*, vol. 2, no. 6 (December 1937), 890–97; Herbert Gans, *The Urban Villagers* (Glencoe, Ill.: Free Press, 1962), p. 342.

The inviting and proffering, selecting and modifying phases may extend through the entire period of fieldwork. Nevertheless, a relative degree of stabilization may emerge based on the definitions as selected and modified.

Stabilizing and Sustaining. This final phase is characterized by a tenuous balance in the mutually accepted definitions of research and life roles. Our experiences with student nurses and that of others suggest that fieldwork roles are constantly being modified in the course of the research. Such stabilization as occurs is best characterized by the seemingly contradictory term "balanced instability."

Stabilization is much influenced by the onward flow of events and by the social rhythms of the research setting, and the movement of persons in roles related to those of the researcher and the actors. It may also be radically affected by crises and other abnormal events, as noted by Rosalie Wax with reference to research in Japanese Relocation Centers during World War II.[12]

Judging from our own experiences, we suspect that the potential for shifts in previously stable definitions may be particularly high in situations where graduated changes in role arrangements are part of the institutional pattern, as in professional schools. In such instances the actors, in particular, are expected at the termination of institutional time to assume roles different from those assumed at the beginning. Student nurses at the outset of schooling are naive laymen; by its termination they presumably are sophisticated professionals.

In situations where shifting role definitions are integrated with institutional expectations, definitions of research or life roles that at the beginning of the research work well enough may not be appropriate later on. In our work we commenced the study by defining ourselves to the students as ignorant laymen who would have to be informed about the hospital, nursing practices, etc.:

> ... as a point of interest at this stage. I find myself slipping into the role of "poor stupid sociologist" who needs to be directed and have things pointed out to her and so on ... (First year notes, November 1960.)

The students accepted this definition, which became somewhat stabilized. As time went by, however, although we did not and could not acquire the depth and range of knowledge of the student nurses themselves, we nevertheless absorbed a good deal of rather specific

12. Rosalie Wax, "Twelve Years Later: An Analysis of Field Work Experiences," in Adams and Preiss, *op. cit.*, p. 173; "Reciprocity in Field Work," in Adams and Preiss, *op. cit.*, p. 97.

technical information about nursing and medical practice. Indeed, the students themselves undertook some specific teaching with us in several instances:

> Yesterday in the operating room one of the scrub nurses had asked me to obtain and open a package containing a sterile vest. I got the package, but did not know how to open it and told her so. Today, when the the instructor was out of the classroom, the students gathered around me and showed me how to open a sterile package. They had me practice this several times. (Second year notes, October 1961.)

To continue to proffer the definition of the ignorant layman, when, in fact, we were somewhat knowledgeable, would have been hypocritical as well as unrealistic, since the students themselves were aware that we were beyond being mere laymen. We thus had to proffer new definitions of ourselves as interested, partially ignorant, somewhat knowledgeable laymen. As an example of how the definition shifted, consider the following exchange in which the student assumed a knowledgeable listener in the person of the researcher:

> As Renata Soldo was discussing this case, I turned to Tanya Wadja and asked her what Renata meant by bone measurement. She then launched into a detailed description of how the age of an individual can be learned through taking samples of bone marrow. It was a beautiful technical description and one which I thought would have done credit to any physiology student. (Third year notes, May 1963.)

Similarly, as the students became more knowledgeable as nurses and as they changed certain life roles, perhaps married and had children, they redefined themselves to us.

Those factors which may tend to disrupt stabilization are counterbalanced by others that make for stability. One such stabilizing element is consistency in expressive gestures, dress and demeanor. We had decided not to wear nurse uniforms because of the problems it would have created for us on the ward. Instead, when we were around the school of nursing, we adopted a rather informal style of student dress: flat shoes, skirts and sweaters. In our dress we symbolized an easy, and we hoped friendly, approach and relationship with the students. (Elsewhere in interaction with colleagues, we dressed more formally, heels, suits or street dresses.) We retained this informal dress throughout the course of the study, supplementing it with a white laboratory coat when we were on the wards, also to bridge the gap between ourselves as laymen and the students as maturing professionals. The usefulness of the laboratory coats for the students and the ward personnel was not lost upon the students, one of whom commented to us in the first year, "You look official in your lab coats." Our management of dress here was similar to the management of behaviors reported by Gerald Berreman, who recalls that he concealed his use of American amenities from the Sirkande villagers.[13] Our adoption of informal, student-like style of clothing, was also akin to Hannah Papanek's use of a sari to affirm her role in Pakistan.[14]

The stabilization of meaningful definitions of roles further depends on the ecological or spatial setting in which roles are developed. In our case we had to be especially alert to the management of ourselves in the space allocated to us at the school, because our offices were part of a faculty complex. Because of this physical proximity to faculty, we strenuously avoided faculty contact whenever possible, side-stepping conversations and withdrawing from interaction. Understandably, this posed strains on our relationships with the faculty, but we felt that it was necessary in order to stabilize the role definition that we early offered students, namely, that we were not "in league" with the faculty. The difficulties of managing these spatial and interactional strains and the physical withdrawal as a stabilizing device are evident in the following:

> As I was departing from the office with Sandra Burnaby and Eleanor Carlson, one of the instructors came up to me . . . I felt frankly very uncomfortable at being approached by a faculty member while I was with students. After briefly acknowledging her comment to me, I quickly moved on with the students. (First year notes, September 1960.)

The actors, too, make efforts to stabilize their role definition.[15] One student, for example, sought from the beginning to stabilize a definition of herself as an intellectual:

> After the conference Georgia Sampson told me about a girl friend of hers who is at the Harvard Law School. Georgia emphasized several times how intelligent this girl is, how this girl was like Georgia's twin. (First year notes, January 1961.)

Although role definitions of both the research and life roles are, as we have noted, prone to shift, some degree of stabilization nevertheless ensues. The mutually achieved viable definitions must then

13. Gerald D. Berreman, *Behind Many Masks*, monograph no. 4 (Society for Applied Anthropology, 1962), p. 21.
14. Hannah Papanek, "The Woman Field Worker in a Purdah Society," *Human Organization*, vol. 23, no. 2 (Summer 1964), 161.
15. Berreman, *op. cit.*, pp. 13–14.

be sustained. We felt it necessary from time to time to reinforce certain definitions of both research and life roles. We termed this reinforcement of one's images, "body-building." For instance, one definition of our research role as investigators was that we were completely open with the students about our work. We periodically vigorously reinforced this definition by deliberately making occasional remarks, or again, by "coaching" our actors to reassimilate this definition of us. For example, in a group dynamics class the instructor remarked on the researcher's presence. Then:

> By this time I felt it was necessary to score some points for the study, so I opened up on the researchers' familiar themes of the openness of the study, of how we tried to be above-board with the students, of our efforts to advise them of our presence and the continual attempts on our part to avoid any secretiveness. (Second year notes, March 1962.)

As we thus sustained certain definitions of our research role, we also engaged in "body-building" of our life roles, recalling to the students that we had lives and concerns beyond those of the study: in short, reminding them of our human qualities. In doing so we invited the students to sustain definitions of themselves in their life roles. We did this on any number of occasions, on the wards, over coffee, in casual hallway encounters. We asked about their interests in dating, hobbies, music, politics and life in general. This transaction was mutual, since the students were "body-building" with us. They frequently questioned us about our families, what we thought of certain new books, what films we had seen, what kinds of new dishes we were cooking. Simultaneously, they volunteered similar information about themselves. Such exchanges served to sustain previous definitions and to maintain the mutual humanizing process.

SUMMARY AND CONCLUSION

We have suggested four more or less distinct phases through which investigators and actors under study move in the course of role-making in any fieldwork that relies heavily on participant observation. Throughout the four phases the process is reciprocal, and subject always to the vagaries of the human and social situation, the press of events, and cycles in the community organization or sociocultural unit in which the research takes place. At best this is a rough outline of a process that seems applicable to a variety of field situations.

With this initial step toward a model for studying the fieldwork process, we can only speculate about the influence of its phases on the kind, amount and quality of the data generated. We offer these as tentative suggestions for extending the work of Robert Janes and others who have begun to study more systematically the types and validity of data obtained in different phases of field studies.[16]

Information gained during role-making in the early phases of a study seems, in our experience, to be more descriptive and more frequently couched in generalities than that which comes to the fore later. This is due partly to the fact that the researcher learns the language, as well as the terms which emerge during fieldwork, which later makes possible communication in more condensed terms. For example, in the early stages of our interaction with student nurses, conversations about their interests in and commitment to nursing contained broad statements about likes, dislikes, motives for entering nursing and the like, all couched in ways exemplified by this conversation:

> I said to Melissa, "Well, if your parents are opposed, why *are* you in nursing?" Whereupon she replied with some heat, "Because I *want* to be." This told me very little about the range of reasons for her choice of nursing, but it did indicate something about the intensity of her feeling. (First year notes, October 1960.)

Later on, however, as roles stabilize and the involved parties have some idea of one another, the information is apt to be more detailed, more specific:

> Hildegarde said that she was eagerly looking forward to working after graduation . . . I asked her if she would devote herself exclusively to being a mother. She replied negatively saying she planned always to be a working woman . . . she told me in reply to my question that she wanted to spend two years in a county health office and then work in Peru. (Third year notes, January 1963.)

We may speculate that the greater specificity of detail in the second conversation can be understood in part by the fact that the researcher-actor role definitions were well stabilized at that point. The researcher had then an opportunity for greater probing into details, and the actor had more opportunity to supply these details. Both researcher and actor had achieved a wider basis for communication.

As role-making developed to increase the familiarity of the re-

16. Janes, *op. cit.*

searchers and the students with each other's special terminologies, some of the information we received in the later phases became highly condensed. Thus, a student comment on a "gung ho" student, of a "nursey-nurse" student, or on "our roles on the wards," or "your [the researcher] role in group dynamics," efficiently and quickly transmitted a wealth of information about student committment to nursing, strains with the staff, the perceptions of the researcher.

While such shorthand terms make for efficient and rapid transmission of data, they suffer the shortcomings of all abstractions or stereotypes by excluding certain sectors of experience and viewpoint. Their persistent use may lead both the researcher and the actors to assume greater mutual knowledge than in fact exists. At the same time the stereotypes may serve the researcher as an indicator of the social distribution of knowledge: The student nurse, for example, who was unaware of the "gung ho" phrase was clearly outside certain student communication circuits.

The use of such condensed symbols raises questions with respect to the types of information generated during role-making. For one thing, by the time roles are stabilized the actors in particular may make certain assumptions about the researchers' omniscience, particularly (as in our case) if ongoing contact with the actors is extensive and intensive:

> Charlotte Jensen talked about an incident involving another student who had had a sticky time with a patient while on a home visit. She seemed to assume that we knew all about this incident, which I knew very well we did not. I therefore had to pussyfoot, saying that of course I had heard of it, but had forgotten the details and asked her to refresh me on these. (Third year notes, February 1963.)

This experience was similar to one reported by Robert Janes who indicates that in the latter stages of his community role, he was treated as if he were fully knowledgeable about local issues and persons.[17]

Equally important, as role-making progresses from initial encounter to stabilizing and sustaining, the researcher-actor interaction may become so fixed on certain themes that information on other issues may rarely, if ever, enter communication.[18] It then becomes difficult for the researcher (or the actor) to steer the conversation to other themes. This suggests that certain sensitive and articulate actors can,

17. Janes, *op. cit.*
18. This point is noted by Arthur Vidich and Joseph Bensman, "The Validity of Field Data," in Adams and Preiss, *op. cit.*, p. 194.

if such over-stabilization occurs, serve nicely as information specialists around the themes so fixed. But it points also to the fact that
during the role-making process, particularly in the proffering and
inviting phase, it is well for the investigator to keep open as many
themes as possible to avoid being later becalmed. Moreover, during
the analysis of such data, it is important to recognize the limits that
the position and personality of the actor may impose on such information, and to remain alert to the representativeness and generalizability of such an actor's statements.

We ourselves were becalmed, albeit pleasantly, with two of our
student actors, who were particularly articulate about the themes of
student life. One girl could talk extensively of almost nothing but the
issues of soul-searching during professional education. The other
regaled us with a catalogue of student leisure activities. Both were
rich sources of these types of information, but neither could easily
have been steered to the special topic of the other, once these
themes were firmly entrenched in our interaction. In our analysis,
therefore, we face the issue of the extent to which such statements,
rich and provocative though they were, are reflective of the state of
mind and the types of activities of other students. Indeed, on one
occasion we were witness to an outright disagreement that occurred
between one of these specialists and a number of her fellow students
on issues of student life in the school:

> I want to put down clearly the dominant flavor of this discussion
> between Kelly Marsh and the other students. I felt rather clearly that
> there was a definite student alignment against Kelly on the complaints
> she aired. She got some support from Rachel Dexter, but the others
> made it clear that Kelly's comments were a bit off base from their
> standpoints. (Third year notes, May 1963.)

Paradoxically, as the interaction between researcher and actors
proceeds through the four phases to what we call the "creation of the
liveable world," the role-making can cordon off information that is
potentially disruptive to the balanced definitions already achieved.[19]
We have, for example, sparse information on the sexual behavior of
our students, although this is presumably relevant in the analysis of
emergent professional and personal identity in a group of young
women of courtship age. Nor do we have data on their personal
finances. In the course of the smooth creation of acceptable roles
through the phases, these topics were only rarely introduced and

19. We have dealt with the "creation of the liveable world" in a volume reporting
results of this study, *The Silent Dialogue: The Social Psychology of Professional
Socialization* (San Francisco, Calif.: Jossey-Bass, 1968).

never pursued either by us or by the students, perhaps because they threatened the viable roles that eventually were stabilized. Such subjects might have been too disruptive to the liveable world we shared with the students. Equally significant for the reciprocities of fieldwork, the students for their part never inquired about our sex lives or personal finances, presumably for the same reasons.

This is not to say that sensitive information never enters into the interaction. It is our impression that such information, if it comes up at all, comes most readily at the time of role stabilization and maintenance. This may be explained, perhaps too easily, on the basis of growing trust. It may also be related to the fact that in the latter stages of role-making, the actors have a greater personal hold on the researcher in the sense of knowing him or her as a person. The actor has then more opportunity to control interaction with the researcher and to impart as much or as little sensitive material as he wishes or, indeed, to steer the interaction in an entirely different direction. In the earlier phase of proffering and inviting, for example, the actor can withdraw from the interaction, but cannot readily control it. We experienced such withdrawal by one student in the early phases of role-making. In a later phase we experienced the following reversal of roles with two students who knew us well enough by then to wrench control of the situation away from us when a sensitive topic was brought up:

> I then chose to take a long shot in the fieldwork and it blew up in my face. Namely, I threw a bit of information on the hot topic of student dropouts to these two students to see if they would give us any more information than we had on Jane Brown who had dropped out. It was instantly apparent that these two did not know who I was talking about, but were more than curious about this. The roles suddenly reversed themselves – I became the interviewee and they became the researchers. I was then put in the old pussyfooting position of telling some things about this sensitive topic, but not too much, particularly about the student who dropped out. (Second year notes, January 1962.)

Admittedly, this excursion into a sensitive area was not a loss with respect to information on the social distribution of student ignorance about this particular topic, but the opportunity to explore the subject more deeply was taken out of our hands by the student actors. In other instances we were able to explore sensitive issues, being fully aware that the students were controlling us just as much as we thought we were controlling them.

Our brief suggestions about the relationship between the role-making process in its several phases and the data from fieldwork demand more systematic scrutiny. Only then will we be able to speak confidently about the plausibility, reliability and validity of data from fieldwork. A start has been made by us and by others, but much more needs to be known about the relation of role-making to the meaning and value of data gathered in this way. Such analysis would be of great help in assisting fieldworkers to capitalize on that most sensitive of instruments and not insignificant source of data: the scientist himself.

25. Problems of Inference and Proof in Participant Observations

HOWARD S. BECKER

THE PARTICIPANT observer gathers data by participating in the daily life of the group or organization he studies.[1] He watches the people he is studying to see what situations they ordinarily meet and how they behave in them. He enters into conversations with some or all of the participants in these situations and discovers their interpretations of the events he has observed.

Let me describe, as one specific instance of observational technique, what my colleagues and I have done in studying a medical school. We went to lectures with students taking their first two years of basic science and frequented the laboratories in which they spend

Reprinted by permission from Howard S. Becker, "Problems of Inference and Proof in Participant Observation," *American Sociological Review*, 23 (December 1958), pp. 652–60. Copyright 1958, American Sociological Association.

1. There is little agreement on the specific referent of the term *participant observation*. See Raymond L. Gold, "Roles in Sociological Field Observations," *Social Forces*, 36 (March, 1958), 217–23, for a useful classification of the various procedures that go by this name. Our own research, from which we have drawn our illustrations, falls under Gold's type, "participant-as-observer." The basic methods discussed here, however, would appear to be similar in other kinds of field situations.

most of their time, watching them and engaging in casual conversations as they dissected cadavers or examined pathology specimens. We followed these students to their fraternity houses and sat around while they discussed their school experiences. We accompanied students in the clinical years on rounds with attending physicans, watched them examine patients on the wards and in the clinics, sat in on discussion groups and oral exams. We ate with the students and took night call with them. We pursued internes and residents through their crowded schedules of teaching and medical work. We stayed with one small group of students on each service for periods ranging from a week to two months, spending many full days with them. The observational situations allowed time for conversation and we took advantage of this to interview students about things that had happened and were about to happen, and about their own backgrounds and aspirations.

Sociologists usually use this method when they are especially interested in understanding a particular organization or substantive problem rather than demonstrating relations between abstractly defined variables. They attempt to make their research theoretically meaningful, but they assume that they do not know enough about the organization *a priori* to identify relevant problems and hypotheses and that they must discover these in the course of the research. Though participant observation can be used to test *a priori* hypotheses, and therefore need not be as unstructured as the example I have given above, this is typically not the case. My discussion refers to the kind of participant observation study which seeks to discover hypotheses as well as to test them.

Observational research produces an immense amount of detailed description; our files contain approximately five thousand single-spaced pages of such material. Faced with such a quantity of "rich" but varied data, the researcher faces the problem of how to analyze it systematically and then to present his conclusions so as to convince other scientists of their validity. Participant observation (indeed, qualitative analysis generally) has not done well with this problem and the full weight of evidence for conclusions and the processes by which they were reached are usually not presented, so that the reader finds it difficult to make his own assessment of them and must rely on his faith in the researcher.

In what follows I try to pull out and describe *the basic analytic operations carried on in participant observation*, for three reasons: to make these operations clear to those unfamiliar with the method; by attempting a more explicit and systematic description, to aid those working with the method in organizing their own research; and, most importantly, in order to propose some changes in analytic procedures and particularly in reporting results which will make the processes by which conclusions are reached and substantiated more accessible to the reader.

The first thing we note about participant observation research is that analysis is carried on *sequentially*,[2] important parts of the analysis being made while the researcher is still gathering his data. This has two obvious consequences: Further data gathering takes its direction from provisional analyses; and the amount and kind of provisional analysis carried on is limited by the exigencies of the field work situation, so that final comprehensive analyses may not be possible until the field work is completed.

We can distinguish three distinct stages of analysis conducted in the field itself, and a fourth stage, carried on after completion of the field work. These stages are differentiated, first, by their logical sequence: Each succeeding stage depends on some analysis in the preceding stage. They are further differentiated by the fact that different kinds of conclusions are arrived at in each stage and that these conclusions are put to different uses in the continuing research. Finally, they are differentiated by the different criteria that are used to assess evidence and to reach conclusions in each stage. The three stages of field analysis are: the selection and definition of problems, concepts, and indices; the check on the frequency and distribution of phenomena; and the incorporation of individual findings into a model of the organization under study.[3] The fourth stage of final analysis involves problems of presentation of evidence and proof.

SELECTION AND DEFINITION OF PROBLEMS, CONCEPTS, AND INDICES

In this stage, the observer looks for problems and concepts that give promise of yielding the greatest understanding of the organization he is studying, and for items which may serve as useful indicators of

2. In this respect, the analytic methods I discuss bear a family resemblance to the technique of *analytic induction*. Cf. Alfred Lindesmith, *Opiate Addiction* (Bloomington: Principia Press, 1947), esp. pp. 5-20, and the subsequent literature cited in Ralph H. Turner, "The Quest for Universals in Sociological Research," *American Sociological Review*, 18 (December 1953), 604-11.

3. My discussion of these stages is abstract and simplified and does not attempt to deal with practical and technical problems of participant observation study. The reader should keep in mind that in practice the research will involve all these operations simultaneously with reference to different particular problems.

facts which are harder to observe. This typical conclusion that his data yield is the simple one that a given phenomenon exists, that a certain event occurred once, or that two phenomena were observed to be related in one instance; the conclusion says nothing about the frequency or distribution of the observed phenomenon.

By placing such an observation in the context of a sociological theory, the observer selects concepts and defines problems for further investigation. He constructs a theoretical model to account for that one case, intending to refine it in the light of subsequent findings. For instance, he might find the following: "Medical student X referred to one of his patients as a 'crock' today."[4] He may then connect this finding with a sociological theory suggesting that occupants of one social category in an institution classify members of other categories by criteria derived from the kinds of problems these other persons raise in the relationship. This combination of observed fact and theory directs him to look for the problems in student-patient interaction indicated by the term "crock." By discovering specifically what students have in mind in using the term, through questioning and continued observation, he may develop specific hypotheses about the nature of these interactional problems.

Conclusions about a single event also lead the observer to decide on specific items which might be used as indicators[5] of less easily observed phenomena. Noting that in at least one instance a given item is closely related to something less easily observable, the researcher discovers possible shortcuts easily enabling him to observe abstractly defined variables. For example, he may decide to investigate the hypothesis that medical freshmen feel they have more work to do than can possibly be managed in the time allowed them. One student, in discussing this problem, says he faces so much work that, in contrast to his undergraduate days, he is forced to study many hours over the weekend and finds that even this is insufficient. The observer decides, on the basis of this one instance, that he may be able to use complaints about weekend work as an indicator of stu-

4. The examples of which our hypothetical observer makes use are drawn from our own current work with medical students.
5. The problem of indicators is discussed by Paul F. Lazarsfeld and Allen Barton, "Qualitative Measurement in the Social Sciences; Classification, Typologies, and Indices," in Daniel Lerner and Harold D. Lasswell, ed., *The Policy Sciences: Recent Developments in Scope and Method* (Stanford: Stanford University Press, 1951), pp. 155–92; "Some Functions of Qualitative Analysis in Sociological Research," *Sociologica*, 1 (1955), 324–61 (this important paper parallels the present discussion in many places); and Patricia L. Kendall and Paul F. Lazarsfeld, "Problems of Survey Analysis," in R. K. Merton and P. F. Lazarsfeld, ed., *Continuities in Social Research* (Glencoe, Ill.: Free Press, 1950), pp. 183–86.

dent perspectives on the amount of work they have to do. The selection of indicators for more abstract variables occurs in two ways: The observer may become aware of some very specific phenomenon first and later see that it may be used as an indicator of some larger class of phenomena; or he may have the larger problem in mind and search for specific indicators to use in studying it.

Whether he is defining problems or selecting concepts and indicators, the researcher at this stage is using his data only to speculate about possibilities. Further operations at later stages may force him to discard most of the provisional hypotheses. Nevertheless, problems of evidence arise even at this point, for the researcher must assess the individual items on which his speculations are based in order not to waste time tracking down false leads. We shall eventually need a systematic statement of canons to be applied to individual items of evidence. Lacking such a statement, let us consider some commonly used tests. (The observer typically applies these tests as seems reasonable to him during this and the succeeding stage in the field. In the final stage, they are used more systematically in an overall assessment of the total evidence for a given conclusion.)

The Credibility of Informants. Many items of evidence consist of statements by members of the group under study about some event which has occurred or is in process. Thus, medical students make statements about faculty behavior which form part of the basis for conclusions about faculty-student relations. These cannot be taken at face value; nor can they be dismissed as valueless. In the first place, the observer can use the statement as evidence *about the event,* if he takes care to evaluate it by the criteria an historian uses in examining a personal document.[6] Does the informant have reason to lie or conceal some of what he sees as the truth? Does vanity or expediency lead him to mis-state his own role in an event or his attitude toward it? Did he actually have an opportunity to witness the occurrence he describes or is heresay the source of his knowledge? Do his feelings about the issues or persons under discussion lead him to alter his story in some way?

Secondly, even when a statement examined in this way proves to be seriously defective as an accurate report of an event, it may still provide useful evidence for a different kind of conclusion. Accepting the sociological position that an individual's statements and descrip-

6. Cf. Louis Gottschalk, Clyde Kluckhohn, and Robert Angell, *The Use of Personal Documents in History, Anthropology, and Sociology* (New York: Social Science Research Council, 1945), pp. 15–27, 38–47.

tions of events are made from a perspective which is a function of his position in the group, the observer can interpret such statements and descriptions as indications of the individual's perspective on the point involved.

Volunteered or Directed Statements. Many items of evidence consist of informants' remarks to the observer about themselves or others or about something which has happened to them; these statements range from those which are a part of the running casual conversation of the group to those arrising in a long intimate tete-a-tete between observer and informant. The researcher assesses the evidential value of such statements quite differently, depending on whether they have been made independently of the observer (volunteered) or have been directed by a question from the observer. A freshman medical student might remark to the observer or to another student that he has more material to study than he has time to master; or the observer might ask, "Do you think you are being given more work than you can handle?" and receive an affirmative answer.

This raises an important question: To what degree is the informant's statement the same one he might give, either spontaneously or in answer to a question, in the absence of the observer? The volunteered statement seems likely to reflect the observer's preoccupations and possible biases less than one which is made in response to some action of the observer, for the observer's very question may direct the informant into giving an answer which might never occur to him otherwise. Thus, in the example above, we are more sure that the students are concerned about the amount of work given them when they mention this of their own accord than we are when the idea may have been stimulated by the observer asking the question.

The Observer-Informant-Group Equation. Let us take two extremes to set the problem. A person may say or do something when alone with the observer or when other members of the group are also present. The evidential value of an observation of this behavior depends on the observer's judgment as to whether the behavior is equally likely to occur in both situations. On the one hand, an informant may say and do things when alone with the observer that accurately reflect his perspective but which would be inhibited by the presence of the group. On the other hand, the presence of others may call forth behavior which reveals more accurately the person's perspective but would not be enacted in the presence of the observer alone. Thus, students in their clinical years may express deeply "idealistic" sentiments about medicine when alone with the observer, but behave and talk in a very "cynical" way when surrounded by fellow students. An alternative to judging one or the other of these situations as more reliable is to view each datum as valuable in itself, but with respect to different conclusions. In the example above, we might conclude that students have "idealistic" sentiments but that group norms may not sanction their expression.[7]

In assessing the value of items of evidence, we must also take into account the observer's role in the group. For the way the subjects of his study define that role affects what they will tell him or let him see. If the observer carries on his research incognito, participating as a full-fledged member of the group, he will be privy to knowledge that would normally be shared by such a member and might be hidden from an outsider. He could properly interpret his own experience as that of a hypothetical "typical" group member. On the other hand, if he is known to be a researcher, he must learn how group members define him and in particular whether or not they believe that certain kinds of information and events should be kept hidden from him. He can interpret evidence more accurately when the answers to these questions are known.

CHECKING THE FREQUENCY AND DISTRIBUTION OF PHENOMENA

The observer, possessing many provisional problems, concepts, and indicators, now wishes to know which of these are worth pursuing as major foci of his study. He does this, in part, by discovering if the events that prompted their development are typical and widespread, and by seeing how these events are distributed among categories of people and organizational sub-units. He reaches conclusions that are essentially quantitative, using them to describe the organization he is studying.

Participant observations have occasionally been gathered in standardized form capable of being transformed into legitimate statistical data.[8] But the exigencies of the field usually prevent the collection of data in such a form as to meet the assumptions of statistical tests, so that the observer deals in what have been called "quasi-statistics."[9]

7. See further, Howard S. Becker, "Interviewing Medical Students," *American Journal of Sociology*, 62 (September 1956), 199–201.

8. See Peter M. Blau, "Co-operation and Competition in a Bureaucracy," *American Journal of Sociology*, 59 (May 1954), 530–35.

9. See the discussion of quais-statistics in Lazarsfeld and Barton, "Some Functions of Qualitative Analysis . . . ," *op. cit.*, pp. 346–48.

His conclusions, while implicitly numerical, do not require precise quantification. For instance, he may conclude that members of freshmen medical fraternities typically sit together during lectures while other students sit in less stable smaller groupings. His observations may indicate such a wide disparity between the two groups in this respect that the inference is warranted without a standardized counting operation. Occasionally, the field situation may permit him to make similar observations or ask similar questions of many people, systematically searching for quasi-statistical support for a conclusion about frequency or distribution.

In assessing the evidence for such a conclusion the observer takes a cue from his statistical colleagues. Instead of arguing that a conclusion is either totally true or false, he decides, if possible, how *likely* it is that his conclusion about the frequency or distribution of some phenomenon is an accurate quasi-statistic, just as the statistician decides, on the basis of the varying values of a correlation coefficient or a significance figure, that his conclusion is more or less likely to be accurate. The kind of evidence may vary considerably and the degree of the observer's confidence in the conclusion will vary accordingly. In arriving at this assessment, he makes use of some of the criteria described above, as well as those adopted from quantitative techniques.

Suppose, for example, that the observer concludes that medical students share the perspective that their school should provide them with the clinical experience and the practice in techniques necessary for a general practitioner. His confidence in the conclusion would vary according to the nature of the evidence which might take any of the following forms: (1) *Every* member of the group said, *in response to a direct question*, that this was the way he looked at the matter. (2) *Every* member of the group *volunteered* to an observer that this was how he viewed the matter. (3) *Some given proportion* of the group's members either *answered* a direct question or *volunteered* the information that he shared this perspective, but none of the others was asked or volunteered information on the subject. (4) Every member of the group was asked or volunteered information, but *some given proportion said* they viewed the matter from the differing perspective of a prospective specialist. (5) No one was asked questions or volunteered information on the subject, but *all members were observed to engage in behavior* or to make other statements from which the analyst *inferred* that the general practitioner perspective was being used by them as a basic, though unstated, premise. For example, all students might have been observed to complain that the

University Hospital received too many cases of rare diseases that general practitioners rarely see. (6) *Some given proportion* of the group *was observed* using the general practitioner perspective as a basic premise in their activities, but *the rest of the group* was not observed engaging in such activities. (7) *Some proportion* of the group *was observed* engaged in activities implying the general practitioner perspective while *the remainder* of the group was observed engaged in activities implying the perspective of the prospective specialist.

The researcher also takes account of the possibility that his observations may give him evidence of different kinds on the point under consideration. Just as he is more convinced if he has many items of evidence than if he has a few, so he is more convinced of a conclusion's validity if he has *many kinds* of evidence.[10] For instance, he may be especially persuaded that a particular norm exists and affects group behavior if the norm is not only described by group members but also if he observes events in which the norm can be "seen" to operate — if, for example, students tell him that they are thinking of becoming general practitioners and he also observes their complaints about the lack of cases of common diseases in University Hospital.

The conclusiveness which comes from the convergence of several kinds of evidence reflects the fact that separate varieties of evidence can be reconceptualized as deductions from a basic proposition which have now been verified in the field. In the above case, the observer might have deduced the desire to have experience with cases like those the general practitioner treats from the desire to practice that style of medicine. Even though the deduction is made after the fact, confirmation of it buttresses the argument that the general practitioner perspective is a group norm.

It should be remembered that these operations, when carried out in the field, may be so interrupted because of imperatives of the field situation that they are not carried on as systematically as they might be. Where this is the case, the overall assessment can be postponed until the final stage of postfield work analysis.

CONSTRUCTION OF SOCIAL SYSTEM MODELS

The final stage of analysis in the field consists of incorporating individual findings into a generalized model of the social system or

10. See Alvin W. Gouldner, *Patterns of Industrial Bureaucracy,* (Glencoe, Ill.: Free Press, 1954), pp. 247–69.

organization under study or some part of that organization.[11] The concept of social system is a basic intellectual tool of modern sociology. The kind of participant observation discussed here is related directly to this concept, explaining particular social facts by explicit reference to their involvement in a complex of interconnected variables that the observer constructs as a theoretical model of the organization. In this final stage, the observer designs a descriptive model which best explains the data he has assembled.

The typical conclusion of this stage of the research is a statement about a set of complicated interrelations among many variables. Although some progress is being made informalizing this operation through use of factor analysis and the relational analysis of survey data,[12] observers usually view currently available statistical techniques as inadequate to express their conceptions and find it necessary to use words. The most common kind of conclusions at this level include:

1. Complex statements of the necessary and sufficient conditions for the existence of some phenomenon. The observer may conclude, for example, that medical students develop consensus about limiting the amount of work they will do because (a) they are faced with a large amount of work, (b) they engage in activities which create communication channels between all members of the class, and (c) they face immediate dangers in the form of examinations set by the faculty.

2. Statements that some phenomenon is an "important" or "basic" element in the organization. Such conclusions, when elaborated, usually point to the fact that this phenomenon exercises a persistent and continuing influence on diverse events. The observer might conclude that the ambition to become a general practitioner is "important" in the medical school under study, meaning that many particular judgments and choices are made by students in terms of this ambition and many features of the school's organization are arranged to take account of it.

11. The relation between theories based on the concept of social system and participant observation was pointed out to me by Alvin W. Gouldner. See his "Some Observations on Systematic Theory, 1945–55," in Hans L. Zetterberg, ed., *Sociology in the United States of America,* (Paris: UNESCO, 1956), pp. 34–42; and "Theoretical Requirements of the Applied Social Sciences," *American Sociological Review,* 22 (February 1957), 92–102.

12. See Alvin W. Gouldner, "Cosmopolitans and Locals: Toward an Analysis of Latent Social Roles," *Administrative Science Quarterly,* 2 (December 1957), 281–306, and 3 (March 1958), pp. 444–80; and James Coleman, "Relational Analysis: The Study of Social Structure with Survey Methods," mimeographed.

3. Statements identifying a situation as an instance of some process or phenomenon described more abstractly in sociological theory. Theories posit relations between many abstractly defined phenomena, and conclusions of this kind imply that relationships posited
in generalized form hold in this particular instance. The observer, for
example, may state that a cultural norm of the medical students is to
express a desire to become a general practitioner; in so doing, he in
effect asserts that the sociological theory about the functions of
norms and the processes by which they are maintained which he
holds to be true in general is true in this case.

In reaching such types of conclusions, the observer characteristically begins by constructing models of parts of the organization as
he comes in contact with them, discovers concepts and problems,
and the frequency and distribution of the phenomena these call to
his attention. After constructing a model specifying the relationships
among various elements of this part of the organization, the observer
seeks greater accuracy by successively refining the model to take
account of evidence which does not fit his previous formulation;[13] by
searching for negative cases (items of evidence which run counter to
the relationships hypothesized in the model) which might force such
revision; and by searching intensively for the interconnections *in vivo*
of the various elements he has conceptualized from his data. While a
provisional model may be shown to be defective by a negative
instance which crops up unexpectedly in the course of the field
work, the observer may infer what kinds of evidence would be likely
to support or to refute his model and may make an intensive search
for such evidence.[14]

After the observer has accumulated several partial-models of this
kind, he seeks connections between them and thus begins to construct an overall model of the entire organization. An example from
our study shows how this operation is carried on during the period of
field work. (The reader will note, in this example, how use is made
of findings typical of earlier stages of analysis.)

When we first heard medical students apply the term "crock" to
paitents we made an effort to learn percisely what they meant by it.
We found, through interviewing students about cases both they and
the observer had seen, that the term referred in a derogatory way to
patients with many subjective symptoms but no discernible physical

13. Note again the resemblance to analytic induction.
14. See Alfred Lindesmith's discussion of this principle in "Comment on W. S.
Robinson's 'The Logical Structure of Analytic Induction,'" *American Sociological
Review*, 17 (August 1952), 492–93.

pathology. Subsequent observations indicated that this usage was a regular feature of student behavior and thus that we should attempt to incorporate this fact into our model of student-patient behavior. The derogatory character of the term suggested in particular that we investigate the reasons students disliked these patients. We found that this dislike was related to what we discovered to be the students' perspective on medical school: the view that they were in school to get experience in recognizing and treating those common diseases most likely to be encountered in general practice. "Crocks," presumably having no disease, could furnish no such experience. We were thus led to specify connections between the student-patient relationship and the student's view of the purpose of his professional education. Questions concerning the genesis of this perspective led to discoveries about the organization of the student body and communication among students, phenomena which we had been assigning to another part-model. Since "crocks" were also disliked because they gave the student no opportunity to assume medical responsibility, we were able to connect this aspect of the student-patient relationship with still another tentative model of the value system and hierarchical organization of the school, in which medical responsibility plays an important role.

Again, it should be noted that analysis of this kind is carried on in the field as time permits. Since the construction of a model is the analytic operation most closely related to the observer's techniques and interests, he usually spends a great deal of time thinking about these problems. But he is usually unable to be as systematic as he would like until he reaches the final stage of analysis.

FINAL ANALYSIS AND THE PRESENTATION OF RESULTS

The final systematic analysis, carried on after the field work is completed, consists of rechecking and rebuilding models as carefully and with as many safeguards as the data will allow. For instance, in checking the accuracy of statements about the frequency and distribution of events, the researcher can index and arrange his material so that every item of information is accessible and taken account of in assessing the accuracy of any given conclusion. He can profit from the observation of Lazarsfeld and Barton that the "analysis of 'quasi-statistical data' can probably be made more systematic than it has been in the past, if the logical structure of quantitative research at least is kept in mind to give general warnings and directions to the qualitative observer."[15]

15. "Some Functions of Qualitative Analysis . . . ," *op. cit.*, p. 348.

An additional criterion for the assessment of this kind of evidence is the state of the observer's conceptualization of the problem at the time the item of evidence was gathered. The observer may have his problem well worked out and be actively looking for evidence to test an hypothesis, or he may not be as yet aware of the problem. The evidential value of items in his field notes will vary accordingly, the basis of consideration being the likelihood of discovering negative cases of the proposition he eventually uses the material to establish. The best evidence may be that gathered in the most unthinking fashion, when the observer has simply recorded the item although it has no place in the system of concepts and hypotheses he is working with at the time, for there might be less bias produced by the wish to substantiate or repudiate a particular idea. On the other hand, a well-formulated hypothesis makes possible a deliberate search for negative cases, particularly when other knowledge suggests likely areas in which to look for such evidence. This kind of search requires advanced conceptualization of the problem, and evidence gathered in this way might carry greater weight for certain kinds of conclusions. Both procedures are relevant at different stages of the research.

In the post field work stage of analysis, the observer carries on the model building operation more systematically. He considers the character of his conclusions and decides on the kind of evidence that might cause their rejection, deriving further tests by deducing logical consequences and ascertaining whether or not the data support the deductions. He considers reasonable alternative hypotheses and whether or not the evidence refutes them.[16] Finally, he completes the job of establishing interconnections between partial models so as to achieve an overall synthesis incorporating all conclusions.

After completing the analysis, the observer faces the knotty problem of how to present his conclusions and the evidence for them. Readers of qualitative research reports commonly and justifiably complain that they are told little or nothing about the evidence for conclusions or the operations by which the evidence has been assessed. A more adequate presentation of the data, of the research operations, and of the researcher's inferences may help to meet this problem.

16. One method of doing this, particularly adapted to testing discrete hypotheses about change in individuals or small social units (though not in principle limited to this application), is "The Technique of Discerning," described by Mirra Komarovsky in Paul F. Lazarsfeld and Morris Rosenberg, eds., *The Language of Social Research*, (Glencoe, Ill.: Free Press, 1955), pp. 449–57. See also the careful discussion of

But qualitative data and analytic procedures, in contrast to quantitative ones, are difficult to present adequately. Statistical data can be summarized in tables, and descriptive measures of various kinds and the methods by which they are handled can often be accurately reported in the space required to print a formula. This is so in part because the methods have been systematized so that they can be referred to in this shorthand fashion and in part because the data have been collected for a fixed, usually small, number of categories — the presentation of data need be nothing more than a report of the number of cases to be found in each category.

The data of participant observation do not lend themselves to such ready summary. They frequently consist of many different kinds of observations which cannot be simply categorized and counted without losing some of their value as evidence — for, as we have seen, many points need to be taken into account in putting each datum to use. Yet it is clearly out of the question to publish all the evidence. Nor is it any solution, as Kluckhohn has suggested for the similar problem of presenting life history materials.[17] to publish a short version and to make available the entire set of materials on microfilm or in some other inexpensive way; this ignores the problem of how to present *proof*.

In working over the material on the medical school study a possible solution to this problem, with which we are experimenting, is a description of the natural history of our conclusions, presenting the evidence as it came to the attention of the observer during the successive stages of his conceptualization of the problem. The term "natural history" implies not the presentation of every datum, but only the characteristic forms data took at each stage of the research. This involves description of the form that data took and any significant exceptions, taking account of the canons discussed above, in presenting the various statements of findings and the inferences and conclusions drawn from them. In this way, evidence is assessed as the substantive analysis is presented. The reader would be able, if this method were used, to follow the details of the analysis and to see how and on what basis any conclusion was reached. This would give the reader, as do present modes of statistical presentation, opportunity to make his own judgment as to the adequacy of the proof and the degree of confidence to be assigned the conclusion.

alternative hypotheses and the use of deduced consequences as further proof in Lindesmith, *Opiate Addiction, passim.*

17. Gottschalk, Kluckhohn, and Angell, *op. cit.*, pp. 150–56.

CONCLUSION

I have tried to describe the analytic field work characteristic of participant observation, first, in order to bring out the fact that the technique consists of something more than merely immersing one-self in data and "having insight". The discussion may also serve to stimulate those who work with this and similar techniques to attempt greater formalization and systematization of the various operations they use, in order that qualitative research may become more a "scientific" and less an "artistic" kind of endeavor. Finally, I have proposed that new modes of reporting results be introduced, so that the reader is given greater access to the data and procedures on which conclusions are based.

PART TEN

The Life History Method

INTRODUCTION

THE LIFE history method has not been much used by contemporary sociologists, a lack reflecting a shift in the methodological stance of the researcher. Rigorous, quantitative, and often experimental designs have become the accepted modes of investigation. This situation is unfortunate because the life history, when properly conceived and employed, can become one of the sociologist's most powerful observational and analytic tools. The life history parallels participant observation. Its basic difference lies in breadth of coverage, not in causal intent. Instead of observing an entire organization, the user of the life history will select for analysis critical informants within an organization. He will piece together those persons' organizational experiences with all data that can be collected. The basic theme of any life history is the construction of a set of explanations that reflect one person's or one group's subjective experiences toward a predetermined set of events. These may range from how one became an organizational member to more specific interests in deviant careers, or immigration experiences. It is important to keep in mind that the basic theme of the life history is the presentation of experience from the perspective of the focal subject or subjects. Their world must be penetrated and understood. Once it is entered, the observer lays out the critical-objective experiences relevant to that world and then has his subject react to those events. In this way the subject's definition of the situation is compared to the objective events. These objective experiences may be sequential periods of incarceration for a delinquent, for example. Among college youth, it might be shifts in perspective that parallel movement through a deviant subculture. For academics, it could be changing attitudes toward colleagues, students, and a professional career as recognition and promotion occur. In addition to recording the objective events and eliciting a subject's definitions of those events, the perspectives of other persons involved in those events will also be recorded. For a delinquent, this could include acquiring data from parents, siblings, and peers. By fitting these different perspectives together, the investigator develops a comprehensive explanation of how his subject's experiences reflect variations in the social situation. Unless a comparative-other-person focus is maintained, the life history only presents one person's point of view. To understand how that persons's perspective came into existence, and to understand its veracity, other interpretations have to be gathered. If they are not, an individualistic-psychologistic analysis is prepared. To be sociologically acceptable, the life history has to move from such interpretation to social structure. The investigator must show how his subject's definitions reflect membership in various units of social organization. These units will range from intimate relationships, small, tightly knit social groups to large organizations, or even total societies. As with *all* methods, the principle of triangulating perspectives must not be forgotten.

ADVANTAGES OF THE LIFE HISTORY

Becker's introduction to *The Jack-Roller* (from which book Shaw's selection, "The Baby Bandhouse," also appears) offers a very useful review of the uses to which life histories can be put, and he also distinguishes the life history from other methods. Noting that life histories often have to be judged within the context of other such works, Becker suggests first that they can serve as critical data for any theory. In this sense they represent intensively analyzed cases that a theory could be held accountable for. Thus Goffman's view of total institutions, also cited by Becker, could be judged by its ability to explain Stanley's experiences. In this context it is relevant to note that Stanley did not feel degraded until he entered the Chicago Parental School. He had been to the Detention Home many times before and found it to be a comfortable setting. Why feelings of degradation did not also appear in the Detention Home suggests that the organization of a total institution can significantly vary even though it fits Goffman's abstract definition of such institutions. Stanley's experiences thus represent a negative case of Goffman's framework.

The basic use of life histories rests on the emphasis given subjective experiences. Many modern theories of organization, deviance, and small groups stress subjective, or attitudinal variables, yet only infrequently do these theories offer data on the nature of such experiences. Questionnaires, interviews, and check-lists in no way give data equal to the statements offered by Stanley in his descriptions of the Detention Home. It comes as a surprise to many investigators to learn that subjects can be literate and vocal when given the chance; the life history gives them this chance.

THE NATURE OF LIFE HISTORY DATA

A good life history reads like a novel. Beginning with the objective facts, the reader is taken through his protagonist's life, one step at a time. The hero's reactions to each critical event are carefully detailed, and often presented in the light of other reactions and interpretations. The central figure in a life history presents the world through his own eyes. We see the tragedy of Stanley's early life and are given the full impact of those early experiences on each of his subsequent acts.

Finally life histories are like novels in that novelists, just as sociologists, interpret the experiences of their subjects within special theoretical frameworks. Thus the fatalism of a Zola, or the exstentialism of Conrad, can be compared to the interactionist perspective guiding Shaw's interpretation of Stanley's life. A sociological life history is at once literary and theoretical. Without a theory to guide the facts, a life history becomes bare description. Good life histories, like good novels, offer the reader a way of interpreting the findings. That interpretative framework may be a theoretical scheme or a philosophical position.

ANALYZING LIFE HISTORY DATA

The preceding remarks have attempted to establish the unique nature of life history materials. It is important to point out that these materials can be assessed in terms of the normal rules of reliability and validity. This is the point of the Cavan, Hauser, and Stouffer article. They show that analysts can reliably code such documents. This finding is important, because frequently users of the life history have been accused of biased or unreliable data. Cavan, Hauser, and Stouffer note that life history findings can serve important exploratory functions for subsequent research, and can also offer interpretations for more quantitative findings that are expressed only in statistical or correlational form.

Suggested Readings. Becker's article cites many of the most relevant sources on the method, and these should be examined. Herbert Blumer's *An Appraisal of Thomas and Zaniecki's, "The Polish Peasant in Europe and America"* (New York: Social Science Research Council, 1939) offers a very good review of the first major life history analysis in sociology. Blumer also attempts to place the life history in proper methodological focus. Gordon W. Allport's *The Use of Personal Documents in Psychological Research* (New York: Social Science Research Council, 1942) is probably the single best source on the method. Although Allport examines personal documents as life history materials, his entire discussion can be framed in the context of the life history method generally. The Louis Gottschalk, *et al.*, *The Use of Personal Documents in History, Anthropology, and Sociology* (New York: Social Science Research Council, 1945), is also very good. Gottschalk presents a review of the historical method in the context of life histories. Angell's discussion in the Gottschalk volume of the history of this method is recommended, and Becker's article can be seen as an extension of Angell's interpretation.

26. The Relevance of Life Histories

HOWARD S. BECKER

THE JACK-ROLLER was first published in 1930 and has enjoyed a continuing and well-deserved popularity ever since. It was not the first published sociological life history. That honor goes to the documents published by Thomas and Znaniecki in *The Polish Peasant*.[1] But it was the first of a series to be published by Clifford Shaw and his associates, and was followed by *The Natural History of a Delinquent Career* and *Brothers in Crime*. During the same period, Edwin Sutherland published the still popular *Professional Thief*. And similar documents have been published occasionally since, most recently *The Fantastic Lodge* and *Hustler*.[2]

Excerpts are reprinted by permission from Howard S. Becker, "Introduction," in Clifford R. Shaw, *The Jack-Roller* (1966 Phoenix edition), pp. v–xviii. Copyright © 1966 by The University of Chicago Press.

1. W. I. Thomas and Florian Znaniecki, *The Polish Peasant in Europe and America* (2d ed., New York: Alfred A. Knopf, 1927), II, 1931–2244.

2. Clifford R. Shaw, *The Natural History of a Delinquent Career*, (Chicago: University of Chicago Press, 1931), and *Brothers in Crime* (Chicago, 1936); Chic Conwell and Edwin H. Sutherland, *The Professional Thief* (Chicago: University of Chicago Press, 1937), Helen MacGill Hughes, ed., *The Fantastic Lodge* (Boston: Houghton Mifflin, 1961); Henry Williamson, *Hustler*, R. Lincoln Keiser, ed., (Garden City, N.Y.: Doubleday and Company, 1965).

The life history is not conventional social science "data," although it has some of the features of that kind of fact, being an attempt to gather material useful in the formulation of general sociological theory. Nor is it a conventional autobiography, although it shares with autobiography its narrative form, its first-point of view and its frankly subjective stance. It is certainly not fiction, although the best life history documents have a sensitivity and pace, a dramatic urgency, that any novelist would be glad to achieve.

The differences between these forms lie both in the perspective from which the work is undertaken and in the methods used. The writer of fiction is not, of course, concerned with fact at all, but rather with dramatic and emotional impact, with form and imagery, with the creation of a symbolic and artistically unified world. Fidelity to the world as it exists is only one of many problems for him, and for many authors it is of little importance.

The autobiographer proposes to explain his life to us and thus commits himself to maintaining a close connection between the story he tells and what an objective investigation might discover. When we read autobiography, however, we are always aware that the author is telling us only part of the story, that he has selected his material so as to present us with the picture of himself he would prefer us to have and that he may have ignored what would be trivia or distasteful to him, though of great interest to us.

As opposed to these more imaginative and humanistic forms, the life history is more down to earth, more devoted to our purposes than those of the author, less concerned with artistic values than with a faithful rendering of the subject's experience and interpretation of the world he lives in. The sociologist who gathers a life history takes steps to ensure that it covers everything we want to know, that no important fact or event is slighted, that what purports to be factual squares with other available evidence and that the subject's interpretations are honestly given. The sociologist keeps the subject oriented to the questions sociology is interested in, asks him about events that require amplification, tries to make the story told jibe with matters of official record and with material furnished by others familiar with the person, event, or place being described. He keeps the game honest for us.

In so doing, he pursues the job from his own perspective, a perspective which emphasizes the value of the person's "own story." This perspective differs from that of some other social scientist in assigning major importance to the interpretations people place on their experience as an explanation for behavior. To understand why someone behaves as he does you must understand how it looked to him, what he thought he had to contend with, what alternatives he saw open to him; you can only understand the effects of opportunity structures, delinquent subcultures, social norms, and other commonly invoked explanations of behavior by seeing them from the actor's point of view.

The image of the mosaic is useful in thinking about such a scientific enterprise. Each piece added to a mosaic adds a little to our understanding of the total picture. When many pieces have been placed we can see, more or less clearly, the objects and the people in the picture and their relation to one another. Different pieces contribute different things to our understanding: Some are useful because of their color, others because they make clear the outline of an object. No one piece has any great job to do; if we do not have its contribution, there are still other ways to come to an understanding of the whole.

Individual studies can be like pieces of mosaic and were so in Park's day. Since the picture in the mosaic was Chicago, the research had an ethnographic, "case history" flavor, even though Chicago itself was seen as somehow representative of all cities. Whether its data were census figures or interviews, questionnaire results or life histories, the research took into account local peculiarities, exploring those things that were distinctively true of Chicago in the 1920's. In so doing, they partially completed a mosaic of great complexity and detail, with the city itself the subject, a "case" which could be used to test a great variety of theories and in which the interconnections of a host of seemingly unrelated phenomena could be seen, however imperfectly.[3]

Our attention today is turned away from local ethnography, from the massing of knowledge about a single place, its parts, and their connections. We emphasize abstract theory-building more than we used to. The national survey is frequently used as a basic mode for data collection. Above all, researchers are increasingly mobile, moving from city to city and university to university every few years, building no fund of specialized local knowledge and passing none on to their students. The trend is away from the community study — there will be no more elaborate programs of coordinated study such as those that produced the *Yankee City Series*[4] or *Black Metropolis*.[5] And a great loss it will be.

3. See Louis Wirth, *The Ghetto* (Chicago: University of Chicago Press, 1928); Harvey W. Zorbaugh, *The Gold Coast and the Slum: A Sociological Study of Chicago's Near North Side* (Chicago: University of Chicago Press, 1929); Frederic M. Thrasher, *The Gang: A study of 1,313 Gangs in Chicago* (Chicago: University of Chicago Press, 1928).

4. Published in several volumes by W. Lloyd Warner and his collaborators.

5. St. Clair Drake and Horace Cayton, *Black Metropolis* (New York: Harper and Row, 1945).

In any case, the scientific contribution of *The Jack-Roller* can be assessed properly only by seeing it in relation to all the studies done under Park's direction, for it drew on and depended on all of them, just as all the later studies of that Golden Age of Chicago sociology depended, a little, on it. Much of the background that any single study would either have to provide in itself or, even worse, about which it would have to make unchecked assumptions, was already at hand for the reader of *The Jack-Roller*. When Stanley speaks of the boyish games of stealing he and his pals engaged in, we know that we can find an extensive and penetrating description of that phenomenon in Thrasher's *The Gang*. And when he speaks of the time he spent on West Madison Street, we know that we can turn to Nels Anderson's *The Hobo*[6] for an understanding of the milieu Stanley then found himself in. If we are concerned about the representativeness of Stanley's case, we have only to turn to the ecological studies carried on by Shaw and McKay[7] to see the same story told on a grand scale in mass statistics. And, similarly, if one wanted to understand the maps and correlations contained in ecological studies of delinquency, one could then turn to *The Jack-Roller* and similar documents for that understanding.

I am not sure what the criteria are by which one judges the contribution of a piece of scientific work considered in its total context, but I know that they are not such currently fashionable criteria as are implied by the model of the controlled experiment. We do not expect, in a large and differentiated program of research, that any one piece of work will give us all the answers or, indeed, all of any one answer. What must be judged is the entire research enterprise in all its parts. (One can, of course, assess *The Jack-Roller* by the criteria appropriate to life histories, perhaps those suggested by Kluckhohn, Angell and Dollard.)[8] Criteria have yet to be established for determining how much one piece of mosaic contributes to the conclusions that are warranted by consideration of the whole, but these are just the kind of criteria that are needed. In their place, we can temporarily install a sympathetic appreciation for some of the functions performed by the kind of work represented by *The Jack-Roller*.

What are some of the functions that can be usefully performed by a life history document? In the first place, *The Jack-Roller* can serve as

6. Nels Anderson, *The Hobo* (Chicago: University of Chicago Press, 1923).
7. Clifford R. Shaw and Henry D. McKay, *Juvenile Delinquency and Urban Areas* (Chicago: University of Chicago, 1942).
8. Clyde Kluckhohn, "The Personal Document in Anthropological Science," in Louis Gottschalk *et al.*, *The Use of Personal Documents in History, Anthropology, and*

a touchstone with which to evaluate theories that purport to deal with phenomena like those of Stanley's delinquent career. Whether it is a theory of the psychological origins of delinquent behavior, a theory of the roots of delinquency in juvenile gangs, or an attempt to explain the distribution of delinquency throughout the city, any theory of delinquency must, if it is to be considered valid, explain or at least be consistent with the facts of Stanley's case as they are reported here. Thus, even though the life history does not in itself provide definite proof of a proposition, it can be a negative case that forces us to decide a proposed theory is inadequate.

To say this is to take an approach to scientific generalization that deserves some comment. We may decide to accept a theory if it explains, let us say, 95 per cent of the cases that fall in its jurisdiction. Many reputable scientists do. In contrast, one can argue that any theory that does not explain all cases is inadequate, that other factors than those the theory specifies must be operating to produce the result we want to explain. It is primarily a question of strategy. If we assume that exceptions to any rule are a normal occurrence, we will perhaps not search as hard for further explanatory factors as we otherwise might. But if we regard exceptions as potential negations of our theory, we will be spurred to search for them.[9]

More importantly, the negative case will respond to careful analysis by suggesting the direction the search should take.[10] Inspection of its features will reveal attributes which differ from those of otherwise similar cases, or processes at work whose steps have not all been fully understood. If we know the case in some detail, as a life history document allows us to know it, our search is more likely to be successful; it is in this sense that the life history is a useful theoretical touchstone.

The life history also helps us in areas of research that touch on it only tangentially. Every piece of research crosses frontiers into new terrain it does not explore thoroughly, areas important to its main concern in which it proceeds more by assumption than in-

Sociology (New York: Social Science Research Council, 1945), pp. 79–173; Robert Angell, "A Critical Review of the Development of the Personal Document Method in Sociology 1920–1940," *ibid.*, pp. 177–232; John Dollard, *Criteria for the Life History* (New Haven: Yale University Press, 1932).

9. See, for instance, George H. Mead, "Scientific Method and Individual Thinker," in John Dewey, *et al.*, *Creative Intelligence* (New York: Henry Holt and Co., 1917), pp. 176–227, and Alfred Lindesmith, *Opiate Addiction* (Bloomington: Principia Press, 1947), pp. 5–20. Lindesmith turns the strategy into a systematic method of inquiry usually referred to as analytic induction.

10. See, for a similar view growing out of the tradition of survey research, Patricia L. Kendall and Katherine M. Wolf, "The Analysis of Deviant Cases in Communications

vestigation.[11] A study of a college, for instance, may make assumptions (indeed, must make them) about the character of the city, state, and region it is located in, about the social class background and experience of its students, and about a host of other matters likely to influence the operation of the school and the way it affects students. A study of a mental hospital or prison will make similarly unchecked assumptions about the character of the families whose members end up in the institution. A life history—although it is not the only kind of information that can do this—provides a basis on which those assumptions can be realistically made, a rough approximation of the direction in which the truth lies.

In addition to these matters of neighboring fact, so to speak, the life history can be particularly useful in giving us insight into the subjective side of much-studied institutional processes, about which unverified assumptions are also often made. Sociologists have lately been concerned with processes of adult socialization and, to take an instance in which Stanley's case is directly relevant, with the processes of degradation and "stripping" associated with socialization into rehabilitative institutions such as prisons and mental hospitals.[12] Although the theories concern themselves with institutional action rather than individual experience, they either assume something about the way people experience such processes or at least raise a question about the nature of that experience. Although Stanley's prison experiences do not, of course, provide fully warranted knowledge of these matters, they give us some basis for making a judgment.

The life history, by virtue again of its wealth of detail, can be important at those times when an area of study has grown stagnant, has pursued the investigation of a few variables with ever-increasing precision but has received dwindling increments of knowledge from the pursuit. When this occurs, investigators might well proceed by gathering personal documents which suggest new variables, new questions, and new processes, using the rich though unsystematic data to provide a needed reorientation of the field.

Beneath these specific contributions which the life history is capable of making lies one more fundamental. The life history, more than any other technique except perhaps participant observation, can

Research," in Paul F. Lazarsfeld and Frank Stanton, eds., *Communications Research 1948– 1949* (New York: Harper and Brothers, 1949), pp. 152– 79.

11. See Max Gluckman, ed., *Closed Systems and Open Minds* (Chicago: University of Chicago Press, 1964).

12. Harold Garfinkel, "Conditions of Successful Degradation Ceremonies," *Ameri-*

give meaning to the overworked notion of *process*. Sociologists like to speak of "ongoing processes" and the like, but their methods usually prevent them from seeing the processes they talk about so glibly.

George Herbert Mead, if we take him seriously, tells us that the reality of social life is a conversation of significant symbols, in the course of which people make tentative moves and then adjust and reorient their activity in the light of the responses (real or imagined) others make to those moves. The formation of the individual act is a process in which conduct is continually reshaped to take account of the expectations of others, as these are expressed in the immediate situation and as the actor supposes they may come to be expressed. Collective activity, of the kind pointed to by concepts like "organization" or "social structure," arises out of a continuous process of mutual adjustment of the actions of all the actors involved. Social process, then, is not an imagined interplay of invisible forces or a vector made up of the interaction of multiple social factors, but an observable process of symbolically mediated interaction.[13]

Observable, yes; but not easily observable, at least not for scientific purposes. To observe social process as Mead described it takes a great deal of time. It poses knotty problems of comparability and objectivity in data gathering. It requires an intimate understanding of the lives of others. So social scientists have, most often, settled for less demanding techniques such as the interview and the questionnaire.

These techniques can, I think, tell us much, but only as we are able to relate them to a vision of the underlying Meadian social process we would know had we more adequate data. We can, for instance, give people a questionnaire at two periods in their life and infer an underlying process of change from the differences in their answers. But our interpretation has significance only if our imagery of the underlying process is accurate. And this accuracy of imagery — this cogruence of theoretically posited process with which we could observe if we took the necessary time and trouble — can be partially achieved by the use of life history documents. For the life history, if it is done well, will give us the details of that process whose character we would otherwise only be able to speculate about, the process to which our data must ultimately be referred if they are to have theoretical and not just an operational and pre-

can Journal of Sociology, 61 (1956), 420–24; and Erving Goffman, *Asylums* (Garden City, N.Y.: Doubleday, 1961), pp. 127–69.

13. See George Herbert Mead, *Mind, Self, and Society* (Chicago: University of Chicago Press, 1934); Herbert Blumer, "Society as Symbolic Interaction," in Arnold

dictive significance. It will describe those crucial interactive epi-
sodes in which new lines of individual and collective activity are
forged, in which new aspects of the self are brought into being. It is
by thus giving a realistic basis to our imagery of the underlying
process that the life history serves the purposes of checking assumptions, illuminating organization, and reorienting stagnant fields.

Given the variety of scientific uses to which the life history may be
put, one must wonder at the relative neglect into which it has fallen.
Sociologists, it is true, have never given it up altogether. But neither
have they made it one of their standard research tools. They read the
documents available and assign them for their students to read. But
they do not ordinarily think of gathering life history documents
themselves or of making the technique part of their research approach.

A number of simultaneous changes probably contributed to the
increasing disuse of the life history method. Sociologists became
more concerned with the development of abstract theory and corre-
spondingly less interested in full and detailed accounts of specific
organizations and communities. They wanted data formulated in the
abstract categories of their own theories rather than in categories that
seemed most relevant to the people they studies. The life history
was well suited to the latter task, but of little immediately apparent
use in the former.

At the same time, sociologists began to separate the field of social
psychology from that of sociology proper, creating two specialties in
place of two emphases within one field, and focused more on "structural" variables and synchronic functional analyses than on those
factors that manifested themselves in the life and experience of the
person. Again, the life history made a clear contribution to the latter
task but seemed unrelated to studies that emphasized group
attributes and their interconnections.

But perhaps the major reason for the relatively infrequent use of
the technique is that it does not produce the kind of "findings" that
sociologists now expect research to produce. As sociology increasingly rigidifies and "professionalizes," more and more emphasis has
come to be placed on what we may, for simplicity's sake, call the
single study. I use the term to refer to research projects that are
conceived of as self-sufficient and self-contained, which provide all
the evidence one needs to accept or reject the conclusions they

Rose, ed., *Human Behavior and Social Processes* (Boston: Houghton-Mifflin, 1962),
pp. 179–92; and Anselm L. Strauss *et al.*, *Psychiatric Ideologies and Institutions* (New
York: Free Press, 1964), pp. 292–315.

proffer, whose findings are to be used as another brick in the growing wall of the mosaic. The single study is intergrated with the main body of knowledge in the following way: It derives its hypotheses from an inspection of what is already known; then, after the research is completed, if those hypotheses have been demonstrated, they are added to the wall of what is already scientifically known and used as the basis for further studies. The important point is that the research-er's hypothesis is either proved or disproved on the basis of what he has discovered in doing that one piece of research.

The customs, traditions, and organizational practices of contempo-rary sociology conspire to make us take this view of research. The journal article of standard length, the most common means of scien-tific communication, is made to order for the presentation of findings that confirm or refute hypotheses. The Ph.D. thesis virtually de-mands that its author have a set of findings, warranted by his own operations, which yield conclusions he can defend before a faculty committee. The research grant proposal, another ubiquitous sociolo-gical literary form, pushes its author to state what his project will have proved when they money has been spent.

If we take the single study as the model of scientific work, we will then use, when we judge research and make decisions about how to organize our research, criteria designed to assure us that the findings of our single study do indeed provide a sound basis on which to accept or reject hypotheses. The canons of inference and proof now in vogue reflect this emphasis. Such methodologists as Stouffer, and others who followed him, developed techniques for assessing hypotheses based on model of the controlled experiment.[14] Compare two groups, those who have been exposed to the effects of a variable and those who have not, before and after the exposure. The multiple comparisons made possible by this technique allow you to test not only your original hypothesis, but also some of the likely alternative explanations of the same results, should they be what you have predicted. This is the approved model. If we cannot achieve it, our study is deficient unless we can devise workable substitutes. If we do achieve it, we can say with assurance that we have produced scientific findings strong enough to bear the weight of still further studies.

Criteria drawn from the experimental model and used to evaluate

14. See the very influential paper by Samuel A. Stouffer, "Some Observations on Study Design," *American Journal of Sociology*, 55 (January 1950), 355–61, and any of a large number of books and articles on method which take essentially the same position.

single studies in isolation, however useful they may be in a variety of contexts, have had one bad by-product. They have led people to ignore the other functions of research and, particularly, to ignore the contribution made by one study to an overall research enterprise even when the study, considered in isolation, produced no definite results of its own. Since, by these criteria, the life history did not produce definitive results, people have been at a loss to make anything of it and by and large have declined to invest the time and effort necessary to acquire life history documents.

We can perhaps hope that a fuller understanding of the complexity of the scientific enterprise will restore sociologists' sense of the versatility and worth of the life history. A new series of personal documents, like those produced by the Chicago School more than a generation ago, might help us in all the ways I have earlier suggested and in ways, too, that we do not now anticipate.

27. The Baby Bandhouse

CLIFFORD R. SHAW

THE DETENTION Home at first seemed like a palace to me.[1] It was clean and in order. The very first night I took a nice bath (the first one I ever had), had a change of clothes, and a good meal. I felt like I'd never want to go back to that "old hole" (home) with my step-mother. I went to bed in a clean little white bed, and I thought, "Well, is this jail? Who ever thought it was so nice?"

Inside the Detention Home I found a motley crowd of aspiring young crooks — young aspirants to the "hall of fame of crookdom." In their own minds they had already achieved fame in the world of crime, and proceeded to impress that fact upon the other boys. The whole thing seemed to be a contest, among young crooks, to see who was the biggest and bravest crook. They loiter about the place,

From Clifford R. Shaw, "The Baby Bandhouse," Chapter V in *The Jack-Roller* (1966 Phoenix edition), pp. 57–64. Copyright 1966 by The University of Chicago Press.

1. This chapter is a description of Stanley's experience and contacts in the Juvenile Detention Home and the Chicago Parental School. The former institution is designed for the detention of dependent and delinquent children, pending the disposition of their cases in the Juvenile Court. The Parental School receives commitments of children charged with truancy from school and other behavior difficulties arising in relation to the school situation.

congregating in small groups, talking about their achievements and ambitions in their common vocation, crime. The older crooks are gods and stand around telling about their exploits. Much of it is bunk, but they succeed in making the other boys, especially the younger ones of more tender feelings and not so wise to the world, believe it. I listened eagerly to the stories and fell into the web myself. I was really awed by the bravery and wisdom of the older crooks. Their stories of adventures fascinated my childish imagination, and I felt drawn to them. My timid spirit (you remember I was only eight) wanted to go out and achieve some of the glories for myself.

Well do I remember how Pat Maloney impressed my childish mind. He was seven years my senior, a big husky Irish lad, and a "master bandit." He was in for stealing automobiles, burglary, and "bumming" from home and school. To him the last-mentioned offenses were only minor infractions of the law. The young guys, me included, looked up to him. He paraded among us like a king on dress parade. My feelings of pride swelled to the breaking point when he picked me out and took a liking to me. He must have pitied me, for I was little and frail and timid. I listened eagerly to his stories of how he ran away from home because of his stepfather (like myself), and how he learned to open locks and break into houses and stores, and how he used to go to the White Sox ball park to watch cars for people, and then pick out a good one and drive it away. He was a wise crook, but he had a kind and tender heart. He sympathized with me and said he knowed why I couldn't live at home with my stepmother, and that I didn't need to, because it wouldn't be hard to make a go of it on my own hook when I got a little wiser and knowed a little more about stealing. He said fellows like us, who didn't have any home, had to steal to make a go of it. He was a good pal of mine, and I felt real sorry when he was taken to court and sentenced to St. Charles. He didn't whimper when the sentence of two years was imposed, and I respected him for his courage and grit. It made me feel shame because I cried about my predicament, but he simply smiled and showed a determined face.

During the times I was in the home I met crooks of every creed and color. They were there for every crime, running away from home, bumming from school, taking automobiles, stealing from parents, shoplifting, breaking into houses and stores, petty stealing, and sex perversions. It was a novelty to learn that there were so many crimes and ways of stealing that I had never heard about. I was green at first, and the boys pitied and petted me, but I was well on the way to Crookdom at the end of my stay in that place.[2]

After a while a policeman came to me and said that I was going home. He warned me about running away again and said that I would be sent away till I was twenty-one if I didn't stay at home. I accepted his advice and started home. As I was on the car I thought of Patty and how brave he was, and made up my mind that I could take care of myself; so I got off the car and started to wander down toward the Loop. I got to West Madison Street and begged money to go to a show. I made up my mind never to go back home, where I always got nagged and beat up. I roamed for two days, and got so hungry that I had to get food out of garbage cans. A policeman saw me picking up garbage in an alley at Madison and Halsted streets, and arrested me and took me to the Detention Home. I was glad to get back to the Home and have a bath, good food, and a clean bed. The next day I was taken home by a woman from the court; I guess they had decided not to trust me to go home alone. On the way home she told me to be a good boy and go to school and not run away from home any more.

The stepmother met us and was all smiles till the lady from the court left, and then she sprang into me with fury, but I escaped her and ran into the alley. I saw the lady from the court waiting for a car at the corner, so I hid in the alley until she left, and then proceeded to get the hell out of the neighborhood. Where would I go, a mere kid, without a home and no friends to help me? My legs naturally carried me to West Madison Street, where I slipped into a show. I fell asleep and was awakened by a policeman, who requested me to accompany him. He took me to the station and then to the Detention Home. I was rather glad to get back, because I was used to the place, and it was far better than being home with my stepmother. I was told that I was becoming a "habitual runaway" and a "bad actor," but they sent me back home again that same day. It was no use, for I had the roaming instinct, and during the next few months I was put in the Detention Home eight more times for running away from my stepmother. Everybody knew me at the Detention Home, and they were always looking for me to come back. They saw that I was hopeless, so they booked me for hearing. Everybody thought there

2. Our case histories indicate rather clearly that the social contacts established in institutional situations are a medium through which delinquent codes and techniques are transmitted from one boy to another. This social process is well illustrated by Stanley's experiences in the Detention Home and the institutions to which he was subsequently committed (see also Cases 5, 6, and 7, pp. 12–14).

was something wrong with me. They had my head examined to see if I was a "dummie," and I guess they found that I was, for they said that I'd have to be "committed." I was becoming a dangerous character, for the teachers at school said I was "a menace to society." Now that was strange, for I was only a harmless little boy of eight years who had a roaming instinct because I couldn't live with a selfish and hell-bent stepmother. But the day of my trial arrived. I was led into the courtroom by a big policeman, who told the judge that I was a bad actor and would not stay at home. The judge said, "Sonny, you are not very large to be away from home. You need to be at home with your parents. They love you, and you must stay with them. I'll give you a chance to go back home and make good. But remember, I'll send you away where you'll have to be good if you come here again." I was too scared to say a word. I was taken back home that day, but found the stepmother as cruel as ever. She started to whip me again, and I slipped through the back door into the alley and was free again.

I wandered away from home and "hitched" a ride on a truck, which carried me several blocks from home. My questless journey led me to a group of boys who were playing games around a church. They saw me and invited me to join them in the game, which I did. It got dark and the other boys were called in by their parents. That left me alone, so I crawled into a corner of the church entrance and soon went to sleep. I was soon awakened by people coming to the church. An Irish woman with a decided Irish brogue saw me and took pity on me. She asked me where I lived. I told her that I had no home. Then she asked me to go home with her and have something to eat.

I followed her to her home, which was on the top floor of an old frame building. She immediately placed a meal before me and I ate with great relish. The home was poorly furnished, but it was warm and cozy. Her many children began to play with me, and soon I was part of the family.

In this family I was happy and contented. I had lots of good things to eat and fun. We played games in the attic. There we played telephone, using the clothesline as the telephone wire. One fellow would be lineman, another switchboard operator, etc. The mother would give us bread, butter, and jam, and cookies between meals. My! but it was a great life and I could have lived there forever.[3]

My stay in this happy home came to an end suddenly after four or

3. Stanley's favorable reaction to this family situation suggests that perhaps placement in a congenial and sympathetic foster-home should have been attempted at that time. As previously indicated, Healy had already repeatedly recommended such a plan of treatment.

five weeks. The end came unexpectedly. The Irish lady had given me some pennies to buy candy with. On my way to the store, two detectives stopped me, who ordered me to go with them, which I did. They took me back to the Juvenile Detention Home and to court, where I was released to live with my stepmother.

I wandered away the same day and stayed on the streets all day, and at night, being hungry and cold, stopped at a settlement house on Halsted Street. A kind lady talked to me and asked me about my parents. I said that my parents were dead and that I didn't have any home. She called the police, and in a few minutes I found myself in the Detention Home again. They knew me at the Home, and said, "Didn't you just leave here this morning?" and I said, "yes, I can't live at home with my stepmother." They said, "You can stay here tonight, and we will let the judge settle your case."

The next day I was summoned to court. I had to be dragged away from the blocks I was playing with in the playroom. I never had them at home, so you can imagine how interested I was in them. I wasn't a bit interested in my case, for I was busy gazing around and satisfying my curiosity. The judge asked my stepmother if she wanted me back home. She refused to take me and told the interpreter that I was incorrigible and leading her children astray, and that a few years in the reform school would do me some good. The judge accepted her suggestion and committed me to the Chicago Parental School for three months. That was when I was about nine years old.

My first night at the Parental School was the first time I experienced real sorrow and homesickness.[4] The institution was surrounded by acres of tilled soil. To a common observer it was a beautiful scene to gaze upon, but to me, a timid boy of nine years, it was something new and lonely. I had never been out of the city before, and the quiet and peaceful surroundings made me very lonesome and sad. It all seemed like a foreign town to me, and it took me several weeks to get used to it. I couldn't sleep the first night, and the first day seemed like an age. The first thing in their procedure was to clip off the hair close to the scalp. We were then given the rules of the institution, which we had to adhere to strictly. If not—punishment was the sure result.

The institution had too much discipline. I was very scared and

4. It should be pointed out that Stanley's description of the Chicago Parental School is not indicative of the present situation in this institution. Subsequent to his commitment, a special investigation of the methods of discipline in the institution was made (1922). As a result of the findings of that investigation, the institution was placed under new management. Mr. O. J. Milliken became superintendent, and under his very excellent management the conditions described in Stanley's story have been eliminated.

frightened, and put into submission from the first till I was released. Physically I was a slave, but mentally I was free, and I took advantage of this freedom and dreamed. I dreamed boyish dreams of the outside world, of my home and friends in the city. Many times I would be rudely awakened from my dreams during the day, and would realize that I was in a realistic world that was full of sorrow for me. Other boys had mothers to visit them and take candy and cookies to them, but I had none, only a selfish stepmother. She visited me once and tried to kiss me, but my soul could not take the caress, even though I tried. That angered her, and she didn't come down any more. Indeed, I did not miss her, for the less I saw of her the better I felt.

During the five month's imprisonment I worked as an errand boy part-time, and went to school. Discipline was so strict throughout the institution that a boy could not even talk, and there wasn't any interesting recreation or diversion. The boys all hated the place, the guards were hard boiled, and severe punishment was inflicted for the least infraction of the rules. For each misdemeanor a boy received a mark against his conduct, and it is removed by strenuous exercise, and if you were slack you would be anointed with cowhide, and they weren't any too gentle about laying it on. The most common kinds of punishment were muscle grinders, squats, benders, standing in corner, whipping, confinement in "the cage," chewing soap, being deprived of food and sleep, strenuous labor, and making the sentence longer. Many times I experienced these forms of torture. Being just a child without friends, I cringed in fear and developed a childish revenge against the cruel institution. Why was I in such a place, and why was I punished, just because fate was against me? I was just a mere child, too weak to strike back and defend myself. My only pleasure was in my childish dreams, which carried me away into the free world outside. I dreamed of my chums, our stealing and roaming in the city, of my pals at the Detention Home, especially Patty Maloney, whose stories of adventure I could not get out of my mind. Some day I'd be big and brave like him, and then I wouldn't worry and have fear of these cruel officials. Other boys had nice mothers and friends to bring boxes of goodies to them, and stood by them in this cold world, but I had only a disgusting stepmother. I got lonely and sullen and full of fear, but my dreams kept me alive, and I dreamed every day. There I started to be a dreamer of dreams. That is one of life's cynical jokes—how I could dream such beautiful dreams in such a hole of strict discipline and drabness. So I dreamed and existed five months and I was paroled to live at home.

When I was on the street again I felt like a tied-up colt that runs and kicks and raises hell in general. Two days after I was out I was abused again. The stepmother treated me like a prince for two days, but then she began to make up for lost time. I began to feel like going a million miles away, just to keep out of her reach. That is how I got the roaming instinct. Now I had more courage and more experience in the world, and knew I could get along some way, so I made up my mind not to take much insult from my stepmother. Other boys could make it on their own hooks, and so could I. Besides, I had a lot of "education" during the last six months. So I left home after a quarrel the third day, and met another kid and we sallied out to forage for ourselves. He was a little green, but I told him about the adventures we could have, and then he was glad to go. I hesitated just a minute, thinking of my trip to the Parental School, but I thought I could get along. We traveled to the Loop, and then to Halsted and Madison—my old haunt. We bummed our way into shows, and having a gnawing at our stomach we "lifted" some fruit off a stand and satisfied our hunger. That night we looked for a place to sleep, and found a spacious front porch that we could hide under and sleep. During the night I was awakened by a tug at my leg. Looking up I saw my old friend, a policeman, standing there, and he bade us to go with him. We were taken to the Detention Home, this being the thirteenth time I had entered its pearly gates. I was an "old timer" there at the early age of ten, and being a kid, felt it was an honor to be so well known. Besides, I was a "habitual or professional runaway" and considered a bad actor. In the home the kids all knew I'd done time and sort'a looked up to me for my wide experience in the world.

After a month I was summoned to court. The policeman said, "Your honor, this is a professional runaway. He will not stay at home and will not attend school. Also, he has a record in the Parental School." Looking at me, the judge said, "Young man, what is the trouble with you? Why don't you stay at home? Don't you remember what I told you when you were here before?" I was too scared to reply. He asked the stepmother if she wanted me, and she said she did not, so the judge said, "I'll enter a St. Charles order; he'll have to stay there." I was elated. I was going out on a train ride, and it would be the first one in my life. My companion was let free because it was his first offense, and his mother cried to take him back home. I thought I was better off than him, then. But I soon got down to earth when I was entered in the St. Charles School for Boys.

28. Note on the Statistical Treatment of Life-History Material

RUTH SHONLE CAVAN, PHILIP M. HAUSER, AND
SAMUEL A. STOUFFER

METHODS of securing life-history materials have been improving
faster perhaps than methods of analyzing them. This is especially
true when a large number of life-history documents are involved.

In the course of a study carried on by the Sub-Committee on the
Function of Home Activities in the Education of the Child under
Section IIIA of the White House Conference on Child Health and
Protection[1] it was felt desirable to analyze a large number of life
history documents. In this connection the problem of the objectivity
of the narratives arose, that is, it was desired to know how much
agreement would result if a number of judges interpreted the documents independently. The writers of this article utilized a simple
way of obtaining the degree of agreement, which is reported here.

Reprinted by permission from *Social Forces*, 9 (1930), pp. 200–03. Copyright 1930,
The University of North Carolina Press.

1. Chairman of Section IIIA, Dr. Louise Stanley, Bureau of Home Economics
Washington, D. C. Chairman of Sub-Committee, Dr. E. W. Burgess, University of
Chicago.

They had no hand in the collection of the materials or in the compilation of the categories on the basis of which the documents were analyzed. The little study here reported is quite independent of the work of the White House Conference.

Among the materials collected by the Sub-Committee were some 600 documents from college students consisting of a questionnaire and a life-history. As a guide for writing the narrative the student was presented with a series of questions as "suggestions for writing a description of home life"; he was asked not to follow the questions slavishly but to write freely. The first two paragraphs follow and illustrate the type of questions asked.

> 1. Describe yourself as a child, the degree to which you were shy or at ease with other children, whether you thought of yourself as beautiful or ugly, bright or stupid, etc.
>
> 2. How popular were you with other children? Kinds of games you played, gangs or play groups? Were you a leader or follower? Reading interests?

Since it was desired to determine the relationship of various factors in the students' lives to other factors and to personality traits, those in charge of the study decided to make a statistical analysis of the life-histories. For this purpose it was necessary to construct a key by means of which each document could be analyzed. For each factor upon which the documents presumably contained data, a series of categories was arranged, graded wherever possible. Thus, with reference to the factor of "social development of child by parents," three categories were used: (1) encouraged, pushed forward, urged on; (2) allowed to follow own tendencies, not encouraged; (3) held back, discouraged. The person who analyzed the document then determined from reading the paper the category into which a particular case fell.[2]

2. As it may be of interest to other sociologists, the following note may be added as to the way in which the original list of factors and their attendant categories were reached. The work on this section of the study was done by a committee of twelve graduate students and the director. Each person read five documents and made a list of the factors found in each, with the terms actually used there to describe the situations involved. The results were then pooled and a sub-committee of three worked out a master list of factors with the attendant categories. In some cases the graded series of categories was filled out logically in order to give at least three classes (high, low and middle). The resulting key was very long, and was shortened by the elimination of factors not immediately pertinent to the purpose of the study, and also of factors found in only a few of the documents used in the preliminary reading. The key which resulted was then given to each member of the committee of twelve persons. One case was read to the committee and was classified by the group according to the key. Working in pairs, the committee next analyzed several cases by the key, and at their next meeting discussed the key. Terms were re-defined and some new

The question at once arose as to the amount of subjective judgment which entered into placing a document in, let us say, category (1) above, "encouraged," rather than in category (2) "allowed to follow own tendencies." The question is especially pertinent when a large number of papers are read by several persons but no paper is read by two persons.

In order to check the reliability of the key and the reliability in general of classifying narrative materials into definite categories for statistical analysis, the writers of this article each read the same random selection of 117 documents, made the classifications into categories independently and then studied the results.

Nine factors in the students' lives were investigated in all. From the independent judgments by the three investigators, twenty-seven tables were made up. Table 28.1 presented here is an example.

Twenty-one of these tables lent themselves to comparable treatment by the contingency method.[3] Table 28.2 summarizes the contingency coefficients found.

It will be noted that contingency coefficients are all high—in some cases indicating almost complete agreement. For example, the factor "attractiveness as a child" had four categories: (1) proud of appearance, thought himself very attractive; (2) considered himself of average attractiveness; (3) never thought about looks; (4) considered himself unattractive or ugly. The highest possible contingency coefficient theoretically would be 0.866. The relationship between the judgements of Cavan and Hauser was 0.81; of Cavan and Stouffer, 0.80; of Stouffer and Hauser, 0.80. The lowest average coefficient found, which was on judgments of "extent to which the child confided in the mother," was high enough, as can be seen from Table 28.2, to indicate sufficiently satisfactory agreement for ordinary working purposes. How high agreement is necessary is, of course, a practical question depending on how the inferences from the life history are to be used.

It should be emphasized that this agreement in inferences from the life histories is no check on the validity of the life histories themselves. Whether the students told the truth is another question.

categories were added to complete certain series. The final key contained 51 factors and 194 categories.

In applying the key the categories were numbered consecutively from 1 to 194. A card was then mimeographed with numbers on it from 1 to 194. One card was used for each case, and the numbers representing categories which seemed to fit the case in question was circled.

3. Two of the factors are omitted, one factor because of the presence of too few cases in two of the arrays and the other because there were only two categgories. The six tables for these two factors showed by inspection apparently as high agreement between judgments as that found on the other factors.

TABLE 28.1. *Comparison of Judgments by Hauser and Stouffer on Family Discord Between Parents as Reported in Life Histories*

	Frequent quarreling	Occasional quarrels	Some difference of opinion but never quarrel	No difference of opinion; unity	Total
No difference of opinion; unity........		1	1	16	18
Some difference of opinion but never quarrel........	1	1	22	11	35
Occasional quarrels........	1	18	9	3	31
Frequent quarreling........	12	2		3	14
Total	14	22	32	30	98

$C = .0757$ (theoretical upper limit, 0.866).

TABLE 28.2. *Raw Coefficients of Contingency Between Judgments of Factors as Reported in Life Histories*

	Categories	Theoretical upper limit*	Cavan and Hauser		Cavan and Stouffer		Stouffer and Hauser		Average contingency coefficient
			Number of cases†	Contingency coefficient	Number of cases†	Contingency coefficient	Number of cases†	Contingency coefficient	
Self-feeling in group of children...	4 × 4	0.866	101	0.780	101	0.749	113	0.790	0.773
Attractiveness as a child............	4 × 4	0.866	66	0.808	65	0.797	75	0.798	0.801
Leadership as a child.............	3 × 3	0.816	90	0.736	85	0.698	92	0.696	0.710
Discord between parents............	4 × 4	0.866	96	0.758	96	0.756	98	0.757	0.757
Confiding in Mother...............	3 × 3	0.816	83	0.680	76	0.740	86	0.707	0.709
Methods of control................	4 × 4	0.866	86	0.736	81	0.795	85	0.732	0.754
Mother's attitude toward child at present.................	3 × 3	0.816	93	0.751	88	0.702	86	0.713	0.722

* Yule, G. U., *An Introduction to the Theory of Statistics*, 7th edition, revised, p. 66.

† The judge made no entry if he felt that the data in the life history were inadequate to warrant a judgment about a particular factor. This accounts for the differences in the number of cases upon which the coefficients of contingency are based.

Furthermore, some of these documents were not life histories in a strict sense, for certain of the students, contrary to instructions, apparently took the easy way out by writing brief, perfunctory answers to the questions in the outline of suggestions. It is possible that the more perfunctory the papers were the less they resembled a smooth flowing narrative the easier it was for the judges to agree in analyzing them. This would be interesting to check quantitatively, if enough time were available.

The writers agree with those who doubt the economy, though not the possibility, of treating life history materials quantitatively in practice. Unpublished studies by one of the present writers[4] and by Everett V. Stonequist[5] show that practically the same results can be obtained by classifying categorical responses to a direct questionnaire as by classifying inferences, obtained with far greater labor, from life histories. This is not to deny the importance of the life history method as a tool of research. As some sociologists have held, a main function of the life history is perhaps to supply insights, hunches, and clews. Some of the most important life history material, dealing with elaborate patterns rather than magnitudes, perhaps should not be forced into a quantitative mould. The insights derived from life histories, moreover, are often essential to the construction of direct questionnaires, and also for an interpretation of the relationships among the answers to the direct questionnaire after the magnitude of the relationships has been determined statistically.

It is more important to know whether inferences from life history materials can have objectivity, for it would seem that the value even of qualitative insights is enhanced if a number of competent observers, reading the same document, should make the same inferences. Furthermore, objectivity of the narrative is especially important if life history materials are to be used in a systematic statistical way as a check on the validity of direct questionnaries filled out by the same writers.

The little investigation has reported tends to give further confidence in the objectivity of life history materials. But it should be borne in mind that agreement on inferences as to a single factor abstracted from a document does not mean that investigators necessarily would agree in their appraisal of a time sequence of causal relations involving a chain of inferences or hypotheses or in their abstraction of a complex pattern of relationships.

4. S. A. Stouffer, *Experimental Comparison of Statistical and Case History Methods in Attitude Research*, Ph.D. thesis, University of Chicago, June, 1930.

5. *The Marginal Man*, Ph.D. thesis, University of Chicago, August, 1930.

PART ELEVEN

The Unobtrusive Method

INTRODUCTION

THE UNOBTRUSIVE method removes the investigator from direct participation in the events at hand. Unnoticed or unseen, he records such behavioral acts as how persons dress, speak, or locate themselves within a situation. He may also analyze private or public archival records—be these love letters, poems, or the budget of Salem, Massachusetts in the 1700's—or, on other occasions he may insert hidden recording equipment in a situation. In all events, a nonreactive observation is being made, and—of equal importance—the behavior being observed is occurring in its natural situation.

The logic underlying the unobtrusive approach is simple: Since known observers create reactive effects, remove them from the situation. But this is not the only reason the unobtrusive approach is used. This method, which formally ranges from physical trace analysis, to archival investigations, to such simple observations as those of dress and language, to hidden electronic hardware, suggests new areas for sociological study. It is as if the taken-for-granted aspects of daily life were now made part of the sociologist's domain. Investigators can seriously undertake language, document, and physical location analyses, and they can do so in an uncontaminated fashion, fitting their findings into a naturalistic, interactionist perspective.

In addition, the unobtrusive approach offers a way of buttressing the findings from the more traditional interview, experimenter, and survey methods. Findings from these reactive methods can be complemented and assessed by the nonreactive findings of the unobtrusive approach.

THE NATURE OF THE UNOBTRUSIVE APPROACH

Webb's paper presents the underlying logic of this approach, stresses the rather unconventional nature of the method, and points in the direction of new, naturalistic sampling models. He offers a convincing argument for a multimethod, or triangulated approach to research and in this sense anticipates the papers on triangulation in Part XII. Webb summarizes his position with a list of some 15 different variables that could jeopardize his findings from any study. These closely parallel Campbell's list of factors influencing internal and external validity. Thus Webb notes the reactive effects that come from the investigator and the subject, the sampling frame, the measuring instrument, and the stability of the observed factors.

He calls for the use of multiple samples drawn from natural areas of everyday life. These remarks should be assessed in the context of Part III on sampling procedures. They are of direct relevance in the study of social organizations, for example.

The paper by Felipe and Sommer illustrates one type of unobtrusive analysis: the physical location method. Felipe and Sommer present unobtrusive data of the experimental variety. An ingenious aspect of their two studies was that subjects in the field were treated as experimental or control subjects, depending on their location in the observational situation. This suggests how quasi-experiments can be designed in the field. Confederate, or stooge subjects were also employed, and it would be interesting to examine irrelevant aspects of the stooge's behavior upon the observer's seating patterns; a point earlier stressed by Leik. What, for example, would be the effect on seating patterns and territorial defenses of varying the dress of the stooge?

PROBLEMS WITH THE UNOBTRUSIVE APPROACH

There are several difficulties with this method. Because he does not make his presence felt, or known, the observer may locate in situations where relevant data do not appear, or may appear only at infrequent intervals. The dross rate may be high. In this case a more public and open method could also be used, perhaps on different samples, to insure the more rapid collection of needed data.

Another basic problem stems from the behavioral nature of the method. Because persons are observed and not questioned, the investigator frequently has only correlations between certain events and certain actions. Why, for example do certain persons not leave when their territory is invaded? Or when is a sufficient level of tension produced to create flight patterns? Or why do certain blacks refuse to sit behind whites?

These examples suggest that the unobtrusive method must be combined, at least for certain kinds of analyses, with *obtrusive* and *reactive* techniques, such as the interview. The interview provides a way of probing the subjective side of social action. The unobtrusive method basically probes the public side. Obviously, for many studies the two methods will have to be combined. Indeed, a full-fledged interactional study demands a merger of the objective and subjective facts. No single strategy or technique will offer all the data, or answer all the questions.

Perhaps the ethical issues involved in using unobtrusive methods represents their most severe problem. There is little consensus on this matter. Some argue for no disguised research, claiming that every act of the sociologist must be public. This position obviously precludes the unobtrusive approach. I sanction the use of any method that is not employed in a way that would harm or discredit a subject, leaving it to the observer to decide whether his observations will or will not harm the subject.

I am fully aware that this position invites criticism. How can you judge harm, if you do not give the subject the right to decline observation? I am not sure you can measure harm even if you do ask the subject, but in any event I place the ethical matter in the observer's hands. In my judgment he – not a board of sociologists – can best judge what should and should not be done in the field. I am not putting this issue to rest; Part XIII takes up the ethics of observation once again.

Suggested Readings. The basic source on this method is Eugene J.

Webb, Donald T. Campbell, Richard D. Schwartz and Lee Sechrest, *Unobtrusive Measures: Nonreactive Research in the Social Sciences,* (Chicago: Rand McNally, 1966).

For a statement on the ethics of disguised observation, Kai T. Erikson's "A Comment on Disguised Observation," *Social Problems,* 14 (Spring 1967), 366–73, should be read. Erikson rules against the disguised approach. My critique of his position, and his response to my argument is given in *Social Problems,* 15 (Spring 1968), 502-6.

29. Unconventionality, Triangulation, and Inference

EUGENE J. WEBB

ALL THREE of the nouns in this paper's title—unconventionality, triangulation, and inference—are imbedded in a more general concept: multiple operationalism as a way of knowing. With educational psychologists making significant contributions, the mistaken belief in the single operational definition of learning, or performance, or of values has been eroded.

Most students today would agree that it is appropriate to draw simultaneously on multiple measures of the same attribute or construct—multiple measures hypothesized to overlap in theoretically relevant components, but which do not overlap on measurement errors specific to individual methods (16, 17, 7, 19, 38).

In 1953 E. G. Boring (3) wrote:

> As long as a new construct has only the single operational definition that it received at birth, it is just a construct. When it gets two alterna-

Reprinted by permission from *Proceedings of the Invitational Conference on Testing Problems*, October 29, 1966, pp. 34–43. Copyright 1966, Educational Testing Service.

tive operational definitions, it is beginning to be validated. When the defining operations, because of proven correlations, are many, then it becomes reified.

The most persuasive evidence and the strongest inference comes from a triangulation of measurement processes. Feigl (14) spoke of fixing a concept by triangulation in logical space, and the partition of the sources of variance can do just that.

But just as we ask if a correlated x and y are more highly correlated with z, it is also reasonable to ask if the components being converged or triangulated are truly complementary. Are we fully accounting for known sources of error variance?

This is a serious question with most of the multimethod studies now available. "Multimethod" has usually been defined as multiple scales or behaviors collected under the condition in which the subject knew he was being tested. Humphreys (19), for example, when talking of multiple measures of reasoning, spoke of "series analogies and classification items." The multiple methods thus have tended to be multiple variants within a *single* measurement class such as the interview.

Every data-gathering class — interviews, questionnaires, observation, performance records, physical evidence — is potentially biased and has specific to it certain validity threats. Ideally, we should like to converge data from several data classes, as well as converge with multiple variants from within a single class.

The methodological literature warned us early of certain recurrent validity threats, and the evidence has markedly accelerated in the last few years. It has been 30 years, for example, since Lorge (20) published his paper on response set, and 20 years since Cronbach (11) published his influential paper on the same topic in *Educational and Psychological Measurement*. Further, there is the more recent work of Orne and his associates on the demand characteristics of a known research setting (24, 25, 27, 26) and Rosenthal's stimulating work (29, 30, 31) on the social psychology of the experiment. All these investigations suggest that reliance on data obtained only in "reactive" settings (9) is equivocal.

As a guide to locating the strengths and weaknesses of individual data classes — to better work the convergent multiple-methods approach — my colleagues at Northwestern and I have tried to develop a list of sources of research invalidity to be considered with any data class (38). An outline of these sources of invalidity is contained in Chart 29.1.

To bring under control some of the reactive measurement effect, we might employ data classes which do not require the cooperation of the student or respondent. By supplementing standard interview or pencil-and-paper measures, more dimensionality is introduced into triangulation.

In a recent paper which described the use of observation methods in the study of racial attitudes, Campbell, Kruskal, and Wallace (8) studies seating aggregations by race. Two colleges were picked in the Chicago area—one noted for the liberal composition of its student body and the other more associated with a traditional point of view. Going into lecture halls, they observed seating patterns and the clustering of Negro and white students during class. With a new

Chart 29.1. Sources of Research Invalidity

I. *Reactive Measurement Effect*
  1. Awareness of being tested
  2. Role playing
  3. Measurement as change
  4. Response sets

II. *Error from Investigator*
  5. Interviewer effects
  6. Change—fatigue/practice

III. *Varieties of Sampling Error*
  7. Population restriction
  8. Population stability over time
  9. Population stability over areas

IV. *Access to Content*
  10. Restrictions on content
  11. Stability of content over time
  12. Stability of content over areas

V. *Operating Ease and Validity Checks*
  13. Dross rate
  14. Access to descriptive cues
  15. Ability to replicate

statistical test developed by Kruskal, they were able to demonstrate a greater racial mixture in the more "liberal" college. They also found, however, that the seating mix in the liberal college was significantly less than that expected by chance.

The linkage of secondary records is another way to develop control over reactivity. An example of this approach is DeCharms and Moeller's (12) study of achievement imagery. They first gathered the number of patents issued by the United States Patent Office from 1800 to 1950. These data (controlled for population) were then matched to achievement imagery found in children's readers for the same period. There was a strong relationship between the level of achievement imagery in their sample of books and the number of patents per million population. Both data series are non-recreative, and although other rival, plausible hypotheses might explain the relationship, it remains as one piece in the inferential puzzle, uncontaminated by awareness of being tested.

For matching of other archival records, we can note Lewis Terman's (37) study estimating Galton's IQ (not far from 200) and Galton's own early studies of heredity genius (15).

Another class of data comes from physical evidence, one example of which is Fredrick Mosteller's creative study of the degree of which different sections of the *International Encyclopedia of the Social Sciences* were read (22). He estimated usage by noting the wear and tear on separate sections: dirty edges of pages, frequency of dirt smudges, finger markings and underlinings on pages. He sampled different libraries and even used the *Encyclopedia Britannica* as a control.

Thus far, the emphasis has been on data sources and overlapping classes of data. We might also profitably explore the possibility of using multiple samples. Again, this is different from the usual definition of multiple samples. In addition to sampling a number of different classrooms, or groups of students or cities, one may ask if there are different types or categories of samples available for the variable under study. Is there a group of natural outcroppings among occupations, already formed social and interest groups, or people who have common experiences? Can we economically exploit for research purposes the broad spectrum of already formed groups which may be organized along some principle of direct substantive applicability to the investigation.

Professor James Bryan of Northwestern and I have been interested in the use of these "outcropping" groups as a middle-level sampling strategy—one that straddles the elegant but cumbersome national probability sample and the more circumscribed "N = 80 volunteer males from the introductory psychology class" populations.

Because one sometimes doesn't know the universe for a study and because of cost restraints, subjects are most often selected because of proximity. Our subjects are typically drawn from the subject pool of the introductory class, from friends, friends of friends, or those un-lucky enough to be members of the same institution as the in-vestigator, be it the school, the hospital, or the prison.

Consider some convenience samples which may supplement con-ventional groups. Becker, Lerner and Carroll (1) used caddies loafing about a golf course waiting for jobs as a subject pool. E. E. Smith (33) suggested firemen in a fire house. They have almost unlimited time available for questioning and offer the very happy situation of a naturally formed, read group, whose members know each other very well. This is a good setting in which to replicate findings derived from experimentally formed groups in laboratories or from natural groups.

Sometimes these convenient aggregates offer a special opportunity to get a high concentration of usable subjects. To study somatotyp-ing among top athletes in different track and field events, Tanner (35, 36) went to the 1960 Olympic Village at Rome. In a study of proposed brand names for new products, in which one of the criteria was relative invulnerability to regional accents, MacNiven (21) sent interviewers to a nearby airport where they asked travellers to read off lists of names while the interviewers noted variable pronuncia-tions.

In trait measurement, one may define altruism by one or by a series of self-report scales. But it may also be profitable to examine extant groups with some face-valid loading on altruism – say, volun-teer blood donors, contributors to charitable causes, or even such groups as those who aided Jews in Nazi Germany.

Bryan and Test (5) have recently reported on a provocative study of the influence of modeling behavior on altruism. Their objective in a field experiment was to see whether or not people stopped to help someone who had a flat tire. The experiment involved two women stranded with flat tires one quarter of a mile apart on a highway and a model, a man who had stopped to help one of them. In one part of the experiment, the traffic passed the woman and the model and then, farther up the highway, passed the other woman. In the other part of the experiment, the traffic passed only one woman and no model.

Other clusters of groups may help to define or locate a particular ability. Occupational categories may be particularly useful here. For studies of superior depth perception there are natural occupational outcroppings such as magnetic core threaders, jugglers, or grand prix automobile drivers.

Each of these groups possesses other attributes, and one might consider the same group of automobile race drivers as a high risk-taking sample and link them with other high risk-taking groups such as sport and military parachute jumpers (13).

Or, for studies of deviance, there are the self-help deviants groups of Alcoholics Anonymous, Gamblers Anonymous, and prisoners who volunteer for therapy. All presumably share a common characteristic, but the setting of the phenomenon is varied.

As an expansion of this idea, consider Ernest Haggard's exemplary chapter on isolation and personality (18). Haggard reviewed studies of isolation: How is personality affected by the restraint of habitual body movement in restricted, monotonous, or otherwise unfamiliar environments? Instead of limiting himself to the laboratory experimentation on sensory deprivation, he went abroad to the large literature of "naturally" occurring isolation. There are research findings on interstate truck drivers, pilots flying missions alone at night or at high altitudes, orthopedic patients in iron lungs, and anecdotal reports of prisoners in solitary confinement, shipwrecked sailors and explorers. Haggard reports the commonalities among these widely *differing* groups, which operlapped on the isolation dimension, and which shared common sensory and personality phenomena. He compares, for example, the anecdotal reports of Admiral Byrd (6) and the scientific investigation of Rohrer (28) on International Geophysical Year personnel, both of whom found the individual cutting back on information input under isolated conditions — even when a mass of material was available to consume.

As an aside on the nature of isolated man, Haggard quoted Bombard's (2, p.x) comments on the sinking of the *Titanic:*

> When the first relief ships arrived, three hours after the liner had disappeared, a number of people had either died or gone mad in the lifeboats. Significantly, no child under the age of ten was included among those who had paid for their terror with madness and for their *madness* with *death.* The children were still at the age of reason.

In another isolation investigation, Sells considered many of the same data in his applied study, "A model for the social system for the multiman extended duration space ship" (32). Thinking of such long journeys as Mars shot, Sells assembled data from many isolated groups, both natural and artificial. His analysis was careful and based on theory. He related the findings from different studies to a general model of an isolated social system — evaluating the degree to which results from the individual studies were likely to transfer to a space vehicle setting. Thus, data from submarine and exploration parties were most applicable, while the findings from shipwreck and disaster studies were least likely to transfer. Naroll (23) has suggested similar procedures to differentially weight data derived from documentary sources of varying credibility, and Stanley (34) has offered a broader approach for treating data in the general multitrait-multimethod matrix format.

In this paper, I have stressed two main points. One is the utility of different data-gathering techniques applied concurrently to the same problem. The other is the laying of these techniques against multiple samples which are natural outcroppings of a phenomenon.

From E. G. Boring (4):

> ... The truth is something you get on toward and never to, and the way is filled with ingenuities and excitements. Don't take the straight and narrow path of the stodgy positivists; be gay and optimistic, like Galton, and you will find yourself more toward than you had ever expected.

REFERENCES

1. BECKER, S., LERNER, M., AND CARROL, JEAN, "*Conformity as a Function of Birth Order, Payoff, and Type of Group Pressure*," Journal of Abnormal and Social Psychology, 69, (1964), 318–23.
2. BOMBARD, A., *The Voyage of the Heretique* (New York: Simon and Schuster, 1953).
3. BORING, E. G., "*The Role of Theory in Experimental Psychology*," American Journal of Psychology, 66 (1953), 169–84.
4. BORING, E. G., personal communication, 1966.
5. BRYAN, J. H. AND TEST, MARY ANN, "*Models and Helping*," unpublished paper, Northwestern University, 1966.
6. BYRD, R. E., *Alone* (New York: Putnam's, 1938).
7. CAMPBELL, D. T. AND FISKE, D. W., "*Convergent and Discriminant Validation by the Multitrait-multimethod Matrix*," Psychological Bulletin, 56, (1959), 81–105.
8. CAMPBELL, D. T., KRUSKAL, W. H., AND WALLACE, W. P., "*Seating Aggregation as an Index of Attitude*," Sociometry, 29, (1966), 1–15.
9. CAMPBELL, D. T. AND STANLEY, J. C., "*Experimental and Quasi-experimental Designs for Research on Teaching*," in N. L. GAGE, ed., Handbook of Research on Teaching (Chicago: Rand McNally, 1963; also published as a supplemental monograph by Rand McNally in 1966).
10. COOK, S. W., AND SELLTIZ, C., "*A Multiple-indicator Approach to Attitude Measurement*," Psychological Bulletin, 62, (1964), 36–55.
11. CRONBACH, L., "*Response Sets and Test Validity*," Educational and Psychological Measurement, 6, (1964), 475–94.

12. DeCharms, R., and Moeller, G., "*Values Expressed in American Children's Readers: 1800-1950*," Journal of Abnormal and Social Psychology, 64, (1962), 136–42.

13. Epstein, S., "*The Measurement of Drive and Conflict in Humans; Theory and Experiment,*"in 1962 Nebraska Symposium on Motivation.

14. Feigl, H., "*The Mental and the Physical,*" in H. Feigl, M. Scriven, and G. Maxwell, eds., Minnesota Studies in the Philosophy of Science, Vol. II. Concepts, Theories and the Mind-body Problem (Minneapolis: University of Minnesota Press, 1958).

15. Galton, F., *Hereditary Genius* (New York: D. Appleton, 1870).

16. Garner, W. R., "*Context Effects and the Validity of Loudness Scales,*" Journal of Experimental Psychology, 48, (1954), 218–24.

17. Garner, W. R., Hake, H. W., and Eriksen, C. W., "*Operationism and the Concept of Perception,*" Psychological Review, 63, (1956), 149–49.

18. Haggard, E. A., "*Isolation and Personality,*" in P. Worchel and D. Byrne, eds., Personality Change (New York: Wiley, 1964).

19. Humphreys, L. G., "*Note on the Multitrait-multimethod Matrix,*" Psychological Bulletin, 57, (1960), 86–88.

20. Lorge, I., "*Gen-like: Halo or Reality,*" Psychological Bulletin, 34, (1937).

21. MacNiven, M., personal communication, 1965.

22. Mosteller, F., "*Use as Evidenced by an Examination of Wear and Tear on Selected Sets of* ESS," in K. Daris, et al., "*A Study of the Need for a New Encyclopedic Treatment of the Social Sciences,*" unpublished manuscript, 1955.

23. Naroll, R., *Data Quality Control*, (Glencoe, Ill.: Free Press, 1962).

24. Orne, M. T., "*The Nature of Hypnosis: Artifact and Essence,*" Journal of Abnormal and Social Psychology, 58, (1959), 277–99.

25. Orne, M. T., "*On the Social Psychology of the Psychological Experiment: With Particular Reference to Demand Characteristics and their Implications,*" American Psychologist, 17, (1962), 776–83.

26. Orne, M. T., and Evans, F. J., "*Social Control in the Psychological Experiment: Antisocial Behavior and Hypnosis,*" Journal of Personality and Social Psychology, 1, (1965), 189–200.

27. Orne, M. T., and Scheibe, K. E., "*The Contribution of Nondeprivation Factors in the Production of Sensory Deprivation Effects: The Psychology of the "Panic Button,*" Journal of Abnormal and Social Psychology, 68 (1964), 3–12.

28. Rohrer, J. H., "*Human Adjustment to Antarctic Isolation,*" Armed Services Technical Information Agency (Publication AD246610, Arlington Hall Station, Arlington, Virginia, 1960).

29. Rosenthal, R., "*On the Social Psychology of the Psychological Experiment: The Experimenter's Hypothesis as Unintended Determinant of Experimental Results,*" American Scientist, 51, (1963), 268–83.

30. Rosenthal, R., "*Experimenter Outcome-orientation and the Results of the Psychological Experiment,*" Psychological Bulletin, 61, (1964), 405–12.

31. ROSENTHAL, R., *"Changing Children's IQ by Changing Teacher's Expectations,"* paper read at American Psychological Association meetings, New York, September 1966.
32. SELLS, S. B., *"A Model for the Social System for the Multiman Extended Duration Space Ship"* (NASA report No. NGR 44-009-008), undated.
33. SMITH, E. E., *"Obtaining Subjects for Research,"* American Psychologist, 17, (1962), 577–78.
34. STANLEY, J. C., *"Analysis of Unreplicated Three-way Classifications, with Applications to Rater Bias and Trait Independence,"* Psychometrika, 26, (1961), 205–19.
35. TANNER, J. M., *The Physique of the Olympic Athlete,* (London: Allen and Unwin, 1964).
36. TANNER, J. M., *"Physique and Athletic Performance,"* in S. A. BARNETT AND ANNE MCLAREN, eds., Penquin Science Survey B: 1965 (Middlesex: Penguin, 1965).
37. TERMAN, L. M., *"The Intelligence Quotients of Francis Galton in Childhood,"* American Journal of Psychology, 28, (1917), 209–15.
38. WEBB, E. J., CAMPBELL, D. T., SCHWARTZ, R. D., AND SECHREST, L., *Unobtrusive Measures* (Chicago: Rand McNally, 1966).

30. Invasions of Personal Space

NANCY JO FELIPE AND ROBERT SOMMER

THE LAST decade has brought an increase in empirical studies of deviance. One line of investigation has used the case study approach with individuals whom society has classified as deviants — prostitutes, drug addicts, homosexuals, mental patients, etc. The other approach, practiced less frequently, has involved staged situations in which one individual, usually the investigator or one of his students, violates the norm or "routine ground" in a given situation and observes the results.[1] The latter approach is in the category of an experiment in that it is the investigator himself who creates the situation he observes and therefore has the possibility of systematically varying the parameters of social intercourse singly or in combinations. From this standpoint these studies have great prom-

Reprinted by permission from *Social Problems*, 14 (Fall 1966), pp. 206–214. Copyright 1966, The Society for the Study of Social Problems.

1. See for example, Harold Garfinkel, "Studies of the Routine Grounds of Everyday Activities," *Social Problems*, 11 (Winter 1964), 225–50.

ise for the development of an experimental sociology following the model set down by Greenwood.[2] With topics such as human migration, collective disturbance, social class, the investigator observes events and phenomena already in existence. Control of conditions refers to modes of observations and is largely on an *ex post facto* statistical or correlational basis. On the other hand, few staged studies of deviance have realized their promise as experimental investigations. Generally they are more in the category of demonstrations, involving single gross variations of one parameter and crude and impressionistic measurement of effect without control data from a matched sample not subject to the norm violation. Of more theoretical importance is the lack of systematic variation in degree and kind of the many facets of norm violation. The reader is left with the impression that deviancy is an all-or-none phenomenon caused by improper dress, impertinent answers, naive questions, etc. It cannot be denied that a graduate student washing her clothes in the town swimming pool is breaking certain norms. But we cannot be sure of the norms that are violated or the sanctions attached to each violation without some attempt at isolating and varying single elements in the situation.

The present paper describes a series of studies of one norm violation, sitting too close to another individual. Conversational distance is affected by many things including room density, the acquaintance of the individuals, the personal relevance of the topic discussed, the cultural backgrounds of the individuals, the personalities of the individuals, etc.[3] There are a dozen studies of conversational distance which have shown that people from Latin countries stand closer together than North Americans,[4] eye contact has important effect on conversational distance,[5] introverts stand farther apart than extroverts,[6] friends place themselves closer together than strangers,[7] and so on, but there is still, under any set of conditions, a range of conversational distance which is considered normal for that situation. Several of these investigators, notably Birdwhistell,[8] Garfinkel,[9]

2. Ernest Greenwood, *Experimental Sociology* (New York: Kings Crown Press, 1945).
3. Edward T. Hall, *The Silent Language* (Garden City, N. Y.: Doubleday, 1959).
4. Edward T. Hall, "The Language of Space," *Landscape*, 10 (Autumn 1960), 41–44.
5. Michael Argyle and Janet Dean, "Eye-Contact, Distance, and Affiliation," *Sociometry*, 28 (September 1965), 289–304.
6. John L. Williams, "Personal Space and its Relation to Extraversion-Introversion," unpublished M.A. thesis, University of Alberta, 1963.
7. Kenneth B. Little, "Personal Space," *Journal of Experimental Social Psychology*, 1 (August 1960), 237–47.
8. Birdwhistell, R. L., *Introduction to Kinesics*, (Washington, D.C.: Foreign Service Institute, 1952).
9. Garfinkel, *op. cit.*

Goffman,[10] and Sommer[11] have described the effects of intruding into this distance or personal space that surrounds each individual. The interest shown in the human spacing mechanisms as well as the possibilities of objective measurement of both norm violation and defensive postures suggests that this is an excellent area in which to systematically study norm violations.

The present paper describes several studies of invasions of personal space that took place over a two-year period. The first was done during the summer of 1963 in a mental hospital. At the time it seemed that systematic studies of spatial invasions could only take place in a "crazy place" where norm violation would escape some of the usual sanctions applied in the outside world. Though there is a strong normative control system that regulates the conduct of mental patients toward one another and toward staff, the rules governing staff conduct toward patients (except cases of brutality, rape, or murder), and particularly higher status staff, such as psychiatrists, physicians, and psychologists, are much less clear. At times, it seems that almost anything can be done in a mental hospital provided it is called research, and one can cite such examples as psychosurgery, various drug experiments, and recent investigations of operant conditioning as instances where unusual and sometimes unproven or even harmful procedures were employed with the blessings of hospital officialdom. To call a procedure "research" is a way of "bracketing" it in time and space and thus excluding it from the usual rules and mores. This is one reason why we supposed that spatial invasions would be more feasible inside a mental hospital than outside. We had visions of a spatial invasion on a Central Park bench resulting in bodily assault or arrest on a sex deviant or "suspicious character" charge. It seemed that some studies of norm violation were deliberately on a one-shot basis to avoid such difficulties. After the first study of spatial invasions in a mental hospital had been completed, however, it became apparent that the method could be adapted for use in more typical settings. We were then able to undertake similar intrusions on a systematic basis in a university library without any untoward consequences, though the possibilities of such problems arising were never far beyond the reaches of consciousness in any of the experimental sessions.

METHOD

The first study took place on the grounds of Mendocino State Hospi-

10. Erving Goffman, *Behavior in Public Places* (Glencoe, Ill.: Free Press, 1963).
11. Robert Sommer, "Studies in Personal Space," *Sociometry*, 22 (September 1959), 247-60.

tal, a 1500-bed mental institution situated in parklike surroundings. Most wards were unlocked and many patients spent considerable time outdoors. In wooded areas it was common to see patients seated underneath trees, one to a bench. Because of the easy access to the outside as well as the number of patients involved in hospital industry, the ward areas were relatively empty during the day. This made it possible for the patients to isolate themselves from other people by finding a deserted area on the grounds or remaining in the almost empty wards. The invasions of personal space took place both indoors and outdoors. The victims were chosen on the basis of these criteria: the victim would be a male, sitting alone, and not engaged in any clearly defined activities such as reading, card playing, etc. All sessions took place near the long stay wards, which meant that newly-admitted patients were largely omitted from the study. When a patient meeting these criteria was located, E walked over and sat beside the patient without saying a word. If the victim moved his chair or moved farther down the bench, E would move a like distance to keep the space between them about six inches. There were two experimental conditions. In one, E sat alongside a patient and took complete notes of what ensued. He also jiggled his keys occasionally and looked at the patient in order to assert his dominance. In the second experimental condition, E simply sat down next to the victim and, three or four times during the 20 minute session, jiggled his keys. Control subjects were selected from other patients seated at some distance from E but still within E's visual field. To be eligible for the control group, a patient had to be sitting by himself and not reading or otherwise engaged in an activity as well as be visible to E.

Each session took a maximum of twenty minutes. There were 64 individual sessions with different patients, 39 involved the procedure in which E took notes and 25 involved no writing.[12] One ward dayroom was chosen for additional, more intensive observations. During the daylight hours this large room was sparsely populated and the same five patients occupied the same chairs. These patients would meet Esser's[13] criteria of territoriality in that each spent more than 75 per cent of his time in one particular area.

12. Four incomplete sessions are omitted from this total. On two occasions a patient was called away by a nurse and on two other occasions the session was terminated when the patient showed signs of acute stress. The intruder in Study One was the junior author, a 35 year old male in slight build. It is likely that invasions by a husky six-footer would have produced more immediate flight reactions.
13. Aristide H. Esser, *et al.*, "Territoriality of Patients on a Research Ward," in Joseph Wortis, ed., *Recent Advances in Biological Psychiatry*, vol. 8 (New York: Plenum Press, 1965).

RESULTS

The major data of the study consist of records of how long each patient remained seated in his chair following the invasion. This can be compared with the length of time the control patients remained seated. Figure 30.1 shows the cumulative number of patients who had departed at each one-minute interval of the 20 minute session. Within two minutes, all of the controls were still seated but 36 per cent of the experimental subjects had been driven away. Within nine minutes fully half of the victims had departed compared with only 8 per cent of the controls. At the end of the 20 minute session, 64 per cent of the experimental subjects had departed compared with 33 per cent of the controls. Further analysis showed that the writing condition was more potent than the no-writing condition but that this difference was significant only at the .10 level ($X^2 = 4.61$, df = 2). The patient's actual departure from his chair was the most obvious reaction to the intrusion. Many more subtle indications of the patient's discomfort were evident. Typically the victim would immediately face away from E, pull in his shoulders, and place his elbows at his sides. Mumbling, irrelevant laughter, and delusional talk also seemed to be used by the victim to keep E at a distance.

Repeated observation of the same patients took place on one particular ward where the patients were extremely territorial in their behavior. Five patients generally inhabited this large room and sat in the same chairs day after day. There were gross differences in the way these particular territorial patients reacted to the writer's presence. In only one case (S_3) was (clearly dominant. At the other extreme with S_1 and S_2, it was like trying to move the Rock of Gibralter. E. invariably left these sessions defeated, with his tail between his legs, often feeling the need to return to his colleagues and drink a cup of coffee before attempting another experimental session. S_5 is a peculiar case in that sometimes he was budged but other times he wasn't.

STUDY TWO

These sessions took place in the study hall of a university library, a large room with high ceilings and book-lined walls. The room contains fourteen large tables in two equal rows. Each table is 4 x 16 feet, and accommodates six chairs on each long side. Because of its use as a study area, students typically try to space themselves as far as possible from others. Each victim was the first female sitting alone in a pre-determined part of the room with at least one book in front

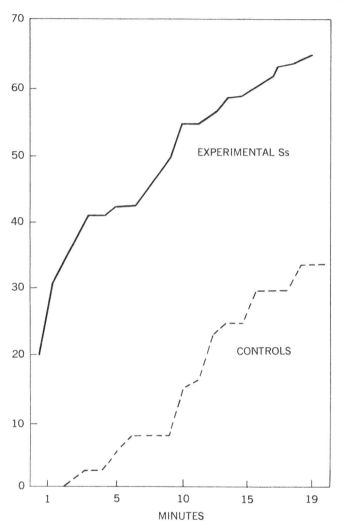

% Ss DEPARTING

MINUTES

Figure 30.1—Cumulative Percentage of Patients Having Departed at Each One-Minute Interval.

of her, two empty chairs on either side (or on one side if she was at the end of the table), and an empty chair across from her. An empty chair was also required to be across from E's point of invasion. The second female to meet these criteria and who was visible to E served as a control. The control was observed from a distance and no invasion was attempted. Sessions took place between the hours of 8-5 on Mondays through Fridays; because of time changes between classes and the subsequent turnover of the library population, the observations began between 5 and 15 minutes after the hour. There were five different experimental conditions.

Condition I: E walked up to an empty chair beside an S, pulling the chair out at an angle, and sat down, completely ignoring S's presence. As E sat down, she unobtrusively moved the chair close to the table and to S, so that the chairs were approximately within three inches from one another. The E would lean over her book, in which she surreptitiously took notes, and tried to maintain constant shoulder distance of about 12 inches between E and S. To use Crook's[14] terms, E tried to maintain the arrival distance, and to keep the S from adjusting to a settled distance. This was sometimes difficult to do because the chairs were 18½ inches wide and an S would sometimes sit on the other half of her chair, utilizing its width as an effective barrier. However, E tried to get as close to the S's as possible without actually having any physical contact. If the S moved her chair away, E would follow by pushing her chair backward at an angle and then forward again, under the pretense of adjusting her skirt. At no time did she consciously acknowledge S's presence. In this condition E took detailed notes of the S's behavior, as well as noting time of departure.

Condition II: E went through the same procedure, except instead of moving the adjacent chair closer to S, E sat in the adjacent chair at the expected distance, which left about 15 inches between the chairs or about two feet between the shoulders of E and S.

Condition III: One empty seat was left between E and S, with a resulting shoulder distance of approximately three and a half feet.

Condition IV: Two empty seats were left between E and S with a resulting shoulder distance of about five feet.

Condition V: E sat directly across from S, a distance of about four feet.

In all conditions E noted the time of initial invasion, the time of the S's departure (or the end of the thirty minute session, depending on which came first), and any observable accommodation to E's presence such as moving books or the chair. For the controls E noted the time the session began and the time of the S's departure if it occurred within thirty minutes after the start of the session.

RESULTS

Figure 30.3 shows the number of subjects remaining after successive

14. J. H. Crook, "The Basis of Flock Organization in Birds," in W. H. Thorpe and O. L. Zangwill, eds., *Current Problems in Animal Behaviour* (Cambridge: Cambridge University Press, 1961).

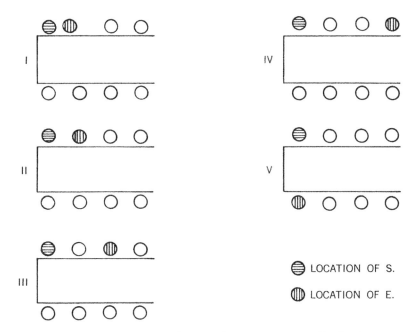

Figure 30.2—Seating of Intruder Vis-à-vis Victim in Each Experimental Condition.

five minute periods. Since there was no significant difference between the scores in Conditions 2-5, these were combined in the analysis. At the end of the thirty minute session, 87 per cent of the controls, 73 per cent of the S's in the combined conditions remained, compared to only 30 per cent of the experimental S's in Condition I. Statistical analysis shows that Condition I produced significantly more flight than any of the other conditions, while there was a slight but also significant difference between the combined conditions (2-5) and the control condition. Although flight was the most clearly defined reaction to the invasion, many more subtle signs of the victim's discomfort were evident. Frequently an S drew in her arm and head, turned away from E exposing her shoulder and back, with her elbow on the table, her face resting on her hand. The victims used objects including books, notebooks, purses, and coats as barriers, and some made the wide chair into a barrier.

DISCUSSION

These results show clearly that spatial invasions have a disruptive

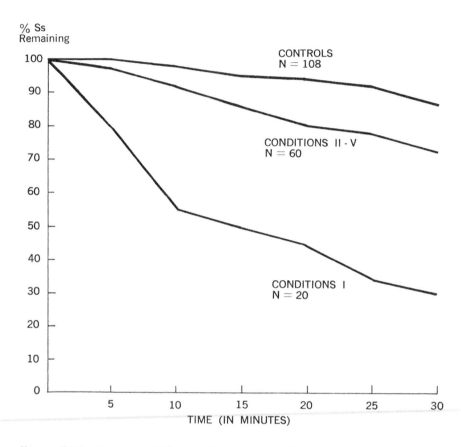

Figure 30.3—Per cent of Victims Remaining at Each Five Minute Interval After the Invasion.

effect and can produce reactions ranging from flight at one extreme to agonistic display at the other. The individual differences in reacting to the invasion are evident; there was no single reaction among our subjects to someone "sitting too close." The victim can attempt to accommodate himself to the invasion in numerous ways, including a shift in position, interposing a barrier between himself and the invader, or moving farther away. If these are precluded by the situation or fail because the invader shifts positions too, the victim may eventually take to flight. The methods we used did not permit the victim to achieve a comfortable *settled distance*. Crook[15] studied the spacing mechanisms in birds, and found three component factors that maintain individual distance, which he defined as the area around an individual within which the approach of a neighboring bird is reacted to with either avoidance or attack. A number of measurements may be taken when studying individual distance – the arrival distance (how far away from settled birds a newcomer will land), settled distance (the resultant distance after adjustments have occurred), and the distance after departure. The conditions in Study One and in Condition I of the second study called for E to maintain the arrival distance, and to keep the victim from adjusting to a settled distance. In these conditions, the victim was unable to increase the arrival distance by moving away (since the invader followed him down the bench in Study One and moved her chair closer in Study Two), and the greatest number of flight reactions was produced by these conditions. McBride,[16] who has studied the spatial behaviors of animals in confinement, has found that avoidance movements and turning aside are common reactions to crowding, particularly when a submissive animal is close to a dominant animal. Literally the dominant bird in a flock has more space and the other birds will move aside and look away when the dominant bird approaches. Looking away to avoid extensive eye contact was also a common reaction in the present studies. This probably would not have occurred if a subordinate or lower status individual had invaded the personal space of a dominant or higher status individual. There was also a dearth of direct verbal responses to the invasions. Only two of the mental patients spoke directly to E although he sat right beside them, and only one of the 80 students victims asked E to move over. This is some support for Hall's view that "we treat space somewhat as we treat sex. It is there but we don't talk about it."[17]

We see then that a violation of expected conversational distance produces, first of all, various accommodations on the part of the victim. The intensity of his reaction is influenced by many factors including territoriality, the dominance-submission relationship between invader and victim, the locus of the invasion, the victim's attribution of sexual motives to the intruder (in this case all victims and intruders were like-sex individuals), etc. All of these factors

15. Crook, *op. cit.*
16. Glen McBride, *A General Theory of Social Organization and Behaviour* (St. Lucia: University of Queensland Press, 1964); also McBride, *et al.*, "Social Forces Determining Spacing and Head Orientation in a Flock of Domestic Hens," *Nature*, 197 (1963), 1272-73.
17. Hall, *The Silent Language, op. cit.*

influence the victim's definition of the situation and consequently his reaction to it. In the present situation the first reaction to the invasion was accommodation or adaption: The individual attempted to "live with" the invasion by turning aside, interposing a notebook between himself and the stranger, and pulling in his elbows. When this failed to relieve the tension produced by the norm violation, flight reactions occurred.

There are other elements in the invasion sequence that can be varied systematically. We have not yet attempted heterosexual invasion sequences, or used invaders of lower social standing, or explored more than two unusual and contrasting environments. We are making a start toward using visual rather than spacial invasions, in this case staring at a person rather than moving too close to him. Preliminary data indicate that visual invasions are relatively ineffective in a library where the victims can easily retreat into their books and avoid a direct visual confrontation. There are many other types of intrusions, including tactile and olfactory, that have intriguing research potentialities. It is important to realize that the use of staged norm violations permits these elements to be varied singly and in combination, and in this sense to go beyond the methods of *ex post facto* or "natural experiments" or single-point demonstrations. It is noteworthy that the area of norm violation provides one of the most fruitful applications for the experimental method.

PART TWELVE

Triangulation:
A Case For
Methodological and
Combination Evaluation

INTRODUCTION

SOME years ago Martin Trow suggested that sociologists should be done with their arguments defending one method over another, "Comment on Participant Observation and Interviewing: A Comparison," *Human Organization*, 16 (1957, 33–35). No single method is always superior. Each has its own special strengths, and weaknesses. It is time for sociologists to recognize this fact and to move on to a position that permits them to approach their problems with all relevant and appropriate methods, to the strategy of methodological triangulation. Webb's paper established the need for this perspective. The papers in this part indicate how multiple methods may be employed. In addition they suggest standards by which different methods may be evaluated.

There is an overwhelming need for a single set of standards by which the methodological act can be evaluated. In my judgment the perspectives of Campbell and Webb furnish these standards. The simultaneous consideration of intrinsic and extrinsic test factors forces every researcher to be self-consciously aware of how his every action can influence subsequent observations. From this perspective research becomes a social act.

VARIETIES OF TRIANGULATION

In addition to the use of multiple methods, there are at least three other varieties of triangulation. *Theoretical triangulation* involves the use of several different perspectives in the analysis of the same set of data. *Data triangulation* attempts to gather observations with multiple sampling strategies. Observations on time, social situations, and persons in various forms of interaction can all be gathered. The use of data triangulation insures that a theory is tested in more than one way, increasing the likelihood that negative cases will be uncovered. *Investigator triangulation* is the use of more than one observer in the field situation. The advantages of multiple observers are obvious: Tests on the reliability of observations can be quickly made, and observer bias can thus be judged.

Methodological triangulation can take two forms. The first is *within-method* and the second is *between-method*. The former is seen when an investigator employs varieties of the same method; for example, three different scales measuring other-directedness. Between-method triangulation is stressed by Zelditch.

The combination of multiple methods, data types, observers and theories in the same investigation is termed multiple triangulation. While it may be difficult for any single investigation to achieve this full combination, it is certainly possible to utilize multiple data levels and methods.

These remarks suggest a standard for evaluating studies: The greater the triangulation, the greater the confidence in the observed findings. The obverse is equally true. The conclusion is evident: Sociologists must move beyond single-method, atheoretical studies.

METHODOLOGICAL COMPARISONS

The three papers in this part examine the problems inherent in experiments, surveys, and participant observation. Zelditch suggests that narrow definitions of participant observation are inadequate. When properly conceived, the method should include observation on the part of the investigator, informant interviewing, and sampling techniques. He thus broadens the conventional view of the method and indicates how triangulation may be implemented with the field technique.

Hovland compares findings on attitude change collected from surveys and experiments. His analysis focuses on the discrepancies yielded by the two methods. He notes two reasons for these: research design and historical factors influencing the interpretation of each method.

Because of their emphasis on natural field settings, many surveys fail to achieve the rigor of laboratory experiments. The survey researcher can not insure that all his subjects were equally exposed to a common stimuli, for example. The strength and size of the stimuli also varies. Surveys typically attempt to assèss the impact of an entire communication, while experiments focus on more narrowly defined communications, a film, for example. The communicators of the stimuli also vary between two methods. In the experiment it may be a lecturer or teacher. In the survey it can be a news broadcaster, a distant relative, or a friend.

Differences in the sampling frame also influence the comparability of findings. Experiments often use captive audiences, such as college sophomores enrolled in introductory psychology. Surveys often examine adults in their homes or places of work. The differences in samples thus preclude many valid comparisons.

On the basis of such factors, Hovland concludes that no contradictions have been established between the data collected with these two methods. The differences can be explained by variations in the communicative situation, the communicator of the message, the audience, and the subjects.

In the second section of his article, Hovland attempts to bring survey and experimental methodologies closer together. Central to his argument is the point that experimenters must learn to recognize the narrowness of the laboratory situation in interpreting the effects of larger communicative processes. The research of Orne, Rosenthal, Friedman, Campbell, and Webb would suggest that the experimenter must also learn to recognize the effects of his own behavior on his results.

On the other hand, survey researchers must understand the limitations inherent in the statistical method. Correlations seldom establish causal relationships. The problems inherent in this mode of analysis were stressed by Hirschi and Selvin.

As a partial solution for the survey problem Hovland suggests greater use of the "panel method," a point similarly stressed by Zeisel in Part VIII. In concluding, Hovland notes that neither method provides all the answers. Both must be combined if a social psychology of communication is to be developed.

Vidich and Shapiro offer a comparison of participant observation and survey data gathered within the same community. They suggest that two distinct approaches can be employed in the evaluation of research methods. The test of *internal consistency* asks if the method produces data which are contradictory. This is seen in checks comparing the results of two sets of questions measuring the same event or object. If the two scales, or indices, produce different results, the investigator must either reject one of them or attempt to reconcile their differences.

The *test of external validity* asks whether the two methods produce comparable data on the same events. Thus this test provides a way of comparing methods, while internal consistency focuses on one method at a time. To avoid confusion with Campbell's use of external validity (which refers to generalizability), it would be better to view Vidich and Shapiro's use of the term as a *test of between-method comparability*. These are two distinct tests. Both are of obvious relevance and of importance.

The Vidich and Shapiro report examines the degree of agreement between the two methods and attempts to assess the amount of bias, or selectivity, introduced by each. For such a test, a common data base is necessary. Vidich and Shapiro utilized prestige ratings of community members which were gathered by sociometric questions with the survey, and the field worker's rating based on the observational approach.

Analysis revealed certain discrepancies between the two methods. While there was a high correspondence between the two ratings of prestige, the observer had not ranked 207 cases covered in the survey questionnaire. The unknown group represented a disproportionate number of those with low prestige. The observer's contacts were biased in the direction of higher-prestige individuals. An important point emerges; without the survey data, this bias would not have been detected. On the other hand, specific data on the nature of prestige rankings were not gathered with the survey method.

The two methods thus buttress one another. Neither was free of bias. It can be concluded that a full understanding of interactions within communities, indeed within any interactional structure, demands the use of more than one method. Without multiple methods assessed against common data bodies, the researcher has no way of judging the reactive and biasing effects of his observations and methods.

AN ADDITIONAL DEFENSE OF THE COMPARATIVE-
TRIANGULATION METHOD

It is commonplace among data analysts that valid casual explanations demand comparisions with groups not exposed to the explanatory variables. This was the central argument underlying Campbell's critique of nonexperimental designs. Unless comparison, or control groups are used, the analyst can only guess as to the effects of his variables.

Paradoxically, this comparative stance has seldom been employed in evaluations of the research act. If comparison groups are needed for causal analysis, then multiple, or comparative methods are needed for methodological evaluation. A new methodological perspective must be adopted in the social sciences. In my opinion, this will be a triangulated perspective. The validity of this conclusion can only be judged by the improved quality of future research.

Suggested Readings. A number of the readings in previous sections have employed the triangulated perspective; for example, the excerpt from *Union Democracy.* Others include Tittle and Hill's evaluation of different attitude measures, and Becker's analysis of participant observation. Another very good example is the previously mentioned Becker, *et al., Boys in White,* (Chicago: The University of Chicago Press, 1961).

31. Reconciling Conflicting Results Derived from Experimental and Survey Studies of Attitude Change

CARL I. HOVLAND

TWO QUITE different types of research design are characteristically used to study the modification of attitudes through communication. In the first type, the *experiment*, individuals are given a controlled exposure to a communication and the effects evaluated in terms of the amount of change in attitude or opinion produced. A base line is provided by means of a control group not exposed to the communication. The study of Gosnell (1927) on the influence of leaflets designed to get voters to the polls is a classic example of the controlled experiment.

In the alternative research design, the *sample survey*, information is secured through interviews or questionnaires both concerning the respondent's exposure to various communications and his attitudes and opinions on various issues. Generalizations are then derived from the correlations obtained between reports of exposure and mea-

Reprinted by permission from *American Psychologist*, 14 (1959), pp. 8–17. Copyright 1959, American Psychological Association.

surements of attitude. In a variant of this method, measurements of attitude and of exposure to communication are obtained during repeated interviews with the same individual over a period of weeks or months. This is the "panel method" extensively utilized in studying the impact of various mass media on political attitudes and on voting behavior (cf., e.g., Kendall & Lazarsfeld, 1950).

Generalizations derived from experimental and from correlational studies of communication effects are usually both reported in chapters on the effects of mass media and in other summaries of research on attitude, typically without much stress on the type of study from which the conclusion was derived. Close scrutiny of the results obtained from the two methods, however, suggests a marked difference in the picture of communication effects obtained from each. The object of my paper is to consider the conclusions derived from these two types of design, to suggest some of the factors responsible for the frequent divergence in results, and then to formulate principles aimed at reconciling some of the apparent conflicts.

DIVERGENCE

The picture of mass communication effects which emerges from correlational studies is one in which few individuals are seen as being affected by communications. One of the most thorough correlational studies of the effects of mass media on attitudes is that of Lazarsfeld, Berelson, and Gaudet published in *The People's Choice* (1944). In this report there is an extensive chapter devoted to the effects of various media, particularly radio, newspapers, and magazines. The authors conclude that few changes in attitudes were produced. They estimate that the political positions of only about 5% of their respondents were changed by the election campaign, and they are inclined to attribute even this small amount of change more to personal influence than to the mass media. A similar evaluation of mass media is made in the recent chapter in the *Handbook of Social Psychology* by Lipset and his collaborators (1954).

Research using experimental procedures, on the other hand, indicates the possibility of considerable modifiability of attitudes through exposure to communication. In both Klapper's survey (1949) and in my chapter in the *Handbook of Social Psychology* (Hovland, 1954) a number of experimental studies are discussed in which the opinions of a third to a half or more of the audience are changed.

The discrepancy between the results derived from these two methodologies raises some fascinating problems for analysis. This divergence in outcome appears to me to be largely attributable to two kinds of factors: one, the difference in research design itself; and, two, the historical and traditional differences in general approach to evaluation characteristic of researchers using the experimental as contrasted with the correlational or survey method. I would like to discuss, first, the influence these factors have on the estimation of overall effects of communications and, then, turn to other divergences in outcome characteristically found by the use of the experimental and survey methodology.

Undoubtedly the most critical and interesting variation in the research *design* involved in the two procedures is that resulting from differences in definition of exposure. In an experiment the audience on whom the effects are being evaluated is one which is fully exposed to the communication. On the other hand, in naturalistic situations with which surveys are typically concerned, the outstanding phenomenon is the limitation of the audience to those who *expose themselves* to the communication. Some of the individuals in a captive audience experiment would, of course, expose themselves in the course of natural events to a communication of the type studied; but many others would not. The group which does expose itself is usually a highly biased one, since most individuals "expose themselves most of the time to the kind of material with which they agree to begin with" (Lipset et al., 1954, p. 1158). Thus one reason for the difference in results between experiments and correlational studies is that experiments describe the effects of exposure on the whole range of individuals studied, some of whom are initially in favor of the position being advocated and some who are opposed, whereas surveys primarily describe the effects produced on those already in favor of the point of view advocated in the communication. The amount of change is thus, of course, much smaller in surveys. Lipset and his collaborators make this same evaluation, stating that:

> As long as we test a program in the laboratory we always find that it has great effect on the attitudes and interests of the experimental subjects. But when we put the program on as a regular broadcast, we then note that the people who are most influenced in the laboratory tests are those who, in a realistic situation, do not listen to the program. The controlled experiment always greatly overrates effects, as compared to those that really occur, because of the self-selection of audiences (Lipset et al., 1954, p. 1158).

Differences in the second category are not inherent in the design of the two alternatives, but are characteristic of the way researchers using the two methods typically proceed.

The first difference within this class is in the size of the communication unit typically studied. In the majority of survey studies the unit evaluated is an entire program of communication. For example, in studies of political behavior an attempt is made to assess the effects of all newspaper reading and television viewing on attitudes toward the major parties. In the typical experiment, on the other hand, the interest is usually in some particular variation in the content of the communications, and experimental evaluations much more frequently involve single communications. On this point results are thus not directly comparable.

Another characteristic difference between the two methods is in the time interval used in evaluation. In the typical experiment the time at which the effect is observed is usually rather soon after exposure to the communication. In the survey study, on the other hand, the time perspective is such that much more remote effects are usually evaluated. When effects decline with the passage of time, the net outcome will, of course, be that of accentuating the effect obtained in experimental studies as compared with those obtained in survey researches. Again it must be stressed that the difference is not inherent in the designs as such. Several experiments, including our own on the effect of motion pictures (Hovland, Lumsdaine, & Sheffield, 1949) and later studies on the "sleeper effect" (Hovland & Weiss, 1951; Kelman & Hovland, 1953), have studied retention over considerable periods of time.

Some of the difference in outcome may be attributable to the types of communicators characteristically used and to the motive-incentive conditions operative in the two situations. In experimental studies communications are frequently presented in a classroom situation. This may involve quite different types of factors from those operative in the more naturalistic communication situation with which the survey researchers are concerned. In the classroom there may be some implicit sponsorship of the communication by the teacher and the school administration. In the survey studies the communicators may often be remote individuals either unfamiliar to the recipients, or outgroupers clearly known to espouse a point of view opposed to that held by many members of the audience. Thus there may be real differences in communicator credibility in laboratory and survey researches. The net effect of the differences will typically be in the direction of increasing the likelihood of change in the experimental as compared with the survey study.

There is sometimes an additional situational difference. Communications of the type studied by survey researchers usually involve reaching the individual in his natural habitat, with consequent supplementary effects produced by discussion with friends and family. In the laboratory studies a classroom situation with low post-communication interaction is more typically involved. Several studies, including one by Harold Kelly reported in our volume on *Communication and Persuasion* (Hovland, Janis, & Kelly, 1953), indicate that when a communication is presented in a situation which makes group membership salient, the individual is typically more resistant to counternorm influence than when the communication is presented under conditions of low salience of group membership (cf. also, Katz & Lazarsfeld, 1955, pp. 48–133).

A difference which is almost wholly adventitious is in the types of populations utilized. In the survey design there is, typically, considerable emphasis on a random sample of the entire population. In the typical experiment, on the other hand, there is a consistent over-representation of high school students and college sophomores, primarily on the basis of their greater accessibility. But as Tolman has said: "College sophomores may not be people." Whether differences in the type of audience studied contribute to the differences in effect obtained with the two methods is not known.

Finally, there is an extremely important difference in the studies of the experimental and correlational variety with respect to the type of issues discussed in the communications. In the typical experiment we are interested in studying a set of factors or conditions which are expected on the basis of theory to influence the extent of effect of the communication. We usually deliberately try to find types of issues involving attitudes which are susceptible to modification through communication. Otherwise, we run the risk of no measurable effects, particularly with small-scale experiments. In the survey procedures, on the other hand, socially significant attitudes which are deeply rooted in prior experience and involve much personal commitment are typically involved. This is especially true in voting studies which have provided us with so many of our present results on social influence. I shall have considerably more to say about this problem a little later.

The differences so far discussed have primarily concerned the extent of overall effectiveness indicated by the two methods: why survey results typically show little modification of attitudes by communication while experiments indicate marked changes. Let me now turn to some of the other differences in generalizations derived from the two alternative designs. Let me take as the second main area of disparate results the research on the effect of varying distances between the position taken by the communicator and that held by the recipient of the communication. Here it is a matter of comparing changes for persons who at the outset closely agree with the communicator with those for others who are mildly or strongly in disagreement with him. In the naturalistic situation studied in surveys the typical procedure is to determine changes in opinion following reported exposure to communication for individuals differing from the communicator by varying amounts. This gives rise to two possible artifacts. When the communication is at one end of a continuum, there is little room for improvement for those who differ from the communication by small amounts, but a great deal of room for movement among those with large discrepancies. This gives rise to a spurious degree of positive relationship between the degree of discrepancy and the amount of change. Regression effects will also operate in the direction of increasing the correlation. What is needed is a situation in which the distance factor can be manipulated independently of the subject's initial position. An attempt to set up these conditions experimentally was made in a study by Pritzker and the writer (1957). The method involved preparing individual communications presented in booklet form so that the position of the communicator could be set at any desired distance from the subject's initial position. Communicators highly acceptable to the subjects were used. A number of different topics were employed, including the likelihood of a cure for cancer within five years, the desirability of compulsory voting, and the adequacy of five hours of sleep per night.

The amount of change for each degree of advocated change is shown in Fig. 31.1. It will be seen that there is a fairly clear progression, such that the greater the amount of change advocated the greater the average amount of opinion change produced. Similar results have been reported by Goldberg (1954) and by French (1956).

But these results are not in line with our hunches as to what would happen in a naturalistic situation with important social issues. We felt that here other types of response than change in attitude would occur. So Muzafer Sherif, O. J. Harvey, and the writer (1957) set up a situation to simulate as closely as possible the conditions typically involved when individuals are exposed to major social issue communications at differing distances from their own position. The issue used was the desirability of prohibition. The study was done in two states (Oklahoma and Texas) where there is prohibition or local option, so that the wet-dry issue is hotly debated. We concentrated on three aspects of the problem: How favorably will the commu-

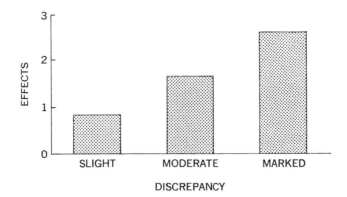

Figure 31.1—Mean opinion change score with three
degrees of discrepancy (deviation between subject's
position and position advocated in communication).
[From Hovland & Pritzker, 1957].

nicator be received when his position is at varying distances from
that of the recipient? How will what the communicator says be
perceived and interpreted by individuals at varying distances from
his position? What will be the amount of opinion change produced
when small and large deviations in position of communication and
recipient are involved?

Three communications, one strongly wet, one strongly dry, and
one moderately wet, were employed. The results bearing on the first
problem, of *reception*, are presented in Fig. 31.2. The positions of
the subjects are indicated on the abscissa in letters from A (extreme
dry) to H (strongly wet). The positions of the communication are also
indicated in the same letters, B indicating a strongly dry communication, H a strongly wet, and F a moderately wet. Along the ordi-
nate there is plotted the percentage of subjects with each position on
the issue who described the communication of distance between the
recipient and the communicator greater influences the evaluation of
the fairness of the communication. When a communication is directed at the pro-dry position, nearly all the dry subjects consider it
fair and impartial, but only a few per cent of the wet subjects consider the identical communication fair. The reverse is true at the other
end of the scale. When an intermediate position is adopted, the

percentages fall off sharply on each side. Thus under the present conditions with a relatively ambiguous communicator one of the ways of dealing with strongly discrepant positions is to *discredit* the communicator, considering him unfair and biased.

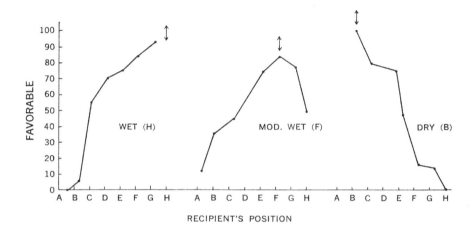

Figure 31.2—Percentage of favorable evaluations ("fair," "unbiased," etc.) of wet (H), *moderately wet* (F), *and dry* (B) *communications for subjects holding various positions on prohibition. Recipients position range from* A *(very dry) to* H *(very wet). Position of communications indicated by arrow.* [*From Hovland, Harvey, & Sherif, 1957*].

A second way in which an individual can deal with discrepancy is by distortion of what is said by the communicator. This is a phenomenon extensively studied by Cooper and Jahoda (1947). In the present study, subjects were asked to state what position they thought was taken by the communicator on the prohibition question. Their evaluation of his position could then be analyzed in relation to their own position. These results are shown in Fig. 31.3 for the moderately wet communication. It will be observed that there is a tendency for individuals whose position is close to that of the communicator to report on the communicator's position quite accurately, for individuals a little bit removed to report his position to be substantially more like their own (which we call an "assimilation effect"), and for those with more discrepant positions to report the communicator's position as more extreme than it really was. This we refer to as a "contrast effect."

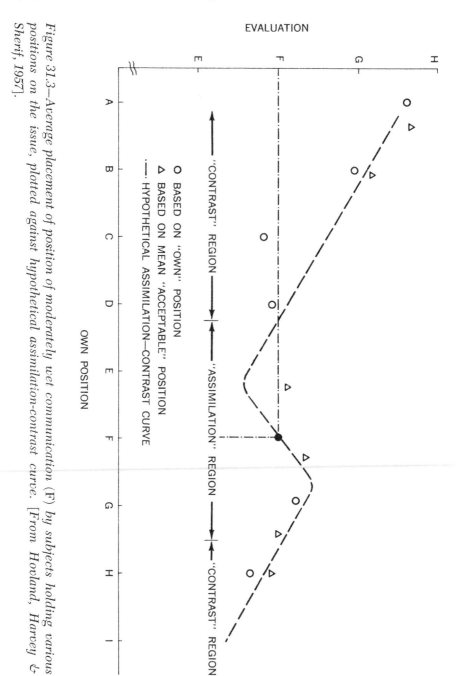

Figure 31.3–*Average placement of position of moderately wet communication (F) by subjects holding various positions on the issue, plotted against hypothetical assimilation-contrast curve.* [*From Hovland, Harvey & Sherif, 1957*].

Now to our primary results on opinion change. It was found that individuals whose position was only slightly discrepant from the communicator's were influenced to a greater extent than those whose positions deviated to a larger extent. When a wet position was espoused, 28% of the middle-of-the-road subjects were changed in the direction of the communicator, as compared with only 4% of the drys. With the dry communication 14% of the middle-of-the-roaders were changed, while only 4% of the wets were changed. Thus, more of the subjects with small discrepancies were changed than were those with large discrepancies.

These results appear to indicate that, under conditions when there is some ambiguity about the credibility of the communicator and when the subject is deeply involved with the issue, the greater the attempt at change the higher the resistance. On the other hand, with highly respected communicators, as in the previous study with Pritzker using issues on lower involvement, the greater the discrepancy the greater the effect. A study related to ours has just been completed by Zimbardo (1959) which indicates that, when an influence attempt is made by a strongly positive communicator (i.e., a close personal friend), the greater the discrepancy the greater the opinion change, even when the experimenter made a point of stressing the great importance of the subject's opinion.

The implication of these results for our primary problem of conflicting results is clear. The types of issues with which most experiments deal are relatively uninvolving and are often of the variety where expert opinion is highly relevant, as for example, on topics of health, science, and the like. Here we should expect that opinion would be considerably affected by communications and furthermore that advocacy of positions quite discrepant from the individual's own position would have a marked effect. On the other hand, the types of issues most often utilized in survey studies are ones which are very basic and involve deep commitment. As a consequence small changes in opinion due to communication would be expected. Here communication may have little effect on those who disagree at the outset and function merely to strengthen the position already held, in line with survey findings.

A third area of research in which somewhat discrepant results are obtained by the experimental and survey methods is in the role of order of presentation. From naturalistic studies the generalization has been widely adopted that primacy is an extremely important factor in persuasion. Numerous writers have reported that what we experience first has a critical role in what we believe. This is particularly stressed in studies of propaganda effects in various countries when the nation getting across its message first is alleged to have a great advantage and in commercial advertising where "getting a beat on the field" is stressed. The importance of primacy in political propaganda is indicated in the following quotation from Doob:

> The propagandist scores an initial advantage whenever his propaganda reaches people before that of his rivals. Readers or listeners are then biased to comprehend, forever after, the event as it has been initially portrayed to them. If they are told in a headline or a flash that the battle has been won, the criminal has been caught, or the bill is certain to pass the legislature, they will usually expect subsequent information to substantiate this first impression. When later facts prove otherwise, they may be loath to abandon what they believe to be true until perhaps the evidence becomes overwhelming (Doob, 1948, pp. 421–422).

A recent study by Katz and Lazarsfeld (1955) utilizing the survey method compares the extent to which respondents attribute major impact on their decisions about fashions and move attendance to the presentations to which they were first exposed. Strong primacy effects are shown in their analyses of the data.

We have ourselves recently completed a series of experiments oriented toward this problem. These are reported in our new monograph on *Order of Presentation in Persuasion* (Hovland, Mandell, Campbell, Brock, Luchins, Cohen, McGuire, Janis, Feierabend, & Anderson, 1957). We find that primacy is often *not* a very significant factor when the relative effectiveness of the first side of an issue is compared experimentally with that of the second. The research suggests that differences in design may account for much of the discrepancy. A key variable is whether there is exposure to both sides or whether only one side is actually received. In naturalistic studies the advantage of the first side is often not only that it is first but that it is often then the only side of the issue to which the individual is exposed. Having once been influenced, many individuals make up their mind and are no longer interested in other communications on the issue. In most experiments on order of presentation, on the other hand, the audience is systematically exposed to both sides. Thus under survey conditions, self-exposure tends to increase the impact of primacy.

Two other factors to which I have already alluded appear significant in determining the amount of primacy effect. One is the nature of the communicator, the other the setting in which the communication is received. In our volume Luchins presents results indicating that, when the same communicator presents contradictory material, the point of view read first has more influence. On the other hand, Mandell and I show that, when two different communicators present opposing views successively, little primacy effect is obtained. The communications setting factor operates similarly. When the issue and the conditions of presentation make clear that the points of view are controversial, little primacy is obtained.

Thus in many of the situations with which there had been great concern as to undesirable effects of primacy, such as in legal trials, election campaigns, and political debate, the role of primacy appears to have been exaggerated, since the conditions there are those least conducive to primacy effects: The issue is clearly defined as controversial, the partisanship of the communicator is usually established, and different communicators present the opposing sides.

Time does not permit me to discuss other divergences in results obtained in survey and experimental studies, such as those concerned with the effects of repetition of presentation, the relationship between level of intelligence and susceptibility to attitude change, or the relative impact of mass media and personal influence. Again, however, I am sure that detailed analysis will reveal differential factors at work which can account for the apparent disparity in the generalizations derived.

INTEGRATION

On the basis of the foregoing survey of results I reach the conclusion that no contradiction has been established between the data provided by experimental and correlational studies. Instead it appears that the seeming divergence can be satisfactorily accounted for on the basis of a different definition of the communication situation (including the phenomenon of self-selection) and differences in the type of communicator, audience, and kind of issue utilized.

But there remains the task of better integrating the findings associated with the two methodologies. This is a problem closely akin to that considered by the members of the recent Social Science Research Council summer seminar on *Narrowing the Gap Between Field Studies and Laboratory Studies in Social Psychology* (Riecken, 1954). Many of their recommendations are pertinent to our present problem.

What seems to me quite apparent is that a genuine understanding of the effects of communications on attitudes requires both the survey and the experimental methodologies. At the same time there appear to be certain inherent limitations of each method which must be understood by the researcher if he is not to be blinded by his preoccupation with one or the other type of design. Integration of the two methodologies will require on the part of the experimentalist an awareness of the narrowness of the laboratory in interpreting the larger and more comprehensive effects of communication. It will require on the part of the survey researcher a great awareness of the limitations of the correlational method as a basis for establishing casual relationships.

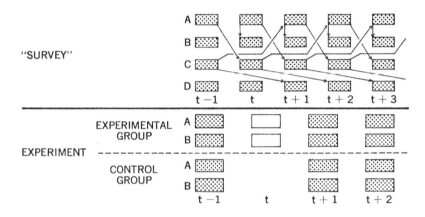

Figure 31.4—top half: "Process analysis" schema used in panel research. (Successive time intervals are indicatedl along abscissa. Letters indicate the variables under observation. Arrows represent relations between the variables.) [From Berelson, Lazarsfeld, & McPhee, 1954].

bottom half: Design of experimental research. (Letters on vertical axis again indicate variables being measured. Unshaded box indicates experimentally manipulated treatment and blank absence of such treatment. Time periods indicated as in top half of chart.)

The framework within which survey research operates is most adequately and explicitly dealt with by Berelson, Lazarsfeld, and McPhee in their book on *Voting* (1954). The model which they use, taken over by them from the economist Tinbergen, is reproduced in the top half of Fig. 31.4. For comparison, the model used by experimentalists is presented in the lower half of the figure. It will be seen that the model used by the survey researcher, particularly when he employs the "panel" method, stresses the large number of simultaneous and interacting influences affecting attitudes and opinions. Even more significant is its provision for a variety of "feedback" phenomena in which consequences wrought by previous influences affect processes normally considered as occurring earlier in the sequence. The various types of interaction are indicated by the placement of arrows showing direction of effect. In contrast the experimentalist frequently tends to view the communication process as one in which some single manipulative variable is the primary determinant of the subsequent attitude change. He is, of course, aware in a general way of the importance of context, and he frequently studies interaction effects as well as main effects; but he still is less attentive than he might be to the complexity of the influence situation and the numerous possibilities for feedback loops. Undoubtedly the real life communication situation is better described in terms of the survey type of model. We are all familiar, for example, with the interactions in which attitudes predispose one to acquire certain types of information, that this often leads to changes in attitude which may result in further acquisition of knowledge, which in turn produces more attitude change, and so on. Certainly the narrow question sometimes posed by experiments as to the effect of knowledge on attitudes greatly underestimates these interactive effects.

But while the conceptualization of the survey researcher is often very valuable, his correlational research design leaves much to be desired. Advocates of correlational analysis often cite the example of a science built on observation exclusively without experiment: astronomy. But here a very limited number of space-time concepts are involved and the number of competing theoretical formulations is relatively small so that it is possible to limit alternative theories rather drastically through correlational evidence. But in the area of communication effects and social psychology generally the variables are so numerous and so interwined that the correlational methodology is primarily useful to suggest hypotheses and not to establish casual relationships (Hovland et al., 1949, pp. 329-340; Maccoby, 1956). Even with the much simpler relationships involved in biological systems there are grave difficulties of which we are all aware these days when we realize how difficult it is to establish through correlation whether eating of fats is or is not a cause of heart disease or whether or not smoking is a cause of lung cancer. In communications research the complexity of the problem makes it inherently difficult to derive causal relationships from correlational analysis where experimental control of exposure is not possible. And I do not agree with my friends the Lazarsfelds (Kendall & Lazarsfeld, 1950) concerning the effectiveness of the panel method in circumventing this problem since parallel difficulties are raised when the relationships occur over a time span.

These difficulties constitute a challenge to the experimentalist in this area of research to utilize the broad framework for studying communication effects suggested by the survey researcher, but to employ well controlled experimental design to work on those aspects of the field which are amenable to experimental manipulation and control. It is, of course, apparent that there are important communication problems which cannot be attacked directly by experimental methods. It is not, for example, feasible to modify voting behavior by manipulation of the issues discussed by the opposed parties during a particular campaign. It is not feasible to assess the effects of communications over a very long span of time. For example, one cannot visualize experimental procedures for answering the question of what has been the impact of the reading of *Das Kapital* or *Uncle Tom's Cabin*. These are questions which can be illuminated by historical and sociological study but cannot be evaluated in any rigorous experimental fashion.

But the scope of problems which do lend themselves to experimental attack is very broad. Even complex interactions can be fruitfully attacked by experiment. The possibilities are clearly shown in studies like that of Sherif and Sherif (1953) on factors influencing cooperative and competitive behavior in a camp for adolescent boys. They were able to bring under manipulative control many of the types of interpersonal relationships ordinarily considered impossible to modify experimentally, and to develop motivations of an intensity characteristic of real-life situations. It should be possible to do similar studies in the communication area with a number of the variables heretofore only investigated in uncontrolled naturalistic settings by survey procedures.

In any case it appears eminently practical to minimize many of the differences which were discussed above as being not inherent in design but more or less adventitiously linked with one or the other method. Thus there is no reason why more complex and deeply-involving social issues cannot be employed in experiments rather than the more superficial ones more commonly used. The resistance to change of socially important issues may be a handicap in studying certain types of attitude change; but, on the other hand, it is important to understand the lack of modifiability of opinion with highly-involving issues. Greater representation of the diverse types of communicators found in naturalistic situations can also be achieved. In addition, it should be possible to do experiments with a wider range of populations to reduce the possibility that many of our present generalizations from experiments are unduly affected by their heavy weighting of college student characteristics, including high literacy, alertness, and rationality.

A more difficult task is that of experimentally evaluating communications under conditions of self-selection of exposure. But this is not at all impossible in theory. It should be possible to assess what demographic and personality factors predispose one to expose oneself to particular communications and then to utilize experimental and control groups having these characteristics. Under some circumstances the evaluation could be made on only those who select themselves, with both experimental and control groups coming from the self-selected audience.

Undoubtedly many of the types of experiments which could be set up involving or simulating naturalistic conditions will be too ambitious and costly to be feasible even if possible in principle. This suggests the continued use of small-scale experiments which seek to isolate some of the key variables operative in complex situations. From synthesis of component factors, prediction of complex outcomes may be practicable. It is to this analytic procedure for narrowing the gap between laboratory and field research that we have devoted major attention in our research program. I will merely indicate briefly here some of the ties between our past work and the present problem.

We have attempted to assess the influence of the communicator by varying his expertness and attractiveness, as in the studies of Kelman, Weiss, and the writer (Hovland & Weiss, 1951; Kelman & Hovland, 1953). Further data on this topic were presented earlier in this paper.

We have also been concerned with evaluating social interaction effects. Some of the experiments on group affiliation as a factor affecting resistance to counternorm communication and the role of salience of group membership of Hal Kelley and others are reported in *Communication and Persuasion* (Hovland et al., 1953).

Starting with the studies carried out during the war on orientation films by Art Lumsdaine, Fred Sheffield, and the writer (1949), we have had a strong interest in the duration of communication effects. Investigation of effects at various time intervals has helped to bridge the gap between assessment of immediate changes with those of longer duration like those involved in survey studies. More recent extensions of this work have indicated the close relationship between the credibility of the communicator and the extent of post-communication increments, or "sleeper effects" (Hovland & Weiss, 1951; Kelman & Hovland, 1953).

The nature of individual differences in susceptibility to persuasion via communication has been the subject of a number of our recent studies. The generality of persuasibility has been investigated by Janis and collaborators and the development of persuasibility in children has been studied by Ableson and Lesser. A volume concerned with these audience factors to which Janis, Ableson, Lesser, Field, Rife, King, Cohen, Linton, Graham, and the writer have contributed will appear under the title *Personality and Persuasibility* (1959).

Lastly, there remains the question on how the nature of the issues used in the communication affect the extent of change in attitude. We have only made a small beginning on these problems. In the research reported in *Experiments on Mass Communication*, we showed that the magnitude of effects was directly related to the type of attitude involved: Film communications had a significant effect on opinions related to straight-forward interpretations of policies and events, but had little or no effect on more deeply intrenched attitudes and motivations. Further work on the nature of issues is represented in the study by Sherif, Harvey, and the writer (1957) which was discussed above. There we found a marked contrast between susceptibility to influence and the amount of ego-involvement in the issue. But the whole concept of ego-involvement is a fuzzy one, and here is an excellent area for further work seeking to determine the theoretical factors involved in different types of issues.

With this brief survey of possible ways to bridge the gap between experiment and survey I must close. I should like to stress in summary the mutual importance of the two approaches to the problem of communication effectiveness. Neither is a royal road to wisdom, but each represents an important emphasis. The challenge of future work is one of fruitfully combining their virtues so that we may develop a social psychology of communication with the conceptual breadth provided by correlation study of process and with the rigorous but more delimited methodology of the experiment.

REFERENCES

BERELSON, B. R., LAZARSFELD, P. F., AND MCPHEE, W. N., *Voting: A Study of Opinion Formation in a Presidential Campaign* (Chicago: University of Chicago Press, 1954).

COOPER, EUNICS, AND JAHODA, MARIE, "*The Evasion of Propaganda: How Prejudiced People Respond to Anti-prejudice Propaganda*," Journal of Psychology, 23, (1947), 15–25.

DOOB, L. W., *Public Opinion and Propaganda* (New York: Holt, 1948).

FRENCH, J. R. P., JR., "*A Formal Theory of Social Power*," Psychology Review, 63, (1956), 181–94.

GOLDBERG, S. C., "*Three Situational Determinants of Conformity to Social Norms*," Journal of Abnormal Social Psychology, 49, (1954), 325–29.

GOSNELL, H. F., *Getting Out the Vote: An Experiment in the Stimulation of Voting* (Chicago: University of Chicago Press, 1927).

HOVLAND, C. I., "*Effects of the Mass Media of Communication*," in G. LINDZEY, ed., Handbook of Social Psychology, vol. II, Special Fields and Applications (Cambridge, Mass.: Addison-Wesley, 1954).

HOVLAND, C. I., HARVEY, O. J., AND SHERIF, M., "*Assimilation and Contrast Effects in Reactions to Communication and Attitude Change*," Journal of Abnormal Social Psychology, 55, (1957), 244–52.

HOVLAND, C. I., JANIS, I. L., AND KELLEY, H. H., *Communication and Persuasion* (New Haven: Yale Univeristy Press, 1953).

HOVLAND, C. I., LUMSDAINE, A. A., AND SHEFFIELD, F. D., *Experiments on Mass Communication* (Princeton: Princeton University Press, 1949).

HOVLAND, C. I., MANDELL, W., CAMPBELL, ENID H., BROCK, T., LUCHINS, A. S., COHEN, A. R., MCGUIRE, W. J., JANIS, I. L., FEIERABEND, ROSALIND L., AND ANDERSON, N. H., *The Order of Presentation in Persuasion* (New Haven: Yale University Press, 1957).

HOVLAND, C. I., AND PRITZKER, H. A., "*Extent of Opinion Changes as a Function of Amount of Change Advocated*," Journal of Abnormal Social Psychology, 54, (1957), 257–61.

HOVLAND, C. I., AND WEISS, W., "*The Influence of Source Credibility on Communication Effectiveness*," Public Opinion Quarterly, 15, (1951), 635–50.

JANIS, I. L., HOVLAND, C. I., FIELD, P. B., LINTON, HARRIETT, GRAHAM, ELAINE, COHEN, A. R., RIFE, D., ABELSON, R. P., LESSER, G. S., AND KING, B. T., *Personality and Persuasibility* (New Haven: Yale University Press, 1959).

KATZ, E., AND LAZARSFELD, P. F., *Personal Influence* (Glencoe, Ill.: Free Press, 1955).

KELMAN, H. C., AND HOVLAND, C. I., "'*Reinstatement*' of the Communicator in Delayed Measurement of Opinion Change," Journal of Abnormal Social Psychology, 48, (1953), 327–35.

KENDALL, PATRICIA L., AND LAZARSFELD, P. F., "*Problems of Survey Analysis*," in R. K. MERTON AND P. F. LAZARSFELD, eds., Continuities in Social Research: Studies in the Scope and Method of "The American Soldier" (Glencoe, Ill.: Free Press, 1950).

KLAPPER, J. T., *The Effects of Mass Media* (New York: Columbia University Bureau of Applied Social Research, 1949), mimeo.

LAZARSFELD, P. F., BERELSON, B., AND GAUDET, HAZEL, *The People's Choice* (New York: Duell, Sloan, and Pearce, 1944).

LIPSET, S. M., LAZARSFELD, P. F., BARTON, A. H., AND LINZ, J., *"The Psychology of Voting: An Analysis of Political Behavior,"* in G. LINDZEY, ed., Handbook of Social Psychology, vol. II, Special Fields and Applications (Cambridge, Mass.: Addison-Wesley, 1954).

MACCOBY, ELEANOR E., *"Pitfalls in the Analysis of Panel Data: A Research Note on Some Technical Aspects of Voting,"* American Journal of Sociology, 59, (1956), 359–62.

RIECKEN, H. W. (Chairman), *"Narrowing the Gap between Field Studies and Laboratory Experiments in Social Psychology: A Statement by the Summer Seminar,"* Items Social Science Research Council, 8, (1954), 37–42.

SHERIF, M., AND SHERIF, CAROLYN W., *Groups in Harmony and Tension: An Integration of Studies on Intergroup Relations* (New York: Harper, 1953).

ZIMBARDO, P. G., *"Involvement and Communication Discrepancy as Determinants of Opinion Change,"* unpublished doctoral dissertation, Yale University, 1959.

32. Some Methodological Problems of Field Studies

MORRIS ZELDITCH, JR.

THE ORIGINAL occasion for this paper was a reflection on the use of sample survey methods in the field: that is, the use of structured interview schedules, probability samples, etc., in what is usually thought of as a participant-observation study.[1] There has been a spirited controversy between, on the one hand, those who have sharply criticized field workers for slipshod sampling, for failing to document assertions quantitavely, and for apparently accepting impressionistic accounts — or accounts that the quantitatively minded could not distinguish from purely impressionistic accounts,[2] and, on

Reprinted by permission from Morris Zelditch, Jr., *American Journal of Sociology,* 67 (March 1962), pp. 566–76. Copyright 1962, The University of Chicago Press.

1. This paper reports part of a more extensive investigation of problems of field methods in which Dr. Reneé Fox is a collaborator. The author gratefully acknowledges the partial support given this investigation by funds from Columbia University's Documentation Project for Advanced Training in Social Research.

2. See, e.g., Harry Alper, "Some Observations on the Sociology of Sampling," *Social Forces,* XXXI (1952), 30–31; Robert C. Hanson, "Evidence and Procedure Characteristics of 'Reliable' Propositions in Social Science," *American Journal of Sociology,* LXIII (1958), 357–63.

the other hand, those who have, sometimes bitterly, been opposed to numbers, to samples, to questionnaires, often on the ground that they destroy the field workers' conception of a social system as an organic whole.[3]

Although there is a tendency among many younger field workers to accent criticisms made from the quantitative point of view,[4] there is reason to believe that the issue itself has been stated falsely. In most cases field methods are discussed as if they were "all of a piece."[5] There is, in fact, a tendency to be either *for* or *against* quantification, as if it were an either/or issue. To some extent the battle lines correlate with a relative concern for "hardness" versus "depth and reality" of data. Quantitative data are often thought of as "hard," and qualitative as "real and deep"; thus if you prefer "hard" data you are for quantification and if you prefer "real, deep" data you

3. See W. L. Warner and P. Lunt, *Social Life of a Modern Community* (New Haven, Conn.: Yale University Press, 1941), p. 55; Conrad Arensberg. "The Community Study Method," *American Journal of Sociology*, LX (1952), 109–24; Howard Becker, "Field Work among Scottish Shepherds and German Peasants," *Social Forces*, XXXV (1956), 10–15; Howard S. Becker and Blanche Geer, "Participant Observation and Interviewing: A Comparison," "*Human Organization*, XVI (1957), 28–34; Solon Kimball, "Problems of Studying American Culture," *American Anthropologist*, LVII (1955), 1131–42; and A. Viditch and J. Bensman, "The Validity of Field Data," *Human Organization*, XIII (1954), 20–27.

4. See particularly Oscar Lewis, "Controls and Experiments in Field Work," in *Anthropology Today* (Chicago: University of Chicago Press, 1953), p. 455 n.; also cf. Howard S. Becker, "Problems of Inference and Proof in Participant Observation," *American Sociological Review*, XXIII (1958), 652–60; Elizabeth Colson, "The Intensive Study of Small Sample Communities," in R. F. Spencer (ed.), *Method and Perspective in Anthropology* (Minneapolis: University of Minnesota Press, 1954), pp. 43–59; Fred Eggan, "Social Anthropology and the Method of Controlled Comparison," *American Anthropologist*, LVI (1954), 743–60; Harold E. Driver, "Statistics in Anthropology," *American Anthropologist*, LV (1953), 42–59; Melville J. Herskovitz, "Some Problems of Method in Ethnography," in R. F. Spencer (ed.), *op. cit.*, pp. 3–24; George Spindler and Walter Goldschmidt, "Experimental Design in the Study of Culture Change," *Southwestern Journal of Anthropology*, VIII (1952), 68–83. And see the section "Field Methods and Techniques" in *Human Organization*, esp. in its early years and its early editorials. Some quantification has been characteristic of "field" monographs for a very long time; cf. Kroeber's *Zuni Kin and Clan* (1916). Such classics as *Middletown* and the *Yankee City* series are studded with tables.

5. A significant exception is a comment by M. Trow directed at Becker and Geer. Becker and Geer, comparing interviewing to participant observation, find participant observation the superior method and seem to imply that it is superior for all purposes. Trow insists that the issue is not correctly formulated, and that one might better ask: "What kinds of problems are best studied through what kind of methods; . . . how can the various methods at our disposal complement one another?" In their reply, Becker and Geer are more or less compelled to agree. See Becker and Geer, "Participant Observation and Interviewing: A Comparison," *op. cit.*, Trow's "Comment" (*Human Organization*, XVI [1957], 33–35), and Becker and Geer's "Rejoinder" (*Human Organization*, XVIII [1958], 39–44).

are for qualitative participant observation. What to do if you prefer data that are real, deep, *and* hard is not immediately apparent.

A more fruitful approach to the issue must certainly recognize that a field study is not a single method gathering a single kind of information. This approach suggests several crucial questions: *What* kinds of methods and *what* kinds of information are relevant? How can the "goodness" of different methods for different purposes be evaluated? Even incomplete and imperfect answers — which are all that we offer here — should be useful, at least in helping to restate the issue. They also pose, order, and to some extent resolve other issues of field method so that in pursuing their implications this paper encompasses a good deal more than its original problem.

THREE TYPES OF INFORMATION

The simplest events are customarily described in statements predicating a single property of a single object at a particular time and in a particular place. From these descriptions one may build up more complex events in at least two ways. The first is by forming a configuration of many properties of the same object at the same time in the same place. This may be called an "incident." A more complex configuration but of the same type would be a sequence of incidents, that is, a "history."

A second way to build up more complex events is by repeating observations of a property over a number of units. Units here can be defined formally, requiring only a way of identifying events as identical. They can be members of a social system or repetitions of the same type of incident at different times or in different places (e.g., descriptions of five funerals). The result is a frequency distribution of some property.

From such information it is possible to deduce certain underlying properties of the system observed, some of which may be summarized as consequences of the "culture" of S (S stands here for a social system under investigation). But at least some portion of this culture can be discovered not only by inference from what is observed but also from verbal reports by members of S — for example, accounts of its principal institutionalized norms and statuses. The rules reported, of course, are to some extent independent of the events actually observed; the norms actually followed may not be correctly reported, and deviance may be concealed. Nevertheless, information difficult to infer can be readily and accurately obtained from verbal reports.

For example, it may take some time to infer that a member occupies a given status but this may readily be discovered by asking either him or other members of S.

We thus combine various types of information into three broad classes.

Type I: Incidents and Histories. — A log of events during a given period, a record of conversations heard, descriptions of a wedding, a funeral, an election, etc. Not only the actions observed, but the "meanings," the explanations, etc., reported by the participants can be regarded as part of the "incident" insofar as they are thought of as data rather than actual explanations.

Type II: Distributions and Frequencies. — Possessions of each member of S, number of members who have a given belief, number of times member *m* is observed talking to member *n*, etc.

Type III: Generally Known Rules and Statuses. — Lists of statuses, lists of persons occupying them, informants' accounts of how rules of exogamy apply, how incest or descent are defined, how political leaders are supposed to be chosen, how political decisions are supposed to be made, etc.

This classification has nothing to do with what is *inferred* from data, despite the way the notion of reported rules and statuses was introduced. In particular, more complex configurations of norms, statuses, events which are "explained" by inferring underlying themes or structures involve a level of inference outside the scope of this paper: The classification covers only information *directly* obtained from reports and observations. Moreover, this classification cuts across the distinction between what is observed by the investigator and what is reported to him. Although Type III consists only of reports, Types I and II include both observations by the investigator himself *and* reports of members of S, insofar as they are treated as data. Later we talk of an event as seen through the eyes of an informant, where the investigator trusts the informant as an accurate observer and thinks of the report as if it were his own observation. Now, however, interest is focused not on the facts of the report but rather on what the report reveals of the perceptions, the motivations, the world of meaning of the informant himself. The report, in this case, does not transmit observational data; it is, itself, the datum and so long as it tells what the person reporting thinks, the factual correctness of what he thinks is irrelevant. (This is sometimes phrased as making a distinction between *informants* and *respondents,* in the survey research sense.) Thus Type I includes both observations (what we see going on) and the statements of members telling what they understand the observed events to mean, which is regarded as part of the event. In a somewhat different way, Type II also includes both reports (e.g., an opinion poll) and observations (e.g., systematically repeated observations with constant coding categories).

THREE TYPES OF METHOD

It is possible to make a pure, logically clear classification of methods of obtaining information in the field, but for the present purpose this would be less useful than one that is, though less precise, rather closer to what a field worker actually does.

Two methods are usually thought of as characteristic of the investigator in the field. He invariably keeps a daily log of events and of relatively casual, informal continuous interviews, both of which go into his field notes. Almost invariably he also develops informants, that is, selected members of S who are willing and able to give him information about practices and rules in S and events he does not directly observe. (They may also supply him with diaries, autobiographies, and their own personal feelings; i.e., they may also function as respondents.) Contrary to popular opinion, almost any well-trained field worker also keeps various forms of census materials, records of systematic observations, etc., including a basic listing of members of S fact-sheet data on them, and systematically repeated observations of certain recurrent events. Many field workers also collect documents; however, we will classify field methods into only three broad classes which we conceive of as primary. These are:

Type I. Participant-observation. — The field worker directly observes and also participates in the sense that he has durable social relations in S. He may or may not play an active part in events, or he may interview participants in events which may be considered part of the process of observation.

Type II. Informant-interviewing. — We prefer a more restricted definition of the informant than most field workers use, namely that he be called an "informant" only where he is reporting information presumed factually correct about others rather than about himself; and his information about events is about events in their absence. Interviewing during the event itself is considered part of participant-observation.

Type III. Enumerations and samples. — This includes both surveys and direct, repeated, countable observations. Observation in this sense may entail minimal participation as compared with that implied in Type I.

This classification excludes documents on the ground that they represent resultants or combinations of primary methods. Many documents, for example, are essentially informant's accounts and are treated exactly as an informant's account is treated: subjected to the same kind of internal and external comparisons, created with the same suspicions, and often in the end, taken as evidence of what occurred at some time and place from which the investigator was absent. The fact that the account is written is hardly important. Many other documents are essentially enumerations; for example, personnel and cost-accounting records of a factory, membership rolls of a union, tax rolls of a community.

TWO CRITERIA OF "GOODNESS"

Criteria according to which the "goodness" of a procedure may be defined are:

1. *Informational adequacy*, meaning accuracy, percision, and completeness of data.
2. *Efficiency*, meaning cost per added input of information.

It may appear arbitrary to exclude validity and reliability. Validity is excluded because it is, in a technical sense, a relation between an indicator and a concept, and similar problems arise whether one obtains information from an informant, a sample, or from direct observation. Construed loosely, validity is often taken to mean "response validity," accuracy of report, and this is caught up in the definition of informational adequacy. Construed more loosely yet, validity is sometimes taken as equivalent to "real, deep" data, but this seems merely to beg the question. Reliability is relevant only tangentially; it is a separate problem that cuts across the issues of this paper.

FUNDAMENTAL STRATEGIES

Certain combinations of method and type of information may be regarded as formal prototypes, in the sense that other combinations may be logically reduced to them. For example: Instead of a sample survey or enumeration, an informant is employed to list dwelling units, or to estimate incomes, or to tell who associates with whom or what each person believes with respect to some issue. The information is obtained from a single informant, but he is treated *as if he himself* had conducted a census or poll. More generally, in every case in which the information obtained is logically reducible to a distribution of the members of S with respect to the property *a*, the implied method of obtaining the information is also logically reducible to an enumeration. The enumeration may be either through direct observation (estimating the number of sheep each Navaho has by actually counting them; establishing the sociometric structure of the community by watching who interacts with whom), or through a questionnaire survey (determining household composition by questioning a member of each household, or administering a sociometric survey to a sample of the community). If an informant is used, it is presumed that he has himself performed the enumeration. We are not at the moment concerned with the validity of this assumption in specific instances but rather in observing that regardless of the actual way in which the information was obtained, the logical and formal character of the procedure is that of a census or survey.

Suppose an informant is asked to describe what went on at a community meeting which the observer is unable to attend; or a sample of respondents is asked to describe a sequence of events which occurred before the observer entered S. In either case his reports are used as substitutes for direct observation. Such evidence may, in fact, be examined critically to establish its accuracy — we begin by assuming the bias of the reports — but it is presumed that, having "passed" the statements they become an objective account of what has occurred in the same sense that the investigator's own reports are treated as objective, once his biases have been taken into account. The informant, one usually says in this case, is the observer's observer; he differs in no way from the investigator himself. It follows that the prototype is direct observation by the observer himself.

The prototype so far is not only a formal model; it is also a "best" method, efficiently yielding the most adequate information. In learning institutionalized rules and statuses it is doubtful that there is a formal prototype and all three methods yield adequate information. Here we may choose the *most efficient* method as defining our standard of procedure. To illustrate: We wish to study the political structure of the United States. We are told that the principal national political figure is called a "president," and we wish to know who he is. We do not ordinarily think of sampling the population of the

United States to obtain the answer; we regard it as sufficient to ask one well-informed member. This question is typical of a large class of questions asked by a field worker in the course of his research.

A second example: Any monograph on the Navaho reports that they are matrilineal and matrilocal. This statement may mean either of two things:

1. All Navaho are socially identified as members of a descent group defined through the mother's line, and all Navaho males move to the camp of their wife's family at marriage.

2. There exists a set of established rules according to which all Navaho are supposed to become socially identified as members of a descent group defined through the mother's line, and to move to the camp of their wife's family at marriage.

The truth of the first interpretation can be established only by an enumeration of the Navaho, or a sample sufficiently representative and sufficiently precise. It is readily falsified by exceptions, in fact there *are* exceptions to both principles. But suppose among thirty Navaho informants at least one says that the Navaho are partilineal and patrilocal. If this is intended to describe institutionalized norms as in (2) above, we are more likely to stop using the informant that we are to state that there are "exceptions" in the sense of (1) above. We might sample a population to discover the motivation to conform to a rule or the actual degree of conformity, but are less likely to do so to establish that the rules *exists*, if we confront institutionalized phenomena. This also constitutes a very large class of questions asked by the field worker.

ADEQUACY OF INFORMANTS FOR VARIOUS PROBLEMS IN THE FIELD

It does not follow from the definition of a prototype method that no other form of obtaining information can suffice; all we intend is that it *does* suffice, and any other method is logically reducible to it. Further, comparison with the prototype is a criterion by which other forms can be evaluated. In considering the adequacy in some given instance of the use of an informant as the field worker's surrogate census, for example, we are interested primarily in whether he is likely to know enough, to recall enough, and to report sufficiently precisely to yield the census that we ourselves would make. Comments below, incidentally, are to be taken as always prefixed with the phrase, "by and large." It is not possible to establish, at least yet, a firm rule which will cover every case.

The informant as a surrogate census-taker. A distinction must again be made between *what* information is obtained and *how* it is obtained. It is one thing to criticize a field worker for not obtaining a frequency distribution where it is required—for instance, for not sampling mothers who are weaning children in order to determine age at weaning—and another to criticize him for not obtaining it *directly* from the mothers. If the field worker reports that the average age at weaning is two years and the grounds for this is that he asked an informant, "About when do they wean children around here?" it is not the fact that he asked an informant but that he asked the wrong question that should be criticized. He should have asked, "How many mothers do you know who are now weaning children? How old are their children?"

The critical issue, therefore, is whether or not the informant can be assumed to have the information that the field worker requires, granting that he asks the proper questions. In many instances he does. In some cases he is an even better source than an enumerator; he either knows better or is less likely to falsify. Dean, for example, reports that workers who are ideologically pro-union, but also have mobility aspirations and are not well integrated into their factory or local unions, are likely to report attending union meetings which they do not in fact attend.[6] She also shows that, when *respondent-reported* attendance is used as a measure of attendance, this tends spuriously to increase correlations of attendance at union meetings with attitudes toward unions in general, and to reduce correlations of attendance at union meetings with attitudes more specifically directed at the local union. The list of those actually attending was obtained by an observer, who, however, had sufficient rapport with officers of the local to obtain it from them.[7] Attendance, largely by "regulars," was stable from meeting to meeting so that the officers could have reproduced it quite accurately.[8]

On the other hand, there are many instances in which an informant is *prima facie* unlikely to be adequate, although no general rule seems to identify these clearly for the investigator. The nature of the information—private versus public, more or less objective, more or less approved—is obviously relevant, yet is often no guide at all. Some private information, for example, is better obtained from informants, some from respondents. The social structure of S, particularly its degree of differentiation and complexity, is also obviously rele-

6. R. Dean, "Interaction, Reported and Observed: The Case of One Local Union," *Human Organization*, XVII (1958), 36–44.

7. *Ibid.*, p. 37, n. 4.

8. *Ibid.*

vant. An informant must be in a position to know the information desired, and if S is highly differential and the informant confined to one part of it, he can hardly enumerate it. Probably to discover attitudes and opinions that are relatively private and heterogeneous in a structure that is relatively differentiated, direct enumeration or sampling should be used.

The informant as a "representative respondent." An "average" of a distribution is sometimes obtained not by asking for an enumeration by the informant, nor even by asking a general question concerning what people typically do; sometimes it is obtained by treating the informant as if he were a "representative respondent." The informant's reports about himself—perhaps deeper, more detailed, "richer," but nevertheless like those of a respondent in a survey rather than an informant in the technical sense—stand in place of a sample. Where a multivariate distribution is thought of, this person is treated as a "quintessential" subject, "typical" in many dimensions. Some field workers speak favorably of using informants in this way, and it is likely that even more of them actually do so.

Since, as yet, we have no really hard and fast rules to follow, it is possible that in some cases this is legitimate; but, by and large, it is the most suspect of ways of using informants. It is simply a bad way of sampling. The legitimate cases are probably of three types: first, as suggestive of leads to follow up; second, as illustration of a point to be made in a report that is verifiable on other grounds. But in this second case the proviso ought to be thought of as rather strict; it is not sufficient to "have a feeling" that the point is true, to assume that it is verifiable on other grounds. The third case is perhaps the most legitimate, but is really a case of using informants to provide information about generally known rules: for example, using informants to collect "typical" genealogies or kinship terms, the assumption being that his kin terms are much like those of others (which is not always true, of course) and his genealogy sufficiently "rich"—this being the basis on which he was chosen—to exhibit a wide range of possibilities.

The informant as the observer's observer. The third common use of the informant is to report events not directly observed by the field worker. Here the investigator substitutes the observations of a member for his own observation. It is not simply interviewing that is involved here, because participant-observation was defined earlier as including interviewing on the spot, in conjunction with direct observation. Thus, some of the most important uses of the informant—to provide the meaning and context of that which we are observing, to provide a running check on variability, etc.—are actually part of participant observation. It is the use of informants as if they were colleagues that we must now consider.

Such a procedure is not only legitimate but absolutely necessary to adequate investigation of any complex structure. In studying a social structure by participant observation there are two problems of bias that override all others, even the much belabored "personal equation." One results from the fact that a single observer cannot be everywhere at the same time, nor can he be "everywhere" in time, for that matter—he has not been in S forever, and will not be there indefinitely—so that, inevitably, something happens that he has not seen, cannot see, or will not see. The second results from the fact that there exist parts of the social structure into which he has not penetrated and probably will not, by virtue of the way he has defined himself to its members, because of limitations on the movement of those who sponsor him, etc. There has never been a participant-observer study in which the observer acquired full knowledge of all roles and statuses through his own direct observation, and for that matter there never will be such a study by a single observer. To have a team of observers is one possible solution; to have informants who stand in the relation of team members to the investigator is another. The virtue of the informant used in this way is to increase the accessibility of S to the investigator.

EFFICIENCY OF SAMPLING FOR VARIOUS
PROBLEMS IN THE FIELD

Sampling to obtain information about institutionalized norms and statuses. It has already been argued that a properly obtained probability sample gives adequate information about institutionalized norms and statuses but is not very efficient. Two things are implied: that such information is *general* information so that any member of S has the same information as any other, and that the truth of such information does not depend solely on the opinions of the respondents—the information is in some sense objective.

The first of these implications is equivalent to assuming that S is homogenous with respect to the property a, so that a sample of one suffices to classify S with respect to it. It then becomes inefficient to continue sampling. The principal defect in such an argument is a practical one: By what criterion can one decide S is homogeneous with respect to a without sampling S? There are two such criteria, neither of which is wholly satisfactory. The first is to use substantive knowledge. We would expect in general that certain norms are invariably institutionalized, such as incest and exogamy, descent, inheritance, marriage procedures, patterns of exchange of goods, formal structure of labor markets, etc. We may assume a priori, for example, that a sample of two hundred Navaho is not required to discover that marriage in one's own clan is incestuous. But the pitfall for the unwary investigator is that he may stray beyond his substantive knowledge or apply it at the wrong time in the wrong place.

A second is to employ a loose form of sequential sampling. Suppose, for example, that we ask an informed male in S whom he may marry, or whom any male may marry. He answers, "All who are A, but no one who is B." We ask a second informant and discover again that he may marry all who are A, but no one who is B. We ask a third, a fourth, a fifth, and each tells us the same rule. We do not need to presume that the rule is actually obeyed; that is quite a different question. But we may certainly begin to believe that we have found an institutionalized norm. Conversely, the more variability we encounter, the more we must investigate further. The pitfall here is that we may be deceived by a homogeneous "pocket" within which all members agree but which does not necessarily represent all structural parts of S. For this reason we try to choose representative informants, each from a different status group. This implies, however, that we are working outward from earlier applications of this dangerous principle; we have used some informants to tell us what statuses there are, thereafter choosing additional informants from the new statuses we have discovered.

The second implication—that in some sense the truth of the information obtained depends not on the opinions of respondents but on something else that is "objective" in nature—simply paraphrases Durkheim: Institutions are "external" to given individuals, even though they exist only "in" individuals; they have a life of their own, are *sui generis*. Illustrating with an extreme case: A "belief" of S's religion can be described by an informant even where neither he nor any living member of S actually believes it, although if no member ever did believe it we might regard the information as trivial. In other words, this type of information does not refer to individuals living at a given time, but rather to culture as a distinct object of abstraction. It is this type of information that we mean by "institutionalized norms and statuses." It bears repeating at this point that if one Navaho informant told us the Navaho were patrilineal and patrilocal, we would be more likely to assume he was wrong than we would be to assume that the Navaho had, for the moment, changed their institutions.

Sampling to obtain information about incidents and histories. If we had the good fortune to have a report from every member of S about what happened in region R at time T, would it really be good fortune? Would we not distinguish between those in a position to observe the events and those not? Among those who had been in the region R itself, would we not also distinguish subregions which provided different vantage points from which to view the event? Among those viewing it from the same vantage point, would we not distinguish more and less credible witnesses? Enumeration or not, we would apply stringent internal and external comparisons to each report in order to establish what truly occurred. Formally, of course, this describes a complex technique of stratification which, if carried out properly, would withstand any quantitative criticism. But if all the elements of a decision as to what is "truth" in such a case are considered, it is a moot point how important enumeration or random sampling is in the process.[9]

Informants with special information. Some things happen that relatively few people know about. A random sample is not a sensible way in which to obtain information about these events, although it is technically possible to define a universe U containing only those who do know and sample from U. A parallel case is the repetitive event in inaccessible parts of a social structure. A social structure is an organized system of relationships, one property of which is that certain parts of it are not readily observed by members located in other parts. There is a considerable amount of relatively esoteric information about S. It may be satisfactory from a formal point of view to regard S as consisting in many universes U, each of which is to be sampled for a different piece of information, but again the usefulness of such conception is questionable, particularly if most U, contain very few numbers.

EFFICIENCY AND ADEQUACY OF PARTICIPANT OBSERVATION FOR VARIOUS PROBLEMS IN THE FIELD

Ex post facto quantitative documentation. Because certain things are observed repeatedly, it sometimes occurs to the field worker to count these repetitions in his log as quantitative documentation of an assertion. In such cases, the information obtained should be subjected to any of the canons by which other quantitative data are evaluated; the care with which the universe is defined and the sense

---

9. *None of this applies to repeated events.* If we are interested in comparing several repetitions of the same event, generalizing as to the course that is typical, care must be taken in sampling the events.

in which the sample is representative are particularly critical. With few exceptions, frequency statements made from field logs will *not* withstand such careful examination.

This sharp stricture applies only to ex post facto enumeration or sampling of field logs, and it is because it is ex post facto that the principal dangers arise. Events and persons represented in field logs will generally be sampled according to convenience rather than rules of probability sampling. The sample is unplanned, contains unknown biases. It is not so much random as haphazard, a distinction which is critical. When, after the fact, the observer attempts to correlate two classes of events in these notes very misleading results will be obtained. If we wish to correlate *a* and *b* it is characteristic of such samples that "*a*" will be more frequently recorded than "*not-a*," and "*a and b*" more frequently than "*not-a and b*" or "*a and not-b*." As a general rule, only those data which the observer actually intended to enumerate should be treated as enumerable.

There are, of course, some valid enumerations contained in field notes. For example a verbatim account kept of all meetings of some organization is a valid enumeration; a record kept, in some small rural community, of all members of it who come to the crossroads hamlet during a year is a valid enumeration. These will tend, however, to be intentional enumerations and not subject to the strictures applicable to ex post facto quantification. A much rarer exception will occur when, looking back through one's notes, one discovers that, without particularly intending it, every member of the community studied has been enumerated with respect to the property *a*, or that almost all of them have. This is likely to be rare because field notes tend not to record those who do *not* have the property *a*, and, of all those omitted in the notes, one does not know how many are *not-a* and how many simply were not observed. If everyone, or almost everyone can be accounted for as either *a* or *not-a*, then a frequency statement is validly made.[10] But, if such information were desired in the first place, participant observation would clearly be a most inefficient means of obtaining it.

Readily verbalized norms and statuses. It is not efficient to use partipant observation to obtain generally known norms and statuses

10. We may make a less stringent requirement of our notes, using what might be called "incomplete" indicator spaces. Briefly, if we wish to classify all members of S with respect to the underlying property A, and behaviors *a*, *b*, *c*, *d* . . . , all indicate A, then it is sufficient for our purpose to have information on *at least one* of these indicators for each member of S. For some we might have only *a*, for some only *b*, etc., but we might have one among the indicators for all members, even though not the same one for all members; and thus be able to enumerate S adequately.

so long as these can be readily stated. It may take a good deal of observation to infer that which an informant can quickly tell you. Participant observation would in such cases be primarily to check what informants say, to get clues to further questions, etc. It is, of course, true that the concurrent interviewing involved in participant observation will provide the information—it is necessary to make sense out of the observations—but it comes in bits and pieces and is less readily checked for accuracy, completeness, consistency, etc.

Information Types	Enumerations and Samples	Participant Observation	Interviewing Informants
Frequency distributions	Prototype and best form	Usually inadequate and inefficient	Often, but not always, inadequate; if adequate it is efficient
Incidents, histories	Not adequate by itself; not efficient	Prototype and best form	Adequate with precautions, and efficient
Institutionalized norms and statuses	Adequate but inefficient	Adequate, but inefficient, except for unverbalized norms	Most efficient and hence best form

Figures 32.1—Methods of Obtaining Information.

Latent phenomena. Not all norms and statuses can be verbalized. Consequently, there remains a special province to which participant observation lays well-justified claims. But certain misleading implications should be avoided in admitting them. Because such phenomena may be described as "latent"—as known to the observer but not the members of S—it may be concluded that *all* latent phenomena are the province of participant observation. This does not follow. The term "latent" is ambiguous; it has several distinct usages, some of which do not even share the core meaning of "known to the observer, unknown to members." Lazarsfeld, for example, refers to a dimension underlying a series of manifest items as a "latent" attribute; it cannot be observed by anyone, and is inferred by the investigator from intercorrelations of observables. But the members of S may also make these inferences. (They infer that a series of statements classify the speaker as "liberal," for example.) The most advanced techniques for searching out such latent phenomena are found in survey research and psychometrics, not in participant observation.

These are matters of inference, not of how data are directly obtained. The same is true of the discovery of "latent functions." Often the observer is aware of connections between events when the members of S are not, even though they are aware of the events themselves. But again, relations among events are not the special province of any one method; we look for such connections in *all* our data. In fact, owing to the paucity of non-comparability of units that often plague the analysis of field notes, it might be argued that participant observation is often incapable of detecting such connections. The great value of participant observation is detecting latent phenomena, then, is in those cases in which members of S are unaware of actually observable events, of some of the things they do, or some of the things that happen around them, which can be directly apprehended by the observer. Any other case requires inference and such inference should be made from *all* available data.

SUMMARY AND CONCLUSION

With respect to the problem with which this paper originated, the following conclusion may be drawn: Because we often treat different methods as concretely different types of study rather than as analytically different aspects of the same study, it is possible to attack a field study on the ground that it ought to be an enumeration and fails if it is not; and to defend it on the ground that it ought to be something *else* and succeeds only if it is. But, however we classify types of information in the future — and the classification suggested here is only tentative — they are not all of one type. True, a field report is unreliable if it gives us, after consulting a haphazard selection of informants or even a carefully planned "representative" selection, a statement such as, "All members of S believe that . . ." or "The average member of S believes that . . ." *and* (1) there is variance in the characteristic reported, (2) this variance is relevant to the problem reported, *and* (3) the informants cannot be seriously thought of as equivalent to a team of pollsters, *or* (4) the investigator has reported what is, essentially, the *"average"* beliefs of his *informants*, as if *they* were a representative, probability sample of respondents. But demand that every piece of information be obtained by a probability sample is to commit the researcher to grossly inefficient procedure and to ignore fundamental differences among various kinds of information. The result is that we create false methodological issues, often suggest quite inappropriate research strategies to novices, and sometimes conceal real methodological issues which deserve more discussion in the literature — such as how to establish institutionalized norms given only questionnaire data. It should be no more satisfactorily rigorous to hear that everything is in some way a sample, and hence must be sampled, than to hear that everything is in some sense "whole" and hence cannot be sampled.

33. A Comparison of Participant Observation and Survey Data

ARTHUR J. VIDICH AND GILBERT SHAPIRO

THERE has been considerable discussion in tne literature concerning the validity of data secured by the informal anthropological research technique designated as "participant observation." The question at issue is to what extent a lone and frequently foreign observer is capable of observing or "absorbing" the culture of a group well enough to render a correct account of its beliefs, attitudes, values and practices. It is clear that any answer to this question must presume some standard of judgment — preferably the results of some different method of investigation — against which the antropological report can be compared. There would be no problem for the social scientist if he could be thoroughly convinced of the absolute validity of the research method used as a standard for the test of participant observation. All discrepancies between the two sets of results could be attributed to the antropological method. Unfortunately, any alternative procedure for the study of culture and social behavior is also subject to serious questions of validity.

In this study, an observer's perception of a community will be compared with data obtained by sample survey techniques. Two distinct approaches are possible for the evaluation of either of the research methods. The most common approach (continually used by the best practitioners in both methods) is the test of internal consistency. The careful anthropologist, for example, will cross-check the reports of one informant against those of another, and will pay careful attention to discrepancies between avowals in one context and facts which are allowed to "slip out" in another. These are "internal" consistency checks because they compare, within the confines of the same method, one observation with another. In a very similar fashion, careful survey technicians check the results they receive on one attitude question by comparison with results on a different question which is supposed to measure the same variable. The various scaling procedures are, in part, designed to test the data for "internal consistency" in our general sense. While such tests of the internal consistency of each method are an admirable first step, we might ask further questions about the *external* validity of each of the methods. For it is perfectly conceivable that either method may present us with a thoroughly *consistent* picture which has little relationship to "reality." One valuable way of testing the external validity of both methods is to examine the degree to which their results correspond to one another in areas where the two methods can be made to yield comparable data.

We see the problem of the validity of the two methods, for present purposes, as twofold; as involving the degree of correspondence between the results and the direction of selectivity introduced in each. While it would be ideal to compare results of the two methods on a large number of variables, we have available measures of only one variable by both methods. The prestige of community members was measured by an anthropological field worker's ratings and by sociometric-type questions in a sample survey of the same community. By "prestige" we mean the generalized attitude of respect and admiration or disdain and condemnation extended by individuals to each other. We feel that the comparison of the prestige measures resulting from the two techniques will throw some light on the correspondence of the methods and the direction of selectivity of each.

The research was conducted in "Springdale," a rural New York state community with a total adult population of about 1500.[1] A sample of the adults in the community was drawn by choosing at random one person between the ages of 20 and 80 from each household in the survey area. Due to lack of cooperation and availability, illness, language barriers and deaths, schedules were not completed in about two hundred households. The "achieved sample" consisting of 547 community residents was, therefore, unrepresentative to some extent, lacking proportional representation of the ill, the busy, and the intransigent. The participant observer's knowledge of the community was based upon one year of intensive contact as a resident, interviewing and observation, and the experience gained in the administration of the survey. Prior to his work in Springdale, he had had previous anthropological field experience in two other cultures and in another rural American community.

The participant observor was assisted in making the prestige ratings by a graduate student who had done field work in Springdale. The task was undertaken to provide a measure of prestige for the purpose of testing a theory of primary social integration.[2] In presenting the task, Shapiro attempted to instruct the raters in such a fashion as to minimize his own influence upon the criteria of rating to be used. A set of cards containing the names of the household heads of the community was given to the raters, and they were asked to classify them according to the "prestige, respect, standing, or general reputation" of the individuals in the "eyes of the community." All further questions about the meaning of these terms were met by asking that the raters use those criteria which, in their experience, were commonly used by community members in evaluating one another. In addition, no effort was made to determine in advance the number of categories or prestige groupings. This effort to keep the task unstructured was intended to utilize to the fullest extent the informal, unconscious understanding of the community developed by the judges over the period of their field experience. The groupings isolated by this method are described below.

1. The Springdale research is sponsored by the Department of Child Development and Family Relationships in the New York State College of Home Economics at Cornell University. This report is a by-product of a larger study of the social and psychological correlates of community activity. The research is supported in part by grants from the National Institute of Mental Health, United States Public Health Service, and the Committee on the Early Identification of Talent on the Social Science Research Council with the aid of funds granted to the council by the John and Mary R. Markle Foundation. Mr. Vidich acted as the participant observer and Mr. Shapiro analyzed the sociometric data introduced in this report.

2. Gilbert Shapiro, "The Formulation and Verification of a Theory of Primary Social Integration," Ph.D. Thesis, Cornell University, 1954.

Descriptions of the Prestige Groupings Provided by the Judges Immediately after the Rating Process, In Order from Low to High Prestige.

(1) Non-entities, on the bottom rung of the financial and social ladder. Many without kin in community. Frequently their existence is unrecognized, at least publicly, by the town. Includes physical and mental wrecks, degenerates, "deadbeats," and the like.

(2) Only slightly higher in prestige than Group 1. More contact with the rest of the community. Economically marginal, unskilled. Includes some moral degenerates, such as alcoholics, as well as some widows with large families.

(3) The lowest group which has a steady income; respectable working folk. Some have risen to this status from Groups 1 and 2; others have fallen to it from higher Groups described below.

(4) Only slightly higher in prestige than Group 3. These are more often recruited from *migration* rather than higher or lower local groups. They are still unskilled occupationally, but are striving to enter the semi-skilled ranks, and to improve their lot generally more than Group 3. The wives of the families in this group sometimes participate in formal organizations (a form of behavior much rarer in local groups). Includes marginal entrepreneurs, such as free-lance truckers, as well as part-time farmers with jobs.

(5) Almost equal in prestige with Group 4. These, however, are people who have risen or fallen to lower middle class respectability and have close kinship ties in the community with relatives in higher and lower positions.

(6) A large, intermediate, and indeterminate catch-all grouping. Neither disdained nor admired by the community. Frequently have both pretensions to much higher standing and skeletons in the family closet.

(7) The lowest group which can be properly considered as having higher than median prestige. Their prestige is based primarily on non-economic characteristics (such as high moral standards, temperance, community activity, church support and membership) although they may, in addition, have money. Extremely conscious of community attitudes towards them. Includes some newcomers.

(8) A separate category for school teachers, including only those teachers who have no community ties other than their jobs and those social activities incumbent upon them because of their occupation. They have positive prestige as teachers. All of their actions, and the evaluation of them by the community, are focused upon their occupation. Prestige slightly higher than Group 7, lower than 9.

(9) Relatively powerless professionals and holders of new wealth deriving from the post-war prosperity. Includes also a scattering of "old names" maintaining their prestige without the income or power which used to buttress it. Some non-professionals (larger farmers, business operators) in this group are hard working "money makers."

(10) The highest ranking group of any size. All of the qualifications of an "upper-upper" in the usual sense, except that they lack the extreme of power, prestige, and money characteristic of the small "X-Family" group described below. Active in organizations, frequently as powers behind the scenes, sometimes openly the leaders of the community. Most economically well off (in terms of local standards). Includes prosperous businessmen and farmers, as well as the upper group of professionals.

(11) The Springdale equivalent of the Middletown X-Family; *the powers, highest in money, prestige, and political control (always behind the scenes).*

(12) Unknown. People whom the raters did not know well enough to classify. This group includes about a third of the total population. Their characteristics will be examined in detail in the discussion of selectivity below.

The survey questions used for the measurement of prestige were in the form of five sociometric type queries:

(1) If some one person were to be selected to represent this particular part of town at a special meeting of the town board, who would *you personally* want to go?

(2) What person do you think most of the people around here would choose to represent them?

(3) When you think of the over-all leadership in this community, who are the three or four people you would think of first?

(4) Are there any women (men) you would think of as leaders in this community? (Asked with reference to sex opposite the respondent's.)

(5) Are there any other people you think have a good deal of influence in the community?

The total number of these five types of choices received is interpreted here as an index of each individual's prestige in the community. It is clear that this interpretation of the score is not immediately given to us by the manifest meaning of the questions asked. In this sense, the sociometric score described is a more *indirect* prestige index than the observer's ratings. The interpretation, on the other hand, is not wholly arbitrary. It is at least reasonable in a rural

American context that those most frequently mentioned as "community leaders," or as desirable neighborhood representatives, have the greatest prestige, general standing, and the highest reputations or "evaluative status" in the community. As compared with the three other sociometric questions in the Springdale survey schedule, these items have the highest degree of concentration of choices received in the population, and the lowest rates of reciprocal choice. These facts and others[3] tend to provide some internal basis for the interpretation of the sociometric score as a measure of overall community prestige, irrespective of any shift in the interpretation of the questions from subject to subject, and such influences as varying interview situations.

An *external* test of the validity of this prestige index, as well as of the validity of the anthropologist's ratings, is the degree of correspondence between the two. Table 33.1 shows the correspondence between prestige, as measured by each of the two methods.

If we had found no correspondence in Table 33.1 between the two methods (or a small correspondence just exceeding chance expectancy), we would have no basis for choosing one method as more "valid" than the other. However, remarkably strong correspondence between the two methods is shown. The correspondence does not "prove" the validity of either method, but it does reinforce willingness on our part to accept both methods of measuring prestige. Since this mutual validation is so strong, we should be willing to accept the survey results for ranking the 207 cases not known by the participant observer.

Aside from the correspondence of the methods, the data of Table 33.1 show that only 12 per cent of those not known by the observer received at least one choice while 36 per cent of those who were known received one or more. This clearly indicates that the unknown group contains a disproportionate number of those with low prestige. Thus, even though the observer had made deliberate efforts to establish contact with lower prestige groups, his knowledge of community members was biased in favor of individuals with higher prestige. Table 33.1 indicates that the observer's efforts to meet and learn about all segments of the community were largely successful—almost two-thirds of the sample was known well enough to be rated. A large number of even the low prestige community members was known. Yet, despite all efforts to counteract the tendency, definite selectivity is indicated, and it would be surprising if this selec-

3. A more complete analysis of the validity of the sociometric measure of prestige, which cannot be provided here, will be found in Shapiro, *op. cit.*

tive association of the observer with the community did not somehow influence his understanding of the local culture. Without the
survey data, the observer could only make reasonable guesses about
his areas of ignorance in the effort to reduce bias. The survey data
give him more exact information regarding the degree and kind of
selectivity operating, and thereby allow him to make better com-
pensatory allowances in planning his observational activities.

*Table 33.1. Correspondence Between Anthropologist's Prestige Rat-
ings and Prestige as Indicated by Number of Choices Received*

	Per Cent of Prestige Grouping								
Number of Choices Received	1–2	3	4	5	6	7	8–9	10–11	Not Known
0	100	87	79	63	64	54	36	7	88
1	0	7	15	21	18	14	10	7	4
2–4	0	7	4	8	14	18	21	27	5
5 or more	0	0	2	8	4	14	33	60	2
(N)	(20)	(61)	(53)	(24)	(72)	(56)	(39)	(15)	(207)

Table 33.2 provides more information about the selectivity of the
anthropological observer's contacts.

As might be expected in a society which segregates the activites of
the sexes in so many contexts, a disproportionate number of those
known by the male observer were males. Age groups, however, were
all fairly equally represented. A clear, consistent relationship is
found between educational level and the probability that a person is
known by the observer. This relationship may be interpreted as a
consequence of educational attainment as such, or of the relationship
between educational level and socio-economic status. Those in the
labor force, whether self-employed or not, are more likely to be
interviewed by the observer than are housewives, retired people,
and the like. Finally, the probability of being known by the observer
increases with the prestige of the individual's occupation as customarily ranked in American society. In short, the observer's status in
the community as an employed male, middle class professional, is
reflected in the types of people with whom he is likely to make
contact. This fact is consistent with the findings of Table 33.1, where
we found that the unknowns contained a disproportionate number of
those who, by survey crtieria, had low prestige.

Finally, we consider the bias introduced by selectivity of respondents in the survey. We compare the background characteristics of

*Table 33.2. Percentage of Various Sub-Groups of
the Springdale Sample Which Were
Known Well Enough to be Rated*

Group	Per Cent Known	Total Number in Group
Entire	62	547
Sex		
Males	70*	265
Females	55*	282
Age		
20–29	65	81
30–39	64	123
40–49	58	106
50–59	66	83
60–69	61	90
70–79	56*	64
Education		
Some grade school	48*	93
Grade school graduate	58	98
Some high school	58	124
High school graduate	66	147
Some college	87*	23
College graduate	84*	49
Employment status		
Retired	56*	36
Not in labor force	55*	205
Self-employed	69*	125
Employed by others	66	178
Occupation		
Manager, proprietors	88*	41
Professionals, semi-prof.	80*	30
Clerical and sales	76*	25
Industrial workers	63	134
Farmers and farm laborers	59	90
Housewives	56*	210

*Starred percentages differ from the per cent known of the entire sample beyond the 1 per cent level of significance.

those in the achieved sample described above with those of the entire adult population of the survey area. Data on the whole population were collected prior to the survey on a typical census basis; every effort was made to get as complete a report as possible on every adult in every household. Occasionally, when members of the household were unavailable, information was collected from neighbors, provided by the participant observer, or pieced together from other sources. For this reason, and because the census schedule was shorter and less personal in content, the census has fewer incomplete schedules and a far lower refusal rate; altogether only 24 out of 765 were not completed. Another reason for the greater completeness of the census data is the fact that any member of the household could give the information required, while the sample survey interview had to be conducted with the household member whose name arose in the random choice. For these reasons we consider the census frequencies to be close approximations of the actual parameters of the population. We can, therefore, measure the bias introduced by the selective failure to interview people whose names arose in the random sample by comparing frequencies in the achieved sample with those in the population. Table 33.3 compares the sample and population frequencies on the same characteristics used in Table 33.2 to find the characteristics of the anthropologist's contacts.

None of the differences between sample and population frequencies shown in Table 33.3 are significant at the 5 per cent level. As contrasted with the findings of Table 33.2, the survey techniques seem to reach the various segments of the population more evenly than the contacts of the anthropological observer. Whatever its comparative defects on other grounds, selectivity of respondents as a source of bias in the collection of data is not present in the achieved random sample to the extent that it is found in our analysis of the observer's contacts.

The selectivity of respondents is only one of a host of potential sources of bias in social research. What the survey method gains in representative coverage of a population is probably no greater methodological significance than the increased *depth* of understanding and interpretation possible with participant observation techniques. This is evident when we contrast the position of a survey analyst and a participant observer when both face the problem of interpreting the *meaning* of a question. The desk chair analyst can give at best an intelligent guess based upon sketchy pretest and tabular data. The observer, in contrast can call upon the wealth of his experience with the linguistic habits, the attitudes, values and beliefs of the group and provide a much richer, and probably sounder interpretation. This is indicated in the present study by the descriptions of the prestige rating categories as compared with the sociometric scores. The latter are mere numbers symbolizing, at best, indices of an abstract variable expressed in a single word—prestige. The prestige

*Table 33.3. Frequencies of Selected Background
Characteristics in the Achieved Sample and
in the Population as Estimated by
Census Interview*

	Per Cent of Sample	Per Cent of Population
Sex		
Male	48	48
Female	52	52
Age		
20–29	15	18
30–39	23	22
40–49	19	18
50–59	15	16
60–69	16	16
70–79	12	9
Education		
None	0	1
Some grade school	17	16
Grade school graduate	18	19
Some high school	23	26
High school graduate	27	24
Some college	4	3
College graduate	9	7
Employment status		
Not in labor force	37	37
Retired	6	6
Unemployed	1	1
Self-employed	24	21
Employed by others	32	35
Occupation		
Housewife	39	38
Managerial, proprietor	7	6
Professional, semi-prof.	5	5
Clerical	3	3
Sales	2	2
Farmer	15	14
Farmer laborer	2	3
Industrial		
Skilled and semi-skilled	18	21
Manual	6	6

rating categories, however, are groups of people with a wealth of specified characteristics which are, for one reason or another, sources of respect in the community. We have an immediate idea from the prestige group descriptions of the important criteria of assigning prestige in Springdale, as well as other clues to the stratification system. These descriptions of the prestige system can be frequently tested with the survey data. This point indicates the techniques of participant observation and the sample survey are not competitive, but, in the well conducted community study, will be complementary. The survey provides representative information which is given meaning by the anthropological observer. Frequently, but not always, survey methods may be used to test hypotheses developed out of the less formal experience of the observer, particularly in those areas where information is admissable at a public level and where replication is both possible and meaningful.

PART THIRTEEN

Contingencies and Problems in the Execution of Social Research

INTRODUCTION

AN INVESTIGATION seldom runs to successful completion. Demands from clients or subjects can alter the nature of field work; problems can arise from the organizations created to do research; coders can misunderstand instructions; interviewers can falsify results or interview the wrong persons; data analysts can employ the wrong statistical tests; political pressures can arise to shift the direction of a project, or to prematurely end it. The list of possible contingencies is endless. In general, however, it is possible to classify such problems under the headings of theory, research methods, investigators, subjects, social demands and pressures, and ethical pressures and decisions. One's theory can create problems if certain hypotheses cannot be tested, or if the theory itself is vague. Research methods and their users create special demand characteristic effects. Subjects can talk back, or refuse to be studied. Pressures from academic, political, and social communities can force actions on the researcher that he would not otherwise take. Ethical contracts made with subjects and value decisions involving who is to be studied and what is to be done with one's findings can also create significant pressures. Any of the above factors can render an investigation less than perfect.

EXTRA-SCIENTIFIC CONTINGENCIES

Hart offers a comprehensive overview of contingencies that lie out-side formal rules of method, or theory construction. He notes that differences in results can arise from preferences for one theory or one method. Because methods and theories reveal different aspects of the empirical world, the very selection of a method or a theory can produce differences between investigations. The auspices under which research is conducted can also influence one's findings. Grant-ing agencies favor certain problems over other, and this often places special demands on the researcher to couch his work in terms of the current vogue.

The sociologist's prejudices, values, and politics can also lead him to study problems that a researcher with different values would not study. His sponsor and major instructor in graduate school can also influence his subsequent conduct; as Hart notes, to have studied under Lundberg as opposed to Park would itself lead a sociologist to view his activity differently.

Hart's remarks complement the statements by Blumer and Hill in Part I. Sociology is a social enterprise. It has a special reward struc-ture that favors certain activities over others.

THE PROBLEMS WITH RESEARCH ORGANIZATIONS

It is fashionable today to conduct research in an organized manner. Grants are frequently sought for the construction of a large research organization in which complex divisions of labor delegate research responsibility. This is best seen in survey and experimental work, where special roles are created for interviewers, coders, data analysts, field directors, and even field observers. It is frequently necessary to create such organizations, since large-scale studies can seldom be conducted by one individual, but such organizations can create problems that detract from the original intent of the study. It is necessary for the researcher to be aware of these potential problems. Roth presents some very troubling data on these issues. His three case studies indicate how observers may cheat in their records, how coders can be inconsistent in analyzing questionnaire responses, and how interviewers may fill in or fabricate answers for respondents.

Roth submits that his case studies are not unique; they represent just a few of the basic problems that occur in social research. Accord-ingly, he suggests that sociologists must learn to apply their insights from research in work settings to their own conduct. He suggests that in any situation where a worker is not responsible for his product, cheating and restrictions in production will be observed. Several factors seem to create this tendency to deviate, including increased size of the work organization, the delegation of authority, the subordination of activity, and reliance on rigid plans. Hired hand research is thus produced. A hired hand becomes a person who feels that he has no stake in the research. Such persons simply carry out assigned work and turn in their results. In Roth's opinion most hired hand research is characterized by restricted production, failures to abide by instructions, avoidance of the unpleasant aspects of the assigned job, and outright cheating.

Roth notes that these problems can arise in one-man studies where the researcher still delegates unpleasant tasks to persons below him. There is no easy solution to this problem. One obvious strategy is to create situations where workers are encouraged to become involved in the activity. These may range from giving graduate students a hand in writing up reports, or even allowing them to carve out their own areas of interest within a larger project. These are partial solutions. Hired hand research will continue to be done, and in many situations it is absolutely necessary, but unless involvement and commitment on the part of hired hand researchers can be obtained, the subsequent productions are likely to share the problems noted by Roth. His conclusion is harsh and cannot be ignored. To the extent that any portion of a study is carried out by hired-hand researchers, these portions of the study should be discounted.

THE ETHICS AND POLITICS OF SOCIAL RESEARCH

As sociology becomes more relevant to society's social problems, demands and pressures will increasingly be brought to bear upon the sociologist's activity. But while many now call for an involved sociology, for a sociology that actively enters into the definition and resolution of social issues, a radical and humanizing sociology, counterforces are appearing to restrict the sociologist's work. Legislation has been passed to screen studies on human subjects. Decisions reached in the White House now prohibit foreign research that might damage the image of the United States. Sociology approaches a critical point: Decisions have to be made regarding the stance to be taken toward political demands. Some resolution of the ethical implications involved in research has to be made. Unless the sociologist self-consciously approaches these problems and attempts his own resolution he will find that others will make the decisions for him.

Horowitz's paper and the following discussion addresses these problems. Voss, in an essay not reprinted here ("Pittfalls in Social Research: A Case Study," *American Sociologist,* 1 [May 1966], 136–40) reported an investigation that so incensed the right-wing segment of a community that the project was cancelled. Horowitz describes the now infamous Project Camelot that was ended by a directive from President Johnson.

Rainwater and Pittman have elsewhere ("Ethical Problems in Studying a Politically Sensitive and Deviant Community," *Social Problems,* 14 [Spring 1967], 357–66), described the touchy ethical issues involved in studying a controversial public housing project. Becker, in another source ("Whose Side Are We On?" *Social Problems,* 14 [Winter 1967], 239–48), forces the sociologist to face up to his problems. It is impossible to escape making value decisions. All that can be done is to state our values from the outset and take the criticism that is sure to come our way.

Voss has reviewed the events that forced the cancellation of a study on high school experience and subsequent drop-out or delinquent behavior. Of central importance are his remarks on the ethics of observation. One reason the study was cancelled was because right-wing oriented persons objected to what they regarded as an invasion of their privacy. Voss's questionnaire touched on intimate interactions in the family and some claimed that he had no right to ask such questions; indeed, at one point Senator Barry Goldwater commented adversely on the nature of this study.

Voss's conclusions call for serious discussion among sociologists of the problem of invasion of privacy. Rules need to be developed concerning the conditions under which subjects should be studied, and strict procedures should be developed to maintain the confidentiality of research findings. In addition, the researcher must protect the rights of his colleagues to engage in research, since every sociological act can produce pressures to close doors for future research.

Voss offers a series of general principles. Researchers should endeavor to receive formal approval of their studies from the highest source possible. This may be a superintendent of a school district or the director of a mental hospital. Open communication between all levels and persons in the field setting should also be maintained. People have to know what is going on among them. If they do not, suspicion, doubt, and rumor can arise and a study may be cancelled simply because subjects misunderstand its intent. Steering committees should be created to inform people of the study. Such committees can also be apprised of the implications of one's research so that they can anticipate reactions the study may produce. Above all, when a researcher makes an agreement with a subject or organization he must uphold it. This means that one has to be very careful in his public statements so as to anticipate all consequences.

Rainwater and Pittman have continued the discussion of ethics by noting how pressures from sponsoring agencies and various groups within the field can arise and often be in conflict. Their study produced demands for public information, many of them from the press. Early in the study they formulated a rule that precluded any and all public statements until the study was complete. This protected their field relations and insured that conclusions were not prematurely drawn.

The problem of confidentiality was raised with respect to Voss's study. Rainwater and Pittman pursue this problem by suggesting that sociologists may not have to grant confidentiality to respondents who are publicly accountable for their role activity. Thus, any information about a person who is publicly or socially accountable can be seen as "open information." This is an important principle because many studies focus on such activities and in these situations the strictures on observation are considerably reduced. Of course variations in methodological strategies may produce ethical problems of another order, especially in long-term studies where respondents or informants come to be friends with the researcher. Implicit demands within the relationship may create counterpressures to hide certain information.

The rule of public accountability demands that such information be avoided; that such relationships not be developed. This may not be attractive always, but it may be the only alternative. This would be the case with high level governmental officials, for example.

SOCIOLOGY'S INTERNATIONAL CONTEXT

Elsewhere I have outlined what I regard as the main implications of Project Camelot (see chap. 13 of my *The Research Act* [Chicago: Aldine Publishing Company, 1970]). I cannot add to Horowitz's analysis, but I wish to repeat his conclusions. Sociologists should never enter into a research relationship where they lose or give up control over their own activities. The researcher, and only the researcher, should decide what is to be studied.

THE FINAL DILEMMA: WHOSE SIDE ARE WE ON?

Becker ["Whose Side Are We On?" *Social Problems* 14 (Winter, 1967), 239–48] has offered an uncomfortable stance for all researchers. Value decisions must be made. Every action in the field is bound to produce biased results because it is impossible to study all sides of an issue. All that can be hoped is that each researcher will publicly state his values so that future researchers may know them. In that ideal scheme of social research, cumulative studies will appear which buttress or counter previous biases. At some point, then, all sides will be unveiled.

In conclusion, no researcher can escape influencing his own findings. The readings in this final part suggest many sources of influence, but ultimately the source is the researcher himself. He is the one who stands against the outside world and through an involved interpretational process constructs his images of how best to be a sociologist. The first step for every sociologist necessarily becomes the self-conscious awareness of his own values, ideologies and biases.

Suggested Readings. Three excellent edited books present statements by sociologists on the social factors involved in doing research. These are Vidich, Bensman, and Stein, *Reflections on Community Studies* (New York: Wiley, 1964); Hammond, *Sociologists at Work* (New York: Basic Books, 1964); and Sjoberg, *Ethics, Politics, and Social Research* (Schenkman, 1967).

The journal *Trans*-action publishes papers addressed to the relationship between sociological findings and applied social issues. This journal is one of the few social science publications with this explicit focus. Recent statements in the *American Sociologist*, a formal journal of the American Sociological Association, have presented findings from the Committee on Ethics which the interested reader should examine.

34. Some Factors Affecting the Organization and Prosecution of Given Research Projects

CLYDE W. HART

RESEARCH methods and procedures are matter to which sociologists have always given a great deal of attention. Few subjects, in fact, have been discussed with as much heat on as many occasions or have accumulated as voluminous a literature. Nearly every text-book writer has felt constrained to warn unwary students against the pitfalls of bias and the methodological errors of his contemporaries in an extended exposition of the requirements of the scientific discipline. Every respectable graduate curriculum includes from one to a half-dozen courses on methodology in which lectures and discussion are supplemented by student reading in an extensive bibliography. As interest in Wissenssociologie has grown, sociologists have even shown a dispostion to examine their own research behavior from the point of view of sociology itself. The more perspicacious among them have perceived that sociology—like a religious sect or a

Reprinted by permission from *American Sociological Review*, 12 (October 1957), pp. 514-19. Copyright 1957, The American Sociological Association.

political party — is a form or aspect of collective behavior, and that the sociologist as a person — like the patriarch, the gangster, or the professional thief — develops within a social and cultural context apart from which he cannot be understood and cannot understand himself.

Despite all this concern about soundness of method and the relevance and validity of various modes of analysis and generalization when we are thinking explicitly about method in the abstract, notwithstanding even the implications of the currently developing sociology of sociological knowledge, most of us, when we embark on a specific research venture of our own, assume that the way we set it up and carry it through to a supposed solution is determined by the nature of the problem itself and by dictates of the scientific method and point of view. We may have been biased in our selection of the project but, from that point on, bias does not enter in, because facts are facts and scientific method is scientific method under all circumstances.

Yet, if several of us were working independently on a *given* problem — the etiology of some form of race prejudice, for example — there would undoubtedly be wide divergences among us in the way we would organize and prosecute our researches and in the general form, if not the specific content, of our solutions. We would differ categorically in the kinds of data we would deem requisite, the techniques we would use in discovering these data, the modes of analysis we would bring to bear upon them, and the kind of generalization that, in our several judgments, would constitute a satisfactory solution. Our sociological acquaintances could make fairly accurate forecasts for each of us in all these respects. Some of us would observe behavior only in its external manifestations and would be distrustful of introspective materials; others while not ignoring overt behavior would consider it relatively valueless as a datum unless the corresponding covert aspects of experience were also known. Some would almost certainly resort to life histories, some would make case studies, some would select samples and proceed statistically, still others would endeavor to construct "controlled experimental situations." The generalizations with which some of us came out would describe within stated limits the behavior of actual persons and groups under the complex circumstances of real life; the conclusions drawn by others would be highly abstract generalizations, rarely descriptive of behavior in the concrete situations of real life because the simplified conditions assumed in the statement of any conclusion are seldom found in real life. And some sociologists would be fairly

sure to discover evidences of the determining effects of class structure; others would find in infantile experiences adequate explanatory
clues; still others would consider their quest ended only when they
had fitted to their data, without too much distortion, a logistic, Gom-
pertz, or other measure of trend.

These wide divergences in the handling of a given research problem would not occur if the procedures we follow and the types of
solution we seek were wholly determined by the nature of the
problem and the requirements of scientific method. Obviously they
are not so determined. We select them, and our selections are restricted or directed by many extra-scientific factors operating upon
and within us in varying combinations and with varying degrees of
intensity.

Some of these extra-scientific factors, external and arbitrary in
their mode of operation and generally not controllable by the student
himself, keep us from selecting the sources of data we would prefer
to tap, impose severe limitations on our use of sources, and make it
impossible for us to employ the analytical methods we deem most
appropriate. Research takes time, costs money, needs competent
personnel with specialized skills, and requires work space, laboratories, and equipment of various sorts. These resources are seldom in
plentiful supply, nor are they equally available to all who need them.
Not infrequently, a research worker cannot attack his problem as he
would like to, but must resort to an inferior method because it takes
less time, money, and equipment, and is within the competence of
available personnel. If he is studying attitudes, for example, he may
have to substitute simple polling questions of the "yes-no" type for
free-answer or "open-ended" questions that encourage respondents
to talk about the issues or values presented to them, and he may, in
addition, have to reduce the number of interviews to a point where
certain desired types of analysis cannot be made.

Moreover, access to and methods of utilizing such resources as are
available may be limited by the predilections and prejudices of those
persons who allocate them. Deans of graduate schools, research committees of university faculties, trustees of foundations, and project
clearance officers in governmental agencies usually review the plans
for accomplishing a research project as well as the value of the
anticipated results, and fully as much consideration is given to proposed methods and techniques as to project justifications. Just as
different universities, research centers, and foundations develop specialized interests in certain types of problem — the growth process of
the child, race relations, international relations, for example — so they

sometimes tend, although in lesser degree, to have specialized methodological preferences. These preferences operate as a continuous
pressure in the selection and implementation of research under-
takings, not only because of discriminations in granting or withholding funds, but also because of the prestige these agencies have in the
community at large as well as in academic circles.

Whether or not the research is undertaken under the auspices of
one of these agencies, it will be judged by them when it is completed and the major material rewards—jobs, publication, and other
forms of professional advancement—bestowed accordingly. Researchers are almost certain to have some part of this audience
before them, consciously or unconsciously, as they devise and carry
on their projects and prepare their reports. Perhaps most of us are
influenced more than we admit, even to ourselves, by our anticipations of the applause or censure we may get from those whose
opinion matters most to us.

Examination of our own research behavior would reveal another
set of extra-scientific factors, also essentially external, that limit or
otherwise influence the selection of research procedures. Research
goes on in an environment of conventions, moral prejudices, institutionalized practices and ideologies, and whenever one of our
projects impinges upon this body of social and cultural fact it may
have to proceed by indirection. Quinn McNemar has suggested that,
because so large a proportion of attitude studies have used college
students as subjects, our present social psychology might better be
called a "social psychology of sophomores." This use of students as
sources of data, though undeniably dictated in most instances by
considerations of convenience and economy, is sometimes done because students are more understanding or tolerant of professorial
curiosities about such delicate subject-matters as the sex mores or
political ideologies. Government research workers are often prohibited from collecting certain types of data because of the fear of Congressional criticism or the fairly certain prospect of vitriolic criticism
in the press and by letter, and have to turn to documentary sources or
some form of indirect evidence.

But conventional and institutional environment affects the availability of data and the way data are or may be collected in still other
important ways. In certain research projects, the student is limited to
types of data that have already been collected and compiled by the
Bureau of the Census, the Public Health Service, or some other
federal, state, or private agency, and may even have to accept many
of the classifications that were devised by the collecting agency for

its own purposes and that are ill suited to the purposes of the project under study. The incidental effects of these limitations are particularly apparent in the field of opinion and attitude research and in other fields where sampling is used. In constructing representative samples of the purposive type the categories used – age, sex, occupation, residence, etc. – are those about which the requisite information is available in recorded sources. In collating the opinion data themselves these same conventional classifications tend to govern the groupings that are abstracted from the total sample in order to get a more detailed picture of the distribution of opinions and attitudes or as an aid to inference about causes. Yet these particular breakdowns may not be helpful to the administrator who wants to use the findings from the study in directing his informational and educational programs; nor are they likely to isolate variables that determine people's opinion.

But more important than the institutional and other essentially external restrictions and pressures are the extra-scientific factors which we ourselves introduce into our research procedures – the premises (usually unstated), the preconceptions, and value judgments of the one who is doing the research. These factors are more important not only because their distorting effects are greater, but also because they are so subtle, so implicit, so deeply rooted that it is difficult for us to discern them in ourselves or, when they are called to attention, to avoid rationalizing them instead of examining them objectively. Most of these biasing assumptions have been called to everyone's attention in courses in method and on other occasions, so that we should be aware of them, but the increase in their prevalence that has accompanied the unfortunate decline of good armchair – *i.e.*, rigorously systematic – sociology suggests a need for recalling them as a basis for a little wholesome self-criticism. In the time I have left, I propose to state with brief comments a few of these personal and subjective extra-scientific, or anti-scientific factors.

1. The assumption that only individuals are real, that all behavior is individual behavior, and that the causes of social and cultural changes are to be found in individual mechanisms. Perhaps few of us think that we are in any degree subject to this nominalistic bias, but I believe that careful scrutiny of our sociological production would convict large numbers of us of being incorrigible nominalists at heart. How many researches in the field of personality development, or how many treatises on the subject, can you cite that clearly and consistently conceive of the person as a role played in a group or

even as a system of roles each of which derives from one of several tangential and intersecting groups? Most of us, in fact, are less successful than a good football coach in avoiding the nominalistic bias. He has no difficulty in abstracting the team as a relatively closed system of interaction within which roles are defined, or in abstracting the role of tackle and explaining it without reference to the peculiar biology or psychology of the individual who happens to be playing it at a given moment in a given game. And his abstract conception of the team and of team play is useful to him as a tool of analysis and means of control just because it is abstract. But we seldom find as consistent abstract analyses of groups and roles (persons) coming from the workshops of the sociologists.

In consequence of the nominalistic bias, we tend to examine individuals and to come out with generalizations about numbers of individuals rather than about groups. Students of attitudes and opinions have been particularly addicted to this bias. In little of their research is there evidence of any organic conception of the public or public opinion. The public is millions of individuals, behaving as individuals because of individual motivation. And public opinion is something that can be got at by collecting a good sample of individual opinions and summating them. As has already been indicated in another connection, the subordinate groups into which the "general public" is broken by the use of such criteria as age, sex, and urban-rural residence do not correspond to functional groups within which issues are defined and discussed, and emotional and ideational unities developed. And it is notable, in this connection, that sociologists have made virtually no contributions in the form of improved criteria to supplement the present ones, which are sociological in only a very elementary sense.

But students of other types of collective behavior exhibit the same bias. In an unrecorded discussion of current social aggressions among minority groups at a recent meeting of District of Columbia sociologists, the causes of aggressions were found to lie in social situations incident to the war. But when attention turned to methods of controlling them, the only suggestions forthcoming involved the utilization of such individual psychological mechanisms as substitution and sublimation; no mention was made of control by way of modifications in the social situations within which, according to the previous analysis of causes, the aggressions were being continuously produced.

2. The assumption that science is technique rather than a systematic body of principles and laws. A variant of this assumption goes

further to identify science with a *specific* technique or group of related techniques—the experimental or the statistical, for example. Though precedent can be cited for this usage of the term, *scientific*, it is confusing and is certainly one of the important reasons why sociologists vary widely, not only in the selection of methods and procedures of research, but also in their conceptions of what constitutes a solution of a research problem.

A statement of the probable frequency with which behavior of a certain kind occurs under the complex conditions of real life, though interesting and useful, is not a scientific statement no matter how valid and reliable the instruments were by means of which it was derived. Nor is a measure of a historic trend or a diagnostic inference. The clinical diagnosis of a patient's condition as arteriosclerosis with specified complications may have been derived by bringing to bear on his case diagnostic techniques of proven reliability. The probability that the diagnosis is correct may approach certainty, and it is unquestionably of great practical importance to him, his wife, and his physician, but it has no scientific interest whatever and no place in a textbook on physiology. Yet sociological textbooks and journals are replete with reports of research findings of corresponding character.

Those who hold this assumption that science is technique, in either its general or its specific form, tend naturally to be chiefly or exclusively preoccupied with improvements in technique. They not only tend to select problems which provide opportunities to use preferred techniques or to devise and test new ones; they may also reshape a problem undertaken for other purposes in order that it may better serve their own technical interest. In any event, they tend to neglect sociological theory, in general or in any of its specific segments, and to become more or less exclusive students of methods and techniques. The development of a theory of public opinion and public behavior, to cite a specific example, gives way to the perfection of a theory of sampling. A year ago, in the first conference of public opinion research personnel, only one or two out of more than thirty prepared contributions presented any research findings about public opinion *per se;* all the others were devoted to sampling methods, questionnaire construction, and other technical and procedural problems.

3. The assumption that a scientific research project aims to derive a generalization that fits a concrete empirical universe, or that the research is ended when such a generalization is derived. In our statistical studies we frequently assume that our job is done when we

have computed rates, measures of trend, measures of central tendency, coefficients of correlation, etc., describing the behavior of some variables — births, deaths, opinions, or attitudes — in a representative sample of people. Findings at this stage of the inquiry may have great practical utility. They may enable us to reduce to a minimum the risk involved in writing life insurance or enable us to forecast the size of the future population, the outcome of an election, or the market for funeral goods and undertakers' services. They may even have some crude predictive value since they would make it possible to calculate the chances that an individual having certain known characteristics, such as type of home background, will become a criminal. From an administrative standpoint they are frequently sufficient so that research need be carried no further.

But from a scientific standpoint, these findings are preliminary; they are significant because they point to possibilities of further study. Frequency distributions are not used as imaginatively as they could be for the purpose of locating instances that could profitably be studied intensively. Moreover, by picking up clues from our initial statistical findings we might be able progressively to restrict the universe from which samples are drawn, thus getting closer approximations of the abstract situations to which strictly scientific generalizations always relate. The difference between the crude initial sort of statistical generalization and a generalization of scientific sort can be easily illustrated by a hypothetical illustration. If we had a frequency distribution of observed instances of freely falling bodies with time as the variable and distance held constant, the extreme instance at the low end of the time axis would more nearly approximate the instance described by the law of falling bodies ($S = \frac{1}{2} Gt_2$) than would the mean, median, or modal instance. The law of falling bodies describes an instance that lies clear outside the frequency distribution.

These are but three of many commonplace assumptions that operate as extra-scientific factors in the selection of research methods and procedures.

Since, when our attention is called to the fact that we ourselves are addicted to any one of these biasing assumptions, we react defensively by trying to defend the assumption on logical grounds, it may help us to achieve a more nearly objective attitude toward them if we realize that our addiction to them is a result of our own differential participation in systems of social interaction generally, and of the historical sociological movement in particular. Our tendencies as research students to select or reject statistical or other modes of analysis and generalization, the nominalistic or realistic conception of the nature of social reality, abstract as opposed to concrete conceptions of sociological knowledge, or sympathetic introspection as opposed to the observations of the external aspects of behavior are, in large degree, resultants of our selective contacts and relations with any one of several sectarian or factional developments in the concrete sociological enterprise. Usually they reveal our student or other affiliations and indentifications in the field of sociology. It makes a great deal of difference in these and other respects whether we studies under, or have otherwise been affiliated with, MacIver, Park, Chapin, Ogburn, Lundberg, Young, Blumer, Reuter, or any one or more of dozens of other scholars. Unless we appreciate this fact we stand little chance of lifting the discussion of methodology and research procedures from the sentimental to the critical level. In the meantime, sociology will continue to be split into sects and factions that may ultimately harden into denominations and parties, the production of our researches will continue to be a heterogeneous mass of discrete inferences scarcely susceptible of systemization, and the ratio of research effort to useful results will continue to be exceedingly high in both the theoretical and the practical realms.

35. Hired Hand Research

JULIUS ROTH

CASE I

After it became obvious how tedious it was to write down numbers on pieces of paper which didn't even fulfill one's own sense of reality and which did not remind one of the goals of the project, we all in little ways started avoiding our work and cheating on the project. It began for example when we were supposed to be observing for hour and a half periods, an hour and a half on the ward and then an hour and a half afterwards to write up or dictate what we had observed, in terms of the category system which the project was supposed to be testing and in terms of a ward diary. We began cutting corners in time. We would arrive a little bit late and leave a little bit early. It began innocently enough, but soon boomeranged into a full cheating syndrome, where we would fake observations for some time slot which were never observed on the ward. Sam, for

Reprinted by permission from *American Sociologist*, 1 (August 1966), pp. 190–96. Copyright 1966, American Sociological Review.

example, in one case, came onto the ward while I was still finishing up an assignment on a study patient and told me that he was supposed to observe for an hour and a half but that he wasn't going to stay because he couldn't stand it anymore. He said he wasn't going to tell anyone that he missed an assignment, but that he would simply write up a report on the basis of what he knew already about the ward and the patients. I was somewhat appalled by Sam's chicanery, and in this sense I was the last one to go. It was three or four weeks after this before I actually cheated in the same manner.

It was also frequent for us to miss observation periods, especially the 8 to 9:30 a.m. ones. We all had a long drive for one thing, and we were all chronic over-sleepers for another. For a while we used to make up the times we missed by coming in the next morning at the same time and submitting our reports with the previous day's date. As time went on, however, we didn't bother to make up the times we'd missed. When we were questioned by our supervisor about the missing reports, we would claim that there had been an error in scheduling and that we did not know that those time slots were supposed to be covered.

There were other ways we would cheat, sometimes inadvertently. For example, one can decide that one can't hear enough of a conversation to record it. People need to think fairly highly of themselves, and when you think that you're a cheat and a liar and that you're not doing your job for which you are receiving high wages, you are likely to find little subconscious ways of getting out of having to accuse yourself of these things. One of the ways is to not be able to hear well. We had a special category in our coding system, a question mark, which we noted by its symbol on our code sheets whenever we could not hear what was going on between two patients. As the purgatory of writing numbers on pieces of paper lengthened, more and more transcripts were passed in with question marks on them, so that even though we had probably actually heard most of the conversations between patients, we were still actually avoiding the work of transcription by deceiving ourselves into believing that we could not hear what was being said. This became a good way of saving yourself work. If you couldn't hear a conversation, it just got one mark in one column of one code sheet, and if you wrote down an elaborate conversation lasting even ten minutes, it might take you up to an hour to code it, one hour of putting numbers in little blocks. In the long run, all of our data became much skimpier. Conversations were incomplete; their duration was strangely diminishing to two or three minutes in length instead of the half-hour talks the patients usually had with each other. We were all defining our own cutting off points, saying to ourselves, "Well, that's enough of that conversation." According to the coding rules, however, a communication can't be considered as ended until the sequence of interaction has been completed and a certain time lapse of silence has ensued.

In order to ensure the reliability of our coding, the research design called for an "Inter-Rater Reliability Check" once every two months, in which each of the four of us would pair up with every other member of the team and be rated on our ability to code jointly the same interaction in terms of the same categories and dimensions. We learned to loathe these checks; we knew that the coding system was inadequate in terms of reliability and that our choice of categories was optional, subjective, and largely according to our own sense of what an interaction is really about, rather than according to the rigid, stylized, and preconceived design into which we were supposed to make a reality fit. We also knew, however, that our principal investigators insisted on an inter-rater reliability coefficient of .70 in order for the research to proceed. When the time came for another check, we met together to discuss and make certain agreements on how to bring our coding habits into conformity for the sake of achieving reliability. In these meetings we would confess our preferences for coding certain things in certain ways and agree on certain concessions to each other for the duration of the check. Depending on what other individual I was to be paired with, for example, I had a very good idea of how I could code in order to achieve nearly the same transcriptions. We didn't end it there. After each phase of a check, each pair of us would meet again to go over our transcriptions and compare our coding, and if there were any gross discrepancies, we corrected them before sending them to the statisticians for analysis. Needless to say, as soon as the reliability checks were over with, we each returned to a coding rationale which we as individuals required in order to do any coding at all—in order to maintain sanity.

CASE II

There didn't appear to be too much concern with the possibility of inconsistency among the coders. Various coders used various methods to determine the code of an open-end question. Toward the end of the coding process, expediency became the keynote, leading to gross inconsistency. The most expedient method of coding a few of the trickier questions was to simply put down a "4" (This was the middle-of-the-road response on the one question that had the most variation.). If the responses were not clear or comprehensible, the coder had two alternatives: on the one hand, he could puzzle over it and ask for other opinions or, on the other hand, he could assign it an arbitrary number or forget the response entirely.

In the beginning, many of us, when in doubt about a response, would ask the supervisor or his assistant. After a while, I noted that quite often the supervisor's opinion would differ when asked twice about the same response and he would often give two different answers in response to the same question. One way the supervisor and his assistant would determine the correct coding for an answer would be to look at the respondent's previous answers and deduce what they should have answered—thereby coding on *what they thought the respondent should have answered*, not on the basis of what he *did* answer. One example that I distinctly remember is the use of magazines regularly read as reported by the respondent being used as a basis on which to judge and code their political views. This, in my opinion, would be a factor in some of the cases, such as the reading of an extreme leftist or extreme rightist magazine, but to use magazines such as *Time* or *Reader's Digest* to form any conclusions about the type of person and his views, I feel is quite arbitrary. Furthermore, I feel questionnaires should be used to see *if* consistent patterns of views exist among respondents and it is not the coder's job to put them in if the respondents fail to!

Some of the coders expected a fixed pattern of response. I, not being sure of what responses meant in a total political profile, treated each response separately—which I feel is the correct way of coding a questionnaire. Others, as I learned through their incessant jabbering, took what they thought was a more sophisticated method of treating an interview. A few would discuss the respondent's answers as if they took one political or social standpoint as an indicator of what all the responses should be. They would laugh over an inconsistency in the respondent's replies, feeling that one answer did not fit the previous pattern of responses.

The final problem leading to gross inconsistency was the factor of time. The supervisor made it clear that the code sheets had to be in the computation center by Saturday. This meant that on Saturday morning and early afternoon the aim of the coders was to code the questionnaires as quickly as possible, and the crucial factor was speed, even at the expense of accuracy. The underlying thought was that there were so many questionnaires coded already (that we *assumed* to be coded consistently and correctly) that the inconsistencies in the remainder would balance themselves out and be of no great importance. I found myself adapting to this way of thinking, and after spending two or three hours there on Saturday morning, I joined in the game of "let's get these damn things out already." It did indeed become a game, with the shibboleth, for one particularly vague and troublesome question, "Oh, give it a four."

CASE III

One of the questions on the interview schedule asked for five reasons why parents had put their child in an institution. I found most people can't think of five reasons. One or two — sometimes three. At first I tried pumping them for more reasons, but I never got any of them up to five. I didn't want (the director) to think I was goofing off on the probing, so I always filled in all five.

Another tough one was the item about how the child's disability affected the family relationships. We were supposed to probe. Probe what? You get so many different kinds of answers, I was never sure what was worth following up. Sometimes I did if the respondent seemed to have something to say. Otherwise I just put down a short answer and made it look as if that was all I could get out of them. Of course, (the director) *did* list a few areas he wanted covered in the probing. One of them was sex relations of the parents. Most of the time I didn't follow up on that. Once in a while I would get somebody who seemed to be able to talk freely without embarrassment. But most of the time I was afraid to ask, so I made up something to fill that space.

Then there was that wide open question at the end. It's vague. Most people don't know what to say. You've been asking them questions for about an hour already. Usually you get a very short answer. I didn't push them. I'd write up a longer answer later. It's easy to do. You have their answer to a lot of other questions to draw on. You just put parts of some of them together, dress it up a little, and add one or two bits of new information which fits in with the rest.

Any reader with research experience can probably recall one or more cases in which he observed, suspected, or participated in some form of cheating, carelessness, distortion, or cutting of corners in the collection or processing of research data. He probably thought of these instances as exceptions — an unfortunate lapse in ethical behavior or a failure of research directors to maintain proper controls. I would like to put forth the thesis that such behavior on the part of hired data collectors and processors is not abnormal or exceptional, but rather is exactly the kind of behavior we should expect from people with their position in a production unit.

The cases I have presented do not constitute proof, of course. Even if I presented ten or twenty more, my efforts could be dismissed as merely an unusually industrious effort to record professional dirty linen (or I might be accused of making them up!) and not at all representative of the many thousands of cases of hired researching carried out every year. Rather than multiply examples, I would like to take a different tack and examine the model we have been using in thinking about research operations and to suggest another model which I believe is more appropriate.

The ideal we hold of the researcher is that of a well-educated scholar pursuing information and ideas on problems in which he has an intrinsic interest. Frequently this ideal may be approximated when an individual scholar is working on his own problem or several colleagues are collaborating on a problem of mutual interest. Presumably such a researcher will endeavor to carry out his data collection and processing in the most accurate and useful way that his skills and time permit.

When a researcher hires others to do the collecting and processing tasks of his research plan, we often assume that these assistants fit the "dedicated scientist" ideal and will lend their efforts to the successful conduct of the over-all study by carrying out their assigned tasks to the best of their ability. As suggested by my examples, I doubt that hired assistants usually behave this way even when they are junior grade scholars themselves. It becomes more doubtful yet when they are even further removed from scholarly tradition and from the direct control of the research directors (e.g., part-time survey interviewers).

It seems to me that we can develop a more accurate expectation of the contribution of the hired research worker who is required to work according to somebody else's plan by applying another model which has been worked out in some detail by sociologists—namely, the work behavior of the hired hand in a production organization. First, let us look at one of the more thorough of these studies, Donald Roy's report on machine shop operators.[1]

Roy's workers made the job easier by loafing when the piece rate did not pay well. They were careful not to go over their informal "quotas" on piece rate jobs because the rate would be cut and their

1. Donald Roy, "Quota Restriction and Goldbricking in a Machine Shop," *American Journal of Sociology*, 57 (March 1952), 427–42.

work would be harder. They faked time sheets so that their actual productive abilities would not be known to management. They cut corners on prescribed job procedures to make the work easier and/or more lucrative even though this sometimes meant that numerous products had to be scrapped. Roy's calculations show that the workers could have produced on the order of twice as much if it had been in their interest to do so.

But it is *not* in their interest to do so. The product the hired hand turns out is not in any sense his. He does not design it, make any of the decisions about producing it or about the conditions under which it will be produced, or what will be done with it after it is produced. The worker is interested in doing just enough to get by. Why should he concern himself about how well the product works or how much time it takes to make it? That is the company's problem. The company is his adversary and fair game for any trickery he can get away with. The worker's aim is to make his job as easy and congenial as the limited resources allow and to make as much money as possible without posing a threat to his fellow workers or to his own future. The company, in turn, is placed in the position of having to establish an inspection system to try to keep the worst of their products from leaving the factory (an effort often unsuccessful—the inspectors are hired hands, too) and of devising some form of supervision to limit the more extreme forms of gold-bricking and careless workmanship.

Almost all the systematic research on "restriction of output" and deviation from assigned duties has been done on factory workers, office clerks, and other low prestige work groups. This is mostly because such work is easier to observe and measure, but also because much of this research has been controlled in part by those in a position of authority who want research done only on their subordinates. However, there is evidence to indicate that work restrictions and deviations in the form of informal group definitions and expectations are probably universal in our society. They can be found among business executives and in the professions, sports, and the creative arts. They are especially likely to crop up when one is working as a hired hand, and almost all productive activities have their hired hand aspects. A professor may work hard on scholarly tasks of his own choosing and perhaps even on teaching a course which he himself has devised, but he becomes notoriously lax when he is assigned to a departmental service course which he does not like—spending little or no time on preparation, avoiding his students as much as possible, turning all the exams over to a graduate assistant, and so on.

"Restriction of production" and deviation from work instructions is no longer regarded by students of the sociology of work as a moral issue or a form of social delinquency. Rather, it is the expected behavior of workers in a production organization. The only problem for an investigator to work practices is discovering the details of cutting corners, falsifying time sheets, defining work quotas, dodging supervision, and ignoring instructions in a given work setting.

There is no reason to believe that a hired hand in the scientific research business will behave any different from those in other areas of productive activity. It is far more reasonable to assume that their behavior will be similar. They want to make as much money as they can and may pad their account or time sheet if they are paid on that basis, but this type of behavior is a minor problem so far as the present discussion is concerned. They also want to avoid difficult, embarrassing, inconvenient, time-consuming situations as well as those activities which make no sense to them. (Thus, they fail to make some assigned observations or to ask some of the interview questions.) At the same time they want to give the right impression to their supervisors—at least right enough so that their material will be accepted and they will be kept on the job. (Thus, they modify or fabricate portions of the reports in order to give the boss what he *seems* to want.) They do not want to "look stupid" by asking too many questions, so they are likely to make a stab at what they think the boss wants—e.g., make a guess at a coding category rather than having it resolved through channels.

Even those who start out with the notion that this is an important piece of work which they must do right will succumb to the hired hand mentality when they realize that their suggestions and criticisms are ignored, that their assignment does not allow for any imagination or creativity, that they will receive no credit for the final product, in short, that they have been hired to do somebody else's dirty work. When this realization has sunk in, they will no longer bother to be careful or accurate or precise. They will cut corners to save time and energy. They will fake parts of their reporting. They will not put themselves out for something in which they have no stake except in so far as extrinsic pressures force them to. Case No. I is an excerpt from the statement of a research worker who started out with enthusiasm and hard work and ended with sloppy work and cheating when she could no longer escape the fact that she was a mere flunky expected to do her duty whether or not it was meaningful. The coders in Case II soon gave up any effort to resolve the ambiguities of their coding operation and followed the easiest path acceptable to their supervisor. In this case, the supervisor himself made little effort to direct the data processing toward supplying answers to meaningful research issues. We must remember that in many research operations the supervisors and directors themselves are hired hands carrying out the requests of a client or superior as expeditiously as possible.

Many of the actions of hired hand researchers are strikingly analogous to restrictive practices of factory operatives. Interviewers who limit probing and observers who limit interaction recording are behaving like workers applying "quota restriction," and with interacting hired hands informal agreements may be reached on the extent of such restrictions. To fabricate portions of a report is a form of goldbricking. The collusion on the reliability check reported in Case I is strikingly similar to the workers' plot to mislead the time-study department. Such similarities are no accident. The relationship of the hired hand to the product and the process of production is the same in each case. The product is not "his." The production process gives him little or no opportunity to express any intrinsic interest he may have in the product. He will sooner or later fall into a pattern of carrying out his work with a minimum of effort, inconvenience, and embarrassment—doing just enough so that his product will get by. If he is part of a large and complex operation where his immediate superiors are also hired hands with no intrinsic interest in the product and where the final authority may be distant and even amorphous, quality control of the product will be mechanical and the minimal effort that will get by can soon be learned and easily applied. The factory production situation has at least one ultimate limitation on the more extreme deviations of the hired hands: The final product must "work" reasonably well in a substantial proportion of cases. In social science research, on the other hand, the product is usually so ambiguous and the field of study so lacking in standards of performance that it is difficult for anyone to say whether it "works" or not.

What is more important is the effect of the hired hand mentality on the *nature* of the product. Workmen not only turn out less than they could if it were in their interest to maximize production, but often produce shoddy and even dangerous products.[2] In the case of research, the inefficiency of hired hands not only causes a study to take

2. I want to emphasize once again that in a business setting, supervisors and executives, as well as production line workmen, participate in aspects of the hired hand mentality. None of them may have an intrinsic interest in the quality of the product. (See, for example, Melvin Dalton, *Men Who Manage* (New York: Wiley, 1959), esp. chaps. 7, 8, and 9.) The same is the case in much large-scale research.

longer or cost more money, but is likely to introduce much dubious data and interpretations into the process of analysis. Our mass production industrial system has opted to sacrifice individual efficiency and product quality for the advantages of a rationalized division of labor. The same approach has been applied to much of our larger scale scientific research and the results, in my opinion, have been much more disastrous than they are in industrial production with little compensating advantages.

When the tasks of a research project are split up into small pieces to be assigned to hired hands, none of these data collectors and processors will ever understand all the complexities and subtleties of the research issues in the same way as the person who conceived of the study. No amount of "training" can take the place of the gradual development of research interests and formulations on the part of the planner. Since the director often cannot be sure what conceptions of the issues the hired hands have as a result of his explanations and "training," he must make dubious guesses about the meaning of much of the data they return to him. If he attempts to deal with this difficulty by narrowly defining the permissible behavior of each hired hand (e.g., demand that all questions on a schedule be asked in a set wording), he merely increases the alienation of the hired hand from his work and thus increases the likelihood of cutting corners and cheating. As he gains in quantity of data, he loses in validity of meaningfulness.[3]

I do not want to give the impression that the hired hand mentality with its attendant difficulties is simply a characteristic of the large-scale on-going research organization. We may find it at all size levels, including the academic man hiring a single student to do his research chores. The argument may be advanced that assignment of specified tasks by the director of a study is essential to getting the job done in the manner that he wants it done. My answer is that such assignments are often not effectively carried out and it is misleading to assume that they are.

Let me illustrate this point. A researcher wants to do a study of the operation of a given institution. He has some definite notion of what aspects of behavior of the institutional personnel he wants informa-

3. In this discussion I am assuming there *is* someone (or a small group of colleagues) who has initially formulated the research problem or area of concern because of intrinsic interest and curiosity. In much of our social science research, we do not have even this saving grace and the research is formulated and carried out for various "political" reasons. In such cases, we cannot count on having anyone interested enough to try to turn the accumulations of data into a meaningful explanatory statement.

tion about and he has some ideas about the manner in which he will go about analysing and interpreting these behaviors. He finds it possible and useful to engage four trained and interested assistants. Let me outline two ways the study might be conducted.

A. Through a series of discussions, general agreement is reached about the nature of the study and the manner in which it might be conducted. Some division of labor is agreed upon in these discussions. However, none of the field workers is held to any particular tasks or foci of interest. Each is allowed to pursue his data collection as he thinks best within the larger framework, although the field workers exchange information frequently and make new agreements so that they can benefit from each other's experience.

B. The director divides up the data collection and processing in a logical manner and assigns a portion to each of the assistants. Each field worker is instructed to obtain information in all the areas assigned to him and to work in a prescribed manner so that his information will be directly comparable to that of the others. The director may use a procedural check such as having each assistant write a report covering given issues or areas at regular intervals.

Which is the preferred approach? Judging from my reading of social science journals, most research directors would say Method B is to be preferred. Method A, they would maintain, produces information on subjects, issues, or events from one field worker which is not directly comparable to that collected by another field worker. They would also object that if each field worker is permitted to follow his own inclinations even in part, the total study will suffer from large gaps. These accusations are quite true — and, I would add, are an inevitable result of dividing a research project among a number of people. What I disagree with, however, is the assumption that Method B would not suffer from these defects (if indeed, they should be regarded as defects.) It is assumed that the assistants in Method B are actually carrying out their assigned tasks in the manner specified. In line with my earlier discussion of the behavior of hired hands, I would consider this highly unlikely. If the information produced by these assistants is indeed closely comparable, it would most likely be because they had reached an agreement on how to restrict production. And, whether the study is carried out by Method A or by Method B, gaps will occur. The difference is that the director of Study A — assuming he had succeeded in making his assistants into collaborating colleagues — would at least know where the gaps are. The director of Study B would have gaps without knowing where they are—or indeed, that they exist—because they have been covered over by the fabrications of his alienated assistants.

It is ironic that established researchers do not ascribe the same motivating forces to their subordinates as they do to themselves. For many years research scientists have been confronting those who pay their salaries and give them their grants with the argument that a scientist can do good research only when he has the freedom to follow his ideas in whatever way seems best. They have been so successful with this argument that university administrations and research organization directorates rarely attempt to dictate—or even suggest—problems or procedures to a researcher on their staff, and the more prominent granting agencies write contracts with almost no strings attached as to the way in which the study will be conducted. Yet research directors fail to apply this same principle to those they hire to carry out data collection and processing. The hired assistant's desire to participate in the task and the creative contribution he might make is ignored with the result that the assistants' creativity is applied instead to convertly changing the nature of the task.

There has been very little discussion in our journals and our books on research methods on the relationship of the hired hand to the data collected. Whatever discussion there *has* been can be found in the survey interview field where there have been some studies of the effect of such demographic factors as age, sex, and race, sometimes measured personality traits, on "interviewer bias." The nature of the interviewer's status in a research organization is seldom discussed in print. The problem of interviewer cheating, although a common subject of informal gossip, is seldom dealt with openly as a serious problem. When Leo Crespi published an article twenty years ago in which he expressed the worry that cheating was seriously affecting the validity of much survey data,[4] those who responded (mostly survey organization executives) stated reassuringly that few interviewers cheated and that they had pretty effective ways of controlling those who did.[5] If the analysis offered in this paper is correct, the first part of this reassurance is almost certainly wrong. The low-level flunky position which most interviewers occupy in survey organizations[6] should lead us to expect widespread deviations from assigned tasks. The survey executives who responded give no con-

4. Leo Crespi, "The Cheater Problem in Polling," *Public Opinion Quarterly* (Winter 1945–1946), pp. 431–45.

5. "Survey on Problems of Interviewer Cheating," *International Journal of Opinion and Attitude Research*, 1 (1947), 93–107.

6. Julius A. Roth, "The Status of Interviewing," *The Midwest Sociologist*, 19 (December 1956), 8–11.

vincing evidence to the contrary. As for the second part of the
assertion, their descriptions of their control measures indicate that
they can hope to block only the cruder, more obvious, and repeated
forms of cheating. The postal card follow-up will catch the interviewer who make contacts, but fabricates demographic data (to fill a
spot-check follow-up interviewing may eventually catch the interviewer who makes contacts, but fabricates demographic data (to
fill a quota sample) or completes only part of the interview and fills
in the rest in a stereotyped manner later on. (Even here, many of his
interviews may be used before he is detected.) However, from the
cases of hired hand interviewing which I am familiar with, I would
say such crude cheating is not the most common form of cutting
corners on the job. Far more common is the kind found in Case III
where the interviewer makes his contact, obtains a fairly complete
interview, but leaves partial gaps here and there because he found it
time-consuming, embarrassing, or troublesome, felt threatened by
the respondent, or simply felt uncertain about how the study director
wanted certain lines of questioning developed. With a little imagination, such gaps can be filled in later on in a way that is very unlikely
to be detected in a follow-up interview. If, for example, a supervisor
in Case III had returned to the respondents and asked them whether
the "five reasons" listed on their interview form were accurate reflections of their opinion, probably most would have said yes, and
the few who objected to one or two of the reasons could have been
dismissed as the degree of change that one expects on re-interview.[7]

Some gimmicks for catching cheaters may even put the finger on
the wrong person. Thus, one approach to detecting cheating is to
compare the data of each interviewer to the group averages and to
assume that if one deviates markedly from the group, he is cheating
or doing his work improperly. This reasoning assumes that cheating
is exceptional and will stand out from the crowd. I have already
suggested that the opposite is often the case. Therefore, if the cheaters are working in the same direction (which is readily possible if
they have reached an informal agreement or if the question is of such
a nature as to suggest distortion in a given direction), it is the
"honest" person who will deviate. In the study alluded to in Case

7. I have even heard the argument that it makes no difference if perceptive interviewers make up parts of the interview responses with the help of information from
other responses because their fabrications will usually closely approximate what the
subject would have said if he could have been prompted to answer. But if we accept
this argument, a large portion of the interview should have been eliminated to begin
with. It means we already claim to know the nature of some of the relationships which
the study is purportedly investigating.

III, for example, one of the interviewers always left spaces open on the "five reasons" item. At one point the director reprimanded him for not obtaining five responses "like the rest of the interviewers." The director preferred to believe that this man was not doing his job right than to believe that all the rest were making up responses.

Large survey organizations have at least made some attempts to control the cruder forms of cheating. In most studies using hired hands, even this limited control is absent. The academic man with one or a few assistants, the research organization study director with one or a few small projects, usually has no routine way of checking on the work of his assistants.If he duplicates much of their work or supervises them very closely, he may as well dispense with their services. If he gives them assignments without checking on them closely, he is in effect assuming that they are conducting their assignment more or less as directed and is accepting their products at face value. This assumption, I assert, is a dubious one. And since it is a common practice nowadays to farm out much of one's research work—quite often to accumulate research grants only to hire others to do the bulk of the work—the dubious nature of hired hand research is a widespread problem in small as well as large scale research, in surveys, in direct observation, and in various forms of data processing.

I do not want to suggest, however, that the major failure of hired hand research is the lack of control of cheating. Rather, the very fact that we are placed in a position of having to think up gimmicks to detect cheating is in itself an admission of failure. It means that we are relying for an important part of our research operation on people who have no concern for the outcome of the study. Such persons cannot have the kind of understanding of the data collection or data-processing procedures which can come only with working out problems in which the researcher has an intrinsic interest and has gone through a process of formulating research questions and relevant ways of collecting and processing data.

I can hear the objection that much social science cannot be done without hired hands. But we should at least be aware of the doubtful nature of some of the information collected in this way and construct our data collection and processing in such a way as to reduce the encouragement of cheating and restriction of production as much as possible (See Crespi's list of "ballot demoralizers."[8]) More important, however, I believe the need for hired hands has been greatly exaggerated. Why, for example, must we so often have large sam-

8. Leo Crespi, *op. cit.*, pp. 437–39.

ples? The large sample is frequently a contrivance for controlling various kinds of "errors" (including the "error" introduced by unreliable hired hands). But if the study were done on a much smaller sample by one person or several colleagues who formulated their own study and conducted it entirely by themselves, much of this error would not enter in the first place. Isn't a sample of fifty which yields data in which we can have a high degree of confidence more useful than a sample of five thousand where we must remain doubtful about what it is that we have collected? Often a large-scale study tries to do too much at one time and so ends up as a hodge-podge affair with no integration of ideas or information ever taking place because it is, in effect, *nobody's* study. How often have you read the report of a massive study expending large amounts of money and employing large numbers of people where you were disappointed at the paucity of the results, especially when compared to a far smaller project on a similar issue conducted entirely by one or a few people?

Let me repeat that I am not singling out large-scale operations as the only villains. The current structure of professional careers is such that often small studies are turned over to hired hands. We tend to be rated on how many studies we can carry on at the same time rather than on how thoroughly and carefully we can carry through a given line of research. Soon we find that we do not have time for all of the projects we have become involved in and must turn some over to others of lower professional status. This might not be so bad if we were willing to turn over the research work wholeheartedly. We might simply act as entrepreneurs to funnel funds to others and to provide them with appropriate clearance and an entré to research settings. We can then leave the specific formulation of the problem and procedure (and the credit for doing the work) to the person we have helped out. Such is often done, of course. However, there are many instances in which the senior researcher believes those he has hired cannot be trusted to formulate their own plans, or professional career competition convinces him that he cannot "afford" to give up any of his studies to others. In such cases he is likely to maintain a semblance of control by mechanically structuring a research plan and making assignments to his assistants. This, as I have indicated, is the way to the hired hand mentality with its attendant distortions of research data.

What is a hired hand? So far I have been talking as if I knew and as if the hired hand could readily be distinguished from one who is not. This, of course, is not true. The issue is a complex one and information on it is, by its very nature, not very accessible. It is a crucial question which deserves study in its own right as part of the more general study of the process of "doing research."

Let me attempt a crude characterization of hired hand research, a characterization which hopefully will be greatly refined and perhaps reformulated with further study. A hired hand is a person who feels that he has no stake in the research that he is working on, that he is simply expected to carry out assigned tasks and turn in results which will "pass inspection." Of course, a hired assistant may not start out with the hired hand mentality, but may develop it if he finds that his talents for creativity are not called upon and that his suggestions and efforts at active participation are ignored.

From specific examples from the research world and by analogy from research on hired hands in other occupational spheres, I am convinced that research tasks carried out by hired hands are characterized, not rarely or occasionally, but *typically*, by restricted production, failure to carry out portions of the task, avoidance of the more unpleasant or difficult aspects of the research, and outright cheating. The results of research done in part or wholly by hired hands should be viewed as a dubious source for information about specific aspects of our social life or for the raw material for developing broader generalizations.

Of course, this leaves open the question of what constitutes a "stake in the research" and how one avoids or reduces the hired hand mentality. Again, I have no specific answers and hope that issue will receive much more attention than it has up to now. A stake may mean different things in various circumstances. For graduate students, a chance to share in planning and in writing and publication may often be important. For interviewers or field workers, the determination of the details of their procedure may be crucial. In an applied setting, the responsibility for the practical consequences of the research findings may be most important.[9]

It would also be worthwhile to examine the conditions which make for hired hand research. Here again, I have little specific to say and this subject, too, needs much more investigation. However, I will suggest a few factors I consider important.

Size. Hired hands can be found in research staffs of all sizes from one on up. However, it is clear that when a very small number of

9. The "human relations in industry" movement has given us some useful suggestions about the circumstances which alienate workers and executives, and also ways in which industrial employees may be given a real stake in their jobs. See, for example, Doublas McGregor, *The Human Side of Enterprise* (New York: McGraw-Hill, 1960), Part 2.

researchers are working together, there is a greater possibility of developing a true colleagueship in which each will be able to formulate some of his own ideas and put them into action. The larger the group, the more difficult this becomes until the point is probably reached where it is virtually impossible, and the organization must be run on the basis of hierarchical staff relations with the lower echelons almost inevitably becoming hired hands.

Subordination. If some members of the research group are distinctly subordinate to others in a given organizational hierarchy or in general social status, it will be more difficult to develop a true colleague working relationship than if their status were more closely equal. The subordinate may hesitate to advance his ideas; the superordinate might be loath to admit that his lower-level co-worker be entitled to inject his ideas into the plans. Formal super-subordinate relationships can of course be muted and sometimes completely overcome in the course of personal contact, but certainly this is an initial, and sometimes permanent, basis for establishing hired hand status.

Adherence to rigid plans. If a researcher believes that good research can be done only if a detailed plan of data collection, processing, and analysis is established in advance and adhered to throughout, he has laid the basis for hired hand research if he makes use of assistance from others who have not participated in the original plan. Sticking to a pre-formed plan means that others cannot openly introduce variations which may make the study more meaningful for them. Any creativity they apply will be of a surreptitious nature.

In their research methods texts, our students are told a great deal about the mechanics of research technique and little about the social process of researching. What little is said on the latter score consists largely of Pollyannaish statements about morale, honesty, and "proper motivation." It should be noted that appeals to morality and patriotism never reduced goldbricking and restriction of production in industry, even during the time of a world war. There is no reason to believe that analogous appeals to interviewers, graduate students, research assistants, and others who serve as hired hands will be any more effective. If we want to avoid the hired hand mentality, we must stop using people as hired hands.

Glaser and Strauss state that we regularly "discount" aspects of many, if not most, of all scientific analyses we read because we consider the research designed onesided, believe that it does not fit the social structure to which it was generalized, or that it does not fit in with our observations in an area where we have had considerable experience.[10]

I would like to suggest another area in which we might consistently apply the "discounting process." When reading a research report, we should pay close attention to the description of how the data were collected, processed, analyzed, interpreted, and written up with an eye to determining what part, if any, was played by hired hands. This will often be a difficult and highly tentative judgment, requiring much reading between the lines with the help of our knowledge of how our colleagues and we ourselves often operate. However, we can get hints from such things as the size of the staff, the nature of the relationship of the staff members, the manner in which the research plans were developed and applied, the organizational setting in which the research was done, mention made of assignment of tasks, and so on. If there is good reason to believe that significant parts of the research has been carried out by hired hands, this would, in my opinion, be a reason for discounting much or all of the results of the study.

10. Barney Glaser and Anselm L. Strauss, "Discovery of Substantive Theory: A Basic Strategy Underlying Qualitative Research," *American Behavioral Scientist*, 8 (February 1965), 5–12.

36. The Life and Death of Project Camelot

IRVING LOUIS HOROWITZ

IN JUNE of this year—in the midst of the crisis over the Dominican Republic—the United States Ambassador to Chile sent an urgent and angry cable to the State Department. Ambassador Ralph Dungan was confronted with a growing outburst of anti-Americanism from Chilean newspapers and intellectuals. Further, left-wing members of the Chilean Senate had accused the United States of espionage.

The anti-American attacks that agitated Dungan had no direct connection with sending US troups to Santo Domingo. Their target was a mysterious and cloudy American research program called Project Camelot.

Dungan wanted to know from the State Department what Project Camelot was all about. Further, whatever Camelot was, he wanted it stopped because it was fast becoming a *cause célébre* in Chile (as it soon would throughout capitals of Latin America and in Washington)

Reprinted by permission from *Trans*-action, November-December 1965. Copyright © by *Trans*-action Magazine, New Brunswick, New Jersey.

and Dungan had not been told anything about it—even though it was sponsored by the US Army and involved the tinderbox subjects of counter-revolution and counter-insurgency in Latin America.

Within a few weeks Project Camelot created repercussions from Capitol Hill to the White House. Senator J. William Fulbright, chairman of the Foreign Relations Committee, registered his personal concern about such projects as Camelot because of their "reactionary, backward-looking policy opposed to change. Implicit in Camelot, as in the concept of 'counter-insurgency,' is an assumption that revolutionary movements are dangerous to the interests of the United States and that the United States must be prepared to assist, if not actually to participate in, measures to repress them."

By mid-June the State Department and Defense Department—which has created and funded Camelot—were in open contention over the project and the jurisdiction each department should have over certain foreign policy operations.

On July 8, Project Camelot was killed by Defense Secretary Robert McNamara's office which has a veto power over the military budget. The decision had been made under the President's direction.

On that same day, the director of Camelot's parent body, the Special Operations Research Organization, told a Congressional committee that the research project on revolution and counter-insurgency had taken its name from King Arthur's mythical domain because "It connotes the right sort of thing—development of a stable society with peace and justice for all." Whatever Camelot's outcome, there should be no mistaking the deep sincerity behind this appeal for an applied social science pertinent to current policy.

However, Camelot left a horizon of disarray in its wake: an open dispute between State and Defense; fuel for the anti-American fires in Latin America; a cut in US Army research appropriations. In addition, serious and perhaps ominous implications for social science research, bordering on censorship, have been raised by the heated reaction of the executive branch of government.

GLOBAL COUNTER-INSURGENCY

What was Project Camelot? Basically, it was a project for measuring and forecasting the causes of revolutions and insurgency in under-developed areas of the world. It also aimed to find ways of eliminating the causes, or coping with the revolutions and insurgencies. Camelot was sponsored by the US Army on a four to six million dollar contract, spaced out over three to four years, with the Special Operations Research Organization (SORO). This agency is nominally under the aegis of American University in Washington, D.C., and does a variety of research for the Army. This includes making analytical surveys of foreign areas; keeping up-to-date information on the military, political, and social complexes of those areas; and maintaining a "rapid response" file for getting immediate information, upon Army request, on any situation deemed militarily important.

Latin America was the first area chosen for concentrated study, but countries on Camelot's four-year list included some in Asia, Africa, and Europe. In a working paper issued on December 5, 1964, at the request of the Office of the Chief of Research and Development, Department of the Army, it was recommended that "comparative historical studies" be made in these countries:

(Latin America) Argentina, Bolivia, Brazil, Colombia, Cuba, Dominican Republic, El Salvador, Guatemala, Mexico, Paraguay, Peru, Venezuela.
(Middle East) Egypt, Iran, Turkey.
(Far East) Korea, Indonesia, Malaysia, Thailand.
(Others) France, Greece, Nigeria.

"Survey research and other field studies" were recommended for Bolivia, Colombia, Ecuador, Paraguay, Peru, Venezuela, Iran, Thailand. Preliminary consideration was also being given to study of the separatist movement in French Canada. It, too, had a code name: Project Revolt.

In a recruiting letter sent to selected scholars all over the world at the end of 1964, Project Camelot's aims were defined as a study to "make it possible to predict and influence politically significant aspects of social change in the developing nations of the world." This would include devising procedures for "assessing the potential for internal war within national societies" and "identify(ing) with increased degrees of confidence, those actions which a government might take to relieve conditions which are assessed as giving rise to a potential for internal war." The letter further stated:

> The US Army has an important mission in the positive and constructive aspects of nation-building in less developed countries as well as a responsibility to assist friendly governments in dealing with active insurgency problems.

Such activities by the US Army were described as "insurgency prophylaxis" rather than the "sometimes misleading label of counter-insurgency."

Project Camelot was conceived in late 1963 by a group of high-ranking Army officers connected with the Army Research Office of the Department of Defense. They were concerned about new types of warfare springing up around the world. Revolutions in Cuba and Yemen and insurgency movements in Vietnam and the Congo were a far cry from the battles of World War II and also different from the envisioned – and planned for – apocalypse of nuclear war. For the first time in modern warfare, military establishments were not in a position to use the immense arsenals at their disposal – but were, instead, compelled by force of a geopolitical stalemate to increasingly engage in primitive forms of armed combat. The questions of moment for the Army were: Why can't the "hardware" be used? And what alternatives can social science "software" provide?

A well-known Latin American area specialist, Rex Hopper, was chosen as director of Project Camelot. Hopper was a professor of sociology and chairman of the department at Brooklyn College. He had been to Latin America many times over a thirty-year span on research projects and lecture tours, including some under government sponsorship. He was highly recommended for the position by his professional associates in Washington and elsewhere. Hopper had a long-standing interest in problems of revolution and saw in this multi-million dollar contract the possibile realization of a life-long scientific ambition.

THE CHILEAN DEBACLE

How did this social science research project create a foreign policy furore? And, at another level, how did such high intentions result in so disastrous an outcome?

The answers involve a network spreading from a professor of anthropology at the University of Pittsburgh, to a professor of sociology at the University of Oslo, and yet a third professor of sociology at the University of Chile in Santiago, Chile. The "showdown" took place in Chile, first within the confines of the university, next on the floor of the Chilean Senate, then in the popular press of Santiago, and finally, behind US embassy walls.

It was ironic that Chile was the scene of wild newspaper tales of spying and academic outrage at scholars being recruited for "spying missions." For the working papers of Project Camelot stipulated as a criterion for study that a country "should show promise of high pay-offs in terms of the kinds of data required." Chile did not meet these requirements – it is not on the preliminary list of nations specified as prospects.

How then did Chile become involved in Project Camelot's affairs? The answer requires consideration of the position of Hugo G. Nutini, assistant professor of anthropology at Pittsburgh, citizen of the United States and former citizen of Chile. His presence in Santiago as a self-identified Camelot representative triggered the climactic chain of events.

Nutini, who inquired about an appointment in Camelot's beginning stages, never was given a regular Camelot appointment. Because he was planning a trip to Chile in April of this year—on other academic business—he was asked to prepare a report concerning possibilities of cooperation from Chilean scholars. In general, it was the kind of survey which has mild results and a modest honorarium attached to it. (Nutini was offered $750). But Nutini had an obviously different notion of his role. Despite the limitations and precautions which Rex Hopper placed on his trip, especially Hooper's insistence on its informal nature, Nutini managed to convey the impression of being an official of Project Camelot with the authority to make proposals to prospective Chilean participants. Here was an opportunity to link the country of his birth with the country of his choice.

At about the same time, Johan Galtung, a Norwegian sociologist famous for his research on conflict and conflict resolution in underdeveloped areas, especially in Latin America, entered the picture. Galtung, who was in Chile at the time and associated with the Latin American Faculty of Social Science (FLACSO), received an invitation to participate in a Camelot planning conference scheduled for Washington, D.C., in August 1965. The fee to social scientists attending the conference would be $2,000 for four weeks. Galtung turned down the invitation. He gave several reasons. He could not accept the role of the US Army as a sponsoring agent in a study of counter-insurgency. He could not accept the notion of the Army as an agency of national development; he saw the Army as managing conflict and even promoting conflict. Finally, he could not accept the asymmetry of the project—he found it difficult to understand why there would be studies of counter-insurgency in Latin-America, but no studies of "counter-intervention" (conditions under which Latin American nations might intervene in the affairs of the United States). Galtung was also deeply concerned about the possibility of European scholars being frozen out of Latin American studies by an inundation of sociologists from the United States. Furthermore, he expressed fears that the scale of Camelot honoraria would competely destroy the social science labor market in Latin America.

Galtung had spoken to others in Oslo, Santiago, and throughout

Latin American about the project, and he had shown the memorandum of December 1964 to many of his colleagues.

Soon after Nutini arrived in Santiago, he had a conference with Vice-Chancellor Alvaro Bunster of the University of Chile to discuss the character of Project Camelot. Their second meeting, arranged by the vice-chancellor, was also attended by Professor Eduardo Fuenzalida, a sociologist. After a half-hour of exposition by Nutini, Fuenzalida asked him pointblank to specify the ultimate aims of the project, its sponsors, and its military implications. Before Nutini could reply, Professor Fuenzalida, apparently with some drama, pulled a copy of the December 4 circular letter from his briefcase and read a prepared Spanish translation. Simultaneously, the authorities at FLACSO turned over the matter to their associates in the Chilean Senate and in the left-wing Chilean press.

In Washington, under the political pressures of State Department officials and Congressional reaction, Project Camelot was halted in midstream, or more precisely, before it ever really got under way. When the ambassador's communication reached Washington, there was already considerable official ferment about Project Camelot. Senators Fulbright, Morse, and McCarthy soon asked for hearings by the Senate Foreign Relations Committee. Only an agreement between Secretary of Defense McNamara and Secretary of State Rusk to settle their differences on future overseas research projects forestalled Senate action. But in the House of Representatives, a hearing was conducted by the Foreign Affairs Committee on July 8. The SORO director, Theodore Vallance, was questioned by committee members on the worth of Camelot and the matter of military intrusion into foreign policy areas.

That morning, even before Vallance was sworn in as a witness — and without his knowledge — the Defense Department issued a terse announcement terminating Project Camelot. President Johnson had decided the issue in favor of the State Department. In a memo to Secretary Rusk on August 5 the President stipulated that "no government sponsorship of foreign area research should be undertaken which in the judgment of the Secretary of State would adversely affect the United States foreign relations."

The State Department had recently established machinery to screen and judge all federally-financed research projects overseas. The policy and research consequences of the Presidential directive will be discussed later.

What effect will the cancellation of Camelot have on the continuing rivalry between Defense and State departments for primacy in foreign policy? How will government sponsorship of future social science research be affected? And was Project Camelot a scholarly protective cover for US Army planning—or a legitimate research operation on a valid research subject independent of sponsorship?

Let us begin with a collective self-portrait of Camelot as the social scientists who directed the project perceived it. There seems to be a general consensus on seven points.

First, the men who went to work for Camelot felt the need for a large-scale, "big picture" project in social science. They wanted to create a sociology of contemporary relevance which would not suffer from the parochial narrowness of vision to which their own professional backgrounds had generally conditioned them. Most of the men viewed Camelot as a bona fide opportunity to do fundamental research with relatively unlimited funds at their disposal. (No social science project ever before had up to $6,000,000 available.) Under such optimal conditions, these scholars tended not to look a gift horse in the mouth. As one of them put it, there was no desire to inquire too deeply as to the source of the funds or the ultimate purpose of the project.

Second, most social scientists affiliated with Camelot felt that there was actually more freedom to do fundamental research under military sponsorship than at a university or college. One man noted that during the 1950's there was far more freedom to do fundamental research in the RAND corporation (an Air Force research organization) than on any campus in America. Indeed, once the protective covering of RAND was adopted, it was almost viewed as a society of Platonist elites of "knowers" permitted to search for truth on behalf of the powerful. In a neoplatonic definition of their situation, the Camelot men hoped that their ideas would be taken seriously by the wielders of power (although, conversely, they were convinced that the armed forces would not accept their preliminary recommendations).

Third, many of the Camelot associates felt distinctly uncomfortable with military sponsorship, especially given the present United States military posture. But their reaction to this discomfort was that "the Army has to be educated." This view was sometimes cast in Freudian terms: the Army's bent toward violence ought to be sublimated. Underlying this theme was the notion of the armed forces as an agency for potential social good—the discipline and the order embodied by an army could be channeled into the process of economic and social development in the United States as well as in Latin America.

Fourth, there was a profound conviction in the perfectibility of mankind; particularly in the possibility of the military establishment performing a major role in the general process of growth. They sought to correct the intellectual paternalism and parochialism under which Pentagon generals, State Department diplomats, and Defense Department planners seemed to operate.

Fifth, a major long-range purpose of Camelot, at least for some of its policy-makers, was to prevent another revolutionary holocaust on a grand scale, such as occurred in Cuba. At the very least, there was a shared belief that *Pax Americana* was severely threatened and its future could be bolstered.

Sixth, none of them viewed their role on the project as spying for the United States government, or for anyone else.

Seventh, the men on Project Camelot felt that they made heavy sacrifices for social science. Their personal and professional risks were much higher than those taken by university academics. Government work, while well-compensated, remains professionally marginal. It can be terminated abruptly (as indeed was the case) and its project directors are subject to public scrutiny not customary behind the walls of ivy.

In the main, there was perhaps a keener desire on the part of the directing members of Camelot not to "sell out" than there is among social scientists with regular academic appointments. This concern with the ethics of social science research seemed to be due largely to daily confrontation of the problems of betrayal, treason, secrecy, and abuse of data, in a critical situation. In contrast, even though a university position may be created by federally-sponsored research, the connection with policy matters is often too remote to cause any *crise de conscience*.

THE INSIDERS' REPORT

Were the men on Camelot critical of any aspects of the project?

Some had doubts from the outset about the character of the work they would be doing and about the conditions under which it would be done. It was pointed out, for example, that the US Army tends to exercise a far more stringent intellectual control of research findings than does the US Air Force. As evidence for this, it was stated that SORO generally had fewer "free-wheeling" aspects to its research designs than did RAND (the Air Force-supported research organization). One critic inside SORO went so far as to say that he knew of no SORO research which had a "playful" or unregimented quality, such as one finds at RAND (where for example, computers are used to plan invasions but also to play chess). One staff member said that "the self-conscious seriousness gets to you after a while." "It was all grim stuff," said another.

Another line of criticism was that pressures on the "reformers" (as the men engaged in Camelot research spoke of themselves) to come up with ideas were much stronger than the pressures on the military to actually bring off any policy changes recommended. The social scientists were expected to be social reformers, while the military adjutants were expected to be conservative. It was further felt that the relationship between sponsors and researchers was not one of equals, but rather one of superordinate military needs and subordinate academic roles. On the other hand, some officials were impressed by the disinterestedness of the military, and thought that far from exercising undue influence, the Army personnel were loath to offer opinions.

Another objection was that if one had to work on policy matters – if research is to have international ramifications – it might better be conducted under conventional State Department sponsorship. "After all," one man said, "they are at least nominally committed to civilian political norms." In other words, there was a considerable reluctance to believe that the Defense Department, despite its superior organization, greater financial affluence, and executive influence, would actually improve upon State Department styles of work, or accept recommendations at variance with Pentagon policies.

There seemed to be few, if any, expressions of disrespect for the intrinsic merit of the work contemplated by Camelot, or of disdain for policy-oriented work in general. The scholars engaged in the Camelot effort used two distinct vocabularies. The various Camelot documents reveal a military vocabulary provided with an array of military justifications; often followed (within the same document) by a social science vocabulary offering social science justifications and rationalizations. The dilemma in the Camelot literature from the preliminary report issued in August 1964 until the more advanced document issued in April 1965 is the same: an incomplete amalgamation of the military and sociological vocabularies. (At an early date the project had the code name SPEARPOINT.)

POLICY CONFLICTS OVER CAMELOT

The directors of SORO are concerned that the cancellation of Camelot might mean the end of SORO as well in a wholesale slash of research funds. For while over $1,000,000 was allotted to Camelot each year, the annual budget of SORO, its parent organization, is a good deal less. Although no such action has taken place, SORO's future is being examined. For example, the Senate and House Appropriations Committee blocked a move by the Army to transfer unused Camelot funds to SORO.

However, the end of Project Camelot does not necessarily imply the end of the Special Operations Research Office, nor does it imply an end to research designs which are similar in character to Project Camelot. In fact, the termination of the contract does not even imply an intellectual change of heart on the part of the originating sponsors or key figures of the project.

One of the characteristics of Project Camelot was the number of antagonistic forces it set in motion on grounds of strategy and timing rather than from what may be called considerations of scientific principles.

The State Department grounded its opposition to Camelot on the basis of the ultimate authority it has in the area of foreign affairs. There is no published report showing serious criticism of the projected research itself.

Congressional opposition seemed to be generated by a concern not to rock any foreign alliances, especially in Latin America. Again, there was no statement about the project's scientific or intellectual grounds.

A third group of skeptics, academic social scientists, generally thought that Project Camelot, and studies of the processes of revolution and war in general, were better left in the control of major university centers, and in this way, kept free of direct military supervision.

The Army, creator of the project, did nothing to contradict McNamara's order cancelling Project Camelot. Army influentials did not only feel that they had to execute the Defense Department's orders, but they are traditionally dubious of the value of "software" research to support "hardware" systems.

Let us take a closer look at each of these groups which voiced opposition to Project Camelot. A number of issues did not so much hinge upon, as swim about, Project Camelot. In particular, the "jurisdictional" dispute between Defense and State loomed largest.

State vs. Defense. In substance, the debate between the Defense Department and the State Department is not unlike that between electricians and bricklayers in the construction of a new apartment house. What union is responsible for which processes? Less generously, the issue is: Who controls what? At the policy level, Camelot was a tool tossed about in a larger power struggle which has been going on in government circles since the end of World War II, when the Defense Department emerged as a competitor for honors as the most powerful bureau of the administrative branch of government.

In some sense, the divisions between Defense and State are outcomes of the rise of ambiguous conflicts such as Korea and Vietnam, in contrast to the more precise and diplomatically controlled "classical" world wars. What are the lines dividing political policy from military posture? Who is the most important representative of the United States abroad: the ambassador or the military attaché in charge of the military mission? When soldiers from foreign lands are sent to the United States for political orientation, should such orientation be within the province of the State Department or of the Defense Department? When undercover activities are conducted, should the direction of such activities belong to military or political authorities? Each of these is a strategic question with little pragmatic or historic precedent. Each of these was entwined in the Project Camelot explosion.

It should be plain therefore that the State Department was not simply responding to the recommendations of Chilean left-wingers in urging the cancellation of Camelot. It merely employed the Chilean hostility to "interventionist" projects as an opportunity to redefine the balance of forces and power with the Defense Department. What is clear from this resistance to such projects is not so much a defense of the sovereignty of the nations where ambassadors are stationed, as it is a contention that conventional political channels are sufficient to yield the information desired or deemed necessary.

Congress. In the main, congressional reaction seems to be that Project Camelot was bad because it rocked the diplomatic boat in a sensitive area. Underlying most congressional criticisms is the plain fact that most congressmen are more sympathetic to State Department control of foreign affairs than they are to Defense Department control. In other words, despite military sponsored world junkets, National Guard and State Guard pressures from the home State, and military training in the backgrounds of many congressmen, the sentiment for political rather than military control is greater. In addition, there is a mounting suspicion in Congress of varying kinds of behavioral science research stemming from hearings into such matters as wire-tapping, uses of lie detectors, and truth-in-packaging.

Social scientists. One reason for the violent response to Project

Camelot, especially among Latin American scholars, is its sponsor-ship by the Department of Defense. The fact is that Latin Americans have become quite accustomed to State Department involvements in the internal affairs of various nations. The Defense Department is a newcomer, a dangerous one, inside the Latin American orbit. The train of thought connected to its activities is in terms of international warfare, spying missions, military manipulations, etc. The State De-partment, for its part, is often a consultative party to shifts in govern-ment, and has played an enormous part in either fending off or bringing about *coups d'état*. This State Department role has by now been accepted and even taken for granted. Not so the Defense Department's role. But it is interesting to conjecture on how mat-ter-of-factly Camelot might have been accepted if it had State De-partment sponsorship.

Social scientists in the United States have, for the most part, been publicly silent on the matter of Camelot. The reasons for this are not hard to find. First, many "giants of the field" are involved in govern-ment contract work in one capacity or another. And few souls are in a position to tamper with the gods. Second, most information on Proj-ect Camelot has thus far been of a newspaper variety; and profes-sional men are not in a habit of criticizing colleagues on the basis of such information. Third, many social scientists doubtless see nothing wrong or immoral in the Project Camelot designs. And they are therefore more likely to be either confused or angered at the Latin American response than at the directors of Project Camelot. (At the time of the blowup, Camelot people spoke about the "Chilean mess" rather than the "Camelot mess.")

The directors of Project Camelot did not "classify" research mate-rials, so that there would be no stigma of secrecy. And they also tried to hire, and even hired away from academic positions, people well known and respected for their independence of mind. The difficulty is that even though the stigma of secrecy was formally erased, it remained in the attitudes of many of the employees and would-be employees of Project Camelot. They unfortunately thought in terms of secrecy, clearance, missions, and the rest of the professional non-sense that so powerfully afflicts the Washington scientific as well as political ambience.

Further, it is apparent that Project Camelot had much greater difficulty hiring a full-time staff of high professional competence, than in getting part-time, summertime, weekend, and sundry assis-tance. Few established figures in academic life were willing to sur-render the advantages of their positions for the risks of the project.

One of the cloudiest aspects to Project Camelot is the role of American University. Its actual supervision of the contract appears to have begun and ended with the 25 per cent overhead on those parts of the contract that a university receives on most federal grants. Thus, while there can be no question as to the "concern and disappointment" of President Hurst R. Anderson of the American University of the demise of Project Camelot, the reasons for this regret do not seem to extend beyond the formal and the financial. No official at American University appears to have been willing to make any statement of responsibility, support, chagrin, opposition, or anything else related to the project. The issues are indeed momentous, and must be faced by all universities at which government sponsored research is conducted: the amount of control a university has over contract work; the role of university officials in the distribution of funds from grants; the relationships that ought to be established once a grant is issued. There is also a major question concerning project directors: Are they members of the faculty, and if so, do they have necessary teaching responsibilities and opportunities for tenure as do other faculty members?

The difficulty with American University is that it seems to be remarkably unlike other universities in its permissiveness. The Special Operations Research Office received neither guidance nor support from university officials. From the outset, there seems to have been a "gentleman's agreement" not to inquire or interfere in Project Camelot, but simply to serve as some sort of camouflage. If American University were genuinely autonomous it might have been able to lend highly supportive aid to Project Camelot during the crisis months. As it is, American University maintained an official silence which preserved it from more congressional or executive criticism. This points up some serious flaws in its administrative and financial policies.

The relationship of Camelot to SORO represented a similarly muddled organizational picture. The director of Project Camelot was nominally autonomous and in charge of an organization surpassing in size and importance the overall SORO operation. Yet at the critical point the organizational blueprint served to protect SORO and sacrifice what nominally was its limb. That Camelot happened to be a vital organ may have hurt, especially when Congress blocked the transfer of unused Camelot funds to SORO.

Military. Military reaction to the cancellation of Camelot varied. It should be borne in mind that expenditures on Camelot were minimal in the Army's overall budget and most military leaders are skeptical, to begin with, about the worth of social science research. So there was no open protest about the demise of Camelot. Those officers who have a positive attitude toward social science materials, or are themselves trained in the social sciences, were dismayed. Some had hoped to find "software" alternatives to the "hardware systems" approach applied by the Secretary of Defense to every military-political contingency. These officers saw the attack on Camelot as a double attack—on their role as officers and on their professional standards. But the Army was so clearly treading in new waters that it could scarcely jeopardize the entire structure of military research to preserve Camelot—a situation threatening to other governmental contracts with social scientists—no doubt impressed many armed forces officers.

The claim is made by the Camelot staff (and various military aides) that the critics of the project played into the hands of those sections of the military predisposed to veto any social science recommendations. Then why did the military offer such a huge support to a social science project to begin with? Because $6,000,000 is actually a trifling sum for the Army in an age of multi-billion dollar military establishment. The amount is significantly more important for the social sciences, where such contract awards remain relatively scarce. Thus, there were differing perspectives of the importance of Camelot: an Army view which considered the contract as one of several forms of "software" investment; a social science perception of Project Camelot as the equivalent of the Manhattan Project.

WAS PROJECT CAMELOT WORKABLE?

While most public opposition to Project Camelot focused on its strategy and timing, a considerable amount of private opposition centered on more basic, though theoretical, questions: Was Camelot scientifically feasible and ethically correct? No public document or statement contested the possibility that, given the successful completion of the data gathering, Camelot could have, indeed, established basic criteria for measuring the level and potential for internal war in a given nation. Thus, by never challenging the feasibility of the work, the political critics of Project Camelot were providing back-handed compliments to the efficacy of the project.

But much more than political considerations are involved. It is clear that some of the most critical problems presented by Project Camelot are scientific. Although, for an extensive analysis of Camelot, the reader would, in fairness, have to be familiar with all of its documents, salient general criticisms can be made without a full reading.

The research design of Camelot was from the outset plagued by ambiguities. It was never quite settled whether the purpose was to study counter-insurgency possibilities, or the revolutionary process. Similarly, it was difficult to determine whether it was to be a study of comparative social structures, a set of case studies of single nations "in depth," or a study of social structure with particular emphasis on the military. In addition, there was a lack of treatment of what indicators were to be used, and whether a given social system in Nation A could be as stable in Nation B.

In one Camelot document there is a general critique of social science for failing to deal with social conflict and social control. While this in itself is admirable, the tenor and context of Camelot's documents make it plain that a "stable society" is considered the norm no less than the desired outcome. The "breakdown of social order" is spoken of accusatively. Stabilizing agencies in developing areas are presumed to be absent. There is no critique of US Army policy in developing areas because the Army is presumed to be a stabilizing agency. The research formulations always assume the legitimacy of Army tasks—"if the US Army is to perform effectively its parts in the US mission of counter-insurgency it must recognize that insurgency represents a breakdown of social order...." But such a proposition has never been doubted—by Army officials or anyone else. The issue is whether such breakdowns are in the nature of the existing system or a product of conspiratorial movements.

The use of hygienic language disguises the anti-revolutionary assumptions under a cloud of powder puff declarations. For example, studies of Paraguay are recommended "because trends in this situation (the Stroessner regime) may also render it 'unique' when analyzed in terms of the transition from 'dictatorship' to political stability." But to speak about changes from dictatorship to stability is an obvious ruse. In this case, it is a tactic to disguise the fact that Paraguay is one of the most vicious, undemocratic (and like most dictatorships, stable) societies in the Western Hemisphere.

There typify the sort of hygienic sociological premises that do not have scientific purposes. They illustrate the confusion of commitments within Project Camelot. Indeed the very absence of emotive words such as revolutionary masses, communism, socialism, and capitalism only serves to intensify the discomfort one must feel on examination of the documents—since the abstract vocabulary disguises, rather than resolves, the problems of international revolution. To have used clearly political rather than military language would not "justify" governmental support. Furthermore, shabby assumptions of academic conventionalism replaced innovative orientations. By adopting a systems approach, the problematic, open-ended aspects of the study of revolutions was largely omitted; and the design of the study became an oppressive curb on the study of the problems inspected.

This points up a critical implication for Camelot (as well as other projects). The importance of the subject being research does not *per se* determine the importance of the project. A sociology of large-scale relevance and reference is all to the good. It is important that scholars be willing to risk something of their shaky reputations in helping resolve major world social problems. But it is no less urgent that in the process of addressing major problems, the autonomous character of the social science disciplines—their own criteria of worthwhile scholarship—should not be abandoned. Project Camelot lost sight of this "autonomous" social science character.

It never seemed to occur to its personnel to inquire into the desirability for successful revolution. This is just as solid a line of inquiry as the one stressed—the conditions under which revolutionary movements will be able to overthrow a government. Furthermore, they seem not to have thought about inquiring into the role of the United States in these countries. This points up the lack of symmetry. The problem should have been phrased to include the study of "us" as well as "them." It is not possible to make a decent analysis of a situation unless one takes into account the role of all the different people and groups involved in it; and there was no room in the design for such contingency analysis.

In discussing the policy impact on a social science research project, we should not overlook the difference between "contract" work and "grants." Project Camelot commenced with the US Army; that is to say, it was initiated for a practical purpose determined by the client. This differs markedly from the typical academic grant in that its sponsorship had "built-in" ends. The scholar usually *seeks* a grant; in this case the donor, the Army, promoted its own aims. In some measure, the hostility for Project Camelot may be an unconscious reflection of this distinction—a dim feeling that there was something "non-academic," and certainly not disinterested, about Project Camelot, irrespective of the quality of the scholars associated with it.

THE ETHICS OF POLICY RESEARCH

The issue of "scientific rights" versus "social myths" is perennial. Some maintain that the scientist ought not penetrate beyond legally or morally sanctioned limits and others argue that such limits cannot exist for science. In treading on the sensitive issues of national sovereignty, Project Camelot reflects the generalized dilemma. In deference to intelligent researchers, in recognition of them as scholars, they should have been invited by Camelot to air their misgivings and qualms about government (and especially Army sponsored) research — to declare their moral conscience. Instead, they were mistakenly approached as skillful, useful potential employees of a higher body, subject to an authority higher than their scientific calling.

What is central is not the political motives of the sponsor. For social scientists were not being enlisted in an intelligence system for "spying" purposes. But given their professional standing, their great sense of intellectual honor and pride, they could not be "employed" without proper deference for their stature. Professional authority should have prevailed from beginning to end with complete command of the right to thrash out the moral and political dilemmas as researchers saw them. The Army, however respectful and protective of free expression, was "hiring help" and not openly and honestly submitting a problem to the higher professional and scientific authority of social science.

The propriety of the Army to define and delimit all questions, which Camelot should have had a right to examine, was never placed in doubt. This is a tragic precedent; it reflects the arrogance of a consumer of intellectual merchandise. And this relationship of inequality corrupted the lines of authority, and profoundly limited the autonomy of the social scientists involved. It became clear that the social scientist savant was not so much functioning as an applied social scientist as he was supplying information to a powerful client.

The question of who sponsors research is not nearly so decisive as the question of ultimate use of such information. The sponsorship of a project, whether by the United States Army or by the Boy Scouts of America, is by itself neither good or bad. Sponsorship is good or bad only insofar as the intended outcomes can be pre-determined and the parameters of those intended outcomes tailored to the sponsor's expectations. Those social scientists critical of the project never really denied its freedom and independence, but questioned instead the purpose and character of its intended results.

It would be a gross oversimplification, if not an outright error, to assume that the theoretical problems of Project Camelot derive from any reactionary character of the project designers. The director went far and wide to select a group of men for the advisory board, the core planning group, the summer study group, and the various conference groupings, who in fact were more liberal in their orientations than any random sampling of the sociological profession would likely turn up.

However, in nearly every page of the various working papers, there are assertions which clearly derive from American military policy objectives rather than scientific method. The steady assumption that internal warfare is damaging disregards the possibility that a government may not be in a position to take actions either to relieve or improve mass conditions, or that such actions as are contemplated may be more concerned with reducing conflict than with improving conditions. The added statements about the United States Army and its "important mission in the positive and constructive aspects of nation building . . . " assumes the reality of such a function in an utterly unquestioning and unconvincing form. The first rule of the scientific game is not to make assumptions about friends and enemies in such a way as to promote the use of different criteria for the former and the latter.

The story of Project Camelot was not a confrontation of good versus evil. Obviously, not all men behaved with equal fidelity or with equal civility. Some men were weaker than others, some more callous, and some more stupid. But all of this is extrinsic to the heart of the problem of Camelot: What are and are not the legitimate functions of a scientist?

In conclusion, two important points must be clearly kept in mind and clearly apart. First, Project Camelot was intellectually, and from my own perspective, ideologically unsound. However, and more significantly, Camelot was not cancelled because of its faulty intellectual approaches. Instead, its cancellation came as an act of government censorship, and an expression of the contempt for social science so prevalent among those who need it most. Thus it was political expedience, rather than its lack of scientific merit, that led to the demise of Camelot because it threatened to rock State Department relations with Latin America.

Second, giving the State Department the right to screen and approve government-funded social science research projects on other countries, as the President has ordered, is a supreme act of censorship. Among the agencies that grant funds for such research are the National Institutes of Mental Health, the National Science Foundation, the National Aeronautics and Space Agency, and the Office of Education. Why should the State Department have veto power over the scientific pursuits of men and projects funded by these and other agencies in order to satisfy the policy needs — or policy failures — of the moment? President Johnson's directive is a gross violation of the autonomous nature of science.

We must be careful not to allow social science projects with which we may vociferously disagree on political and ideological grounds to be decimated or dismantled by government fiat. Across the ideological divide is a common social science understanding that the contemporary expression of reason in politics today is applied social science, and that the cancellation of Camelot, however pleasing it may be on political grounds to advocates of a civilian solution to Latin American affairs, represents a decisive setback for social science research.

Epilogue

I have no doubt that much sociology will continue to violate the principles set forth in the readings in this book. For as I have repeatedly argued, sociology is a social enterprise. It is not easy to change cherished values, to redefine well-loved roles, or to confront the troublesome issues of ethics and politics.

Yet I am convinced that such a confrontation is necessary if sociology is to be relevant to the empirical world. Once this empirical world is openly approached, many political and ethical issues will be resolved. Only a science firmly grounded in the empirical world can offer prescriptions for social action.

It is not sufficient to state that we take value-laden stances; these lead to an amorality, or an immortality, that favors only the discipline. Black militants, drug users, and homosexuals warrant more consideration than a public rendering of their codes, ideologies, and political views. A value-laden sociology relevant to what happens in the empirical world must become relevant for those studied. If situations of social injustice are uncovered they must be revealed, and alternative lines of action must be specified.

A final principle can be offered. Sociology will not become a full-fledged science until its practitioners learn to analyze their own activity self-consciously. Such an appraisal may lead to the development of a set of rules and guidelines to evaluate all aspects of the sociological act.

Index

Name Index

Subject Index

Printed by Amazon Italia Logistica S.r.l.
Torrazza Piemonte (TO), Italy

67468175R00338